R00873 01487

ENCYCLOPEDIA OF MORTGAGE & REAL ESTATE FINANCE

OVER 1,000
TERMS DEFINED,
EXPLAINED AND
ILLUSTRATED

■

James Newell
Albert Santi ■ Chip Mitchell

PROBUS PUBLISHING COMPANY
Chicago, Illinois

This publication is designed to provide accurate and authoritative information in
regard to the subject matter covered. It is sold with the understanding that the
publisher is not engaged in rendering legal, accounting or other professional
service.

Library of Congress Cataloging in Publication Data Available

ISBN 1-55738-123-2

Printed in the United States of America

KP

1 2 3 4 5 6 7 8 9 0

ACKNOWLEDGMENTS

Albert Santi edited, wrote, and rewrote most of the material for this book.

James Newell supplied nearly all the secondary marketing terms, particularly those involving commitments, hedging and transactions with securities. Chip Mitchell did much of the proofreading and editing of this book. Ms. Charlotte C. Monteith, V.P. of the South Carolina Federal Savings Bank, Columbia; Ms. Margaret C. England, V.P., attorney for 1st Wachovia at Winston-Salem; and Ms. Dee McLandlish, EVP of the Mortgage Bankers Association of the Carolinas, allowed the use of their UNIFORM CLOSING INSTRUCTIONS for the terms LOAN ORIGINATION PROCESS (Step 5), SURVEY, and TITLE INSURANCE.

Many thanks to Karen Biafora of VMP for supplying many of the forms copied for this book. The Mortgage Bankers Association of America is the source for much of the information in the terms COMPUTERIZED LOAN ORIGINATION (CLO), DELIN-QUENCY, NO-BID, SOLDIERS' AND SAILORS' CIVIL RELIEF ACT OF 1940, and the HOME MORTGAGE DISCLOSURE ACT.

INTRODUCTION

Most people think that you have to be good at math to understand finance. A quick review of some real estate exam books in your local library will show you that about 90 percent of the chapters devoted to finance have questions that relate to *terms* and not numbers. In reality, real estate finance has its own language, and you must understand it to understand the subject.

Let us look at a short summary of a simple real estate transaction. John and Mary sold their house to Bill and Sue. John and Mary made Bill and Sue a second mortgage to help finance the sale. How many real estate terms can you think of that relate to just the part of John and Mary in the transaction?

First, since John and Mary are the sellers, that makes them the **vendors** or **grantors**. Since John and Mary made Bill and Sue a mortgage loan, John and Mary are the **mortgagees**. Now let us consider the type of mortgage loan made to Bill and Sue. The purpose of the mortgage was to help Bill and Sue buy the house; therefore, the mortgage loan is a **purchase-money mortgage**. We said the mortgage was a **second mortgage**, which means it is a **junior mortgage** and is **subordinate** to the **senior** or **primary mortgage**. Now, Bill and Sue could have made a standard second mortgage or they could have made a **wrap-around mortgage**. If they used a wrap-around mortgage, they probably used an **all-inclusive trust deed**. Of course, if a **trust deed** was used for either a standard second mortgage or a wrap-around mortgage, this means that John and Mary probably live in a **title-theory state**. To use a trust deed, John and Mary named a **trustee**. John and Mary were careful in selecting the trustee because the trustee holds **title** to the **property** and has the right to exercise the **acceleration clause**, or the **due-on-sale clause** if Bill and Sue do something that is an **alienation** to the **conditions** of the mortgage causing the trustee to declare the mortgage in **default** and to begin a **foreclosure** on the property. Since the trustee has legal title, a **non-judicial foreclosure** can began anytime Bill and Sue are in default. Bill and Sue have **equitable title** and in the mortgage there is a **defeasance** clause giving them the right to claim legal title when there is a **release** with the **satisfaction of a mortgage**. John and Mary were careful in not lending on a high **loan-to-value ratio** because in most states, if foreclosure happens with a purchase-money mortgage, the **mortgagors** are exempt from **personal liability**; it is the same as a **non-recourse** or an **exculpatory clause** in the mortgage. John and Mary should always make sure the primary lender knows how to get in touch with them if there is a default in the first mortgage. If notice comes to John and Mary after Bill and Sue miss three payments, John and Mary have the right to **advance** the payments and add them to the **principal** balance. If rates fall and Bill and Sue want to **refinance** their first mortgage which they took by an **assumption of the mortgage**, they can ask John and Mary to sign a **subordination agreement** so the second will not become a first when the first is paid off with the refinancing.

Now count the terms that relate to the *simple* transaction of selling a house and making a second mortgage loan described above. Altogether there are thirty-seven terms. We can make the count an even number by saying that John and Mary got a **release of liability** when they sold their house. All the terms relating to John and Mary are in this book, plus over 2,000 more, including acronyms. Did you notice that not one math function or term appeared? The first step to understanding real estate finance is to know its *language*.

A

"A" FRAME

"A" Frame. In this style, the frame is the shape of one or more "A's."

AAA TENANT A rating given to a prime tenant with the highest credit rating. It is often used to describe the credit rating of a retail store. For example, a developer who plans to build a shopping center will seek a triple "A" tenant to help secure financing.

See ANCHOR TENANT.

1

ABANDONMENT OF PROPERTY The surrender, relinquishment, of property owned or leased without intending to resume or reclaim ownership and without naming a successor. The property usually reverts to the prior owner or to the state if there is no owner found. Abandonment does not release the owner or tenant from liability. In an example of a mortgagor "mailing the keys" to the lender, there may be abandonment, but it does not release the mortgagor from liability.

See DISTRAINT.

ABATEMENT A reduction or termination of a debt or obligation. The reduction or termination can occur from an actual payment, legal action, or by contract. Examples of abatement are: forgiving rent because a building is temporarily uninhabitable due to a fire; reducing real estate taxes because of an appraisal that is proven to be too high.

ABSENTEE OWNERSHIP An owner of income property who does not manage or reside at the subject property. The term can be critical in deciding tax deductions, e.g., allowing a tax deduction if ownership is not *absentee*. Generally, the IRS rules favorably for real estate and allows absentee owners to claim loses from real estate investments.

ABSOLUTE AUCTION An auction where property is sold to the highest bidder despite the minimum price or the final bid price.

See BID, BID-IN, UPSET PRICE.

ABSOLUTE TITLE *See* FEE SIMPLE.

ABSORPTION RATE A rate that is a forecast of how quickly properties can be sold or leased in a given area. For example, if a developer can lease 20% of the units available to the market in a given area for a given time, the absorption rate is 20%. You can usually find this term in feasibility studies.

See FEASIBILITY STUDY.

ABSTRACT OF TITLE A condensed history of the title of a property. An abstract of title should be a chronological history of recorded instruments that affect the title of the subject property. In some states, an attorney does a title search using an abstract. After a title search, the attorney issues an opinion that can be used to obtain title insurance.

The abstract does not guarantee or assure the validity of title. The abstract only reveals what is of public record. It does not protect against forgery or fraud as will title insurance.

The person preparing the abstract is the *abstractor*. The abstractor summarizes details of the abstract in the chronological order of recording, beginning with the original grant of title. The abstract will list all public records searched and not searched, including the information from the county recorder, county registrar, circuit court, and any other official source.

See CERTIFICATE OF TITLE, TITLE INSURANCE, TITLE REPORT.

ABUT Connect or join. If two pieces of property touch each other, they *abut* each other. Synonymous with adjoin.

See ADJOIN, CONTIGUOUS.

ABUTMENT A load bearing vertical member of a structure. A wall or a column are examples of abutments.

See LOAD-BEARING WALL, NON-BEARING WALL.

AC *See* ACRE.

ACC *See* ANNUAL CONTRIBUTIONS CONTRACT.

ACCELERATED REMITTANCE CYCLE (ARC) An option available to Freddie Mac's seller/servicers allowing the lender to decrease the management and guarantee fee in return for remitting principal and interest payments early. Freddie Mac seller/servicers may take advantage of this feature by an option in either the regular guarantor contract or under the ARC contract. The ARC contract offers a five or six point basis spread reduction with a lender's advanced remittance of interest and principal (to qualify for the lower fees).

ACCELERATION CLAUSE A clause in a note, bond, mortgage, or deed of trust giving the lender the right to demand the remaining balance due and payable before its original date because of some event that has an adverse effect on the lender. Without an acceleration clause, a default occurs only in the matured and unpaid portion to the debt. Examples of an adverse effect causing a lender to use the acceleration clause are:

(1) Failure to pay the PITI (Principal, Interest, Taxes, and Insurance).

(2) Placing additional liens on the property without the consent of the lender when said consent is required (FNMA requires its consent in certain cases).

(3) Events that can affect the lender's security such as extreme abuse or deterioration of the improvement.

The following is typical of acceleration clauses found in mortgage contracts:

In the event any failure to pay an installment of this note when due, time being of the essence, and such installment remains unpaid for thirty (30) days, the Holder of this Note may, at its option, without notice or demand, declare the entire principal sum, with secured interest and late charges thereon, immediately due and payable. The lender may without further notice or demand invoke the power of sale and any other remedies permitted by applicable law.

Note the use of the phrase *without notice* above. When this phrase is legal in the borrower's state, the borrower waives the right to notice. In other words, they have given up the right to be notified of some occurrence, e.g., a missed payment. If a borrower has waived the right to notice of delinquency or default and makes a late payment, action may be initiated against such mortgagor before being told. Additionally, the mortgagee may begin foreclosure proceedings. While a common clause, its legality must be determined on a state-by-state basis.

See CALL, FORECLOSURE.

ACCEPTANCE The consent or act of accepting an offer to enter a contract. Acceptance is binding and legal when a seller and purchaser agree to the initial terms or after all counter offers are made and accepted by both parties. The acceptance must be made to the person making the offer. Depending on what is being sold (real or personal property) the acceptance may not have to be in writing. A contract to purchase personal property does not normally have to be in writing. A contract to purchase real property should be in writing.

See CONTRACT.

ACCESS Every property should be entitled to a way of entrance onto itself. The right is *access*. Normally this means the property owner is due the right of having access to and from a public street or highway. The method of entry is *ingress* and the method of exiting is *egress*. This right includes access to and from a body of water that borders the property. Access can be implied or expressed.

Most state laws maintain that a landlord has access onto their property for the purposes of safeguarding the property and making repairs or improvements. Access allows the landlord entry for the purposes of showing the property to interested third parties such as: lenders, purchasers, and a new tenant. The landlord should make an appointment with the tenant to gain entry, and only in an emergency should the landlord enter the property without the tenant's prior approval.

ACCESSION The right of an owner to claim property added or joined to their property by natural means or by labor or material of another party. If a prop-

erty owner accidently builds part of a garage onto a neighbor's property, the neighbor will be the owner unless the neighbor has otherwise agreed.
See ACCRETION, ALLUVION, ANNEX, TACKING.

ACCESSORY BUILDING A building or structure detached from but on the same property as a main building. Examples of an accessory building are: garages, storage buildings, and guest houses.

ACCIDENT AND HEALTH PREMIUM A premium paid by a mortgagor for an insurance policy to ensure the continuance of mortgage payments if the borrower is disabeled or ill.

ACCOMMODATION PARTY One who accommodates another by signing a note or a bill without receiving compensation. A *note* being a negotiable instrument such as a promissory note.

ACCOUNTING NET YIELD The net yield rate of interest that a servicer of mortgage loans remits monthly to the investor.

ACCRETION PROCESS (1) Accretion is the addition of value over time. In CMO accrual bonds, it is the accumulation of accrued coupon payments that represent increased principal. The CMO bond (as an accrual type) is also known as a bond of compound interest. The accretion process comes into play with accrued interest increasing in quantity for the principal other than in cash applied, as such. The accretion process remains active in coupon bonds of the accrual type periodically over its life, as opposed to coupon bonds conforming to a standard zero coupon. (2) An addition to property by a gradual deposit of soil or an increase of exposed land by a permanent receding of the water.
See ACCESSION, ANNEX, TACKING.

ACCRUAL BASIS For federal income tax purposes, it is an accounting method for counting income and expenses when earned or applicable as opposed to counting income and expenses received or paid.
See CASH BASIS.

ACCRUED INTEREST Interest earned but not paid since the last due date. This term is heard frequently in discussions of adjustable rate mortgages that allow negative amortization. The negative amortization for an ARM loan is the accrued interest.
See NEGATIVE AMORTIZATION.

ACH *See* AUTOMATED CLEARING HOUSE.

ACKNOWLEDGEMENT A written certification or declaration stating that an execution of an instrument, such as a deed or note, is of a person's own free will. An acknowledgment is a declaration or certification usually made before a notary public or an attesting officer.
See AFFIDAVIT, ATTESTATION, CERTIFICATION, NOTARIZE.

ACOUSTICAL TILE Tile that absorbs sound. Acoustical tile is often used in the ceilings of apartment units and offices.

ACQUISITION COST *See* FHA - ACQUISITION COST.

ACRE (AC) Land that measures 43,560 square feet. A lot 208.71' × 208.71' is: 4,840 square yards, 4,047 square meters, 160 square rods, 0.4047 hectare, and 43,560 square feet.

ACT OF GOD An event that causes damage by nature such as a flood, earthquake, or winds; an occurrence not caused by man.

ACTION TO QUIET TITLE A court action to establish ownership of real property. This court action usually removes any interest or claim to title of real estate. The *action* results in removing any cloud on the title. Normally a lender will not commit to a mortgage with a cloud on the title. If the complainant is successful in the court action, the title is made quiet or is clean.

ACTUARY A mathematical expert who calculates insurance risks and, therefore, the premiums to cover those risks.

ADAPTIVE REUSE An older but sound structure made useful by providing a new use for the building. An example would be an abandoned warehouse converted into commercial space or residential condominiums.

ADDENDUM An agreement or list added to a contract or agreement or other document such as a letter of intent. FHA and VA require that you include it as an addendum or incorporate it in any sales contract written before the appraisal. People refer to the addendum as the *amendatory language*.
See FHA AMENDATORY LANGUAGE and VA AMENDATORY LANGUAGE.

ADD-ON INTEREST Interest added to the amount of the loan on the front end or beginning of the loan repayment period. The balance is then paid by installments. This form of interest is much more expensive than simple interest paid on the entire amount for the entire term of the loan. Car loans use add-on interest.

AD-HOC TRANSACTION For this exclusive loan transaction.

ADJOIN Connect or join. If two pieces of property touch each other, they *adjoin* or *abut* each other.
See ABUT, CONTIGUOUS.

ADJUDICATION A court decision or judgment.

ADJUSTABLE RATE MORTGAGE (ARM) **(For the FHA ARM loan, see FHA - ADJUSTABLE MORTGAGE** A mortgage with an interest rate that adjusts and is not fixed. Loans without a fixed rate are commonly called ARMs or Adjustable Mortgage Loans (AMLs). They are also known as a Flexible Rate Mortgage or Variable Rate Mortgage and there is an almost infinite variety of these mortgages. With an ARM loan, part of the interest rate risk transfers to the borrower and away from the lender. ARM loans will have a lower rate than fixed rate loans because of the risk transfer feature.

Adjustable rate mortgages have an interest rate that increases or decreases over the life of the loan based upon market conditions. In most adjustable rate loans the starting rate, or initial interest rate, is lower than the rate offered on a standard fixed rate mortgage. A financial index governs the changes in the interest rate. When the index rises, so will the interest rate; the opposite happens when the index falls. Examples of these indices include the Federal Home Loan Bank Board's national average mortgage rate and the U.S. Treasury bill rate. Generally, the more sensitive the index is to market changes, the more frequently the rate can increase or decrease.

Adjustable Rate Mortgages have two important terms, the index and the margin. An index is the benchmark used to adjust the interest rate at specified times in the future. For example, a one-year adjustable rate mortgage may have a one-year Treasury bill as the index. If the one year T-bill is the index, each yearly adjustment period of the rate will involve the price of a one-year Treasury bill and will usually be a price determined by a weekly or monthly average over a specified time.

Margin is the lender's profit. To decide the interest rate for an adjustable rate loan, add the margin to the index. Example: Assuming the index is 10% and the margin is 2.5%, the rate will be 12.5%. One word of caution: do not assume that the lower the margin, the lower the lender's profit. A lender may charge a low margin, but have a high measure for an index or have shorter adjustment periods. Adjustable rate mortgages must be looked at in their entirety; what a lender gives on one feature may be more than taken back by another.

Some ARM loans advertise an option of converting from an adjustable rate loan to a fixed rate loan. The option is a *conversion feature*. A conversion feature sounds like an answer to a prayer, but it can be an illusion. Before concluding that you can offset risks with an ARM loan by simply getting out of it with a conversion feature, you should check of the following points:

(1)   Is there a prepayment penalty during the life of the loan?

(2)   Is there a charge for the conversion? If so, how much?

(3)   What is the formula for determining the fixed rate?

Lenders use *payment caps* or *rate caps* to make adjustable rate loans somewhat predictable and limit the amount an interest rate may change. These provisions limit the borrower's risk. However, if there are no payment or rate caps, the interest rate and monthly payments will fluctuate according to the index.

Adjustable rate mortgages may incorporate payment caps that limit the rise of monthly payments. For instance, though the interest rate may increase on an adjustable rate loan, the monthly payment may not increase by the full amount required by the index. This may occur because the payments themselves are capped. For example, if the ARM loan provides for unlimited changes in the interest rate but the loan has a $50 per year cap on payment increases, a borrower who started with a 14% rate on 9/1/82 on a $50,000 mortgage and a monthly payment of $592.44 will experience only $50 annual payment increases despite the index movement. In this example, the index increased 2 percentage points in the first year and the rate increased to 16%. Payments should have risen to $671.80. However, due to the payment cap, monthly increases rose only to $642.44.

But, payment-capped loans do not require the borrower to pay the difference between the cap and the interest rate. Negative amortization usually takes place with payment-capped loans to ensure that the lender eventually receives the full amount of the principal plus interest. In most payment-capped mortgages, the amount of principal increases when interest rates rise. Thus, the borrower now owes (and eventually will pay) interest on interest.

Rate caps limit the increase or decrease in the interest rate of the mortgage. There are usually rate caps for each adjustment period and rate caps for the life of the loan. Rate caps prevent negative amortization.

Assume an initial rate of 7%, annual rate caps of 2%, a lifetime cap of 5%, a margin of 2.75%, the one year T-bill as the index and the T-bill is 6.5%. Assuming the T-bill rate in the second year is 7.5%, the new rate should be 10.25% (the total of the index plus the margin) but the rate is 9% because of the 2% cap limitation. Assuming a T-bill rate of 8.5% in the third year, the new rate should be 11.25 (8.5 + 2.75), but the rate is 11% because of the 2% cap. Assuming a T-bill rate of 9.5% in the fourth year, the rate should be 12.25%, but the rate is capped at 12% because of the 5% lifetime cap. Assuming a T-bill rate of 7% in the fifth year, the rate should be 9.75%, but it is 10% because of the 2% cap in the upward or downward adjustment in the rate.

The following offers a summary of the above numbers:

Year	Rate	Margin	Index Rate + Margin	Rate
1	6.5%	2.75	9.25%	7%
2	7.5%	2.75	10.25%	9%
3	8.5%	2.75	11.25%	11%
4	9.5%	2.75	12.25%	12%
5	7.0%	2.75	9.75%	10%

Use the following check list to make a comparison of Adjustable Rate Mortgage Loans. At the end of the list you count the number of times A or B "wins."

Lenders will use a form like the one in Exhibit 1 to make disclosures about ARM loans.

Use the following checklist to make a comparison of Adjustable Rate Mortgages.

	Mortgage A	Mortgage B	Wins (A or B)
Start Rate			
Fully Indexed Rate (Index + Margin)	_____	_____	_____
Initial Monthly Payment	_____	_____	_____
Fully Indexed Payment (Index + Margin)	_____	_____	_____
Current Index Rate	_____	_____	_____
Margin	_____	_____	_____
Adjustment Period	_____	_____	_____
Type of Index	_____	_____	_____
If Index is different; which is less volatile? (refer to page 344-347)	_____	_____	_____
Method used for Adjustments i.e., monthly or weekly average?	_____	_____	_____

	Mortgage A	Mortgage B	Wins (A or B)
Discounted Rate Period	_____	_____	_____
Rate Cap per Adjustment	_____	_____	_____
Life Time Rate Cap	_____	_____	_____
Cost of Buydowns	_____	_____	_____
Is Buydown Short Term or Permanent?	_____	_____	_____
Cost of Mortgage Insurance	_____	_____	_____
Cost of Title Insurance	_____	_____	_____

If ARM has a Conversion Feature, what would rate be today?

Cost for conversion	_____	_____	_____
Prepayment Feature	_____	_____	_____
Closing Costs	_____	_____	_____
Points	_____	_____	_____
Assumable?	_____	_____	_____
Can Terms change on Assumption?	_____	_____	_____
Negative Amortization	_____	_____	_____

For ARM loans with the possibility of Negative Amortization:

Payment Caps	_____	_____	_____
Cap for Negative Amortization	_____	_____	_____
If deferred interest involved, does it accumulate on a interest or non-interest bearing basis?	_____	_____	_____
Special Requirements for Mortgage, Title, Hazard Insurance	_____	_____	_____

Amount of "Wins" by: A_____ B_____

See COMPUTERIZED LOAN ORIGINATIONS for a comparison of an ARM loan with a Fixed Rate Mortgage. *See* NEGATIVE AMORTIZATION.

Exhibit 1

VMP MORTGAGE FORMS • (313)293-8100 • (800)521-7291

-790 (8807)

☐ VARIABLE RATE MORTGAGE PROGRAM DISCLOSURE
(This is neither a contract nor a commitment to lend.)

LENDER:

VARIABLE RATE MORTGAGE PROGRAM:

This Variable Rate Mortgage Program Disclosure describes the features of the adjustable rate mortgage (ARM) you are considering. Information on other variable rate mortgage programs is available upon request.

HOW YOUR INTEREST RATE AND PAYMENT ARE DETERMINED

☐ Your interest rate will be based on an index plus a margin.

☐ This variable rate mortgage loan has a discount feature, and your initial interest rate will not be based on the index used for later adjustments. Please ask about our current discount amount.

☐ This type of ARM loan carries a provision for a change in: ☐ the Interest Rate ☐ the Monthly Payment ☐ the Loan Term.

Your payment will be based on the interest rate, loan balance and loan term.

The index used to determine your initial interest rate and/or all adjustments is:

NOTE: If the index for your variable rate mortgage loan is no longer available, the Lender will choose a new index which is based on comparable information.

Information about the index can be found:

Your interest rate will be equal to

Ask us for our current interest rate and margin.

HOW YOUR INTEREST RATE CAN CHANGE

Your interest rate can change	, and every thereafter.
Your interest rate cannot increase more than	percentage point(s) at each adjustment.
Your interest rate cannot decrease more than	percentage point(s) at each adjustment.
Your interest rate cannot increase more than	percentage point(s) over the term of the loan.
Your interest rate cannot decrease more than	percentage point(s) over the term of the loan.

Your interest rate will be rounded off to ☐ the nearest ☐ next highest ☐ next lowest   % at each adjustment.

☐ This variable rate loan utilizes interest rate carryover.
EXAMPLE:

HOW YOUR PAYMENT CAN CHANGE

Your payment can change , and every thereafter, based on changes in the interest rate.

☐ Your payment will not increase more than percentage point(s) or $, at each adjustment.

You will be notified in writing days before the due date of a payment at a new level. This notice will contain information about your interest rates, payment amount and loan balance.

EXAMPLE: On a $10,000, year loan with an initial interest rate of percent, (the rate shown in the interest rate column for the year), the maximum amount that the interest rate can rise under this program is percentage points, to %, and the payment can rise from a first year payment of $ to a maximum of $ in the year.

Any increase in interest will take the form of ☐ a larger amount due at maturity ☐ higher payment amount or ☐ more payments of the same amount.

☐ This variable rate loan program has a negative amortization feature. An increase in your interest rate will result in your loan being negatively amortized, and the following will apply:

YOUR INTEREST RATE CONVERSION OPTION

☐ This variable rate mortgage loan program has an option for you to convert your variable interest rate to a fixed interest rate. You should be aware that if you exercise this option, the interest rate may be increased from the variable rate you have been paying. If you choose this conversion option, you may only convert if certain conditions are met. These conditions are:
1.
2.
3.
4.
5.

Page 1

1. Complete page one.
2. Remove this stub (bottom), and extract carbon.
3. Turn over and complete page two.

Exhibit 1 (continued)

- 790 (8807)   VMP MORTGAGE FORMS • (313)293-8100 • (800)521-7291

⌋

You may only convert to a fixed interest rate on _ , and only during
the following time period: _

Your new fixed interest rate will be determined by: _

ADDITIONAL FEATURES OF YOUR VARIABLE RATE MORTGAGE PROGRAM

Someone buying this property ☐ cannot assume the remaining balance due under original mortgage terms ☐ may assume, subject to lender's conditions, the remaining balance due under original mortgage terms.

This Variable Rate Mortgage Program Disclosure ☐ does ☐ does not have a Demand Feature.

The Demand Feature is subject to the following:

Other additional features:

HISTORIC EXAMPLE

The example below shows how your payments would have changed under this variable rate mortgage program based on actual changes in the index from   to   . This does not necessarily indicate how your index will change in the future. The example is based on the following assumptions:

Amount . . . . $10,000   Caps   periodic interest rate cap
Term . . . .   lifetime interest rate cap
Change Date . . . .   payment cap
Payment Adjustment . . . .   Interest rate carryover
Interest Adjustment . . . .   Negative amortization
Margin* . . . .   Interest rate discount****
                                                                        Index

Year (as of)	Index (%)	Margin (percentage pts.)	Interest Rate (%)	Monthly Payment ($)	Remaining Balance ($)

To see what your payments would have been during that period, divide your mortgage amount by $10,000; then multiply the
payment by that amount. (For example, in   the   would be $ payment for
a mortgage amount of $ taken out in   × $10,000
=   =

    * This is a margin we have used recently; your margin may be different.
   ** This interest rate reflects a   percentage point annual interest rate cap.
  *** This interest rate reflects a   percentage point lifetime interest rate cap.
 **** This is a discount we have used recently; your discount may be different.

I/We hereby acknowledge receipt of this Variable Rate Mortgage Program Disclosure and a copy of the Consumer Handbook on Adjustable Rate Mortgages on the date indicated below.

_____   _____
Borrower/Date   Borrower/Date

Exhibit 2
Common Adjustable Rate Mortgage Indices

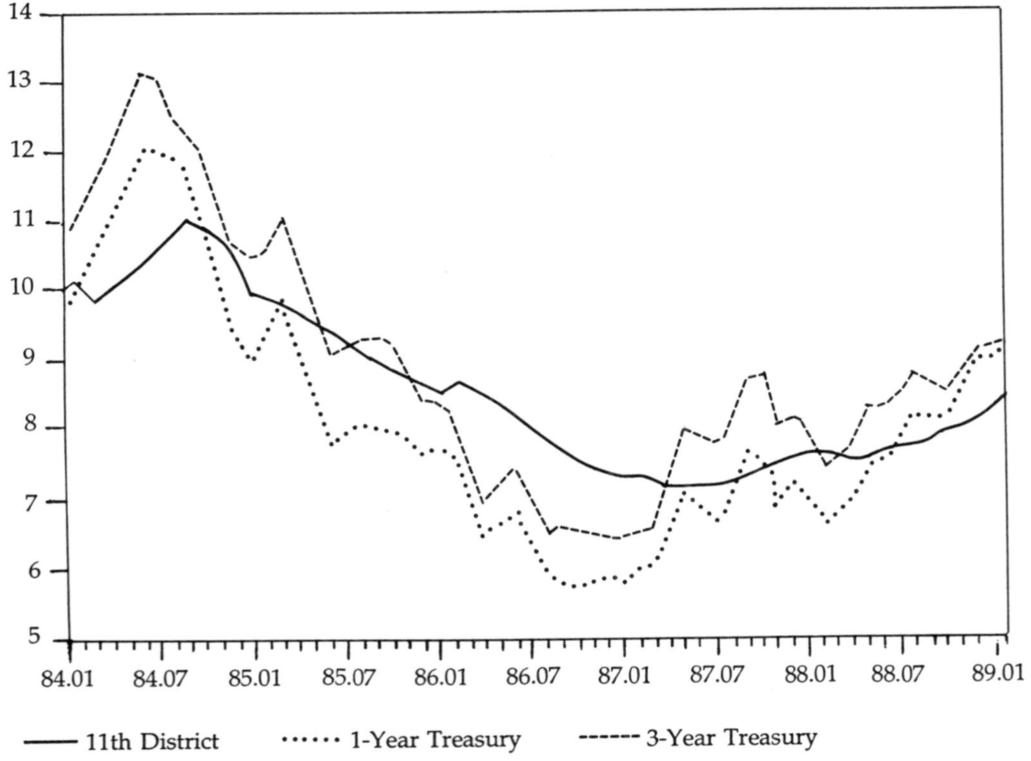

———— 11th District ⋯⋯⋯⋯ 1-Year Treasury - - - - - 3-Year Treasury

Exhibit 3
A Recent History of Several Major Indices

6 Month T-bills (Discount Basis)

	1973	1974	1975	1976	1977	1978	1979	1980
JAN	5.53	7.63	6.53	5.24	4.78	6.69	9.50	11.85
FEB	5.75	6.87	5.67	5.14	4.90	6.74	9.35	12.72
MAR	6.43	7.83	5.64	5.49	4.88	6.64	9.46	15.10
APR	6.53	8.17	6.01	5.20	4.79	6.70	9.50	13.62
MAY	6.62	8.50	5.65	5.60	5.19	7.02	9.53	9.15
JUN	7.23	8.23	5.46	5.78	5.20	7.20	9.06	7.22
JUL	8.08	8.03	6.49	5.60	5.35	7.47	9.19	8.10
AUG	8.70	8.85	6.94	5.42	5.81	7.36	9.45	9.44
SEP	8.54	8.60	6.87	5.31	5.99	7.95	10.13	10.55
OCT	7.26	7.56	6.39	5.07	6.41	8.49	11.34	11.57
NOV	7.82	7.55	5.75	4.94	6.43	9.20	11.86	13.61
DEC	7.44	7.09	5.93	4.51	6.38	9.40	11.85	14.77

	1981	1982	1983	1984	1985	1986	1987	1988
JAN	13.88	12.93	7.90	9.06	8.03	7.13	5.47	6.31
FEB	14.13	13.71	8.23	9.13	8.34	7.08	5.60	5.96
MAR	12.98	12.62	8.33	9.58	8.92	6.60	5.56	5.91
APR	13.43	12.68	8.34	9.83	8.31	6.07	5.93	6.21
MAY	15.33	12.22	8.20	10.31	7.75	6.16	6.11	6.53
JUN	13.95	12.31	8.89	10.55	7.16	6.28	5.99	6.76
JUL	14.40	12.24	9.29	10.58	7.35	5.85	5.86	6.97
AUG	15.55	10.11	9.53	10.65	7.27	5.58	6.14	7.36
SEP	15.06	9.54	9.19	10.51	7.27	5.31	6.57	7.43
OCT	14.01	8.30	8.90	10.05	7.32	5.26	6.86	7.50
NOV	11.53	8.32	8.89	8.99	7.26	5.42	6.23	7.76
DEC	11.47	8.23	9.14	8.36	7.09	5.53	6.36	8.24

1 Year Treasury

	1973	1974	1975	1976	1977	1978	1979	1980
JAN	5.89	7.42	6.83	5.81	5.29	7.28	10.41	12.06
FEB	6.19	6.88	5.98	5.91	5.47	7.34	10.24	13.92
MAR	6.85	7.76	6.11	6.21	5.50	7.31	10.25	15.82
APR	6.85	8.62	6.90	5.92	5.44	7.45	10.12	13.30
MAY	6.89	8.78	6.39	6.40	5.84	7.82	10.12	9.39
JUN	7.31	8.67	6.29	6.52	5.80	8.09	9.57	8.16
JUL	8.39	8.79	7.11	6.20	5.94	8.39	9.64	8.65
AUG	8.82	9.36	7.70	6.00	6.37	8.31	9.98	10.24
SEP	8.31	8.87	7.75	5.84	6.53	8.64	10.84	11.52
OCT	7.40	8.05	6.95	5.50	6.97	9.14	12.44	12.49
NOV	7.57	7.66	6.49	5.29	6.95	10.01	12.39	14.15
DEC	7.27	7.31	6.60	4.89	6.96	10.30	11.98	14.88

	1981	1982	1983	1984	1985	1986	1987	1988
JAN	14.08	14.32	8.62	9.90	9.02	7.73	5.78	6.99
FEB	14.57	14.73	8.92	10.04	9.29	7.61	5.96	6.64
MAR	13.71	13.95	9.04	10.59	9.86	7.03	6.03	6.71
APR	14.32	13.98	8.98	10.90	9.14	6.44	6.50	7.01
MAY	16.20	13.34	8.90	11.66	8.46	6.65	7.00	7.40
JUN	14.86	14.07	9.66	12.08	7.80	6.73	6.80	7.49
JUL	15.72	13.24	10.20	12.03	7.86	6.27	6.68	7.75
AUG	16.72	11.43	10.53	11.82	8.05	5.93	7.03	8.17
SEP	16.52	10.85	10.16	11.58	8.07	5.77	7.67	8.09
OCT	15.38	9.32	9.81	10.90	8.01	5.72	7.59	8.11
NOV	12.41	9.16	9.94	9.82	7.88	5.80	6.96	8.48
DEC	12.85	8.91	10.11	9.33	7.68	5.87	7.17	8.99

Exhibit 3 (continued)

3 Year Treasury

	1973	1974	1975	1976	1977	1978	1979	1980
JAN	6.27	6.96	7.23	6.99	6.22	7.61	9.50	10.88
FEB	6.58	6.76	6.65	7.06	6.44	7.67	9.29	12.84
MAR	6.86	7.35	6.81	7.13	6.47	7.70	9.38	14.05
APR	6.78	8.05	7.76	6.84	6.32	7.85	9.43	12.02
MAY	6.83	8.27	7.39	7.27	6.55	8.07	9.42	9.44
JUN	6.83	8.15	7.17	7.31	6.39	8.30	8.95	8.91
JUL	7.54	8.41	7.72	7.12	6.51	8.54	8.94	9.27
AUG	7.89	8.66	8.16	6.86	6.79	8.33	9.14	10.63
SEP	7.25	8.41	8.29	6.66	6.84	8.41	9.69	11.57
OCT	6.81	8.00	7.81	6.24	7.19	8.62	10.95	12.01
NOV	7.00	7.61	7.46	6.09	7.22	9.04	11.18	13.31
DEC	6.81	7.24	7.44	5.68	7.30	9.33	10.71	13.65

	1981	1982	1983	1984	1985	1986	1987	1988
JAN	13.01	14.64	9.64	10.93	10.43	8.41	6.41	7.87
FEB	13.65	14.73	9.91	11.05	10.55	8.10	6.56	7.38
MAR	13.51	14.13	9.84	11.59	11.05	7.30	6.58	7.50
APR	14.09	14.18	9.76	11.98	10.49	6.86	7.32	7.83
MAY	15.08	13.77	9.66	12.75	9.75	7.27	8.02	8.24
JUN	14.29	14.48	10.32	13.18	9.05	7.41	7.82	8.22
JUL	15.15	14.00	10.90	13.08	9.18	6.86	7.74	8.44
AUG	16.00	12.62	11.30	12.50	9.31	6.49	8.03	8.77
SEP	16.22	12.03	11.07	12.34	9.37	6.62	8.67	8.57
OCT	15.50	10.62	10.87	11.85	9.25	6.56	8.75	8.43
NOV	13.11	9.98	10.96	10.90	8.88	6.46	7.99	8.72
DEC	13.66	9.88	11.13	10.56	8.40	6.43	8.13	9.11

5 Year Treasury

	1973	1974	1975	1976	1977	1978	1979	1980
JAN	6.34	6.95	7.41	7.46	6.58	7.77	9.20	10.74
FEB	6.60	6.82	7.11	7.45	6.83	7.83	9.13	12.60
MAR	6.81	7.31	7.30	7.49	6.93	7.86	9.20	13.47
APR	6.67	7.92	7.99	7.25	6.79	7.98	9.25	11.84
MAY	6.80	8.18	7.72	7.59	6.94	8.18	9.24	9.95
JUN	6.69	8.10	7.51	7.61	6.76	8.36	8.85	9.21
JUL	7.33	8.38	7.92	7.49	6.84	8.54	8.90	9.53
AUG	7.63	8.63	8.33	7.31	7.03	8.33	9.06	10.84
SEP	7.05	8.37	8.37	7.13	7.04	8.43	9.41	11.62
OCT	6.77	7.97	7.97	6.75	7.32	8.61	10.63	11.86
NOV	6.92	7.68	7.80	6.52	7.34	8.84	10.93	12.83
DEC	6.80	7.31	7.76	6.10	7.48	9.08	10.42	13.25

	1981	1982	1983	1984	1985	1986	1987	1988
JAN	12.77	14.65	10.03	11.37	10.93	8.68	6.64	8.18
FEB	13.41	14.54	10.26	11.54	11.13	8.34	6.79	7.71
MAR	13.41	13.98	10.08	12.02	11.52	7.46	6.79	7.83
APR	13.99	14.00	10.02	12.37	11.01	7.05	7.57	8.19
MAY	14.63	13.75	10.03	13.17	10.34	7.52	8.26	8.58
JUN	13.95	14.43	10.63	13.48	9.60	7.64	8.02	8.49
JUL	14.79	14.07	11.21	13.27	9.70	7.06	8.01	8.66
AUG	15.56	13.00	11.63	12.68	9.81	6.80	8.32	8.94
SEP	15.93	12.25	11.43	12.53	9.81	6.92	8.94	8.69
OCT	15.41	10.80	11.28	12.06	9.69	6.83	9.08	8.51
NOV	13.38	10.38	11.41	11.33	9.28	6.76	8.35	8.79
DEC	13.60	10.22	11.54	11.07	8.73	6.67	8.45	9.09

Exhibit 3 (continued)

National Median Cost of Funds

	*1979	1980	1981	1982	1983	1984	1985	1986
JAN	—	8.09	9.50	11.44	10.14	9.89	9.75	8.50
FEB	—	8.29	9.82	11.26	9.75	9.73	9.40	8.29
MAR	—	7.95	10.24	11.37	9.72	9.73	9.36	8.35
APR	—	8.79	10.40	11.35	9.62	9.64	9.29	8.22
MAY	7.35	9.50	10.59	11.39	9.62	9.74	9.19	8.12
JUN	7.27	9.41	10.79	11.38	9.54	9.67	8.95	7.95
JUL	7.44	9.18	10.92	11.54	9.65	9.90	8.87	7.94
AUG	7.49	8.98	10.76	11.50	9.81	10.01	8.77	7.80
SEP	7.38	8.78	11.02	11.17	9.74	9.93	8.63	7.59
OCT	7.47	8.60	11.53	10.91	9.85	10.15	8.59	7.50
NOV	7.77	8.68	11.68	10.62	9.82	10.04	8.50	7.33
DEC	7.87	8.84	11.58	10.43	9.90	9.92	8.48	7.28

	1987	1988
JAN	7.22	7.12
FEB	7.02	7.11
MAR	6.99	7.13
APR	6.93	7.12
MAY	6.92	7.11
JUN	6.90	7.11
JUL	6.96	7.14
AUG	6.95	7.21
SEP	6.93	7.21
OCT	7.03	7.29
NOV	7.04	
DEC	7.11	

11th District Cost of Funds

	*1978	1979	1980	1981	1982	1983	1984	1985
JAN	6.49	7.25	8.76	10.45	11.95	10.46	10.03	10.22
FEB	7.10	7.92	9.65	11.16	12.34	10.42	10.17	10.16
MAR	6.51	7.42	8.86	10.95	12.14	9.87	9.98	9.98
APR	6.68	7.67	9.82	11.14	12.17	9.81	10.14	9.97
MAY	6.61	7.67	10.41	11.43	12.17	9.63	10.26	9.70
JUN	6.75	7.76	10.08	12.14	12.67	9.82	10.43	9.57
JUL	6.69	7.68	9.67	11.85	12.23	9.68	10.71	9.37
AUG	6.71	7.77	9.39	12.03	11.96	9.97	10.86	9.27
SEP	6.89	7.91	9.29	12.33	11.77	10.00	11.04	9.13
OCT	6.83	7.79	9.11	12.29	11.29	10.00	10.99	9.03
NOV	7.11	8.42	9.52	12.47	11.04	10.03	10.89	9.04
DEC	7.04	8.65	9.63	12.18	11.09	10.19	10.52	8.88

	1986	1987	1988
JAN	8.77	7.40	7.615
FEB	8.96	7.45	7.647
MAR	8.74	7.31	7.509
APR	8.59	7.25	7.519
MAY	8.44	7.22	7.497
JUN	8.37	7.27	7.618
JUL	8.20	7.28	7.593
AUG	8.02	7.28	7.659
SEP	7.90	7.39	7.847
OCT	7.72	7.44	7.828
NOV	7.60	7.56	7.914
DEC	7.51	7.65	

Exhibit 3 (continued)

FHLBB Contract Rate

	1973	1974	1975	1976	1977	1978	1979	1980
JAN	7.53	8.47	9.32	9.07	8.84	8.95	10.08	11.78
FEB	7.55	8.53	9.19	9.03	8.80	8.99	10.14	12.30
MAR	7.54	8.47	9.07	8.92	8.76	9.04	10.22	12.56
APR	7.55	8.43	8.92	8.85	8.74	9.14	10.29	13.21
MAY	7.62	8.49	8.85	8.84	8.75	9.17	10.35	13.74
JUN	7.64	8.66	8.86	8.82	8.78	9.27	10.46	12.88
JUL	7.70	8.82	8.89	8.85	8.83	9.41	10.67	12.23
AUG	7.87	8.95	8.95	8.91	8.86	9.55	10.88	11.89
SEP	8.10	9.15	8.93	8.94	8.86	9.62	10.94	12.00
OCT	8.35	9.31	8.97	8.94	8.88	9.68	11.01	12.31
NOV	8.42	9.37	9.09	8.91	8.89	9.74	11.23	12.85
DEC	8.46	9.39	9.09	8.90	8.93	9.85	11.59	13.15

	1981	1982	1983	1984	1985	1986	1987	1988
JAN	13.24	15.37	13.04	11.70	12.09	10.40	9.19	8.92
FEB	13.73	15.22	12.88	11.73	11.90	10.46	8.89	8.84
MAR	13.91	15.07	12.61	11.69	11.72	10.24	8.80	8.84
APR	13.99	15.39	12.42	11.61	11.62	10.00	8.79	8.93
MAY	14.19	15.57	12.36	11.63	11.62	9.80	8.93	8.90
JUN	14.40	15.01	12.21	11.79	11.29	9.83	9.02	8.98
JUL	14.77	14.96	12.18	12.03	11.02	9.88	9.05	8.98
AUG	15.03	15.03	12.25	12.24	10.87	9.88	9.05	9.00
SEP	15.38	14.71	12.38	12.43	10.76	9.71	8.91	8.98
OCT	15.47	14.37	12.19	12.52	10.86	9.59	8.86	9.11
NOV	15.80	13.74	12.11	12.38	10.80	9.48	8.89	9.16
DEC	15.53	13.44	11.94	12.26	10.70	9.29	8.86	9.31

Source: Telerate
*Data not available prior to this date.

ADJUSTED BASIS The original cost of the property plus improvements (including what it cost to sell the property), less depreciation. Calculate the gain on the sale by subtracting the adjusted basis from the sale price.

ADJUSTABLE RATE PREFERRED STOCK (ARPS) Variable rate securities that can reduce a firm's interest rate risk.

AD LITEM Legal term that describes a guardian appointed to prosecute or defend a lawsuit for a minor or an incompetent individual.

ADMINISTRATOR A person appointed by an appropriate court of law to settle the estate of a person who died without a will (intestate). The specific duty of the administrator decides the type of administrator, there are many kinds of administrators.

ADMINISTRATRIX A female administrator.

ADOBE

Adobe. A home made of adobe brick with projecting roof beams called "viga."

AD VALOREM A method of taxation using a fixed proportion of property value; for example, real estate taxes collected at the rate of a specific dollar amount of appraised value or assessment. People use the Ad Valorem method as a formula to decide how much tax to pay the government. A commonly used formula for computing taxes is as follows: (assumptions: properties are assessed at 25% of valuation, appraisal is $100,000, and the tax rate is $7.50 per $100). The formula for deciding the tax amount is as follows:

$$\$100,000 \times 25\% = \$25,000 \div \$100 = 250 \ (\$100 \text{ units}), \ 250 \times \$7.50 =$$
$$\$1,875 \div \ 12 \ (12 \text{ months}) = \$156.25 \text{ per month.}$$

See PROPERTY TAX.

ADVANCE To give someone a draw or payment by making them a loan. For savings institutions it is usually a loan from a Federal Home Loan Bank to a member institution. Advances in real estate may refer to a partial disbursement of funds under a note written as a construction loan.

Advance can mean a payment by a party not under obligation to do so but who pays the obligation to protect their interest. An example is the owner of a second mortgage paying back payments on the first mortgage to keep the first mortgagee from foreclosing. The person or institution making the advance adds it to the balance of the second mortgage.

See DRAW, GUARANTY PERFORMANCE.

ADVANCE COMMITMENT (Conditional) See FORWARD DELIVERY COMMITMENTS.

ADVERSE POSSESSION A method of acquiring title to property by the possession of the property for a statutory time in an open, notorious, continuous, exclusive, and adverse manner. The burden of proof is upon the party claiming adverse possession. The are several conditions to claim title by this method. The claim must be actual, it must be open so that anyone could see the claimant using the property, it must be continuous, it must be hostile and against the claim of any other party. The claim must be contrary to property owners who make periodic inspections of their property and issue written notices to people telling them to vacate property they occupy without the consent of the owner.

See COLOR OF TITLE, NOTORIOUS POSSESSION, QUIET TITLE ACTION.

AEOLIAN SOIL Soil composed of materials deposited by the wind. See the topical index for other types of soil.

AESTHETIC VALUE The value attributable to beauty created by improvements and natural surroundings. A densely wooded lot can add aesthetic value to the property.

AFFIDAVIT A written statement sworn before a notary public or an officer with authority to administer an oath. An affidavit is an instrument by itself. A certification or an acknowledgement is always part of another instrument.
See ATTESTATION.

AFFIDAVIT OF TITLE A sworn statement by a seller that: (1) says the title conveyed is free from any clouds or defects, (2) identifies the owner and the owner's marital status, and (3) verifies that the owner is in possession of the property.

AFFINITY Relationship other than by blood. It usually means a relationship by marriage, but can mean a group organized for a specific purpose such as a club or a business relationship. For example, a credit union uses a mortgage banking company to originate residential loans for their members. The credit union and mortgage banking company are in an affinity relationship to each other.
See FHA - SECTION 221, SHARED EQUITY.

AFFIRMATIVE MARKETING AGREEMENT A method used by HUD to assure minorities of a fair housing plan. Authority for the program began with Title VIII of the Civil Rights Act of 1968.

AFTER-ACQUIRED CLAUSE A provision in a mortgage that allows the lien to apply to any additional property acquired by the mortgagor. The lender is further protected by the after-acquired clause that serves as a vehicle to create additional collateral for the loan as the mortgagor acquires more property.

AFTER-TAX CASH FLOW Cash flow minus income taxes.

AGENCY The relationship between an Agent and a Principal. Agencies can be specific or general.
An example of a *general agency* is a landlord giving a property manager the right to manage property. The property manager, according to a management contract, can rent to individuals, evict tenants, authorize repairs, and perform many other duties.
An example of a *specific agency* is a property owner giving a real estate agent a listing to find a buyer for the owner's property. The real estate agent is confined to finding a ready, willing, and able buyer.
In mortgage lending, *agency* also means an affiliated agency of the government, e.g., FHA, VA, FNMA, FHLMC.
See INVESTOR.

AGENT A person authorized to represent or act for another person (the principal) in negotiations with third parties. The authority may be expressed or implied. The principal difference between an agent and an employee is the agent can bind the principal to a contract, according to an agreement between principal and agent. An employee cannot bind an employer unless given specific authority.

See RESPONDEAT SUPERIOR.

AGRARIAN Something that relates to land or to a distribution or division of land.

AGREEMENT OF SALE *See* CONTRACT.

AIA *See* AMERICAN INSTITUTE OF ARCHITECTS.

AICPA *See* AMERICAN INSTITUTE OF CERTIFIED PUBLIC ACCOUNTANTS.

AIR RIGHTS The right to use the space or air above the ground but not the ground itself. Air rights can be sold or leased.

Ownership of land includes air rights above the property. Some use of air rights, such as traveling through air space by airplane, no longer require the approval of the property owner.

AITD *See* ALL-INCLUSIVE TRUST DEED.

ALCOVE A recessed room connected to a main or larger room.

ALIENATION A transfer or conveyance of property. Alienation is voluntary when it is with the consent of the owner. Involuntary alienation is a transfer of property without the consent of the owner, as in a foreclosure, adverse possession, and eminent domain.

ALIENATION CLAUSE A clause closely associated in meaning with DUE-ON-SALE CLAUSE, and ACCELERATION CLAUSE. An alienation clause in a mortgage can give the lender the option to call the loan (declare the entire balance due) when the property owner transfers ownership, title, or interest, without the lender's consent.

ALL-INCLUSIVE TRUST DEED (AITD) A new deed of trust securing a balance due on an existing note plus new funds advanced. This technique is similar to a wraparound mortgage.

See WRAPAROUND MORTGAGE.

ALLODIAL SYSTEM Ownership of land with the owner having full and absolute dominion over the property. This system is the basis for our property rights in the United States. A contrasting system is the feudal system that gives ownership to the king or sovereign who gives rights to the citizenry to occupy land for a time.

ALLOTMENT Reservation of funds for the purchase of mortgages within a specified time. An allotment is when a mortgage lender has found a permanent investor but does not have a formal commitment with the investor.

ALLOWANCE FOR VACANCY AND INCOME LOSS An allowance used on pro-forma or profit and loss projections for income properties. You subtract an allowance for vacancy from gross income to decide net effective income (income before expenses). An investor cannot use rental that is 100% of occupancy. Depending on the market area, the vacancy allowance for income properties such as apartments is usually from 5% to 10% of the gross rental.

ALLUVION The opposite of diluvion. Soil gradually builds because of deposits from a waterway.

ALTERNATIVE DOCUMENTATION The reduction of processing time as a marketing tool has been long needed in the secondary and primary mortgage markets.

Occasionally called low documentation, low-doc, no qualifiers, easy qualifiers or priority loans. Alternative documentation programs normally require a 25% downpayment and a good credit rating. Since this approach first appeared in California, Fannie Mae and Freddie Mac have developed alternative documentation programs and now permit underwriters to use the approach in reducing time consuming verifications. This time reduction loan program, with large downpayments, is not used often because of competition from low down payment loans.

The borrower usually signs a form like or similar to Exhibit 4.

See PRIORITY MORTGAGE.

ALTERNATIVE MORTGAGE INSTRUMENT (AMI) A mortgage without a level payment. A mortgage such as an adjustable rate mortgage, graduated payment mortgage, growing equity mortgage, early retirement mortgage, are all an example of an alternative mortgage instrument.

ALLUVIAL, ALLUVION, OR ALLUVIUM Soil deposited by accretion along the shore or bank of a river.

Exhibit 4

 FannieMae

Borrower's Certification & Authorization
(TimeSaver Plus Documentation Program)

Certification

The undersigned certify the following:

1. I/We have applied for a mortgage loan from _(lender)_. In applying for the loan, I/we completed a loan application containing various information on the purpose of the loan, the amount and source of the down payment, employment and income information, and assets and liabilities. I/We certify that all of the information is true and complete. I/We made no misrepresentations in the loan application or other documents, nor did I/we omit any pertinent information.

2. I/We understand and agree that _(lender)_ reserves the right to change the mortgage loan review process to a full documentation program. This may include verifying the information provided on the application with the employer and/or the financial institution.

3. I/We fully understand that it is a Federal crime punishable by fine or imprisonment, or both, to knowingly make any false statements when applying for this mortgage, as applicable under the provisions of Title 18, United States Code, Section 1014.

Authorization to Release Information

To Whom It May Concern:

1. I/We have applied for a mortgage loan from _(lender)_. As part of the application process, _(lender)_ and the mortgage guaranty insurer (if any), may verify information contained in my/our loan application and in other documents required in connection with the loan, either before the loan is closed or as part of its quality control program.

2. I/We authorize you to provide to _(lender)_, and to any investor to whom _(lender)_ may sell my mortgage, and to the mortgage guaranty insurer (if any), any and all information and documentation that they request. Such information includes, but is not limited to, employment history and income; bank, money market, and similar account balances; credit history; and copies of income tax returns.

3. _(lender)_ or any investor that purchases the mortgage, or the mortgage guaranty insurer (if any), may address this authorization to any party named in the loan application.

4. A copy of this authorization may be accepted as an original.

5. Your prompt reply to _(lender)_, the investor that purchased the mortgage, or the mortgage guaranty insurer (if any) is appreciated.

6. Mortgage guaranty insurer (if any):

_____ _____
(Borrower's Signature) (Social Security Number)

_____ _____
(Borrower's Signature) (Social Security Number)

-1134 (9008)   VMP MORTGAGE FORMS • (313)293-8100 • (800)521-7291   Fannie Mae
Form 1097 Apr. 90

ALTA AMERICAN LAND TITLE ASSOCIATION.

A/M *See* ASSIGNMENT OF MORTGAGE.

AMA *See* AFFIRMATIVE MARKETING AGREEMENT.

AMENDATORY LANGUAGE *See* FHA - AMENDATORY LANGUAGE and VA -AMENDATORY LANGUAGE.

AMENITY A natural or man-made feature that increases the value of property. Examples would be a view of a golf course or the ocean or a beautifully landscaped yard.
See AESTHETIC VALUE.

AMERICAN BANKERS ASSOCIATION (ABA) A professional organization of banks based in Washington, D.C. that lobbies the federal government and monitors federal and state laws and regulations on issues pertinent to the banking industry. The association provides many membership services, including educational programs, seminars and publications.

AMERICAN INSTITUTE OF ARCHITECTS (AIA) A professional organizations of architects. All registered architects subscribe to the Standards of Ethical Practice.

AMERICAN INSTITUTE OF CERTIFIED PUBLIC ACCOUNTANTS A professional organization of certified public accountants. The AICPA is responsible for developing "GAAP" accounting - Generally Accepted Accounting Principles. The GAAP accounting method is considered decisive in absence of accounting methods. The AICPA awards the designation "CPA."

AMERICAN INSTITUTE OF REAL ESTATE APPRAISERS (AIREA) Formerly, a member organization of the National Association of REALTORS (NAR). The Institute, formed in 1932, has 22,000 members and candidates. Designations were MAI (Member of the Appraisal Institute) and RM (Residential Member). In 1990, the Institute severed their affiliation with the NAR and they merged with the Society of Real Estate Appraisers to form The Appraisal Institute. The AIREA officially began operation on January 1, 1991.

AMERICAN LAND TITLE ASSOCIATION (ALTA) An organization comprised of title insurance companies, abstractors and attorneys specializing in real property law. The ALTA has adopted many title insurance policy forms that standardize coverage nationally for property owners and lenders. Many states require the ALTA standardized title insurance policies.

See LOAN ORIGINATION PROCESS, Step 5.

AMERICAN MANSARD

American Mansard. A nineteenth century style house mainly distinguished by the mansard roof design. There are dormers protruding through the roof. The style features french doors, much decorative iron work and massive cornice and supporting brackets.

AMI *See* ALTERNATIVE MORTGAGE INSTRUMENT.

AML An acronym for Adjustable Mortgage Loan.
See ADJUSTABLE RATE MORTGAGE.

AMORTIZATION Loan amortization is paying off debt or mortgage, usually by monthly payments. Whether a loan is a level payment mortgage, graduated payment mortgage, adjustable graduated mortgage or variable rate mortgage, if it is an amortized loan, there will be a portion for interest and for principal reduction in every payment of the loan.

A Monthly Payment Amortization Factor Table (Exhibit 5) gives the various factors on a per $1,000 basis for interests rates from 8% to 19.5%. To use the table, multiply a loan amount by the factor, e.g., $89,235 @ 9.5% for 30 years = a monthly P&I payment of $750.33. Multiplying 89.235 × 8.4085 = $750.33.

See STANDING MORTGAGE.

Exhibit 5

Principal and Interest

Monthly Payment Amortization Factors
per $1,000 from 8% to 19.5% In
1/2% Increments for 30-Year and 15-Year Loans

30 Years		15 Years	
Rate	Factor	Rate	Factor
8%	7.3376	8%	9.5565
8.5	7.6891	8.5	9.8474
9.0	8.0462	9	10.1427
9.5	8.4085	9.5	10.4422
10	8.7757	10	10.7461
10.5	9.1474	10.5	11.0540
11	9.5232	11	11.3660
11.5	9.9029	11.5	11.6819
12	10.2861	12	12.0017
12.5	10.6726	12.5	12.3252
13	11.0620	13	12.6524
13.5	11.4541	13.5	12.9832
14	11.8487	14	13.3174
14.5	12.2456	14.5	13.6550
15	12.6444	15	13.9959
15.5	13.0452	15.5	14.3399
16	13.4476	16	14.6870
16.5	13.8515	16.5	15.0371
17	14.2568	17	15.3900
17.5	14.6633	17.5	15.7458
18	15.0709	18	16.1042
18.5	15.4794	18.5	16.4652
19	15.8889	19	16.8288
19.5	16.2992	19.5	17.1947

AMORTIZATION SCHEDULE A list showing the payment number, interest payment, principal payment, total payment and unpaid principal balance. People sometimes call an amortization schedule a *curtail schedule.*

AMOUNT FINANCED The base loan amount without regard to closing costs, discount points, or mortgage insurance premiums. This dollar amount is associated with a disclosure statement used in compliance with the Truth in Lending Act.
You can use the form in Exhibit 6 to disclose the amount financed.

AMOUNT TO MAKE THE PROPERTY OPERATIONAL (AMPO) An allowance that can be included in a HUD mortgage to provide a non-profit sponsor with required working capital to make a project operational.

AMPERE Measure of electrical current equal to the current produced by the force of one volt through the resistance of one ohm.

ANACONDA MORTGAGE A mortgage that uses the subject property as collateral for all debts from various loans owed to the lender. Courts may disagree with what a Anaconda Mortgage intends since they may require a direct relationship between each loan and the collateral acquired by the loan proceeds.
See DRAGNET CLAUSE, MOTHER HUBBARD CLAUSE.

ANCHOR BOLT A bolt that attaches the sill of a house to the foundation wall.

ANCHOR TENANT A retail store in a shopping center used as a major draw to the center. The presence of an anchor tenant helps secure financing of the center and enhances the chance of success for other tenants as it draws the public to its store. The store is normally part of a major chain and is a name easily recognized by the public. Depending on the size of the shopping center, there can be several anchor tenants.
See SATELLITE TENANT.

ANCILLARY INCOME Income that is secondary in nature and not the main reason for being in the business. Income that an investor would not receive if they were not in a particular business.
A prime example of ancillary income is related income from servicing mortgage loans. A lender receives a fee for servicing loans (collecting the monthly principal, interest, taxes and insurance premiums) that is normally a percentage of the loan balance. But, in servicing a loan, the lender has an

Exhibit 6

70819A

VMP_-16 (8802)   VMP MORTGAGE FORMS • (313)293-8100 • (800)521-7291

AMOUNT FINANCED ITEMIZATION

DATE
LENDER: LOAN NO.
                                                                           TYPE
                              BORROWERS
                              ADDRESS
                           CITY/STATE/ZIP
                              PROPERTY

ITEMIZATION OF THE AMOUNT FINANCED

$_____

$_____   AMOUNT GIVEN TO YOU DIRECTLY

$_____   AMOUNT PAID ON YOUR ACCOUNT

AMOUNTS PAID TO OTHERS ON YOUR BEHALF:

        AMOUNT   PAYEE/FOR

$_____   _____

$_____   _____

$_____   _____

$_____   _____

$_____   _____

$_____   _____

$_____   _____

$_____   _____

$_____   _____

$_____   _____

$_____   PRE PAID FINANCE CHARGE

I/WE ACKNOWLEDGE RECEIPT OF AMOUNT FINANCED ITEMIZATION, AND AUTHORIZE DIRECT DISBURSEMENT AS
SET FORTH IN THIS AMOUNT FINANCED ITEMIZATION.

_____   _____   _____   _____
        BORROWER   DATE   BORROWER   DATE

E = ESTIMATED
VMP_-16 (8802)   VMP MORTGAGE FORMS • (313)293-8100 • (800)521-7291

opportunity to sell the homeowner many services. The lender who services loans has a regular communication with the homeowners who mail in their payments. Some examples of services a lender can sell are: checking accounts, savings accounts, mortgage life insurance, disability insurance, car loans, boat loans, and many more.

ANNEX To attach or add; to add to something else.

ANNUAL CONTRIBUTIONS CONTRACT (ACC) Debt service payments made by HUD to public housing units or rent subsidies and administrative costs for the Section 8 Housing Assistance Payments Program. The number of families housed decides the amount of payments.

ANNUAL HOUSING SURVEY (AHS) An annual census by HUD and the Census Bureau to study housing units and trends in the movement of owners and renters.

ANNUAL PERCENTAGE RATE (APR) A method for calculating an interest rate to the interest collected, discount points charged to either purchaser or seller or both, and certain costs related to closing, and mortgage insurance premiums.

An Annual Percentage Rate represents the percentage relationship of the total finance charge to the amount of the loan on an accrual basis. You calculate the APR by using a standardized actuarial method. The Truth-in-Lending Act (provided by the Consumer Credit Protection Act of 1968, Public Law 90-321; Title 15, U.S. Code 1601 et seq.) includes Payment Tables that represent the APR after subtracting the amount of credit a borrower will have for actual use (the Amount Financed) and the Finance Charge (consisting of the interest, besides other fees and charges) expressed as a dollar amount financed and as an Annual Percentage Rate.

In addition, Truth-in-Lending regulations, set up by Regulation Z, enable a borrower, within three days following the loan transaction, to rescind a closed-end credit transaction if the loan is secured by a lien on the borrower's principal dwelling.

The Board of Governors of the Federal Reserve System implemented regulations interpreting the Truth-in-Lending Act under Regulation Z (12 CFR 226). Nine Federal agencies share enforcement of Truth-in-Lending and Regulation Z. The text of Regulation Z and the Truth-in-Lending Act are presented in an informative pamphlet, *What You Ought to Know About Regulation Z, Truth in Lending, Consumer Credit Cost Disclosure* that can be obtained from any Federal Reserve Bank or from the Board of Governors of the Federal Reserve System in Washington, D.C. The basic interest rate is rarely the only finance charge. Service charges, carrying charges or any charge of any kind on any single transaction, besides the interest, must be totaled under Truth-in-Lending regulations. This total sum is the finance charge that is then listed as the annual percentage rate of the total charge for the credit transaction. Regulation Z provides a tolerance in deviation from the Annual Percentage Rate of 1/8% for regular transactions and 1/4% for irregular transactions.

Lenders will use forms like that in Exhibit 7 to disclose the APR.

In South Carolina, a lender will use the form in Exhibit 8 to disclose the APR.

See REAL ESTATE SETTLEMENT PROCEDURES ACT (RESPA).

ANNUITY An assured income for life or a given time. This term normally relates to the insurance industry but is sometimes used in comparison with certain kinds of high-quality income from real estate investments. Annuity tables such as the Inwood Table will provide a factor that when multiplied by the income will give the value of income property.

See NET PRESENT VALUE ANALYSIS.

APPLICATION *See* LOAN APPLICATION.

APPOINTMENTS Decorative items such as furnishings and equipment in a building.

APPORTIONMENT A division of expenses, liabilities, responsibilities, or property among individuals.

APR *See* ANNUAL PERCENTAGE RATE.

APPRAISAL An opinion of estimated value for a specific purpose of a described property on a given date. An appraisal can be either written or verbal.

See APPRAISED VALUE.

APPRAISAL INSTITUTE An organization that began January 1, 1991. THE APPRAISAL INSTITUTE is the result of a merger of the former American Institute of Real Estate Appraisers (AIREA) and The Society of Real Estate Appraisers. The surviving designations are the MAI, member of the Appraisal Institute and SRA, Senior Residential Appraiser.

APPRAISAL REPORT A written opinion of value. The report will contain the estimate of value, date of valuation, certification and signature of the appraiser, the purpose, qualifying conditions, description of the subject property and its

Exhibit 7

⬤-784 (8807)   VMP MORTGAGE FORMS • (313)293-8100 • (800)521-7291

FEDERAL TRUTH-IN LENDING STATEMENT
(THIS IS NEITHER A CONTRACT NOR A COMMITMENT TO LEND)

Creditor:

Date: Loan Number:

Check box if applicable:

ANNUAL PERCENTAGE RATE	FINANCE CHARGE	Amount Financed	Total of Payments	☐ Total Sale Price
The cost of your credit as a yearly rate.	The dollar amount the credit will cost you.	The amount of credit provided to you or on your behalf.	The amount you will have paid after you have made all payments as scheduled.	The Total cost of your purchase on credit including your down-payment of $
%	$	$	$	$

☐ REQUIRED DEPOSIT: The annual percentage rate does not take into account your required deposit.

PAYMENTS: Your payment schedule will be:

Number of Payments	Amount of Payments	When Payments Are Due	Number of Payments	Amount of Payments	When Payments Are Due	Number of Payments	Amount of Payments	When Payments Are Due
		Monthly Beginning:			Monthly Beginning:			Monthly Beginning:

☐ DEMAND FEATURE: This obligation has a demand feature.

☐ VARIABLE RATE: This loan has a Variable Rate Feature. Variable Rate Disclosures have been provided to you earlier.

INSURANCE: The following insurance is required to obtain credit:

☐ Credit life insurance and credit disability   ☐ Property Insurance   ☐ Flood Insurance

You may obtain the insurance from anyone you want that is acceptable to creditor.

☐ If you purchase ☐ property ☐ flood insurance from creditor you will pay $ for a one year term.

SECURITY: You are giving a security interest in:

☐ The goods or property being purchased   ☐ Real property you already own.

FILING FEES: $

LATE CHARGE: If a payment is more than   days late, you will be charged   % of the payment.

PREPAYMENT: If you pay off early, you

☐ may   ☐ will not   have to pay a penalty.

☐ may   ☐ will not   be entitled to a refund of part of the finance charge.

ASSUMPTION: Someone buying your property

☐ may   ☐ may, subject to conditions   ☐ may not   assume the remainder of your loan on the original terms:

See your contract documents for any additional information about nonpayment, default, any required repayment in full before the scheduled date and prepayment refunds and penalties.

* means an estimate   ☐ all dates and numerical disclosures except the late payment disclosures are estimates.

The undersigned acknowledge receiving and reading a completed copy of this disclosure.
Neither you nor the creditor previously has become obligated to make or accept this loan, nor is any such obligation made by the delivery or signing of this disclosure.

(Applicant) _____ (Date) _____ (Applicant) _____ (Date) _____

(Applicant) _____ (Date) _____ (Applicant) _____ (Date) _____

NOTE: Payments shown above do not include reserve deposits for taxes, assessments, and property or flood insurance.

Exhibit 8

-788(SC) (9001)   VMP MORTGAGE FORMS • (313)293-8100 • (800)521-7291   67,513-E

TRUTH IN LENDING DISCLOSURE STATEMENT
(THIS IS NEITHER A CONTRACT NOR A COMMITMENT TO LEND)

LENDER: ☐ Preliminary   ☐ Final

DATE

BORROWERS   LOAN NO.

Type of Loan

ADDRESS
CITY STATE/ZIP
PROPERTY

ANNUAL PERCENTAGE RATE The cost of your credit as a yearly rate.	FINANCE CHARGE The dollar amount the credit will cost you.	Amount Financed The amount of credit provided to you or on your behalf.	Total of Payments The amount you will have paid after you have made all payments as scheduled.
%	$	$	$

PAYMENT SCHEDULE:

NUMBER OF PAYMENTS	AMOUNT OF PAYMENTS	PAYMENTS ARE DUE BEGINNING	NUMBER OF PAYMENTS	AMOUNT OF PAYMENTS	PAYMENTS ARE DUE BEGINNING

DEMAND FEATURE: ☐ This loan does not have a Demand Feature. ☐ This loan has a Demand Feature as follows:

VARIABLE RATE FEATURE:
☐ This Loan has a Variable Rate Feature. Variable Rate Disclosures have been provided to you earlier.

SECURITY: You are giving a security interest in the property located at:

ASSUMPTION: Someone buying this property ☐ cannot assume the remaining balance due under original mortgage terms
☐ may assume, subject to lender's conditions, the remaining balance due under original mortgage terms.

FILING / RECORDING FEES: $

PROPERTY INSURANCE: ☐ Property hazard insurance in the amount of $ with a loss payable clause to the lender is a required condition of this loan. Borrower may purchase this insurance from any insurance company acceptable to the lender.
Hazard insurance ☐ is ☐ is not available through the lender at an estimated cost of   for a   year term.

LATE CHARGES: If your payment is more than   days late, you will be charged a late charge of   % of the overdue payment.

PREPAYMENT: If you pay off your loan early, you

☐ may   ☐ will not   have to pay a penalty.
☐ may   ☐ will not   be entitled to a refund of part of the finance charge.

See your contract documents for any additional information regarding non-payment, default, required prepayment in full before scheduled date, and prepayment refunds and penalties.
e means estimate

ASSUMPTION NOTICE - THE DEBT SECURED HEREBY IS SUBJECT TO CALL IN FULL OR THE TERMS THEREOF BEING MODIFIED IN THE EVENT THE REAL ESTATE SECURING THE DEBT IS SOLD, CONVEYED OR OTHERWISE TRANSFERRED.

I/We hereby acknowledge reading and receiving a complete copy of this disclosure.

_____   _____
BORROWER / DATE   BORROWER / DATE

_____   _____
BORROWER / DATE   BORROWER / DATE

-788(SC) (9001)   VMP MORTGAGE FORMS • (313)293-8100 • (800)521-7291   1/90
© 1988 Consolidated Business Forms, Inc. The contents of this form in whole or in part are protected under the copyright laws of the United States.

ownership, neighborhood description, the approaches to value, and the final determination of value.

Several appraisal groups have agreed to form a standard appraisal board patterned after the Financial Accounting Standards Board (FASB) where appropriate appraisal theories would be applied to the R-41C clarifications. A synopsis of the clarifications serve to clarify four areas of R-41C that have been subject to repeated misinterpretations. The following represents the official interpretive views of the Federal Home Loan Bank System, Office of Regulatory Policy:

(1) Compliance with Freddie Mac and Fannie Mae appraisals and appraisal reporting guidelines and standard form reports is sufficient for appraisals on *existing* one-to-four family dwellings and on multi-family properties.

(2) To help in controlling the cost of appraisal services and to encourage the establishment of uniform appraisal standards, the use of other standardized forms will be permitted eventually, provided they are consistent with generally accepted and established written appraisal practices and are pre-approved by the Bank Board.

(3) The appraiser does not need to become enmeshed in aspects of the underwriting process other than those necessary to do the appraisal.

(4) An appraiser shall report the present market value for existing properties and proposed developments. The appraiser may report a value as of the conclusion of construction and as of the projected date when stabilized occupancy is achieved.

APPRAISED VALUE The dollar amount of value given to the property appraised. There are three major approaches to estimating value for real estate. The market approach bases value on the sales of other comparable properties. The cost approach bases value on what it will cost to replace the property. The income approach bases value on the income produced by owning the property. In most appraisals all three approaches will be used with the appraiser stating what approach was most influential in making the final determination of value. For existing single-family dwellings, the market approach has the most influence in determining the appraised value. For newly constructed single-family dwellings, the cost approach is most important. The income approach is most influential for any income property.

See COST APPROACH, INCOME APPROACH, MARKET APPROACH.

APPRAISER One who estimates value on a professional level. Many appraisers have designations such as: ASA, MAI, SRA, SREA, and SRPA.

A lender will probably want the appraiser to make a certification like the one in Exhibit 9.

A lender will probably want the appraiser to make a certification like the one in Exhibit 9.

See APPRAISAL INSTITUTE, FEE APPRAISER.

APPRECIATION An increase in the value of property. The opposite of depreciation.

APPROPRIATION The private taking of property and dedicating it to public use. It is also the dedication of public land for a private use, such as a public park or a school.

APPURTENANCE Item attributable to the land such as improvements or an easement. Something that comes from outside the property but is considered part of the property and transfers with the property upon sale or other transfer. A utility easement is an example of an appurtenance.

APPURTENANT Something that belongs to the property and transfers with it. The common area in a condominium or a PUD is an example of an appurtenant.

APRON Something that connects such as the entrance to a driveway or the concrete portion around a swimming pool.

AR An abbreviation for a type of adjustable payment mortgage pool or loan package. Lenders use the multiple issuer pool approach to issue the package. The interest rates and the monthly payments for the included mortgages adjust annually based on the average weekly yield of U.S. Treasury securities adjusted to a constant maturity of one year as described in GNMA Handbook 5500.2.

ARBITRAGE (1) The buying and selling of mortgages, futures, contracts, or mortgage-backed securities in various markets to create a profit from the differences in price. (2) The spread in interest rates as in a wrap-around mortgage.

See WRAP-AROUND MORTGAGE.

ARC *See* ACCELERATED REMITTANCE CYCLE.

Exhibit 9

DEFINITION OF MARKET VALUE: The most probable price which a property should bring in a competitive and open market under all conditions requisite to a fair sale, the buyer and seller, each acting prudently, knowledgeably and assuming the price is not affected by undue stimulus. Implicit in this definition is the consummation of a sale as of a specified date and the passing of title from seller to buyer under conditions whereby: (1) buyer and seller are typically motivated; (2) both parties are well informed or well advised, and each acting in what he considers his own best interest; (3) a reasonable time is allowed for exposure in the open market; (4) payment is made in terms of cash in U.S. dollars or in terms of financial arrangements comparable thereto; and (5) the price represents the normal consideration for the property sold unaffected by special or creative financing or sales concessions* granted by anyone associated with the sale.

*Adjustments to the comparables must be made for special or creative financing or sales concessions. No adjustments are necessary for those costs which are normally paid by sellers as a result of tradition or law in a market area; these costs are readily identifiable since the seller pays these costs in virtually all sales transactions. Special or creative financing adjustments can be made to the comparable property by comparisons to financing terms offered by a third party institutional lender that is not already involved in the property or transaction. Any adjustment should not be calculated on a mechanical dollar for dollar cost of the financing or concession but the dollar amount of any adjustment should approximate the market's reaction to the financing or concessions based on the appraiser's judgment.

CERTIFICATION AND STATEMENT OF LIMITING CONDITIONS

CERTIFICATION: The Appraiser certifies and agrees that:

1. The Appraiser has no present or contemplated future interest in the property appraised; and neither the employment to make the appraisal, nor the compensation for it, is contingent upon the appraised value of the property.

2. The Appraiser has no personal interest in or bias with respect to the subject matter of the appraisal report or the participants to the sale. The "Estimate of Market Value" in the appraisal report is not based in whole or in part upon the race, color, or national origin of the prospective owners or occupants of the property appraised, or upon the race, color or national origin of the present owners or occupants of the properties in the vicinity of the property appraised.

3. The Appraiser has personally inspected the property, both inside and out, and has made an exterior inspection of all comparable sales listed in the report. To the best of the Appraiser's knowledge and belief, all statements and information in this report are true and correct, and the Appraiser has not knowingly withheld any significant information.

4. All contingent and limiting conditions are contained herein (imposed by the terms of the assignment or by the undersigned affecting the analyses, opinions, and conclusions contained in the report).

5. This appraisal report has been made in conformity with and is subject to the requirements of the Code of Professional Ethics and Standards of Professional Conduct of the appraisal organizations with which the Appraiser is affiliated.

6. All conclusions and opinions concerning the real estate that are set forth in the appraisal report were prepared by the Appraiser whose signature appears on the appraisal report, unless indicated as "Review Appraiser." No change of any item in the appraisal report shall be made by anyone other than the Appraiser, and the Appraiser shall have no responsibility for any such unauthorized change.

CONTINGENT AND LIMITING CONDITIONS: The certification of the Appraiser appearing in the appraisal report is subject to the following conditions and to such other specific and limiting conditions as are set forth by the Appraiser in the report.

1. The Appraiser assumes no responsibility for matters of a legal nature affecting the property appraised or the title thereto, nor does the Appraiser render any opinion as to the title, which is assumed to be good and marketable. The property is appraised as though under responsible ownership.

2. Any sketch in the report may show approximate dimensions and is included to assist the reader in visualizing the property. The Appraiser has made no survey of the property.

3. The Appraiser is not required to give testimony or appear in court because of having made the appraisal with reference to the property in question, unless arrangements have been previously made therefor.

4. Any distribution of the valuation in the report between land and improvements applies only under the existing program of utilization. The separate valuations for land and building must not be used in conjunction with any other appraisal and are invalid if so used.

5. The Appraiser assumes that there are no hidden or unapparent conditions of the property, subsoil, or structures, which would render it more or less valuable. The Appraiser assumes no responsibility for such conditions, or for engineering which might be required to discover such factors.

6. Information, estimates, and opinions furnished to the Appraiser, and contained in the report, were obtained from sources considered reliable and believed to be true and correct. However, no responsibility for accuracy of such items furnished the Appraiser can be assumed by the Appraiser.

7. Disclosure of the contents of the appraisal report is governed by the Bylaws and Regulations of the professional appraisal organizations with which the Appraiser is affiliated.

8. Neither all, nor any part of the content of the report, or copy thereof (including conclusions as to the property value, the identity of the Appraiser, professional designations, reference to any professional appraisal organizations, or the firm with which the Appraiser is connected), shall be used for any purposes by anyone but the client specified in the report, the borrower if appraisal fee paid by same, the mortgagee or its successors and assigns, mortgage insurers, consultants, professional appraisal organizations, any state or federally approved financial institution, any department, agency, or instrumentality of the United States or any state or the District of Columbia, without the previous written consent of the Appraiser; nor shall it be conveyed by anyone to the public through advertising, public relations, news, sales, or other media, without the written consent and approval of the Appraiser.

9. On all appraisals, subject to satisfactory completion, repairs, or alterations, the appraisal report and value conclusion are contingent upon completion of the improvements in a workmanlike manner.

Date ....   Appraiser(s) ....

Freddie Mac
Form 439   JUL 86
⟨VMP⟩_ -22B (8805)

VMP MORTGAGE FORMS • (313)293-8100 • (800)521-7291

Fannie Mae
Form 1004B   JUL 86

Exhibit 9 (continued)

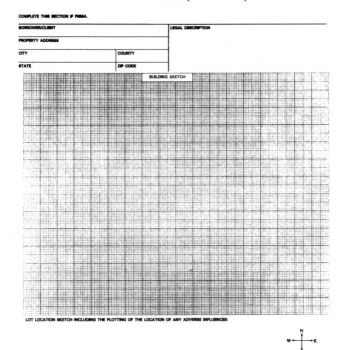

ARCADIAN FARMHOUSE

Arcadian Farmhouse. This house features the "raised cottage" architecture, wide front and rear covered porches, farmhouse-styled railings and plain square columns. The house is usually made out of clapboard siding. There will be shutters on the windows and dormers on the roof.

ARCADIAN or GREEK REVIVAL

Arcadian or Greek Revival. This home is of deep southern design with columns reflecting a modified Greek Revival style. It is commonly called a "raised cottage." Usually features wide front and rear covered porches and often has dormers on roof.

ARM *See* ADJUSTABLE RATE MORTGAGE.

ARM GUARANTOR PROGRAM (FHLMC) An adjustable rate guarantor or swap program offered by Freddie Mac with competitive pricing available by swapping one or two percent annual rate-capped ARMs for participating certificates (PCs). The rate-capped ARMs will be Treasury-indexed to one year Treasury interest rates. Freddie Mac urges lenders to arrange cost of funds (COF) ARM swaps adjusted to the index of the Federal Home Loan Banks by negotiation. Thus, ARM securities can be converted into borrowings, such as collateral for repurchase agreements (repos). The PCs can be sold, traded or repurchased with the help of Freddie Mac's security sales and trading group.

ARM'S LENGTH TRANSACTION A transaction between individuals who do not have a conflict of interest or reason for collusion. The parties are as strangers to each other. The value of property should be questioned for fairness or accuracy if there is not an arm's length transaction between the seller and buyer. An appraiser should not use comparable sales not closed by an arm's length transaction in the market approach to value.

ARPS *See* ADJUSTABLE RATE PREFERRED STOCK.

ARREARS At the end of a period. You pay interest on home mortgages in arrears. You pay rent in advance. Example: a mortgage payment due May 1st is for the interest for April; rent due May 1st is for the month of May. The term can pertain to delinquent mortgage payments. A mortgage loan that is three months delinquent can be said to be three months in arrears.

ARTESIAN WELL A deep well where water rises to the surface by natural pressure.

AS-IS Property sold in its present condition with no warranties made about the plumbing, heating, electrical, or infestation of termites.

ASSEMBLAGE Combining pieces of property to make one large, attractive property. The added value is *plottage*. People often use option contracts with the practice of assemblage.

ASSESSED VALUATION The dollar amount or value on what real estate taxes are levied. If a property worth $100,000 is assessed for tax purposes at 50% of value, the assessed valuation is $50,000. County or township tax assessors normally make appraisals for tax reasons. Many state laws require properties to be reappraised periodically. If the taxpayer disagrees with the appraisal they can appeal to a board of appeal or board of equalization.
See AD VALOREM for math computation for real estate taxes.

ASSESSMENT (1) The fair market value of property for tax purposes, (2) an expense appropriated to a unit of a whole such as a condominium assessment for common grounds, maintenance, or an additional charge for improvement (3) a levy for adding a product or services to a neighborhood, such as curbs or sewers, and (4) a value given to a property owner for the taking of the property by the process of condemnation.

ASSESSOR Commonly called a tax assessor, it is that individual charged with determining the fair market value for tax purposes. Tax assessors do not set the tax rate, they merely set the value for tax purposes.

ASSIGN The act of transferring rights or property to another.

ASSIGNEE One who receives rights or property. An assignee stands in the place of the assignor for rights, liabilities, and interest in the property.

ASSIGNMENT OF MORTGAGE (A/M) A transfer of a mortgage from one mortgagee to another. Sometimes, FHA will accept an assignment of a mortgage to help a qualified, distressed mortgagor.

ASSIGNMENT OF SERVICING A process of assigning the servicing rights from one lender to another.

ASSIGNOR One who assigns rights or property.

ASSUMPTION OF MORTGAGE Today there are four ways to handle a loan assumption.

(1) A lender can allow an assumption of a mortgage without pre-qualifying and not raise the interest rate.

(2) A lender can allow an assumption of a mortgage subject to the approval of the buyer and not raise the interest rate.

(3) A lender can allow an assumption of a mortgage subject to approval of the buyer and raise the interest rate. With FHA and VA loans, approval of the buyer for a loan assumption automatically releases the seller from liability. This is not necessarily the case with conventional loans.

(4) A lender can forbid an assumption of a mortgage.

You must get approval from a lender before assuming a loan. If a loan assumption takes place without lender approval, the lender can call the loan (require the entire loan balance due). If the assumptor cannot pay the loan off, the lender can begin foreclosure proceedings.

Good advice to follow about the subject of assumption rights is that everything a lender can do or can't do in an assumption is in the deed of trust or mortgage, and any addendum or disclosures signed by the original borrower. Today, when someone says that a mortgage is *completely assumable* they mean that a mortgage can be assumed without pre-qualification and without a change in the interest rate.

The processing work required decides the cost of the loan assumption. In general, FHA and VA loans that do not require pre-qualification (ones made before December 1, 1986 for FHA and loans made before March 1, 1988 for VA) are the least expensive to assume and have the best terms.

A sale by loan assumption relieves the seller from primary liability; but, unless there is a release of liability, the original mortgagor has a potential liability. FHA is now asking lenders to list all assumed mortgages as a liability unless the seller obtained a release of liability.

See ACCELERATION CLAUSE, ALIENATION CLAUSE, DUE-ON-SALE CLAUSE, FHA - RELEASE OF LIABILITY, RELEASE OF LIABILITY, SUBJECT TO, VA - RELEASE OF LIABILITY.

AT RISK For income tax purposes, it is the limit of deductible loss. This limit equals the cash amount invested plus the loan(s) the owner is personally liable.

ATRIUM Usually a space in the center of a building with a translucent ceiling and sometimes decorated with such amenities as a water fountain and tropical plants.

AT-THE-MONEY When the underlying security of an option is selling at the exercise price of the option. An option striking price equivalent to forward prices on an underlying security. The holder is then in a neutral position when options are at-the-money at the closing price date, on exercising or not exercising the option in effect.

ATTACHMENT The actual taking of property into the custody of a court to serve as collateral for a judgement sought in an impending suit. Law creates the lien and not private consent. This form of legal action is not available for obligations secured by collateral, as is the case of a mortgage.

ATTESTATION The act of witnessing a signature on an instrument.

ATTIC The portion of the house between the ceiling of the top floor and the underside of the roof. There must be access to an attic. By inspecting an attic you can check for signs of structural problems with rafters and joists and assure that there is adequate ventilation.

ATTORNEY-IN-FACT *See* POWER OF ATTORNEY.

ATTORNMENT A tenant's formal recognition of a new landlord. A mortgagee who becomes an owner by foreclosure, with the tenant recognizing the mortgagee as the new landlord, has a defense against claims for rent by the defaulting mortgagor. Attornment starts a new tenancy between the new owner and the tenant.

ATTRACTIVE NUISANCE DOCTRINE A legal doctrine holding that a property owner must protect children from injuring themselves by an attractive danger such as a swimming pool. In adhering to this doctrine, a property owner should build a fence around a swimming pool, or board-up an abandoned building.

AUCTION A process occasionally used in the secondary market to sell mortgage-backed securities or whole loan mortgages previously withheld from sale. Sellers lower their prices until a buyer accepts, while buyers raise their prices until a seller accepts.

An auction can be a public sale of property or property rights where bidders bid against each other. The highest bid offer will purchase the property. Auctions are frequently used to dispose of bulk quantities of real estate owned property (REO).

See ABSOLUTE AUCTION.

AUDIT Examination of records by a third party to decide if regulations have been followed. An investigation of a lender by a HUD investigator (for FHA loans), or a FBI agent (for VA loans) is said to be undergoing an *audit*. For example, a HUD investigator who examines a lender's records is said to be under a HUD-audit. FNMA and FHLMC have investigators for conventional lending practices.

AUTOMATED CLEARING HOUSE (ACH) A check clearing facility operated for the convenience of the banks in a particular region, generally through the regional Federal Reserve Bank. Besides processing interbank credits and debits electronically, they handle the electronic transfer of government securities. GNMA Handbook 5500.2 contains detailed information on automated debits from an issuer's central P&I account for GNMA IIs.

AVERAGE LIFE OF A MORTGAGE The average number of years one dollar of principal investment remains outstanding in a mortgage loan. The average life is used in deciding the true yield of a mortgage. A 30-year mortgage is said to have an average life of twelve years; a 10- to 15-year mortgage has an average life of seven years. Investors base the yield of a mortgage on the average life as opposed to the original term.

See DISCOUNTED YIELD.

AVULSION The sudden removal of land by action of a body of water or a river.

AZ An abbreviation for a type of adjustable payment mortgage pool with payments that are adjustable, in a manner acceptable to FHA or VA, other than in the manner applicable for AR pools. The mortgages may include indexed (also known as price level adjustment), shared appreciation, partially amortizing and other similar loans as described in GNMA Handbook 5500.2.

B

BBB, BB, B, Baa, Ba, B *See* MOODY'S AND STANDARD & POOR'S.

BACKFILLING The act of putting back dirt removed for construction. You backfill by filling the gap between the foundation wall and yard so that water will drain away from the house.

BACKUP CONTRACT A term often used with contracts to buy real estate. It is a contract that will replace a prior contract in the event of failure to perform or close by the parties of the prior contract. The seller should get a release from the buyer on the first contract before canceling the contract and proceeding with the second or backup contract.

BALLOON MORTGAGE A mortgage loan with periodic payments of principal and interest that do not completely amortize the loan. The balance of this type of mortgage loan is all due and payable in a lump sum at a specified time in the future. The borrower pays interest regularly, but may or may not make small principal repayments during the loan period. The unpaid balance, is due at a specific time in the future as stated in the mortgage or Deed of Trust.

For example, if you borrow $30,000 for five years or 60 months and the interest rate is 15%, your monthly payments will be only $375. But, the payments cover interest only with the entire principal due at maturity in five years. Thus, the borrower must make 59 equal monthly payments of $375 and a final balloon payment of $30,375 (the principal plus the last interest payment). If the borrower cannot make the final payment, the borrower must refinance (if refinancing is available) or sell the property.

Some lenders guarantee refinancing when the balloon payment is due, although they do not commit to a specified interest rate. The rate, at refinancing, could be much higher than the borrower's current rate. Other lenders do not offer automatic refinancing. Without such a guarantee, the borrower could be forced to start the whole business of shopping for mortgage funds again, besides paying closing costs and front-end charges a second time. A balloon mortgage can be a senior or a junior mortgage, i.e., first or second mortgage.
See BULLET LOANS.

BALLOON PAYMENT The final payment in a balloon mortgage. The balloon payment ends the mortgage, the mortgage is paid in full. This final payment is called the *balloon* or *bullet*.

BALUSTER The support for the rail in a staircase; one of a series of upright posts.

BANK HOLDING COMPANY (BHC) A corporation that owns interests in one or more banks.

BANKRUPT A corporation, firm, or person who files for relief from the courts and surrenders all assets. It is a condition when liabilities exceed assets and the person or business is unable to pay the creditors. Bankruptcy may be voluntary or involuntary. Involuntary bankruptcy is when a creditor forces payment of a debt of $1,000 or more and the debtor cannot pay.

There are several chapters of bankruptcy. A lender will most likely encounter the following chapters:

(1)   Chapter 7 - covers liquidation of the debtor's assets.

(2)   Chapter 11 - covers reorganization of a bankrupt business.

(3)   Chapter 13 - covers repayment of debts by individuals (commonly called wage-earner). Some plans may provide for full payment of debts while others arrange for payment of reduced debts.

Under Chapter 7 and 11 dismissal of bankruptcy means that the debts, but not the liens, are dismissed. The courts must close the bankruptcy to release the liens. Under Chapter 13, dismissal means that the court has thrown you out of bankruptcy. You are no longer under its protection and you are subject to the action of creditors.

In reviewing a loan application from a person who has taken bankruptcy, lenders look at two important points: (1) the reason for bankruptcy, e.g., unable to work due to bad health, an accident, etc., (2) the type of bankruptcy taken (the chapter), and (3) compensating factors.

BASEBOARD A board that runs along the base of the wall where it meets the floor.

BASEMENT The space that is below the first floor. Basements are usually wholly or partly below the exterior grade. You should check basements for signs of water leakage. Dampness in corners is a sign of moisture problems, and water marks along the base of walls or any cabinets suggest that there is or has been some serious water leakage.

BASEMENT WINDOW *See* WINDOW.

BASE LINE A surveyor's term used to show an east-west line.

BASE LOAN For FHA and VA loans it is the amount that does not include any borrowed MIP for FHA loans or funding fee for VA loans. FHA allows the borrower to 100% finance any one-time mortgage insurance premium. VA allows the veteran-borrower to 100% finance the funding fee.
See LOAN ORIGINATION FEE.

BASIS An unadjusted basis is the cost of the property minus the land value. Cost plus capital spent to modify the improvements minus the land value is the *adjusted basis*. For the purposes of determining capital gain or loss, it is the total cost of the property compared to the sales price minus the costs of the sale.

BASIS POINTS A term used in relationship to interest rates. One basis point is equal to one 100th of one percent. Basis points are used to describe the yield of a debt instrument, including mortgages. The difference between 9% and 9.5% is 50 basis points.
See DISCOUNT YIELD.

BASIS RISK The risk that the price of a hedge tool does not move as expected relative to the increase or decrease in the market value of the hedged loan. While hedging with substitute sales helps reduce exposure to market rate movements, it can introduce risks of its own basis risks. The basis is the relationship between the price of the item being hedged (like a mortgage pipeline) and that of the hedge tool (e.g., Treasury Bond futures). The risk is that the price of the hedge tool does not move as expected relative to the increase or decrease in the market price of the hedged loan.

BASKET PROVISION Regulatory authority permitting insurance companies, savings and loan associations, and mutual savings banks to put some of their total assets in investments not otherwise allowed by regulatory acts.

BATT The strip of insulation placed between the studs of a wall or joists of a ceiling or floor.

BATTEN A narrow board normally used to cover a joint or space between boards, often called a batten board.

BD The designation for a pool consisting entirely of buydown mortgages as described in GNMA Handbook 5500.1.

BEAM A load-bearing support that can be made of wood, iron, stone, or other strong material.

BEARER BOND A coupon bond payable to the individual who has possession of the bond.

BEARING WALL See LOAD-BEARING WALL.

BEDROCK Solid rock for a foundation of a large building.

BEDROOM COMMUNITY OR SUBURB Residential area for commuters who work at a nearby large city or employment center.

BEFORE-TAX INCOME Income used to decide yield from an investment before it becomes taxable to the investor. It is income used in an offering of an investment without regard to the investor's taxable income bracket used in filing income tax returns.

BELLY-UP A project, business, or venture that has failed is said to have gone *belly-up* (as a capsized ship).

BENCH MARK A mark etched on a durable substance such as a rock or metal. A bench mark will show the elevation above sea level.

BENCHMARK An indication of a measure of quality or performance in an industry. Treasury bills are the benchmarks for many Adjustable Rate Mortgage loans.

BENEFICIAL ESTATE Equitable title or estate; a condition when legal title has not yet passed. Examples would be a person who owns a valid sales contract or a person who has a contract for land.

BENEFICIARY STATEMENT The statement from a lender that shows the remaining principal balance and other information about a loan. It is usually obtained when an owner wishes to sell or refinance. It is often called a *bene statement, offset statement* or *estoppel certificate* and is requested by escrow or title companies.

BENEFICIARY A person who receives a benefit from certain acts such as through a will or proceeds from an insurance policy. A lender is a beneficiary with a deed of trust or a note as security for a loan.

BEQUEATH The giving of property by a will.

BETTERMENT Improvement to real estate; something that is more substantial than ordinary repairs. The increase in the value of the improvement measures the *betterment*, and not the cost.

BIANNUAL Biannual is an event that occurs twice a year or semi-annual.

BID The price offered to acquire a mortgage or real estate. A pool of mortgages may be offered to various investors. Depending upon the yield of the investment, buyers may want to offer or bid to buy the mortgages at a discount so that the yield will increase. The price offered and any conditions attached to the offer will be considered by the seller. The winning bid is the investor who submits a bid that is acceptable to the seller.
See DISCOUNT YIELD.

BID AND ASKED PRICE The bid price is a quotation or quote that represents a price a buyer declares they will pay for mortgage-backed securities at a given time. The asked price is the offering price declared by the seller at the same time.
See TAKEOUT BID.

BID IN If a lender states a price at a foreclosure sale that will cover the unpaid balance plus allowable costs, the lender is said to have bid in his price. Subject to laws in various states, any amount received above the winning bid (from the lender or any other bidder) is given to the owner of the property.

BIENNIAL An event that occurs every two years.

BILATERAL CONTRACT A contract with each party promising to perform an act in exchange for the other party's promise to perform.

BILL AND STATEMENT A method of recording loan payments. A financial institution sends the borrower a monthly bill for the next payment due and, at the end of each accounting period (usually semiannually or annually), a statement of activity in the account during the period.

BILL OF SALE A written account of the sale of personal property. An investor may want a bill of sale to certify the cost paid for personal property associated with a purchase of real estate. One reason for requesting a bill of sale is to decide cost for depreciation purposes. The write-off period for personal property is much faster when compared to real property.

BINDER (1) In real estate, this term is often used with title insurance. A binder is a report on certain real estate as of a certain date. It is different from a title insurance policy, but you can use it to obtain a policy. A binder is less costly than a policy and it will often meet a lender's title insurance requirement on a short-term loan, such as a construction loan. A binder covers a specific time. (2) In hazard insurance, it is agreeing to insure for a specific time. (3) In real estate contract law, it is a preliminary agreement between the seller and purchaser.

BIRD DOG A person who hunts for a lead on a good buy for an investor or a prospect or listing for a real estate agent. The *bird dog* earns a fee if the lead turns into a purchase, listing, or something of benefit to the end user who pays the fee.

BI-LEVEL

Bi-Level. A house built on two levels with the entrance being in between both levels. The entryway has a landing with stairs leading to the upper level and another set of stairs leading down to the lower level.

BI-WEEKLY MORTGAGE A mortgage requiring 26 payments per year as opposed to a monthly payment. Each payment is only half the size of the required regular monthly payment and the resulting effect is quicker loan amortization and reduced interest cost.

A bi-weekly mortgage usually pays out in 18 to 20 years as opposed to monthly payments for 30 years.

Biweekly mortgages have met with a fair amount of popularity among borrowers who find it convenient to make loan payments twice monthly and lenders who, in turn, have fewer delinquencies. The secondary mortgage market now carries biweekly mortgages and Fannie Mae and Freddie Mac sponsor such programs.

An example for calculating biweekly mortgage payments with the HP-12C Calculator for a $100,000 mortgage is shown below:

BIWEEKLY LOAN COMPUTATION PLAN
(with HP-12C Key Strokes)

Scenario: $100,000 over 30 years at 11% interest biweekly amortized payments credited to the mortgagor instead of monthly amortization payments.

Factors: Monthly payments would be $952.32, but when paid every two weeks the amount becomes $476.16, indicating the division of loan payments by one-half $952.32.

	Key Strokes	Display	Explanation
Step 1.	(f)CLEARREG	0.00	REGISTER CLEAR.
Step 2.	30 (g) (n)	360.00	Computes months.
Step 3.	11 (g) (i)	0.92	Computes annual rate of interest into a monthly rate of interest.
Step 4.	100,000(PV)	100,000	Stores Present value.
Step 5.	(PMT)	–952.32	Computes the monthly payment. The minus represents an amount paid out.
Step 6.*	2 (+)	–476.16	Computes biweekly payment.
Step 7.	(PMT)	–476.16	Stores biweekly payment.
Step 8.	11 (ENTER)	11.00	Stores annual interest.
Step 9.	26 (+)	0.42	Recurring interest rate.
Step 10.	(i)	0.42	Stores interest rate.
Step 11.**	(n)	520.00	Computes payments to payoff.
Step 12.	26 (+)	20.00	Computes payoff in years.

*Lender receives $476.16 biweekly from mortgagor.
**Mortgage paid off in 20 years.

Biweekly mortgages can be offered in any mortgage amount and term, at a given interest rate. Shorter payment intervals accelerate equity through faster amortization which will shorten the loan maturity. The interest rate controls biweeklies as to maturity of a loan (at 10% the biweekly payment is $438.79 and will mature in 20.96 years while at 11% maturity is attained in 20). Higher interest rates reflect shorter mortgage maturity in a biweekly plan; thus, a lower rate will increase the maturity of the loan.

NOTE: The above HP-12C Biweekly Plan is a procedural guide only and is not unfailing in the number of payments as it is synchronized for monthly payments. It is recommended, therefore, that the appropriate HP-12C programming be created for accurate determination of biweeklies.

BLACKTOP A paving surface usually made of asphalt.

BLANKET MORTGAGE A single mortgage used to secure a debt for money loaned on several properties such as the lots a builder owns in a subdivision. It is important for the borrower (mortgagor) to ask for a *partial release* clause in the blanket mortgage. A partial release clause will release each lot that is sold for a stated amount that is a portion of the entire debt. Without a partial release clause the entire debt will have to be paid before the mortgage is released.

BLENDED RATE (1) A first mortgage lender can use it in an advertisement to induce his mortgagors to refinance and pay off the old low-interest-rate first mortgage. The first mortgage lender could offer a 10% interest loan as compared to the going rate of 12% if the mortgagor will refinance the existing mortgage that is at 8%. (2) A second mortgage lender or a wrap-around lender will advertize not to pay off the old mortgage with the low rate and short term remaining, but instead, place a second mortgage or wrap-around loan behind the first and have a blended rate below market interest rates for first mortgage loans.

BLIGHTED AREA Usually an inner city area where property values are falling and buildings are deteriorating.

BLOCKBUSTING An illegal practice of promoting panic selling in an all-white neighborhood because someone of a minority or ethnic background has moved into or is said to be moving into the neighborhood. The blockbuster will try to gain illegally from depressed prices either by buying or listing the properties at far below market values.

BLS *See* BUREAU OF LABOR STATISTICS.

BLUE-SKY LAWS State laws to protect the public against fraud in the offer and sale of securities. The intent of these laws is to protect the public from unscrupulous practices by dealers selling securities on promises that are untrue. Blue-sky laws normally require you to register securities in the state you offer the security and the offerings follow stated guidelines in making full disclosure to the public. The securities most commonly seen deal with partnerships, bonds, and syndications.

BOARD AND BATTEN Siding with batten boards nailed over cracks between wider boards.

BOARD FOOT A piece of wood that is one foot square by one inch thick; 144 cubic inches = 1' × 1' × 1.''

BOARD OF ADJUSTMENT A government body that hears appeals concerning zoning matters. A Board of Adjustment can grant zoning variances.

BOARD OF EQUALIZATION A government body that hears appeals concerning real estate tax assessments. If a property owner thinks the assessment is too high, they can appeal to the board of equalization. This board can lower assessments causing a lower real estate tax.

BOARD OF REALTORS The local association of REALTORS who belong to the State and National Association of REALTORS.

BOARD OF REVIEW See Board of Equalization.

BOILER PLATING Standard language found in contracts, deeds or deeds of trust, and in Covenants, Conditions, and Restrictions (CC&R's).

BONA FIDE Genuine, sincere, in good faith. The term can be used in a sentence such as: "This is a bona fide offer to purchase your real estate."

BOND A formal certificate that evidences a debt and outlines the terms. It is a formal promise to pay a lender a specified sum of money at a future date, with or without collateral. The promise must be in writing and signed and sealed by the maker (borrower). The balance owed is paid on a future date with a series of interest payments in the interval.

BOND EQUIVALENT YIELD (BEY) A measurement of the rate of return on a security sold on a discount basis that assumes actual days to maturity and a a 365-day year. As used in Fannie Mae's Hedging Guide ARM examples, the BEY is the yield on a 1-year Treasury Bill (quoted on a discount basis) that would be equal to the yield of a Treasury coupon security with a maturity of one year.

BOND-TYPE SECURITY An investment security, especially a mortgage-based one, that has the characteristics of a typical corporate bond, including a long-term, fixed rate of return and repayment of principal at maturity.

BOND VALUE The mortgage bond's cash flow (or underlying collateral) that upholds the value of the bond. The mortgage bond's value is restricted to the mortgage loan's unpaid balance.

BOOK VALUE An accounting term used to show the value of a business as a whole or any particular asset, such as real estate. You show the value by accounting records that normally give the cost of the assets plus any improvement minus depreciation. It is the net value of an asset. Depending on the reason for valuation, book value may be marked down for a distress sale but it is normally never marked up to reflect an increase in value.

BOOT Something of value given to even the exchange of like properties. Parcel A is worth $100,000 and is exchanged for parcel B worth $80,000 and $20,000 in cash. The boot is the $20,000 in cash.

BORING TEST Using samples obtained by boring deep holes in the ground to decide the strength of the subsoil for construction purposes.

BOROUGH A section of a city, similar to an incorporated village, that has control over local matters. New York City has five boroughs.

BOTTOM LAND Low land situated near a body of water.

BOTTOM LINE A phrase that means the net result such as after-tax cash flow or the result or final consequence.

BREACH OF CONTRACT Failure to perform according to the terms of a contract. The party who has not breached the contract can rescind the agreement and sue for damages or for performance.

BREACH OF TRUST Abuse of the responsibilities or authority as set forth in a trust agreement.

BREAK-EVEN POINT A point when gross income will cover operating expenses and the debt service.

BREAK-EVEN RATE OF PREPAYMENT The demanded flow of cash creating a pass-through-mortgage-backed security that produces a rate of prepayment that justifies the investment at a projected break-even point.

BRIDGE FINANCING OR BRIDGE LOAN Short-term mortgage financing between the end of one loan and the beginning of another. A bridge loan is usually based on the amount of equity in the borrower's current home with the proceeds going toward the purchase of a new home. The loan helps to *bridge* the gap between one home to another without the benefit of cash proceeds from the sale of a previous home. People sometimes call a bridge loan a *swing loan*.

BRIDGING Placing boards between floor or ceiling joists to prevent them from twisting.

BRITISH THERMAL UNIT (BTU) A unit used to measure the efficiency or capacity of heating or cooling systems. A unit of heat required to raise one pound of water one degree Fahrenheit at sea level.

BROKER An agent who may be a member of a stock exchange firm or a stock exchange member individually and who handles the public's orders to buy and sell securities and earns a commission for this service.

A real estate broker, on the other hand, is nearly always an independent contractor under agency rules of law that ordinarily describes him or her as a special contractor dealing in real estate for the broker's principal. They are a properly licensed agent who, for a fee or valuable consideration, serves as an agent for owners in helping with the sale or lease of their property. A broker can be incorporated or act as a partnership; but, the salespeople hired by the broker must act as individuals. A broker usually works for the seller who pays their commission.

A very important element when establishing oneself as an independent contractor is the fact that the broker selects a procedure for finding a buyer for his employer, without the controlling custody of agency matters under the laws of the agency. Some states and other jurisdictional entities, as in California, consider a real estate salesperson as an employee of the broker under whom he or she is licensed and, as such, cannot assume an independent contractor designation. Questions relating to how other governmental agencies view the broker-salesperson relationship should be referred to those agencies. It should be remembered, however, that the broker/salesperson status under one law does not establish what that status is under different laws, rules or circumstances. For purposes of federal income tax, worker's compensation, unemployment insurance or other matters outside the scope of various governmental agencies license laws and regulations, the relationship of broker and salesperson is a question of fact common to all.

See MORTGAGE BROKER.

BTU *See* BRITISH THERMAL UNIT.

BUFFER STRIP OR ZONE Land between two areas of different use such as commercial and residential.

BUILDER BONDS First issued in 1981, when thrifts were hit with disintermediation due to higher interest rates, large builders resorted to issuing this type of mortgage-backed bond when confronted with a shortage of mortgage credit to provide financing for home buyers. Builders of one-to-four family homes are the primary issuers of these mortgage pay-through bonds. Builder bonds emphasize pay-through bonds collateralized by GNMA pools, FNMAs and FHLMC PCs.

BUILDER BOND CMO Builder bonds are mortgage-collateralized securities issued by a homebuilder. They were first issued in 1981 and, initially, most were pass-through bonds that matched the underlying mortgages very closely. Volume was slow until 1983 when CMOs appeared. The underlying mortgages of these bonds consist of about 30% GNMAs, FNMAs or FHLMCs and 70% AAA-rated whole loans. These programs can be split so that some bonds are backed 100% by whole loans and some entirely by GNMAs. Bonds are structured so that residuals, the difference between the amount of the mortgages and the amount of the bonds, are used either to pay the bond down faster or to go back to the issuer. Nearly all the mortgages underlying builder bond CMOs are on new homes, with interest generally slightly lower than the current coupon mortgages. Payoff rates in the early years are lower on new homes than others; although, they rise in the fifth to seventh years.

BUILDER'S AND SPONSOR'S PROFIT AND RISK ALLOWANCE (BSPRA) Credit given by HUD/FHA insurance programs for services provided by the developer, said credit is used against the required equity contribution.

BUILDER'S RISK INSURANCE Used to protect builders against fire and special risks while they have houses under construction. It increases as the building progresses and ends at completion of construction.

BUILDING AND LOAN ASSOCIATION A savings and loan association.

BUILDING CODE Standards for constructing buildings that are established by city, county, state or municipal governments. In most areas these codes are modeled after national standards. The codes establish many minimum requirements for construction of buildings. Some points covered by the codes are: design, quality of construction, use and occupancy, location of the building on the site, safety and health. The codes are enforced by issuing permits and are followed up by inspections. Organizations such as Building Officials and Code Administrators (BOCA) play a major role in setting standards for building codes.

BUILDING LINE A line established by law for city lots that serves to establish a minimum distance between the front of a building and the front of a lot or a minimum distance between the sides of a building and the sides of a lot.

BUILDING PERMIT Permission in writing from local authority to build, demolish, repair, or improve a specific building at a designated lot.

BULLET Interim financing used for income property when the construction loan has expired and acceptable permanent financing is not available. These are interest-only loans for two to ten years and cannot be prepaid. When income property borrowers raise money through construction loan borrowings and subsequently refinance the construction loan (on five or ten year bullet loans), they do so in the hope that interest rates will drop even further. But when interest rates increase, it may be too late to apply for a permanent fixed-rate mortgage. Thus, less loan money is available, e.g., the size of the loan will be less to an income property borrower. The size of the loan is never established by the down payment nor the price availability of an income property, but with rental revenues (less operating expenses) in arriving at the available amount for the loan payments. A lender then calculates the minimum ratio required between the ratio and amount of loan payments (ratio of debt service coverage) before the minimum loan payment is determined. Consequently, high mortgage rates control the amount of available funds. In an income property loan, the lender is an investor who purchases the mortgage loan.

Income property borrowers with small equity in the property (or liquidity) may face an uneasy time in refinancing the bullet loan as it approaches expiration. In this situation, more equity is required. The construction lender faces a threat of holding an open-ended mortgage loan for several months, not to mention income property with a large percentage of vacancies. The bullet loan is thus characterized as a fixed-rate, semi-permanent (five to ten year), multi-purpose commercial loan amount with a balloon payment on the principal at the end of its term. A permanent lender is usually a life insurance company who obtains the money on contract from pension funds for a specific time. The Guaranteed Income Contract (GIC) carries an interest rate commensurate with the marketing agreement negotiated with the life insurance company. Insurance companies then re-invest the funds to the borrower at 70-155 basis points over the contract rate as negotiated with the pension fund.

BUNDLE OF RIGHTS A theory adhering to the idea that when one buys real estate one buys all the rights inherent in that property except what is limited or reserved by the sale. The rights to sell, lease, mortgage, bequeath, enjoy, share, and restrict property are supported by the Bundle of Rights theory.

BUREAU OF LABOR STATISTICS (BLS) A Labor Department bureau that issues various statistics associated with the country's labor force. For real estate purposes, the most widely used statistic is the Consumer Price Index (CPI). Landlords often use this index to increase the rent. Reports are issued on a monthly, quarterly, and an annual basis. The reports contain information on labor economics, such as: labor requisites, work forces, unemployment and employment data, labor hours, employee wages, relation status of management to labor, price levels, living conditions, research and development products, health and safety occupational hazards, patterns of economic expansion or deflation.

BUSINESS DAY Monday through Friday excluding holidays. Also known as *working days*. For Secondary Marketing, it is any calendar day when the New York City branch offices of the transfer agent are open to the public for business as described in GNMA Handbook 5500.1.

BUTTERFLY ROOF *See* ROOF.

BUY-BACK AGREEMENT A seller agreeing to buy back a property at a specific price for specific conditions. Normally used by builders as a sales inducement.

BUYDOWN A level payment mortgage with funds provided to reduce the borrower's monthly payments during the early years of the mortgage as described in GNMA Handbook 5500.1. A buydown is an incentive sometimes used by sellers and even lenders to attract the consumer. For example, if interest rates are at 12%, you may read adds for 9% or 10% interest or a 3-2-1 buydown. A buydown plan involves a party buying down the interest rate on either a temporary or a permanent basis. A 3-2-1 temporary buydown will result in a rate of 9% for the first year, 10% for the second year, 11% in the third year, and 12% in the fourth and remaining year. Using the rates in the example you can decide the cost with one of the three methods below.

(1) The addition of 3+2+1 equaling a 6% (or point) discount.

(2) The total difference in the monthly principal and interest payments at 9%,10%, and 11% as compared to 12%.

(3) A discount on the buydown for what is, in effect, prepaid interest. Example: A lender could give a 1.5% discount on a 3-2-1 buydown, making the total cost 4.5% instead of 6%.

A permanent buydown is costly. You bring the rate down for the life of the loan by paying additional discount points. For example, the following FHA, VA or conventional loan quotes all have the same yield: 12% at par (no discount), 11.75% with a 1.5% discount, and 11.5% with a 3% discount. It is expensive to buydown an interest rate on a permanent basis.

Investors and the Agencies have become very cautious about the use of buydowns. FHA is in the mortgage insurance business. As a mortgage insurer, it is important to insure loans based on true market values. In the way of an acknowledgement, the "TV gurus" and real estate investment authors are correct when they assert "any property can be sold for the right terms." FHA has been listening. On 8 August 1986, FHA issued guidelines for "seller buydowns" more than 5% of the sales price. The 5% limit was later raised to 6% on 22 October 1987. In general, FHA defines a buydown as any inducement to influence a buyer to buy when they would not do so under normal circumstances. More importantly, for insuring purposes, buydowns are abusive when they influence the buyer to accept a price higher than a true market value.
Some examples of what FHA defines as a seller buydowns are as follows:

(1) Payments for discount points.

(2) Any type of interest payment, i.e., 3-2-1 plans.

(3) A payment of a closing cost that the buyer normally pays, e.g., the 1% origination fee.

(4) Monthly payments to principal.

(5) Gifts such as: trips, maid service, any non-realty items.

(6) Payments for condo or homeowner association dues.

If the seller buydowns exceed 6% of the sales price, the amount over 6% will be deducted from the sales price and the LTV will be based on the lowered sales price. If the seller buydowns pertain to interest (3-2-1 buydown), the purchaser must qualify at no less than 2% below the note rate. If the note rate is 10%, the purchaser must qualify at a rate not less than 8%. VA has a 4% limit for buydowns; FHLMC and FNMA have limits of from 3% to 6% depending upon the LTVR. Most lenders do not allow buydowns on a refinance loan.

Adjustable rate mortgage rates can be bought down in the same manner as a fixed rate loan. A temporary buydown can be calculated by using the above examples. A permanent buydown requires buying down the margin for the life of the loan. The permanent buydown of a margin is decided just the same as buying down a fixed rate for the life of a loan.

Buydowns are best used in periods of high interest rates. A subsidy of the mortgage interest rate helps the buyer meet the payments during the first few years of the loan. Suppose a new home sells for $150,000. After a down payment of $75,000, the buyer still needs to finance another $75,000. A 30-year first mortgage is available for 17%. The monthly payment is $1,069.26 and is, in this case, beyond the buyer's reach. However, a buydown is available. For the first three years, the developer will subsidize the buyer's payments, bringing down the interest rate to 14%. This means the payment is only $888.65, and the buyer can afford it.

Buydowns raise several issues. First, payments after the first few years (if a fixed rate loan) will jump to the rate originally made (17% in the above example) and total more than $1,000. If a flexible rate loan and the index to which the rate is tied has risen since the loan was made, the payments could rise even more. Second, if the subsidy is provided separately by the builder, the lender can still hold the borrower liable for the full interest rate (17% in the example) even if the builder backs out of the deal or goes out of business. Finally, the $150,000 sales price may have been increased to cover the builder's interest subsidy. A comparable home around the corner may, in fact, be available at a lower sales price. At the same time, competition may have encouraged the builder to offer his buyer a genuine savings.

There exist plans called consumer buydowns. In these loans, the buyer makes a sizable down payment; in turn, the interest granted is below market. In other words, in exchange for a large payment at the beginning of the loan, the buyer may qualify for a lower rate on the amount borrowed. Frequently, this type of mortgage has a shorter term than those written at current market rates. The consumer buydowns may apply to first-time buyers who need help with a starter home that may cost upwards of $150,000. Some help with the down payment may be possible from relatives (with proper documentation for the lending institution as in a Gift Letter).

See GIFT LETTER.

BUYER'S MARKET Economic conditions when demand for housing is at a low level.

BUY-SELL AGREEMENT Parties in a partnership agree to buy the interest of a party who leaves the partnership and the departing partner agrees to sell to the remaining party or parties. The parties can agree to provide for an option to buy or sell. It is recommended to have this type of agreement between parties in closely held corporation or partnership in case a key party dies or becomes disabled.

BYLAWS The rules, laws, and regulations for a condominium. Bylaws regulate the management and operation of the condominium. The developer sets forth the bylaws, but they are later subject to change by the condominium association.

C

CCC, CC, C, Caa, Ca, C *See* MOODY'S AND STANDARD & POOR'S.

CADASTRAL MAP A map with legal boundaries and ownership of real property used for title recording. A cadastral program is a complete inventory of property within a government jurisdiction (city or county) and sometimes called a reassessment.

CAISSON A water-tight chamber for men to work underwater or in an open excavation where there is danger of walls caving in.

CALL (1) In a mortgage, a *call provision* is the right of a lender to accelerate or demand the entire loan balance due and payable. (2) An option to buy real estate, a right given in an option contract. (3) An option to buy a specific security at a specified price within a designated period. (4) A demand for payment of an installment due on the purchase of stocks or bonds. (5) In bonds, a call provision is the issuer's right to redeem the bond before maturity. (6) A reference in a survey to a monument.
See ACCELERATION CLAUSE.

CAFMV *See* COMMISSIONER'S ADJUSTED FAIR MARKET VALUE (CAFMV).

CALIFORNIA CONTEMPORARY

California Contemporary. A modern-styled home featuring many large windows, skylights, vaulted ceilings and sloping roof lines. The exterior is usually made of wood and there are many angles and box shapes. Often-times the gable is glassed. Most of these homes have one or more wood decks.

CALIFORNIA RANCH

California Ranch. A one-story, ground-hugging, usually long house with a low pitched roof. There will be many contemporary styled windows.

CALIFORNIA VETERANS AFFAIRS (CAL-VET) A ground-breaking program administered by the California State Department of Veterans Affairs for the direct financing of farm and home purchases by eligible California veterans of the armed forces. The Cal-Vet farm and home purchase program, originally created by the Legislature in 1921, allows the State Department of Veterans Affairs to help qualified California veterans to acquire farm or home property at low financing costs. It is a complete loan program. The Department originates, processes, funds and services the loan.

Funds are obtained through state bond issues authorized by the Legislature and approved by the voting public. The veteran buys the property and repays the loan at a low interest rate with level monthly payments over the life of the loan. These monthly payments cover all costs, including bond issuance, redemption and interest to bond holders and the cost of administering the program. Thus, the program involves no expense to the taxpayers.

Since the Department purchases the property directly from the seller with no other lenders involved, costs to the buyer are small. There are no appraisal fees, loan charges or discount points. It is like a cash transaction to the seller. The Department takes title to the property and, in turn, sells it to the veteran via a purchase contract. Although the Department holds legal title, the veteran has equitable title and full use of the property as a personal residence. The loan process decides eligibility. The applicant's discharge documents must show a California home of record at time of entry, a California place of entry and registration with a California Selective Service Board. If any of the items suggest an out-of-state entry, Cal-Vet will require additional documentation.

Veterans who have more than one qualifying period of service with a definite break between the periods may be eligible for more than one loan. However, only one loan may be active at a time. Any period of service that a veteran has received a benefit or bonus from another state may not be used to qualify for a Cal-Vet loan.

Construction requirements are, in general, equivalent to those of the FHA under Title II, Section 203(b). Some exceptions may be approved where state and local building codes are complied with and general acceptance and marketability, present and future, are indicated. There are no arrangements made with the secondary mortgage market conduits such as Ginnie Mae in the Cal-Vet program. The program is subject to legislative and administrative changes during the year, including maximum loan amount increases. Mobile home loans are available if the mobile home is in an approved park.

CALLABLE DEBT A security that the issuer can redeem before its maturity. The issuance of long-term callable debt lowers prepayment and basis risk simultaneously (a good hedging tool for thrifts and banks). A possible financing vehicle, besides long-term callable debt, is a Letter of Credit (LOC) advance by the FHLB that has a 5-year maximum maturity, 10-year debt, callable after a 5-year limitation. Thrifts might choose to issue a 10-year bond with a call option of five years, effective if the LOC is non-renewable. Credit problems can be circumvented by exercising other callable approaches, such as mortgage-backed bonds. Other possibilities are the financing subsidiaries, but these approaches require possible over-collateralization. Many thrifts and banks need strategies to raise their credit ratings, thus limit their costs of debt issues.

CALL OPTION A short-term contract that gives the holder the right, but not the obligation, to purchase securities at a pre-arranged price within a specified time. Used in hedging mortgage pipelines.

CALL PROTECTION A guaranty to not call a security, or retire it, for a stated time. Money managers, particularly those for pension funds and life insurance companies, seek to protect an investment from early retirement so that the yield will be protected for a time. An obstacle in investing in home mortgages is the unexpected retirement of debt due to a homeowner's need to relocate, refinance, or rapidly reduce the loan balance by prepaying the mortgage.

CANADIAN ROLLOVER MORTGAGE An adjustable rate mortgage with terms that are renegotiated every five years.
See RENEGOTIABLE RATE MORTGAGE.

CANDLE A measure of light intensity that is approximately equal to the intensity of light from a seven-eighths inch sperm candle burning at the rate of 120 grains per hour.

CANDLE HOUR A measure of light equal to one candle burning for one hour.

CANDLE POWER Luminous intensity of a light expressed in candles.

CANTILEVER The part of a structural member that extends beyond its support and can support loads and resist lateral pressure by virtue of its rigidity and material strength. Examples of a cantilever are a bay window and a balcony.

CANTILEVER BRIDGE A bridge supported by two cantilevered members extending out toward each other and connecting with each other or to a suspended span.

CAP Limits on how much the interest rate or the monthly payment of an Adjustable Rate Mortgage can change, either at each adjustment or during the life of the mortgage. ARMs may contain one or more types of caps.

Payment caps limit the amount of increase in the monthly payment. They do not limit the amount of interest the lender is charging. Payment caps can cause negative amortization.

A rate cap is the limit upon the increase in the interest rate for an Adjustable Rate Mortgages. There are generally two types of rate caps. The rate cap per adjustment period and the rate cap for the life of the loan.

See ADJUSTABLE RATE MORTGAGE, PAYMENT SHOCK.

CAPE COD

Cape Cod. A Colonial style, usually 1-1/2 in story height. The house is small and compact with a single centered front entrance. The entrance usually has one or two windows on each side of the front door and is symmetrical. The chimney is often in the center of the house, and the roof is a steep gable made of shingles. You will often see this style home with a picket fence for adornment.

CAPITAL The net worth of a business or an individual; accumulated wealth used to produce goods or more wealth.

CAPITAL ASSET As defined by the IRS, it is an asset that can receive favorable tax treatment upon sale. Assets excluded would be inventory, property held for resale, or property used in a trade or business.

CAPITAL GAIN The taxable profit from the sale of a capital asset. The gain is the difference from the basis for the capital asset and the value received less adjustments for the cost of the sale, e.g., sales commissions, discount points, and closing costs.

See RECAPTURE.

CAPITAL IMPROVEMENT A permanent improvement that increases the value of real property and extends the useful life of the property. It is an expenditure that is different from a necessary repair expense. Painting a house is a maintenance or repair expense whereas the installation of vinyl or aluminum siding is a capital improvement.

CAPITALIZATION (1) The procedure of recording interest on a mortgage loan with interest recorded on the due date whether or not a payment is received. Interest is added to the principal balance. Any overdue interest is, therefore, an asset to the lender. (2) The process used in the income approach to value.

See CAPITALIZATION RATE.

CAPITALIZATION RATE Commonly called the *cap rate*, you can use it as a division factor to decide the capital value. The net income from an investment divided by the cap rate will equal the capital value or value. The cap rate is a combination of a return or recapture of the investment and a return on the investment.

The economic life of a building decides the recapture rate. If a building has an economic life of 50 years, then the recapture rate is 2% per year.

Yields available to investors decides the rate of return. If a life insurance company is lending commercial loans at a 9% interest rate, the rate of return is 9% interest. You decide the cap rate by combing the recapture rate and the rate of return. You use the cap rate in the income approach to value. A cap rate is essentially a discount rate used to find the present value of a series of future cash flows. If a building produces $50,000 in net income and the cap rate is 11%, the value is $454,545.

See INWOOD ORDINARY ANNUITY COEFFICIENT and REVERSION FACTOR.

CARDS *See* CERTIFICATES FOR AMORTIZING REVOLVING DEBT.

CARRYBACK FINANCING When the seller helps to finance the sale of property.
See PURCHASE-MONEY MORTGAGE.

CARS *See* CERTIFICATE FOR AUTOMOBILE RECEIVABLES.

CASEMENT WINDOW *See* WINDOW.

CASH BASIS OF ACCOUNTING The method of reporting income and expenditures as they are received. A way of deciding the net profit or loss of a business based solely on income received minus expenses paid.

CASH FLOW Income from an investment after deducting expenses and debt service from gross income and before depreciation and income taxes. Net income minus debt service equals cash flow.
See INTERNAL RATE OF RETURN.

CASH FLOW YIELD An internal monthly yield computed on a mortgage-related security based on an assumed prepayment rate on the underlying mortgages.

CASH-ON-CASH RETURN Rate of return based on cash returned to the investor on his cash investment. The cash-on-cash return is the relationship of the cash returned to the cash invested.

CASH MARKET A market where mortgages or mortgage-backed securities are bought and sold for immediate or forward delivery. The cash market is a part of the secondary market.

CASH-TO-FUTURES BASIS (CFB) The price of a Ginnie Mae or Treasury futures contract relative to changes in prices of their underlying cash market securities. The cash-to-future basis reflects price changes in Ginnie Mae or Treasury futures contracts relative to the change of price of the underlying market for these cash securities. As with other basis factors, some changes can be anticipated with the risk that this component moves contrary to expectations.

CASING A door or window frame.

(CATS) *See* CERTIFICATES OF ACCRUAL ON TREASURY SECURITIES.

CAULKING Flexible putty used to seal a crack or seam in a building and thus prevent passage of air and moisture.

CAUSE OF ACTION Grounds for initiating legal proceedings to seek legal relief from another.

CAVEAT EMPTOR Latin phrase that means "Let the buyer beware." A doctrine that means the buyer should examine the property thoroughly to satisfy any doubts about the condition of the improvements. Caveat emptor is diminishing greatly in the eyes of the courts.

CBOT *See* CHICAGO BOARD OF TRADE.

CC&Rs *See* COVENANTS, CONDITIONS, AND RESTRICTIONS.

CD An Abbreviation for concurrent dates pools only; for GNMA I issuers in pool administration procedures, i.e., pool advances to investors. The concurrent date method is also called the 15 day procedure. For example, The Issuer collects payments from borrowers with an April 1st due date. Payment to the security holders is mandated to be April 15. The Issuer only has 15 days to collect and remit, resulting in advances from corporate funds to remit principal and interest payments due security holders on due but unpaid installments.

CENTRAL PAYING AND TRANSFER AGENT (CPTA) The   institution that Ginnie Mae employs to act on its behalf as: (1) paying agent, by debiting the central P&I accounts of individual issuers and by making payments to holders in connection with GNMA II pools and loan packages; (2) transfer agent, by preparing certificates for mortgage-backed securities issued under the Ginnie Mae program, canceling and re-registering certificates tendered in good form by or for holders and maintaining a central registry of holders for all pools issued under the GNMA II program; and (3) pool processing agent, by reviewing pool and loan package document submissions from issuers in connection with the initial certification under the Ginnie Mae program. Ginnie Mae has appointed Chemical Bank of New York to act as its CPTA (as described in GNMA Handbook 5500.2).

CEASE AND DESIST An order from a governing authority directing a person to stop violating an ordinance. For example, a builder that discriminates in hiring practices can be given a cease and desist order to stop practicing discrimination.

CENTRAL P&I ACCOUNT An issuer's non-interest-bearing account that the CPTA debits monthly via an automated clearinghouse transaction. An issuer can have only one such account as described in GNMA Handbook 5500.2.

CERTIFICATE FOR AMORTIZING REVOLVING DEBT (CARDS)
Credit card-backed securities that give the owner a pro-rata share in a fixed pool of credit card accounts.

CERTIFICATE FOR AUTOMOBILE RECEIVABLES (CARS) Similar to a CMO, but backed by a pool of automobile loans.

CERTIFICATE OF ACCRUAL ON TREASURY SECURITIES (CATS)
An ownership in an investment backed by U.S. Treasury notes and bonds.

CERTIFICATE OF CLAIM A contingent promise to reimburse an insured lender for costs arising from a foreclosure. It is contingent upon the proceeds from the foreclosure sale being sufficient to cover the lender's claim.

CERTIFICATE OF COMMITMENT *See* FHA - CERTIFICATE OF COMMITMENT.

CERTIFICATE OF COMPLETION A document issued by an architect or an engineer certifying that a construction project has been completed according to the terms, conditions, and approved plans and specifications.

CERTIFICATE OF DEPOSIT (CD) A written document provided by a financial institution to evidence a deposit and the rate of interest it shall earn.

CERTIFICATE OF ELIGIBILITY *See* VA - CERTIFICATE OF ELIGIBILITY.

CERTIFICATE OF INSURANCE Proof that insurance is in force. The certificate shows the type of insurance, the amount of coverage, the date coverage, and the expiration date.

CERTIFICATE OF NO DEFENSE *See* ESTOPPEL.

CERTIFICATE OF OCCUPANCY (CO) Official document by governing authority stating that a structure complies with the building code and may be occupied legally.

CERTIFICATE OF REASONABLE VALUE (CRV) *See* VA - CERTIFICATE OF REASONABLE VALUE.

CERTIFICATE OF SALE A certificate issued to the buyer of real property at a judicial sale.

CERTIFICATE OF TITLE A written opinion on the status of the title to real property based on public records. The opinion can be written by a title company, licensed abstractor, or an attorney. A certificate of title does not guarantee the title, it merely gives an opinion of the title. Title insurance guarantees title. The certificate of title certifies the condition of title as of a specified date based on a search of public records maintained by a recorder of deeds, a county clerk, a city clerk, and clerks of different courts of record. The certificate deals with what is only of record. Claims not recorded are beyond the scope of a certificate of title. For this reason, for unrecorded claims, you need title insurance.

CERTIFICATION Refers to a statement used in loan processing. When using a copy of a document and not the original, the lender must certify to the authenticity. For example, a copy of a sales contract must have the following statement: "We hereby certify this copy to be a true and exact copy of the original we have in our possession." The *certification* statement must be signed by the lender. The lender should be aware that any auditor can always ask to see the original; therefore, care should be taken to have possession of the original.

In accepting information provided by loan applicants, lenders can use the following certifications: "WARNING: It is a crime to knowingly make false statements to the United States on this or any other similar form. Penalties upon conviction can include a fine or imprisonment. For details see Title 18 U.S. Code Section 1001 and Section 1010. For FHA loans, lenders can use the following: Section 1010 of Title 18, U.S.C., "Federal Housing Administration Transactions," Provides: "Whoever, for the purpose of—influencing in any way the action of such administration—makes, passes, utter, or publishes any statement, knowing the same to be false—shall be fined not more than $5,000 or imprisoned not more than two years, or both."

See APPRAISER.

CERTIFIED CHECK A check guaranteed to be good by the issuing bank. A stop payment cannot be issued against a certified check. For real estate closings, a certified check is what is normally required to close the transaction.

CERTIFIED COPY A true copy of the original and certified or attested to that fact by the holder of the original.

CERTIFIED MORTGAGE BANKER (CMB) A professional designation awarded by the Mortgage Bankers Association of America to those in the industry who prove superior knowledge and skills in the field of real estate finance. Membership qualifications for the CMB requires the successful completion of a written examination plus an oral exam administered by other CMBs who are selected from the MBA staff. This panel of interviewers test candidates for loan production knowledge in single-family and income property matters such as underwriting, servicing, marketing, appraisals, and corporate strategy. The panel's approach is to pin-point strengths where qualification is justified, not to search for weakness in details of a technical nature. The written exam takes eight hours to complete. The candidate chooses five subject areas out of eight for the questions on real estate finance. The knowledge and professional propensity necessary for a CMB designation is similar to the MAI designation in the appraisal industry. A CMB designation is not assurance that the recipient has reached a level of success in mortgage banking but it helps to establish the member's knowledge needed for success in mortgage banking.

CESSION DEED A deed used to transfer rights to a government authority. A subdivision developer will use a cession deed to transfer control of streets in a subdivision.

CHAIN OF TITLE *See* ABSTRACT OF TITLE.

CHANGE ORDER A form used by a builder to specify changes from the approved original plans or blueprints used to construct a building.

CHATTEL MORTGAGE A lien on personal property that is not permanently attached; something other than real estate.

CHEAP A security having an apparently undervalued price compared to its historical price. A mortgage-backed security may be underpriced according to an investor.
See RICH.

CHICAGO BOARD OF TRADE (CBOT) An organized futures market where investors can competitively trade contracts to buy or sell agreed upon amounts of securities at a negotiated price at a specified future date. For mortgage lenders, institutions can pass along interest rate risks of dealing in these securities to speculators who gamble on interest rate trends. Ginnie Mae financial futures contracts were the first of these futures contracts offered by the CBOT.

CHILD CARE EXPENSE Lenders are now requiring borrowers to disclose information on the cost to care for their children if the parents or single parent is away from the children while at work. The lender considers the cost to be an expense and uses it to decide the qualification ratios.

CIRCLE HEAD WINDOW *See* WINDOW.

CISTERN A tank for storing rainwater.

CIVIL RIGHTS ACT OF 1866 This act was the first federal law to prohibit any type of discrimination based on race.

CIVIL RIGHTS ACT OF 1968 Title VIII prohibits discrimination in mortgage applications and loans because of race or ethnic background.

CL The designation for a pool consisting of a mortgage on a project under construction as described in GNMA Handbook 5500.1.

CLAPBOARD A board used for exterior siding. A clapboard is a long, thin board with edges graduated in thickness from one end to the other. Clapboards overlap each other when in place.

CLEAN-OUT DOOR The door at the base of the chimney. Cleaning a chimney is much easier when there is a clean-out door.

CLEARING ACCOUNT A bank account kept by a mortgage banker for the deposit of mortgage payments that are later cleared out for transmittal to the investor. A clearing account can be used for the deposit of escrow funds.

CLEAR TITLE Title that is free of any clouds and is marketable. Title that is free of any liens, claims, defects, and encumbrances except those agreed to by the buyer or lender, for a mortgage loan.

CLOSED-END MORTGAGE A fixed mortgage amount that cannot be increased.

CLOSED PERIOD A period in the term of a mortgage that prevents a prepayment. This period can be described as a *lock-in* period. Lenders of large commercial loans use the lock-in period to insure the investor (owner of the mortgage) an undisturbed flow of cash for a period of time. Life insurance or pension funds who make large commercial loans favor a commercial loan with a closed period so they need not worry about an unexpected amount of cash returned from an investment.

CLOSING The actual transfer of title from seller to purchaser. People use this term to mean an event when transfer of title will occur such as, "We will meet you at the closing."

Depending upon state law, closing can be handled by an attorney, escrow companies, lenders, brokers, or the parties themselves.

See LOAN ORIGINATION, Step 5, PRE-CLOSING, ESCROW AGENT, and LOAN CLOSER.

CLOSING COSTS All costs related to closing except the prepaid or escrow items. Some examples of closing costs are: loan origination fee, discount points, sales commission, attorney fees, charge for a survey, title insurance premiums, appraisal fee, credit report, cost of a termite report, cost of a loan amortization schedule, recording fees, document preparation fee, mortgage insurance premiums, the VA funding fee, and loan transfer or assumption fee.

A partial list of closing costs allowed to be paid by the buyer on FHA loans include the following:

- the mortgagee's origination fee;
- cost of title search;
- charges for preparation of deed and mortgage documents;
- mortgage tax;
- recording fees;
- a home inspection fee of up to $200;
- an appraisal fee;
- credit report fee; and other similar items.

Besides these acceptable closing costs, the FHA Central office policy is for each FHA office to maintain their list of other acceptable charges and a list of unacceptable closing costs. FHA allows the seller to pay the prepaid items for a purchaser, but the charge will be deducted from the acquisition cost (resulting in a lowering of the maximum loan) since it is viewed as a sales concession.

Each VA Regional Office has an established schedule of allowable fees and charges. The VA list should include prohibited fees and charges.

A list of allowable charges the veteran can pay, according to the VA Central office, includes:

- the appraisal fee;
- recording fees or recording taxes;
- credit report charge;
- proration of taxes or assessments;
- hazard insurance premium;
- survey charges;
- title examination and title insurance premiums;
- a loan origination fee charged by the lender of up to 1% of the loan amount; any allowable discount points;
- and the funding fee charged by the veteran administration (said fee may be financed).

Examples of costs the veteran may not pay are:

- Loan discount or commitment fees, except where the VA has approved payment by the veteran;
- Appraisal fee, except if the veteran's name appears on the Certificate of Reasonable Value;
- Inspection fees for inspections made before the date of the sales contract;
- Photograph fees;
- Repair inspections, pest inspections, and fees for any repairs required by the pest inspection;
- Sales/brokerage commission;
- Settlement or closing fee, document preparation or notary fees (items 1101, 1105, 1106, and 1107 respectively on HUD-1, the uniform settlement statement);
- Recording fees for mortgage release, mortgage assignment;
- Seller's pro-rata share of taxes for the year that the loan is closed;
- Charges for copying, mailing, long distance charges, etc.;
- Excessive charges for survey, title examination, etc.;
- Tax Service fee; and
- IRS Reporting form fees.

CLOSING STATEMENT *See* SETTLEMENT STATEMENT.

CLOUD ON TITLE An existence of a claim or encumbrance that impairs the owner's claim for clear title but usually can be removed by judicial procedure. *See* QUIET TITLE ACTION, QUITCLAIM DEED.

CLUSTER HOUSING A planned subdivision development with dwelling units grouped in close proximity and sharing an open space or other recreation areas such as swimming pool, tennis courts, etc.

CMB *See* CERTIFIED MORTGAGE BANKER.

CMO - COLLATERALIZED MORTGAGE OBLIGATION A corporate pass-through bond that places payments made into a trusteed pool causing the pool of loans to pay principal and interest to security holders on a class-by-class basis where one class is completely paid off before any principal is repaid to the next greater maturity class. Freddie Mac also uses CMOs as call protection for pension fund managers and others with similar investment characteristics. In the early stages of development, CMOs were issued to arbitrage the yield differentials that were apparent between pass-throughs and Treasury bills. This arbitrage profit was an immediately recognized business transaction attributed to the accelerated expansion of markets for CMOs.

A CMO is an amortizing debt instrument collateralized by mortgages or mortgage-backed securities and characterized by cash flow sizing techniques and differential allocation of cash flows to investors. A CMO provides payment predictability with respect to mortgages that are pooled and packaged into mortgage-backed securities (MBS).

CMO TRANCHE A tranche is a portion or series of a bond issue, typically a CMO, that shares documentation with other parts but has different maturities. In a CMO one tranche may have a maturity of five years while another tranche may mature in ten years. *See* PSA EXPERIENCE and FHA EXPERIENCE.

CODE A set of laws or regulations governing subjects such as building regulations or codes and criminal laws or codes.

CODE OF ETHICS A guideline of acceptable practices or behavior subscribed to by an organization such as the National Association of REALTORS.

CODICIL Alteration of an existing will.

COINSURANCE For hazard insurance purposes, it is the requirement of insuring to a minimum percentage of value, usually 80%, so that if there is a loss the insured can collect the full benefit from the loss. If the insured does not meet the minimum percentage, then, if there is a loss, the insurance company will pay for only a percentage of the loss and not 100% of the loss minus the deductible.

For title insurance purposes, coinsurance is the sharing of risks by more than one insurance company. A large commercial project may be too big of a risk for one title company to insure. Instead of passing up the opportunity of writing a policy, the title company will ask other title companies to share in the policy and divide the risk but earn a premium.

See REINSURANCE.

COLD CANVAS A door-to-door solicitation for a specific purpose such as listings for a real estate agent. Agents use this method to establish an area in which they want to be active in listing houses. The area of emphasis is a *farm area*.

COLLATERAL Property that serves as security for a loan. If the borrower does not pay the mortgage, the collateral belongs to the lender.

COLLATERALIZED DEPOSITORY RECEIPT (CDR) The instrument delivered in fulfillment of the Chicago Board of Trade GNMA-CRD, a popular GNMA futures contract.

COLLECTION REPORT An itemized statement showing collection of payments on a debt or mortgage and payments made according to instructions from the investor (owner of the debt). Examples of payments are: real estate taxes, hazard insurance premiums, mortgage term insurance, and disability insurance. The person or company providing the collection service gets paid a stated amount or a percentage of the amount collected.

COLLUSION Two or more parties agree to perform an illegal act. A seller agreeing to reimburse a buyer for the prepaid items on a conventional loan, without having informed the lender, is guilty of committing collusion with the buyer and of entering into a dual contract.

See DUAL CONTRACT.

COLONIAL ARCHITECTURE A home of traditional design, usually two stories, with emphasis on details such as small window panes, balanced openings, shutters, and dormer windows.

See DUTCH COLONIAL, SALT BOX COLONIAL, SOUTHERN COLONIAL.

COLOR OF TITLE Title that appears to be good or clear but has a defect. Color of title is used in cases of adverse possession. If a buyer believed he was buying a property with clear title, as was represented to the buyer by the seller, then the buyer has performed in good faith and through adverse possession can become the true owner with clear title.
See ADVERSE POSSESSION.

COLORADO, OKLAHOMA, LOUISIANA, TEXAS, STATES (COLTS) Starting in 1987, this term was commonly used in Secondary Marketing. Many investors refused to buy mortgage-related assets from these states because of their troubled economies caused by oil related or energy related industries.

COMMERCIAL BANK A privately-owned and operated financial institution chartered by a state or federal agency for stimulating commerce and providing a safe repository for deposited funds. These funds can be disbursed or transferred by check or line of credit. Banks primarily make consumer or short-term loans. These types of institutions offer checking accounts, credit cards, savings, and other consumer or business-related services. Commercial banks are an excellent source for construction loans. Commercial mortgage loans secured by property or other collateral such as pools of loans pledged by mortgage bankers and income producing property are made.

COMMERCIAL PAPER A short-term, unsecured note used to raise capital. Many second mortgage lenders use commercial paper as an excellent primary source for funds to be used for their lending purposes.

CO-MINGLED FUNDS Money mixed into an account deemed improper or illegal. For example, a broker must keep a separate account for earnest money received on deposit. It is illegal or unlawful for the broker to mix those funds with their personal or business account.
For financial institutions, the term *co-mingled funds* relates to money in a single account but separately accounted for and owned.

COMMISSION The compensation for the sale of an asset or a service.

COMMISSIONER'S ADJUSTED FAIR MARKET VALUE (CAFMV) A system adopted by HUD in dealing with pre-foreclosure actions. When the local HUD office receives the appraisal, it will calculate a foreclosure bid price by deducting from the appraised value the estimated costs for holding and reselling the property that HUD would incur if it acquired the property. Requirements are thus set for the way originating lenders must bid at foreclosure sales.

The bid must include notification of the anticipated sale date, the name of the fee appraiser, and the bid price that a lender must offer to retain the option to convey title to HUD. If a lender bids an amount more than the CAFMV, the right to convey the property to HUD is forfeited unless existing state law dictates that lenders can bid more than the CAFMV. In this case, a claim without conveyance of title to HUD is mandatory.

COMMITMENT An agreement to lend money to a borrower at a stated rate within a certain time, subject to compliance with certain conditions. Also, a written agreement between a lender and an investor stating the terms, rates, and conditions under which the investor will purchase loans or mortgage-backed securities from the lender.

A lender's risk position is the key element that creates the need for interest rate commitments. The lender must issue a forward commitment to eliminate the interest rate risk. However, this exposes the lender to new risks if the loan to be delivered to the forward commitment does not close.

A commitment to swap, however, does not affect a lender's risk position. The swap only causes a conversion of securities for eventual sale in the secondary market; instead of cash, lenders are paid in securities issued by Fannie Mae or Freddie Mac under their PC programs. The lender then sells the securities to investors.

See LOAN COMMITMENT.

COMMITMENT FEE A deposit or a reservation fee paid for future use of money. Normally, the deposit or reservation is placed at the time the commitment is rendered. For a loan to a borrower, the commitment fee may be refunded upon the closing of the loan. A commitment letter should be issued upon receipt of the fee. The commitment letter is a written agreement outlining a future commitment by a lender to reserve funds for a borrower subject to terms and conditions.

In secondary marketing there are several types of commitment fees. (1) A straight commitment fee may be paid to investors or prospective investors and may or may not be refundable for a commitment to purchase mortgage-backed securities or whole loans. (2) A standby or gap commitment fee is a non-refundable amount obtained from the sale or purchase of standby whole loan or mortgage-backed security commitments.

COMMON AREAS and COMMON ELEMENTS Reference to property used by owners or tenants; those portions or areas of a condominium used by all the owners. Examples of common areas are: a courtyard, playground area, tennis courts, swimming pools, and recreational facilities.

COMMON LAW A body of laws originating from common or customary practices that developed in England.

COMMUNITY ASSOCIATION A group composed of property owners that serves to protect and maintain a neighborhood or commonly owned properties.

COMMUNITY DEVELOPMENT BLOCK GRANT A federal community development funding program created by Title I of the Housing and Community Development Act of 1974. These grants replace category funding for several grants with a grant that allows communities to choose how to spend the money. This form of grant eliminates the paper work involved in getting HUD approval for individual projects that could be approved in one large grant.

COMMUNITY PROPERTY Ownership of property in common by husband and wife. In states where community property laws exist, each spouse is viewed as an equal and a concurrent owner. Depending on state laws, in case of death the surviving spouse inherits the property.

COMMUNITY REINVESTMENT ACT (CRA) In 1978, Congress enacted CRA to encourage lenders to meet the credit needs of their local communities. The main thrust of the law requires lenders to display a CRA notice, maintain a public comment file, delineate their local communities, and periodic reporting of loan application disposition.
See HOME MORTGAGE DISCLOSURE ACT.

CO-MORTGAGOR An individual who joins in the mortgage loan and ownership of the property. A co-mortgagor is jointly and individually liable for the indebtedness. A common error loan applicants, and sometimes real estate agents, make is to assume that when a loan is denied because of insufficient income, a relative or close friend can overcome this obstacle by serving as a co-mortgagor. For example, a loan application is rejected and the lender explains that the applicant's income is lacking by $100 per month. Often, the applicant assumes that all is needed for loan approval is to find a relative or friend earning $100 per month to act as a co-mortgagor. No. The co-mortgagor must have $100 or more, based on our example, of disposable income *after* all deductions for living expenses. Of course, living expenses includes any mortgage payment, rent payment, all recurring charges - all the same type of deductions and liabilities used for loan qualification. *If* the relative or friend has disposable income in the amount needed for loan application, then the loan applicant has a worthy candidate for a co-mortgagor.

Any co-mortgagor must understand that they are jointly and individually liable. Citibank uses plain language to underline the liability risk to a co-maker.

"If I'm signing this note as a co-maker, I agree to be equally responsible with the borrower. You don't have to notify me that this note hasn't been paid."

The above statement is clear and it reflects two important points about mortgage loans. The first point is that a co-mortgagor is just as liable as the mortgagor. Second, it is not the duty of the lender to inform a mortgagor or co-mortgagor of the duty to pay a mortgage. This second point applies to a mortgagor who allows a buyer to assume a mortgage without a release of liability, or to take title subject to the mortgage. It is not the duty of the lender to notify the original mortgagor of a pending foreclosure on an assumptor.

Since a co-mortgagor is wholly liable for a mortgage there is an immediate harmful effect on their balance sheet. Simply put, liabilities increase by 100% of the amount of the loan, but assets may increase only by 50% of the value of the property. The percentage of ownership depends on how the purchasers agree on the way title is to be taken. It is wise to explore the possibilities of a shared equity loan because liability is limited to the portion of the property owned or shared.

See CO-SIGNER, FHA - RELEASE OF LIABILITY, RELEASE OF LIABILITY, SHARED EQUITY, SURETY, VA - RELEASE OF LIABILITY.

COMPARABLES Properties that are similar or comparable to the subject property. Comparable sales are sales used in the market approach to value. One should take care in using comparables to justify value. Always compare "apples to apples, oranges to oranges" -meaning don't use sales on three-bedroom houses to justify value for a two-bedroom house. Don't use two-story houses as comparison to a one-story house. Keep all comparables in a close area and use recent transfers.

See MARKET APPROACH TO VALUE for a comparable sales chart.

COMPENDIUM *See* FHA - COMPENDIUM, VA - DVB CIRCULARS.

COMPENSATING BALANCES A practice used by banks in the absence of security or collateral for a loan. This method will require a borrower, as a condition for obtaining a loan, to maintain a minimum average balance in an account with the lending institution, said balance normally being a minimum of 20% of the loan amount.

Compensating balances is also used to describe a credit line with an interest rate that is below the prime rate. For example, Company A has a non-interest-bearing bank account that averages nine million dollars. With the bank not having to pay interest on such a large balance, the bank may extend Company A a line of credit at three percent below its prime rate.

COMPENSATING FACTORS In mortgage loan underwriting, exceptions can be made to guidelines established for income ratios for loan qualification. FHA lists examples of the most often encountered compensating factors.

(1) The borrower has a conservative attitude toward the use of credit and has show an ability to accumulate money that results in a minimum reserve of three months mortgage payments after closing.

(2) The borrower has a minimum of ten percent investment in the property.

(3) There is only a small increase in the housing expense, not more than ten percent.

(4) The borrower receives compensation not reflected in effective income, but directly affecting the ability to pay the mortgage and all other obligations.

(5) A considerable amount of effective income is from non-taxable sources.

(6) Income of a temporary nature that cannot be considered as effective, but may be considered available to meet short-term, non-recurring charges.

(7) The term of the mortgage is less than the maximum available, by five years or more.

(8) Smaller families whose living needs permit them to live on less than larger families, or families whose needs are expanding.

(9) Energy-efficient housing.

See INCOME ANALYSIS.

COMPETENT Legally capable of entering a contract; includes being of legal age, mentally competent, and not a drunkard.

COMPLETION BONDS Bonds submitted by contractors to lenders to guarantee completion of construction under certain plans and specifications. Contractors must meet certain experience and knowledge qualifications and post a bond or cash deposit to the state involved in jurisdictional construction matters. The deposit is for the benefit of persons damaged because of contractors violating the State Contractors' License Law.

COMPLIANCE INSPECTION REPORT A written report showing the satisfactory or unsatisfactory completion of work on a building for code requirements or appraisal requirements. An FHA compliance inspection is a certification by an approved inspector that construction work has been done in a workman-like fashion to comply with FHA requirements.

COMPONENT DEPRECIATION An accounting method used to depreciate individual parts or components of a structure or improvement. A practice of dividing components of a structure or improvement into separate depreciating schedules. Examples of components would be electrical, plumbing, heating, air conditioning, roofing, floor covering, and permanently attached appliances. *See* DEPRECIATION.

COMPOUND INTEREST Interest paid on the balance plus accumulated unpaid interest. The interest is immediately added to the balance and then the process begins anew. It is interest upon interest. The method of compounding may be daily, weekly, monthly, quarterly, annually, almost any predetermined time.

COMPROMISE SALES AGREEMENT (CSA) When a borrower is deeply in default and cannot repay the amount due, the lender and borrower can agree to sell the home and turn over the proceeds to the lender. Lenders find compromise agreements helpful in avoiding foreclosure costs and the costs of carry real estate owned property.

For VA loans, the Veterans Administration, through the applicable VA regional office, must approve all compromise sales agreements. Before the VA will approve a compromise agreement, certain documents must be submitted: (1) statement of account as of the estimated closing date; (2) a copy of the sales contract; (3) a recent appraisal; (4) a liability release package if a VA loan is to be assumed; and (5) veteran's acknowledgment for the compromise claim.

The following events are typical in a CSA: a VA borrower will sell their property at the fair market value but if the selling price is too low to clear the existing loan entirely, the VA then makes up this difference in a pay-off to the VA lender. A liability agreement must be made to remain in debt to the government by the borrower, in that this pay-off by the VA to the lender is absolute. The compromise agreement is a possible way to avoid foreclosure by the lender where a negative equity situation exists or where delinquent interest has caused an increase in the remaining balance of the mortgage, above the value of the veteran's property.

Inquiries regarding the compromise agreement process should be addressed to the local regional office of the VA. *See* DEED-IN-LIEU OF FORECLOSURE.

COMPTROLLER OF THE CURRENCY (OCC) Official appointed by the President. The Office of the Comptroller of the Currency is responsible for chartering, examining, supervising and liquidating national banks.

COMPUTERIZED LOAN ORIGINATION SYSTEM (CLO) An electronic system that furnishes subscribers with the latest data on available loan programs at a variety of lending institutions. A CLO may offer buyer pre-qualifications or mortgage information services. Some CLO systems can process loan applications, underwrite loans and make commitments of funds. MIDANET and LASER are Freddie Mac's and Fannie Mae's automated loan delivery and accounting vehicles, respectively.

Clos inevitably raise the problem of referral fees paid to real estate agents using this development in technology. Some lenders have offered CLO systems to real estate agents and will pay them a fee for using the system and referring loans to the lender. In the past, before the fall of 1990, the MBA has aggressively contested the payment of referral fees to real estate agents who provide nothing more than basic loan information to borrowers. The MBA believes that some referral fees violate Section 8 (a) of RESPA. On September 18, 1990, HUD General Counsel Frank Keating testified before the House Subcommittee on Housing and Community Development on several issues involving RESPA, including the payment of referral fees for real estate agents that use a computerized loan origination system (CLO). HUD believes consumers are interested in the services provided by these systems; namely, access to the interest rates and loan terms of multiple lenders. The agency intends to propose that all real estate agents who offer CLOs must offer the products of multiple lenders. In addition, the real estate agent will be required to disclose to the homebuyer that the agent will receive a fee for the CLO service and further that there are other lenders, not on the system, that may offer more favorable terms. The maximum referral fee allowed is not established at the time of this writing, but it is projected to be a top of from $250 to $300. The settling of the issue of referral fees is a welcome relief by all participates in the mortgage industry. Some lenders, such as Citicorp with their Mortgage Power program, had been paying referral fees to real estate agents, mortgage brokers, accountants, attorneys and others who were paid participants in their CLO program. Citicorp operated this program under a "private opinion letter." The program gave Citicorp an unfair advantage of sorts since others in the industry could not imitate it without seeking a similar private opinion letter, which is very expense in legal costs. Mr. Keating noted during the week's hearing that the effect of the opinion letter was to help create a monopoly through Citicorp. "We should speak in a generic manner to the industry, not to one person," said Keating. In further testimony, Keating said: "If technology has reached the point where loan origination and loan information can be provided by real estate brokers efficiently and economically, then in our view it is in the interest of the homebuyer to use this service. By shutting the door on CLO systems before they have had a chance to develop, we would be denying the existence of a new technology and ensuring that consumers could never realize any of the potential benefits of a carefully regulated CLO system." Keating addressed the issue of conflict of interest as it applies to real estate brokers. Keating said HUD does not consider this a legitimate concern. "Although the broker, in short, is not the representative of the buyer, he has an obligation to deal with the buyer professionally and ethically. Use of a CLO is, in this respect, no different than a standard real estate transaction, in which the broker usually represents the seller. The key to ensuring that this process protects the consumer and allows effective enforcement is full disclosure, and to that principle the secretary is fully committed." HUD proposes that disclosure be made on the good faith estimate and the real estate settlement statement (HUD-1). Mr. Keating noted that currently, section 8 (a) of RESPA prohibits giving and accepting "any fee, kickback or thing of value" for the referral of business, and section 8 (b) prohibits the giving and acceptance of any portion of funds paid by the borrower of settlement services "other than for services actually performed."

Let us now look at a CLO system. The author, Albert Santi, is the exclusive FHA/VA and Conventional Consultant for CDI, incorporated. The CDI *Qualification Commander* is the only software to be tested and recommended by the Commercial Investment Real Estate (CCIM) and Residential Sales (RS) councils of the National Association of REALTORS. Since this software has been sold to many lenders, particularly by the author, it is important to note that the following CLO demonstration is FOR USE BY A LOAN OFFICER OR A REAL ESTATE AGENT. Used in the demonstration is the *Closing Module* and *Buy v. Rent. Qualification Commander* retails for $249.95, the *Closing Module* is $89.95, and *Buy v. Rent* is $89.95.

Estimated Maximum Loans for Tim Norwood

CONVENTIONAL LOAN

RATE	10.000 %
ESTIMATED MAXIMUM LOAN:	$ 46397.95
MONTHLY PAYMENT:	$ 407.18
ESTIMATED TAX SAVINGS—:	$ 0.00
Actual Top Loan Ratio—:	15.42%
Actual Bottom Ratio—:	36.00%

Limiting Loan Ratio is the Bottom Ratio.

VA INSURED LOAN

RATE:	9.500%
ESTIMATED MAXIMUM LOAN:	$121100.00
MONTHLY PAYMENT:	$ 1018.27
LOAN RATIO:	55.35%
ESTIMATED TAX SAVINGS—:	$ 76.87
ESTIMATED LOAN AT 41%—:	$ 69048.17
MONTHLY PAYMENT:	$ 580.59

FHA INSURED LOAN

RATE:	9.500%
ESTIMATED MAXIMUM LOAN:	$ 67207.39
MONTHLY PAYMENT:	$ 565.12
ESTIMATED TAX SAVINGS—:	$ 0.00
Actual Top Loan Ratio—:	20.42%
Actual Bottom Ratio—:	41.00%

Limiting Loan Ratio is the Bottom Ratio.

ALL INFORMATION WILL BE KEPT CONFIDENTIAL
THIS IS ONLY AN ESTIMATE, AND IS BASED ON 1990 TAX DATA.

Step 1. Tim Norwood calls a lender or real estate agent and asks about qualifying for a home loan. A loan officer, named Sue, tells Tim that for a quick qualification, Tim must give his income and the sum of his monthly debts. Tim explains that he is in the Air Force and the income is somewhat different from a salaried person. Sue asks: "What is your pay grade?" Tim answers: "I am an officer, pay grade 02 and I have an off-base housing allowance of $400." Sue asks: "How long have you been in service?" Tim replies: "For ten years." Sue then asks about his monthly debts. Tim tells her that he has the following monthly payments: car—$250, Visa—$150, Sears—$250.

While Tim has been giving Sue answers to her questions she has entered the information in her computer. When Tim said he was an officer, Sue changed the setting on her quick qualification menu form Mr. to 02. When Sue entered 10 (for length of service) the computer automatically gave her Tim's monthly income (QC will do this for any branch and for any pay grade). She entered the debts and then pressed her F9 key for "DONE." The computer then showed her this printout on the screen. That's it! In less than one minute, Sue can tell Tim the maximum loan he qualified on all three loan types, Conventional, VA, and FHA.

Detailed Estimated of a FHA Loan for Tim Norwood

LOAN INTEREST RATE:	9.500%
LOAN TERM:	30 years
THE MAXIMUM FHA LOAN IS	$ 67200.00
THE MONTHLY PAYMENT IS	$ 565.05
TOTAL BUYER INCOME:	$ 3158.82
× BOTTOM LOAN RATIO:	41.00%

=	$ 1295.12
– LONG TERM DEBTS:	$ 650.00

= REMAINING BALANCE:	$ 645.12
TOTAL BUYER INCOME:	$ 3158.82
× TOP LOAN RATIO:	29.00%

= PROPOSED PITI:	$ 916.06
FUNDS AVAIL FOR PITI:	$ 645.12
– ESTIMATED INSURANCE:	$ 30.00

= AVAILABLE FOR PIT:	$ 615.12
– ESTIMATED PROP. TAX:	$ 50.00

= AVAILABLE FOR P & I	$ 565.12

The Actual Top Ratio is 20.42%
The Actual Bottom Ratio is 41.00%
The maximum loan is limited by the Bottom Ratio.

ALL INFORMATION WILL BE KEPT CONFIDENTIAL
THIS IS ONLY AN ESTIMATE, AND IS BASED ON 1990 TAX DATA.

Step 2. Tim says he does not want to use his VA eligibility at this time. He asks if he can have a copy of the quick qualification. Sue tells Tim that she will not only give him a printout but she also can give him a detailed estimate of an FHA qualification. Step 2 is the FHA detailed estimate.

FHA Loan Income Estimate for a Family of 4

Prepared By: Mary Smith
Home For ⇒ 2800 Dogwood Lane
Sale at ⇒ Mountain Top, TN

Loan Rate: 9.50%
Loan Term: 30 years
Ratios: 29.0/41.0

This home has three bedrooms, two baths, a den with fireplace, cent. heat and air, and a 2-car garage. The exterior is brick.

Loan Information:

Sale Price of Home:	$	80000.00
− Amount of Price Financed:	$	78750.00
= Minimum Downpayment:	$	1250.00
Amount of Price Financed:	$	78750.00
+ FHA Loan Insurance:	$	2950.00
= Total Financed:	$	81700.00
Mo. Principal/Interest:	$	686.98
+ Mo. Property Tax:	$	50.00
+ Mo. Hazard Insurance Cost:	$	360.00
+ Mo. Homeowner Fees:	$	0.00
= Total for PITI & Fees:	$	1096.98
− Estimated Tax Savings:	$	40.10
= Net Monthly Payment:	$	1056.88
ESTIMATED INCOME TO QUALIFY:	$	3782.69 ⇐
Maximum Debt at This income:	$	453.92

THIS IS ONLY AN ESTIMATE, AND IS BASED ON 1990 TAX DATA.

Step 3. Tim looks at an open house over the weekend and finds one he likes. A REALTOR® gives him a print out of a *reverse qualification* income estimate she gave to everyone that looked at the listing. Tim has never before seen an estimate like the one the agent gave him. The agent explained to Tim that she has a software program named *Qualification Commander* that allows her to give any loan amount and receive the required income and maximum debts to qualify for a FHA, VA, or Conventional loan. With this feature the user does not need to know the income and debts to be given a loan amount. **Step 3** is the reverse qualification for an FHA, Conventional, and a VA loan.

Step 3 continued
FHA Loan Income Estimate for a Family of 4

Prepared By: Mary Smith   Loan Rate: 9.50%
Home For ⇒ 2800 Dogwood Lane   Loan Term: 30 years
Sale at ⇒ Mountain Top, TN   Ratios: 29.0/41.0

This home has three bedrooms, two baths, a den with fireplace, cent. heat and air, and a 2-car garage. The exterior is brick.

BUYDOWN Loan Information:

Note: Assumes the first year interest rate is bought down 3 points

	Sale Price of Home:	$	80000.00
–	Amount of Price Financed:	$	78750.00
=	Minimum Downpayment:	$	1250.00
	Amount of Price Financed:	$	78750.00
+	FHA Loan Insurance:	$	2950.00
=	Total Financed:	$	81700.00
	Mo. Principal/Interest:	$	516.40
+	Mo. Property Tax:	$	50.00
+	Mo. Hazard Insurance Cost:	$	360.00
+	Mo. Homeowner Fees:	$	0.00
=	Total for PITI & Fees:	$	926.40
–	Estimated Tax Savings:	$	0.00
=	Net Monthly Payment:	$	926.40
	ESTIMATED INCOME TO QUALIFY:	$	3194.48 ⇐
	Maximum Debt at This Income:	$	383.34
	Cost of the Buydown:	$	4140.88

THIS IS ONLY AN ESTIMATE, AND IS BASED ON 1990 TAX DATA.

Step 3 continued
VA Guaranteed Loan Income Estimate for a Family of 4

Prepared By: Mary Smith
Home For ⇒   2800 Dogwood Lane
Sale at ⇒   Mountain Top, TN

Loan Rate: 9.50%
Loan Term: 30 years

This home has three bedrooms, two baths, a den with fireplace, cent. heat and air, and a 2-car garage. The exterior is brick.

Loan Information

Sale Price of Home:	$ 80000.00	
− Amount of Price Financed:	$ 80000.00	
= Minimum Downpayment:	$ 0.00	
Amount of Price Financed:	$ 80000.00	
+ VA Loan Funding Fee:	$ 1000.00	
= Total Financed:	$ 81000.00	

Projected tax savings is based on tiemizing mortgage interest, property tax, and state tax.

This income analysis is based on income ratio, not minimum balance. The minimum balance required for this home is $893.00

Mo. Principal/Interest:	$ 681.09
+ Mo. Property Tax:	$ 50.00
+ Mo. Hazard Insurance Cost:	$ 360.00
+ Mo. Homeowner Fees:	$ 0.00
= Total for PITI & Fees:	$ 1091.09
− Estimated Tax Savings:	$ 25.63 (Using Debt = 300)
= Net Monthly Payment:	$ 1065.45

Example ESTIMATED Income Profiles to Qualify (based on differing debt):

AMOUNT OF EST. DEBT ⇒	$ 0.00	100.00	300.00	500.00
+ Monthly Federal Tax:	$ 256.96	285.72	358.23	452.39
+ Monthly State Tax:	$ 0.00	0.00	0.00	0.00
+ Monthly Soc. Sec Tax:	$ 204.97	219.64	256.62	293.60
+ Total Home Expenses*:	$ 1321.09	1321.09	1321.09	1321.09
= Total Expenses:	$ 1783.02	1926.45	2235.94	2567.08
EST. INCOME TO QUALIFY:	$ 2679.39	2871.09	3354.49	3837.89
− Total Expenses:	$ 1783.02	1926.45	2235.94	2567.08
= Balance for Support:	$ 896.37	944.64	1118.55	1270.81
= Estimated Tax Savings:	$ 25.62	25.63	25.63	47.28
= Est Balance w/Savings:	$ 922.00	970.27	1144.18	1318.09
Income Ratio**	40.72	41.49	41.47	41.46

* Total home expense includes PITI, monthly utility, maintenance, and fees.
** You must meet the income ratio test to qualify without additional justification. This makes the income ratio a good test of qualification.

THIS IS ONLY AN ESTIMATE, AND IS BASED ON 1990 TAX DATA.

Step 3 continued
Conventional Fixed Rate Loan Income Estimate for a Family of 4

Prepared By:	Mary Smith	Loan Rate:	10.00%
Home For ⇒	2800 Dogwood Lane	Loan Term:	30 years
Sale at ⇒	Mountain Top, TN	Ratios:	28.0/36.0

This home has three bedrooms, two baths, a den with fireplace, cent. heat and air, and a 2-car garage. The exterior is brick.

Loan Information:

	20% DOWN	10% DOWN	5% DOWN
Sale Price of Home:	$ 80000.00	80000.00	80000.00
− Mortgage Amount:	$ 64000.00	72000.00	76000.00
= Minimum Downpayment:	$ 16000.00	8000.00	4000.00
Mo. Principal/Interest:	$ 561.65	631.85	666.95
+ Mo. Property Tax:	$ 50.00	50.00	50.00
+ Mo. Hazard Insurance Cost:	$ 360.00	360.00	360.00
+ Mo. Homeowner Fees:	$ 0.00	0.00	0.00
+ Mo. Mortgage Insurance Cost:	$ 0.00	20.40	31.03
= Total for PITI & Fees:	$ 971.65	1062.25	1107.98
− Estimated Tax Savings:	$ 0.00	41.54	47.83
= Net Monthly Payment:	$ 971.65	1020.71	1060.15
ESTIMATED INCOME TO QUALIFY:	$ 3470.18	3793.75	3957.08
Maximum Debt at This Income:	$ 277.61	303.50	316.57
PMI Factor Used in Analysis:	0.00	0.00340	0.00490

THIS IS ONLY AN ESTIMATE, AND IS BASED ON 1990 TAX DATA.

Step 3 continued
Financing Estimate Spreadsheet for a Family of 4

Prepared By: Mary Smith
Home For ⇒   2800 Dogwood Lane
Sale at ⇒   Mountain Top, TN

This home has three bedrooms, two baths, a den with fireplace, cent. heat and air, and a 2-car garage. The exterior is brick.

Loan Information:

Loan Program: Type of Financing:		Conv Fixed	FHA Fixed	FHA Fixed	VA Fixed
		5% Down		3% Buydown	
Loan Interest Rate:	%	10.000	9.500	9.500	9.500
Loan Term:		30	30	30	30
Sale Price of Home:	$	80000.00	80000.00	80000.00	80000.00
− Mortgage Amount:	$	76000.00	78750.00	78750.00	80000.00
= Minimum Downpayment:	$	4000.00	1250.00	1250.00	0.00
FHA Mortgage Insurance:	$	0.00	2950.00	2950.00	0.00
+ VA Funding Fee (financed):	$	0.00	0.00	0.00	1000.00
+ Mortgage Amount:	$	76000.00	78750.00	78750.00	80000.00
= Total Financed:	$	76000.00	81700.00	81700.00	81000.00
Mo. Principal/Interest:	$	666.95	686.98	516.40	681.09
+ Mo. Property Tax:	$	50.00	50.00	50.00	50.00
+ Mo. Hazard Insurance Cost:	$	360.00	360.00	360.00	360.00
+ Mo. Homeowner Fees:	$	0.00	0.00	0.00	0.00
+ Mo. Mortgage Insurance Cost:	$	31.03	0.00	0.00	0.00
= Total for PITI & Fees:	$	1107.98	1096.98	926.40	1091.09
− Estimated Tax Savings:	$	47.83	40.10	0.00	25.63
= Net Monthly Payment:	$	1060.15	1056.88	926.40	1065.46
ESTIMATED INCOME TO QUALIFY:	$	3957.08	3782.69	3194.48	3354.49
Maximum Debt at This Income:	$	316.57	453.92	383.34	300.00

THIS IS ONLY AN ESTIMATE, AND IS BASED ON 1990 TAX DATA.

FHA Insured Loan Qualification

SALE PRICE OF HOME: $ 80000.00
AMOUNT OF MORTGAGE: $ 81327.00 (M.I.P. FINANCED)

FIXED RATE AT 9.500%

Name : TIM NORWOOD
Title   : 02

BUYER INCOME DATA:

Buyer's Monthly Income:	$ 3158.82
Total Tax Free Income:	$ 946.62
Spouse's Monthly Income:	$ 0.00
Other Monthly Income:	$ 0.00
Total Monthly Income:	$ 3158.82

QUALIFICATION SUMMARY:

29.00% of Monthly Income:	$ 916.06
41.00% of Monthly Income:	$1295.12

CALCULATIONS:

41.00% of Monthly Income:	$ 1295.12
Total Mo. Long-Term Debt:	$650.00
Remaining Balance:	$645.12

Remaining Balance Is Less than 29.00% of Income.

Remaining Balance:	$645.12
Total for Housing Expenses:	$763.84
	−118.72

Actual Ratios: 24.18/44.76

THE BUYER IS NOT QUALIFIED

ALL INFORMATION WILL BE KEPT CONFIDENTIAL
THIS IS ONLY AN ESTIMATE, AND IS BASED ON 1990 TAX DATA.

Step 4. When Tim looked at the information in Step 3, he saw there would be trouble qualifying for a loan to buy the house because he had more debts than the maximum listed on the *reverse qualification* sheet. But he decides to call Sue, the loan officer. Sue tells Tim that she recommended the QC software to the REALTOR® and there wasn't much doubt that the numbers are correct. But she agreed to run the numbers and see what QC says. The bad news is just after the actual ratios on this printout.

Step 4 continued
FHA Insured Loan Qualification

FAMILY INCOME SUMMARY FOR TIM NORWOOD

DEBT HISTORY:	# OBLIGATIONS	PAYMENT
	1. Car	250.00
	2. Visa	150.00
	3. Sears	250.00
	4.	0.00
	5.	0.00
	6.	0.00
	7.	0.00
	8.	0.00
	9.	0.00
	10.	0.00
		650.00

INCOMING CASH:

Buyer's Monthly Income:	$ 3158.82
Spouse's Monthly Income:	$ 0.00
Other Monthly Income:	$ 0.00
Withholding Tax Savings:	$ 25.62
Total Monthly Income:	$ 3184.44

OUTGOING CASH:

Monthly Federal Income Tax:	$ 186.88 (4 ALLOWANCES)
Monthly State Income Tax:	$ 0.00
Monthly Social Security Tax:	$ 169.23
Monthly Property Tax:	$ 50.00
Monthly Hazard Insurance:	$ 30.00
Monthly Mortgage Payment:	$ 683.84
Total Mo. Long-Term Debt:	$ 650.00
Monthly Homeowner's Assoc.:	0.00
Maintenance + Utility Costs:	$ 120.00
Total Monthly Costs:	$ 1889.95
Total Monthly Income:	$ 3184.44
Total Monthly Costs:	$ 1889.95
Balance for Family Support:	$1294.49

DOWNPAYMENT + LOAN COSTS (MIP) + CLOSING COSTS= $3641.20
REQUIRED

ALL INFORMATION WILL BE KEPT CONFIDENTIAL
THIS IS ONLY AN ESTIMATE, AND IS BASED ON 1990 TAX DATA.

FHA Insured Loan Qualification

SALE PRICE OF HOME: $ 80000.00
AMOUNT OF MORTGAGE: $ 81327.00 (M.I.P. FINANCED)

FIXED RATE AT 9.500%

Name : TIM NORWOOD
Title   : 02

BUYER INCOME DATA:
Buyer's Monthly Income: $ 3158.82
Total Tax Free Income: $ 946.62
Spouse's Monthly Income: $ 0.00
Other Monthly Income: $ 0.00
                             _____
Total Monthly Income: $ 3158.82

QUALIFICATION SUMMARY:
29.00% of Monthly Income: $ 916.06
41.00% of Monthly Income: $ 1295.12

CALCULATIONS:
41.00% of Monthly Income: $ 1295.12
Total Mo. Long-Term Debt: $ 400.00
                             _____
Remaining Balance: $ 895.12

Remaining Balance Is Less than 29.00% of Income.

Remaining Balance: $ 895.12
Total for Housing Expenses: $ 763.84
                             _____
                                131.28
Actual Ratios: 24.18/36.84

THE BUYER IS QUALIFIED

ALL INFORMATION WILL BE KEPT CONFIDENTIAL
THIS IS ONLY AN ESTIMATE, AND IS BASED ON 1990 TAX DATA.

Step 5. Sue decides to do a little counseling. She asks Tim if he can pay off the bill to Sears. He says he can. Sue presses the F3 key and deletes the Sears bill, then presses F9 for "DONE." After the actual ratios, the good news appears!

Step 5 continued
FHA Insured Loan Qualification

FAMILY INCOME SUMMARY FOR TIM NORWOOD

DEBT HISTORY:	# OBLIGATIONS	PAYMENT
	1. Car	250.00
	2. Visa	150.00
	3.	0.00
	4.	0.00
	5.	0.00
	6.	0.00
	7.	0.00
	8.	0.00
	9.	0.00
	10.	0.00
		400.00

INCOMING CASH:

Buyer's Monthly Income:	$ 3158.82
Spouse's Monthly Income:	$ 0.00
Other Monthly Income:	$ 0.00
Withholding Tax Savings:	$ 25.62
Total Monthly Income:	$ 3184.44

OUTGOING CASH:

Monthly Federal Income Tax:	$ 186.88
Monthly State Income Tax:	$ 0.00
Monthly Social Security Tax:	$ 169.23
Monthly Property Tax:	$ 50.00
Monthly Hazard Insurance:	$ 30.00
Monthly Mortgage Payment:	$ 683.84
Total Mo. Long-Term Debt:	$ 400.00
Monthly Homeowner's Assoc.:	$ 0.00
Maintenance + Utility Costs:	$ 120.00
Total Monthly Costs:	$ 1639.95
Total Monthly Income:	$ 3184.44
Total Monthly Costs:	$ 1639.95
Balance for Family Support:	$ 1544.49

DOWNPAYMENT + LOAN COSTS (MIP) + CLOSING COSTS $3641.20
REQUIRED

ALL INFORMATION WILL BE KEPT CONFIDENTIAL
THIS IS ONLY AN ESTIMATE, AND IS BASED ON 1990 TAX DATA.

Good Faith Estimate of the Buyer's Closing Costs

Prepared by: Sue
Property Address: 2800 Dogwood Lane
Mountain Top, TN
Sale Price: $80000
Mortgage Amount: $81327
(Mortgage includes $2977 for the financed MIP)

Prepared for: TIM NORWOOD
Downpayment: $1650
Rate: 9.500%
Term: 30 years

ESTIMATED CLOSING COSTS:

HUD-1	ITEM		
801	Loan Origination Fee:	$ 783.50	
802	Loan Discount Points (1.0):	$ 813.27	
803	Appraisal Fee:	$ 200.00	
804	Credit Report:	$ 35.00	
805	Miscellaneous Lender Fees:	$ 50.00	
806	Prepaid PMI Insurance:	$ 0.30	
807	Assumption Fee:	$ 0.00	800 Series Total: $1882.07
901	Pre-Paid Interest (3 days):	$ 63.48	
903	1 Year's Hazard Insurance:	$ 360.00	900 Series Total: $423.48
1001	Hazard Insurance Escrow:	$ 60.00	
1002	PMI Escrow:	$ 0.00	
1003/4	Property Tax Escrow:	$ 100.00	1000 Series Total: $160.00
1107–7	Attorney Fees:	$ 250.00	
1108–10	Title Insurance:	$ 213.32	1100 Series Total: $463.32
1201/3	Recording Fee (Deed):	$ 210.00	
1201/3	Recording Fee (Mortgage):	$ 213.32	1200 Series Total: $423.32
Other	Misc. Other Costs:	$ 0.00	
1301	Survey:	$ 300.00	
1303	Misc. Settlement Charge:	$ 200.00	1300 Series Total: $500.00

Tot. Closing Costs: $3852.19

TOTAL CASH DUE AT SETTLEMENT:

	Closing Costs:	$ 3852.19
+	Downpayment:	$ 1650.00
=		$ 5502.19
–	Deposit:	$ 0.00
-	Paid by Seller:	$ 0.00
=	Estimated Due:	$ 5502.19

Purchaser:_____   :_____
Sales Associate:_____

Note: This estimate of closing costs is provided in good faith. The actual costs will be calculated at the closing and may be different than estimated here. Attorney fees, surveys, lender fees, etc., all vary. We believe these figures to be a reasonable estimate, but they cannot be guaranteed. The interest charge is based on three days at $21.16 per day.

Step 6. Tim wants to know how much the settlement requirements will be, including the closing costs.

Compare Two Loans

> Loan #1 Type: ADJUSTABLE <

Mortgage Amount: $81327   Mortgage Term: 30   Mortgage Rate: 7.750%
Adjustment Period: 12 Mo.   Adjust. Cap: 2.00%   Life Cap: 5.0

> Loan #1 Type: FIXED RATE <

Mortgage Amount: $81327   Mortgage Term: 30   Mortgage Rate: 9.500%
Biweekly? <Y/N>: N

TOTAL PAYMENTS

YEAR	ADJ 7.750%	FIX 9.500%	CUMULATIVE SAVINGS
1	6992	8206	1214
2	15352	16412	1060
3	25133	24618	515
4	35637	32824	-2812
5	46140	41030	-5110
6	56644	49236	-7408
7	67148	57443	-9706
8	77652	65649	-12003
9	88156	73855	-14301
10	98660	82061	-16599
11	109164	90267	-18897
12	119667	98473	-21194
13	130171	106679	-23492
14	140675	114885	-25790
15	151179	123091	-28088
16	161683	131297	-30385
17	172187	139503	-32683
18	182690	147709	-34981
19	193194	155916	-37279
20	203698	164122	-39576

Mo. Payments at Start of Loan Are:

ADJ	FIX	Savings
582.64	683.84	101.20

Breakeven Point Occurs at:
2 Years, 8.1 Months

Payment Increase Scenario:

MONTH	ADJ	FIX	Savings
1	582.64	683.84	101.20
12	696.68	683.84	-12.84
24	815.08	683.84	-131.24
36	875.32	683.84	-191.48

These numbers have been computed in good faith.
All risk associated with their use rests with the user.

Step 7. Tim now asks about an ARM loan; Sue gives him the rates. He asks if it will be better to go with a 7.75% ARM or to stick with a 9.5% FHA loan. Does Sue get frustrated? Never! Sue knows that "QC" can tell Tim the answer in one of four ways: (1) worst case scenario, (2) first year after tax, (3) breakeven analysis, and (4) amortization basis. This printout is based on a breakeven analysis and shows the breakeven point occurring at 2 years, 8.1 months—after which Tim will be better off with a fixed rate

Income vs Payment Analysis
Adjustable Rate Loan

BASELINE DATA		RATE OF INCREASE DATA	
Total Mo. Income:	$ 3158	Income Increases	4.0% per year
Mortgage Amount:	$81327	Prop Tax Increases	2.0% per year
Mortgage Term:	30 Years	Insurance Increases	2.0% per year
Mortgage Rate:	7.750%	Adjustment Period:	12 months
Mo. Property Tax:	$ 50.00	Adj. Period Cap:	2.00 max increase
Mo. Insurance:	$ 30.00	Life of Loan Cap:	5.0% max increase

YR	Monthly Payment	Property Tax	Insurance	Total	Monthly Income	Total as % of Income
1	$ 582.64	$ 50.00	$ 30.00	$ 662.64	$ 3158.00	20.98%
2	$ 696.67	$ 51.00	$ 30.60	$ 778.27	$ 3284.32	23.70%
3	$ 815.07	$ 52.02	$ 31.21	$ 898.30	$ 3415.69	26.30%
4	$ 875.31	$ 53.06	$ 31.84	$ 960.21	$ 3552.32	27.03%
5	$ 875.31	$ 54.12	$ 32.47	$ 961.91	$ 3694.41	26.04%

These numbers have been computed in good faith.
All risk associated with their use rests with the user.

Step 8. Tim openly worries about keeping up with the payment increases if the interest adjusts to the maximum each year. Sue tells him that she can print a five-year forecast based on given parameters. Together, they select the percentage increases listed in the brackets under RATE OF INCREASE DATA. Sue says "Tim, your total PITI to your monthly income starts at 20.98%, reaches a high of 27.03% in the fourth year and is 26.06% in the fifth year. The percentage of the PITI to your monthly income is less than a 6% increase at the end of four years." Tim decides to take the fixed rate loan.

Tax Savings
Withholding Tax Method

MORTGAGE BACKGROUND		INCOME BACKGROUND	

MORTGAGE BACKGROUND

Mortgage Amount:	$81327
Mortgage Term:	30 Years
Mortgage Rate:	9.500%
Property Tax:	$ 50.00 Mo.

Results in (1st Year):

| Monthly Payment: | $ 683.84 |
| × | 12 |

| = Annual Payment: | $ 8206.10 |
| − Principal Paid: | $ 501.50 |

| = Interest Paid → | $ 7704.60 |

INCOME BACKGROUND

Current Situation:

| Filing Status <S/M>: | M |
| Total Income (Monthly): | $ 3158 |

Number of Withholding
| Allowances Claimed: | 4 |
| Federal Withholding Tax: | $ 328.75 |

Estimated Tax Savings

The Mortgage Interest and Property Tax permits One More Allowance to Be Claimed for a Monthly Tax Savings of: $25.62

These numbers have been computed in good faith.
All risk associated with their use rests with the user.

Step 9. Tim now wants to know how the interest rate deduction will affect his income tax status. Sue doesn't say to herself: "I'm not a CPA! What more does this guy want?" Sue does not get upset because she knows that in a matter of minutes "OC" can furnish the answer. Sue informs Tim that she can give a "good faith attempt" at answering his question with the assistance of the computer. After Sue tells Tim that he can claim one more allowance and increase his monthly paycheck by $25.62, she advises Tim that he should later consult with a tax expert for final results. If Sue forgets to tell Tim about seeking professional advice, it is not a problem since the printout comes with a disclaimer statement.

Refinance Worksheet

This analysis is based on the assumption that you will stay in your current home for an additional 60 months.

Background Data:

Discount Rate:	6.00%
Date of First Payment:	05/01/1991
Effective Date of New Loan:	04/01/1991
Tax Bracket:	28.0%

ORIGINAL LOAN INFORMATION

Mortgage Amount:	$81327
Mortgage Term:	30 years
Mortgage Rate:	9.500%
Monthly Payment:	$ 683.84

NEW LOAN INFORMATION

Mortgage Amount:	$81367
Mortgage Term:	360 months
Mortgage Rate:	7.500%
Monthly Payment:	$ 568.93

REFINANCING COSTS

Closing Costs (5.0%):	$4068.35
2.0 Loan Discount Points:	$1627.34
Present Value of Add'l Income Tax:	$1989.29
Total Refinancing Costs:	$7684.98

Step 10. Tim now wonders if he selects the 9.5% FHA loan and rates come down, at what point will it be worthwhile to refinance? Tim says: "I understand that anytime the rate is more than 2% below your present rate, it is worthwhile to refinance." Sue says: "That rule of thumb is not always accurate. Let us assume you will own the home for five years, which is about the national average for the length of time a homeowner resells. Let us also assume a new loan is available at 7.5%, which is 2% less than the 9.5% rate, and that you will pay a 2% discount and 5% in closing costs. With these assumptions, you will lose $1,741.20 if you follow the 2% rule of thumb. You will have to own the home for 95 months before you breakeven from refinancing (shown on the printout). The best way to refinance is by taking a rate that is higher than the going rate, even as small as of 1%, for example 8% instead of 7.5%, and have the lender pay your closing costs and any discount points. With this type of refinancing it will pay you to refinance even when the rate is less than a 2% decrease in your existing rate."

Step 10 continued

Analysis:
Original Loan Projection (60 months):
    Total Interest Paid: $37997.32   Breakeven Point
    Total Principal Paid: $ 3033.08   Is 95 Months

New Loan Projection (60 months):
    Total Interest Paid: $29756.19
    Total Principal Paid: $ 4379.61

	Present Value of the Original Loan Payments:	$ 35372.01
–	Present Value of the New Loan Payments:	$ 29428.22
=	Gross New Loan Savings:	$ 5943.78
–	Total Refinancing Cost:	$ 7684.98
=	Net Savings Associated with the New Loan:	$ –1741.20

Mortgage Accelerator Analysis

Mortgage Amount:	$ 81327	Monthly Payment:	$ 683.84
Interest Rate:	9.500%	+ Additional Principal:	$ 50.00
Term in Years:	30		

= Increased Mo.   733.84
   Payment:

The Loan Will Be Paid Off in 267 Payments

Normal Monthly Payment: $ 683.84
× Term in Months: 360 months

= Total Amount Paid with Normal Payment   > $ 246183

Increased Payment: $ 733.84
× Term in Months: 267 months

= Total Amount Paid with Increased Payment   > $ 195288
       (Last payment was: $ 86.25)
   The Savings with the Increased Payment is   > $ 50895

These numbers have been computed in good faith.
All risk associated with their use rests with the user.

Step 11. Tim tells Sue that he has recently read some articles about how much interest he can save by prepaying a mortgage. Tim: "Sue, can you help me figure how much I will save by prepaying this mortgage?" Sue: "I sure can. Do you think you can afford to prepay $50 per month?" Tim: "Go ahead and use that figure, I want to see how much it will save me." Sue uses QC again for the answer. She tells Tim that by prepaying $50 per month he will save $50,895 and his mortgage will be paid in 267 months or 22.25 years.

Homeowner's Analysis

Purchase Price:	$80000	Mortgage Rate:	9.500%
× Percent Down Payment:	2.00%	Mortgage Term:	30 years
= Cash Down Payment:	$ 1600		

= Mortgage Amount:	$78400

1st Year Mortgage Interest:	$ 7427.31		Mortgage Principal:	$ 483.45
+ Annual Property Taxes:	$ 600.00	+	Mortgage Interest:	$ 7427.31
= Total Tax Deductible Items:	$ 8027.31			
× Owner's Federal Tax Rate:	28.0%		= 1st Year Payment:	$ 7910.76

= Annual Federal Tax Savings:	$2247.65	Monthly Tax Savings: $ 187.30	

Monthly Payment (PI):	$ 659.23		
+ Monthly Property Tax:	$ 50.00		
+ Monthly Hazard Insurance:	$ 30.00	Appreciation Rate:	4.00%
= Monthly PITI:	$ 739.23	Number of Years:	5
− Monthly Tax Savings:	$ 187.30	Projected Value:	$97680

= Net Monthly Payment:	$ 551.93	Total Appreciation:	$17680

These numbers have been computed in good faith.
All risk associated with their use rests with the user.

Step 12. Tim now wonders about what the house will be worth five years from now. He asks Sue if she has any idea how homes have been appreciating in the area he has picked and does she have any words of wisdom about his decision to buy? Again, Sue does not get frustrated. She does not say to herself: Now this guy wants me to be an investment consultant! Sue says: "I can make a good faith estimate based on information you give me." Together they decide on a 4% appreciation rate and use 5 years as the length of time for owning the home. Sue cautions Tim that the information in this printout assumes Tim has enough other tax deductions to allow all the loan interest and property tax expense to be fully deductible. The conservative option is available in the tax savings printout, Step 9.

Step 13. Right before saying "I do," Tim has one more question. "All this financing is so complex, I wonder if it is better for me to keep on renting?" Sue does not throw her hands up! She asks Tim if he would like to know in what year it will be better to buy than to rent? Tim asks her to repeat the question, because he can't believe what he heard. Sue assures Tim that with another program from CDI, and some information from Tim, she can tell him at what point in time owning will be better than renting. Together they give the computer the information and the answer is that buying is better than renting at the beginning of the third year.

Tim says: "Sue, you and QC make an unbeatable team. I have asked you some tough questions, but all of answers are very important to me. For me, you have been a mortgage financing expert, and the equivalent of a CPA and a financial consultant. Who knows how much *time* it would have taken me to get the answers to all the questions I asked you? I appreciate your patience and assistance, it has been a real pleasure to talk to you. I feel confident that you have advised me about what loan is best for my needs. You can be sure that you will be handling my loan transactions. Thank you."

After Sue hangs up she thinks back to the old days, before a CLO system like QC, and wonders how much time it would have taken her to answer all of Tim's questions, and she knows that she could not have answered some of them at all.

CLO with QC—an idea whose time has come!

Analysis Variables:

"Buy Option" Variables:

Home Price:	$80000
Downpayment:	$ 1600
Mortgage Amount:	$81327
Mortgage Rate:	9.500%
Mortgage Term:	30 years
Property Taxes:	$ 50.00 (mo.)
Hazard Insurance:	$ 30.00 (mo.)
Utility Cost:	$ 150.00
Maintenance:	$ 55.00 (mo.)
Closing Costs:	4.0%
Selling Costs:	7.0%

"Rent Option" Variables:

Rental Expense:	$800.00
Utility Cost:	$150.00
Maintenance:	$ 20.00
Total Deposits:	$800.00

Other Variables:

Years to Analyze:	5
Tax Bracket:	28.0%
Appreciation Rate:	4.0% (yr.)
Investment Return:	6.0% (yr.)
Inflation Rate:	4.0% (yr.)

Summary of Analysis Procedure:

Step 1:   Calculate total cost of renting.

Step 2:   Calculate total cost of buying the home.

Step 3:   Subtract the tax savings from the total cost of buying.

Step 4:   Compare the cash differences of renting and buying.
Calculate: Step 1 (Total Cost) - Step 3 (Net for Buy).
Positive numbers mean buying is preferred.

Step 5:   Calculate the return on the downpayment + closing costs if invested.
Also calculate the net (including appreciation) if you sold at the end of
the year.

Step 6:   Calculate the difference between the investment growth and the net
on the home (after appreciation and selling costs) A positive number
means buying is preferred.

Step 7:   Add the results from Step 4 and Step 6.
A positive result means buying is preferred by that amount. A
negative number means you lose that much money by buying. You
should note the year in which the number ("cumulative" row) becomes
positive to determine how long to hold the home and how much it
would have to appreciate to beat renting.

Step 14:   Sue takes the application.

Step 14 continued

Year Number:	1	2	3	4	5

Step 1: Calculate Total Cost of Renting.
Rental Cash Flow Analysis

Annual Rent:	9600	9984	10383	10799	11231
Annual Utility:	1800	1872	1947	2025	2106
Ann. Maint:	240	250	260	270	281
Total Cost:	11640	12106	12590	13093	13617

Step 2: Calculate Total Cost of Buying the Home.
Home Purchase Cash Flow Analysis

Annual Paymt:	8206	8206	8206	8206	8206
Prop. Taxes:	600	624	649	675	702
Insurance:	360	374	389	405	421
Ann. Utility:	1800	1872	1947	2025	2106
Ann. Maint:	660	686	714	742	772
Total Cost:	11626	11763	11905	12053	12207

Step 3: Subtract the Tax Savings from the Total Cost of Buying.

Tax Savings:	2325	2318	2310	2300	2289
Net for Buy:	9301	9445	9595	9753	9918

Step 4: Calculate: Step 1 (Total Cost) — Step 3 (Net for Buy).
Cash Difference (Rent—Buy)

Each Year:	2339	2661	2994	3340	3699
Cumulative:	2339	5000	7994	11335	15034

Step 5: Calculate the Return for Both Options.
Capital Gains Analysis

Investment:	4240	4494	4764	5050	5353
Net if Sell:	−6650	−3003	822	4835	9049

Step 6: Using the Step 5 Numbers, Calculate Net if Sell—Investment.

Net Capital:	−10890	−7498	−3942	−215	3696

Step 7: Add the Results from Steps 4 and 6.
Summary Analysis (Cash + Capital)

Each Year:	−8550	−4837	−948	3126	7396
Cumulative:	−8550	−2498	4052	11120	18730
Decision:	RENT	RENT	BUY	BUY	BUY

Miscellaneous Background Information

Principal:	501	551	606	666	732
Interest:	7705	7655	7600	7540	7474
Appreciation:	3200	6528	9989	13589	17332

If, in the past, you have opposed paying real estate agents a referral fee, you now have an opportunity to reexamine your position. After reading this demonstration, use Sue as a real estate agent instead of a loan officer and ask yourself this question; Is what Sue did worth $250-$300? I think so. Particularly, if Sue bought the software and hardware with her money and invested her time in becoming efficient in the use of the new technology.

In the past real estate agents have been told: "Financing is the key to real estate sales." They may soon be able to decide how much it is worth when they total referral fees paid to them by lenders.

COMPUTER RECORD-KEEPING Calculations for amortization payments, taxes, insurance collections on defaults and other administrative servicing information is best stored in computers. Secondary marketing can then furnish more efficient progress for originated loans when servicing the loan portfolios. Computer record-keeping enhances portfolio expansion and mortgages are more easily sold into the secondary market.

CONCESSIONARY ITEMS/CONCESSIONS Items that are paid for or given by a seller to induce a buyer to purchase or lease real estate. Normally, a loan underwriter will deduct concessions from a purchaser's acquisition cost, thereby reducing the maximum loan amount. Concessions are different than buydowns. If, for example, a builder advertises that the person that buys his house will be given a free trip to Hawaii, the cost of the trip is a concession. The trip cost will be fully deductible from the buyer's acquisition cost, thereby reducing the loan.

Another meaning of this term is the right to conduct a business within another's premises. For example, a concession stand operated on a football stadium parking lot.

See BUYDOWN.

CONDEMNATION Property that is taken by the powers of eminent domain. A public authority or government can compensate an owner and take his property for a public use. Examples of public use would be parks, schools, streets, fire stations, and police stations. A second use of the term would be to designate a building or structure unfit for occupancy.

CONDENSATION The process of moisture in the air turning into water. In a building, condensation occurs when air moves from the interior through the wall and comes into contact with air on the outside that is opposite in temperature, e.g., warm/cold and cold/hot.

For houses with a veneer wall (which is true for nearly all residential dwellings), the point of contact is in the space between the interior and exterior walls.

Excess condensation, called *sweating*, can become a major problem. In extreme cases, excess condensation can cause a dwelling to be inhabitable. Sweating can cause health and structural problems.

See VAPOR BARRIER, VENEER, WEEP HOLE.

CONDITION A qualification or restriction attached to the transfer of property. An example is a property limited to residential purposes. A condition is also a provision or stipulation in a sales contract requiring certain events to take place or be followed before a sale can close.

In mortgage lending, loans can be approved subject to completion or compliance with a condition of loan approval. For example, loan approval is given subject to the payoff of a mortgage by the sale of the applicant's home. At or before loan closing, the applicant must submit proof that the loan was paid, something that is usually done by providing a copy of the settlement statement or some type of documentary evidence.

See GUARANTY PERFORMANCE.

CONDITIONAL COMMITMENT *See* FHA CONDITIONAL COMMITMENT.

CONDITIONAL SALES CONTRACT *See* CONTRACT FOR DEED.

CONDOMINIUM A joint ownership of property improved by multiple dwellings. It is an estate in real property that is an individual interest in an apartment or commercial building and an undivided interest in the common areas. Each condominium unit may be mortgaged, sold, foreclosed upon, or taxed, and it is treated as an individual unit separate and apart from the other units. State laws vary, but most condominiums must have a master deed, a condominium declaration accompanied by bylaws, map, floor plans, and elevations. A condominium association of owners is formed to enforce the condominium by-laws.

In closing a loan transaction with a condominium or a PUD as the secured asset, a lender will want all components of the unit estate to be described in the Security Instrument and title policy. If the security property is part of a PUD, fee simple title to the common areas must be vested in the name of the Owner's Association. Unless permitted by the lender, the common areas of a PUD or condominium may not be subject to any liens, including tax liens, statutory liens for labor or materials arising from any improvement on the common areas commenced before the date of closing, or liens arising under or created by any document specifically referred to in Schedule B of the title policy. Standard ALTA endorsements should be issued with the title policies on PUDs and Condominiums. For Condominiums it is ALTA Endorsement #4, for PUDs it is ALTA Endorsement #5. A copy of the recorded map showing the location of the unit will be required if the lender does not already have one on file.

See FIDELITY OR SURETY BOND.

CONDUIT (1) In the Secondary Mortgage Market, the term is used to describe a flow of mortgages from the originating lender to the investor. A *conduit program* is an investor approving lenders and setting forth guidelines that loans will be purchased. The conduit purchaser would then re-market the loans through various securitization processes. Government or private institutions act as conduits when they standardize mortgage investments to convert them into mortgage-backed securities. A conduit will stand behind the securities in the event of a default. When conduits purchase loans, the servicing may be retained by the originating lender or by a central servicer. CMO conduits dealing in the multi-layered structures through which mortgages are channeled are slightly different. They re-work the mortgage collateral into various classes and then into multi-class, mortgage-backed bonds that are issued to investors.

(2) A channel or pipe used to convey and protect wires, water, or other materials.

CONDUIT PURCHASING POLICY LIMITS The maximum original loan amounts that Fannie Mae and Freddie Mac will purchase mortgages (after 1/1/90) was limited to:

One-family dwellings:	$187,450
Two-family dwellings:	$239,750
Three-family dwellings:	$289,750
Four-family dwellings:	$360,150

The formula by which the maximum mortgage loan amount is calculated was provided for in the Housing and Community Development Act of 1980. Limits for properties in the states of Alaska, Hawaii and Guam are 50% higher than the above-noted limits. These limits are determined by the Federal Home Loan Bank Board according to their Mortgage Interest Rate Survey (MIRS).

CONDUITS CONVENTIONAL MBS POOL The structure and documentation of each conventional pool (unlike Ginnie Mae MBSs) is tailored to the requirements of the issuer, trustee/custodian, and underwriter. Conventional mortgage-backed securities are pooled so that weighted average interest rates of the pooled loans exceed the coupon rates of the securities. Pass-through rates, generally, do not exceed the lowest rates of any pool of mortgages. A procedure of this kind protects security holders and allows the issuer to earn service fee income. Fixed or variable-rate mortgage pools may be collateralized in this way.

CONFESSION OF JUDGEMENT A debtor permits a creditor to enter a judgement without a court procedure proving the judgement. The debtor confesses in writing the details of the judgement.

CONFIRMATION OF SALE The court approval of a sale of property by an executor, administrator, guardian, conservator, or commissioner in a foreclosure sale.

CONFORMING In secondary marketing, this word applies to conventional mortgages with loan amounts and underwriting guidelines that are in conformity to those used by FHLMC and FNMA. Conventional mortgages are classified as non-conforming if the loan amounts are too large or if underwriting guidelines used are unacceptable to FHLMC or FNMA.

CONFORMITY The subject property being appraised is in like use, as compared to other properties in the same area. Example: A commercial establishment would be in conforming use in a commercial area. On the other hand, a commercial building would be in a non-conforming use in a single-family neighborhood. Conformity can apply to size, style, land area, and the age of a property.

CONSANGUINITY Blood relationship as distinguished from legal relationship.

COUNSELING The 1990 Housing bill requires lenders to notify homeowners of the availability of homeownership counseling no later than 45 days after an FHA-insured loan becomes delinquent. The bill provides for a four-year demonstration program in three cities where pre-purchase counseling would be provided to first-time FHA borrowers.
See DELINQUENCY.

CONSERVATOR A party appointed by court to act as a guardian for a legally incompetent individual (usually an adult) to ensure that their property is managed properly.

CONSIDERATION Something of value, not necessarily money, given to make a contract legal and binding.

CONSISTENT PAYMENT RATE (CPR) The principal balances of mortgage pools are paid down at a rate consistent with the established coupon rate on a basis of annual maturities of the pool. This is the weighted average coupon rate of individual note rates for each group of loans being made up for a pool by the originating lender, called WACs. This is not a single monthly mortality rate (SMM) as found in FHA experience rates relative to outstanding mortgages on a monthly basis for pools; it is not the original amount loaned, nor is it considered the prepayment rate of an individual loan.

Prepayment rates in FHA statistical experience percentage reference to residential loans are considered as models by many investors.

See WEIGHTED AVERAGE COUPON (WAC).

CONSOLIDATED OBLIGATION A debt security issued from Federal Home Loan Banks over the signature of the FHLBB chairman; the financing needs of the various regional Banks are consolidated into larger issues for the capital markets.

CONSTANT An equal annual payment, expressed in a percentage, that will amortize the principal and pay interest over the life of the mortgage. A constant payment is the dollar amount given when the percentage is applied to the principal balance. To decide a monthly percentage or payment you simply divide by twelve.

CONSTANT PREPAYMENT RATE (CPR) The rate that the principal balance on a pool of mortgages is being paid down. The rate is stated on an annualized basis.

See CONSISTENT PAYMENT RATE.

CONSTRUCTION LOAN A short-term loan intended for the construction of an improvement, such as a house. A construction loan often includes the funds for land acquisition. The loan may include provisions for permanent long-term financing besides partial disbursements in stages as construction progresses. A three-party agreement is sometimes made in the form of a document executed by the borrower, lender, and contractor outlining the amount of funds for construction, the permitted uses of the loan money, and the construction according to approved plans and specifications.

Construction mortgage loans are known as building and loan agreements. The flow of funds to building projects should be estimated accurately so that a sum of money is withheld from the progress payments disbursement. The progress payments are made periodically according to the owner/contractor's arrangement with the lender. The lender then schedules advances to the borrower (or builder) as work proceeds on the project. The mortgagee makes periodic inspections, writes a final inspection report on the completed construction, and then makes final disbursement. Depending on the type of construction (residential or commercial), the three primary sources of conventional construction loans are savings and loan associations, commercial banks, and mortgage companies. Life insurance companies are active in commercial construction loans. In the secondary market, it is usually the mortgage banker who originates the construction loan and then assigns or sells the loan to investors.

CONSTRUCTIVE NOTICE Legal assumption that information is available to everyone by virtue of its being in the public records or published in a newspaper rather than delivering it in person to all concerned.

CONSUMER CREDIT PROTECTION ACT *See* TRUTH IN LENDING ACT.

CONSUMER CREDIT REPORTING ACT (FAIR CREDIT REPORTING ACT)
Federal law that protects consumers from abuse by parties preparing and using credit reports. If additional information on a borrower is given to a financial institution then a lender must provide the applicant with direct access to the information. The applicant has the right to ask that any information not verified or that is obsolete be deleted from the file. The purpose of the act is to insure that the consumer reporting agencies undertake their responsibilities with fairness, impartiality, and respect for the consumer's right to privacy.
See CREDIT REPORT, FAIR CREDIT REPORTING ACT.

CONSUMER LENDING Loans made for personal property, such as automobiles and appliances.

CONSUMER PRICE INDEX (CPI) A measure of changes in the cost of goods and services. This statistical information is furnished by the Bureau of Labor Statistics of the Department of Labor. The CPI is often used as an index in leasing.

CONSUMMATION Regulation Z defines the term consummation as meaning the actual time that a contractual relationship is created between borrower and lender, despite the performance of such relationship in a particular transaction. Depending upon the law of contracts in the state governing a particular institution, consummation may occur at the time a loan is closed, at the time a lender accepts (as distinct from receives) a borrower's loan application, or at the time a firm commitment is given to make a mortgage loan.
See LOAN ORIGINATION PROCESS, Step 5.

CONTIGUOUS A word used to describe properties that touch each other; it is especially important when assembling small parcels to find out if property lines are actually touching. The term is used in a different way for FHA investor loans.

See FHA -INVESTOR LOAN.

CONTINGENCY *See* CONDITION.

CONTOUR MAP A topographical map showing elevations of the land.

CONTRACT In real estate there are several kinds of contracts; there are: listings, contract of sale, options, assignments, deeds, contract for deed, loan commitments, escrow agreements, and servicing contracts.

For a contract to be legal and binding, there must be a legal purpose, normally the contract must be in writing, a description of the property, a consideration, acceptance, competent parties, and usually required signatures of all parties involved.

A contract is an agreement between two or more parties, enforceable by law, that creates or modifies a relationship. If a contract is ambiguous due to numbers and words not agreeing or other conflicting information in the contract, it is important to note that: words take precedence over numerals, handwriting takes precedence over type, and type takes precedence over pre-printed type.

CONTRACT FOR DEED Title to the property remains in the seller's name while the buyer receives equity title and possession of the property and assumes the obligation to purchase the property. When conditions of the contract are fulfilled, legal title passes to the purchaser.

See LAND CONTRACT.

CONTRACT OF SALE When used in the acquisition of real estate, it is a written agreement between two or more parties stating the contract or sales price and the terms or conditions of the sale. It is normally called a *sales contract*. For a contract to be legal and binding, there must be an offer in writing, acceptance, a legal purpose, a consideration, a description of the property, competent parties, and signatures. It is preferred that all parties involved sign a sales contract, but is not mandatory. A spouse can fail to sign a sales contact, but join in the deed to release any dower or curtesy right.

A contract is an agreement between two or more parties, enforceable by law, that creates or modifies a relationship. To be enforceable a contract must

be in writing and there must be an offer and acceptance. Consideration, something of value, may be required in some states.
See EQUITABLE TITLE.

CONTRACT RENT The rent for a property according to an existing lease.

CONVECTION For heating purposes, it is natural and forced circulatory motion.

CONVENTIONAL FOUNDATION A foundation for a house made of floor joists and not a concrete slab. A house with a conventional foundation has either has a crawl space or a basement. There should be adequate foundation vents and an access door. You will want to check to see what is used to cover the vents in cold weather.

For a house without a basement, there should be an access door and no moisture problems. There should be a minimum clearance of 18 inches between the floor joists and the ground.
See CRAWL SPACE.

CONVENTIONAL LOAN A real estate mortgage not affiliated with FHA or VA. It is called a conventional loan because it adheres to conventional standards within legal limits by mutual consent of the lender and borrower. It is the type of loan most commonly made by thrift institutions and is usually privately insured. Although it is not mandatory and even if the loan amounts are more than conforming guidelines, most conventional loans are made to conform with FHLMC or FNMA guidelines.

A list of underwriting guidelines for conventional loans will not be universal. Any investor can write his guidelines for a conventional loan. However, as explained above, most lenders conform to FNMA and FHLMC (Fannie Mae and Freddie Mac) guidelines for underwriting. Together, FNMA and FHLMC comprise the largest purchasing group for conventional residential loans in the world. These two corporations (Fannie and Freddie) have such an impact on the lending industry that loans not intended for a later sale to these two giants will most likely be underwritten in conformity to their guidelines. It should be noted that the guidelines listed below may differ for a lender who has negotiated a special commitment with Fannie or Freddie.

The following is a list of general underwriting guidelines for Fannie Mae and Freddie Mac.

1.   The borrower must pay any initial prepaid or escrow items.

2. Buyer's closing cost, buydown fees and discounts paid by a seller will be limited in relationship to the type of loan in question and the loan-to-value (LTV) ratio. The limitation is a percentage of the sales price or appraised value, whichever is lesser.

   a. For fixed rate loans and ARMs with a LTV ratio of more than 90%, the seller contribution cannot be more than 3%.

   b. For fixed rate loans and ARMs with a LTV ratio of 90% or less, the seller contribution cannot be more than 6%.

3. If the limits described above are exceeded, the amount of excess will be viewed as a sales concession and, therefore, will be deducted from the lower of either the sales price or the appraised value in determining the maximum loan amount.

4. Buydowns for adjustable rate mortgages are not allowed.

5. The maximum LTV for an adjustable rate mortgage (ARM) is 95%.

6. Qualifying ratios for fixed rate loans should be 25–28% and 35–38%, exceptions may be possible for excellent applicants — check with your lender.

7. Co-mortgagors will be required to take title and occupy the property if the LTV ratio is greater than 90%. For LTV ratio of 90% or less, the co-mortgagor does not have to occupy the property. All co-mortgagors must sign the deed and the note. At least 5% of the required downpayment must come from the mortgagor.

8. Gifts for settlement requirements are acceptable from family members provided certain conditions are met. There must be verification that a donor has the money to give and the funds must be verified in the applicant's account. On mortgages with a LTV greater than 80%, a gift is permitted but the mortgagor must contribute a minimum of a 5% downpayment from their assets.

CONVENTIONAL MORTGAGE-BACKED SECURITY Mortgage-backed securities not guaranteed by a federal agency. Conventional MBSs are collateralized by conventional home loans with private mortgage insurance. Individually pooled loans usually carry more than the standard 80% loan-to-value ratio. Each public issue is required to be registered with the Securities and Exchange Commission and payments to the security holders take place on the 25th of each month. Private conventional issues provide for the direct pass-through of interest and principal less servicing fees.

Private mortgage insurance (PMI) issuers provide a pool insurance policy with a five percent indemnity on the pool plus special policy hazards on one percent of the pool. Pool insurance arrangements cover shortfall amounts due on mortgages uncollected as of the date of distribution. They are distributed subject to the policy terms. The guarantee to the registered holders by private companies, as opposed to the federal government or quasi-government sponsored institutions, is in the nature of guarantees offered.

CONVERTIBLE BOND ISSUE A convertible is a fixed interest type of bond, where holders have rights or options to exchange the bonds for an appropriate number of shares of common stock, customarily at any given time during the bond's life. Convertibles are not like bonds with warrants since a choice to convert the shares to stock issues are an option built in a convertible. *See* PARITY.

CONVERTIBLE BOND OPTION (CBO) A right to exchange a convertible bond option for shares of common stock. During the life of the convertible the holder may choose to convert a bond to a given number of shares. (Bonds with warrants do not permit an exchange option.)

CONVERTIBLE MORTGAGE (1) A mortgage used for ownership interest of the lender. As payments to the principal balance are due the lender increases his ownership in lieu of the principal payments. It is used as a joint venture vehicle between the property owner and the lender. The payments to principal or for an increase in ownership in lieu of the principal payments is at the option of the lender. (2) An adjustable mortgage giving the borrower an option to convert to a fixed rate mortgage at specified periods during the term of the loan.

CONVERTIBLE STANDBY COMMITMENT A commitment from FNMA to purchase mortgages that can be converted to the same yield as offered in the most recent Free Market Auction.

CONVEYANCE It is the transfer of title or interest in real property by a written instrument. The instrument (except a will) used to transfer title to real property.

COOPERATING BROKER OR SALE A sale involving two or more agents.

COOPERATIVE (CO-OP) Ownership of real estate through stock in a corporation; an apartment unit owned by shares in a cooperative. The owner of the shares receives a proprietary lease granting use of a specific unit in the apartment building. The co-op owner has a leasehold right of occupancy under a proprietary lease. The cooperative is based on ownership of personal property,

proprietary lease. The cooperative is based on ownership of personal property, the lease, and is not based on ownership of a specific unit as with a condominium. The individual owning shares in a cooperative may deduct real estate taxes and mortgage interest that is applicable to the share of ownership. There are some disadvantages to ownership in a co-op as compared to a condominium. Because of the form of ownership, permanent financing is hard to find. There is no separate mortgage for each unit, as in a condo. Since there is but one mortgage, and one tax bill, there is a danger of other owners not being able to pay their share of the mortgage or taxes.

CORNICE Top course or ornamental crowning member of a wall where it meets the roof under the eaves.

CORRELATION In the final steps of an appraisal. The appraiser correlates or reconciles the three approaches to value, cost, income, and market, into a final estimate of value.

See APPRAISED VALUE, COST APPROACH, INCOME APPROACH, and MARKET APPROACH.

CORRESPONDENT A lender whose normal practice is to sell all loans originated to a particular investor or a group of investors. Another similar meaning is an approved FHA lender that is not a fully licensed FHA mortgagee. The net worth requirements and conditions of becoming a FHA approved correspondent are much less stringent as compared to a licensed FHA mortgagee.

CO-SIGNER An individual who lends his name and therefore his character and credit to another individual in hopes that it will help obtain credit. A co-signer is one who can be called upon to help in times of a financial emergency. The co-signer signs the loan application form and the note, but does not sign the deed of trust or mortgage. Typically, the income of a co-signer cannot be included in income analysis of an applicant. This term is different than *co-mortgagor*. The co-signer is liable for the loan, but does not share in the ownership.

See CO-MORTGAGOR.

COST APPROACH One of three approaches to value, it emphasizes the cost or replacement value of the permanent improvements. The cost approach answers the question of how much it will cost to reproduce the improvements. This approach is most often used in appraising new construction such as newly built homes. The steps to value with this approach are: (1) estimate the land value, (2) estimate the cost to reproduce the permanent improvements (the building), (3) deduct depreciation from the permanent improvements, and (4) add the land value to the value of the improvements after depreciation is considered. The cost approach to value is frequently used in appraising special purpose buildings were there are not many or any comparables.

COST CERTIFICATION A formal affidavit attesting to the true cost to construct permanent improvements. Because loans are based on cost or appraised value, whichever is the less, it is important for the lender to decide what is "cost" for loans on new construction loans. The cost certification can be in the form of an itemized statement backed by canceled checks and receipts showing the actual money spent to acquire the land and build the improvements. This type of certification can be required by any lender operating within conventional, FHA, or VA guidelines. In 1990 FHA ceased the practice of requiring cost certification for a single-family dwelling built by an owner for occupancy as a principal residence.

COST OF FUNDS (COF) An index referring to the cost lenders pay for attracting funds. The 11th District Cost of Funds is the weighted average interest rate paid by the 11th Federal Home Loan Bank District members for their source of funds. The Monthly Median Cost of Funds is the median average interest rate paid by all FSLIC-insured institutions on their sources of funds. *See* ADJUSTABLE RATE MORTGAGE for how these COF affect ARM loans.

COST-OF-LIVING INDEX *See* CONSUMER PRICE INDEX.

COTENANCY A form of co-ownership of property such as tenancy in common, joint tenancy, tenancy-by-the-entirety, or other forms of co-ownership of property. It is a concurrent property ownership interest in the same property.

COUNCIL OF STATE HOUSING AGENCIES (CSHA) The CSHA is a state housing finance agency organization based in Washington, D.C. that is made up of state housing agencies. These state agencies are generally responsive to local conditions and attempt to meet housing needs in efficiently managed programs that involve private business and grass roots efforts. They create jobs and sometimes are a principal source of support to the construction industry and allied trades in the communities they serve. State housing finance agencies fill single-family and multi-family housing needs. While they are created independent of the U.S. Department of Housing and Urban Development, they are not purely private entities either. They draw upon the resources of the private mortgage lending industry and developers to form a link between government and private enterprise to create low-income housing.

COUNTER OFFER Refers to an alteration of an original offer to buy or sell real estate. A new offer is made in response to the original offer. The common practice is to make changes on the original offer by lining through existing text and writing in new text (the changes) then having all parties date and initial the change(s).

See CONTRACT.

COUPON BOND Bearer bond; not registered in the name of the owner. A bond with coupons for each interest installment.

See BEARER BOND.

COUPON RATE Rate of interest paid on a bond or the rate of interest for a pool of mortgages. It is the rate of annual interest on a debt instrument, such as a mortgage-backed security, stated as a percentage of its face value.

See WEIGHTED AVERAGE COUPON RATE.

COVENANT A promise written into a deed to perform or not perform certain acts. It can refer to the existence or non-existence of certain facts related to the title of the property. An example of a covenant not to perform is a deed restriction prohibiting the subdividing of the land. A seller representing property that it is free of any outstanding claims is an example of a covenant.

COVENANT, CONDITIONS, AND RESTRICTIONS (CC&Rs) Private conditions upon the use of property. CC&Rs are usually restrictions to the use of property by conveyance in a deed.

CPI *See* CONSUMER PRICE INDEX.

CPR *See* CONSISTENT PAYMENT RATE.

CPTA *See* CENTRAL PAYING AND TRANSFER AGENT.

CRA *See* CERTIFIED REVIEW APPRAISER.

CRAWL SPACE Automatically implies a house built on a conventional foundation as opposed to a concrete slab. This term implies a house without a basement, just as it does with a slab foundation. It is an area beneath the floor of a house big enough for a person to crawl in and make an inspection. In cold climates, crawl spaces should be insulated.

See CONVENTIONAL FOUNDATION.

CREATIVE FINANCING A term that has come to mean financing other than the traditional sources. Creative financing can take the forms of seller financing, wrap-around financing, balloon mortgages, sale/leaseback, substitution of collateral, and other alternative mortgage instruments.

CREDIT ANALYSIS A determination of the risk inherent in extending credit to a particular person or business. Credit analysis considers a loan applicant's income, expenses, liabilities, assets, and past use of credit and general business acumen to manage their financial affairs.

CREDIT LIFE INSURANCE Insurance on the life of a mortgagor that pays off the mortgage debt if he or she dies; also known as mortgage life insurance.

CREDIT MARKETS The credit markets (or debt market) are comprised of bonds, short-term non-equity securities, and non-securitized debt obligations - all part of the secondary market. This market has grown drastically in the last decade because of the phenomenal popularity of mortgage-backed securities as investment vehicles. The secondary mortgage markets are a source of available mortgage funding and serve many types of lending institutions such as: mortgage bankers, savings and loan institutions, savings banks, commercial banks, pension funds, and life insurance companies. The expansion of Fannie Mae, Freddie Mac, and Ginnie Mae has served many in the secondary market growth.

Traditionally, mortgages were funded with savings account deposits. Portfolio lenders then maintained these loans in their investment portfolios. When depositors began moving their savings to higher interest bearing funds (outside the savings institution), savings and loan mortgage funds became scarce. The credit market for mortgages has become a significant source of funds since the mid-1980s.

CREDIT RATING *See* MOODY'S and STANDARD & POOR'S.

CREDIT REPORT A written report that helps the lender decide the credit worthiness of a prospective borrower. Residential credit reports are different than those issued on a business.

All agencies (FHA, VA, FHLMC, FNMA) have guidelines for what a residential credit report must disclose. A standard Factual Data Report must show:

(1)   legal information for the past seven years;
(2)   the terms, balances, and ratings for all debts on the credit application;
(3)   any adverse credit over 30 days;

(4) debts that are not disclosed on the credit application;

(5) all recent inquiries;

(6) any matters of record in the local recorder's office that may adversely affect the mortgage loan, i.e., judgements, garnishments, liens, pending lawsuits, prison term, etc..

CROSS-DEFAULT CLAUSE A provision in a junior mortgage making the mortgagor in default on all mortgages if a default occurs on just one mortgage. The cross-default clause allows a lender to foreclose if the borrower is in default on just one mortgage.

CRV *See* CERTIFICATE OF REASONABLE VALUE.

CSA *See* COMPROMISE SALES AGREEMENT.

CSHA *See* COUNCIL OF STATE HOUSING AGENCIES.

CTLVR Combined Total Loan-to-Value Ratio. See TLVR.

CUL-DE-SAC A street that is closed at one end with a circular area big enough for cars to turn around.

CULVERT Underground ditch that carries drainage water such as under a highway.

CURRENT PRODUCTION A term normally used to describe loans that have been originated within the past 12 months. Loans that have *aged* or been in existence for more than 1 year are sometimes called *seasoned loans*.

CURRENT YIELD A yield obtained by dividing the security price (or cost) into the coupon's current return.

CURTAIL SCHEDULE *See* AMORTIZATION SCHEDULE.

CURTAILMENT Any unscheduled payment (other than a full prepayment or prepaid installment) that reduces the loan balance of a mortgage, e.g., insurance payments or liquidation payments.

CURTSEY Common-law right of a husband to a life estate in all or part of his deceased wife's property. This right may not exist in some states and those that do recognize it may have different interpretations.

CUSTODIAN (1) A financial institution that holds documents relating to the pooled mortgages for the life of the pool or loan package. A specific number of mortgages will be accumulated in a pool that is sent to an approved custodian (or a commercial bank) who certifies them. Upon examination and appropriate documentation, Ginnie Mae, Fannie Mae, or Freddie Mac will issue a mortgage-backed security. The actual mortgages and related documents are held in safekeeping by the custodian.

(2) A financial institution that holds specific documents, such as original notes, in trust for another institution. Frequently used in connection with mortgage-backed securities, such as GNMA.

CUSTOM BUILDER An individual who normally pre-sells houses as opposed to a builder who builds for the speculative market.

CUSTOM POOL A pool issued under the GNMA II program. This pool has only one issuer and is assembled under a single Commitment to Guarantee issued by Ginnie Mae as described in GNMA Handbook 5500.2.

D

D *See* STANDARD & POOR'S.

DAILY PRICE LIMITS The maximum number of points a contract can rise above or fall below the previous day's settlement price. If the maximum limit is exceeded, all trading for the day ceases. The maximum price change allowed by the exchange for a futures contract.

DAMAGES Compensation for injuries or damages by another to an individual or their property. In a real estate contract, often times the seller will keep a buyer's earnest money as damages for failure to comply with the terms of the contract. Another meaning of *damages* is a lessening of the value of property remaining after part of it has been taken by eminent domain.

The burden of proof of damages is on the plaintiff. There are several kinds of *damages*.

Liquidated damages is a predetermined estimate of the damages set forth in a contract. The party that breaches the contract knows how much will be assessed for damages.

Under the doctrine of *mitigation of damages*, the injured party must lessen or eliminate the damages. For example, a landlord is responsible for pursuing a replacement tenant for one who has breached a lease.

Punitive damages are those given for suffering from fraudulent practices and it's purpose is more for punishing the party more than just awarding the injured party. Damages more than actual loss suffered is the result of punitive damages.

Severance damage is the loss in value caused by a condemnation procedure. The property is not as valuable or useful after condemnation as it was before. The drop in value is due to a partial taking by condemnation.

DAMPER Adjustable device in a fireplace, stove, or furnace used to regulate the draft caused by the fire.

DATA PROCESSING A method of processing information by electronic methods. Used in the processing of mortgage loans.

DATUM A reference point used in determining heights or depths. *See* BENCH MARK.

DEALER (1) In the lending profession, a dealer is in the business of buying and selling mortgage-backed securities as a principal and not as an agent. A dealer buys for his or her account normally, then sells to customers out of the inventory. The dealer's profit or loss is the difference between the price paid and the price received for the trade. The assignment contact must disclose to the buyer that the dealer acted as principal. At times this individual or firm may operate as an investment banker.

(2) An individual who buys property for resale to the public in the regular course of business. The same person may buy property as an investor.

See MORTGAGE BROKER.

DEBENTURE A broad term for any unsecured, long-term debt instrument. Corporations use debenture bonds to raise capital. Municipal bonds are debenture bonds.

DEBT RATIO See INCOME ANALYSIS.

DEBT COVERAGE RATIO A factor used to express the amount of difference between net operating income and the debt service. If the net income from an apartment building is $125,000 and the debt service is $100,000, the debt service is 1.25. Lenders use debt coverage ratios as a broad classification to pre-qualify various projects. For example, a lender may require apartment projects to have a minimum debt coverage ratio of 1.25, and may require shopping centers to have a minimum of 1.10.

DEBT/EQUITY RATIO The ratio between loans outstanding and the capital account (the investment plus undistributed profits) of the shareholders or partners. In real estate companies it is not unusual to see a ratio that far exceeds non-real estate enterprises. The reason is that real estate represents excellent collateral as compared to personal property.

DEBT ISSUE The financing of Fannie Mae's operations include general obligations of the corporation. Funding sources for operations comes from cash flow from the mortgages it already owns and debt issue. Long-term and short-term debt is issued in the form of debentures and short-term notes to raise debt. They have been classified as having *agency status* so that the debt issues generally yield investors a rate of return higher than Treasury issues and less than corporate offerings.

DEBT SERVICE The payment due on a mortgage. If the mortgage is an amortized loan then the debt service will consist of principal and interest. You base the debt service on the repayment schedule, e.g., monthly, quarterly, or annual payments.

DEBT INSTRUMENT A document that evidences a debt. A mortgage note is a debt instrument.

DECEDENT A deceased person.

DECK The flat, wooden surface of a roof or a patio.

DECLARATION Information about a condominium. A declaration of condominium is the master deed. This instrument requires the developer to meet certain state laws in describing the condominium project. The description in a declaration normally includes: a description of the units, the common property, any restrictive use of the units, and any other information pertinent to the development.

DECLARATION OF TRUST An instrument that identifies property held by a trustee for another individual.

DECREE An order or judgement of a court.

DEDICATION Property or an easement transferred to the public for its use.

DEED An instrument used to transfer ownership of property. The recording of a deed ends ownership of one party and starts ownership for another.

To be valid a deed must have: a grantor, a grantee, consideration, signature by the grantor, words of conveyance, and delivery. Some states require the signature of the grantor to be acknowledged or witnessed. A legal description is not necessary, but to obtain title insurance you may need one. If the grantee is assuming a mortgage or is abiding by a restrictive provision in the deed, then the grantee must sign the deed. A deed must be delivered to be valid.

An *exception* in a deed excludes part of the property. A *reservation* in a deed, such as an easement, retains a right in the property.

DEED COVENANTS *See* DEED RESTRICTIONS.

DEED-IN-LIEU OF FORECLOSURE With the approval of the lender, the owner deeds the property to the lender to avoid foreclosure. This procedure saves the borrower from having a foreclosure on their credit history. This type of transfer of title posses risk to the lender as it does not wipe out all claims to the title as is true of foreclosures in most states.

DEED OF RECONVEYANCE An instrument used to convey property from a trustee to the borrower after paying a mortgage according to the terms of a deed of trust.

See DEED OF TRUST, RELEASE.

DEED OF TRUST A Deed of Trust has three parties: the borrower, the trustee, and the lender. The borrower transfers title to property to a trustee for the duration of a loan.

The trustee holds legal title. People sometimes call the legal title held by a trustee a *naked legal title*. The mortgagor has equitable title. When the mortgagor pays the debt, the trustee conveys legal title to the owner by the way of a deed of reconveyance.

If the mortgagor violates the terms of the mortgage, the trustee has the power to sell the property without having permission from a judicial process. Statutory right of redemption is usually waived by a deed of trust.

See DEFEASANCE, RELEASE, SATISFACTION OF A MORTGAGE, TITLE THEORY.

DEED RESTRICTIONS Restrictions or limitations to the use of property as noted in the deed. If a deed restriction is violated, the proper legal remedy is to seek an injunction. Some communities control use of property by Deed Restrictions instead of using zoning ordinances. The city of Houston is an example of property use control by Deed Restriction. Deed restrictions are known as deed covenants.

DE FACTO Latin for *in fact*.

DEFAULT Failure to perform a legal obligation. In residential mortgages, a borrower who fails to pay the mortgage payment is in default. A borrower is in default if a term in the Deed of Trust or the mortgage is violated. Default gives the lender the right to begin foreclosure proceedings. There can be conditions other than failure to pay that constitute a default in the mortgage. For example, failure to maintain the property can be considered as a default in the mortgage. The lender wants the property used as security for the loan to be properly maintained so that the lender's security is not lessened in value. Depending on State law and the conditions in a Deed of Trust or Mortgage, a delinquent loan that is more than 30 days past due is considered to be in default. Once a lender considers a loan to be in default, the lender can call the loan by exercising the rights given in the acceleration clause (the outstanding balance is considered due and payable).

See CALL.

DEFEASANCE The right given to a borrower to defeat a claim in a mortgage. In title theory states, title is given to a trustee upon execution of a mortgage. Although the mortgagor owns the property and has an equitable title, the trustee has the power to sell the property if the mortgage becomes *in default*. The defeasance clause gives the borrower the right to reclaim, or claim full and complete title to the property when the mortgage debt is paid in full. There is usually a requirement that a release deed or a satisfaction of the mortgage be issued before the trustee relinquishes all rights to the property.

DEFECTIVE TITLE Title that is not clear.

DEFENDANT Party who is defending or denying in a legal action.

DEFERRED INTEREST Interest due but unpaid. Mortgages that permit negative amortization (GPMs, and ARMs without a rate cap) will allow deferred interest.

DEFERRED MAINTENANCE Depreciation caused by failure to maintain property properly; sometimes called curable physical depreciation.

DEFICIENCY In the event of a foreclosure, there is a deficiency when the highest bid in a foreclosure sale is less than the outstanding balance plus foreclosure-related costs.

DEFICIENCY JUDGEMENT A judgement allowing the lender to pursue any legal measure to recover a loss created by a deficiency. It is a legal decision obtained by a lender when the sale of a foreclosed property does not furnish proceeds sufficient to cover the total payment of the mortgage debt. This judgment allows the lender to pursue legal remedies to collect the balance from the borrower. The basic obligation of the buyer may arise in two ways: (1) there may be an actual loan of money; or (2) there may merely exist an extension of credit by a seller who takes a note and trust deed (or mortgage) as part of the purchase price. In the second case, if there is a default by the buyer on the promise to pay on the note, the seller cannot get a deficiency judgment. The seller can foreclose the trust deed or mortgage but if the sale under foreclosure does not bring enough to pay off the note, the seller cannot sue for the balance. In contrast, one who lends money (a hard money loan) can get a deficiency judgment under some circumstances. However, if an actual loan of money is made specifically for the purchase of buying the property, and it is so used, a deficiency judgment cannot be leveled, with exception. A third party lender may secure a deficiency judgment when the purchase money loan was made on a dwelling designed for housing more than four families. In summary, defia dwelling designed for housing more than four families. In summary, deficiency judgments cannot exist when there is a purchase money mortgage or trust deed except as noted above.

A purchase money mortgage or trust deed includes the extending of credit by a seller and the lending of money, specifically for buying property. It should be noted that a purchase money mortgage or trust deed given for all or part of the purchase of real property at the time of its conveyance has priority over all other private liens created by or against the purchaser, subject to the operation of the recording laws. This rule protects even third persons who furnish money, but when it is only loaned for buying the property. It may, of course, be necessary for the mortgagee to record the mortgage before other liens are recorded to sustain priority in some states.

Local and federal government agencies each view deficiency laws differently and questions should be referred to the appropriate agency having jurisdiction over the real estate mortgage loan disposition. FHA and VA now pursue deficiency judgements.

See JUDGEMENT.

DEFLATING THE MORTGAGE A method of reducing the principal balance of a mortgage and increasing the interest rate so that the mortgagee gets the same dollars and the mortgagor gets a greater tax deduction.

DELAY DELIVERY CONTRACT An agreement between underwriters of a new issue and persons or institutions to pay for and take delivery of various amounts of a new security on various dates after the original offering.

DELAY PERIOD The time between the record date and the payment date. For pass-through securities, the delay is: 45 days for GNMAs, 54 days for FNMAs and 75 days for FHLMC PCs. The penalty or *actual delay* is less time than a *stated delay* by 30 days. A delay is the time between the homeowner's regular payment schedules and the time that servicing institutions pay investors in pass-through securities. This time is normal or *actual* delay, rather than *stated* delay. Different types of pass-through securities call for different pay schedules: 14 days for GNMA I, 19 days for GNMA IIs, 24 days for FNMAs and 44 days for FHLMC PCs.

DELINQUENCY When a mortgage payment is not paid on the due date, it is delinquent. FHA and VA loans are due on the first of the month. If the mortgage payment on a FHA or VA loan is received on or after the 16th of the month the mortgagor must pay a late fee. The late fee for FHA and VA loans is 4% of the total of the principal and interest payment. Because of when the late fee is due, many people assume that it is acceptable to make the payment after the 1st but before the 16th, this is an erroneous assumption. To insure an excellent credit rating, mortgage payments should be made on the due date. Most lenders will not give a credit rating based on when mortgage payments are made, but they will give a past 12 months history of when they received the mortgage payment on a loan. The past 12 months report is usually broken down into number of times paid on the due date, and then the number of times paid between certain periods such as five to ten days, ten to fifteen days, or the lender may give the exact date each payment was received.

Conventional loans have due dates that can vary but they normally have the same number of days (15 days) before a late fee can be assessed. The late fee for a conventional loan is usually 5% of the total monthly principal and interest payment.

The 1990 Housing Bill prohibits servicers from charging late fees for 60 days following a servicing transfer to borrowers who have made payments to the wrong servicer.

The payment record of a mortgagor can be critical in a tight underwriting situation. If a loan application is borderline, the underwriter will take a close look at how the applicant has paid mortgage payments (or rental payments) in the past. If the applicant has a history of slow payments for housing, then an underwriter can ask the question: "If they don't pay their present mortgagee (or landlord) on time, why should they start with us?"

Lender can use the form below to verify a mortgage account or the rent.

See COUNSELING.

DELINQUENCY RATIO Number of loans past-due in relationship to number of loans serviced. This is a very important ratio for the lender. A valuable asset of the lender is the right to service loans. At times, the lender will sell rights to service a group of loans. Potential buyers will closely scrutinize the delinquency ratio, particularly for the past 12 months and will look at the various times the lender says the loan payments are received. Delinquency ratios for loan pools are stated as a percentage of loans paid within 30-60-90 days from the due date. The price a lender receives for the servicing right is affected by the delinquency ratio. The lower the ratio, the better price paid for servicing rights.

The Tables below show a percentage of about 14.5 million loans (about 1/3 of all loans) serviced in the United States. The source of information for these Tables is the MBA Economics Department.

Exhibit 10

VMP MORTGAGE FORMS • (313)293-8100 • (800)521-7291

INSTRUCTIONS TO LENDER:
1. FILL OUT PART I - REQUEST
2. HAVE APPLICANT(S) SIGN EACH COPY (No Carbon Signatures)
3. PULL YELLOW COPY AND FILE FOR FOLLOW-UP
4. FORWARD OTHER 2 COPIES (CARBON INTACT) TO LANDLORD/CREDITOR

INSTRUCTIONS TO LANDLORD/CREDITOR:
1. COMPLETE PART II AND III
2. RETURN BOTH COMPLETED COPIES TO LENDER

70,013-B

Request for Verification of Rent or Mortgage Account

Privacy Act Notice: This information is to be used by the agency collecting it or its assignees in determining whether you qualify as a prospective mortgagor under its program. It will not be disclosed outside the agency except as required and permitted by law. You do not have to provide this information, but if you do not your application for approval as a prospective mortgagor or borrower may be delayed or rejected. The information requested in this form is authorized by Title 38, USC, Chapter 37 (if VA); by 12 USC, Section 1701 et. seq. (if HUD/FHA); by 42 USC, Section 1452b (if HUD/CPD); and Title 42 USC, 1471 et. seq., or 7 USC, 1921 et. seq. (if USDA/FmHA).

Instructions: Lender - Complete items 1 through 8. Have applicant(s) complete item 9. Forward directly to creditor named in item 1.
Landlord/Creditor - Please complete items 10 through 18 and return directly to lender named in item 2.
The form is to be transmitted directly to the lender and is not to be transmitted through the applicant(s) or any other party.

Part I - Request

1. To (Name and address of landlord/creditor)	2. From (Name and address of lender)

I certify that this verification has been sent directly to the landlord/creditor and has not passed through the hands of the applicant or any other party.

3. Signature of Lender	4. Title	5. Date	6. Lender's Number (Optional)

FOLD

7. Information To Be Verified

Property Address	Account in the Name of	Account Number
	☐ Mortgage ☐ Rental	
	☐ Land Contract	

I have applied for a mortgage loan. My signature below authorizes verification of mortgage or rent information.

8. Name and Address of Applicant(s)	9. Signature of Applicant(s)
	X _____
	X _____

Part II - To be Completed by Landlord/Creditor

We have received an application for a loan from the above, to whom we understand you rent or have extended a loan. In addition to the information requested below please furnish us with any information you might have that will assist us in processing of the loan.

☐ Rental Account   ☐ Mortgage Account or ☐ Land Contract

10. Tenant rented from _____
to _____
Amount of rent $ _____ per _____
Number of late payments _____ *
Is account satisfactory? ☐ Yes ☐ No

FOLD

11. Date account opened _____
Original contract amount $ _____
Current account balance $ _____
Monthly payment P & I only $ _____
Payment with taxes & ins. $ _____
Is account current? ☐ Yes ☐ No
Was loan assumed? ☐ Yes ☐ No
Satisfactory account? ☐ Yes ☐ No

12. Interest rate _____ %
☐ FIXED   ☐ ARM
☐ FHA   ☐ VA
☐ CONV   ☐ OTHER _____
Next pay date _____
No. of late payments _____ *
No. of late charges _____

*Payment History for the previous 12 months must be provided in order to comply with secondary mortgage market requirements.

13. Additional information which may be of assistance in determination of credit worthiness

Part III - Authorized Signature - Federal statutes provide severe penalties for any fraud, intentional misrepresentation, or criminal connivance or conspiracy purposed to influence the issuance of any guaranty or insurance by the VA Secretary, the USDA, FmHA/FHA Commissioner, or the HUD/CPD Assistant Secretary.

14. Signature of Landlord/Creditor Representative	15. Title (Please print or type)	16. Date

17. Print or type name signed in item 14

18. Phone No.

7/90

DELINQUENCY RATES OF ALL 1- TO 4-UNIT RESIDENTIAL MORTGAGE LOANS

End of Quarter	Total % Past Due	30 Days	60 Days	90+ Days	Foreclosure Started
1989					
1st	4.64	3.13	0.74	0.77	0.32
2nd	4.56	3.06	0.74	0.76	0.36
3rd	4.99	3.44	0.78	0.77	0.33
4th	4.96	3.45	0.76	0.75	0.32
1990					
1st	4.41	3.03	0.70	0.68	0.31
2nd	4.52	3.13	0.70	0.69	0.31

DELINQUENCY RATES FOR CONVENTIONAL 1- TO 4-UNIT RESIDENTIAL MORTGAGE LOANS

End of Quarter	Total % Past Due	30 Days	60 Days	90+ Days	Foreclosure Started
1989					
1st	2.92	2.03	0.42	0.47	0.20
2nd	2.92	2.02	0.43	0.47	0.23
3rd	3.24	2.30	0.46	0.48	0.21
4th	3.14	2.25	0.44	0.45	0.21
1990					
1st	2.76	1.98	0.41	0.37	0.21
2nd	2.85	2.07	0.42	0.36	0.21

DELINQUENCY RATES FOR VA 1-TO 4-UNIT RESIDENTIAL MORTGAGE LOANS

End of Quarter	Total % Past Due	30 Days	60 Days	90+ Days	Foreclosure Started
1989					
1st	6.13	4.06	1.02	1.05	0.40
2nd	6.22	4.08	1.06	1.08	0.49
3rd	6.59	4.41	1.10	1.08	0.42
4th	6.56	4.50	1.04	1.02	0.42
1990					
1st	5.98	4.00	0.99	0.99	0.38
2nd	6.24	4.20	1.01	1.03	0.39

DELINQUENCY RATES FOR FHA 1- TO 4-UNIT RESIDENTIAL MORTGAGE LOANS

End of Quarter	Total % Past Due	30 Days	60 Days	90+ Days	Foreclosure Started
1989					
1st	6.38	4.25	1.07	1.06	0.46
2nd	6.29	4.19	1.05	1.05	0.50
3rd	6.99	4.76	1.14	1.09	0.46
4th	6.97	4.78	1.11	1.08	0.47
1990					
1st	6.26	4.24	1.01	1.01	0.44
2nd	6.58	4.44	1.05	1.09	0.43

Tables below show delinquency rates for the first six months of 1990 by census regions. The census regions, followed by the states included, are: **NEW ENGLAND:** CT, ME, MA, NH, RI, VT; **MID-ATLANTIC:** NJ, NY, PA; **E.N. CENTRAL:** IL, IN, MI, OH, WI; **W.N. CENTRAL:** IA, KS, MN, MO, NE, ND, SD; **S. ATLANTIC:** DE, D.C., FL, GA, MD, N.C, S.C., VA, WV; **E.S. CENTRAL:** AL, KY, MS, TN; **W.S. CENTRAL:** AR, LA, OK, TX; **MOUNTAIN:** AZ, CO, ID, MT, NV, NM, UT, WY; **PACIFIC:** AK, CA, HI, OR, WA; and **PUERTO RICO.**

DELINQUENCY RATES OF ALL 1- TO 4-UNIT RESIDENTIAL MORTGAGE LOANS FOR THE FIRST SIX MONTHS OF 1990, BY CENSUS REGION

Census Region	Number of Loans	Total % Past Due	30 Days	60 Days	90+ Days
New England	667,419	3.10	2.13	0.51	0.46
Mid-Atlantic	1,868,061	4.03	2.85	0.59	0.59
N. Central	1,878,557	4.67	3.30	0.71	0.66
W.N. Central	816,775	3.65	2.57	0.56	0.52
S. Atlantic	2,998,606	4.29	3.05	0.64	0.60
E.S. Central	630,375	5.90	3.95	0.86	1.09
W.S. Central	1,315,061	5.98	3.85	0.90	1.23
Mountain	1,082,234	4.67	3.13	0.72	0.82
Pacific	2,696,422	2.85	2.11	0.41	0.33
Puerto Rico	119,975	8.35	5.58	1.63	1.14
U.S. Total	14,542,491	4.25	2.96	0.64	0.65

DELINQUENCY RATES OF ALL 1- TO 4-UNIT CONVENTIONAL RESIDENTIAL MORTGAGE LOANS FOR THE FIRST SIX MONTHS OF 1990, BY CENSUS REGION

Census Region	Number of Loans	Total % Past Due	30 Days	60 Days	90+ Days
New England	608,888	2.90	1.98	0.48	0.44
Mid-Atlantic	1,434,292	3.02	2.21	0.43	0.38
N. Central	1,035,409	2.45	1.83	0.34	0.28
W.N. Central	371,976	2.32	1.75	0.33	0.24
S. Atlantic	1,433,665	2.72	2.07	0.36	0.29
E.S. Central	184,440	3.55	2.78	0.39	0.38
W.S. Central	483,443	4.21	2.72	0.60	0.89
Mountain	299,033	2.67	1.86	0.38	0.43
Pacific	1,552,673	1.61	1.25	0.22	0.14
Puerto Rico	32,679	9.48	6.70	1.60	1.18
U.S. Total	7,727,164	2.69	1.97	0.38	0.34

DELINQUENCY RATES OF ALL 1- TO 4-UNIT VA RESIDENTIAL MORTGAGE LOANS FOR THE FIRST SIX MONTHS OF 1990, BY CENSUS REGION

Census Region	Number of Loans	Total % Past Due	30 Days	60 Days	90+ Days
New England	26,180	5.17	3.66	0.78	0.73
Mid-Atlantic	129,667	6.95	4.73	1.03	1.19
N. Central	283,338	7.26	4.98	1.16	1.12
W.N. Central	141,631	4.99	3.35	0.82	0.82
S. Atlantic	650,043	5.51	3.75	0.88	0.88
E.S. Central	154,454	6.23	4.09	0.97	1.17
W.S. Central	306,720	6.78	4.35	1.07	1.36
Mountain	243,860	5.20	3.44	0.82	0.94
Pacific	385,385	4.38	3.17	0.64	0.57
Puerto Rico	11,129	8.68	6.04	1.73	0.91
U.S. Total	2,393,218	5.79	3.92	0.91	0.96

DELINQUENCY RATES OF ALL 1- TO 4-UNIT FHA RESIDENTIAL MORTGAGE LOANS FOR THE FIRST SIX MONTHS OF 1990, BY CENSUS REGION

Census Region	Number of Loans	Total % Past Due	30 Days	60 Days	90+ Days
New England	32,351	5.25	3.67	0.90	0.68
Mid-Atlantic	304,102	7.49	5.08	1.14	1.27
N. Central	559,810	7.45	5.16	1.17	1.12
W.N. Central	303,168	4.67	3.21	0.73	0.73
S. Atlantic	914,898	5.84	4.07	0.89	0.88
E.S. Central	291,481	7.22	4.62	1.10	1.50
W.S. Central	524,898	7.15	4.61	1.08	1.46
Mountain	539,341	5.54	3.70	0.86	0.98
Pacific	758,364	4.60	3.33	0.67	0.60
Puerto Rico	76,167	7.82	5.03	1.63	1.16
U.S. Total	4,422,109	6.14	4.18	0.95	1.01

See SERVICING AGREEMENT OR SALE AND SERVICING AGREEMENT.

DELIVERY The handing over of legal documents so that the recipient becomes the owner of property described in said documents. For a delivery to be legal, the grantor must competent at the time of execution of the papers and at the time of delivery. Delivery is complete when the recipient accepts the documents.

See ACCEPTANCE.

DELIVERY DATE The date the Central Paying and Transfer Agent (CPTA) releases securities to the issuer's agent at the CPTA's window or places the securities in the mail to the issuer. The Central Paying and Transfer Agent is a Ginnie Mae employee.

DEMAND NOTE A debt instrument that allows the lender to call the balance due at any time without prior notice.

DEMOGRAPHICS Statistical information concerning population growth and trends.

DENSITY A measure of the number of dwelling units per component size of land, such as an acre.

DEPARTMENT OF HOUSING AND URBAN DEVELOPMENT (HUD)
A cabinet-level department of the federal government charged with the responsibility for Federal Housing programs and urban affairs. HUD administers the Federal Housing Administration (FHA) insurance and Ginnie Mae programs. The agency was established by the Housing and Urban Development Act of 1965 with the purpose of the implementation and administration of government housing and urban development programs.

Below is a list of HUD Handbooks.

1060s	Regulations
4000.2	Mortgagee's Guide, Application through Insurance
4000.4	Mortgagee's Guide to Direct Endorsement
4000.5	Direct Endorsement
4010.1	Definitions, Policy Statements and General Rulings
4020.1	HUD/FHA Underwriting Analysis
4050.1	Records Control Handbook
4060.1	Mortgagee Approval Handbook
4060.2	Mortgagee Review Board Handbook
4060.3	Field Office Guide for Mortgagee Reviews
4065.1	Previous Participation Handbook
4070.1	Construction Complaints and Section 518(a)
4080.1	Compliance Handbook
4110.1	Fiscal and ADP Handbook
4110.2	Mortgagee's Guide, Fiscal Instructions
4115.1	Administrative Instructions and Procedures
4115.3	Master Conditional Commitment Procedures
4125.1	Underwriting - Technical Directions
4135.1	Proposed Construction in New Subdivisions
4145.1	Architectural Processing and Inspections
4150.1	Valuation Analysis
4155.1	Mortgage Credit Analysis. Revision 1 through 3.
4160.1	Reconsideration before Endorsement
4165.1	Insurance Endorsement
4170.1	Reconsideration after Endorsement
4190.1	Underwriting Reports and Forms Catalog
4205.1	Coinsurance
4210.1	Section 235(i)
4240.1	Section 203(h) and Section 203(i)
4240.2	Section 245
4240.3	Section 203(n)
4240.4	Section 203(k)
4245.1	Section 220(d)(3)(A) and Section 220(h)

See FEDERAL HOUSING ADMINISTRATION (FHA).

DEPOSIT Money or an item of value placed in good faith to express the need to abide by the terms of an agreement or contract. A deposit is subject to being returned.

See EARNEST MONEY.

DEPOSITORY INSTITUTION A financial intermediary that accepts savings or demand deposits from the public and invests the funds in consumer loans, e.g., a bank.

DEPOSITORY INSTITUTIONS DEREGULATION ACT (DIDA) 1980 legislation that deregulated depository financial institutions, mandatorily authorized equalization of thrift interest paid to depositors, and phased out interest rate ceiling deposits on savings accounts in 1986.

DEPRECIATION (1) For federal income tax purposes, it is the assumption that permanently attached improvements always lessen in value, even if market conditions show the improvements are increasing in value. Depreciation is a major reason for investing in real estate. While the real estate may be increasing in value, depreciation, for tax reasons, means the real estate is always decreasing in value. For income tax purposes, depreciation is an expense deduction that allows for the recovery of the cost of the investment.

(2) In appraising real estate there are three types of real depreciation that contribute to a loss in value, they are: economic obsolescence, functional obsolescence, and physical deterioration.

See COMPONENT DEPRECIATION, ECONOMIC OBSOLESCENCE, FUNCTIONAL OBSOLESCENCE, and PHYSICAL DETERIORATION, RECAPTURE.

DERAIGN To trace a title to prove ownership of land.

DEREGULATION To loosen governmental control. A specific form of deregulation is found when thrift institution interest was deregulated (DIDA): before this act, 1/4 of 1% more interest was paid to thrift depositors by thrift institutions than commercial banks paid to their customers. On 1/1/84 a law was passed that ended this practice. The equalization was intended to help savings institutions attract funds for housing since they could now offer the full range of consumer financial services that banks could offer.

DERIVATIVE SECURITIES Market instruments that have underlying security or are created from other securities, including mortgage-backed securities in the form of strips and CMO residuals.

DESCENT The act of transferring property upon death according to state law. State laws that govern inheritance of property.
See DEVISE.

DESCRIPTION In real estate, this term commonly refers to the property address or its legal description. Legal documents, such as deeds and leases, must have a full description to be valid. A street address is sufficient description for certain other documents, such as a sales contract.
See LEGAL DESCRIPTION.

DETACHED SINGLE-FAMILY DWELLING A house with yard space in the front, sides, and rear.

DETAILS Part of a window.
See WINDOW.

DEVELOPMENT LOAN A short-term loan used for the acquisition of land intended for the development of building sites. The development loan proceeds go for improvements for such items as grading, streets, and utilities.

DEVISE The act of transferring property upon death by a will.
See DESCENT.

DILUVION The opposite of alluvion. Soil gradually washes away because of an erosion caused by a waterway.

DIRECT ENDORSEMENT *See* FHA - DIRECT ENDORSEMENT.

DIRECT REDUCTION MORTGAGE A mortgage, usually between individuals, requiring level payments of principal. Payment will vary as interest lessens with the declining balance.

DISBURSEMENT Cash payment for a draw according to the terms and provisions of a loan, usually a construction loan; the payment of items as reflected on a settlement statement at a closing.

DISCHARGE OF BANKRUPTCY The date a bankruptcy is finally discharged. This date is important for loan underwriting purposes since certain programs require a minimum amount of time to have transpired from the date of bankruptcy before an application can be considered for approval.

DISCLOSURE The-Truth-in-Lending Act requires lenders to disclose or inform borrowers what the true cost of borrowing money is, what the closing costs will be, and special conditions of a mortgage. *Disclosure* is a broad term used to describe a form used to inform the borrower of certain costs or conditions of obtaining a loan.

Developers must disclose certain information to prospective purchasers of real estate such as: condominium units, time shares, and resort property.

FHLBB regulated or FSLIC insured institutions must use the form in Exhibit 11.

See ANNUAL PERCENTAGE RATE (APR), GOOD FAITH ESTIMATE, PROSPECTUS.

DISCOUNT The difference between par or 100% of the face value of a note or obligation and the actual bid price for said obligation. The purpose of a discount is to increase the yield of a mortgage or debt instrument. For example, if a mortgage of $100,000 sells for $95,000, the loan discount is 5% or $5,000. The term *discount* refers to a dollar amount expressed as a percentage of the loan amount. In the above example, the discount would be $5,000. A *point* is 1% of the loan amount; two points is 2% of the loan amount, etc. In the above example, the discount can be expressed as 5% or 5 points. If a loan is sold without a discount, it is sold at par.

The 1990 Housing Bill established a limit on discount points for lower loan amounts - see the last paragraph of FHA - LOAN AMOUNTS.

See ELLWOOD TABLE and INWOOD ORDINARY ANNUITY COEFFICIENT.

DISCOUNT NOTE A short-term debt security sold at less than face value but redeemed at maturity at full value; the difference between the purchase price and redemption amount is the equivalent of interest paid for the funds. The discount note is most popular in the world of mortgages as security for real estate sales in the housing market. The principal and interest payments are

Exhibit 11

FIXED RATE AND VARIABLE RATE LOAN PROGRAM DISCLOSURE

DUE ON SALE

☐ Your loan documents do not contain a "due-on-sale" clause.

☐ Your loan documents contain a "due-on-sale" clause. A "due-on-sale" clause states that if you sell or transfer the mortgaged property without the Note Holder's prior written consent, all sums owed under the promissory note and the other loan documents (including the outstanding principal balance) could become immediately due and payable. The loan documents will set forth in detail what would constitute a sale or transfer.

LATE PAYMENTS

If you fail to make your loan payments within _____ days after the due date, the Note Holder may charge a late payment charge equal to _____ percent (_____ %) of the missed payment of principal and interest.

PREPAYMENT

If you pay off your loan early, you

☐ may ☐ will ☐ will not   have to pay a penalty.

The amount of any prepayment penalty will be equal to_____
_____
_____ .

PAYMENTS OF ESCROW ITEMS

Your total monthly payment will also include an escrow payment, paid together with your monthly payments of principal and interest (subject to applicable state law). These escrow payments will be put into an escrow account so that the Note Holder can pay large semi-annual or annual expenses associated with your property when they are due. These expenses can include yearly property taxes, assessments, ground rents, and yearly mortgage and hazard insurance premiums, as applicable to your property. The escrow payment is calculated as the estimated annual total of these Escrow Expenses divided by the number of payments that are due per year.

If you fail to make an escrow payment when due, the Note Holder will have the right to deduct it from your monthly payment and require you to make up the difference. The Note Holder may also reject any monthly payment which is less than the amount of the principal, interest, and monthly escrow payment due, and exercise the rights provided in the contract regarding default for late or delinquent payments.

Once a year, your escrow account will be analyzed to assure that the proper amount of funds is being collected monthly. At this time, a new escrow payment will be calculated by comparing the current escrow account balance with the estimated annual total of your current Escrow Expenses divided by the number of payments that are due per year.

If insufficient funds are available in the escrow account to pay necessary Escrow Expenses, the Note Holder may advance the money as needed to cover those expenses and bill you for the amounts advanced. You will be required to pay the amounts advanced immediately upon receipt of the bill.

Any surplus in escrow payments will be returned to the borrower in the form of_____
_____ .

NOTICE OF MATURITY

At the time of maturity (termination period of your Note), the Note Holder will send a statement to you _____ days in advance, notifying you of your loan's maturity. The statement will include all pertinent information regarding the maturity of your loan.

This loan ☐ is ☐ is not partially or non-amortized. This could result in a larger final payment at the time of loan maturity or upon call of the loan. The loan maturity notice will indicate the amount of the final loan payment.

The final payment may be large enough to warrant refinancing of the loan.

This institution ☐ does ☐ does not unconditionally obligate itself to refinance the amount of the final payment at the time of loan maturity.

Additional Features contained in the notice of maturity:
_____
_____
_____
_____

I/We acknowledge that I/we have received this disclosure.

_____   _____
Borrower   Date

_____   _____
Borrower   Date

VMP-791 (8809/01)   VMP MORTGAGE FORMS • (313)293-8100 • (800)521-7291   9/88
(For use with FHLBB regulated or FSLIC insured institutions.)

submitted periodically during a time agreed upon by the buyer and the seller, the same way the buyer makes installments on their first mortgage. The junior or second mortgage (or trust deed) is a credit extended to the buyer usually on a discounted note (sold in escrow for cash). This procedure is fairly standard when making a low down payment in a home purchase.

Appraisers, on the other hand (regardless of the sale price), reflect fair market value as the criteria for cash worth of real property, especially many county assessors who use equivalent cash value for real property taxes.

DISCOUNT POINTS The amount of discount expressed as a point or a percentage. For example: A discount of five points would be 5% of the loan amount; one point equals 1% of the loan amount.

See DISCOUNTED YIELD.

DISCOUNT RATE (1) The rate that banks discount a negotiable instrument such as a note, acceptance, and bills of exchange. (2) The rate charged by the Federal Reserve to member banks for borrowed funds.

DISCOUNTED CASH FLOW ANALYSIS The method of applying an appropriate discount to cash to be received in the future to arrive at the present value of those future earnings.

See DISCOUNTED YIELD.

DISCOUNTED YIELD The purpose of a loan discount is to increase the yield of a mortgage. Yield is the net interest a mortgagee (investor) receives from the loan. In nearly all cases, loans are sold in the secondary market and the rate of a loan must meet the yield requirement of an investor. If the rate is below the yield requirement, the loan must be discounted.

To convert a discount point into interest or yield, one can use a rule of thumb of 1.5% in discount equals 1/4% increase in yield based on a 12-year average life for a 30-year loan. A more accurate estimate of a discount yield can be decided by using a Discount Yield Table, or a HP-12C calculator.

Originators of mortgage loans for the secondary market calculate a discount required on the sale akin to calculating other cash flows. Secondary market participants and other lenders/investors who buy the originated mortgages establish their required net yields (RNYs). The buyer's RNY usually includes servicing as a part of the calculation on a gross to gross basis. The omission of servicing from the calculations would require net to net yields since a rate on the mortgage to be purchased is lower than the RNY established. The gross to gross application is found necessary because servicing is involved in both cases. The theory assumes a mortgage will be active for 12 years (a standard time in the industry). A mortgagor is expected to prepay fully a 25-year, fixed rate loan in 12 years because of selling the property or refinancing the loan.

The following cash flow discount that an originating lender considers marketing is cash flow on an origination transaction for a 25-year, fixed rate mortgage of $72,000 at 11%. The lender estimates a time to a prepayment assumption of 12 years. Selling it to a buyer whose RNY (required net yield) is 11.25 (servicing included) will consequently discount the new loan for $1,118.50 (0.0155%).

DISCOUNTING THE CASH FLOWS
(with the HP-12C Calculator)

	Keystrokes	Display	Explanations
Step 1.	(f)CLEAR(REG)	0.00	
Step 2.	25 (g) (n)	300.00	calculates and stores months
Step 3.	11 (g) (i)	.92	calculates annual interest
Step 4.	-72,000 (CHS) (PV)		minus sign stores -72,000 PV
Step 5.	(PMT)	705.68	calculates monthly payment
Step 6.	12 (g) (n)	144.00	prepay assumption in months
Step 7.	(FV)	58,440.20	calculates prepay balance
Step 8.	11.25 (g) (i)	.94	buyer RNY
Step 9.	(PV)	-70,881.50	calculates buyer's present value
Step 10.	72,000 (+)	1,118.50	calculates new cash discount

To ensure this cash flow discount on a sale, the loan originator may assume less severe consequences in such a decision to sell (if appointed) to the .3750 point fee for servicing. This 3/8 point fee is the criteria accepted by the industry (in this case $90 monthly, besides the up-front points charged to the borrower). Profits from a sale to a secondary market conduit depend upon various factors, i.e., delivery schedule performance, float considerations, etc.

A discount yield table helps to decide the effective yield of a discounted mortgage. The Discount Yield Table (Exhibit 12) shows what the true interest or yield is after a loan has been discounted. A discount or points can be charged so that the true yield or interest is actually higher than that reported on

Exhibit 12

Discount Yield Table

Rate of Interest	Bid Price	5 Years	10 Years	15 Years	20 Years	25 Years	30 Years
9%	95	11.22	10.21	9.89	9.73	9.64	9.58
	96	10.76	9.96	9.70	9.58	9.51	9.46
	97	10.31	9.72	9.52	9.43	9.38	9.34
	98	9.87	9.48	9.35	9.28	9.25	9.23
	99	9.43	9.24	9.17	9.14	9.12	9.11
9⅛%	95	11.34	10.34	10.01	9.86	9.77	9.71
	96	10.89	10.09	9.83	9.71	9.63	9.59
	97	10.44	9.84	9.65	9.56	9.50	9.47
	98	9.99	9.60	9.47	9.41	9.38	9.35
	99	9.56	9.36	9.30	9.27	9.25	9.24
9¼%	95	11.47	10.47	10.14	9.99	9.90	9.84
	96	11.01	10.22	9.96	9.83	9.76	9.72
	97	10.56	9.97	9.78	9.68	9.63	9.60
	98	10.12	9.73	9.60	9.54	9.50	9.48
	99	9.68	9.49	9.42	9.39	9.38	9.36
9⅜%	95	11.60	10.60	10.27	10.11	10.03	9.97
	96	11.14	10.35	10.09	9.96	9.89	9.85
	97	10.69	10.10	9.90	9.81	9.76	9.73
	98	10.25	9.85	9.73	9.66	9.63	9.61
	99	9.81	9.61	9.55	9.52	9.50	9.49
9½%	95	11.73	10.73	10.40	10.24	10.16	10.10
	96	11.27	10.47	10.21	10.09	10.02	9.98
	97	10.82	10.22	10.03	9.94	9.89	9.85
	98	10.37	9.98	9.85	9.79	9.76	9.73
	99	9.93	9.74	9.67	9.64	9.63	9.62
9⅝%	95	11.86	10.85	10.53	10.37	10.28	10.23
	96	11.40	10.60	10.34	10.22	10.15	10.11
	97	10.94	10.35	10.16	10.07	10.01	9.98
	98	10.50	10.11	9.98	9.92	9.88	9.86
	99	10.06	9.86	9.80	9.77	9.75	9.74
9¾%	95	11.98	10.98	10.66	10.50	10.41	10.36
	96	11.52	10.73	10.47	10.35	10.28	10.23
	97	11.07	10.48	10.29	10.19	10.14	10.11
	98	10.62	10.23	10.10	10.04	10.01	9.99
	99	10.18	9.99	9.93	9.90	9.88	9.87
9⅞%	95	12.11	11.11	10.78	10.63	10.54	10.49
	96	11.65	10.86	10.60	10.47	10.40	10.36
	97	11.20	10.61	10.41	10.32	10.27	10.24
	98	10.75	10.36	10.23	10.17	10.14	10.11
	99	10.31	10.11	10.05	10.02	10.00	9.99
10%	95	12.24	11.24	10.91	10.76	10.67	10.62
	96	11.78	10.98	10.72	10.60	10.53	10.49
	97	11.32	10.73	10.54	10.45	10.40	10.37
	98	10.88	10.48	10.36	10.30	10.26	10.24
	99	10.43	10.24	10.18	10.15	10.13	10.12
10⅛%	95	12.37	11.37	11.04	10.89	10.80	10.75
	96	11.90	11.11	10.85	10.73	10.66	10.62
	97	11.45	10.86	10.67	10.57	10.52	10.49
	98	11.00	10.61	10.48	10.42	10.39	10.37
	99	10.56	10.37	10.30	10.27	10.26	10.25

Exhibit 12 (continued)

Discount Yield Table

Rate of Interest	Bid Price	5 Years	10 Years	15 Years	20 Years	25 Years	30 Years
10¼%	95	12.49	11.50	11.17	11.02	10.93	10.88
	96	12.03	11.24	10.98	10.86	10.79	10.75
	97	11.58	10.99	10.79	10.70	10.65	10.62
	98	11.13	10.74	10.61	10.55	10.52	10.50
	99	10.69	10.49	10.43	10.40	10.38	10.37
10⅜%	95	12.62	11.62	11.30	11.15	11.06	11.01
	96	12.16	11.37	11.11	10.99	10.92	10.88
	97	11.70	11.11	10.92	10.83	10.78	10.75
	98	11.25	10.86	10.74	10.68	10.64	10.62
	99	10.81	10.62	10.55	10.52	10.51	10.50
10½%	95	12.75	11.75	11.43	11.27	11.19	11.14
	96	12.29	11.49	11.24	11.11	11.05	11.01
	97	11.83	11.24	11.05	10.96	10.91	10.88
	98	11.38	10.99	10.86	10.80	10.77	10.75
	99	10.94	10.74	10.68	10.65	10.63	10.62
10⅝%	95	12.88	11.88	11.56	11.40	11.32	11.27
	96	12.41	11.62	11.36	11.24	11.18	11.14
	97	11.96	11.37	11.17	11.08	11.03	11.00
	98	11.51	11.12	10.99	10.93	10.90	10.88
	99	11.06	10.87	10.81	10.78	10.76	10.75
10¾%	95	13.01	12.01	11.68	11.53	11.45	11.40
	96	12.54	11.75	11.49	11.37	11.30	11.26
	97	12.08	11.49	11.30	11.21	11.16	11.13
	98	11.63	11.24	11.11	11.06	11.02	11.00
	99	11.19	10.99	10.93	10.90	10.89	10.88
10⅞%	95	13.13	12.14	11.81	11.66	11.58	11.53
	96	12.67	11.88	11.62	11.50	11.43	11.39
	97	12.21	11.62	11.43	11.34	11.29	11.26
	98	11.76	11.37	11.24	11.18	11.15	11.13
	99	11.31	11.12	11.06	11.03	11.01	11.00
11%	95	13.26	12.26	11.94	11.79	11.71	11.66
	96	12.80	12.00	11.75	11.63	11.56	11.52
	97	12.34	11.75	11.56	11.47	11.42	11.39
	98	11.88	11.49	11.37	11.31	11.28	11.26
	99	11.44	11.25	11.18	11.15	11.14	11.13
11⅛%	95	13.39	12.39	12.07	11.92	11.84	11.79
	96	12.92	12.13	11.88	11.76	11.69	11.65
	97	12.46	11.87	11.68	11.59	11.54	11.52
	98	12.01	11.62	11.49	11.43	11.40	11.38
	99	11.56	11.37	11.31	11.28	11.26	11.25
11¼%	95	13.52	12.52	12.20	12.05	11.97	11.92
	96	13.05	12.26	12.00	11.88	11.82	11.78
	97	12.59	12.00	11.81	11.72	11.67	11.64
	98	12.14	11.75	11.62	11.56	11.53	11.51
	99	11.69	11.50	11.43	11.40	11.39	11.38
11⅜%	95	13.64	12.65	12.33	12.18	12.10	12.05
	96	13.18	12.39	12.13	12.01	11.95	11.91
	97	12.72	12.13	11.94	11.85	11.80	11.77
	98	12.26	11.87	11.75	11.69	11.66	11.64
	99	11.82	11.62	11.56	11.53	11.51	11.50

Exhibit 12 (continued)

Discount Yield Table

Rate of Interest	Bid Price	5 Years	10 Years	15 Years	20 Years	25 Years	30 Years
11½%	95	13.77	12.78	12.46	12.31	12.23	12.18
	96	13.30	12.51	12.26	12.14	12.08	12.04
	97	12.84	12.25	12.06	11.98	11.93	11.90
	98	12.39	12.00	11.87	11.81	11.78	11.76
	99	11.94	11.75	11.69	11.66	11.64	11.63
11⅝%	95	13.90	12.90	12.58	12.44	12.36	12.31
	96	13.43	12.64	12.39	12.27	12.20	12.17
	97	12.97	12.38	12.19	12.10	12.06	12.03
	98	12.51	12.13	12.00	11.94	11.91	11.89
	99	12.07	11.87	11.81	11.78	11.77	11.76
11¾%	95	14.03	13.03	12.71	12.57	12.49	12.44
	96	13.56	12.77	12.51	12.40	12.33	12.30
	97	13.10	12.51	12.32	12.23	12.18	12.16
	98	12.64	12.25	12.13	12.07	12.04	12.02
	99	12.19	12.00	11.94	11.91	11.89	11.88
11⅞%	95	14.16	13.16	12.84	12.69	12.62	12.57
	96	13.69	12.90	12.64	12.52	12.46	12.43
	97	13.22	12.63	12.45	12.36	12.31	12.28
	98	12.77	12.38	12.25	12.19	12.16	12.15
	99	12.32	12.12	12.06	12.03	12.02	12.01
12%	95	14.28	13.29	12.97	12.82	12.74	12.70
	96	13.81	13.02	12.77	12.65	12.59	12.55
	97	13.35	12.76	12.57	12.49	12.44	12.41
	98	12.89	12.50	12.38	12.32	12.29	12.27
	99	12.44	12.25	12.19	12.16	12.14	12.13
12⅛%	95	14.41	13.42	13.10	12.95	12.87	12.83
	96	13.94	13.15	12.90	12.78	12.72	12.68
	97	13.48	12.89	12.70	12.61	12.57	12.54
	98	13.02	12.63	12.51	12.45	12.42	12.40
	99	12.57	12.38	12.31	12.29	12.27	12.26
12¼%	95	14.54	13.55	13.23	13.08	13.00	12.96
	96	14.07	13.28	13.03	12.91	12.85	12.81
	97	13.60	13.02	12.83	12.74	12.69	12.67
	98	13.15	12.76	12.63	12.57	12.54	12.53
	99	12.69	12.50	12.44	12.41	12.40	12.39
12⅜%	95	14.67	13.67	13.36	13.21	13.13	13.09
	96	14.19	13.41	13.15	13.04	12.98	12.94
	97	13.73	13.14	12.95	12.87	12.82	12.80
	98	13.27	12.88	12.76	12.70	12.67	12.65
	99	12.82	12.63	12.57	12.54	12.52	12.51
12½%	95	14.79	13.80	13.49	13.34	13.26	13.22
	96	14.32	13.53	13.28	13.17	13.11	13.07
	97	13.86	13.27	13.08	13.00	12.95	12.92
	98	13.40	13.01	12.88	12.83	12.80	12.78
	99	12.95	12.75	12.69	12.66	12.65	12.64
12⅝%	95	14.92	13.93	13.61	13.47	13.39	13.35
	96	14.45	13.66	13.41	13.30	13.23	13.20
	97	13.98	13.40	13.21	13.12	13.08	13.05
	98	13.52	13.14	13.01	12.95	12.92	12.91
	99	13.07	12.88	12.82	12.79	12.77	12.76

the debt instrument. For example, a mortgage note of $100,000 at an 11 1/2% rate for a 30-year term was sold for $95,000. The discount was 5% or 5 points and the true yield or interest would be raised to 12.18%. If this 30-year loan matured (paid out) in 12 years the yield would be approximately 1/2 the distance between the 10 and 15 year yields or 12.62%. FHA, VA and Conventional mortgages with a 30-year term are considered to have an average maturity of 12 years.

See ELLWOOD TABLE, INWOOD ORDINARY ANNUITY COEFFICIENT, and YIELDS.

DISINTERMEDIATION Depositors withdrawing funds from a savings and loan institution to work their money at higher yields in other deposits or investments. It is an observable event occurring when rates being paid by certain depository intermediaries cannot compete with rates being paid by others, e.g., U.S. Treasury Bills. Imbalances occur for deposits held by thrifts, for instance, that cannot pay the higher interest rates on savings deposits.

DISPOSSESS See EVICTION.

DISSEISIN This term has the same meaning as DISPOSSESS and EVICTION. *See* EVICTION.

DISTRAINT The right of a landlord, subject to a court order, to seize personal property belonging to a tenant in satisfaction of rent not paid.
See ABANDONMENT, REPLEVIN.

DISTRESSED PROPERTY Term that denotes property in trouble due to one of several reasons such as: cost overrun, insufficient income, poor management, or any other conditions that affect the mortgagor's ability to repay the loan on a timely basis.

DIVIDED INTEREST An interest in a part of the whole property. A mortgagee or a lessee has a divided interest in the mortgaged or leased property.

DOCUMENTS Legal instruments. Examples are: a mortgage, deed, contract, lease, and an option.

DOCUMENTARY EVIDENCE Written evidence in support of claim.

DOCUMENTARY TAX STAMPS *See* TAX STAMPS.

DOLLAR VALUE OF A BASIS POINT The price change in a given debt instrument resulting from a one basis point (.01%) change in its yield. It is calculated as the amount of the price discount (premium) required to equate the cash flows of an instrument with a given rate to a like instrument yielding one basis point more (or less).

DOMICILE The apparently permanent home of an individual. A person may have several residences but only one domicile.

DORMER A dormer window projects from the slope of a roof and has an appearance of a house in itself.
See CAPE COD.

DOUBLE-GLAZED WINDOW Two panes of glass or transparent plastic separated by an open space of approximately one inch. The open space serves as an insulating pocket that temporarily traps and warms the cold air, or cools the warm air, coming in from the outside. People sometimes call a double-glaze window a: double-pane window or an insulated window or a storm window.

DOUBLE-HUNG WINDOW *See* WINDOW.

DOUBLE-PITCH ROOF *See* ROOF.

DOUBLE-PLATE Two horizontal boards that form a plate on top of a row of studs. Rafters rest on top of the plates.

DOUBLE-WHAMMY The practice of exercising a due-on-sale clause and charging a prepayment penalty on the same loan.

DOWER Common-law right of a wife to part of her deceased husband's property.
See CURTSEY.

DOWNPAYMENT The difference between the loan amount and the cost to acquire a property. If the purchase price for a property is $100,000 and the loan amount is $75,000, the downpayment is $25,000. For home loans, the source of downpayment should be in the form of cash derived from earnings. There are generally two exceptions to the source rule for downpayments.

(1) Most lenders will allow a downpayment that is borrowed if the loan is secured against an asset and not a signature loan. The asset serving as collateral should not be the borrower's personal possessions nor principal mode of transportation. The lender cannot be the seller of the property nor the real estate broker or agent involved in the sale.

(2) The downpayment is in the form of a gift that is not to be repaid to the donor or their estate in any form or fashion. The donor has verified funds to make the gift.

DOWNSPOUT A part of a gutter system that is in a vertical position.
See GUTTER SYSTEM.

DOWNZONING Land that is rezoned to a lesser use, e.g., commercial to residential, or a lower density.

DRAGNET CLAUSE A clause in a mortgage that uses the subject property as collateral for all debts from various loans owed to the lender. Courts may disagree with what a dragnet clause intends since they may require a direct relationship between each loan and the collateral acquired by the loan proceeds.
See ANACONDA MORTGAGE, MOTHER HUBBARD CLAUSE.

DRAW In mortgage terms, it implies a cash payment from the lender to the contractor or builder according to the terms and conditions of a construction loan.

DRIP CAP A projection over a door or window that forces rainwater to fall away from the building.

DROP SIDING Exterior siding applied to the framing structure by the *tongue & groove* method.

DRY CLOSING The act of closing without distribution of funds. Reasons for delay in funding are normally unfulfilled conditions of loan approval or lack of a satisfactory final inspection of the subject property. Once the condition(s) is satisfied, cash disbursement occurs.
See PRECLOSING.

DRY ROT *See* ROT.

DRYWALL Wall board that is not plaster. Examples are sheetrock, plywood paneling, plasterboard, and wood paneling.

DUAL AGENCY Representation of the buyer and the seller in the same transaction. Dual agency is illegal in most states. In real estate sales, an agent should make clear what party they represent. It is illogical and conflicting to strive earnestly to get the highest price for the seller, while negotiating for the lowest price for the buyer. In recent times there has been a new emergence of the real estate agent representing the buyer.

DUAL CONTRACT An illegal practice of a seller and a purchaser agreeing to perform acts different from what is disclosed to a lender. A dual contract can be either written or oral. A dual contact is illegal and subject to penalties as described by Section 1010 of Title 18 that provides for a maximum of a $5,000 fine or imprisonment for a maximum of 2 years, or both.

An example of a dual contract is discount paid by a buyer on an FHA loan made before 1 December 1983. Before that date, the purchaser could not pay discount points on purchase transactions. Many dual contracts were discovered when the buyer reimbursed the seller for discount points the seller had to pay in compliance with FHA regulations.

Contracts are very important in dual contract situations. The sales contract given the lender must be the only agreement between the parties involved. Charges on the settlement statement that conflict with the agreements in the contract are *red flags* for the existence of a dual contract.

Often times closing instructions will include the following:

Other than in the case of a refinanced loan, each loan has been processed and approved by the Lender according to the terms of the sales contract. A copy of this contract will be included in the closed loan package. If the borrower receives any credit from the seller that reduces the agreed upon sales price, or if the terms of the loan transaction differ from the terms of the sales contract, you must notify the Lender prior to closing.

DUCTS Conduits or pipes used in heating and air conditioning systems.

DUE BILL A promissory note delivered to an investor by a broker or dealer in place of corporate securities. Due bills must be replaced by actual securities on a specific date in the future.

DUE DATE The date when a mortgage payment is due. Payments made after the due date are delinquent though they may not involve a delinquent fee. Lenders prefer (for many reasons) the first payment to become due on the first day of the second month following the date of execution of the loan documents and not the date of disbursement. For example, if the loan closing documents are executed anytime in March, the payment due date will be the first day of May.

See DELINQUENCY.

DUE-ON-SALE CLAUSE A sale (or transfer of title) of a mortgage loan generally requires full payment of the remaining balance of the loan upon sale by virtue of a clause generally found in loan agreements. Law governs window periods. Due-on-sale clauses have been included in most mortgage contracts for years. The following is an example of a due-on-sale clause:

If all or any part of the Property or an interest therein is sold or transferred by Borrower without Lender's prior written consent . . . Lender may, at Lender's option, declare all the sums secured by this Mortgage to be immediately due and payable.

Lenders use the due-on-sale clause when a buyer tries to assume a sellers' existing low rate mortgage. In these cases, the courts have frequently upheld the lender's right to raise the interest rate to the prevailing market level. Thus, buyers should tread with care when assuming a mortgage with a due-on-sale clause. If the seller's mortgage contains a due-on-sale provision, written permission to assume the mortgage should be obtained from the lender. Otherwise, an assumption could be illegal and the existing mortgagor could be liable for thousands of additional dollars.

It is important to know whether the buyer and seller of property have a clear understanding in advance of such risks. The broker or an attorney should check state law to decide if the due-on-sale provision is legal. When consummating a mortgage, a borrower should carefully read the fine print; otherwise it may be impossible to have a buyer assume the mortgage at a later date.

FHA loans originated after December 1, 1986 have a due-on-sale clause requiring the borrower to pre-qualify before assuming the loan. VA loans originated after March 1, 1988 contain a similar due-on-sale clause. It is important to note that neither FHA or VA due-on-sale clauses provide for an escalation of the interest rate as do conventional loans. FHA and VA loans can be assumed (subject to approval of the assumptor on loans originated after the above mentioned dates) repeatedly without increasing the interest rate.

The best way to avoid a due-on-sale clause that allows the interest rate to escalate upon loan assumption is to get an FHA or a VA loan.

See DUE-ON-SALE WINDOW PERIOD.

DUE-ON-SALE WINDOW PERIOD A three-year period when the window period states were authorized to reimpose due-on-sale limits and expiring October 15, 1985.

DUPLEX A two-family dwelling.

DURATION The calculation of the weighted average of time cycles when obtaining present values of cash flow from an investment. This calculation is called a measure of a loan's price to possible yield changes. Even more precise than average life, although similar, is years to bond maturity as an estimate of the investment's duration. Investors find it desirable to quantify the effective lifetime of a pool in a way that accounts for its principal paydowns. Duration is calculated as the weighted average remaining time to repayments of security on all the principal (or interest) using as weights the dollar amounts to final security payments. The greater the security payment, the heavier the weight. Passthrough prepayment assumption is directly related to cash flows estimated by investors. Pass-throughs generally return more dollars in their early years than in their later years and modify yield, average mortgage life and duration. When these future payments are converted to present value equivalents and summed up, the result should be the known market price. Yield (or more properly, yield to maturity) is the discount rate that makes this relationship true. A discount rate that applies yield to maturity (or other qualifying rate), that forces a definite cash flow into the yield calculation, should decide a current market price. The weights used establish the present values of the payments (yield to maturity).

For instance, when a pool is priced by using a discount to par, a fast-pay pool of prepayments will produce higher yield, a lower duration or lower average life; however, a fast-pay pool at a premium price will produce a lower yield and a lower duration for the investor.

DURESS Compulsion, force, or pressure forcing an individual to perform an act.

DUTCH COLONIAL An architectural style of home design that features a gable roof.

Dutch Colonial. The home is of Early American design featuring a gambrel roof and eaves that flare outward. The chimney is off-center and there are many small pane windows.

DWELLING A person's residence. Commonly used to imply a single-family dwelling or a house.

See the heading "Home" in the topical index.

E

EARNEST MONEY A cash deposit that accompanies a sales contract to show good faith in abiding by the terms and conditions set forth in the contract. If the buyer does not abide by the conditions of the purchase agreement (sales contract, offer and acceptance, etc.) the earnest money can be forfeited. The term *earnest money* is sometimes called *good faith deposit.* The amount of earnest money used as a deposit can vary, usually it is from 5% to 10% of the purchase price. At the closing, the earnest money is credited as a partial payment or a part of the downpayment if there is a loan.

See DAMAGES.

EARNEST MONEY CONTRACT *See* CONTRACT.

EARTHEN HOME

Earthen Home. The approach to the front of this house is at street level, but the side walls are under the earth and the back of the house comes out to an open wall with clerestory windows for cooling purposes.

EASEMENT A right in property that is less than a right in possession. This term is commonly used to refer to a right that a party has in relationship to another party's property.

Easements are usually described in Schedule B of title policies. The lender will want to check the easements in the title policy against the survey for any encroachment or violation. Any negative or adverse easements must be brought to the lender's attention before closing.

EASTLAKE

Eastlake. A nineteenth century style home similar to the Queen Anne or Carpenter Gothic. The Eastlake is distinct because of the ornamentation made by the chisel gouge and lathe rather than the scroll saw. The style features a tower or turret, a single covered gable roof and an open front porch. The ornamentation resembles furniture parts.

EAVE The lower portion of a roof that projects out and over the side walls of a building.

ECOA *See* EQUAL CREDIT OPPORTUNITY ACT.

ECOLOGY A study that shows the impact of the environment on living things.

ECONOMIC INDICATORS Investors should watch these leading indicators:

- average workweek of production workers in manufacturing;
- average weekly initial claims for state unemployment insurance;
- new orders for durable goods industries;

- Index of net business formation;
- Contracts and orders for plants and equipment;
- New building permits;
- Change in manufacturing and trade inventories;
- Industrial material prices;
- Changes in consumer installment debt;
- Corporate after tax profits; and
- Ratio of price to unit labor cost for manufacturing.

Roughly Coincident Indicators

- Employees on agricultural payroll;
- Total unemployment rate;
- GNP in current dollars;
- Industrial production;
- Personal income;
- Manufacturing and trade sales; and
- Retail store sales.

Lagging Indicators

- Unemployment rate for 15 weeks and over;
- Business expenditures for new plants and equipment;
- Book value for manufacturing and trade inventories;
- Labor cost per unit of output for manufacturing;
- Commercial and industrial loans outstanding; and
- Bank rates on short-term business loans.

The Federal Reserve System reports monthly, semi-annual, and annual studies on statistical trends.

ECONOMIC LIFE That period when a property has a useful life; a time when use of the property is economically feasible. For VA loans, the term of the loan is normally limited to the number of years of economic life shown on the VA appraisal or CRV.

ECONOMIC OBSOLESCENCE Changes in the surrounding area making real estate less valuable. Examples are: a deteriorating neighborhood, a zoning change, a movement in the population such as leaving the inner city and moving to the suburb.

ECONOMIC RENT The rent a property would normally bring if leased. In most loan underwriting circumstances, an investor with multiple properties can claim an economic rent on a unit that happens to be temporarily vacant at the time of loan application.

EFFECTIVE AGE An appraisal term that is an age to a property other than its actual age. For example, a fifty-year-old house that has been renovated recently and had the installation of new plumbing, electrical, heating, kitchen appliances, cabinets, etc., may have an effective age of 15 years.
See REHABILITATION.

EFFECTIVE GROSS INCOME For income or investment properties effective gross income is gross income minus a vacancy allowance and collection loss. The term is often found in a pro-forma or profit and loss projection for an income property. Effective gross income is income before any deductions for expenses.
See ALLOWANCE FOR VACANCY AND INCOME LOSS.

EFFECTIVE INTEREST RATE *See* ANNUAL PERCENTAGE RATE (ARR).

EFFECTIVE YIELD The yield of a mortgage or note after it has been purchased at a discount or a premium. *See* DISCOUNTED YIELD to decide the effective yield of a discounted mortgage.

EFFLUENCE A seeping from a soil absorption waste system, such as a septic tank, on to the top soil, or river, or lake.

EGRESS The right to exit a property.

ELEVATION The height of land above sea level. In a set of blueprints, elevation designates drawings of side views of a structure; for example, a front elevation shows the appearance of the front of a building.
See ELEVATION.

ELECTRICAL SYSTEM The normal minimum requirement for a residential dwelling is a 60-amp, 3-wire, 240-volt service. Houses with central heating and air-conditioning need a minimum of 100-150 amps. The utility meter will state the volt and wire service. On the utility meter look for something such as

240V, 3W, which means 240-volt, 3-wire service. FHA will not accept a 120-volt, 2-wire service. Check the electrical panel to decide if the amp service available. An electrical panel can be a clue to wiring problems. Place your hand on the panel cover, if it is extremely warm, this can be a sign of a shortage or an overload.

If you are concerned about aluminum wiring, simply take off a light switch cover plate and observe the metal used for wiring. All light switches and receptacles should be checked for adequacy and to assure that they are secured tightly and are in working condition.

See AMPERE, VOLT.

ELIGIBILITY *See* VA LOAN and VA - CERTIFICATE OF ELIGIBILITY.

ELLWOOD TABLE See Exhibit 13. The keystrokes on the HP-12C for the Ellwood Table are as follows:

Column 1:   5n (5 years), 9i (interest rate), 1 CHS PV, FV = 1.538624

Column 2:   5n, 9i, 1 CHS PMT, FV = 5.984711

Column 3:   5n, 9i, 1 FV, PMT = .167092

Column 4:   5n, 9i, 1 FV, PV = .649931

Column 5:   5n, 9i, 1 PMT, PV = 3.889651

Column 6:   1 PV, 9i, 5n, PMT. = .257092

See HEWLETT-PACKARD 12C (HP-12C).

EMBLEMENT A farmer's crop resulting from labor. The farmer has a right to remove the crop though it may not mature before the end of the tenancy.

EMERGING ISSUES TASK FORCE An arm of the Financial Accounting Standards Board that deals with *emerging issues* and develops rules for new accounting standards. The Task Force is a fairly recent development; it is important within FASB and its voluntary recommendations carry significant influence.

EMINENT DOMAIN The right of public authority to take property back by an exercise of its powers of condemnation. The property taken must be for public use, and the owner must be compensated justly. The public authority can be

Exhibit 13

	1	2	3	4	5	6	
9% RATE i	AMOUNT OF $1	AMOUNT OF $1 PER PERIOD	SINKING FUND FACTOR	PRESENT WORTH OF $1	PRESENT WORTH OF $1 PER PERIOD	PARTIAL PAYMENT	RATE i
n	The amount to which $1 will grow with compound interest	The amount to which $1 per period will grow with compound interest	The amount per period which will grow with compound interest to $1	What $1 due in the future is worth today	What $1 payable periodically is worth today	The installment to repay $1 with interest	n
1	1.090 000	1.000 000	1.000 000	.917 431	.917 431	1.090 000	1
2	1.188 100	2.090 000	.478 469	.841 680	1.759 111	.568 469	2
3	1.295 029	3.278 100	.305 055	.772 183	2.531 295	.395 055	3
4	1.411 582	4.573 129	.218 669	.708 425	3.239 720	.308 669	4
5	1.538 624	5.984 711	.167 092	.649 931	3.889 651	.257 092	5
6	1.677 100	7.523 335	.132 920	.596 267	4.485 919	.222 920	6
7	1.828 039	9.200 435	.108 691	.547 034	5.032 953	.198 691	7
8	1.992 563	11.028 474	.090 674	.501 866	5.534 819	.180 674	8
9	2.171 893	13.021 036	.076 799	.460 428	5.995 247	.166 799	9
10	2.367 364	15.192 930	.065 820	.422 411	6.417 658	.155 820	10
11	2.580 426	17.560 293	.056 947	.387 533	6.805 191	.146 947	11
12	2.812 665	20.140 720	.049 651	.355 535	7.160 725	.139 651	12
13	3.065 805	22.953 385	.043 567	.326 179	7.486 904	.133 567	13
14	3.341 727	26.019 189	.038 433	.299 246	7.786 150	.128 433	14
15	3.642 482	29.360 916	.034 059	.274 538	8.060 688	.124 059	15
16	3.970 306	33.003 399	.030 300	.251 870	8.312 558	.120 300	16
17	4.327 633	36.973 705	.027 046	.231 073	8.543 631	.117 046	17
18	4.717 120	41.301 338	.024 212	.211 994	8.755 625	.114 212	18
19	5.141 661	46.018 458	.021 730	.194 490	8.950 115	.111 730	19
20	5.604 411	51.160 120	.019 546	.178 431	9.128 546	.109 546	20
21	6.108 808	56.764 530	.017 617	.163 698	9.292 244	.107 617	21
22	6.658 600	62.873 338	.015 905	.150 182	9.442 425	.105 905	22
23	7.257 874	69.531 939	.014 382	.137 781	9.580 207	.104 382	23
24	7.911 083	76.789 813	.013 023	.126 405	9.706 612	.103 023	24
25	8.623 081	84.700 896	.011 806	.115 968	9.822 580	.101 806	25
26	9.399 158	93.323 977	.010 715	.106 393	9.928 972	.100 715	26
27	10.245 082	102.723 135	.009 735	.097 608	10.026 580	.099 735	27
28	11.167 140	112.968 217	.008 852	.089 548	10.116 128	.098 852	28
29	12.172 182	124.135 356	.008 056	.082 155	10.198 283	.098 056	29
30	13.267 678	136.307 539	.007 336	.075 371	10.273 654	.097 336	30
31	14.461 770	149.575 217	.006 686	.069 148	10.342 802	.096 686	31
32	15.763 329	164.036 987	.006 096	.063 438	10.406 240	.096 096	32
33	17.182 028	179.800 315	.005 562	.058 200	10.464 441	.095 562	33
34	18.728 411	196.982 344	.005 077	.053 395	10.517 835	.095 077	34
35	20.413 968	215.710 755	.004 636	.048 986	10.566 821	.094 636	35
36	22.251 225	236.124 723	.004 235	.044 941	10.611 763	.094 235	36
37	24.253 835	258.375 948	.003 870	.041 231	10.652 993	.093 870	37
38	26.436 680	282.629 783	.003 538	.037 826	10.690 820	.093 538	38
39	28.815 982	309.066 463	.003 236	.034 703	10.725 523	.093 236	39
40	31.409 420	337.882 445	.002 960	.031 838	10.757 360	.092 960	40
41	34.236 268	369.291 865	.002 708	.029 209	10.786 569	.092 708	41
42	37.317 532	403.528 133	.002 478	.026 797	10.813 366	.092 478	42
43	40.676 110	440.845 665	.002 268	.024 584	10.837 950	.092 268	43
44	44.336 960	481.521 715	.002 077	.022 555	10.860 505	.092 077	44
45	48.327 286	525.858 734	.001 902	.020 692	10.881 197	.091 902	45
46	52.676 742	574.186 021	.001 742	.018 984	10.900 181	.091 742	46
47	57.417 649	626.862 762	.001 595	.017 416	10.917 597	.091 595	47
48	62.585 237	684.280 411	.001 461	.015 978	10.933 575	.091 461	48
49	68.217 908	746.865 648	.001 339	.014 659	10.948 234	.091 339	49
50	74.357 520	815.083 556	.001 227	.013 449	10.961 683	.091 227	50
51	81.049 697	889.441 076	.001 124	.012 338	10.974 021	.091 124	51
52	88.344 170	970.490 773	.001 030	.011 319	10.985 340	.091 030	52
53	96.295 145	1058.834 943	.000 944	.010 385	10.995 725	.090 944	53
54	104.961 708	1155.130 088	.000 866	.009 527	11.005 252	.090 866	54
55	114.408 262	1260.091 796	.000 794	.008 741	11.013 993	.090 794	55
56	124.705 005	1374.500 057	.000 728	.008 019	11.022 012	.090 728	56
57	135.928 456	1499.205 063	.000 667	.007 357	11.029 369	.090 667	57
58	148.162 017	1635.133 518	.000 612	.006 749	11.036 118	.090 612	58
59	161.496 598	1783.295 535	.000 561	.006 192	11.042 310	.090 561	59
60	176.031 292	1944.792 133	.000 514	.005 681	11.047 991	.090 514	60

$$S^n = (1+i)^n \qquad S_{\overline{n}|} = \frac{S^n - 1}{i} \qquad \frac{1}{S_{\overline{n}|}} = \frac{i}{S^n - 1} \qquad \frac{1}{S^n} = \frac{1}{(1+i)^n} \qquad a_{\overline{n}|} = \frac{1 - 1/S^n}{i} \qquad \frac{1}{a_{\overline{n}|}} = \frac{i}{1 - 1/S^n}$$

$$S = 1 + i$$

can be state, federal, and public corporations such as school districts, public utilities, and public service corporations such as railroad and power companies. Normally, any profit to an owner of property that has been taken by eminent domain can be deferred if similar property is purchased within three years.
See CONDEMNATION.

EMPLOYEE RETIREMENT INCOME SECURITY ACT (ERISA) This act regulates the investments made by pension and profit-sharing plans and the conduct of the fiduciaries associated with pension funds.

EMPTY NESTERS A couple whose children have grown and left their home. A term frequently used in marketing analyses to measure the demand for housing by couples categorized as empty nesters.

ENCROACHMENT An overlapping or trespassing of a structure or construction on one property onto an adjoining property. For example, part of a building or a driveway extending over onto the adjoining property is an encroachment.

ENCUMBRANCE An outstanding claim or lien on a property. A property with a mortgage is said to be encumbered by a mortgage. It is a legal right or interest in land that affects a good or clear title and thereby diminishes the land's value. It can take many forms, e.g., zoning ordinances, easement rights, claims, mortgages, liens, charges, pending legal actions, unpaid taxes or restrictive covenants.

An encumbrance does not legally prevent transfer of a property from one owner to another. Encumbrances are generally revealed in title searches. It is up to the buyer to decide whether the encumbrance interferes with their plans and to have it removed. If a mortgage is required to purchase a property, the lender will dictate what encumbrances must be removed.
See EASEMENT, LIEN.

ENDORSEMENT (1) Transferring title to a negotiable instrument, e.g., a check, or a note, (2) a change to a document to remedy or clarify a matter addressed in the instrument. An endorsement can restrict or add benefits addressed in an instrument such as a title policy.
See FHA - FINAL ENDORSEMENT.

END LOAN A permanent loan placed on a property at the end of development or construction.
See PERMANENT LOAN.

ENERGY-EFFICIENT HOUSING Housing built with advanced technology that reduces home energy costs. An energy consultant or an appraiser completes the first part of the form shown in Exhibit 14; an appraiser completes the second part.

ENGLISH TUDOR

English Tudor. English styled home made mostly out of stone. The exterior will feature some stucco, brick, half-timbers and a massive chimney. The house will have a fortress-like appearance, there will be molded stone trim and small leaded casement windows.

ENGLISH TUDOR RANCH

English Tudor Ranch. Tudor styled one-story home of brick or stone. The home will feature many of the trademarks of the English Tudor such as: stone, stucco, brick, half-timbers, small casement windows and a massive chimney.

ENJOINED Forbidden or regulated by a court order.

ENTITLEMENT *See* VA - LOAN GUARANTY.

ENTITY A form of ownership that can be a partnership, corporation, limited partnership, or an individual.

Exhibit 14

ENERGY ADDENDUM

This energy addendum is a two-part optional report designed to assist lenders in underwriting energy-efficient properties. Each part has a particular use, and the parts are to be treated as separate reports.

Part I of this addendum is for rating the energy efficiency of the subject property. It must be completed by an energy consultant or an appraiser. An energy-efficient rating of "high" is required to justify additional consideration in the credit underwriting process.

Part 2 of this addendum is for estimating the value of energy-efficient items only when adequate comparable market data are not available. It must be completed by an appraiser.

Borrower: _____

Property Address: _____

Part 1 — Energy checklist

In this section, the energy consultant or appraiser should note the energy-efficient characteristics of the subject property and use these characteristics as a basis for rating the property's overall energy efficiency (high, adequate, or low). Generally, a dwelling should contain energy-efficient features for insulation, windows and doors, and heating and cooling to receive a "high" rating.

The comments sections should be used to describe the specific features and the quality and adequacy of the installation of the energy-efficient item(s) or technique(s). For example, if the energy-efficient furnace box is checked in the heating and cooling section below, those features that make the furnace "energy efficient" should be explained. In addition, the estimated monthly savings * from the energy-efficient items should be noted (* not required by Fannie Mae). The estimated monthly savings should be calculated as follows:

* for existing homes: the actual dollar difference between the current energy costs for an existing item and the estimated energy costs for the proposed energy-efficient item or the actual dollar difference between the current energy costs for an existing item and the estimated energy costs for whatever is prevalent for that item in the subject neighborhood ("neighborhood norm").

* for new homes: the actual dollar difference between the energy costs of the builder's base item and the estimated energy costs of the proposed energy-efficient item (if no base exists with which to compare, the base would be the neighborhood norm).

A. Insulation (check if present, state "R" value if known)

☐ Attic/roof: R- _____
☐ Ceiling: R- _____
☐ Exterior walls: R- _____
☐ Floors: R- _____

☐ Slab/perimeter: R- _____
☐ Foundation walls: R- _____
☐ Insulated water heater ☐ Insulation wrap: R- _____
☐ Insulated heat/cooling ducts or pipes: R- _____

Comments (describe quality and adequacy): _____

_____

*Estimated monthly savings $ _____

B. Windows and doors

☐ Double (storm)/triple glazed windows
☐ Storm doors: On _____ of _____ doors
☐ Insulated doors

☐ Weatherstripping
☐ Caulking
☐ Other: _____

Comments (describe quality and adequacy): _____

_____

*Estimated monthly savings $ _____

C. Heating and cooling

1. Conventional equipment

☐ Automatic setback thermostat
☐ Automatic flue damper
☐ Energy efficient furnace
☐ Energy-efficient air conditioner
☐ Energy-efficient heat pump

☐ Energy-efficient hot water heater
☐ Special fireplace devices/features (describe in comments)
☐ Wood burning stove
☐ Outside combustion air for fireplace or woodstove
☐ Other: _____

Efficient heating and cooling systems include such things as a high efficiency oil or gas furnace with an Annual Fuel Utilization Efficiency (AFUE) rating of 80% or higher, a high efficiency heat pump with a Seasonal Energy Efficiency Ratio (SEER) measure of 9.0 or greater and a Heating Seasonal Performance Factor (HSPF) of 7.0 or greater, and a central air conditioner with a SEER rating of 9.0 or greater.

Energy-efficient modifications to an existing system include such things as a flame retention oil burner, vent dampers for oil and gas furnaces, pilotless ignition for gas furnaces, and a secondary condensing heat exchanger for gas and oil furnaces.

Comments (describe quality and adequacy): _____

_____

*Estimated monthly savings $ _____

2. Solar equipment or design

☐ Passive solar design/landscaping — exterior (describe features below)
☐ Passive solar design — interior (describe features below)
☐ Solar space heating/cooling
☐ Back-up heating/cooling system

☐ Solar electric panels
☐ Solar hot water heating
☐ Earth-sheltered housing design
☐ Other: _____

Comments (describe quality and adequacy): _____

_____

*Estimated monthly savings $ _____

Energy rating

Has an energy audit/rating been performed on the subject property?

☐ Yes (attach, if available) ☐ No ☐ Unknown

Energy efficiency appears:

☐ High ☐ Adequate ☐ Low

Comments: (including sources of above data and specifications) _____

_____

*Total estimated monthly savings of energy-efficient features $ _____

SIGNATURE _____

COMPANY
NAME _____

NAME _____

DATE _____

Exhibit 14 (continued)

Part 2 — Estimate of value of energy-efficient items

This section can be used to help estimate the value of energy-efficient items only when adequate comparable market data are not available.

In such cases, the value of the energy-efficient items should be the lesser of

(a) the present worth of the estimated savings in utility costs, as determined by capitalizing the savings at an interest rate that is not less than the current interest rate for home mortgages for a period that does not exceed the lesser of the item's expected physical life or seven years, or

(b) the installed cost of the energy-efficient item or construction technique, less any physical, functional, and external depreciation.

For example, if the subject property is an existing house with inadequate insulation and infiltration barriers — such as one without storm windows, caulking, and weatherstripping — and the estimated savings per month is $35 for upgrading the property (based on an energy audit/rating), the appraiser could use the following calculations as a guide.

Installed cost (less depreciation)	$2,500	
Expected life	7 + years	
Expected monthly savings	$35 per month	$420 x 4.789 = $2,011.38
Expected annual savings	$420 per year	
Present value factor (annual compound interest at 10.5% for 7 years)	4.789	

For this example, it would appear reasonable (only if adequate comparable data were not available) that a typical purchaser might pay a premium of $2,000 for the property as improved with the suggested energy-related items.

Value calculations (Use additional forms if more than three items)

1. Description of item or construction technique _____

_____

Estimated monthly savings $ _____   Expected life:_____ years

Source(s) of savings estimate: _____

Use this space to show all calculations

a. Present worth of estimated savings $_____

b. Installed cost of item or technique (less any depreciation) $_____

Estimated value of item (the lesser of a or b) $_____ (1)

2. Description of item or construction technique _____

_____

Estimated monthly savings $_____   Expected life:_____ years

Source(s) of savings estimate _____

Use this space to show all calculations

a. Present worth of estimated savings $_____

b. Installed cost of item or technique (less any depreciation) $_____

Estimated value of item (the lesser of a or b) $_____ (2)

3. Description of item or construction technique_____

_____

Estimated monthly savings $_____   Expected life:_____years

Source(s) of savings estimate _____

Use this space to show all calculations

a. Present worth of estimated savings $_____

b. Installed cost of item or technique (less any depreciation) $_____

Estimated value of item (the lesser of a or b) $_____ (3)

Estimated total value of item(s) or technique(s) (the sum of (1), (2), (3) above) $_____

I have used acceptable valuation methodology in this analysis to estimate the present worth of the items and techniques contributing to the energy efficiency of the property. The results are subject to variance based on the effective use and maintenance of the items and the lifestyle of the occupants of the property.

COMPANY
NAME

Appraiser   SIGNATURE _____

NAME _____   DATE _____

ENVIRONMENTAL IMPACT STATEMENT (EIS) Used by developers of raw land and submitted to a federal, state, or local agency. The statement documents the impact or change a development will have on the environment or geographic region. The statement evaluates the effects of the development on a physical, social, and economic level. The analysis covers effects that cannot be avoided, alternatives to the proposed change, short-term productivity, irreversible commitments of resources, and the benefits to be derived.

EOLIAN SOIL *See* AEOLIAN SOIL.

EQUAL CREDIT OPPORTUNITY ACT (ECOA) A federal law enacted in 1975 to prohibit any lender from discriminating against any purchaser because of race, sex, color, religion, national origin, marital status, age or receipt of public assistance or the exercise of rights under the Consumer Credit Protection Act.

The law has four main purposes.

(1) The applicant must be notified of action taken on their application.

(2) Credit history must be reported in the names of both spouses.

(3) Information about an applicant's race and other personal characteristics must be collected for monitoring purposes on dwelling loans.

(4) Records of loan applications must be retained.

A lender may not require a spouse to repay the debt of a borrower. But, ECOA does permit a lender extending secured credit to require the signature of any person necessary to perfect the lender's first lien position, including anyone who has any interest in the property arising out of conveyance, dower, marital rights or any other rights based on the laws of the state for the property.

Any lender who fails to comply with this act is subject to civil liability for actual and punitive damages in individual or class actions. Violating the act or regulation means other federal laws are violated. Liability or punitive damages are restricted to non-governmental entities and are limited to $10,000 in individual actions and the lesser of $500,000 or 1 percent of the lender's net worth for class action suits.

The lender will complete a form like the one in Exhibit 15 if there is a denial, termination, or change in the application.

EQUALIZATION BOARD An entity vested with the authority to review tax assessments and to lower them if they are excessive. The review process is

Exhibit 15

-30 (2 PLY) (9006)   VMP MORTGAGE FORMS • (313)293-8100 • (800)521-7291   6/90

STATEMENT OF CREDIT DENIAL, TERMINATION, OR CHANGE

Applicant(s): (Type Full Name and Address)   Description of Account, Transaction or Requested Credit:

Date:

Description of Action Taken:

PART I. Principal reason(s) for credit denial, termination or other action taken concerning credit. In compliance with Regulation "B" (Equal Credit Opportunity Act), you are advised that your recent application for an extension or renewal of credit has been declined. The decision to deny your application was based on the following reason(s):

A. CREDIT
- ☐ No Credit File
- ☐ Insufficient Number of Credit References Provided
- ☐ Insufficient Credit File
- ☐ Limited Credit Experience
- ☐ Unable to Verify Credit References
- ☐ Garnishment, Attachment, Foreclosure, Collection Action or Judgment Repossession or Suit
- ☐ Excessive Obligations in Relation to Income
- ☐ Unacceptable Payment Record on Previous Mortgage
- ☐ Lack of Cash Reserves
- ☐ Delinquent Past or Present Credit Obligations with Others
- ☐ Bankruptcy Past or Present
- ☐ Information From a Consumer Reporting Agency
- ☐ Unacceptable Type of Credit References Provided
- ☐ Poor Credit Performance with Us

B. EMPLOYMENT STATUS
- ☐ Unable to Verify Employment
- ☐ Length of Employment
- ☐ Temporary or Irregular Employment

C. INCOME
- ☐ Insufficient Income for Amount of Credit Requested
- ☐ Unable to Verify Income
- ☐ Excessive Obligations in Relation to Income

D. RESIDENCY
- ☐ Temporary Residence
- ☐ Length of Residence
- ☐ Unable to Verify Residence

E. INSURANCE, GUARANTY or PURCHASE DENIED BY:
- ☐ Department of Housing and Urban Development
- ☐ Veterans Administration
- ☐ Federal National Mortgage Association
- ☐ Federal Home Loan Mortgage Corporation

F. OTHER
- ☐ Insufficient Funds to Close the Loan
- ☐ Credit Application Incomplete
- ☐ Value or Type of Collateral not Sufficient
- ☐ Unacceptable Property
- ☐ Insufficient Data - Property
- ☐ Unacceptable Appraisal
- ☐ Unacceptable Leasehold Estate
- ☐ We do not grant credit to any applicant on the terms and conditions you have requested.

PART II. Disclosure of use of information obtained from an outside source.
- ☐ Our credit decision was based in whole or in part on information obtained in a report from the consumer reporting agency listed below. You have a right under the Fair Credit Reporting Act to know the information contained in your credit file at the consumer reporting agency.

Name:
Address:

Telephone Number:

- ☐ Our credit decision was based in whole or in part on information obtained from an outside source other than a consumer reporting agency. Under the Fair Credit Reporting Act, you have the right to make a written request, no later than 60 days after you receive this notice, for disclosure of the nature of this information.

This information is obtained as a routine matter in connection with a mortgage application. Any question you may have concerning this information should be addressed to the consumer reporting agency shown above rather than the lender.

If you have any questions regarding this notice, you should contact:
Creditor's Name:
Creditor's Address:
Creditor's Telephone Number:

The federal Equal Credit Opportunity Act prohibits creditors from discriminating against credit applicants on the basis of race, color, religion, national origin, sex, marital status, age (provided that the applicant has the capacity to enter into a binding contract); because all or part of the applicant's income derives from any public assistance program; or because the applicant has in good faith exercised any right under the Consumer Credit Protection Act. The federal agency that administers compliance with this law concerning this creditor is the

Should you have any additional information which might assist us in evaluating your creditworthiness, please let us know.
Thank you for applying.

(Lender)

By: _____

Notice: ☐ Mailed   Date:_____
       ☐ Delivered

-30 (2 PLY) (9006)   VMP MORTGAGE FORMS • (313)293-8100 • (800)521-7291

focused on what the tax assessors believes is the fair market value versus a lower valuation contended by the owner.

EQUITABLE CONVERSION *See* EQUITABLE TITLE.

EQUITABLE MORTGAGE A lien created by a written contract showing the intent of the parties to encumber a particular property as collateral for a debt or an obligation. Depending on state law, a seller allowing a purchaser to assume a mortgage with little or no equity can protect himself by creating a second mortgage (an equitable mortgage) on the promise or obligation to pay the first mortgage on a timely basis. Failure to perform the obligation will result in a default of the second mortgage that will allow the seller to foreclose and regain the property. In so doing, the seller avoids having to appear at a foreclosure held by the first mortgage lender that will require an all cash payment for the balance of the first mortgage.

See GUARANTY PERFORMANCE.

EQUITABLE TITLE The interest in a property a purchaser has through being a party in a sales contract, contract for deed, an installment purchase agreement, a deed of trust, or any other instrument that gives a buyer the right to purchase legal title to the property in question. It is an interest that the buyer can protect by legal action if necessary. For example, suing a seller for specific performance of a sales contract so that the buyer can become the legal owner.

See DEED OF TRUST, CONTRACT OF SALE.

EQUITY The value of a homeowner's unencumbered interest in real estate. Equity is computed by subtracting from the property's fair market value the total of the unpaid mortgage balance and any outstanding liens or other debts against the property. A homeowner's equity increases as the mortgage is reduced or the property appreciates. When the mortgage and all other debts against the property are paid in full, the homeowner will have 100% equity in the property.

EQUITY ACCRUAL BASIS The growing equity mortgage (GEM) is based on the equity accrual basis. A GEM mortgage combines a fixed interest rate with a changing monthly payment. The interest rate is usually a few percentage points below market. Although the mortgage term may run for 30 years, the loan is frequently paid in less than 15 years as payment increases are applied entirely to the principal.

Monthly payment changes are based on an agreed-upon schedule of increases or an index. For example, the U.S. Department of Commerce index may be used (pending borrower agreement) that will increase the payments at a specified portion of the change in this index, thereby applying this increase to the mortgagor's principal and thus shortening the term of the loan. If the index change amounts to 75%, for instance, and the borrower is paying $500/month, the specified portion they will be obliged to pay is calculated on the following Equity Accrual Basis:

Original Value or Sales Price of Property	$77,500
Original Amount Borrowed on a GEM	$62,000
Original Interest Rate Amortized	9%
Original Mortgage Established	360 months
Original Payment Rate Established	$498.88 PI
Original Commerce Department Increase	8%

For the sake of demonstration, we will use the original payment rate as $500 (instead of $498.88). The Commerce Department increased the index by 8% in the payment rate. The borrower will now pay 75% of that or 6% additional. The payments will increase to $530, but the additional $30 is applied to the principal.

9% Equity Accrual Basis 30 Years

$500 divided by 92%	$543.48
$543.48 multiplied by 75%	$407.61
$407.61 divided by 94%	$433.63
$433.63 divided by $407.61	1.06%
$500.00 multiplied by 1.06%	$530.00*

Remaining balance for $62,000. 9%-30 years 10 yrs. $5,542.80
Equivalent age in months applied to principal 120 mo. $3600.00

Remaining balance for $62,000. 9%-30 yrs. 12 yrs. $5,325.80
Equivalent age in months applied to principal 144 mo. $4,320.00

Remaining balance for $62,000. 9%-30 yrs. 14 yrs. $5,065.40
Equivalent age in months applied to principal 168 mo. $5,040.00*

Remaining balance for $62,000. 9%-30 yrs. 15 yrs. $4,916.60
Equivalent age in months applied to principal 180 mo. $5,400.00

* The payoff point is realized in 168 months with $4.60 difference in overpayment by the GEM borrower on the loan.

See GROWING EQUITY MORTGAGE.

EQUITY OF REDEMPTION A right given to a property owner to reclaim property lost before a foreclosure. The property owner must pay the full debt plus interest and costs. Statutory redemption is the right, given in some states, to redeem the property after foreclosure.

See FORECLOSURE.

EQUITY PARTICIPATION (1) A loan in which the lender participates in the ownership of the equity. For being given a share in the equity, the lender usually makes concessions such as; a higher loan-to-value ratio loan, a below-market interest rate, or the lender makes the loan when it would normally be rejected as a high-risk loan.

(2) A developer offers an investor part of the equity if the investor will put up *seed money* for many needs such as: feasibility costs, option money, downpayment, development front-end cost, closing costs, or even part of the mortgage payment.

See FEASIBILITY STUDY, and SEED MONEY.

EQUITY SHARING LOAN *See* SHARED EQUITY LOAN.

EQUITY SKIMMING The practice of collecting rent and not applying it to the repayment of the mortgage. Unscrupulous investors have become aware that certain mortgages can be assumed without qualifying for the loan. These investors assume non-qualifying loans and then keep all the rents and make no repairs on the properties purchased nor do they make payments on the mortgage. The new Housing Bill has an increased penalty for equity skimming with FHA loans, it is: five (5) years imprisonment and $250,000 in fines.

EQUITY TRUST A real estate investment trust (REIT) that acquires income producing properties, as contrasted with a mortgage REIT, that makes or purchases loans on real estate.

See REAL ESTATE INVESTMENT TRUST (REIT).

ERISA *See* EMPLOYEE RETIREMENT INCOME SECURITY ACT.

EROSION The gradual waste or depletion of land through natural causes.

ESCALATOR CLAUSE A clause in a lease that requires an increase in rent due to increase in cost. Examples of increases in cost are property taxes and hazard insurance. Another method of making the lease sensitive to cost increases and inflation is to have escalator clause tied to the Cost-of-Living Index.

ESCAPE CLAUSE A clause in a contract allowing parties to amend or cancel an agreement.
See FHA and VA AMENDATORY LANGUAGE.

ESCHEAT The act of property reverting to the state when an owner dies without leaving a will (intestate) and has no legal heirs. Abandoned property reverts to the state.

ESCROW ACCOUNT A deposit of valuable considerations such as money or documents with an impartial third party. An escrow account is used for the separation of money between parties that are due money and parties that owe money. Two examples of *parties* are a seller and a buyer, or a lender and a borrower. Funds held in escrow are to be deposited in an account maintained solely for the safekeeping of money by an impartial third party. An escrow account can be used to hold items of value to assure the successful compliance of an agreement such as a contract of sale.

The predominant use of the words *escrow account* is related to home mortgages that have a provision of having an account for the monthly payment of taxes, and hazard insurance. Other types of services or premiums (disability insurance, mortgage term insurance, condo assessments) can be collected on a monthly basis and held in an escrow account. In recent times there has been much attention by consumer advocates to how money held in an escrow account is treated. Many states have passed laws requiring lenders to pay interest on money held in escrow accounts for home loans. There has been attention drawn to the use of balances in escrow accounts for financial gain for the lender. A major item of concern for a lender servicing home loans are the restrictions placed on money held in escrow accounts.

ESCROW AGENT A third party acting as agent between buyer and seller who performs according to the instructions of the principals and assumes responsibilities of handling paperwork. The agent, usually a corporation or attorney, then disburses the funds for loan settlement. Loan settlement is sometimes called loan closing. This "loan closer" reviews the funding items with the borrower such as the deposit of funds required for proration of taxes, hazard insurance premiums, etc. Before the borrower can receive the loan, title searches, surveys and recording fees must be handled. Before loan closing the borrower should receive an orientation booklet and an itemized statement that shows the full amount of the loan, all deductions from that amount and the net amount available. Too often the proposed mortgagor will think light of a closing and loan cost. Frequently, prospective purchasers who buy real estate assume the costs are minor extras, but actually they are considerable, up to five percent of the purchase price of the property for single-family housing purchases.

If there is no binding commitment, the mortgage in some states does not become a lien on the property until the date that the loan is actually paid out to the mortgagor. This "binding commitment" by the lender may be a present date for availability of the proceeds as shown on the application, the day the title policy is issued or another agreed upon date. If there are no binding commitments, the lien is established on the date of disbursement. Lenders will use either in-house escrow department or may arrange for an outside escrow agent who accepts the note and mortgage from the borrower and the funds from the lender. The escrow agent pays over to the borrower the proceeds of the loan when it is found to be a good lien. In this way the funds are placed beyond recall by the lender at the time the mortgage is recorded and documented as a lien from the date of the mortgage recording. Some states require an attorney's confirmation of clear title rather than a title insurance policy that protects the lender from any loss due to a faulty lien.

It is important to receive a letter of demand that clears an existing mortgage so the new loan can be placed on the property for any sale escrow. The loan closer will correspond with the existing mortgagee or mortgagees (if there is more than one) so the new loan will stand as a first lien.

Additional collateral such as a savings account can be used as a pledge; the closer will then see that the pledge agreement is signed at settlement. Savings department personnel or the loan closer will prepare the collateral pledge.

Escrow expenses for services rendered are shared by the buyer and seller according to the signed agreement (in some jurisdictions).

When performing sales escrow instructions, the escrow holder or agent is usually executing the transaction between the seller and buyer together with a loan transaction between the lender and buyer, with the seller not directly involved. Simultaneously, the agent follows the sale escrow instructions of the seller and buyer and the loan escrow instructions of the borrower (purchaser) and the lender. The escrow holder must furnish the lender with a certified copy of the signed instructions for such sale, with possible amendments accompanying the instructions and other documents the lender may require. Since there is a difference between sales and loan processing, buyers will sometimes confuse the two types of transactions.

Escrow handlers are disinterested parties, by law, and are charged with honesty and integrity in all agency services for principals. The escrow handler may be called upon to review several reports (that must be approved by the principals). The usual reports cover the following documents:

(1) Title Report: showing condition of the title, claims against the title, conditions, covenants, restrictions, encumbrances, etc.

(2) Appraisal Report: shows an objective fair market concept of value in accordance with lender's loan risk.

(3) Survey Report: showing the condition of the soil and sub-soil conditions, topography, flood and slide hazards, etc.

(4) Demand or Beneficiary Statement: if an existing loan is to be paid off, a Demand Statement of the exact amount due as of the pay off date. If an existing loan is to remain, a Beneficiary Statement is needed to verify existing loan terms, etc.

(5) Tax Report: the exact amount of taxes due as of escrow closing date if the property in question is being sold to the borrower. This is for purposes of determining exact proration. Often this is part of the title report. (*See* TAX REPORT).

(6) Insurance report: for proration purposes.

(7) Rent Statement: if income property, a statement of rents paid in advance, security deposits, etc. for proration purposes.

(8) Contractor's Report: if new construction is involved, a copy of contractor's contract, cost breakdown, building plans and specifications, etc.

(9) Geologic Hazard Report: a special study zone with property locations.

(10) Structural Pest Control Report: showing any visible infestation of termite damage.

The escrow agent is often instructed to gather all necessary documents, properly executed and notarized, such as the promissory note, the trust deed or mortgage and do everything necessary to close and record the sale and loan transaction.

When ownership of real property is about to change hands, it is customary to adjust or prorate (fairly divide) between the seller and buyer certain ongoing expenses and profits in connection with the ownership. The seller is paid either in advance or in arrears on these items, or the seller has collected either in advance or in arrears on benefits owned by the seller (rents).

The seller's escrow account is credited with the value of amounts paid in advance by the seller and that the seller will receive no benefit after transfer of ownership. The buyer's escrow account is debited (charged) with that amount because the buyer will get the benefit of those things that the seller already paid (to a third party). If the seller owes money to a third party (tax collector) and has not paid it out (because the tax bill has not been submitted by the tax collector, for instance), the buyer must pay this "seller's" debt in the future; thus, the seller's account is debited in escrow (the money is taken away from seller) and given to the buyer in the form of a credit. This account process means that the buyer will bring less money to close the escrow, but the buyer will pay it out of private funds later after the title is transferred and a new tax bill becomes available. All payments of real property taxes and special or supplemental assessments should be current before closing the loan. Any exception in the title policy regarding these items is acceptable only if they are "not yet due and payable" and if the title policy states this fact. Adequate escrow funds should be established to ensure payment in full of all taxes and assessments by the due date.

Where rents are collected on the first of the month in advance and title to the property is transferred on the 15th of the month, the purchaser usually is entitled to receive the adjustment of a two week rent credit. Tenants, under such circumstances, have already paid rent for the entire current month to the seller/owner. Title to the property, however, is transferred as of the 15th. The owner is entitled to rent only up to the 15th of the month, so the owner's account is charged for the rent from the 15th to the first of the next month and the buyer's account is credited for this sum. Interest payments on loans are adjusted in favor of the purchaser from the date of the last interest payment to the date of the transfer. The prior owner is charged interest for the time the seller owned the property. Thereafter, the buyer will pay the mortgagee the interest from the date of the last payment made to the next due payment. In an amortized loan, if paid monthly, the borrower pays interest for use of the funds at the month's end.

An initial amount to establish the escrow account should be based on actual insurance premiums, tax valuations, and assessment rates. The closing agent must consider expected increases in valuations and rates for the next tax payment period. For example, if the current tax value is based on a vacant lot or partial completion of construction, the monthly escrow deposits should be based on 100 percent completion for the next tax payment period. The Specific Closing Instructions will specify the type of escrow and exact number of months escrow deposit that must be collected at closing.

Any escrow for the completion of improvements must be approved by the lender before closing to escrow the funds necessary for the completion of improvements. If approved, an escrow agreement must be executed by all affected parties and included in the closed loan package.

See CLOSING, LOAN CLOSER, and LOAN ORIGINATION PROCESS (Step 5).

ESCROW ANALYSIS A periodic accounting to decide if deposits in the escrow account are adequate to pay obligations when due and a disclosure of items paid from the account.

An escrow analysis for a home loan is sent to the borrower on a minimum of once a year, usually at the beginning of each year. Some of the items an analysis will show (on a calendar basis) are as follows: interest paid, the outstanding principal balance, taxes paid, insurance premiums paid, and any other payments deducted from the account, such as a condo assessment or homeowners assessment.

Often there is an escrow overage or shortage. If there is an overage, the lender will remit the excess funds to the borrower. If there is a shortage than there is not enough for successful operation of the escrow account. If the analysis shows there is not enough funds being collected to offset an increase in a tax or a premium or any other obligation that must be paid from the account, there will be an increase in the monthly payment.

ESCROW OVERAGE OR SHORTAGE Funds that are more than or not enough for the balance required for the successful function of the escrow account.

ESCROW PAYMENT The portion of the monthly payment applied to obligations other than the principal and interest required of the mortgage.

ESTATE (1) The interest a person has in real property. Estate refers to the ownership interest a person has in real property. The estate can vary as to the degree, quantity, nature, and extent of ownership. Estate does not refer to the physical quantity of land. There are many types of estates, each giving a different degree of ownership. To constitute an estate, the interest must be one that is measured in time. A *freehold estate* or *life estate* is one that has an uncertain period. A *leasehold estate* is one that can be measured by a period. Estates created by operation of the law are known as *legal estates*, estates that are created by the free will of parties are *conventional estates*.

(2) For federal income tax purposes, it is the total value of real and personal property an individual possesses at the time of their death.

ESTOP Obstruct or prevent.

ESTOPPEL A legal doctrine preventing one from contending that because of prior facts and circumstances, present conditions are untrue. If a person signs a certificate acknowledging a balance owed on a mortgage of $50,000, the Doctrine of Estoppel will prevent that person from later contending that the balance owed was only $25,000. The document signed by a party acknowledging the balance of a debt is termed an Estoppel Certificate or a Certificate of No Defense.
See REDUCTION CERTIFICATE.

ESTOPPEL CERTIFICATE *See* ESTOPPEL.

ET AL Latin for "and others."

ETHICS *See* CODE OF ETHICS.

ET UX Latin for "and wife."

ET VIR Latin for "and husband."

EVICTION A legal proceeding for a landlord to regain possession of real property.

EVIDENCE OF TITLE Legal documents that support ownership of real property. A deed is evidence of title.
See CERTIFICATE OF TITLE.

EXACT INTEREST Interest calculated on a 365 day year. Interest on a per diem basis.

EXCEPTION A term normally used in connection with title insurance for matters that are *excepted* from coverage against loss. Title insurance policies will usually make an exception to a public utility easement. Exceptions can limit the owner's rights by easement, lien, or deed restriction.

EXCESS SERVICING This trading action involves "sales of mortgages in markets where rates become lower than the rates on the loans being traded." Excess servicing is income above the required net yield due Fannie Mae and Freddie Mac that the two corporations require their seller/servicers to collect. Excess servicing income is deemed a capitalized asset rather than cash flow income. Fannie Mae and Freddie Mac ruled against the policy on March 23, 1987, in servicing and MBS guidelines that prohibited such a sale of servicing compensation. Mortgage loan "cash flows" in Ginnie Mae's policies are even more prohibitive where excess servicing is contemplated by servicers. Laws enacted by government legislation specifically state this disclaimer in lending institutions that issue Ginnie Mae mortgage securities.

EXCESS YIELD AND BUYDOWN FUNDS The funds are retained by the lender under the Mortgage Characteristics of FNMA Highlights for FHA/VA mortgage loans.

EXCLUSIVE AGENCY *See* EXCLUSIVE LISTING.

EXCLUSIVE LISTING A written exclusive right to sell property for a specific period. There are two types of exclusive listings, *exclusive agency* and *exclusive right to sell.*
   An exclusive agency is a written agreement giving one agent the right to sell for a stated period, but allowing the property to sell *by owner* without the

agent being paid a commission. The only way an agent can collect a commission in an exclusive agency agreement is if the agent or anyone else other than the owner sells the property.

An exclusive right to sell is a written listing agreement giving a broker the exclusive right to sell a specific property for a stated period. If the property sells, the listing broker is entitled to a commission regardless of who sells the property.

EXCLUSIVE RIGHT TO SELL *See* EXCLUSIVE LISTING.

EXCULPATORY LANGUAGE Language in a note meaning the same as non-recourse. The creditor will seek satisfaction from the security used for the debt and not from income or assets belonging to the debtor. In the event of foreclosure, the lender cannot pursue a deficiency against the borrower.

EXECUTE To perform in such a way as to make a document legally valid.

EXECUTOR An individual or trust company designated in a will to carry out the instructions for disposal of property. The roles of an executor and an administrator are similar. An executor is named in a will, and an administrator is appointed if a party dies without a will or intestate.

EXECUTRIX A woman named as an executor.

EXEMPLARY DAMAGES Damages awarded to a plaintiff beyond what was sought for as compensations from an actual loss for injuries. The excess damages charge is used as an example of the punishment that can be rendered because of gross or deliberate negligence.

EXERCISE Requesting the option writer to buy or sell mortgage related securities by an option holder in their efforts to hedge a pipeline of mortgages.

EXPERIENCE A prepayment rate, generally measured by a standard or norm, in the pass-through market. For example, "200% FHA experience" means that prepayments occur at twice the rate determined by the FHA model.
See FHA EXPERIENCE and PSA EXPERIENCE.

EXPIRATION DATE The notification date or the last day that an option can be exercised for U.S.-offered options; in a European option, the expiration date is the only day that a mortgage-related security option can be exercised in hedge planning for mortgages or pools of mortgages.

EXTENDED COVERAGE (EC) That part of a standard fire insurance policy that extends coverage to other perils such as wind, lightning, hail, etc. Extended coverage is that beyond what the normal policy affords.

EXTENSION DATE The window date or first expiration date that a split-fee option holder must notify the option writer of plans for exercising their right to buy the underlying option.

F

FACADE Usually the front wall of a building.

FACE INTEREST The amount of interest stated on a mortgage or a note.

FACE VALUE The par value of an instrument such as a mortgage, bond, or note. It is an amount an issuer promises to pay when the bond matures. The original principal amount of a mortgage-backed security, bond or similar security that is noted on the face of the certificate.

FACTOR The ratio of the outstanding principal amount of a pass-through pool to its original principal. A figure, calculated monthly by Ginnie Mae, that represents the proportion of an original principal amount of a securities issuance that remains outstanding; also used in conventional whole loans.

FACTORY BUILT HOUSING *See* MANUFACTURED HOUSING.

FADA *See* FEDERAL ASSET DISPOSITION ASSOCIATION.

FAIR CREDIT REPORTING ACT The Fair Credit Reporting Act became effective on April 25, 1971. The act is designed:

(1) to regulate the consumer reporting industry;

(2) to place disclosure obligations on users of consumer reports; and

(3) to ensure fair, timely, and accurate reporting of credit information.

This act does not apply to commercial transactions. It restricts the use of reports on consumers, and, in certain situations, requires the deletion of obsolete information. A report containing information about only transactions and experiences between the consumer and the institution making the report is *not* a consumer report.

This act provides for a fine of not more than $5,000 or imprisonment of not more than one year, or both, for any person who willfully and knowingly obtains information from a consumer reporting agency under false pretenses. The same criminal penalty can be imposed upon any officer or employee of a financial institution that is a consumer reporting agency who willfully and knowingly provides information from a financial institution's files about a consumer to a person not authorized to receive it.

See CREDIT REPORT, CONSUMER CREDIT REPORTING ACT.

FAIR HOUSING ACT The Federal Fair Housing Act provides that it is unlawful to discriminate based on of race, color, creed, sex or national origin when selling or leasing residential property.
It prohibits the following discriminatory acts:

(1) refusing to see, rent or negotiate with any person;

(2) changing terms, conditions or services for individuals in practicing discrimination;

(3) practicing discrimination through any statement or advertisement that restricts the sale or rental of residential property;

(4) representing to any person as a means of discrimination, that a dwelling is not available for sale or rental;

(5) making a profit by inducing owners of housing to sell or rent because of the prospective entry into the neighborhood of persons of a particular race, color, religion or national origin;

(6) altering the terms or conditions for a home loan to any person who wishes to purchase or repair a dwelling; or

(7) denying persons membership in any multiple listing service or real estate brokers organization.

In 1972, an amendment to the Federal Fair Housing Act started the use of an equal housing opportunity poster. This 11 x 14 inch poster, available through HUD, features:

(1) the equal housing opportunity slogan;

(2) an equal housing statement pledging adherence to the Fair Housing Act;

(3) support of affirmative marketing and advertising programs; and

(4) the equal housing opportunity logo.

The Office of Equal Opportunity (OEO), under the direction of HUD, is in charge of administrating the regulations of the Fair Housing Act.

FAIR, JUST AND EQUITABLE STANDARD The standard a sponsor's compensation meets before Commissioner of Corporations allows a security offering in the commissioner's jurisdiction. The current federal income tax laws are considered in state or federal jurisdiction.

FAIR MARKET RENT *See* ECONOMIC RENT.

FAIR MARKET VALUE The price a property will sell for after it has been on the market for a reasonable length of time and with a willing and informed seller and a willing and informed buyer and with neither being under any duress. A comparable sale will not be considered for supporting the market value of a property if there was not an arms-length-transaction due to an uninformed buyer or seller or because of a forced sale. A reason for selling, such as to avoid a foreclosure, is classified as a distress sale and such sales will not be considered as a fair market value sale.

FALLOUT RISK The risk incurred by the lender that a borrower will not close on a loan after filing an application or than an investor will renege on a contract to purchase the loan as agreed. Borrower fallout, however, is the risk most likely to occur if a pipeline is hedged against price risk during the production cycle. This risk occurs in "1-1" or "2-1" pipelines where the terms of the loan sale to the secondary market have been established before the loan has closed. Furthermore, the lender's forward sale or other hedge requires that the loan be delivered, while the origination commitment is generally not binding on the borrower.

Borrowers fail to close for many reasons. It is common for them to do so when rates fall and opportunities arise for more advantageous forms of financing. Thus, when lenders hedge against price risk to protect against rising rates, they set themselves up for possible losses if rates fall. Of course, lenders avoid fallout risk if they remain at risk on prices. Protecting against borrower fallout risk is a matter of creating an additional hedge to be placed in tandem with the forward or substitute sale. This is an option not to deliver under the terms of the original sale or hedge.

As described in Fannie Mae's Hedging Guide, "Managing Your Mortgage Pipeline," there are two types of fallout that introduce risk into the mortgage pipeline. These risks occur in pipelines with simultaneous commitments to borrowers and investors ("1-1" or "2-1" pipelines) that are often created because of having constructed hedges against price risk. Since borrower fallout has already been covered on a loan not closed after filing the application, lenders can experience investor fallout in a "1-1" or "2-2" pipeline. In a "1-1" pipeline, lenders commit loan terms to the borrowers and get commitments from investors at the time of application. In a "2- 2" pipeline, sets of terms are made at closing. If interest rates rise subsequently, investors may renege on their promises to buy lower yielding mortgages at par. Lenders, therefore, should be certain of the investor's ability and willingness to live up to their commitments.

FANNIE MAE A nickname for the Federal National Mortgage Association (FNMA).
See FEDERAL NATIONAL MORTGAGE ASSOCIATION.

FANNIE MAJOR POOLS (FMP) A new multiple-lender MBS program for non-conforming loans. Similar to Multi-Issuer pools formed under GNMA II but not conforming to FHA or VA standards, these Fannie Mae "first issues" pooled $250 million with 60 lenders contributing from $300,000 to $26,600,000. Mortgage lenders of all sizes participated in and agreed to these criteria: 1) higher prices to lenders for larger pools with more geographic diversity; 2) lower minimum submission ($250,000 vs. the usual $1 million); 3) pools of $1 million or more may realize higher prices; 4) loan eligibility comprises most 25-30-year loans less than 12 months old.

FARM Normally used to describe large acreage used for growing crops or certain animals or fish for sale. Real estate agents use "farm" to describe a selected area in which a concentrated effort is made to get listings.

FARMER MAC *See* FEDERAL AGRICULTURAL MORTGAGE CORPORATION.

FARMERS HOME ADMINISTRATION (FmHA) A federal agency formed under the Farmers Home Administration Act of 1946. It provides mortgage financing to farmers and other qualified borrowers who cannot find mortgage loans elsewhere. It participates in, makes, and insures loans for rural housing and similar properties.

FARMHOUSE ADAPTION

Farmhouse Adaption. Modern two-story house with wood clapboard siding, a wrap-a-round porch and a country-style door.

FARM MORTGAGE BANKERS ASSOCIATION The founding organization of the present Mortgage Bankers Association. The Farm Mortgage Bankers Association was founded in 1914 and changed its name to The Mortgage Bankers Association in 1923.

See MORTGAGE BANKERS ASSOCIATION.

FASB *See* FINANCIAL ACCOUNTING STANDARD BOARD.

FASCIA Flat, horizontal board used to cover the ends of rafters.

FDIC *See* FEDERAL DEPOSIT INSURANCE CORPORATION.

FEASIBILITY STUDY An analysis of the viability of a proposed investment project. Experts familiar with certain properties can be hired to furnish a written report about the probability for the success of a proposed project. The study will be a detailed report about the nature of the project. Included in the report will be information about the risks and the benefits for the type of proposed project, the existing competition, any proposed competition, the availability of money, land, material, and customers to make the project a success.

See ABSORPTION RATE.

FEDERAL AGRICULTURAL MORTGAGE CORPORATION (Farmer Mac) The farm mortgage credit system created to help agriculturally-based farm lands or buildings, or both, is now a part of the secondary mortgage market as of the signing of the Agricultural Credit Act of 1987.

This law authorizes a single secondary market for originating mortgages for portfolio servicing and pools by originations interested in such originations or by lenders of specialty type financial mortgage-backed securities. This includes all mortgage-related operations of most companies, commercial banks, and other finance-oriented firms. An original non-exemption from the SEC, a perquisite for exemption, was not applied to Farmer Mac (but was enjoyed by Fannie Mae and Freddie Mac in their securities issuances).

FEDERAL ASSET DISPOSITION ASSOCIATION (FADA) A private corporation chartered by the FHLBB in 1985 to dispose of assets held in receivership by the FSLIC. Currently, it has a portfolio of about $1.8 billion. FADA handles the management, liquidation, and workout of a substantial amount of savings institution failures encountered by the FSLIC. The justification for the creation of FADA, therefore, is to recover capital asset receivables or recapture reserves resulting from the failure of savings institutions, through such liquidation.

FEDERAL ASSOCIATION A thrift institution chartered and regulated by the Federal Home Loan Bank Board (FHLBB).

FEDERAL DEPOSIT INSURANCE CORPORATION (FDIC) The   FDIC insures most commercial banks and savings banks in the U.S. Until passage of the Garn-St. Germain Act, the FDIC was the only federal insuring agency for savings banks; most savings banks are still insured by the FDIC.

Federal savings associations are required by law to have their savings accounts insured by the FSLIC. Insurance of accounts may be optional for state-chartered institutions. Some federally-chartered savings banks belong to the FSLIC. FSLIC- and FDIC-insured institutions pay a regular insurance premium or assessment for deposit protection. In addition, they must comply with a host of regulations that govern their operations.

State insurance funds have been established under special statutes in many states. Savings banks may belong to the FDIC and a state fund; the state fund insures excess deposits over the FDIC's $100,000 maximum. Savings associations, on the other hand, may not maintain such dual memberships.

FEDERAL DEPOSIT INSURANCE CORPORATION
550 17TH STREET, N.W.
WASHINGTON, DC 20429
(202) 393-8400

Bank Insurance Fund (BIF)
(202) 898-3542

Savings Association Insurance Fund (SAIF)
(202) 898-3542

The eight offices and the states in their region are:

Atlanta Regional Office   Alabama, Florida, Georgia, North Carolina,
Marquis One Building   South Carolina, Virginia, West Virginia.
Suite 1200
245 Peachtree Center Ave., N.E.
Atlanta, GA 30303
(404) 525-0308

Dallas Regional Office   Colorado, New Mexico, Oklahoma, Texas.
1910 Pacific Avenue
Suite 1900
Dallas, TX 75201
(214) 220-3342

Memphis Regional Office   Arkansas, Kentucky, Louisiana, Mississippi,
5100 Poplar Avenue   Tennessee.
Suite 1900
Memphis, TN 38137
(901) 685-1603

San Francisco   Alaska, Arizona, California, Guam, Hawaii,
  Regional Office   Idaho, Montana, Nevada, Oregon, Utah,
25 Ecker Street, Suite 2300   Washington, Wyoming.
San Francisco, CA 94105
(415) 546-0160

Boston Regional Office   Connecticut, Maine, Massachusetts, New
160 Gould Street   Hampshire, Rhode Island, Vermont.
Needham, MA 02194
(617) 449-9080

Chicago Regional Office   Illinois, Indiana, Michigan, Ohio, Wisconsin.
30 S. Wacker Drive
Suite 3100
Chicago, IL 60606
(312) 207-0210

Kansas City Regional Office   Iowa, Kansas, Minnesota, Missouri, Nebraska,
2345 Grand Avenue   North Dakota, South Dakota.
Suite 1500
Kansas City, MO 64108
(816) 234-8000

New York Regional Office   Delaware, District of Columbia, Maryland,
452 Fifth Avenue, 21st Fl.   New Jersey, New York, Pennsylvania, Puerto
New York, NY 10018   Rico, Virgin Islands.
(212) 704-1200

FEDERAL FARM CREDIT SYSTEM The Federal Farm Credit System, through its Federal Land Banks, holds approximately 53% of institutionally-held farm real estate debt; commercial banks hold approximately 16% and insurance companies about 15%. The Farm Credit System is essentially a farm mortgage credit system created to help agriculturally-based farm land or buildings or both. It is not affiliated with secondary market investment capital at this time.

FEDERAL HOME LOAN BANK One of twelve federally-chartered regional banks that comprise the Federal Home Loan Bank System. The Federal Home Loan Bank exists to supply credit to member banks at an indexed rate. The prime rate is controlled by the FHLBB, while individual banks establish their profit margin over the cost of funds index (COF). A consumer rate on home mortgages, for instance, stood at 10.01% on February 14, 1987 based on a

Loan Banks adjust COF indexes to comply with specific origination costs for ARMs.
See INDEX.

FEDERAL HOME LOAN BANK BOARD (FHLBB) A board established to charter and regulate federal savings and loans institutions. The Board oversees the operations of FSLIC and FHLMC and banks in ascertaining the cost of borrowing from the FHLBB national median cost of funds. The cost of funds index generally reflects the trend of the prime rate registered from May 1979 to July 1985 as a current cost to member banks.

Prime rate is controlled by the FHLBB, while individual banks establish their profit margins over a cost of funds index. Changes in the interest rate are usually governed by a financial index that may rise or fall. Examples of these indexes are the FHLBB's national average mortgage rate and the U.S. Treasury bill rate. Generally, the more sensitive the index is to market changes, the more frequently interest rates can increase or decrease. The average cost of funds for savings and loans that are insured by the FSLIC (or how much lending institutions are paying on the money that they borrow) will reflect the profit margin. The Prime Rate on cost of funds was lowered from 9.50% (2/4/86) to 8.50% on 4/21/86. For example, assuming a starting interest rate of 8.50% on 4/21/86 is lowered again by 1 percent on 1/5/87, then a new loan will also be lowered by 1 percentage point. The FHLBB regulates federally-chartered savings and loans and overviews the operations of the FSLIC, Freddie Mac and the 12 Federal Home Loan Banks.

FEDERAL HOME LOAN MORTGAGE CORPORATION (FHLMC) A private corporation authorized by Congress whose primary purpose is to establish a secondary market for conventional home loans. FHLMC is known as "Freddie Mac" and the "Mortgage Corporation." It is also called "The Corporation." It is the secondary market arm of the Federal Home Loan Bank System. Freddie Mac sells participation sales certificates secured by pools of conventional mortgage loans whose principal and interest carry a guarantee by the federal government through Freddie Mac. It has sold Ginnie Mae bonds to raise funds to finance the purchase of mortgages.

The Corporation is congressionally chartered and operates on shares of non-voting stock totaling $1 million, invested for the Federal Home Loan Banks. The agency formed actively preferred stock in 1984. This preferred stock can be properly priced by federally chartered finance corporations. The directors, as appointed by the U.S. President, consist of three members of the board who serve on the FHLBB. Freddie Mac's 1989 mortgage limits were $187,450 to $360,150 for one-to-four unit residential dwellings, in the October to October index.

Freddie Mac's Mortgage Participation Certificates (PCs) were the first securities backed by conventional mortgages. Created in 1971, they are not guaranteed by the U.S. government but do carry the Freddie Mac warranty. In
1982, the Guarantor or *swap* program, began as thrifts, sold low-yielding conventional FHA and VA mortgages at par, exchanging their portfolios for more
liquid PCs. The PCs are immediately repurchased by thrift originators upon
selling these swapped mortgages. These PCs represent the value of the original
loans sold either for cash or in certificate form. The approved sellers/servicers
are supervised by Freddie Mac in servicing all mortgages purchased. Delivery
in the mandatory and optional programs include single-family, multi-family,
and second mortgages, as offered on a daily basis. Freddie Mac's purchasing
and selling activities cover thrift institutions engaged in mortgage lending and
are approved by HUD. Some FHA and VA mortgage-backed securities are
marketed on a smaller scale than other pass-through securities. The conventional mortgage pass-throughs are sold as undivided interests.

Due to the ongoing interest in convertible adjustable rate mortgages
(CARMs), Freddie Mac may purchase CARMs and issue securities backed by
convertible ARMs. The ARM participation certificate as collateralized by
CARMs is to be issued under the guarantor or swap program.

Until this plan is realized by Freddie Mac, however, mortgage loan originators who sell to Freddie Mac on an approved basis can expect a borrower to
anticipate a servicing fee as a negotiable or arbitrary net yield. A mortgage
loan commitment based on 30 years is currently 37 1/2 basis points to service a
Freddie Mac fixed-rate or adjustable-rate loan. The required net yield, therefore, must be delivered before a 30-day period in order for the corporation to
execute a purchase.

Freddie Mac purchases up to 100% of home improvement loans, or a 50%
to 95% interest in such loans. Formerly, Freddie Mac only purchased participation interests up to 80% of the improvement mortgages.

FEDERAL HOUSING ADMINISTRATION (FHA) A division of the U.S.
Department of Housing and Urban Development established under the provisions of the National Housing Act as approved on June 27, 1934. This government agency is the innovator of the long-term, amortized, minimum
down-payment home mortgage common in today's market. An FHA loan is a
real estate mortgage insured by the Federal Housing Administration and available to anyone purchasing or refinancing property that has an appraisal acceptable to the Federal Housing Administration. In general, an FHA loan is: a long
term, high loan-to-value ratio, fixed or adjustable rate mortgage with a limited
due-on-sale clause for 1-4 single family dwellings. First mortgage loans are
authorized by Title II of the 1934 National Housing Act, as amended, and, as
such, are sometimes called Title II loans. FHA does not lend money, it insures

mortgages made by approved lenders. The purpose of FHA is to provide housing for low and moderate income families.

Citizenship of the United States is not required in order for a borrower to be eligible for an FHA loan. The property that is the subject of the application must either be the occupying borrower's principal residence or their principal residence must be located in the United States. Principal residence requirement is defined as the dwelling where the borrower maintains, or will maintain, a permanent place of abode and typically spends, or will spend, the majority of the calendar year. A borrower can have only one principal residence.

FHA has an outstanding record of being a self-supported government agency. The Mutual Mortgage Insurance fund provides nearly all the income for FHA by collecting insurance premiums. The most often heard acronym concerning the Insurance program is MIP. This acronym stands for "mortgage insurance premium" and refers to the insurance premium paid to FHA for insuring a loan. In exchange for the premiums collected, FHA insurance will compensate a lender for a loss from a foreclosure of a FHA loan. Today we take for granted the features in a standard mortgage:

(1) Low down payment, often at 3%;

(2) Long-term amortization;

(3) A fixed interest rate;

(4) Loan assumability;

(5) Uniform and fair loan qualification guidelines;

(6) Minimum property standards; and

(7) Uniform property appraisals

All the features above were FHA innovations.

Before the creation of FHA, mortgage terms were not very attractive. If you could get a home mortgage, the terms were likely to be:

(1) An adjustable rate of interest;

(2) A down payment of 25% or more; and

(3) A term of ten years or less.

Loans were made on an interest-only basis that required periodic payments to principal or a balloon payment at the end. Of course, there were no nationwide uniform guidelines for credit or property approval.

There are several advantages to an FHA loan.

(1) A high loan-to-value mortgage is available. FHA purchasers may buy a home with as little as a 3% investment.

(2) Mortgagors may borrow a portion of the closing costs they pay.

(3) All the mortgage insurance premium may be financed.

(4) FHA interest rates are usually comparable to VA rates. Because FHA/VA loans are *enhanced* (insured or guaranteed by U.S. government), rates are usually better than conventional rates.

(5) Various programs are available. Program types include fixed rate, adjustable rate, graduated payment, shared equity and many more programs.

(6) FHA Loans are assumable. Loans originated after 1 December 1986, have a limited due-on-sale clause. Loans assumed after the December date require loan assumption approval for evaluating the borrower's ability to repay the loan.

(7) You may refinance, and there is no prepayment penalty. Homeowners may take advantage of any lower rate by refinancing without penalties. Current regulations allow for a "streamline" method of loan approval for refinancing to a lower monthly payment.

(8) Other mortgages may be placed behind an FHA first mortgage, i.e., second mortgages and wrap-around mortgages.

Beyond a doubt, the biggest advantage to the public is that the interest rate remains unchanged upon loan assumption.

See FHA - SECTION for a listing of the various kinds of FHA loans.

FHA *See* FEDERAL HOUSING ADMINISTRATION.

FHA - ACQUISITION COST The cost to acquire the property. In lending practices the maximum Conventional, FHA, and VA loan is dependent upon the lesser of either the acquisition cost or the appraised value. Establishing the true acquisition cost helps lenders ensure they are not making a loan for more than their established loan-to-value guidelines.

FHA - ADJUSTABLE RATE MORTGAGE *See* FHA - SECTION 251.

FHA - AMENDATORY LANGUAGE If a sales contract incorporating the use of an FHA loan is written before an FHA or a VA appraisal has been issued, the following amendatory language must be inserted in the contract.

It is expressly agreed that, notwithstanding any other provisions of this contract, the purchaser shall not be obligated to complete the purchase of the property described herein or to incur any penalty by forfeiture of the earnest money deposits or otherwise unless the seller has delivered to the purchaser a written statement issued by the Federal Housing Commissioner or a Direct Endorsement lender setting forth the appraised value of the property (excluding closing costs) of not less than $_____ which statement the seller hereby agrees to deliver to the purchaser promptly after such appraised value statement is made available to the seller. The purchaser shall, however, have the privilege and option of proceeding with the consummation of the contract without regard to the amount of the appraised valuation. The appraised valuation is arrived at to decide the maximum mortgage the Department of Housing and Urban Development will insure. HUD does not warrant the value or the condition of the property. The purchaser should satisfy himself/herself that the price and condition of the property are acceptable.

FHA no longer has a prevailing rate, and discounts can be paid by the purchaser; therefore, the contract should cover the subject of rate and who will pay the points.

FHA - ASSUMPTION *See* FHA - RELEASE OF LIABILITY.

FHA - CLOSING COSTS *See* CLOSING COSTS.

FHA - COMPENDIUM A topical index of FHA directives, memos, mortgagee letters, and HUD Handbooks. The index contains a brief description of the subject matter addressed by a letter, memo, directive or handbook. One might be able to obtain this listing from the FHA Central Office, or a Regional Office.

Here is an example on the topic of "Interest Buydowns":

HUD Handbook 4155.1 Rev - 2, 3-27.

6-12-81 *Mortgagee Letter 81-23.* Where seller deposits money in an escrow account with monthly releases to reduce borrower's payments, no longer reduce acquisition cost. Specific criteria regarding terms of buydown, buydown agreement, handling escrow, applicable programs.

4-2-84 *Memorandum from Alan Kappeler,* Director, Ofc of SF Hsg. Any interest only buydown may be used, provided funds are escrowed. In order for HUD to qualify buyer on reduced payment, agreement must comply with Mortgagee Letters 81-3 and 82-7 and Handbook 4155.1 pg. 3-28-3. Buydown never affects sales price of property. Any other buyer expense paid by seller is deducted from acquisition cost. Buydowns can be used in any HUD program including the GPM plans, but if a GPM is used, we qualify buyer on reduced payment for 245(a) plan IV only. If buydown plan does not meet our requirements, treated as a compensating factor.

3-13-85   *Processing Directive #17* (item 1). Qualify borrower on 3-2-1 buydown if: (1) buydown agreement submitted with application. (2) minimum term of three years, (3) level adjustments annually. For example: 5-3-1, 4-2-2. On 2-1 buydown, use 2% reduction to qualify borrower. On 1%, one year buydown, use 1% reduction to qualify borrower. See Handbook 4155.1 regarding establishing buydown account, payment of monthly proportionate share. Signed copy of escrow agreement must be submitted with request for endorsement.

8-8-86   *Mortgagee Letter 86-15 and Processing Directive #36.*
Effective 8-15-86, firm applications received (and Direct Endorsement applications processed - worksheet signed) that use a temporary buydown will no longer be processed at the first year buydown interest rate but will be processed at the note rate.

8-13-86   *Processing Directive #38.* Effective date changed: New instructions on underwriting at note rate apply if sales contract signed *after* 8-15-86.

10-22-87   *Mortgagee Letter 87-35.* Effective immediately, can qualify borrower on buydown, not exceeding two percent in the first year, on level payment, fixed rate mortgage. On larger buydowns, qualify borrower at interest rate no more than two percent less than note rate (buydown must have level annual adjustments and final year of buydown cannot exceed 1 percent.)

12-1-88   *Mortgagee Letter 88-37* emphasizes buydown agreement may not result in more than a 1% increase in the effective interest rate each year.

Interest Buydowns - 245(a)

4-1-84   *Memorandum from Philip Abrams,* General DAS

6-22-82   *Mortgagee Letter 82-10*

4-2-84   *Memorandum from Alan Kappeler, Director,* Ofc of SF Hsg.
Buydowns permitted in any program, but if a GPM is used, we qualify buyer on reduced payment only for 245(a) plan IV.

8-8-86   *Mortgagee Letter 86-15 and Processing Directive #36.*
Buydowns treated as compensating factors only.

Interest Buydowns - ADP Suffix Codes and Program ID

11-14-84   *Direct Endorsement Update #7.* Only use the buydown ADP
codes if the loan is underwritten at bought down rate to qualify borrower.

8-8-86   *Mortgagee Letter 86-15 and Processing Directive #36.*
For all firm applications received (and D.E. applications processed) starting
8-15-86, buydown will be treated as compensating factor only — therefore, discontinue using these suffix codes.

8-13-86   *Processing Directive #38.* Effective date changed: New instructions on underwriting at note rate apply if sales contract signed *after* 8-15-86.

1-22-87   *Mortgagee Letter 87-35.* Where underwriting at bought down
rate, use buydown ADP code.

Interest Buydown Escrow Accounts

5-6-82   *Mortgagee Letter 82-7.* Third party must maintain and administer
escrow account. Subsidiaries or affiliates may administer only if they are separate corporate entities with no common officers, etc.

5-6-82   *Mortgagee Letter 82-7.* No objection to mortgagee holding and
administering escrow for up to 60 days when there is an outstanding forward
commitment to sell the mortgage. Mortgagee's intention indicated at time of
application for firm. Letter required with closing package.

8-6-82   *Memorandum from G.H. Bowers,* DAS, SF Housing.
Federal or state supervised savings institutions, savings and loans, and banks
can hold the buydown funds, provided they agree to administer the accounts
according to the agreement.

Interest Buydown Escrow Accounts - At Prepayment

5-6-82   *Mortgagee Letter 82-7.* Any undisbursed escrow funds may be
applied to the balance due on the mortgage at the time the mortgage is prepaid
in full for any reason.

8-31-87   *Mortgagee Letter 87-24.* When refinancing mortgages with undistributed, temporary interest buydown funds where the unexpended funds are available to the mortgagor, they must be used to offset such items as negative amortization (Sec. 245), closing costs, etc., or to reduce the remaining principal balance. Unexpended funds may not be provided to the mortgagor as a cash refund.

FHA - DIRECT ENDORSEMENT A program that allows lenders to approve FHA loans without submitting them to FHA for approval. The intent of the program is to shift more of the credit approval process over to the lender and reduce time for loan approval. Lenders must submit to an approval process to become a direct endorsement lender. The endorsement of an FHA loan insures the loan under the National Housing Act.

FHA - FINAL ENDORSEMENT The date FHA endorses the loan for mortgage insurance purposes. The endorsement gives the FHA insurance to the loan. If a loan does not receive FHA endorsement then the lender has made a very high loan-to-value ratio conventional loan. Most lenders have written commitments obligating all parties to a loan closing to cooperate with eliminating any obstacles in obtaining the FHA endorsement, either before or after the loan closing.

FHA - GRADUATED PAYMENT MORTGAGE (GPM) *See* FHA - SECTION 251.

FHA - HANDBOOKS *See* DEPARTMENT OF HOUSING AND URBAN DEVELOPMENT.

FHA - INSURED LOAN Insurance is available to cover losses incurred from a foreclosure. This is often called private mortgage insurance (PMI for conventional loans) or mortgage insurance (MI) for FHA loans.

When FHA was established by The National Housing Act of 1934, it was to become self-supporting by income derived primarily from a 1/2 of 1% insurance charge. The insurance charge is commonly called Mortgage Insurance Premium (MIP). In earlier days the insurance had been called Mutual Mortgage Insurance (MMI). Revenues and costs of FHA's permanent loan program are still accounted for in the Mutual Mortgage Fund. Throughout the history of FHA, it has been self-supporting concerning its unsubsidized programs.

On 1 September 1983, FHA altered the collection procedure for the Mortgage Insurance Premium. On most FHA Sections, the entire Mortgage Insurance Premium is collected up front at the closing by charging a one-time premium. Reasons given by FHA were: (a) increased cash flow now is better than later payments, and (b) in a benevolent gesture, FHA wanted to lessen the paperwork burden for the lenders. A rumor gave a third reason: FHA was avoiding the gigantic task of maintaining or supervising the annual collections and balancing of the premiums for all outstanding FHA loans.

Not all FHA loans were included in the policy change. The policy change was effective for all FHA appraisals issued after 1 September 1983. The guidelines have changed since its inception, and it appears that the FHA sections affected are 203, 245, 251 (adjustable rate mortgage) for detached housing. Mortgages secured by condominiums required that the insurance be collected by the monthly payment method, that used before the 1 September change. The one-time premium, a method starting 1 September, can be borrowed or paid in full. If the MIP is financed, the seller cannot contribute or reimburse the mortgagor for any portion of the financed MIP. The present cost of a MIP for the one-time premium on a 30-year loan is 3.8% of the loan amount or 3.661% if paid in cash. For a 15-year loan the MIP cost is 2.4% if financed or 2.344% if paid in cash.

The 1990 Housing Bill passed by the Congress on October 27 made another change in the collection of MIP. According to the new bill, borrowers pay an up-front premium of 3.8% for loans originated in 1991 and 1992, 3.0% on loans originated in 1993 and 1994, and 2.25% on loans originated in 1995 and thereafter. In addition, all borrowers must pay an annual premium of at least .5% of the loan amount for many years varying with the loan-to-value ratio. In 1991 a loan with less than 5% downpayment will require a .5% annual premium for 10 years; a loan with a downpayment of from 5% to 10% will require a .5% premium for 8 years; and a loan with greater than 10% downpayment will require an extra .5% premium for 5 years.

For premiums collected on a monthly basis, it is important to note that the MIP is not amortized monthly. The 1/2% MIP is charged on the average scheduled balance of loan principal outstanding during the year. Simply stated, the MIP is based on an annual calculation, and therefore, will be slightly higher than adding 1/2% (as in monthly P & I) to the FHA rate.

Insurance refunds are allowed for FHA loans that are paid off before the end of the term of the loan. There are conditions for an insurance refund, they are:

(1) The FHA loan was a Section 203(b).

(2) Premium income has been collected for ten years or paid up front with a one-time premium payment.

(3) The Mutual Mortgage Insurance fund has income more than expenses at the time the insurance is stopped.

(4) The insurance is stopped because of full payment of the mortgage or a request of termination by the lender.

Only certain sections of FHA loans are eligible for refunds. Other sections, such as Section 221, are not eligible.

Once a loan is paid off, the Housing and Urban Development (HUD) will normally forward a Form HUD-2042 to an eligible party within 60 days from the termination of the FHA insurance. Disbursement is usually 45 days from HUD receipt of the completed HUD-2042. If this does not occur, contact your lender or write to:

U.S. Department of Housing and Urban Development
Director, Mortgage Insurance Accounting, OFA
Attn: Home Mortgage Branch
Washington, DC 20410

Include the FHA case number, property address, and the date the loan was paid in full or the date the property was sold. Any refundable insurance is payable to the last owner of record. There have been situations where someone else paid the 1/2 of 1% MIP over a long period and the owner of last record, which may be an ownership of months compared to years, received the entire insurance refund. Any refund is payable to the owner of last record.

As this book goes to press, FHA has not yet published guidelines for refunds on premiums paid according to the change in the 1990 Housing Bill.

FHA - LENDER OPTION If a subject property is within 25 miles of an FHA office, but subject property is not within that FHA office's jurisdiction, you may not have to do business with the nearest authorized FHA office that might be 300 miles away. FHA has developed a program called Lender Option. Before Lender Option, in certain areas of our country, situations exist where a lender's office may be within 100 miles of various properties, but due to geographical boundaries (mostly state boundaries) the lender was forced to deal with three FHA offices.

FHA now gives their offices permission to deal within other FHA office jurisdictions, if the lender opts to take this course and if the property location is within certain boundaries (usually established by counties). For example, a lender in Memphis, Tennessee can use the Memphis FHA office for properties located in certain counties in the states of Kentucky, Missouri, Arkansas, and Mississippi, rather than being forced to communicate with FHA offices located in Lexington, KY; St. Louis, MO; Little Rock, AR; or Jackson, MS. It is much easier for the lender to communicate with one FHA Regional Office as compared to four offices, as in the Memphis example.

FHA - LOAN AMOUNTS FHA establishes maximum loan amounts by location and number of units:

(1) The statutory limit for a single-family residence is $67,500, but may be increased to $124,875 in certain high-cost locations.

(2) A two-family residence has a maximum loan of $76,000, but may be increased to $140,600 for high-cost areas.

(3) A three-family residence has a maximum loan of $92,000, but may be increased to $170,200.

(4) A four-family residence has a maximum loan of $107,000, but may be increased to $197,500.

These FHA limits may be increased an additional 1/2 of the highest amounts given if the properties are located in Alaska, Hawaii, or Guam.

There are a few FHA sections that have lower maximum loan amounts than those listed above. The maximum loan amounts can be increase up to the highest amounts mentioned above, if the property is deemed to be in a high-cost location. Maximum FHA loans are usually listed by counties. For the maximum FHA loan in your area, check with your nearest FHA office or an approved FHA lender.

In 1989, HUD decided to do something about the common practice of lenders establishing minimum loan amounts. HUD reminded lenders that they may not establish their own minimum loan amount. Lenders are in non-compliance with FHA regulations if they require a minimum loan amount as a condition of providing an FHA - VA has similar regulations for VA loans. Another common practice, lenders charging higher discount points for smaller loan amounts, was addressed by the 1990 Housing Act. The bill has a provision prohibiting tiered pricing of FHA-insured loans. Under the bill, the fees (including discount points and origination fees) charged on different sized FHA-insured loans within a given area (SMSA or county, whichever is smaller) cannot vary by more than 2% of the initial principal amount of the mortgage. For any differential in price (within the 2% range allowed), lenders may be required to document to HUD that the difference is justified due to differences in costs. Where HUD decides that a mortgagee is not complying, the Secretary shall refer the matter to the Mortgagee Review Board.

FHA - INVESTOR LOANS An FHA loan to a borrower who does not occupy the property used as collateral for the loan as their principal place of residence. The "Department of Housing and Urban Development Reform Act of 1989" gave the "death blow" to investor loans. This Act was signed by the President on December 15, 1989. The principal focus of this Mortgagee Letter is the elimination of private investors. Investors are no longer eligible for FHA loans except in certain situations. In summary, the ban on investors is effective for mortgages insured with a conditional or master commitment, appraisal report

port or master appraisal report, a CRV or master CRV issued on or after December 15, 1989. Exceptions: 1) investors that are State or local nonprofit agencies that met HUD guidelines, 2) investors applying under the 203(k) section - permits an 85% LTV for private investors, 3) investors purchasing HUD-owned property being sold by PD (Property Disposition) - a 75% LTV is allowed for single family, 85% LTV is allowed for two to four family, 4) investors **assuming** FHA loans originated before the December 1989 Act, 5) streamline refinancing that reduces HUD's insuring risk, 6) investors that are members of an Indian tribe as provided in Section 248, 7) a service person unable to occupy as provided in Section 216 or subsection (b) (4) or (f) of Section 222. Lenders are reminded that no more than 20% of HUD-insured mortgages in condos can be investor loans.

Often times you hear the question, "Is there a restriction on how many FHA loans an individual may have?" The answer is yes, but at this time the author, Santi, wishes to point out that for some unknown reason the interpretation of the regulations varies from region to region. The answer from FHA in Washington is that an individual may have no more than seven non-occupant/owner units per subdivision including any adjacent or contiguous subdivisions. The limit of seven units includes any financial interest an applicant may have in a property, despite the type of ownership or the type of mortgage involved in any unit. Financial interest includes any form of interest: fee simple, interest in a partnership, a corporation, or a trust. The property can be free of any liens, or financed by a VA or a conventional mortgage, it still counts in the seven unit rule.

FHA - LOAN APPROVAL, THE FIRM COMMITMENT Approval of the credit or loan is termed a firm commitment. If a firm commitment is issued before the expiration date of the conditional commitment (appraisal), there will be a three-month term granted for the firm commitment, or the firm commitment will be valid for the remaining life of the conditional commitment, whichever is greater. There are times, however, when FHA will extend a firm commitment to allow closing. An extension of a firm commitment is discretionary and must be for good cause.

See COMPUTERIZED LOAN ORIGINATION, INCOME ANALYSIS.

FHA - MORTGAGE CREDIT CONDITION (MC) An FHA condition of loan approval that must be satisfied before loan closing. Some examples are: sale of a previous home, payment of a debt, and any verification of a condition that did not exist at the time of loan submission.

FHA - MORTGAGE INSURANCE PREMIUM *See* FHA - INSURED LOAN.

FHA - PROPERTY DISPOSITION (PD) A department within FHA vested with the sale of property acquired by FHA. PD manages and sales property acquired from FHA approved lenders. The FHA lenders acquire the properties through foreclosure then later convey the property to FHA. PD can sell property to the public by an auction or a sealed bid.

FHA - REFINANCE FHA will refinance acceptable properties with what will be a maximum loan of 85% of Total Acquisition for an owner/occupant. Refinance loans to investors or a non-owner/occupant are no longer available except for a rate reduction. Usually, the FHA Section 203(b) is used for new loans that are refinances. Other Sections, such as 245 (GPM) and 251 (ARM), can be used to refinance a temporary loan to a permanent loan, or to refinance with the same Section if it is for purposes of obtaining a lower interest rate.

The 85% maximum LTV rule mentioned above can be exceeded if the total of the outstanding lien (loan) or liens plus the discount points and closing costs associated with the refinance surpasses the amount equivalent to 85% of Total Acquisition and if the loan is to an owner/occupant. In no event can an FHA refinance loan exceed the maximum loan amount available to an owner/occupant purchaser in an FHA section used to process the loan. FHA has a paper reduction or *streamline* method for refinancing to a lower interest rate. In cases where refinancing is for a rate reduction only, it is recommended that you check with lenders for guidelines on streamline refinancing, some lenders are more stringent than others (some require an appraisal and some do not).

FHA - RELEASE OF LIABILITY On 7 January 1989 FHA, in a mortgagee letter, instructed lenders to release sellers from liability when the seller requests the release and: 1) the credit of the purchaser has been approved by HUD or a Direct Endorsement (DE) lender, 2) the purchaser has executed an agreement to assume and pay the mortgage debt and become the substitute mortgagor, and 3) if an investor assumes the mortgage, it must be paid down according to guidelines for FHA sections. If an investor assumed a loan that was made from a conditional commitment issued on or after February 5, 1988, the loan must be reduced to 75% of the original balance (or a 75% LTV).

If an investor assumed a loan that was made from a commitment issued before February 5, 1988, the loan would not have to be reduced to 75% of the original balance. This policy applies to all HUD-insured mortgages, no matter when the mortgage was originated, closed or endorsed. The release must be processed within 45 calendar days from the date the lender receives all necessary documents for processing.

If a seller, whose mortgage was originated from a conditional commitment issued on or after February 5, 1988, does not obtain a release from liability and the purchaser assumes the loan, then the seller and the purchaser are liable for five years. After the five years is completed, only the purchaser will be liable. If the purchaser assumes the loan subject to the mortgage, then the seller is liable for the entire life of the loan. If a purchaser applies for a new FHA loan and has sold a home that was acquired with an FHA loan to an investor by a loan assumption within the past five years from date of loan application, and did not obtain a release of liability or the loan is not reduced to 75% of the original balance or 75% of value based on an acceptable appraisal, that purchaser could be denied a new FHA loan if the applicant does not have enough income to offset the new loan payment and the old loan payment (payment on home sold in past five years with an FHA loan). The old loan payment (from the FHA loan) is considered as a contingent liability if the seller was not released from liability.

See GUARANTY PERFORMANCE, SURETY.

FHA - SECTION FHA identifies their loan programs by section numbers.

Section 203   Mutual Mortgage Insurance and Improvement Loans.

Section 203(b)   One-to-Four Family Housing. The (bv) section is commonly called the FHA/VA loan.

Section 203(h)   Single Family Housing for Disaster Victims.
                   Section 203(i) Rural Housing, One Family Non-farm or Farm Housing.
                   Section 203(k) Rehabilitation Loan for One-to-Four Family Housing.
                   Section 203(m) Second Homes, Vacation Homes.
Section 207   Multifamily Housing Mortgage Insurance.
                   Rental Housing for eight or more units.
                   Mobile Home Parks.

Section 213   Cooperative Housing Mortgage Insurance.
                   Dwelling Unit Released from a Cooperative Project.
                   Management-Type Cooperative Projects for five or more units.
                   Sales-Type Cooperative Projects for five or more units.
                   Investor-Sponsored

Section 220   Urban Renewal Mortgage Insurance and Insured Improvement Loans.
                   One-to-Eleven Family Housing in Urban Renewal Area.
                   Construction of Two or More Units in Approved Urban Area.

Section 221   Low-Cost and Moderate Income Mortgage Insurance.
Section 221(d)(2) One-to-Four Family Housing, Low and
Moderate Income, and Displaced families.
Section 221(h) Individual Units Released from 222(h) Project
Mortgage.
Section 221(i) Conversion of 221(d)(3) Below-Market Interest
Rate Rental Project into Condominium Plan.
Section 221(d)(3) Housing Projects, Below-Market Interest
Rate for Housing Moderate-Income Families, Individuals 62
or Older, or Handicapped. The Program was available with
a Rate and a Rental Subsidy.
Section 221(d)(4) Housing Projects for Moderate-Income
Families. Market Interest Rate Program for Profit-motivated
Sponsors.
Section 221(h) Substandard Housing for Subsequent Resale
after Rehabilitation.

Section 222   Servicemen's Mortgage Insurance paid by Department of
Defense. For single family housing only. This program is
currently not funded for any Department except Transportation and the Coast Guard.
See the term: FHA - SECTION 222.

Section 223   Miscellaneous Housing Insurance.
Housing and Mortgage Insurance for Housing in Declining
Neighborhoods.
Insurance for Government-Acquired Properties.

Section 231   Mortgage Insurance Housing the Elderly.
Housing Project of Eight or More Units for Occupancy by Elderly or Handicapped.

Section 232   Mortgage Insurance for Nursing Homes and Intermediate Care
Facilities.
Housing for 20 or More Patients.

Section 233   Experimental Housing Mortgage Insurance.
Proposed or Rehabilitated Housing Using Advanced Technol-
ogy.
Rental Housing Using Advanced Technology.

Section 234   Condominium Housing Mortgage Insurance.
Section 234(c) Individual Units in Condominium Projects.

Section 234(d) Condominium Projects with Four or More
Units.

Section 240   Mortgage Insurance on Loans for Title Purchase.
                 Purchase of Fee Simple Title.

Section 241   Supplementary Financing for FHA Project Mortgages.

Section 242   Mortgage Insurance for Hospitals.

Section 244   Mortgage Coinsurance.

Section 245   Graduated Payment Mortgage. Plan I graduates at 2.5% per
                 year, Plan II graduates at 5% per year, and Plan III grad-
                 uates at 7.5% per year. Plans IV and V normally not offered
                 to the public by lenders.

Section 251   Adjustable Rate Mortgage.

Section 255   Home Equity Conversion Mortgage (reverse mortgages).

Section 809   One-to-Four Family Housing for Civilian Employees at or near
                 R & D Installations.

Section 810(f)   Rental Housing with Eight or More Units for Military or Civil-
                 ian Personnel.

Section 810(g)   Resale of 810(f) as Single Family Housing.
Section 810(h)   Individual Units Released from 810(g) Multifamily Mortgage.

In the definitions below there is a brief description of the common sections
used in daily loan transactions.

FHA - SECTION 203 This section is the standard for nearly all the FHA residential loan sections. Loan amounts and down payments will vary for a few
other sections. FHA maximum loan amounts are adapted to new construction
built with FHA or VA inspections, or to new construction insured by an acceptable homeowner warranty program, or to an existing dwelling more than
one year old. If the subject property does not meet the above criteria, the maximum loan will be penalized and reduced to 90% of the total acquisition.

There are at least four ways to arrive at maximum loan amounts using the
203(b) formula: (1) the purchasers pay their closing costs and prepaid items (2)
the sellers pay all the purchaser's closing costs (3) the sellers pay all the

purchaser's closing costs and prepaid items (4) the sellers pay a portion of the purchaser's closing costs.

The maximum loan amount for a one-to-four family dwelling is decided by taking applicable percentages of the total acquisition. Once you decide total acquisition, all you need do is multiply by an applicable percentage. Applications must be on an owner/occupant basis to obtain maximum loan-to-value ratio.

Total Acquisition refers to the lesser of (1) the "cost to the purchaser," which is the same as "the cost to acquire" and *Acquisition Cost* or (2) the FHA estimate of value plus the estimate of closing costs. The "cost to the purchaser" or "the cost to acquire," normally means the sales price, any repairs the purchaser is paying for, and closing costs the purchaser pays as noted in the closing cost schedule. As we later will see, cost to the purchaser can be the above, minus sales concessions or excessive buydowns. A portion of the closing costs may be financed *only if* the purchasers are paying their closing costs.

You must round your loan amounts down to the nearest $50 increment if the mortgagor is paying the MIP in cash. You do not have to round down if the MIP will be financed. I repeat, you do not have to round down if the MIP is financed. A lender, as a matter of preference, may require the loan amount to be rounded down — but FHA does not require it when the MIP is financed.

If total acquisition cost is $50,000 or less, the maximum loan amount can be determined by multiplying the total acquisition by 97%. If total acquisition exceeds $50,000, the maximum loan amount would be determined by multiplying the first $25,000 by 97% and then multiplying the remainder by 95%.

Allow me to illustrate by examples: assume the sales price and FHA value are $48,750, and the purchasers are paying all their closing costs, which FHA estimates to be $1,250. The formula for the maximum loan would be $48,750 + $1,250 = $50,000 x 97% = $48,500. If the total acquisition is above $50,000, say $70,000, the formula would be: $70,000 + $1,800 (FHA's estimate of closing cost) = $71,800; 97% of the first $25,000 = $24,250, 95% of the remaining $46,800 ($71,800 minus $25,000 = $46,800) = $44,460; $24,250 + $44,460 = the maximum loan of $68,710 or $68,700 if rounded down to the nearest $50. There is a short-cut formula for total acquisition cost more than $50,000, see the Table below.

The 1990 Housing Bill made a small change in the calculation of the maximum loan amount. There is one extra step to decide the maximum loan amount. Put the extra step first. Using the FHA appraised value and disregarding closing costs, multiply 97.75% (if the appraisal is over $50,000) or 98.75% (if the appraisal is under $50,000) to decide your maximum loan amount. THE NEW EXTRA STEP SETS THE MAXIMUM LOAN AMOUNT. Continue with the normal way to decide the maximum loan amount (as above). Choose the lower of the two ways, i.e., the old way (before the Housing Act) or the new way.

It is important to note that the maximum loan amount can include closing costs only if they are paid by the purchaser. A simple way to remember this rule is to think of it as "one cannot borrow what one does not pay." If purchasers do not pay their closing costs, then they cannot borrow money for their closing costs. Purchasers do not have to pay all their closing costs to have them included in the loan amount. If purchasers pay half their closing cost, then half the closing cost can be included in the calculation to decided maximum loan amount. The dollar amount for closing costs comes from a Good Faith Estimate of Closing Cost furnished by the lender.

Any Estimate of Closing Costs does not include prepaid items. Prepaid items are usually real estate taxes and hazard insurance premiums paid at closing or put into an escrow account at the time of closing.

See PREPAID ITEMS.

FHA - SECTION 203(bv) - (FHA/VA LOAN) This loan is used mainly by reservists who have served more than 90 consecutive days on active duty for training purposes and were discharged under conditions other than dishonorable, or by veterans who have used their eligibility or want to preserve the eligibility for later use. Usage of the FHA/VA loan does not involve the veteran's entitlement. Reservists or veterans can use this program as often as they wish.

An FHA/VA loan is a Section 203 loan with a change in the formula for deriving maximum loan amount. The maximum loan amount is calculated as follows: 100% of the first $25,000 of FHA total value and 95% of the remainder. One can decide the maximum loan by taking 95% of the total acquisition and adding back $1,250. Only single-family homes are eligible. There is one supporting document all applicants must obtain, a Certificate of Veteran Status. This Certificate is furnished by request from the Veteran's Administration. A purchaser can have less than a 3% investment when buying with an FHA/VA loan.

If FHA deems an applicant to be a short-term occupant of the property, the normal FHA Section 203 down payment will be required. An example of a short-term occupant would be a service person subject to transfer.

Discharged veterans are eligible for this loan if there has been 90 days of active duty and if the veteran enlisted before 8 September 1980, or if the veteran was an officer enlisted before 14 October 1982. A discharged veteran who was not an officer and entered service after 7 September 1980, must have served 24 months of active duty to be eligible if enlistment was after 14 October 1982. An exception to the above would be a veteran discharged because of disability or hardship. Reservists who served at least 90 days of active duty for training purposes continue to be eligible for this, despite the entry day of service.

Exhibit 16

Four Ways to Determine Maximum Loan Amounts Using the FHA Section 203(b) Formula.

Begin by making a comparison between two totals. The first of two totals is the FHA appraised value plus FHA closing costs. The second total is the contract price plus the FHA closing cost the purchaser pays. The second total can also be the contract price, minus any concession items, plus the FHA closing cost paid by the buyer. Before you begin determining the loan amount you must choose the lower of the two totals. On each example below the first figure ($70,000) is termed the *acquisition cost*. The number below the $70,000 is the FHA closing cost paid by the buyer. The total of the acquisition cost and the FHA closing cost paid by the buyer is the *total acquisition*. Once you correctly determine the total acquisition, you simply use the short-cut formula shown below. In example I, the two totals would be the same. In example II, the total of the acquisition cost plus the FHA closing cost paid by the buyer (nothing) is the lower of the two totals. In example III, the total of the acquisition minus the concession is the lower of the two totals. In example IV, the total of the acquisition cost plus the FHA closing cost paid by the buyer (1/2) is the lower of the two totals. If you do not understand the meaning of the "lower of the two totals," go back and reread the first four sentences of this paragraph.

Total Acquisition Below $50,000

If the total acquisition is below $50,000, you simply multiply by 97% to determine the loan amount. A word of caution! If the total acquisition exceeds $50,000 by $1, you must use the 97% - 95% formula or the short-cut formula.

Assuming a sales price and FHA value of $70,000 and $1,800 for the FHA estimate of closing cost.

I. Purchasers are paying their own closing cost and prepaid items:

$70,000	$71,800	$25,000	$46,800	$24,250
+ 1,800	-25,000	× 97%	× 95%	+44,460
$71,800	$46,800	$24,250	$44,460	$68,710

Maximum Loan is $68,700
(Short-cut: $71,800 × 95% = $68,210 + $500 = $68,710 = $68,700)

Exhibit 16 (continued)

II. Sellers are paying all of the purchaser's closing cost:

$70,000	$70,000	$25,000	$45,000	$24,250
+ -0-	-25,000	× 97%	× 95%	+42,750
$70,000	$45,000	$24,250	$42,750	$67,000

Maximum loan is $67,000
(Short-cut: $70,000 × 95% = $66,500 + $500 = $67,000)

III. Sellers are paying all of the purchasers' closing cost and prepaid items:

$70,000	$69,300	$69,300	$25,000	$44,300	$24,250
- 700*	+ -0-	-25,000	× 97%	× 95%	+42,085
$69,300	$69,300	$44,300	$24,250	$42,085	$66,335

Maximum loan is $66,300
(Short -cut: $69,300 × 95% = $65,835 + $500 = $66,335 =$66,300)

*FHA can view prepaid items paid by the seller as a sales concession. In this example, the $700 is an estimate for prepaid items which is deducted from the sales price as a concession paid by the seller.

IV. Sellers are paying a portion of the closing cost:

$70,000	$70,900	$25,000	$45,900	$24,250
+ 900*	-25,000	× 97%	× 95%	+43,605
$70,900	$45,900	$24,250	$43,605	$67,855

Maximum loan is $67,850
(Short-cut: $70,900 × 95% = $67,355 + $500 = $67,855 =$67,850)

*In this example, we assumed the seller was paying one half of the purchaser's closing cost (FHA estimate is $1,800 divided by 2 = $900).

This answer reminds me of two true or false statements usually included in an exam I use at some of my seminars. The first is: "An FHA/VA loan is a VA loan." The other is: "An individual purchasing a duplex with an FHA/VA loan was rejected. The reason for rejection had to be problems with either the appraisal, income, or credit of the purchaser." I usually put the first question in the VA section, and many students will answer "True." Answers to the second question give me a feeling of wanting to put up a big sign reading: "YOU CAN'T GET AN FHA/VA LOAN ON ANYTHING OTHER THAN A SINGLE-FAMILY DWELLING!" Though the book mentions this fact, many students still answer this question incorrectly.

The second true or false question has the word "rejection." To understand the importance of this question, consider the repercussions if the error is not caught until loan submission. Based on normal situations, this occurs after the sales agent has gone through all the efforts of making the sale, after the purchaser has made a loan application, after the appraisal fee and credit report fee has been paid, and the worst part . . . after roughly 30 days of loan processing! Now, who is going to tell whom, "Sorry, you can't get an FHA/VA loan on a duplex." This scenario should come with a warning beforehand: "The following is based on a true story except the name of the loan officer, processor, and REALTOR have been changed to protect the *guilty*." Better yet, the names have been changed to protect the uninformed from the buyer.

Only single-family properties are eligible for: FHA/VA, Graduated Payment Mortgage (GPM), and Section 222.

FHA - SECTION 203(k)   A section that insures mortgages for the purchase and rehabilitating one to four-unit dwellings or to refinance existing indebtedness and rehabilitating. The loan-to-value ratios and loan amounts are the same as Section 203(b), except for an investor loan. An investor can be approved for an 85% LTV under Section 203(k).

This loan is a much favored Section in the eyes of FHA. Once you become familiar with the guidelines, it is easy to appreciate how this Section helps to meet the goals of affordable housing in areas where there is need for substantial rehabilitation of the existing housing.

Section 203(k) is the only FHA mortgage that will allow closing without requiring a final inspection. Closing without a final inspection is a unique trait of this section. FHA, VA, and Conventional loans normally require a final inspection before closing, even when using an escrow for unfinished work.

FHA will issue two values, an *as is* value and a *finished* value. Funds are disbursed in agreement with Section 203(b) guidelines for both values. Funds used for the acquisition or refinancing will be disbursed initially. Remaining funds for the rehabilitation will be placed in an escrow account and disbursed upon completion of the work. Rehabilitation (a) must begin within 60 days of closing; (b) must not stop for more than 45 days; (c) will be allowed 18 months for completion; (d) can involve up to 5 draws that will include the final. Rehabilitation funds placed in escrow must draw interest at the minimum rate of 5%.

There are additional costs associated with Section 203(k). The appraisal fee is equal to 150% of the normal costs and a supplemental origination fee is equal to the greater of 1-1/2% of the cost of rehabilitation or $350. The supplemental origination fee and discount applying to the rehabilitation cost may be included in the loan amount.

FHA - SECTION 221 This loan is for families of low and moderate income. The real benefit is a lower down payment requirement. Only families are eligible, with an exception for handicapped persons or an elderly person 62 years of age or older. There are no limitations on income, but there are limitations for maximum loan amounts. The maximum FHA 221 loan amount is derived by multiplying 97% of the "Total Acquisition," which can include prepaid items for Section 221. The maximum "221" loan amounts can never exceed the FHA estimate of value excluding closing costs. Displaced families applying for a "221" loan may receive a loan equal to value, closing costs, and prepaid expenses, less $200 per family dwelling unit. The $200 investment per family dwelling unit will satisfy the minimum investment required for displaced families.

Maximum loan amounts are as follows:

(1) A single-family dwelling is $31,000, but may be increased to $36,000 in certain designated locations.

(2) A two-family dwelling is $35,000, but may be increased to $42,000.

(3) A three-family dwelling is $48,600, but may be increased to $57,600.

(4) A four-family structure is $59,400, but may be increased to $68,400.

Families of five or more members are eligible for single-family dwellings with four or more bedrooms with increased limits of $36,000, that can be increased to $42,000 in certain designated locations.

FHA - SECTION 222 This was an often used loan in an area with a military base. There is one distinct feature of this FHA loan: payment of an FHA 1/2 of 1% monthly insurance premium by a government agency. Only single-family dwellings are eligible. Down payment guidelines are the same as for Section 203. The service person must have been on active duty for more than 2 years, and the Commanding Officer must certify that housing is required for the service person or their family. A Certificate of Eligibility (DD Form 802) must accompany the application to FHA. The 1/2 of 1% premium is paid by a government agency while the service person is on active duty, owns the home, and uses it for their primary residence. If the service person dies, the premium will continue to be paid for up to 2 years or until the sale of the home, whichever occurs first. A service person eligible for this section may assume an FHA loan of another section and have that loan changed to a Section 222, thereby eliminating any required monthly payment of mortgage insurance.

Today most departments of service and government agencies have not been funded for payment of the MIP. Exceptions are certain sections of the Department of Transportation and the Coast Guard.

FHA - SECTION 234(c) A Section 203 loan for a condominium. All maximum loan calculations are the same as the "203" program. Other than the type of dwelling allowed for the sections, the main difference between "203" and "234" is the MIP on "234" must be paid on a monthly basis.

FHA - SECTION 245 FHA designed the 245 mortgage as a way to help people buy homes that they normally could not afford now but can afford in the future. An initial low monthly payment allows the borrower to qualify then a series of increasing payments allows amortization of the loan. This loan is often called a GPM loan (Graduated Payment Mortgage). There are five types of FHA GPM loans. As the name implies, a GPM begins with payments that gradually increase over time. Specifically, the FHA GPM Plans, I, II, and III graduate from years 1 through 5, then remain constant for the life of the loan. Plans IV and V increase over a period of 10 years, then remain constant. Because of Secondary Market reasons, Plans IV and V are not normally offered to the public. FHA 245 GPM loans have certain characteristics:

(1) FHA will qualify the applicant on the first year payment to decide that income is sufficient. This is a distinct advantage of Plan III, since the payment rate is equivalent to more than 2% below the note rate. FHA does not permit qualification based on more than 2% below the note rate - except 245 Plan III.

(2) There is negative amortization. In the early years the loan balance increases instead of decreases. This will normally occur in any loan that has a payment rate in the beginning that is lower than the rate of interest or mortgage rate.

(3) There is a payment rate. The monthly payment can be expressed as an interest rate percentage. For example, a 12.25% Plan III will have a monthly payment in year 1 that is equal to an interest rate equivalent to approximately 3% below the mortgage rate or, specifically, equivalent to an interest rate of 9.04%. The interest rate, however, is

not 9.04%, as this is the payment rate. The interest rate is the mortgage rate or note rate, which in the above example was 12.25%.

(4) The mortgage rate or note rate is the actual rate of interest for the mortgage.

(5) After the graduations are completed, the payment rate will be higher than the mortgage rate for the rest of the term, (13.67% in the example above) so that amortization of the loan will occur in 30 years.

(6) 245's can be used only for single-family dwellings.

(7) 245's cannot be used for refinancing a permanent home mortgage, except to refinance an existing 245 loan to a lower rate.

(8) Discount points or the mortgage rate normally will be higher as compared to the other FHA Sections.

The impact of the FHA GPM program is best understood by using a comparison of a level payment mortgage to a graduated payment mortgage. Please turn your attention to Exhibit 17. Take a highlighter or a pen and mark each first-year payment on Plans I, II, and III. Now consider a loan amount of $100,000 at 11.5% for 30 years with a monthly payment of $990.29. On a level payment mortgage, the monthly principal and interest payment will be $990.29. With the FHA GPM, the first year payments will be: $906.31 for Plan I, $829.60 for Plan II, and $759.60 for Plan III. Comparing the monthly payment between a level payment loan and Plan III, there is a savings of $230.69, per month! Of course, there are the negatives to this mortgage. The negatives are:

(1) Negative amortization.

(2) Once positive amortization occurs, monthly payments will end up higher compared with a Level Payment Loan.

(3) An approximate 10% downpayment is required for Plan III.

See BUYDOWN, NEGATIVE AMORTIZATION.

Another very good feature of Plan III, as compared to creative financing in the form of short-term or permanent buydowns, is the front end savings offered by Plan III when compared to a buydown plan. A 3-2-1 buydown can offer better front end monthly payments as compared to Plans I and II, without negative amortization. But, Plan III payments are equal to a 3-2-1 buydown without the cost of buying down the interest rate. For example: A short-term buydown of 3-2-1 (3% for the first year, 2% second year, and 1% third year) may compare with Plan III first year monthly payment; but the cost to the seller will be approximately 6% (3+2+1) plus the discount points. The buydown cost does

Exhibit 17
FHA Section 245 and VA GPM
Principal and Interest
Monthly Payment Amortization Factors per $1,000

Plan I—With increasing payment for 5 years at 2.50 percent each year

Int. Yr.	8.00	8.25	8.50	8.75	9.00	9.25	9.50	9.75	10.00	10.25	10.50	10.75	11.00	11.25
1	6.6651	6.8277	6.9918	7.1574	7.3244	7.4928	7.6625	7.8335	8.0057	8.1791	8.3537	8.5295	8.7063	8.8842
2	6.8317	6.9984	7.1666	7.3364	7.5075	7.6801	7.8541	8.0293	8.2058	8.3836	8.5626	8.7427	8.9240	9.1063
3	7.0025	7.1733	7.3458	7.5198	7.6952	7.8721	8.0504	8.2300	8.4110	8.5932	8.7767	8.9613	9.1471	9.3340
4	7.1775	7.3527	7.5294	7.7078	7.8876	8.0689	8.2517	8.4358	8.6213	8.8080	8.9961	9.1853	9.3757	9.5673
5	7.3570	7.5365	7.7177	7.9005	8.0848	8.2706	8.4580	8.6467	8.8368	9.0282	9.2210	9.4150	9.6101	9.8065

Plan II—With increasing payment for 5 years at 5.0 percent each year.

Int. Yr.	8.00	8.25	8.50	8.75	9.00	9.25	9.50	9.75	10.00	10.25	10.50	10.75	11.00	11.25
1	6.0579	6.2089	6.3613	6.5153	6.6706	6.8274	6.9856	7.1451	7.3059	7.4679	7.6312	7.7957	7.9613	8.1281
2	6.3608	6.5193	6.6794	6.8410	7.0042	7.1688	7.3349	7.5023	7.6712	7.8413	8.0128	8.1855	8.3594	8.5345
3	6.6789	6.8453	7.0134	7.1831	7.3544	7.5272	7.7016	7.8775	8.0547	8.2334	8.4134	8.5948	8.7774	8.9612
4	7.0128	7.1875	7.3640	7.5422	7.7221	7.9036	8.0867	8.2713	8.4575	8.6451	8.8341	9.0245	9.2162	9.4093
5	7.3634	7.5469	7.7322	7.9193	8.1082	8.2988	8.4910	8.6849	8.8804	9.0773	9.2758	9.4757	9.6771	9.8798

Plan III—With increasing payment for 5 years at 7.50 percent each year
Note: Plan III Factors also apply to the VA GPM Program.

Int. Yr.	8.00	8.25	8.50	8.75	9.00	9.25	9.50	9.75	10.00	10.25	10.50	10.75	11.00	11.25
1	5.5101	5.6500	5.7915	5.9344	6.0788	6.2246	6.3719	6.5204	6.6704	6.8216	6.9740	7.1277	7.2826	7.4387
2	5.9233	6.0738	6.2258	6.3795	6.5347	6.6915	6.8498	7.0095	7.1706	7.3332	7.4971	7.6623	7.8288	7.9966
3	6.3676	6.5293	6.6928	6.8580	7.0248	7.1934	7.3635	7.5352	7.7084	7.8832	8.0594	8.2370	8.4160	8.5964
4	6.8452	7.0190	7.1947	7.3723	7.5517	7.7329	7.9158	8.1003	8.2866	8.4744	8.6638	8.8548	9.0472	9.2411
5	7.3585	7.5454	7.7343	7.9252	8.1181	8.3128	8.5094	8.7079	8.9081	9.1100	9.3136	9.5189	9.7257	9.9342

Example: A Plan III mortgage amount of $65,750 at 10% rate would have a monthly principal and interest amount of $438.58 (6.6704 x 65.75). The P & I amounts for the succeeding years could be derived by either multiplying the factor times the loan amount or by simply adding 7.5% to the preceding year's monthly payment (7.1706 x 65.75 = $471.47 or $438.58 x 7.5% = $471.47).

Exhibit 17 (continued)

Plan I—With increasing payment for 5 years at 2.50 percent each year

Int.	11.50	11.75	12.00	12.25	12.50	12.75	13.00	13.25	13.50	13.75	14.00	14.25	14.50	14.75
Yr.														
1	9.0631	9.2430	9.4238	9.6056	9.7882	9.9717	10.1560	10.2411	10.5269	10.7135	10.9008	11.0888	11.2775	11.4667
2	9.2897	9.4740	9.6594	9.8457	10.0329	10.2210	10.4099	10.5996	10.7901	10.0814	11.1734	11.3660	11.5594	11.7534
3	9.5219	9.7109	9.9009	10.0918	10.2837	10.4765	10.6701	10.8646	11.0599	11.2559	11.4527	11.6502	11.8484	12.0472
4	9.7600	9.9537	10.1484	10.2441	10.5408	10.7384	10.9369	11.1362	11.3364	11.5373	11.7390	11.9415	12.1146	12.3484
5	10.0040	10.2025	10.4021	10.6027	10.8043	11.0069	11.2103	11.4146	11.6198	11.8257	12.0325	12.2400	12.4482	12.6571
6	10.2541	10.4576	10.6622	10.8678	11.0744	11.2820	11.4906	11.7000	11.9103	12.1214	12.3333	12.5460	12.7594	12.9736

Plan II—With increasing payment for 5 years at 5.0 percent each year.

Int.	11.50	11.75	12.00	12.25	12.50	12.75	13.00	13.25	13.50	13.75	14.00	14.25	14.50	14.75
Yr.														
1	8.2960	8.4649	8.6348	8.8058	8.9777	9.1505	9.3243	9.4990	9.6745	9.8508	10.0279	10.2059	10.3845	10.5639
2	8.7108	8.8881	9.0666	9.2461	9.4266	9.6081	9.7905	9.9739	10.1582	10.3433	10.5293	10.7161	10.9038	11.0921
3	9.1463	9.3325	9.5199	9.7084	9.8979	10.0885	10.2800	10.4726	10.6661	10.8605	11.0558	11.2520	11.4489	11.6467
4	9.6036	9.7992	9.9959	10.1938	10.3928	10.5929	10.7940	10.9962	11.1994	11.4035	11.6086	11.8145	12.0214	12.2291
5	10.0838	10.2891	10.4957	10.7035	10.9124	11.1225	11.3338	11.5460	11.7594	11.9737	12.1890	12.4053	12.6225	12.8405
6	10.5880	10.8036	11.0205	11.2386	11.4581	11.6787	11.9004	12.1233	12.3473	12.5724	12.7985	13.0255	13.2536	13.4826

Plan III—With increasing payment for 5 years at 7.50 percent each year

Note: Plan III factors also apply to the VA GPM Program

Int.	11.50	11.75	12.00	12.25	12.50	12.75	13.00	13.25	13.50	13.75	14.00	14.25	14.50	14.75
Yr.														
1	7.5960	7.7543	7.9138	8.0743	8.2358	8.3983	8.5618	8.7263	8.8917	9.0580	9.2252	9.3933	9.5621	9.7318
2	8.1657	8.3359	8.5073	8.6798	8.8535	9.0282	9.2040	9.3808	9.5586	9.7374	9.9171	10.0978	10.2793	10.4617
3	8.7781	8.9611	9.1453	9.3308	9.5175	9.7053	9.8943	10.0843	10.2755	10.4677	10.6609	10.8551	11.0502	11.2464
4	9.4364	9.6332	9.8312	10.0306	10.2313	10.4332	10.6363	10.8407	11.0461	11.2528	11.4604	11.6692	11.8790	12.0898
5	10.1442	10.3556	10.5686	10.7829	10.9986	11.2157	11.4341	11.6537	11.8746	12.0967	12.3200	12.5444	12.7699	12.9966
6	10.9050	11.1323	11.3612	11.5916	11.8235	12.0569	12.2916	12.5277	12.7652	13.0040	13.2440	13.4852	13.7277	13.9713

Example: A Plan III mortgage amount of $65,750 at 12.25% rate would have a monthly principal and interest amount of $530.89 (8.0743 × 65.75). The P & I amounts for the succeeding years could be derived by either multiplying the factor times the loan amount or by simply adding 7.5% to the preceding year's monthly payment (8.6798 × 65.75 = $570.70 or $530.89 × 7.5% = $570.71).

Reprinted by permission, from Doris Sowell, *Fundamentals of Finance* © 1981.

not fare very well when compared to a 245 Plan III, which requires only discount points to be paid. A permanent buydown would be even more expensive as it would require buying the rate down for the life of the loan. Although the approximate 10% downpayment with a Plan III is costly, it is a downpayment and not bought down interest.

Another very important comparison, between a buydown and a GPM, is what FHA will use for the first year payment. As we have mentioned before, for income analysis purposes, FHA will not allow the first year buydown payment to be less than 2% below the note rate, but as we have already seen, the first payment could be more than 3% below the note rate with a Plan III. For clarification purposes, FHA will allow a buydown of up to 3% in the first year, but for loan qualification purposes, the monthly payment will be based on a rate that is not less than 2% below the note rate.

For loan qualifying purposes, a quick rule of thumb is a borrower must earn 4 times the monthly payment. Based on that assumption, a Plan III monthly payment $200 lower than a fixed rate amortized loan will result in a purchaser qualifying with $800 less monthly income. A real estate agent can sell the same house to a buyer making $9,600 less per year compared to a buyer financing the purchase with the same loan amount, same interest rate, but with a level payment amortization. Today, the 245 Plan is not as attractive compared to when it was first introduced in 1978. When the program first began, interest rates were in the single digits (8.75-9.5%) and the values of homes were increasing in the double digits. It was possible for an individual to purchase a home in 1978 with a payment rate as low as 5.75%, and the value of the home growing at a 12%, or higher, annual rate. Monthly payments in Plan III are approximately 3% less in the first year, but when the increases are over, the payment rate levels off at approximately 1.5% over the note rate in year six and stays that way for the duration of the loan. Furthermore, Plan III requires an approximate 10% downpayment.

To decide a maximum 245 loan, simply multiply the factor, listed in Exhibit 18 below, times the Total Acquisition. For example: on a $60,000 Total Acquisition cost, the maximum loan amount for a 13% Plan III should be $53,400 ($60,000 × .89004).

Plan I monthly payments graduate at 2-1/2% per year, Plan II at 5% per year, and Plan III at 7-1/2% per year, Plan IV at 2% per year (10 years) and Plan V at 3% per year (10 years).

FHA - SECTION 251 A section for insuring adjustable rate mortgages. This section follows the same guidelines as for the FHA 203(b). The only difference, of course, is the adjustable rate feature. The maximum rate change will be limited to 1% per year and a maximum rate increase or decrease of no more than 5% from the initial rate.

Exhibit 18

FHA Section 245
Factors to Determine Loan Amounts
and Highest Outstanding Balance

	8.00%	8.25%	8.50%	8.75%	9.00%	9.25%	9.50%
Plan I	.96998	.96943	.96889	.96837	.96777	.96679	.96586
Plan II	.95768	.95569	.95376	.95187	.95003	.94824	.94621
Plan III	.94087	.93792	.93505	.93224	.92951	.92684	.92424

	9.75%	10.00%	10.25%	10.50%	10.75%	11.00%	11.25%
Plan I	.96495	.96407	.96312	.96188	.96069	.95954	.95843
Plan II	.94401	.94186	.93979	.93777	.93580	.93388	.93201
Plan III	.92168	.91920	.91677	.91441	.91200	.90932	.90670

Highest Outstanding Balance Factors

	8.00%	8.25%	8.50%	8.75%	9.00%	9.25%	9.50%
Plan I	1000.0201	1000.5896	1001.1418	1001.6772	1002.3079	1003.3129	1004.2877
Plan II	1012.8612	1014.9708	1017.0324	1019.0469	1021.0152	1022.9385	1025.1491
Plan III	1030.9556	1034.1948	1037.3747	1040.4962	1043.5603	1046.5880	1049.5206

	9.75%	10.00%	10.25%	10.50%	10.75%	11.00%	11.25%
Plan I	1005.2331	1006.1499	1007.1468	1008.4360	1009.6867	1010.9001	1012.0773
Plan II	1027.5353	1029.8670	1032.1457	1034.3725	1036.5488	1038.6758	1040.7549
Plan III	1052.4189	1055.2642	1058.0575	1060.7999	1063.5966	1066.7321	1069.8097

Reprinted, by permission from Doris Sowell *Fundamentals of Finance* © 1981

Exhibit 18 (continued)

FHA Section 245
Factors to Determine Loan Amounts and Highest Outstanding Balance *

	11.50%	11.75%	12.00%	12.25%	12.50%	12.75%	13.00%
Plan I	.95734	.95630	.95522	.95392	.95267	.95145	.95028
Plan II	.93020	.92843	.92671	.92502	.92306	.92115	.91929
Plan III	.90415	.90166	.89922	.89685	.89452	.89226	.89004
Plan IV	.93827	.93606	.93393	.93150	.92916	.92686	.92466
Plan V	.90706	.90413	.90094	.89778	.89471	.89175	.88887

	13.25%	13.50%	13.75%	14%	14.25%	14.50%	14.75%
Plan I	.94914	.94803	.94697	.94593	.94492	.94395	.94300
Plan II	.91749	.91572	.91401	.91233	.91070	.90911	.90756
Plan III	.88787	.88574	.88367	.88164	.87966	.87771	.87581
Plan IV	.92253	.92047	.91834	.91610	.91394	.91185	.90982
Plan V	.88608	.88338	.88706	.87822	.87545	.87274	.87012

Highest Outstanding Balance Factors

	11.50%	11.75%	12.00%	12.25%	12.50%	12.75%	13.00%
Plan I	1013.2195	1014.3277	1015.4743	1016.8540	1018.1930	1019.4929	1020.7547
Plan II	1042.7873	1044.7742	1046.7169	1048.6314	1050.8562	1053.0311	1055.1576
Plan III	1072.8307	1075.7964	1078.7082	1081.5673	1084.3752	1087.1331	1089.8422
Plan IV	1033.8188	1036.2553	1038.6198	1041.3283	1043.9734	1046.5419	1049.0358
Plan V	1069.3910	1072.8549	1076.6526	1080.4449	1084.4449	1087.7544	1091.2753

	13.25%	13.50%	13.75%	14.00%	14.25%	14.50%	14.75%
Plan I	1021.9798	1023.1694	1024.3247	1025.4470	1026.5373	1027.5968	1028.6266
Plan II	1057.2370	1059.2707	1061.2602	1063.2066	1065.1115	1066.9759	1068.8012
Plan III	1092.5039	1095.1195	1097.6900	1100.2169	1102.7012	1105.1441	1107.5468
Plan IV	1051.4571	1053.8076	1056.2509	1058.8317	1061.3389	1063.7745	1066.1403
Plan V	1094.7095	1098.0588	1101.3253	1104.5107	1108.0046	1111.4367	1114.7854

Reprinted, by permission from Doris Sowell *Fundamentals of Finance* © 1981

*Refer to RSP^{TM} Section for lower rates.

Only loans insurable under 203(b), 203(k) (only first mortgages), and 234(c) (condominium loans), are eligible for the ARM provision in 251.

One-to-four family dwellings are eligible properties for section 251. One unit must be occupied by the owner.

You may refinance a fixed rate mortgage with an adjustable rate mortgage, if you are an owner/occupant. Furthermore, any approved FHA section may be refinanced to an adjustable rate provided the mortgagor is an owner/occupant.

The index is the weekly average yield on United States Treasury Securities adjusted to a constant maturity of one year. FHA will not decide the margin; this item will be set by laws of "supply and demand" or, more specifically, by the GNMA mortgage-backed securities program. FHA will require the margin to be constant for the life of the loan.

The FHA adjustable loan is assumable with the FHA limited due-on-sale clause. The ARM loans have the same assumption requirements as any of the unsubsidized FHA loans.

One-time mortgage insurance is a requirement for the adjustable rate mortgage. Loans on condominiums still require monthly payment of the MIP.

Another advantage of the FHA adjustable mortgage is rate caps that prohibit negative amortization.

FHA - SHARED EQUITY See SHARED EQUITY.

FHA - TOTAL ACQUISITION The lesser of, a) the "cost to the purchaser," plus closing costs the purchaser is paying, or b) the FHA estimate of value plus the estimate of closing costs. The "cost to the purchaser" normally means the sales price, any repairs the purchaser is paying for, and closing cost the purchaser pays.

FHA - VALUATION CONDITION (VC) A condition of the FHA appraisal that must be met before closing or insurance of the loan.

FHA - VALUE, THE CONDITIONAL COMMITMENT The property appraisal. This commitment normally has a life of six months for existing dwellings and twelve months for proposed construction or substantial rehabilitation. In certain economically distressed areas, a shorter validation period is used for the appraisals. If you live in a "COLT" state (Colorado, Oklahoma, Louisiana, or Texas), check with your local FHA office for the validation periods for appraisals. There is no extension for existing dwellings, but if a sales contract was signed before the expiration date, the lender will be allowed 30 days to submit an application for loan approval. If the application is rejected, there will be time allowed for resubmission. If the application involves a new borrower, it must be treated as a new case. An extension for new construction or substantial rehabilitation is allowed.

Uniform guidelines for FHA appraisals are as follows:

(1) The term for an FHA appraisal is *conditional commitment.*

(2) An FHA appraisal on an existing dwelling is valid for six months and on new construction for twelve months, there are some exceptions.

(3) An extension of a conditional commitment is available for new construction with an updated appraisal. Any extension of a conditional commitment is subject to the FHA appraiser's updating the appraisal and making a field review.

(4) A requested value is necessary.

(5) Eligible dwellings include detached, semi-detached, row and end-row dwellings, or an improved property deemed eligible for an FHA home loan consisting of one to four units.

(6) The size of the site is a concern for FHA. The size of the lot, in most cases, is not a concern for VA. The land should be minimized in size to provide a reasonable yard for the improvements. This guideline may waiver in rural areas. If the site is too large, FHA may suggest that a reasonable site be subdivided from the tract so that the improvements have nothing more than an adequate yard or area. VA, on the other hand, has no objections to a veteran purchasing a home with acreage, provided the bulk of the value consists of the improvements for the home. Check with your local FHA and VA offices for their opinions on excess land.

(7) To obtain the maximum FHA loan-to-value ratios, new construction must have had plans and specifications submitted for approval and have undergone periodic inspections, or have an approved extended homeowners warranty program acceptable to FHA. If, however, the above outlined procedure is not the case, the property may still be eligible, but the loan may be penalized by placing a maximum of a 90% loan-to-value ratio. Of course, this is not a problem if the total value or total acquisition of the home equals or exceeds maximum FHA loan amount divided by 90%.

(8) Subject to confirmation by your local FHA office, VA appraisals are acceptable to FHA.

Guidelines in this answer are general by necessity. Specific appraisal requirements such as minimum specifications for insulation, weather stripping, heating, and air conditioning will vary throughout the country due to weather conditions. The requirements for insulation and heating for dwellings in Minnesota will not be the same for dwellings in Florida. New construction regulations are now closely tied to local building codes and inspections that vary according to weather related factors and soil conditions.

An FHA appraisal does not warrant the condition of the property. The FHA appraisal is an estimate of value. Although an appraiser performs a site inspection, FHA does not warrant the condition of the appraised property. On 19 May 1988 FHA began to allow borrowing part of the cost of a professional inspection. A maximum of $200 can be added to the FHA estimate of closing costs that will result in borrowing approximately 97% of the cost. This new policy is not available for new construction inspected by FHA or VA or insured by an acceptable 10-year Homeowner Warranty program.

FEDERAL LAND BANK A source of a long-term mortgage loans for rural properties featuring a variable interest rate with a maximum loan-to-value ratio of 85%. There are twelve of these banks.

FEDERAL NATIONAL MORTGAGE ASSOCIATION (FNMA) (FANNIE MAE) A corporation that provides a secondary market for FHA, VA, and conventional loans. Fannie Mae is the nation's largest private investor in American home mortgages. With assets of more than $90 billion, Fannie Mae is the third largest corporation in the United States. Although stock is now publicly owned, the president of the United States still has the authority to appoint five of the fifteen directors.

Fannie Mae is an entity of partially owned interests. Private shareholders benefit from a part of the corporation while the federal government benefits from another part. The change from the individual government corporation came in 1954 (Congress had declared Fannie Mae a government agency in 1938). Then, in 1968, it was separated in adaptation with Title III of the National Housing Act, 12 U.S.C. 1716, emerging into Ginnie Mae and Fannie Mae. Now, Fannie Mae entitlement is by shareholders. Although federally-chartered, Fannie Mae is a for-profit corporation, its purpose is to help finance housing by supplementing the supply of funds as a major purpose of secondary market operations. The goals of Fannie Mae are as follows:

- To generate earning sufficient to attract the equity and borrowed capital necessary to finance its operations, as required by its charter;

- To promote the stability of funds available for mortgage investment, therefore making available adequate liquidity to investors for the improvement of capital distribution for construction financing and sales of single-family housing and to carry on its activities at the lowest cost to the home buyer;

- To provide leadership in the housing and home finance industry through the development of new programs and techniques for housing finance. 1988 legislation eliminates new user fees on Fannie Mae programs;

- To purchase 1-4 family, multi-family FHA-insured, VA guaranteed mortgages, and conventional mortgage loans. Conventionals were authorized in 1970;

- To invest in long-term home loans and operate mortgage- backed securities programs in conventional, FHA and VA loans;

- To offer support in secondary markets to federal housing assistance program initiatives in the purchase of mortgages under these initiatives originated at prices dictated by the marketplace;

- To purchase second loans on single-family property;

- To purchase bi-weekly loans on single-family property.

The 1990 Fannie Mae mortgage limit was $187,450 based on previous October limits. Fannie Mae is open to purchase commitment on a negotiated basis but still offers its standard purchase programs to its sellers/servicers.

Supervision and servicing of FHA multi-family mortgages is conducted in-house but the approved lenders, under strict Fannie Mae supervision, service the single-family or conventional multi-family loans or both. Savings and loan institutions, mortgage banking companies, mutual savings banks, commercial banks, credit unions and other approved lenders are the sellers/servicers.

Junior mortgages (2nds) are serviced by finance companies when approved as seller/servicers.

Fannie Mae can use a backstop line of credit of $2.5 billion to the U.S. Treasury. Guaranteed mortgage-backed securities issued by Fannie Mae are backed by mortgage loans purchased by Fannie Mae that were pooled by its lenders from the portfolio maintained by the agency. These pass-throughs have coupons that may vary by a 200 basis point range in a fixed rate pool of underlying loans of 8-30 years.

Fannie Mae's mortgage portfolio is its major source of income and revenues are derived from debenture issuances, interest payments, discounts on short-term notes, and publicly-traded Fannie Mae stock. Within statutory limits, Fannie Mae may require sellers of mortgages to the corporation to buy its stock subject to the approval of the HUD Secretary.

Fee income is further derived from issuing mortgage purchase commitments and warranty fees from operating in mortgage-backed securities and the selling of conventional, FHA, and VA mortgage pass-through securities. It is exempt from federal securities law.

Fannie Mae approved seller/servicers can expect a borrower to anticipate a servicing fee as a negotiable or arbitrary net yield. A mortgage loan commitment based on 30 years is currently 37 1/2 basis points to service a Fannie Mae fixed rate loan. Adjustable rate loans call for a current 50 basis points to service these types of mortgages on a net yield basis. A required net yield, therefore, must be delivered before a 30-day period in order for Fannie Mae to execute a purchase.

Required net yields, when sold to Fannie Mae on a 30-year loan basis at face value, are called "purchase price at par" meaning that the mortgagee must write the mortgage with an interest rate conforming to par value yield with an added quantity for the necessary servicing. A mortgagee realizes a lower amount from the sale should an interest rate bear less than the "purchase price at par."

Interest rates vary on loans being pooled for sale to Fannie Mae or Freddie Mac by lenders in the bellwether state of California. As of July 24, 1988, borrowers are quoted rates, costs for obtaining loans, annual percentage rates, loan-to-value ratios, factors applied as adjustments for adjustable-rate mortgages, margins added to indexes on ARMs, the CAP rate change maximums for life of loan, term of loan, and programs designed for class of ownership as follows:

Amount: Mortgage maximum that is allowed in finance program groups.

Rate: Beginning rate of interest on the face of a note.

Cost: Points are a charge based on one percent of original loan amount as indicated.

APR: Annual percentage rate. The measure applied to credit costs covering interest, points, fees, and terms of loan amount (excepting mortgage insurance).

Factor: Mortgage amount multiplied by the factor and divided by 1000.

Margin: Rate adjustments are made by adding margin to the indexes.

X: Index. ARMs are adjusted by the index used by lenders.

LVR: Loan-to-value ratio is a property's value vs. the loan amount assigned.

CAP: An upper limit of changes in interest rates for the duration of the loan.

Class: Owner occupied (O), Non-owner occupied (N), Purchase (P), Refinance (R), Assumable (A).

FEDERAL RESERVE BANK One of twelve banks in the Federal Reserve System that operates in one of twelve Federal Reserve Districts. They are known as central, reserve, and regional banks. The table below gives the address, phone number and jurisdiction for each bank.

Boston
600 Atlantic Avenue
Boston, MA 02106
(617) 973-3000

Connecticut, (all but Fairfield County), Maine, Massachusetts, New Hampshire, Rhode Island, and Vermont.

Philadelphia
Ten Independence Mall
(P.O. Box 66)
Philadelphia, PA 19105
(215) 574-6000

Delaware, New Jersey (nine southern counties), Pennsylvania (48 counties in eastern two-thirds.

Richmond
701 East Byrd Street
Richmond, VA 23219
(804) 697-8000

District of Columbia, Maryland, North Carolina, South Carolina, Virginia, West Virginia (49 counties).

Chicago
230 South LaSalle Street
(P.O. Box 834)
Chicago, IL 60690
(312) 322-5322

Illinois (50 northern counties), Indiana (68 northern counties), Iowa, Michigan (68 southern counties), Wisconsin (46 southern counties).

New York
33 Liberty Street
Federal Reserve Postal Station
New York, NY 10045
(212) 720-5000

Connecticut, (Fairfield County), New Jersey (12 northern counties), New York.

Cleveland
1455 East Sixth Street
Cleveland, OH 44114
(216) 579-2000

Kentucky (56 eastern counties), Ohio, Pennsylvania (19 western counties), West Virginia (six northern counties).

Atlanta
104 Marietta Street, N.W.
Atlanta, GA 30303-2713
(404) 521-8500

Alabama, Florida, Georgia, Louisiana (38 southern parishes), Mississippi (43 southern counties), Tennessee (74 counties in eastern two-thirds).

St. Louis
411 Locust Street
(P.O. Box 442)
St. Louis, MO 63166
(314) 444-8444

Arkansas, Illinois (44 southern counties), Indiana (24 southern counties), Kentucky (64 western counties), Mississippi (39 northern counties), Missouri (71 central and eastern counties and the city of St. Louis), Tennessee (21 western counties).

Minneapolis
250 Marquette Avenue
Minneapolis, MN 55480
(612) 340-2345

Michigan (15 northern counties), Minnesota, Montana, North Dakota, South Dakota, Wisconsin (26 northern counties).

Dallas
400 South Akard Street
Station K
Dallas, TX 75222
(214) 651-6111

Louisiana (26 northern parishes), New Mexico (18 southern counties), Texas.

Kansas City
925 Grand Avenue
Federal Reserve Bank
Kansas City, MO 64198
(816) 881-2000

Colorado, Kansas, Missouri (43 western counties), Nebraska, New Mexico (14 northern counties), Oklahoma, Wyoming.

San Francisco
101 Market Street
(P.O. Box 7702)
San Francisco, CA 94120
(415) 974-2000

Alaska, Arizona, California, Hawaii, Idaho, Nevada, Oregon, Utah, Washington.

FEDERAL RESERVE SYSTEM (FRS) The Federal Reserve System is responsible for regulating availability of money as part of total monetary policies affecting credit. The Federal Reserve System controls the volume of bank deposits (the money supply) in order to control inflation while maintaining economic growth. All national as well as most state banks are members of the Federal Reserve System. The Federal Reserve system consists of 12 regional Federal Reserve Banks. The System is controlled by a Board of Governors charged with issuing rules and regulations that:

(1) Establish the total of reserves that member banks are required to sustain (subject to announced changes);

(2) Set maximum limits on interest rates to be paid on time and savings deposits for member banks;

(3) Regulate the discount rates, adjusting the credit in open markets for the issuance of securities, purchasing securities, and the holding of same for investment purposes; and

(4) Control the index used by member banks in ascertaining the cost of borrowing from the Federal Home Loan Bank Board national medium cost of funds.

FEDERAL SAVINGS AND LOAN ASSOCIATION A financial institution that is a member of the Federal Home Loan Bank System and the Federal Savings and Loan and Insurance Corporation.

FEDERAL SAVINGS AND LOAN INSURANCE CORPORATION (FSLIC) An agency of the federal government that insures the savings accounts of federally-chartered thrift institutions. Private companies may insure savings and loan associations without the backing of the federal government.

FEDERAL TRADE COMMISSION (FTC) Federal agency charged with the regulation of advertisements and promotions of companies engaged in interstate commerce. It is responsible for enforcing the truth-in-lending regulations.

FEDWIRE The system of book-entry settlement that is used for GNMA mortgage-backed securities in recording the new owner entitled to receive principal and interest payments. Fannie Mae and Freddie Mac are on the FedWire, as well as member banks of the Federal Home Loan Bank System. FedWire differs from the MBSCC Depository that features book-entry settlement through the depository that settles GNMA mortgage-backed securities.

FEE *See* COMMITMENT FEE.

FEE APPRAISER An appraiser who makes appraisals on a professional basis and charges a fee. An appraiser who operates as an independent contractor and is not part of a company staff.

Fee appraisers that are approved by FHA are said to be on the "HUD fee panel." For FHA loans, the 1990 Housing Bill allows lenders to select their appraisers rather than use an appraiser assigned by HUD.

See STAFF APPRAISER.

FEE SIMPLE Ownership of property that is believed to be unrestricted subject to certain powers such as police, eminent domain, or certain other restrictions for public benefit. It is the maximum form of ownership of a property.

Being unrestricted does not necessarily mean being free of encumbrances. For example, a mortgage on property that is owned in fee simple is an encumbrance.

Fee simple and a life estate are the only kinds of freehold estates. Besides a fee owner, there is no other form of ownership that gives the owner the right to place future restrictions on the property's use that goes beyond their interests.

FELONY A crime punishable by imprisonment in a state or federal prison. A felony usually is punishable by imprisonment for one year or more.

FELT Fibrous material used for sheathing on walls and roof. It is a highly absorbent insulation against heat, cold, and dampness.

FHA EXPERIENCE RATE The series of statistics portraying ratios and proportionate loans that exist a stated number of years from initial consummation. The series is adjusted from time to time.

FHLBB *See* FEDERAL HOME LOAN BANK BOARD.

FHLMC *See* FEDERAL HOME LOAN MORTGAGE CORPORATION.

FHLMC GUARANTOR POOLS Pools as low as $250,000 are available to smaller volume lenders for convenience and expediency. This feature helps those wishing not to mix coupon rates in a pool. The guarantor or "swap" PC program now guarantees the timely payment of principal like GNMA and FNMA MBSs.

Formerly, PCs guaranteed the ultimate payment of principal. Additionally, lenders can now designate the coupon rate of a participation certificate to three decimal places. The exact basis point participation certificate now replaces the rule of pegging participation certificates at quarter percent intervals. Small pools are known as baby pools.

FIDELITY OR SURETY BOND A bond-type of insurance used with condominiums and PUDs. The insurance applies to the project as a whole as opposed to the insurance needed by an owner of a unit.

Before buying a loan on a condo or a PUD, an investor will usually require a lender to certify that they have reviewed the insurance for the project. The form in Exhibit 19 is to be completed by the lender. *See* LOAN ORIGINATION, STEP 5.

FIDUCIARY One who acts in a financial role for the benefit of another.

FINAL CLOSING The date a permanent loan is closed. A loan for new construction usually involves two closing. The first closing is for the construction or short term loan. The second closing or final closing is for the permanent long term loan.

FINANCIAL ACCOUNTING STANDARDS BOARD (FASB) Created in 1973, FASB is a private independent entity that sets standards for financial accounting and reporting. It is a national board consisting of seven leading accountants from diverse backgrounds who work full time in developing or modifying accounting standards. This board establishes standards and policies for financial accounting practices. The Securities and Exchange Act of 1934 gave the SEC the authority to promulgate GAAP; but for the most part, the SEC has relied on the FASB and its predecessor, the Accounting Principle Board of the American Institute of Certified Public Accountants.

FINANCIAL FUTURES Futures contracts with mortgages or financial instruments as the underlying security. By nature, they are sensitive to interest rates and are sometimes called interest rate futures. Futures contracts are legally enforceable agreements for either the purchase or sale of a commodity for delivery at a future date and at an agreed-upon price.

There are two advantages of using interest rate futures. First, only price is decided by buyers and sellers or the exchange floor permitting quickly concluded transactions without negotiating terms. Second, they permit increased liquidity and the opportunity for offset since all contracts for delivery in the same month are identical permitting easy exchange.

People using financial futures are classified as follows: *Speculators* who focus on price change profit potential; *Hedgers* who focus on the avoidance of loss from price changes; *Arbitragers* who focus on price change profit potential without the assumption of financial risk.

FINANCIAL INSTITUTIONS REFORM, RECOVERY AND ENFORCE-MENT ACT OF 1989 (FIRREA) HR 1278 - PL 101-73, the most sweeping overhaul of laws governing savings and loan institutions in 55 years. President Bush signed the bailout measure August 9, 1989, promising an end to the thrift crisis and renewed stability for the nation's financial system. The new law

Exhibit 19

 FannieMae

Statement of Insurance and Fidelity Bond Coverage

Name of Project	Address of Project

Phase/Section	Type of Project (Condominium or PUD)

The following insurance information has been obtained by physical review of the insurance policies related to the above project.	Yes	No
1. Is Master or Blanket Type Fire and Extended Coverage Insurance in Force?		
Is the amount of insurance equal to 100% of the current replacement cost of the insurable improvements (if a condominium project) or 100% of the current replacement cost of the insurable improvements to the common areas (if a PUD)?		
The amount of such insurance in force is $_____		
The policy includes:		
Special Condominium Endorsement		
Standard Mortgage Clause or Equivalent		
Agreed Amount Endorsement		
Inflation Guard Endorsement		
Replacement Cost Endorsement		
Other Special Endorsement		
_____		
_____		
_____		
Is the project subject to a substantial construction code change that would be operative in the event of partial destruction of the project by an insured hazard?		
If yes, is this exposure protected by the appropriate endorsement?		

2. If a condominium, is there an insurance trustee? If yes, give name and address.

3. If the project contains a steam boiler, is a boiler insurance policy in effect?	4. Is a public liability insurance policy in force?	5. Is flood insurance in force?
☐ Yes ☐ No $	☐ Yes ☐ No $	☐ Yes ☐ No $

6. Are fidelity bonds in force in an amount at least equal to the estimated maximum amount of funds that will be in the custody of the Owners' Association or its management agent at any time during the term of each bond? ☐ Yes ☐ No

If "no," are the financial controls that justify a lesser amount among those specified in the Fannie Mae Selling Guide and is the coverage at least equal to the sum of three months' assessments on all units in the project? ☐ Yes ☐ No

Association $ Management Company $

7. Do the constituent documents of the project require the Owners' Association to maintain the insurance and fidelity bond coverage required by Fannie Mae? ☐ Yes ☐ No

I have reviewed the insurance policies applicable to the above project and certify to the best of my knowledge and belief that all of Fannie Mae's requirements on this subject as set out in the Fannie Mae Selling Guide have been met, except as indicated in the attachment hereto.

By (Signature)	Date

Name and Title of Lender's Underwriter	Lender's Name and Address

Fannie Mae Lender Number

abolished the independent Federal Home Loan Bank Board that had supervised the thrift industry and it dismantled the bankrupt Federal Savings and Loan Insurance Corporation (FSLIC) that had insured thrift deposits. The law created a new agency in the Treasury to charter and supervise thrifts. The FDIC now supervises the thrifts with a new insurance fund. The law requires thrifts to maintain a higher net worth.

In 1988, M. Danny Wall, chairman of the FHLBB, testified that a taxpayer bailout was not necessary. Mr. Wall said that all was needed was a $10.8 billion infusion of capital into the FSLIC. As the crises unfolded, it became apparent to all that the situation was much more serious than earlier projections. When the bailout was projected to be in excess of $200 billion, USA TODAY said the money needed was enough to send every man, woman, and child in Asia on a three-day trip to Disneyworld. Now the taxpayer bailout is estimated to cost in excess of $500 billion.

The final provisions of the bill are as follows:

- **Capital Standards.** The bill requires thrifts to have 3% core capital as required for banks, half must be in tangible assets, such as cash. Thrifts that had goodwill must write it off over five years. Thrifts that do not meet the capital standards will be subject to limits on asset growth and loss of insurance.

- **Financing.** The Resolution Funding Corporation (RFC), an off-budget agency, will fund the bailout by selling bonds. The Treasury will pay a part of the RFC borrowing, but part will be paid by earnings from the FHLB and from the sale of assets acquired from failed thrifts. The cost of the RFC is included in the budget but the increase to the deficit will not be included for Gramm-Rudman purposes. The Resolution Trust Corporation (RTC), a new on-Budget agency, took possession of all thrifts declared insolvent on January 1, 1989 and not in the receivership of the FSLIC.

- **Regulatory Changes.** Before FIRREA, all thrift regulatory and insurance functions were under the FHLBB and the FSLIC. After a short transition time, these two agencies will be abolished. The new regulatory structure for the thrift industry is as follows:

TREASURY

Office of Thrift Supervision

- charters federal thrifts;
- supervises state thrifts; and
- supervises thrift holding companies.

FEDERAL DEPOSIT INSURANCE CORPORATION (FDIC)

Savings Association Insurance Fund (SAIF)

- insures thrift deposits; and
- manages assets, liabilities of thrifts insolvent after 1992.

FSLIC Resolution Fund

- manages remaining assets and liabilities of FSLIC until assets are sold off.

RESOLUTION TRUST CORPORATION (RTC)

- manages assets, liabilities of thrifts insolvent before 1993 and operated by the FDIC; subject to oversight from five-member board chaired by the Treasury secretary, with secretary of Housing and Urban Development and chairman of the Federal Reserve Board as members;
- uses $50 billion provided by Treasury and the Resolution Funding Corporation; and
- terminates after 1996.

RESOLUTION FUNDING CORPORATION (RFC)

- borrows $30 billion from pubic to give to the RTC;
- purchases zero-coupon bonds using thrift industry money to repay principal on $30 billion; and
- pays interest on $30 billion using receipts from RTC, industry contributions and Treasury funds.

FEDERAL HOUSING FINANCE BOARD

- oversees Home Loan Bank System.

- **Junk Bonds.** Banned all junk bond investments by thrifts, but permits them by a separately capitalized affiliate of the thrift. Thrifts were given five years to sell off their holdings.
- **Quarterly Tests.** Quarterly requirements are stiffened to focus the thrift industry on home loans. Thrifts must have 55% of their assets in residential mortgage and construction loans and 70% in a broader basket that includes consumer loans.

- **Consumer and Housing Issues.** FIRREA expanded the Home Mortgage Disclosure Act of 1975 (HMDA) to require all mortgage lenders to collect and report information on the race, gender and income level of loan applicants and recipients. The Community Reinvestment Act of 1977 (CRA) was amended to require federal financial regulators to disclose summary evaluations and descriptive ratings of institutions under the act. FIRREA requires bank and thrift regulatory agencies to establish minimum standards for the performance of real-estate appraisals.

- **Freddie Mac and Fannie Mae.** FIRREA placed the FHLMC under a new, 18-member board similar to the board that governed its sister secondary-mortgage market institution, FNMA. FHLMC had been under the control of the FHLBB. Both Freddie Mac and Fannie Mae will be subject to oversight by the secretaries of the Treasury and of HUD.

FIRREA (HR 1278 - PL 101-73), the most sweeping overhaul of laws governing savings and loan institutions in 55 years.

See COMMUNITY REINVESTMENT ACT (CRA), HOME MORTGAGE DISCLOSURE ACT (HMDA), RESOLUTION TRUST CORPORATION (RTC).

FINANCIAL INTERMEDIARY The financial establishment that acts as a mediating agency between savers and borrowers by accepting monetary savings from the public and, in turn, lending the accumulated funds to borrowers in its own name. This class of intermediary institutions covers savings and loan associations, commercial banks, mutual savings banks, life insurance companies, credit unions, and pension funds.

FINDER'S FEE A fee that is paid to a party that finds a seller or a buyer for a real estate transaction. Some states prohibit a party from getting a finder's fee without being licensed to sell real estate. A finder's fee is called a referral fee. Most lenders have restrictions against paying a finder's fee to someone that refers a customer to them for a loan.

See BIRD DOG, and REAL ESTATE SETTLEMENT PROCEDURES ACT.

FIRE WALL A brick or incombustible wall built between buildings or part of a building whose main purpose is to stop the spreading of fire. The wall should rise three feet above roof level.

FIRM COMMITMENT *See* FHA - LOAN APPROVAL, THE FIRM COMMITMENT.

FIRREA *See* FINANCIAL INSTITUTIONS REFORM, RECOVERY AND ENFORCE-MENT ACT OF 1989 (FIRREA).

FIRST LIEN LETTER *See* REAL ESTATE SETTLEMENT PROCEDURE ACT (RESPA).

FIRST MORTGAGE A primary "original" mortgage loan that takes priority over all prior liens that are junior to the first mortgage debt. The real property security, as collateral for this primary mortgage, is evidence of the full appraised value at the precise time the loan is made. The only other lien taking priority over a first mortgage debt may conceivably be a mechanics lien. *See* MECHANICS LIEN.

FIXED BAY A window type. See WINDOW.

FIXED BOW A window type. See WINDOW.

FIXED RATE MORTGAGE (FRM) A term that once meant a mortgage made at a predetermined rate of interest that does not change over the life of the mortgage contract. Accrued interest affects the principal at a fixed rate of interest either monthly, quarterly, or semi-annually on an annually amortized basis. Each periodic installment on whatever basis is chosen, reduces the principal accordingly over the life of the loan. Traditionally these mortgages are long term. For example, a lender that makes a loan to a borrower for $50,000 at 15% for 30 years. The borrower makes monthly payments of $632.22. Over 30 years the borrower's total obligation for principal and interest would never exceed a fixed amount, but will gradually build equity.

Most people today define a fixed rate mortgage as follows: "If the interest rate remains the same for the term of your mortgage, you have an FRM" (fixed rate mortgage). The key word is *term*. If you have a conventional fixed-rate mortgage with a due-on-sale-clause, YOU DO NOT have a fixed-rate mortgage for the *term* of the loan. With a fixed-rate conventional loan it is possible for the loan to be assumed many times and *the interest rate raised each time. The conventional fixed-rate loan is fixed for only the period you own the house. Only FHA and VA loans* have fixed rates that remain the same for the *term* of the loan. This is a very important feature and one that may one day be taken away because the vast majority of the public, even real estate educators do not recognize this very important advantage of FHA and VA loans.

FIXTURE Personal property for improvements that are permanently affixed to the property so that it becomes real property. Built-in dishwashers, ovens, and microwaves are fixtures.

FLASHING Non-corrosive metal used around angles or junctions in roofs and exterior walls to insulate against leaks. Flashing is used around chimneys, vents, dormer windows, or valleys between two sections of a roof.

FLAT An apartment or one floor of a building used for rental purposes.

FLAT LEASE A lease that requires fixed level payments on an agreed upon time.

FLAT ROOF *See* ROOF.

FLEXIBLE LOAN INSURANCE PLAN (FLIP) A graduated payment mortgage with a pledged account. The account is set up as a reserve to offset the effects of payments that increase due to the graduated feature of the mortgage.

Usually, the lender holding the pledged account will pay interest on the funds. As the monthly payments increase, the pledged account can be drawn upon to either (1) lower the increase in the payments, (2) pay all the increase in the monthly payments, or (3) pay the negative amortization in the mortgage. If (3) is the case, the monthly payments will increase but there will be no negative amortization.

FLEXIBLE PAYMENT MORTGAGE (FPM) A loan that allows payment of interest only for a specific period, then combines principal and interest sufficient to amortize the mortgage.

FLIP *See* FLEXIBLE LOAN INSURANCE PLAN.

FLOATING RATE CMO A collateralized mortgage obligation with one or more tranches that pay a floating rate of interest.

FLOATING RATE TRANCHE These CMO innovations expanding the mortgage securities market by some secondary market conduits and mortgage bankers are the floating rate tranches formed by Wall Street firms in 1986. This vehicle, among others, is used primarily for selling old mortgages and promises to profit the issuer through arbitrage activities and thereby finances new mortgage production of 1-4 family homes. Most new mortgage production securities are jumbo loan conventional security not eligible for sale to Fannie Mae or Freddie Mac because of their size.

Potential MBS investors must be alert to the myriad of combinations being created. The structure, and other Wall Street innovations, will lower mortgage rates to the borrowers (according to some issuers) by at least one-fourth of one percent. They may be attributable to conventional mortgage rate spreads narrowing to Treasury bond rates as reported in recent trading activity. The creation of MBSs carry possible risks, an artificial yield not found in mortgage products of the past in customary terms of reference because of the REMIC bandwagon trend. CMO floaters earn 50 basis points above the LIBOR.

FLOOD INSURANCE Federal flood legislation states that a lender must require flood insurance on properties located in Special Flood Hazard Areas (SFHA) after such areas have been identified and coverage has become available through community participation in the program. The legislation further states that lenders *may not* make federally-related loans on properties in SFHA if the community does not qualify for participation in the program within a specified time after the areas are identified. The lender should make every effort to keep informed of the activity in mapping and community participation so that they can decide the location of a property within the SFHA. A lender should require the certification of a surveyor as an aid in making this determination. Compliance with the SFHA legislation is very important.

If the property is in a SFHA, the lender should require a copy of the application for flood insurance and the paid receipt for the first year's premium. Where flood insurance is required, the names, address of the property, and the loss payable clause should be the same as on the hazard insurance policy. Flood insurance should be a standard policy issued by members of the National Flood Insurers Association. The minimum amount of flood insurance is the lower of (1) 100 percent of the replacement value of the improvements; or (2) the maximum insurance available under the appropriate National Flood Insurance Administration program.

If the property is or will be in a flood zone, the borrower should sign the form shown in Exhibit 20.

FLOOR AREA RATIO The ratio of total floor area of a building to the total area of a site.

FLOOR JOIST The framing that supports the floor. The normal size for the floor joist is either "2 × 8" or "2 × 10."

FLOOR LOAN A mortgage with an initial funding based upon completion of a project with an additional funding occurring upon a specific condition, such as achievement of an occupancy level or a cash-flow requirement. A floor loan is an amount that is below the maximum loan.

FLOOR-TO-CEILING LOAN A loan used for construction of a project that can be increased upon reaching cash flow or occupancy requirements. It is a

Exhibit 20

70,994-N

1) Mail or deliver this notice as soon as feasible but not less than 10 days prior to settlement.
2) Obtain signed copy by borrower of this notice prior to settlement.

NOTICE TO BORROWER OF
SPECIAL FLOOD HAZARD AND
FEDERAL DISASTER ASSISTANCE

Date
Borrowers Name(s)

Mail Address

Property Address

Lender

Notice to Borrower of Special Flood Hazard

You are hereby notified that the improved real estate or mobile home described above is or will be located in an area designated by the Director of Federal Emergency Management Agency as a special flood hazard area. This area is delineated on _____'s Flood Insurance Rate Map (FIRM) or, if the FIRM is unavailable, on the Flood Hazard Boundary Rate Map (FHBM). This area has a 1% chance of being flooded within any given year. The risk of exceeding the 1% chance increases with time periods longer than one year. For example, during the life of a 30 year mortgage, a structure located in a special flood hazard area has a 26% chance of being flooded.

Notice to Borrower About Federal Flood Disaster Assistance
(Lender Check One)

☐ Notice in Participating Communities

The improved real estate or mobile home securing your loan is or will be located in a community which is now participating in the National Flood Insurance Program. In the event your property is damaged by flooding in a Federally declared disaster, Federal disaster relief may be available. However, such relief will be unavailable if your community is not participating in the National Flood Insurance Program at the time such assistance would be approved (assuming your community has been identified as flood-prone for at least one year). This assistance, usually in the form of a loan with a favorable interest rate, may be available for damages incurred in excess of your flood insurance.

☐ Notice in Non-participating Communities

The improved real estate or mobile home securing your loan is or will be located in a community which is not participating in the National Flood Insurance Program. This means that you are not eligible for Federal flood insurance. In the event your property is damaged by flooding in a Federally declared disaster, Federal disaster relief will be unavailable (assuming your community has been identified as flood-prone for at least one year). Federal flood disaster relief will be available only if your community is participating in the National Flood Insurance Program at the time such assistance would be approved.

Acknowledgement by Borrower

Delivery of these notices is hereby acknowledged.

Borrower's Signature:_____ Date_____

Borrower's Signature:_____ Date_____

VMP-525 (8911)   VMP MORTGAGE FORMS • (313)293-8100 • (800)521-7291   11/89

loan involving two closing. The first closing is upon completion of construction, the second is upon reaching an occupancy or rent level.

FLOW SALE A negotiated agreement to sell particular amounts of servicing on a monthly delivery schedule at an agreed price. Large mortgage servicing pool portfolios are not necessary in flow sale arrangements where the servicing price is predetermined rather than a price determined for a pooled package or bloc transaction.

FHA/VA loans are eligible when servicing is released to the buyer on a co-issuer plan with the seller handling marketing arrangements for the insured/guaranty type of mortgage. A servicing released fee is paid on a monthly basis.

FLUE A duct or pipe for the passage of air, smoke, or gases. Smoke passes through a flue in a chimney.

FMHA *See* FARMERS HOME ADMINISTRATION.

FMP *See* FANNIE MAJOR POOLS.

FNMA *See* FEDERAL NATIONAL MORTGAGE ASSOCIATION.

FNMA OFFERS Fannie Mae offers steep discounts on some loans so that lenders may sell seven-year-balloon mortgages to Fannie Mae at 30 basis points below the required net yield on 15-year-fixed-rate loans and may sell 10-year-fully-amortizing mortgages at 25 basis points below 15-year loans under Fannie Mae intermediate- term standby (ITS) commitments established in March 1986.

Fannie Mae added four products to its regular programs with the ITS commitments: seven- and ten-year balloon mortgages with 30-year amortization schedules and 10- and 20-year fully amortizing fixed rate mortgages. To these products, growing equity mortgages and 15-year-fixed-rate mortgages were added to complete the ITS offering.

ITS is available through Fannie Mae regional offices on a negotiated basis. It covers only fixed rate mortgages to be purchased for the Fannie Mae portfolio. Lenders may continue to sell 15-year loans through Fannie Mae's standard programs. There is no initial fee for the ITS. It is optional except for a fee of 25 basis points of any unused amount payable at the end of the six-month term.

Converting the commitment costs .25% for 10-year-fixed-rate mortgages; .50% for balloon loans and 15-year mortgages; .75% for 20-year loans; and 1% for GEMs. Upon conversion, lenders obtain mandatory commitments for delivery in 10, 30, or 90 days. Only one product may be included in each conversion that must be in amounts of $100,000 or more. Lenders may choose the amounts of each six products to convert and deliver within the total commitment figure.

Net yields required by Fannie Mae are pegged to the standard yield for 15-year-fixed-rate mortgages on the day of each conversion. As noted above, lenders can lock in a spread of 30 basis points below the 15-year rate for seven-year balloons and 25 basis points below the 15-year rate for 10-year-fully-amortizing mortgages. The current conversion yield for 10-year balloons is the same as the 15-year rate. The current yield for GEMs is 10-15 basis points above the 15-year rate; for 20-year loans, the yield is 20 basis points above the 15-year rate.

Fannie Mae will not make a commitment to borrowers to supply financing when balloon loans come due. A balloon loan without such a commitment may be illegal in some states. Balloon loans may have special disclosure requirements for national banks. Fannie Mae is developing policies and guidelines for lenders on these matters. Fannie Mae is developing borrower profile for new products. Currently, lenders are reporting that borrowers asking for 10-year loans are similar to those wanting 15-year loans.

Differences between 30- and 10-year mortgages are similar to but more pronounced than the differences between 30- and 15-year mortgages. The benefits to the borrower of 10-year loans are faster equity build-up and substantial interest savings. The drawback is a higher monthly payment. Fannie Mae says that intermediate-term mortgages have been steadily gaining consumer popularity. In 1986, it purchased 15,000 10-, 20- and 25-year loans and placed them into 15- and 30-year pools. From 1985 to 1986, according to the National Association of Realtors, loans of 20-25 years gained market share from seven percent to eight percent of fixed rate conventional loans, while 10-year loans lost market share, from two percent to one percent.

Characteristics of 15-year borrowers, expected in 10-year borrowers as well, include higher than average income; the need to be free of mortgage payments when paying children's college bills or before retirement; past experience as a home borrower (including many refinance borrowers); sophisticated borrowers who like the lower interest rate; and many young professionals, move-up buyers, and empty nesters.

Twenty-year mortgages may have strong appeal to borrowers who would like a 15-year loan but do not qualify or do not feel that they can properly budget the required monthly payments. On a $65,920 loan, monthly payments on a 20-year loan are $58 more than on a 30-year loan. Payments on a 15-year loan are $66 more than on a 20-year loan.

Fannie Mae now purchases bi-weekly mortgages. They attract borrowers similar to those that take other intermediate-term loans. At current rates, 30-year bi-weeklies pay off in about 22 years. Two major advantages of intermediate-term loans for Fannie Mae are lower delinquencies and shorter average duration before payoff, allowing Fannie Mae to match the loan with slightly shorter-term debt.

FOOTING The base of a foundation wall. A footing distributes the weight of a superstructure over a greater area to resist shifting or settling. *See* FOUNDATION WALL.

FORBEARANCE AGREEMENT In an attempt to avoid foreclosure, a lender *may* follow accepted rules of forbearance when a borrower has become delinquent in monthly payments. Forbearance agreements are usually in writing and should be watched carefully to ensure that they are complied with in accordance to the Equal Credit Opportunity Act (ECOA) and the Consumer Credit Protection Act.

FHA and VA list certain conditions for written forbearance agreements with mortgagors on insured or guaranteed loans or both. The default must have occurred through no fault of the borrower - - curtailment of income, inadequate insurance coverage for damages suffered to the property resulting in financial hardship to the borrower or illness, deaths, or other uncontrollable problems. Loan installments can be waived, but must not exceed specified limits set by the FHA Commissioner.

Besides the forbearance determination, a lending institution, under salvage powers, is permitted to arrange specific agreements with mortgagors that extend far past its usual operations. For example, an institution that is controlled by state charter must follow state regulations in the determination of salvage powers. For instance, in a loan on a single-family-existing home, where an owner has paid the installments for five years on a 30-year loan and becomes disabled on the job and cannot meet the monthly housing obligations, federal S&L salvage powers enable the lender to reduce payments to whatever extended loan term is prudent under the circumstances. This may conceivably mean a new mortgage term of 45 years—a 20-year spread for meeting the new income.

FORECLOSURE The legal action allowing a mortgagee to sell a mortgagor's property in an attempt to satisfy the debt. The lawful course of action taken by a mortgagee under the provisions of a mortgage or deed of trust when a mortgagor has become delinquent and all attempted agreements to bring the loan current have failed. Foreclosure, as it is expensive to the lender, is generally pursued as a last resort to recover, in whole or in part, the remaining loan balance.

There are three types of foreclosure, judicial foreclosure, non-judicial, and strict foreclosure.

In *judicial foreclosure* there is no provision in the mortgage giving the lender the right to foreclose without court action. The property will be sold by a court order.

In *non-judicial foreclosure* the lender has the power of sale in the mortgage documents. If there is a deed of trust, the trustee sells the property. If there is just the mortgage, the lender sells the property. The lender or the trustee is required to give sufficient public notice.

In *strict foreclosure* the lender asks the court for permission to take the property used as collateral. After a time, established by the court, if the borrower has not satisfied the debt, the court awards the property to the lender. There is no deficiency judgement in a strict foreclosure.

Lenders normally have established guidelines for starting a foreclosure. For FHA and VA loans, the agencies (FHA or VA) have great influence on when foreclosure proceedings can begin. As noted in FORBEARANCE AGREEMENT, agencies have alternative plans for the homeowner that is having a hardship beyond their control.

See LIEN THEORY and TITLE THEORY.

FORECLOSURE PAYMENT Proceeds made to owners of mortgage-backed securities from a property liquidation after foreclosure. The funds from prepayments will equal the principal balances on the foreclosed mortgage loans.

FORFEITURE Loss of money or valuable consideration because of failure to perform under the terms of an agreement.

See DAMAGES.

FORMICA A plastic material most commonly used for kitchen cabinet tops.

FORWARD DELIVERY COMMITMENT A written promise to make an investment at some point in the future providing that specified conditions are met. Generally, a written contract for the sale of many mortgages, mortgage-backed securities or other securities at a given price or yield within a specified time. Securities are typically traded on a 60 to 120 day forward-delivery basis while whole loan mortgages are usually sold under commitments of at least six months, and they may be of longer duration.

FORWARD COMMITMENT A commitment by a lender to purchase or make a loan in the future. A definite promise to do something in the future in a specified time. To promise a loan or to buy a mortgage is a forward commitment.

FORWARD DELIVERY The purchase or sale of mortgages and mortgage-backed securities for forward delivery. Selling under a forward delivery commitment affords the mortgage banker the necessary opportunity to sell the commitment before funding, hedging against changes in interest rates. The purchaser can lock-in a preferred investment rate before the mortgage assets are available for purchase.

FORWARD SALE An agreement between a lender and an investor to sell particular kinds of loans at a specified price in the future. The most common type of forward sale is a mandatory delivery commitment (or similar such contract) with a dealer or investor.

FOUNDATION WALL A wall of poured concrete or concrete blocks that rests on top of the footing. The weight of the house rests on top of the foundation wall that rests on top of the footing. Check foundation walls for bowing, crumbling, and cracks. If any of these signs appear there could be serious structure problems, minor hairline cracks in the masonry wall of the foundation being a possible exception.
See FOOTING.

FOYER Hallway or open area at the entrance of a building.

FPM *See* FLEXIBLE PAYMENT MORTGAGE.

FRANCHISE The authorization or license to do business and operate under the methods of another.

FRAUD Intending to misrepresent facts or figures purposely to deceive another party such as a creditor.
See DUAL CONTRACT, RECOVERY FUND.

FREDDIE MAC Nickname for Federal Home Loan Mortgage Corporation.
See FEDERAL HOME LOAN MORTGAGE CORPORATION.

FREEHOLD Estate that is free of a time limitation.

FRENCH PROVINCIAL

French Provincial. A French style 1 to 2 1/2 story house that has a steep hip roof, usually a chimney in the center of the house and arched windows.

FRM *See* FIXED RATE MORTGAGE.

FRONT FEE A buyer of a split-fee option pays an initial fee when executing a trade in pipeline hedging. The characteristics of the underlying mortgage pipeline effects the front fee size of the date of the first expiration (or window date). The two variables are important to the lender and investor as they prepare to tailor mortgage pipelines in over-the-counter (OTC) options on mortgage-related securities. Hedging interest rate risk is the compensating goal.

FRONT FOOTAGE The linear measurement along the front portion of a parcel that adjoins a major street or walkway.

FRONT MONEY Money needed to start a project that is generally furnished by the developer or owner as their capital contribution.

FROST LINE The depth that soil freezes. Footings should be dug lower than the frost line to prevent settling.

FRS *See* FEDERAL RESERVE SYSTEM.

FSLIC *See* FEDERAL SAVINGS AND LOAN INSURANCE CORPORATION.

FULLY-INDEXED RATE An interest rate on an Adjustable Rate Mortgage that equals the index plus the margin.

FULLY MODIFIED Pass-through MBSs called fully modified are those securities that pass to investors bearing all scheduled interest and principal payments on the mortgages underlying the security. Issuers are accountable for replacing delinquent installments and therefore responsive to pass-throughs required by the GNMA program, including principal prepayments as received by the issuer.

FUNCTIONAL OBSOLESCENCE A loss of value created by causes within the property. Structure, equipment, or floor plan that has become inefficient because of innovative changes that have occurred since its construction.

FUNDING DATE Mortgage banker language for stating a date that the mortgage banker funds new issues of mortgage-backed securities.

FUNDING FEE *See* VA - FUNDING FEE.

FURRING Narrow strips of wood used to level up a pad of a wall or floor or between a wall and plaster to provide air space.

G

GAAP *See* GENERALLY ACCEPTED ACCOUNTING PRINCIPALS.

GABLE ROOF A ridged roof, triangular in shape.
See ROOF.

GAMBREL ROOF A ridged roof with four slopes in total.
See ROOF.

GAP FINANCING Financing used by contractors to close the gap between the floor loan and the construction loan (see floor loan and construction loan). What normally triggers the need for gap financing is when the construction lender will not advance anymore funds unless the permanent lender issues a commitment large enough to payoff the construction loan. The permanent lender won't issue the commitment the construction lender wants until the project has been completed and certain conditions have been met, such as a minimum rent-up level. This impasse leaves the developer in need of a gap loan that usually comes in the form of a second mortgage.

In residential lending, buyers sometimes have the need for a bridge or swing loan to close a loan while they wait on a previous home to sell.
See BRIDGE FINANCING.

GARNISHMENT A legal action that enables a creditor to have an employer withhold an employee's wages to be used in payment of a debt.

GEM *See* GROWING EQUITY MORTGAGE.

GENERALLY ACCEPTED ACCOUNTING PRINCIPLES (GAAP) An approach to accounting or reporting a true portfolio sale that gives recognition to either a profit or a loss. These principles are issued by the AICPA. GAAP is specifically determined and mandated by the Financial Accounting Standards Board as standards set forth in procedures for comparing financial results in statements. For example, in accounting for profits from sales of real property under GAAP, the gain is calculated by various economic considerations, unlike the gains reported for tax determination. In GAAP, accounting gains include a purchaser's first and recurring cash investment plus the property's power to perform cash flow to service debt as furnished by the seller upon actual sale. As of January 1, 1989, federally-chartered thrifts must use GAAP.

GAAP accounting is the reporting of financial accounting information according to the rules and conventions, called Generally Accepted Accounting

Principles, as promulgated by the Financial Accounting Standards Board (FASB). The purpose of GAAP is to provide assurance to outside users of financial statements that they are prepared according to a generally understood set of rules. For example, GAAP provides for the use of the lower of cost or market valuation with respect to loans held in inventory for sale. Since these assets possess characteristics akin to accounts receivable and merchandise inventory, GAAP mandates reduction in book values to the lower of cost or market for these inventories.

GENERAL CONTRACTOR The general contractor or prime contractor is the party engaged either to construct or to supervise a construction project. A general contractor may hire other contractors known as subcontractors.

GENERAL PARTNER A partner who acts for a limited partnership. The general partner has the power to bind the partnership to contracts and other obligations, and is fully liable for the debts of the partnership. The general partner can be a corporation or an individual.

GENERAL PARTNERSHIP A form of business where two or more owners, or partners, conduct a business for a profit. All owners share fully in the profits or losses of the business. A general partnership is subject to dissolution if one partner dies, withdraws, or files bankruptcy.

GENERAL WARRANTY DEED *See* WARRANTY DEED.

GESTATION REPO A repurchase agreement covering the time between the date an issuer submits documents to the GNMA for the final pool approval and the date the new security is issued. The normal gestation repo period is twenty calendar days.

GIC *See* GUARANTEED INVESTMENT CONTRACT.

G.I. LOAN *See* VA LOAN.

GIFT LETTER Most lenders allow a borrower to provide all or at least some of the required downpayment for a loan in the form of a gift from a third party. The guidelines for using a gift as a source for the downpayment may vary in detail but most will have the following requirements:

(1) Any donor must be a related or interest party, such as a member of the family.

(2) The gift must be a genuine gift, there can be no provisions for repayment at a later date.

(3) The donor must have the available funds to make the gift. The donor is not allowed to borrow the money to make the gift. An exception to this guideline is borrowing against a secured asset such as a CD that has not matured.

(4) The donor must state the source of the gift, e.g., bank, CD, credit union, etc.

Depending upon the type of loan and the investor requirements, the lender will usually ask for verification, by a VOD, of the source of funds for the donor and the receipt of funds by the borrower. Lenders can use the form in Exhibit 21 when a borrower uses a gift for a downpayment.

GINGERBREAD Excessive ornamentation on a house. Used with Victorian-style houses.

GINNIE MAE Nickname for Government National Mortgage Association. *See* GOVERNMENT NATIONAL MORTGAGE ASSOCIATION.

GINNIE MAE GUARANTY FEE A guaranty fee that issuers pay for GNMA securities. If it becomes necessary for a raise in the fee because of a rise in costs to the agency, GNMA must notify Congress within 90 days before raising the fee. The fee guarantees the full faith and credit of the federal government in guaranteeing the timely payment of principal and interest plus prepayments of GNMA mortgage-backed securities. The current guaranty fee is six basis points. Fees are imposed in the purchase of FNMA and FHLMC guarantees but do not carry the full faith and credit of the federal government that GNMAs do and are subject to agency control.

GMC *See* GUARANTEED MORTGAGE CERTIFICATE.

GNMA *See* GOVERNMENT NATIONAL MORTGAGE ASSOCIATION.

GNMA I A security issued by GNMA and backed by a pool of FHA or VA mortgages with timely payment of principal and interest guaranteed by GNMA. Issuers approved by GNMA are required to pay the MBS holders directly. This program is governed under provisions contained in GNMA Handbook 5500.1. See the table at the end of the definition of GOVERNMENT NATIONAL MORTGAGE ASSOCIATION.

Exhibit 21

INSTRUCTIONS TO LENDER:
1. Fill out Part I - Request
2. Pull yellow copy & file for follow up
3. Forward other 2 copies (carbon intact) to Donor

INSTRUCTIONS TO DONOR:
1. Complete Part II
2. Return both completed copies to Lender

INSTRUCTIONS TO DEPOSITORY:
1. Complete Part III
2. Return both completed copies to lender

 -24G (8902) 01

VMP MORTGAGE FORMS • (313)293-8100 • (800)521-7291

REQUEST FOR VERIFICATION OF GIFT/GIFT LETTER

INSTRUCTIONS: Lender - Complete Items 1 through 6 and mail to Donor listed in Item 1.

PART I - REQUEST

1. TO (Name and Address of Donor)	2. FROM (Name and Address of Lender)		
3. Signature of Lender	4. Title	5. Date	6. Loan Number

We have been advised that you are the donor of a monetary gift to the applicant(s) for the purpose of a home purchase. Please complete Part II below.

PART II - TO BE COMPLETED BY DONOR (Donor - Please complete Part II and return to Lender listed in Item 2 above.)

7. Dollar Amount of Gift	8. Donor's Phone Number	9. Relationship to Applicant(s)

10. Donor's Statement and Signature
    I/We state that no repayment of this gift is expected.

(signature)

11.

Funds have been transferred to applicant
Date Transferred:
(complete Items 12 and 13)

Funds currently held in my account
(complete Items 12 through 15)

12. Name of Donor's Depository	13. Account Number
14. Address of Depository	15. Authorization to Verify this Information

(signature)

PART III - TO BE COMPLETED BY DEPOSITORY (Depository - Please complete Part III and return to Lender in Item 2 above.)

16. Account Number	17. Current Balance	
18. Signature of Depository	19. Title	20. Date

The confidentiality of the information you have furnished will be preserved except where disclosure of this information is required by applicable law. The form is to be transmitted directly to the lender and is not to be transmitted through the applicant(s) or any other party.

-24G (8902) 01   VMP MORTGAGE FORMS • (313)293-8100 • (800)521-7291   2/89

DONOR/DEPOSITORY-RETURN BOTH COPIES TO LENDER
LENDER-DETACH THIS COPY AND FILE FOR FOLLOW-UP

GNMA II A security issued by GNMA backed by a pool of FHA or VA mortgages where GNMA relies on a central paying agent, rather than the issuer, for making the principal and interest payments to holders of the securities. This program is governed by the provisions outlined in GNMA Handbook 5500.2. See the table at the end of the definition of GOVERNMENT NATIONAL MORTGAGE ASSOCIATION.

GNMA REPURCHASE AGREEMENT A financing technique, commonly called repos, involving the sale of GNMA pass-throughs to a dealer while, at the same time, the seller agrees to repurchase them at a later date at an agreed upon price. There is no recorded transfer and the dealer holds the GNMA certificate.

GNMA WARRANT Warrants are used by MBS holders as a hedging strategy to limit prepayment risk involving Ginnie Mae pass-through securities. Warrants, which are similar to options, serve more efficiently. They are essentially certificates that enable the holder to purchase a security at a specified or "strike" price at a future date. A warrant contract is unlike a futures contract in that exercising the deal on time depends on whether or not the buyer will honor the warrant.

If the strike price is less than the market price, the issuer is still obligated to deliver the warrant holder's security at this lower contract price. On the other hand, the warrant expires valueless if the market price proves less than the strike price.

Additionally, options expire in six months or less while warrants are usually valid for one year or longer. The analogous due date structure of GNMAs resemble European options in that they must be acted upon during a date assigned before expiration. The scheduled date for the performance of same is an important part of the futures delivery contract. The warrant structure of GNMAs represents an option modeled after European investments rather than options modeled after American standards that can be acted upon at any time during the investment life. The European option refers to a time for performance. It does not refer to any particular investment vehicle in a foreign nation; thus, an investment in an American concern may have a European option while the American option can be placed on an investment in European interests as to the time of performance.

GOING LONG A lender originates loans before arranging a commitment from an investor to buy the loans.

GOING SHORT A lender finds an investor to buy loans before they are originated.

GOOD FAITH ESTIMATE A good faith estimate, or disclosure, of the settlement charges the mortgagor will incur at closing. A good faith estimate of settlement charges is required by the Real Estate Settlement Procedures Act.
Below are good faith estimate forms.
In Florida, a lender will use the good faith estimate form shown in Exhibit 26.
Below is a Uniform Mortgage Loan Cost Worksheet.
See REAL ESTATE SETTLEMENT PROCEDURES ACT.

GOTHIC

Gothic. A nineteenth century style house featuring: steep roofs, much gingerbread molding and trim, many different shapes and angles, ornate windows and doors, exposed framing members and extremely pointed gables.

GOVERNMENT NATIONAL MORTGAGE ASSOCIATION (GNMA)
The Government National Mortgage Association, known as "GNMA" or "Ginnie Mae," is a wholly-owned corporate instrumentality of the United States Government within the Department of Housing and Urban Development. It was created by Congress in 1968 through federal legislation.
GNMA's role as a federal corporation is to support the government's housing objectives by establishing secondary market facilities for residential mortgages, using private capital to the maximum extent feasible. Through its mortgage-backed securities programs, GNMA serves to increase the supply of

Exhibit 22

TRUTH-IN-LENDING ADDENDUM

Borrower: _____   Date: _____

_____   Loan No.: _____

Property: _____

_____

Listed below is the GOOD FAITH ESTIMATE OF SETTLEMENT CHARGES made pursuant to the requirements of the REAL ESTATE SETTLEMENT PROCEDURES ACT (RESPA). These figures are only estimates and the actual charges due at settlement may be different. This is not a commitment to make a loan. For a further explanation of the charges, consult the enclosed Special Information Booklet, SETTLEMENT COSTS AND YOU.

This form does not cover all items you will be required to pay in cash at settlement, for example, deposits in escrow for real estate taxes and insurance may be different. You may wish to inquire as to the amounts of such other items. You may be required to pay other additional amounts at settlement.

(   ) If checked, all disclosures below are estimates.

ITEMIZATION OF THE AMOUNT FINANCED: LOAN AMOUNT $ _____

+ **Prepaid Finance Charges:**

Origination Fee @_____ % $ _____

Discount Fee @_____ %   _____

_____   _____

_____   _____

_____   _____

_____   _____

Prepaid Interest (_____ Days)   _____

@ _____ % Per Annum   _____

_____   _____

PREPAID FINANCE CHARGES: (_____)

AMOUNT FINANCED: $ _____

+ **Amount Paid To Others On Your Behalf:**

Appraisal Fees $ _____

Credit Report   _____

Lender's Inspection Fee   _____

_____   _____

_____   _____

Closing or Escrow Fee   _____

Abstract and/or Title Search   _____

Title Examination   _____

Title Insurance Binder   _____

Attorney Fees   _____

Title Insurance   _____

_____   _____

Recording Fees   _____

Document Taxes   _____

Recording Notice of Commencement   _____

Survey (required by Lender)   _____

Pest Inspection   _____

Const. Disbursing or Inspection Agent Fee   _____

1st Year's Hazard and/or Flood Insurance Premiums   _____

AMOUNT PAID TO OTHERS ON YOUR BEHALF: (_____)

+ **Amount Paid On Your Account:**

Real Estate Tax Escrow (_____ Mos) $ _____

Hazard Insurance Escrow (_____ Mos)   _____

Other Escrows_____   (_____ Mos)   _____

AMOUNT PAID ON YOUR ACCOUNT: (_____)

AMOUNT GIVEN TO YOU DIRECTLY: $ _____

The undersigned hereby acknowledges receiving and reading a completed copy of this Disclosure prior to the consummation of the loan. Neither you nor the Lender previously has become obligated to make or accept this loan, nor is any such obligation made by the delivery or signing of this Disclosure.

_____   _____
VMP-16B (8709)   Date   Date
TM
VMP MORTGAGE FORMS • (313)293-8100 • (800)521-7291

Exhibit 23

-17 (8903)   VMP MORTGAGE FORMS • (313)293-8100 • (800)521-7291

GOOD FAITH ESTIMATE — RESPA

		AMOUNT
APPLICANT(S)		**OF SALE**
PROPERTY ADDRESS		☐ FHA ☐ VA ☐ CONVENTIONAL
		LOAN AMOUNT **INTEREST RATE**

This list gives an estimate of most of the charges you will have to pay at the settlement of your loan. The figures shown as estimates, are subject to change. The figures shown are computed based on sales price and proposed mortgage amount as stated on your loan application.

ESTIMATED SETTLEMENT CHARGES

NUMBERS FROM HUD-1 FORM	DESCRIPTION OF CHARGES	ESTIMATED AMOUNT OR RANGE From	To
801	LOAN ORIGINATION FEE	$	to
802	LOAN DISCOUNT	$	to
803	APPRAISAL FEE	$	to
804	CREDIT REPORT	$	to
805	INSPECTION FEE	$	to
806	MORTGAGE INSURANCE APPLICATION FEE	$	to
807	ASSUMPTION FEE	$	to
808	UNDERWRITING FEE	$	to
		$	
		$	
901	INTEREST ADJUSTMENT	$	to
902	MORTGAGE INSURANCE PREMIUM	$	to
		$	to
1101	SETTLEMENT OR CLOSING FEE	$	to
1105	DOCUMENT PREPARATION FEE	$	to
1107	ATTORNEY'S FEES	$	to
1108	TITLE INSURANCE	$	to
1201	RECORDING FEES	$	to
1202	CITY/COUNTY TAX/STAMPS	$	to
1203	STATE TAX/STAMPS	$	to
1301	SURVEY	$	to
1302	PEST INSPECTIONS	$	to
OTHERS		$	to
		$	to
		$	to
1400 & 103	ESTIMATED SETTLEMENT CHARGES		
	TOTAL EST. CHARGES		

(FROM / ABOVE) * This interest calculation represents the greatest amount of interest you could be required to pay at settlement. The actual amount will be determined by which day of the month your settlement is conducted. To determine the amount you will have to pay, multiply the number of days remaining in the month in which you settle times $ _____ , which is the daily interest charge for your loan.

"THIS FORM DOES NOT COVER ALL ITEMS YOU WILL BE REQUIRED TO PAY IN CASH AT SETTLEMENT, FOR EXAMPLE, DEPOSIT IN ESCROW FOR REAL ESTATE TAXES AND INSURANCE. YOU MAY WISH TO INQUIRE AS TO THE AMOUNTS OF SUCH OTHER ITEMS." YOU MAY BE REQUIRED TO PAY OTHER ADDITIONAL AMOUNTS AT SETTLEMENT.

1. The Undersigned Acknowledges Receipt of This Good Faith Estimate of Charges.
2. The HUD Guide for Home Buyers, entitled, Settlement Costs.

APPLICANT _____ BY _____

APPLICANT _____ PER _____ DATE _____

REV. (4/78)

-17 (8903)   VMP MORTGAGE FORMS • (313)293-8100 • (800)521-7291

Exhibit 24

68810H

○-17P (2 PLY) (8903)   VMP MORTGAGE FORMS • (313)293-8100 • (800)521-7291

GOOD FAITH ESTIMATE — RESPA

APPLICANT(S) _____

AMOUNT
OF SALE

PROPERTY
ADDRESS _____

☐ FHA   ☐ VA   ☐ CONVENTIONAL

LOAN
AMOUNT

INTEREST
RATE

This list gives an estimate of most of the charges you will have to pay at the settlement of your loan. The figures shown as estimates, are subject to change. The figures shown are computed based on sales price and proposed mortgage amount as stated on your loan application.

ESTIMATED SETTLEMENT CHARGES

NUMBERS FROM HUD-1 FORM	DESCRIPTION OF CHARGES	DESIGNATED PROVIDER REFERENCE	ESTIMATED AMOUNT OR RANGE From	To
801.	LOAN ORIGINATION FEE		$	to
802.	LOAN DISCOUNT		$	to
803.	APPRAISAL FEE		$	to
804.	CREDIT REPORT		$	to
805.	INSPECTION FEE		$	to
806.	MORTGAGE INSURANCE APPLICATION FEE		$	to
807.	ASSUMPTION FEE		$	to
808.	UNDERWRITING FEE		$	to
			$	to
			$	
(SEE BELOW)* 901.	INTEREST ADJUSTMENT		$	to
902.	MORTGAGE INSURANCE PREMIUM		$	to
			$	to
1101.	SETTLEMENT OR CLOSING FEE		$	to
1105.	DOCUMENT PREPARATION FEE		$	to
1107.	ATTORNEY'S FEES		$	to
1108.	TITLE INSURANCE		$	to
1201.	RECORDING FEES		$	to
1202.	CITY/COUNTY TAX/STAMPS		$	to
1203.	STATE TAX/STAMPS		$	to
1301.	SURVEY		$	to
1302.	PEST INSPECTIONS		$	to
OTHERS: _____	_____		$	to
_____	_____		$	to
			$	to
1400 & 103	ESTIMATED SETTLEMENT CHARGES		▓▓▓▓▓	

TOTAL EST. CHARGES

(FROM ABOVE) * This interest calculation represents the greatest amount of interest you could be required to pay at settlement. The actual amount will be determined by which day of the month your settlement is conducted. To determine the amount you will have to pay, multiply the number of days remaining in the month in which you settle times $ _____ , which is the daily interest charge for your loan.

"THIS FORM DOES NOT COVER ALL ITEMS YOU WILL BE REQUIRED TO PAY IN CASH AT SETTLEMENT, FOR EXAMPLE, DEPOSIT IN ESCROW FOR REAL ESTATE TAXES AND INSURANCE. YOU MAY WISH TO INQUIRE AS TO THE AMOUNTS OF SUCH OTHER ITEMS." YOU MAY BE REQUIRED TO PAY OTHER ADDITIONAL AMOUNTS AT SETTLEMENT.

THIS SECTION TO BE COMPLETED BY LENDER ONLY IF A PARTICULAR PROVIDER OF SERVICE IS REQUIRED

Listed below are providers of service which we require you use. The charges or range indicated in the Good Faith Estimate above are based upon the corresponding charge of the below designated numbers.

DESIGNATED CHARGE ITEM NO. _____   PROV. REF. NO.   DESIGNATED CHARGE ITEM NO. _____   PROV. REF. NO.   DESIGNATED CHARGE ITEM NO. _____   PROV. REF. NO.

Service Provided: _____

Providers Name: _____

Address: _____

City, State, Zip: _____

Telephone No.: _____

We ☐ do, ☐ do not have a business relationship with the above named provider.   We ☐ do, ☐ do not have a business relationship with the above named provider.   We ☐ do, ☐ do not have a business relationship with the above named provider.

1. The Undersigned Acknowledges Receipt of This Good Faith Estimate of Charges.
2. The HUD Guide for Home Buyers, entitled, Settlement Costs.

APPLICANT _____ BY _____

APPLICANT _____ PER _____ DATE _____

REV. (4/78) ○-17P (2 PLY) (8903)   VMP MORTGAGE FORMS • (313)293-8100 • (800)521-7291

Exhibit 25

 -770 (8810) 01   VMP MORTGAGE FORMS • (313)293-8100 • (800)521-7291

OF BORROWER'S SETTLEMENT COSTS

Applicant(s):

Sales Price:

Property Address:

Loan Amount:

Type of Loan:

Date Prepared:

This form does not cover all items you will be required to pay in cash at settlement, for example, deposit and escrow real estate taxes and insurance. You may wish to inquire as to the amounts of such items. You may be required to pay other additional amounts at settlement.

Listed below is the GOOD FAITH ESTIMATE OF SETTLEMENT CHARGES MADE pursuant to the requirements of the REAL ESTATE SETTLEMENT PROCEDURES ACT (RESPA). These figures are only estimates and the actual charges due at settlement may be different.

800. ITEMS PAYABLE IN CONNECTION WITH LOAN:

801.	Loan Origination Fee %	$
802.	Loan Discount %	$
803.	Appraisal Fee	$
804.	Credit Report	$
805.	Lender's Inspection Fee	$
806.	Mortgage Insurance Application Fee	$
807.	Assumption Fee	$
808.		$
809.		$
810.		$
811.		$
812.		$
813.		$

900. ITEMS REQUIRED BY LENDER TO BE PAID IN ADVANCE:

901.	Interest From to @ /Day	$
902.	Mortgage Insurance Premium	$
904.		$

1100. TITLE CHARGES:

1101.	Closing or Escrow Fee	$
1102.	Abstract or Title Search	$
1103.	Title Examination	$
1104.	Title Insurance Binder	$
1107.	Attorney Fees	$
1108.	Title Insurance	$
1111.		$
1112.		$

1200. GOVERNMENT RECORDING & TRANSFER CHARGES:

1201.	Recording Fees: Deed: $; Mortgage: $; Release: $	$
1202.	City/County Tax/Stamps: Deed: $; Mortgage: $; Release: $	$
1203.	State Tax/Stamps: Deed: $; Mortgage: $	$
1204.		$
1205.	Recording Notice of Commencement	$

1300. ADDITIONAL SETTLEMENT CHARGES:

1301.	Survey	$
1302.	Pest Inspection	$
1303.		$
1305.	Construction Disbursing or Inspection Agent Fee	$
1306.		$
TOTAL ESTIMATED SETTLEMENT CHARGES		$

Monthly Payment Estimate:	Principal and Interest	$
Interest Rate:	Taxes/Insurance	
Term:	PMI	
	TOTAL	$

THIS SECTION TO BE COMPLETED BY LENDER ONLY IF A PARTICULAR PROVIDER OF SERVICE IS REQUIRED. Listed below are providers of service which we require you use. The charges or ranges indicated in the Good Faith Estimate above are based upon the corresponding charge of the below designated providers.

ITEM NO.	NAME & ADDRESS OF PROVIDER	TELEPHONE NO.	BUSINESS RELATION-SHIP EXISTS?
			☐ Yes ☐ No
			☐ Yes ☐ No
			☐ Yes ☐ No

AGREEMENT:

I/We acknowledge I/we have received a copy of the booklet "Settlement Costs", and if applicable the Consumer Handbook on ARM Mortgages, and I/we fully understand the amounts indicated above are **estimates only** and may vary from the actual settlement charges I/we will be required to pay at closing. Further, I/we fully understand that the loan origination fee, interest rate, loan term, and monthly payment indicated above are subject to change at any time and without notice **prior to** the issuance of a formal written loan commitment by the lender.

Applicant _____   Applicant _____

Date _____   Date _____

-770 (8810) 01   VMP MORTGAGE FORMS • (313)293-8100 • (800)521-7291   **10/87**

Exhibit 26

 -770(FL)(8709)   VMP MORTGAGE FORMS • (313)293-8100 • (800)521-7291

53,487-F

**GOOD FAITH ESTIMATE
OF BORROWER'S SETTLEMENT COSTS**

Applicant(s):

Property Address:

Sales Price:

Loan Amount:

Type of Loan:

Date Prepared:

This form does not cover all items you will be required to pay in cash at settlement, for example, deposit and escrow real estate taxes and insurance. You may wish to inquire as to the amounts of such items. You may be required to pay other additional amounts at settlement.

Listed below is the GOOD FAITH ESTIMATE OF SETTLEMENT CHARGES MADE pursuant to the requirements of the REAL ESTATE SETTLEMENT PROCEDURES ACT (RESPA). These figures are only estimates and the actual charges due at settlement may be different.

800. ITEMS PAYABLE IN CONNECTION WITH LOAN:

801.	Loan Origination Fee %	$
802.	Loan Discount %	$
803.	Appraisal Fee	$
804.	Credit Report	$
805.	Lender's Inspection Fee	$
806.	Mortgage Insurance Application Fee	$
807.	Assumption Fee	$
808.		$
809.		$
810.		$
811.		$
812.		$
813.		$

900. ITEMS REQUIRED BY LENDER TO BE PAID IN ADVANCE:

901.	Interest From to @ /Day	$
902.	Mortgage Insurance Premium	$
904.		$

1100. TITLE CHARGES:

1101.	Closing or Escrow Fee	$
1102.	Abstract or Title Search	$
1103.	Title Examination	$
1104.	Title Insurance Binder	$
1107.	Attorney Fees	$
1108.	Title Insurance	$
1111.		$
1112.		$

1200. GOVERNMENT RECORDING & TRANSFER CHARGES:

1201.	Recording Fees: Deed: $; Mortgage: $; Release: $	$
1202.	City/County Tax/Stamps: Deed: $; Mortgage: $; Release: $	$
1203.	State Tax/Stamps: Deed: $; Mortgage: $	$
1204.		$
1205.	Recording Notice of Commencement	$

1300. ADDITIONAL SETTLEMENT CHARGES:

1301.	Survey	$
1302.	Pest Inspection	$
1303.		$
1305.	Construction Disbursing or Inspection Agent Fee	$
1306.		$

TOTAL ESTIMATED SETTLEMENT CHARGES $

Monthly Payment Estimate:	Principal and Interest	$
Interest Rate:	Taxes/Insurance	
Term:	PMI	
	TOTAL	$

THIS SECTION TO BE COMPLETED BY LENDER ONLY IF A PARTICULAR PROVIDER OF SERVICE IS REQUIRED. Listed below are providers of service which we require you use. The charges or ranges indicated in the Good Faith Estimate above are based upon the corresponding charge of the below designated providers.

ITEM NO.	NAME & ADDRESS OF PROVIDER	TELEPHONE NO.	**BUSINESS RELATION-SHIP EXISTS?**
			☐ Yes ☐ No
			☐ Yes ☐ No
			☐ Yes ☐ No

AGREEMENT:

I/We acknowledge I/we have received a copy of the booklet "Settlement Costs", and if applicable the Consumer Handbook on ARM Mortgages, and I/we fully understand the amounts indicated above are **estimates only** and may vary from the actual settlement charges you will be required to pay at closing. Further, I/we fully understand that the loan origination fee, interest rate, loan term, and monthly payment indicated above are subject to change at any time and without notice **prior to** the issuance of a formal written loan commitment by the lender.

_____   _____
Applicant   Applicant

_____   _____
Date   Date

This transaction is subject to the protection of the Mortgage Brokerage Guaranty Fund pursuant to Section 494.043, Florida Statutes. Recovery from the fund is limited to a maximum of $20,000 per individual claim, and is further limited to an aggregate of $100,000 against any one licensed mortgage broker or registered mortgage brokerage business.

Date: _____   By: _____ .

-770(FL)(8709) VMP MORTGAGE FORMS • (313)293-8100 • (800)521-7291   Brokers License Number: _____ .

Exhibit 27

UNIFORM MORTGAGE LOAN COST WORKSHEET

CLOSING AND SETTLEMENT COSTS MAY VARY AMONG MORTGAGE LENDERS.
YOU MAY WISH TO COMPARE THESE CHARGES IN CONSIDERING THE TOTAL COST OF YOUR MORTGAGE.

FEE	EXAMPLE *	YOUR LOAN

Application Fee
Origination Fee   = Loan Amount X .01 X [Number of Points] =
(Points)
Appraisal Fee
Credit Report
Title Insurance:
  Lender's   = Loan Amount X [Estimated Rate] =
  Coverage

Abstract or Title Search
Title Examination
Documentation Preparation
Attorney's Fees
Private Mortgage   If 5% down payment:
  Insurance (PMI)   Loan amount X [Estimated PMI Rate]
                        or   =
                        If 10% down payment:
                        Loan amount X [Estimated PMI Rate]

Recording/Transfer Fees
Survey or Plot Plan

SUBTOTAL ESTIMATED $ SUBTOTAL ESTIMATED $
CLOSING COSTS   CLOSING COSTS

OTHER POTENTIAL CLOSING COSTS

There may be additional substantial charges payable at closing such   Real Estate Taxes
as deposits in escrow for real estate taxes and insurance and   Property Insurance
prepaid interest which could range from 0 to 30 times the daily   Interest paid
rate, depending on the date of closing. Inquire as to the amounts of   in advance
these items.   Owner's Title
                                                                            Insurance Coverage
                                                                        Other Charges

TOTAL ESTIMATED CLOSING COSTS $

* Example based on $100,000 fixed rate loan with
  a 20% downpayment and a sales price of $125,000.

I/We acknowledge receipt of the following:

1. Uniform Mortgage Loan Cost Worksheet
2. Uniform Mortgage Information Disclosure Statement
   entitled "Consumers' Guide to Obtaining a Home Mortgage"

Borrower _____ Date _____   Borrower _____ Date _____

Borrower _____ Date _____   Borrower _____ Date _____

VMP -956(MA) (8806)   VMP MORTGAGE FORMS • (313)293-8100 • (800)521-7291

mortgage credit available for housing by providing a vehicle for channeling funds from the securities markets into the mortgage market. GNMA guarantees privately issued securities backed by pools of government insured or guaranteed mortgages. Holders of the securities (the investors) receive a monthly "pass-through" of principal and interest payments due on the pooled mortgages, whether or not such payments are made by the borrowers. The GNMA guaranty assures securities holders of receiving timely payment of scheduled monthly principal and interest as well as any prepayments and early recoveries of principal on the underlying mortgages.

GNMA securities offer safety of principal coupled with liquidity and high yield. The securities provide investors with a guaranteed monthly stream of income in the form of interest and principal repayment.

Safety

There is no credit risk to the holders of GNMA mortgage-backed securities. Full and timely payment of all monthly principal and interest payments due investors, under the terms of the securities, are guaranteed by GNMA. The GNMA guaranty carries the full faith and credit of the United States Government. However, as with any fixed rate instrument, the securities may lose value if market conditions change and if they are sold before maturity.

Liquidity

GNMA securities enjoy an active and well established secondary market. Section 446 of The 1987 Housing Bill sets forth a credit ceiling for GNMA of $150,000,000 for fiscal 1988 and $156,000,000 for 1989. GNMA securities are the most widely held and traded mortgage-backed securities in the world.

Yield

The yield of GNMA mortgage-backed securities is decided primarily by the face interest rate on the securities, the price they are sold, and the rate of recovery of principal on the underlying mortgages. Unscheduled prepayments of principal may be made to securities holders from time to time because, among other things, homeowners may sell their homes and pay off the mortgages, or they may refinance their loans, or foreclosures may occur. In each such instance, the pro rata share of principal repayment is passed through to the holders. It is possible that one or more of the pooled mortgages will run until final maturity and that, consequently, some of the investor's funds will be outstanding until the maturity date of the securities.

Pricing

The pricing of GNMA securities is a function of supply and demand factors in the market place. Prices typically are quoted in increments of 1/32 of 1 percent of par and the securities are marketed at a discount or premium from par, depending on market conditions at the time they are sold. The securities can be bought or sold for immediate or delayed delivery.

Representative price quotations for GNMA securities can be found in the *Wall Street Journal* and other publications and can be obtained by contacting a securities dealer.

Trading

GNMA securities are traded within the United States in the "over the counter" market as government guaranteed securities. Unlike U.S. Treasury obligations, GNMA securities are issued by private firms and cannot be purchased directly from the government. Most Securities firms that are licensed by the National Association of Securities Dealers buy and sell GNMA securities.

Tax Status

The income derived from GNMA mortgage-backed securities is *not* exempt from Federal income, estate, or gift taxes under the Internal Revenue Code. Further, neither the Code nor the GNMA Charter Act contains an exemption from State or Local taxes. It is suggested that purchasers, residing in States that impose intangible property or income taxes, consult an advisor about the tax status of the securities.

Investment Amounts

The minimum certificate denomination available for newly issued GNMA securities is $25,000. Beyond the $25,000 minimum, the securities are available in increments of $5,000.

Though $25,000 is the minimum original face value available to investors, it is possible to make investments of less than $25,000 by purchasing GNMA pools that are either selling at a discount (because their interest rate is below current market) or have paid down (reduced) their principal substantially.

Interests in GNMA securities can be purchased in much lesser amounts (as low as $100) by buying units or shares in investment trusts or mutual funds that have invested in GNMA securities.

GNMA MORTGAGE-BACKED SECURITIES

GNMA mortgage-backed securities are an investment instrument representing an undivided interest in a pool of mortgages. Payments of principal and interest on the pooled mortgages are passed through to the securities holders and such payments are guaranteed, as to their amount and timeliness, by GNMA.

GNMA administers two mortgage-backed securities programs with each one having several sub-programs. The GNMA I program was initiated in 1970. The GNMA II program was introduced in July 1983 and takes advantage of many technological improvements that have emerged since the first GNMA I securities were introduced. The key features of the GNMA II program include the use of a central paying agent and the availability of larger geographically dispersed multiple issuer pools. The central paying agent provides consolidated monthly payments (one check to each investor for all GNMA II holdings of that investor). GNMA II multiple issuer pools provide investors with improved prepayment consistency.

HOW THE GNMA MORTGAGE-BACKED SECURITIES PROGRAMS WORK

(1) A mortgage lender applies to GNMA for approval to become an issuer of GNMA mortgage-backed securities and for a commitment for the guaranty of a securities issuance.

(2) The GNMA issuer originates or acquires government insured or guaranteed mortgages and assembles them into a pool or loan package of mortgages. The mortgages within a pool must be of the same type, have similar maturities, be less than 12 months old and, in GNMA I pools, they all must have the same interest rate. Mortgages in a GNMA II pool may have interest rates that vary within a one percent range. The minimum pool size is typically $1 million.

(3) The issuer submits pool mortgage documents, representing the mortgages in a pool, to a private financial institution that serves as document custodian.

(4) GNMA reviews document submissions from the issuer and authorizes its transfer agent (Chemical Bank) to prepare and deliver securities to investors.

(5) The securities bear a fixed interest rate, except for adjustable rate securities. The rate for GNMA I securities is 50 basis points, but not more than 150 basis points, below the interest rates of the pooled mortgages. The rate for adjustable rate securities may adjust annually as a function of market changes. There is a 1% floor and ceiling on annual rate changes and a 5% interest adjustment cap over the life of the securities.

(6) The issuer is fully responsible for the marketing and administration of the securities. In the GNMA I program the issuer makes the monthly payment of principal and interest to investors. In the GNMA II program the issuer remits principal and interest payments to GNMA's central paying agent, which in turn pays the holders. The issuer in both programs carries out mortgage servicing and prepares periodic reports to GNMA.

(7) For its role as guarantor, GNMA earns a guaranty fee of 6 basis points annually computed on the outstanding balance of the securities issued. The remaining difference between the securities interest rate and the interest rate on the underlying mortgages, is earned monthly by the issuer as a servicing fee.

Modified "Pass-Through" Securities

GNMA securities are modified pass-through securities. This means registered holders of the securities receive monthly pass-through (payments) of interest, at the rate shown on the securities, plus principal as scheduled on the pooled mortgages, whether or not such payments are made by the borrowers. Issuers are responsible for providing the funds needed to cover any shortfalls in collections from borrowers. Holders receive pass-through of any early (unscheduled) recoveries of principal-and ultimately receive a full repayment, at par, of all principal outstanding on the securities. All payments to holders are guaranteed by GNMA.

GNMA'S Guaranty

GNMA guarantees, with the full faith and credit of the United States Government, the timely payment of principal and interest to the registered holders of the securities. GNMA's guaranty warrants the performance of the issuer and assures the holder of receiving all scheduled monthly payments, as well as prepayments and early recoveries of principal, in a timely manner.

Issuers of GNMA Securities

Issuers of GNMA securities are private firms involved in the origination or acquisition of residential mortgage loans. The typical GNMA issuer is a mortgage banking company, savings institution, or commercial bank. There are approximately 1,200 approved GNMA issuers.

All GNMA issuers are FHA approved mortgagees, have a net worth acceptable to GNMA, and have adequate experience, management capability, and facilities to issue and service mortgage-backed securities.

Pool Composition

GNMA securities are backed by pools of government insured or guaranteed mortgages: mortgages that are insured by the Federal Housing Administration (FHA), which is a part of the U.S. Department of Housing and Urban Development, or are insured by the Farmer's Home Administration (FmHA), or are guaranteed by the Veterans Administration (VA).

Each pool is composed of a group of mortgages of the same type. There are eight distinct pool types or sub-programs. They are:

(1) Single family level payment mortgages (SF).

(2) Graduated payment mortgages (GPM).

(3) Adjustable rate mortgages [GNMA II only] (AR).

(4) Growing equity mortgages (GEM).

(5) Manufactured home loans (MH).

(6) Construction loans - multifamily [GNMA I only] (CL).

(7) Project loans - multifamily [GNMA I only] (PL).

(8) Buydown loans [GNMA I only] (BD).

FEATURES OF GNMA
MORTGAGE-BACKED SECURITIES

	GNMA I	GNMA II
Issuer	GNMA approved mortgage lender (single issuer)	GNMA approved mortgage lender(s) (single & multiple issuers)
Underlying	Government insured or guaranteed loans (FHA, VA & FmHA)	Government insured or Mortgages guaranteed loans (FHA, VA & FmHA)

	GNMA I	GNMA II
Pool Types	SF, GPM, GEM, MH, CL, PL, & BD	SF, GPM, GEM, MH, & AR
Interest rate on underlying mortgages	All mortgages in a pool have the same interest (except manufactured home pools)	Mortgages in a pool may have interest rates that vary within a one percent range (except manufactured home pools)
Guaranty	Full and timely payment of principal and of principal and interest, plus prepayments	Full and timely payment of principal and of principal and interest, plus prepayments
Guarantor	GNMA (full faith and credit of U.S. Gov't)	GNMA (full faith and credit of U.S. Gov't)
Principal and Interest	Paid monthly to holders	Paid monthly to holders
Payment Date	15th	20th
Maturity	Maximum 30 yrs., project loans 40 years	Maximum 30 yrs.
Minimum Certificate Size	$25,000	$25,000
Transfer Agent	Chemical Bank	Chemical Bank
Paying Agent	Individual Issuers send checks to Investors	Central Paying Agent-Chemical Bank sends check to investors

GOVERNMENT SPONSORED ENTERPRISE (GSE) The Federal National Mortgage Association and the Federal Home Loan Mortgage Corporation are government sponsored credit enterprises, while the Government National Mortgage Association remains a government-owned and operated credit enterprise with the full faith and credit guarantees against possible default by the federal government.

GPARM *See* GRADUATED PAYMENT ADJUSTABLE RATE MORTGAGE.

GPM *See* GRADUATED PAYMENT MORTGAGE.

GRACE PERIOD A period, after the deadline, when one can act without penalty, i.e., as in making a loan payment or redeeming a time deposit.

GRADE The elevation or ground level. The grade elevation means the elevation of the ground in relationship to the building. For ideal drainage, every house should be built on the top of a hill. Since this is not always possible, you should check all around to see that the earth slopes away from the house. Grade also means to prepare a smooth surface for a building site.

GRADUATED   PAYMENT   ADJUSTABLE   RATE   MORTGAGE (GPARM) Most GPM loans are fixed rate loans. With a GPARM, payments are graduated but the interest rate is based on an adjustable rate mortgage. These loans are normally used to lower the monthly payment, which helps the applicant qualify for the loan. These loans normally involve negative amortization.

GRADUATED PAYMENT MORTGAGE (GPM) A mortgage loan designed for borrowers who expect to be able to make larger monthly payments in the near future. A GPM has a fixed interest rate; payments rise gradually for the first few years then level off for the duration of the loan. Though the payments change, the interest rate is fixed. During the early years, the borrower's payments are lower than the amount dictated by the interest rate. During the later years, the difference is made up by higher payments. At the end of the loan, the borrower will have paid the entire debt. One variation of the GPM is the graduated-payment, adjustable-rate mortgage. This loan type carries graduated payments early in the loan. But, like other adjustable rate loans, it ties the borrower's interest to changes in an agreed-upon index. If interest rates climb after the initial period, the payments rise. This variation adds increased risk for the borrower; however, if interest rates decline during the life of the loan, the borrower's payments may decline as well.

Ginnie Mae and Fannie Mae are active in graduated-payment, mortgage-backed pass-throughs in FHA/VA, owner-occupied, one-to-four family dwellings. The GPM loans are 30-year loans (in most cases) and are usually issued by mortgage bankers who deal mostly in this FHA designed GPM as well as other government-insure MBSs.

See FHA - GRADUATED MORTGAGE and VA - GRADUATED MORTGAGE.

GRANDFATHER CLAUSE A term meaning to allow the continuance of a use or a practice that is now forbidden by new legislation; the practice or use being allowed under the old legislation.

GRANTEE That party who is the recipient of property.

GRANTOR That party who transfers title to another party.

GRANTOR TRUST A legal trust that allows investors to hold interests in the trust and be taxed as if they owned their share of the trust assets directly. The trust buys assets from originators and insures debt securities collateralized by the assets.

Grantor trusts are used in security pass-throughs and pass interest and principal through to investors. Under REMICs, tax provisions for cash flows from a pool of mortgages can be arranged and re-arranged into variations without double taxation, which is their most desirable feature. This is a mortgage-backed security format for strip transactions. This "trust" classification directs income tax liabilities to the certificate owner's level and therefore identifies such transactions as sales.

Grantor trust assumes title to the mortgages as relinquished by the private pass-through issuer who then services the mortgages while collecting fees. Investors own an undivided interest in the mortgage pools with a pro rata share of cash flows representing monthly pass-throughs of mortgage payments. Payments of interest and principal (whether schedule or unscheduled) in a grantor trust advance possible delinquencies to the investor.

See REMIC.

GREEK REVIVAL *See* Arcadian.

GROSS AREA The square footage of a building as measured by the outside walls.

GROSS RENT MULTIPLIER (GRM) A rule of thumb used to decide value by dividing the sales price by the gross rental income. If a property sells for $60,000 and the annual gross rent income is $10,000, the Gross Rent Multiplier is six. GRM can be decided on a monthly basis.

GROUND LEASE A lease of the ground or land and none of the improvements.

GROUT A thin mortar used to fill joints between bricks or blocks.

GROWING EQUITY MORTGAGE (GEM) A structured prepayment of a mortgage. Mortgage payments increase, usually on an annual bases, for a specified period of time. After the period of increases, the payments level off and early prepayment of the mortgage is achieved. GEM or Early Retirement Mortgage (ERM) loans usually start with a first year payment based on a 30-year amortized mortgage. The lender will usually qualify the borrower on the first year's monthly payment, particularly if it is feasible for the borrower to absorb the future increase.

A 15-1/2% VA loan with increases in the monthly payment of 7-1/2% per year will have a maturity date of less than 10 years. A 15% loan with an increase in the monthly payments of 5% per year will mature in 12.469 years. A loan at 15.1/2% with a 3% increase in the monthly payment from years 1 through 9, then a constant payment from year 10, will mature in 14 years, 8 months.

Any existing loan without a prepayment penalty can be converted to a GEM method of payment. A loan of any age can be paid out early by prepaying the loan at a schedule selected by the mortgagor. The GEM idea is a marketing idea; any loan without a prepayment penalty may be treated as a GEM type of amortization by prepaying the loan.

See EQUITY ACCRUAL BASIS.

GUARANTEED MORTGAGE CERTIFICATE (GMC) The bond-like instrument issued by the FHLMC representing ownership in a large pool of residential mortgages. Principal is returned annually and interest is paid semi-annually.

GUARANTEE BONDS A credit instrument with principal and interest payments supported by a letter of credit from a financial institution or other sources of funds. Guarantee bonds have been used to ease the financing of residential and income properties.

GUARANTEED COUPON A commitment to buy or sell mortgage-backed securities at an agreed upon interest rate.

GUARANTEED INVESTMENT CONTRACT (GIC) A GIC is a commercial, fixed-rate mortgage that insurance companies obtain from pension funds. Unsteady rates tend to increase attention for GICs.

GUARANTEED MORTGAGE CERTIFICATE (GMC) First offered in 1975, GMCs are bonds issued by Freddie Mac. The GMC represents an undivided interest in a pool of mortgages that are purchased according to Freddie Mac's quality standards. These securities are distinguishable in that the schedule of principal and interest payments has been arranged to avoid the problems associated with receiving and reinvesting monthly payments.

Specifically, the GMC pays interest on the certificate semiannually and principal is returned annually. To reduce prepayment risk, Freddie Mac provides a guaranteed schedule of minimum principal repayments. If actual prepayments exceed this, Freddie Mac provides a notice of the actual amounts in advance of the annual payment date. Timely payment of interest and full payment of principal are guaranteed by Freddie Mac.

GMC was designed specifically to appeal to institutional investors by providing an instrument with more of the attributes of corporate bonds and fewer of the attributes of mortgages. Besides the guaranteed schedule of principal repayment already mentioned, a rather very attractive feature is that Freddie Mac stands ready to repurchase the remaining outstanding balance at par after a specified number of years, usually 15 years. Security dealers provide a market for GMCs. No GMCs have been issued since 1979; however, at the end of 1982, $1.8 billion in GMCs were outstanding.

GUARANTEED MORTGAGE LOAN *See* VA LOAN GUARANTY.

GUARANTOR FEE The fee paid monthly by a servicer to an investor for the right to service a mortgage loan under the related mortgage-backed securities program.

GUARANTOR PROGRAM (FREDDIE MAC) The Guarantor or Swap program is one of two pass-through programs offered by Freddie Mac. A single issuer can form a pool that may qualify for the swap by accumulating mortgage collateral consisting of seasoned or current mortgage loans. Swap participation certificates (PCs) are exchanged by Freddie Mac for these loans that may vary in maturity as the pool is made up of current and seasoned mortgages.

In addition, the Guarantor program may differ from pass-through rates by 200 basis points between pool mortgage rates and pass-through rates. A second Standard (cash) program is described elsewhere. Other pass-through programs are offered by Freddie Mac, although on a more limited basis compared to its Guarantor Program. The Guarantor PC program now guarantees a timely payment of principal rather than the former ultimate payment of principal to investors in pass-throughs. This system of payments is similar to the Ginnie Mae and Fannie Mae procedures.

In addition, the Guarantor pools have sizes as small as $250,000, reduced from a minimum of $1 million in tradeable Guarantor participation certificates. This reduction benefits the smaller volume lender who would not be able to pool $1 million worth of loans in order to pledge the loans in shorter periods of time as well as those not wishing to mix the coupon rates in a pool.

GUARANTY *See* VA - GUARANTY.

GUARANTY PERFORMANCE A technique used to prevent liability through a foreclosure. An original mortgagor is ultimately liable on a mortgage that is assumed unless there is a release of liability granted to the original mortgagor. For example, a veteran applies for a VA loan and in the process an application is made for a Certificate of Eligibility. When the VA researches the records of the veteran, they discover that the veteran had a loan that was foreclosed 15 years ago and there was a $10,000 deficiency from the foreclosure. The veteran is notified and given a bill for $10,000 PLUS ACCRUED INTEREST! After the veteran faints, the first thing he/she does when they come to is to say: "That was not my foreclosure, I sold that house years ago and the loan was assumed. As a matter of fact, I heard that the person that bought the house from me sold it to another." Then the veteran hears the bad news. The original veteran is responsible for the loan and should have asked for a release from liability when they sold their house. The veteran now must pay the bill.

Unfortunately, the story above has happened often to unsuspecting mortgagors. It is not limited to just VA loans, it can happen with any lender that pursues deficiency judgements. How can a seller prevent being liable for a deficiency? One way is to show up at the court house steps (or other place where foreclosures are held) and bid-in the amount owed. The amount asked for will usually be the balance of the loan plus accrued interest and costs related to the foreclosure (advertising fees, attorney fees, and any court cost). The former owner will then regain the property and liability from a deficiency is avoided. As you can imagine this process can be rather costly. At foreclosure, the normal method of payment is with cash or a certified check.

To have the same results without the cash problem, the seller can require a guaranty performance agreement to be executed by the assumptor and secured by a second mortgage. A guaranty agreement can serve as sufficient collateral for a second mortgage; the veteran/seller does not have to lend money to the purchaser. Foreclosure by the owner of the second mortgage may occur if the obligations of the first mortgage are not being fulfilled. The owner of the second mortgage will then have a legal right to buy the property back by foreclosing the second mortgage. The second mortgagee forecloses on the second, becomes the owner of the property, makes the back payments on the first, saves thousands of dollars of cash in the process, and avoids being liable from a deficiency. Another advantage of this method is that most state laws require the owner of a second mortgage to be put on notice of any pending foreclosure by the owner of the first mortgage. With a second mortgage, the chances of knowing about a pending foreclosure on a property a veteran has an interest in is far greater than just watching for a public notice in a local newspaper. As already stated, many states require the holder of a junior mortgage to be notified of a foreclosure by a senior mortgage.

Not all states allow a junior mortgage to be created with a guaranty performance. If this is the case in your state, you may want to check with your attorney about the feasibility of lending a nominal sum and making a second mortgage with lock-out protection. You will find that many states will allow this method. Remember, a lender can foreclose for reasons other than failure to make the payments. For example, if a lender observes the collateral for the loan, which is primarily the improvements to the property (the house for a residential loan) is being devalued by such acts as: alteration that is harmful to the improvements, waste, abuse, improper maintenance, improper use of the improvements - any or all of these and more, the lender has the right to foreclose and regain the property to protect the lender's interest. As a seller, you have your credit and net worth to protect on a loan assumption without a release of liability. If the buyer is willing to have the seller released from liability but the process is too lengthy, try this second or junior mortgage method and later cancel the second when the release from liability has been granted.

See EQUITABLE MORTGAGE, DEFAULT, GUARANTY PERFORMANCE, LOCK-OUT PROTECTION.

GUARDIAN AD LITEM The party appointed by a court to represent the interests of a minor or incompetent in a lawsuit.

GUTTER SYSTEM A channel for carrying off rainwater. Gutters should be free of rust, tightly secured to the structure, and slanted enough so that water will drain and not become stagnant. Downspouts should not empty at the base of the foundation wall but should have either splash blocks or elbow extensions to prevent basement leaks and soil erosion from the foundation walls and flower and shrub beds.

HABENDUM CLAUSE The clause in a deed that defines or limits the extent of ownership. It begins with the words: "To have and to hold" and it follows the granting clause.

HALF LIFE A measure of the initial "principal amount" of a pool when repaid by one half. The half life of a security is the number of years that must elapse before half the principal is repaid.

The half life concept is simply explained by the use of the following example where an FHA yield measurement of 200% is present: the half life of a security would be 6 1/2 years on a horizontal scale in 0-30 year increments where the total principal payments (amortization plus pre-payments) that would be received from a 30-year, 9.5% GNMA security of 200% FHA experience on $1 million. The principal payments per month (in dollars) of 0-8 thousand dollars on a vertical scale are estimated at $7,500. The half life of this security running parallel with a vertical scale will indicate a half life of 6 1/2 years on a graph dividing two equal portions. In other words, half the issue is retired by the end of 6 1/2 years according to the FHA experience curve.

HALF-TIMBERED Walls with timber frames exposed for decorative purposes.

HANGOUT The remaining term of a loan when it is beyond the term of a lease. A 20-year mortgage on a building that is leased for 15 years has a hangout of 5 years.

HARD COST The cost of land acquisition and improvement.
See SITE DEVELOPMENT COST.

HARD MONEY A mortgage loan given for the purposes of obtaining cash as opposed to financing the purchase of real estate. A home equity loan or a second mortgage loan based on equity to pay personal bills are examples of "hard money" loans.

HAZARD INSURANCE Insurance that covers physical damage to property. Hazard insurance premiums must be paid when due. To avoid possible cancellation and to ensure that policies are fully adjusted for renewal as coverage expires, guidelines are established by the lending institution for the minimum coverages required to protect the security.

The loan servicing department of a lending institution carries the responsibility of following company policy for property insurance claims filed by property owners (borrowers). A lender will accept a hazard insurance policy for the remaining balance of an individual loan or for the property's value, but never less than the remaining balance. A mortgagor is expected to protect against the hazard of fire and casualties by estimating limits of necessary insurance individually, and not rely on lender's guidelines.

Hazard insurance covers necessary improvements on real property resulting from not only fire, but may include any other coverage required by the lender, which may include damage resulting from malicious conduct of others or vandalism. Hazard insurance coverage is estimated not by only an amount equal to the mortgage encumbrance but also by the appraised value of improvements to the land. If a dwelling is insured for more than its value, that amount would not be reimbursed to the insured - even if the home were destroyed entirely.

At closing, the lender will want the original hazard insurance policy with proof that the first year's premium has been paid. Hazard insurance should be written by companies bearing a Best's rating of B-III or better. Most lenders will want the policy to contain minimum coverage for fire, extended coverage and other perils, and provide for settlement of any loss or damage on a replacement cost basis. The property should be insured in an amount equal to 100 percent of the insurable replacement value of improvements (cost value of appraisal minus the lot value). The policy should be prepaid for a minimum of one year and it should not be a deferred payment or a financed policy. The policy should not contain any coinsurance clause. The policy date should be effective no later than the date of closing. A lender will usually not accept an insurance binder.

A recommended mortgagee clause for use in the policy is as follows: "(name of lender), its successors and /or assigns as their respective interests may appear." Unless a higher maximum amount is required by state law, the maximum deductible clause should be the lesser of $1,000 or one percent of the policy face amount. It is normal for the deductible clause to apply on either fire or extended coverage or to both. The name of the insured should correspond to the names of the actual title holders and the property address should correspond to the property description in the loan documents.

For Planned Unit Developments (PUDs) the lender should want evidence that the PUD Owner's Association has adequate hazard and liability coverage in force for the common areas. If the project has more than 20 units, the lender should consider requiring fidelity bond coverage on the Owner's Association.

For Condominiums the lender should want evidence that the following coverages exist.

(1) A "Master" or "Blanket" policy of property insurance equal to 100 percent of the current replacement cost of the condominium project

affording coverage for loss or damage by fire and other hazards to general and limited common elements, building service equipment, and common personal property.

(2) A comprehensive policy of public liability insurance covering all of the common areas and commercial spaces owned by the Owner's Association. The lender should require coverage of at least $1 million for bodily injury and property damage for any single occurrence.

(3) The lender should require a "Certificate of Insurance" from the insurance carrier as to the specific unit in the condominium project.

(4) If the project has more than 20 units, the lender should require that adequate fidelity bond coverage on the condominium project's Owner's Association must be in force to protect against dishonest acts by its officers, directors, trustees, employees, and all others who are responsible for handling funds of the Association.

(5) The named insured should be the Owner's Association of the condominium project.

(6) If the Master Policy does not specifically cover the limited common elements (interior walls, ceiling, floors, etc.), the borrower should be required to purchase additional coverage to protect the mortgagee. Evidence of the additional coverage and payment of the first year's premium should be provided at closing.

HEADERS Double wood boards supporting joists or windows or doors so that the weight is transferred to the studs. Another term for *headers* is *head casing*.

HEARTH The floor of a fireplace.

HEDGE An action taken to reduce risk or market exposure. In the secondary mortgage market, hedging is designed to neutralize the risk that rate movements pose to an existing pipeline. The production segment of the mortgage pipeline begins when the borrower submits an application and ends when the loan is closed.

There is generally no production period risk if a lender can avoid setting the terms of loan origination (the interest rate) until closing. However, most lenders, for competitive reasons, set the interest rate and the discount rate at the time of application. Thus, lenders purchase mortgage futures contracts to offset cash market transactions to be made at a later date.

HEDGING POSITION A strategy used when hedging mortgage loans, as in the following example:

Situation: USA Mortgage Company purchases a $1 million commitment on June 1, 1983 to deliver GNMA Mbss on September 1, 1983.

Problem: In order to fill this commitment, mortgages must be originated during June and July. As mortgages are assembled for the pool, interest rate changes could cause a profit or loss to be generated when the commitment is closed out. Since the company's objective is not to loose money on the sale of its originations, a hedge is needed.

HEIR An individual who inherits property.

HEREDITAMENT Real property; property that can be inherited.

HEWLETT-PACKARD 12C (HP-12C) A popular financial calculator that is often used by people in the real estate and investment banking industry. In today's rapidly advancing technological world, it is especially difficult to have a consistent high demand for the same product since 1981 - Hewlett Packard has accomplished that feat with its HP-12C. (*The HP-12C Real Estate Solutions Manual*, written by Albert Santi and published by Probus Publishing, is an easy-to-use, step-by-step guide for the real estate professional. The book is in paperback and retails for $14.95.)

See ELLWOOD TABLE, INWOOD ORDINARY ANNUITY COEFFICIENT, REVERSION FACTOR, SINKING FUND FACTOR, SIX FUNCTIONS OF A DOLLAR.

HIDDEN DEFECT Cloud on a title that is not found by a search of public records.

HIGHEST AND BEST USE An appraisal term used to describe the best use of a property. If a property is in a residentially zoned subdivision, its highest and best use would be as a residence.

HIP ROOF A roof with four sides sloping upward to a ridge.
See ROOF.

HOLDBACK A provision whereby money is withheld until certain performance is made. For income properties the holdback could be a portion of the permanent loan held back until certain rent levels are achieved. With a construction loan or interim loan the holdback can be a required completion of the project before more funds are advanced. Often an estimate of 10% of the construction cost is held back until the project is fully completed and there is assurance of no mechanics liens.

HOLDER Any legal entity that is the owner of any mortgage-backed security issued under GNMA I or II programs or mortgage related products that are recognized as legitimate mortgage securities. Buyers of mortgage related securities in the options market are called holders.

HOLDER IN DUE COURSE A doctrine allowing a person who acquires a bearer instrument in good faith to keep said instrument free of certain claims.

HOLD HARMLESS CLAUSE A provision in a contract whereby a party is protected from claims.

HOLOGRAPHIC WILL A written will that is not witnessed. Some states allow the use of a holographic will on the basis that the handwriting of the testator (person who made the will) can be verified.

HOMAC *See* HOME MORTGAGE ACCESS CORPORATION.

HOME EQUITY LINE OF CREDIT A second mortgage with a floating loan balance that has an upper limit. A homeowner may have equity of $40,000 and wishes to establish a line of credit with a lender. Normally, the lender will loan 80% of the equity in the form of a second mortgage.

The borrower, however, is not required to draw the entire $32,000 and begin interest payments on the loan. The borrower can use the loan as a line of credit to access cash that is needed for whatever reason, such as an investment or to pay an obligation.

Often this loan will require interest-only payments with periodic payments to the principal. There can be interest only for a stated period and the funds advanced can be for personal reasons; an equity line of credit.

See SECOND MORTGAGE.

HOME EQUITY LOAN A second mortgage of a decided amount based on the equity in a home. The loan will normally have a repayment schedule that will include interest and principal. Proceeds from home equity loans usually go towards an addition or an improvement to the home.

See SECOND MORTGAGE.

HOME MAINTENANCE SERVICE AGREEMENTS Service contracts or agreements for homes are becoming a popular item. Before entering into a contract, you may want these questions answered:

1. **Where is the home office located?** A local office location is a convenience factor.

2. **How do you get service?** Companies that have toll-free numbers may not be as attractive as a local contact.

3. **Who performs the service work?** Many service companies subcontract their work. Companies that have their technicians may be available.

4. **Who inspects the equipment before initiation of a service contract?** This answer will be a big shock to many homebuyers. Some of your big-name companies use real estate agents to make the home inspections. A home inspection should be done by licensed and bonded technicians who can render professional evaluations of heating, air-conditioning, plumbing, and electrical systems.

5. **Does the company refuse to pay claims due to pre-existing conditions?** Most companies will refuse to pay a claim if the repair needed is due to a pre-existing condition—one that was not picked up at the time of inspection.

6. **Does the company offer 24-hour emergency service?** Most will, but on only a limited basis. Examples would be heating only or heating and plumbing only. Find out what qualifies for an emergency.

7. **Is there a deductible?** Deductibles can render the contract of no benefit. You will want to avoid high deductibles or deductibles for each call.

8. **Who pays for the cost of repairs?** Some companies pay all, other companies pay all above $100, others require the homeowner to pay all and then get reimbursed at a later date.

9. **Does the company cover: a) swimming pool, spa; b) boiler heating; c) window air-conditioning units; and d) personal appliances?** You will find the type of coverage will vary.

10. **Does the company offer total replacement of equipment that is beyond repair?** Some companies will; others offer only equal value for worn-out parts.

11. **What is the base price?** Shop the prices, but remember the services provided.

12. **Is the service contract transferable?** You will find that most are not.

The home service contract business is a relatively new member of the service industry and it should have a big future. Currently, there are very few states that regulate such companies so be careful in your selection.

HOME MORTGAGE DISCLOSURE ACT (HMDA) The purpose of the Home Mortgage Disclosure Act (HMDA) and the Federal Reserve's Regulation C is to provide the public with information that will help show whether depository institutions are serving the housing credit needs of the neighborhoods and communities in which they are located. Another purpose is to help public officials distribute public sector investments in a way that will attract private investments in neighborhoods where they are needed.

As its name implies, the HMDA is a disclosure act, and relies upon public scrutiny for its effects. It does not prohibit any activity, and it is not intended to encourage the allocation of credit or any unsound lending practices.

Congress enacted the HMDA in 1975. The act became effective along with Regulation C, on June 28, 1976. In 1980, the act was amended and extended for a five-year period under provisions of the Housing and Community Development Act. A corresponding revision of Regulation C was published by the Board in July 1981.

A depository institution that is subject to Regulation C must compile and disclose data about home purchase and home improvement loans that it originates or purchase during each calendar year.

Covered institutions are required to make their HMDA disclosures available to the public. They must post a notice of the availability of the disclosures in their public lobbies. Finally, the institutions must send two copies of their HMDA disclosures to the regional office of their federal financial supervisory agency. The regulators will forward one copy of the statement to a central data repository in each standard metropolitan statistical area (SMSA), and another to the Federal Financial Institutions Examination Council (FFIEC) in Washington, D.C. for aggregation of the loan data. The FFIEC will produce individual disclosure statements for each reporting institution plus aggregate tables for each Metropolitan Statistical Area using the information from the loan registers.

On December 15, 1989 (Federal Register, Vol. 54, No. 240, page 51357), The Federal Reserve Board issued the final regulations changing Regulation C. The result of the enactment by the Fed is the Financial Institutions Reform, Recovery, and Enforcement Act of 1989 (FIRREA). This new act expanded HMDA to include other mortgage lenders besides those affiliated with depository institutions or holding companies. Privately owned mortgage banking companies are now included in HMDA. The Act requires reporting of information regarding the loan applicants as well as information on loan originations. The lender must report the race, sex, and income level of applicants. There are two cases when the applicant information is not mandatory: (1) purchased loans, and (2) lenders with assets under $30 million. The Act requires lenders to identify the class of the investor to whom they sell their mortgages. The lender is allowed the basis for making lending decisions. The new regulations are effective January 1, 1990 and first reports are due by March 1, 1991. The new HMDA regulations require lenders to use a "register form" for reporting the required information. On the form, lenders will record information for each application without regard as to whether the application was granted, denied or withdrawn. If a loan application is withdrawn or cannot be processed because of lack of information, there is a separate category to report such cases. Refinances of home purchase loans are to be included in the report even if they involve the original borrower and the original lender. The information gathered by the lender is submitted to their supervisory agency at the close of the calendar year.

Lenders with assets under ten million dollars are exempt from HMDA, *but* assets of any parent institution must be combined with those of the subsidiary mortgage lender. Banks, savings institutions, and credit unions are exempt if their assets are under ten million without counting any assets of affiliated mortgage lending operations. If a lending institution does not have a home or branch office in an Metropolitan Statistical Area they are exempt from HMDA. If a lending institution had less than ten percent of its loan volume in home purchase loan originations, they are exempt from HMDA. In complying with the ten percent rule, subsidiaries of depository institutions are considered as independent entities.

HMDA considers a completed application when a lender receives an *oral* or *written* request for a mortgage or home improvement loan that is made according to established procedures of the lender. This interpretation by HMDA means that it considers an application to be "complete" without an approval from an agency (FHA/VA), secondary entities (FNMA/FHLMC) or from private insurers and investors.

For privately owned mortgage companies, a branch office not just a physical presence, it is wherever a lender receives applications for, originates, or purchases five or more home purchase or home improvement loans.

INSTITUTION	WHERE TO REPORT *
National banks and their subsidiaries.	District office of the Office of the Comptroller of the Currency serving the district that the national bank or subsidiary is located.
State member banks of the Federal Reserve System, their subsidiaries, and subsidiaries of bank holding companies.	Federal Reserve Bank serving the district in which the state member bank or subsidiary is located.
Nonmember insured banks (except for federal savings banks) and their subsidiaries.	Regional Director of the Federal Deposit Insurance Corporation for the region in which the bank or subsidiary is located.

INSTITUTION	WHERE TO REPORT *
Savings institutions insured under the Savings Association Insurance Fund of the FDIC: federally-chartered savings banks insured under the Bank Insurance Fund of the FDIC (but not including state-chartered savings banks insured under the Bank Insurance Fund), their subsidiaries, and subsidiaries of savings institutions holding companies.	To the District or other office specified by the Office of Thrift Supervision.
Credit Unions.	National Credit Union Administration, Office of Examination and Insurance, 1776 G Street, N.W., Washington, D.C. 20456.
Other depository institutions.	Regional Director of the FDIC for the region in which the institution is located.
Other Mortgage Lending Institutions, e.g. Independent or Mortgage Banking Companies.	Assistant Secretary for Housing, HMDA Reporting - Room 9233, U.S. Department of Housing and Urban Development, 451 7th Street, S.W. Washington, D.C. 20410.

* FHA issued MORTGAGEE LETTER 90-25 advising that HUD has no way of knowing which mortgagees are required to report to a Federal supervisory agency specified in Regulation C, mortgagees reporting to such agencies must report to HUD the required information with regard to their originations and purchases of mortgage loans insured by FHA, and applications for FHA insured loans. These mortgagees shall report (1) if the indicated data were included in a report to a Federal supervisory agency pursuant to Regulation C, and (2) the name of the agency to which the report was made. Reports relating to FHA-insured mortgages and applications for FHA-insured mortgages submitted to HUD will not be sent to the Federal Financial Institutions Examination Council, and mortgagees are not required to have this information available for public use.

See Exhibits 28-30.

Lenders must use the prescribed format but are not required to use the forms themselves; computer printouts are acceptable.

Exhibit 28

Loan/Application Register for Institutions Subject to 12 CFR 528

Section I (Required by 12 CFR 203 and 12 CFR 528.6 (d) (2))

LOAN/APPLICATION REGISTER   Page _____ of _____

Form FR HMDA-LAR
Control number (agency use only)

Name of Reporting Institution   City and State

Section II (Required by 12 CFR 528.6 (d)(3))

Applicant or Loan Information				Action Taken		Property Location				Applicant Information A = Applicant CA = Co-Applicant					Type of Purchaser of Loan	Reason(s) for Denial	In CRA Delin.	Marital Status		Age		Purchase Price in thousands	Appraised Value in thousands	L/V Ratio	Int. Rate	Year Built	Maturity
Application or Loan Number	Date Application Received (mm/dd/yy)	Type	Pur-pose	Occu-pancy	Amount in thousands	Type	Date (mm/dd/yy)	MSA Number	State Code	County Code	Census Tract	Race or National Origin	Sex	Income in thousands													
												A	CA	A	CA	A	CA				A	CA	A	CA				

SAMPLE

597 (9002) 01   VMP MORTGAGE FORMS • (313) 293-8100 • (800) 521-7291

OTS Form 1498, December 1989
OMB No. 1550-0021

Exhibit 29

LOAN/APPLICATION REGISTER

Page ____ of ____

Name of Reporting Institution _____

City and State _____

Application or Loan Information							Action Taken		Property Location				Applicant Information A = Applicant CA = Co-Applicant							
Application or Loan Number	Date Application Received (mm/dd/yy)	Type	Purpose	Occu-pancy	Amount in thousands		Type	Date (mm/dd/yy)	MSA Number	State Code	County Code	Census Tract	Race or National Origin		Sex		Income in thou-sands	Type of Purchaser of Loan	Reason(s) for Denial (Optional)
													A	CA	A	CA	A CA		

SAMPLE

Exhibit 30

LOAN/APPLICATION REGISTER

Form FR HMDA-LAR
OMB No. 7100-0247. Approval expires December 31, 1992
Hours per response: 10-750 (120 Average)
This report is required by law (12 USC 2801-2810 and 12 CFR 203)

TRANSMITTAL SHEET

Control Number (agency use only)

| | | | | | | | | | | | - | |

You must complete this transmittal sheet (please type or print) and attach it to the Loan/Application Register, required by the Home Mortgage Disclosure Act, that you submit to your supervisory agency.

The Loan/Application Register that is attached covers activity during 19   and contains a total of   pages.

Enter the name and address of your institution. The disclosure statement that is produced by the Federal Financial Institutions Examination Council will be mailed to the address you supply below:

_____
Name

_____
Address

_____
City, State, ZIP

Enter the name and telephone number of a person who may be contacted if questions arise regarding your report:

_____ _____
Name   Telephone Number

If your institution is a subsidiary of another institution or corporation, enter the name of your parent:

_____
Name

_____
Address

_____
City, State, ZIP

Enter the name and address of your supervisory agency:

_____
Name

_____
Address

_____
City, State, ZIP

An officer of your institution must complete the following section.
I certify to the accuracy of this report.

_____ _____ _____
Name of Officer   Signature   Date

-596A (8912)   VMP MORTGAGE FORMS • (313)293-8100 • (800)521-7291   **12/89**

Lenders may obtain further guidance from the "Guide to HMDA." The guide can be obtained by writing to:

Dr. William F. Shaw, Director
Information Systems Division
Room 9241
Department of Housing and Urban Development
Washington, D.C. 20410

HOMEOWNER'S ASSOCIATION An organization of owners in a condominium, planned unit development, or subdivision. The purpose of a Homeowner's Association is to enforce deed restrictions and manage common elements of their development.

A lender may want a homeowner's association to complete a form like the one shown in Exhibit 31.

HOMEOWNER'S POLICY *See* HAZARD INSURANCE.

HOMEOWNER'S WARRANTY PROGRAM (HOW) An insurance program used by builders to give warranty against defects in the house for a specific period of time. Extended coverage is provided beyond the normal one-year warranty period for new homes.

HOMESTEAD Laws in some states that protect a person's principal residence against judgments up to certain amounts. Depending upon state law, certain judgements are not protected by homestead, and homestead can be waived.

HOMESTEAD EXEMPTION Favorable treatment in some states for a person's principal residence in relationship to the assessed valuation.

HONEST-TO-GOD CASH FLOW YIELDS (HTG) Coined by First Boston, HTG Yields are computed monthly on mortgage-related securities based on an *actual* or *assumed* prepayment rate on the underlying mortgages. The term HTG was intended to suggest a superior estimate to the true yield of a passthrough. Unlike mortgage yield, there is more than one HTG yield for a given pass-through at a given price. In fact, there are infinitely many HTG yields, depending on the prepayment assumption used; no one prepayment model or experience multiple is cast as the standard although market conditions inevitably make some assumptions that appear to be more reasonable that others. Perhaps the greatest asset of HTG yield is its ability to evolve in a changing market. Recent street practices have all but eliminated FHA experience models;

Exhibit 31

ANALYSIS OF ANNUAL INCOME AND EXPENSES – OPERATING BUDGET

For FNMA submissions complete both pages of this form. For FHLMC submissions complete this side only. Note: If developer control has terminated and the Home Owners Association has been controlled by Unit Owners for two or more years, FHLMC does not require this form.

TO BE COMPLETED BY SELLER/SERVICER, OWNERS ASSOCIATION OR MANAGEMENT AGENT

Project Name ______

Address or Location ______ City ______ State ______ Zip ______

STATEMENT OF ANNUAL PROJECT OPERATING BUDGET AND RESERVES FOR THE YEAR 19 ______

COMPLETE ONLY THOSE ITEMS WHICH ARE PAID BY OWNERS ASSOCIATION WHICH INCLUDES SUBJECT UNIT.

Budget below is for: ☐ Entire project ☐ Phase No. ______

ADMINISTRATIVE EXPENSES

Office expenses, supplies, equipment rental, etc. . . . $ ______

Telephone . . . . ______

Office salaries (itemize) ______

Management fee (name of management firm) ______

Legal and audit . . . . ______

______ . . . . ______

OPERATING EXPENSES

Fuel . . . . ______

Utilities (Gas $ ______ Electricity $ ______ Water & Sewer $ ______) . . . . ______

Trash & Garbage Removal . . . . ______

Exterminating . . . . ______

Supplies . . . . ______

______ . . . . ______

REPAIRS AND MAINTENANCE

Decorating (exterior and interior) . . . . ______

Cleaning expenses and supplies . . . . ______

Snow removal . . . . ______

Building maintenance and repairs . . . . ______

Elevator maintenance and repairs . . . . ______

Heating and air conditioning maintenance and repairs . . . . ______

Pool maintenance and repairs . . . . ______

Parking area maintenance and repairs . . . . ______

Private street maintenance and repairs . . . . ______

Gardening and yard maintenance and repairs including shrub replacement . . . . ______

Other (specify) ______

Salaries (itemize including employee benefits and payroll taxes)

______

______

______

FIXED EXPENSES

Real estate taxes (if PUD) . . . . ______

Other (Taxes $ ______ Assessments $ ______ Regime Fees $ ______) . . . . ______

Licenses . . . . ______

Insurance premiums . . . . ______

Ground rent . . . . ______

Recreational or other facilities rental . . . . ______

______ . . . . ______

TOTAL EXPENSES . . . . ______

REPLACEMENT RESERVES

List Each Item	Yrs. of Estimated Remaining Life	Expected Replacement Cost	Average Yearly Cost
		$	$

TOTAL REPLACEMENT RESERVES . . . . $ ______

TOTAL ANNUAL EXPENSES AND REPLACEMENT RESERVES . . . . $ ______

Project Annual Income from: Condo/PUD charges $ ______ Other $ ______ Total $ ______

Itemize other income ______

______

If the income is less than the budget, discuss deficit ______

______

______

Actual funds now held: for payment of operating expenses $ ______ in Replacement Reserve fund $ ______

No. of Unit Owners over 30 days delinquent in Association charges ______ in Special Assessment charges ______

Explain any indebtedness or leases on the common area or parking, utilities or other facilities (if none, so state) ______

______

______

Certified Correct: Organization ______

Date ______ By ______ Title ______

Seller/Servicer's Use Only

I certify that I have analyzed the above Statement of Operating Budget and Reserves. In my opinion, except as stated below, the items as set forth in this Budget appear sufficient to maintain the project, including replacement of major items, in a manner adequate to protect its marketability.

Comments on Budget and Reserves ______

______

______

______

______

Date ______ 19 ______ Organization ______

By ______ Title ______

FHLMC Form 465 ADDENDUM B 9/80 VMP MORTGAGE FORMS • (313)293-8100 • (800)521-7291 VMP-37B (8704) FNMA Form 1073A 9/80

models; for the most part, the Public Securities Association's (PSA) prepayment model has been adopted as being more dependable. This cash flow yield differs from mortgage yield in that the underlying cash flow is made to be as realistic as possible. This means accounting for all known factors, such as the age of the underlying mortgages, as well as projecting reasonable estimates for future prepayments. Prepayments are usually specified in the form of a percentage of the FHA or SMM experience rate.

HORIZONTAL PROPERTY ACT Legislation that allows condominium ownership of property.

HOT WATER TANK A tank used to heat water. In making a home inspection, you should check the hot water tank for age and capacity. Hot water tanks should have a minimum capacity of 40 gallons and the normal life-expectancy is 10 years. Rust or leaks at the bottom of the tank are signs of future problems. Check for a pressure-relief valve and be sure it is on the hot water line. Heating elements and thermostats can be checked for proper operation by filling a bathtub with hot water. An average bathtub filled to within an inch of the overflow drain will contain approximately 35 to 40 gallons of water. If the hot water tank is functioning properly, you should have continuous hot water up to the overflow drain.

HOUSEHOLD All persons occupying a distinct housing unit that has either direct access to the outside or a public area or separate cooking facilities, regardless of whether the members are legally related or not.

HOUSING AUTHORITY LOANS See HOUSING FINANCE AGENCY.

HOUSING AND URBAN DEVELOPMENT (HUD) See DEPARTMENT OF HOUSING AND URBAN DEVELOPMENT.

HOUSING CODE Municipal ordinances that regulate roofing requirements, siding, room sizes, floor plans, ventilation, electrical systems, heating equipment, plumbing, occupancy, and maintenance.
See BUILDING CODES.

HOUSING DEVELOPMENT CORPORATION A private enterprise created to serve a particular area with multi-family housing needs. The corporation can serve a city, county, state, or a region. Civic leaders and private entrepreneurs are enlisted in helping the housing needs of the poor on a non-profit bases. It can help many in securing federal grants or it can provide a grant or "seed money" to get a project started.

HOUSING FINANCE AGENCY Usually a state agency that raises money by the sale of tax free bonds which is then invested in home mortgage loans. Because of the tax free status, the home loan interest rates are below what is widely available to homebuyers. Because the loans are enhanced, with reduced rates by government assistance, purchasers must qualify according to special guidelines. There is usually a limit to the family income, assets, previous ownership of a house, and size or price limit of the house.

Unlike standard loans, the borrower may become ineligible if their income exceeds a certain amount or if the composition of the household changes between the time of making application and loan closing. Lenders should warn closing agents that if they have reason to believe any such change in income or household composition has occurred since the borrower made application for the loan, the agent should reveal those facts to the lender before closing so the lender may decide if the loan will be eligible for delivery to the Housing Agency. For example, a single applicant may apply for a loan and, prior to closing, marry a person with income in an amount that could make the loan ineligible for delivery to the Agency.

HOUSING VOUCHER A program under HUD's authority that helps low-income families in affording the difference between 30% of the family's income per month and rent for a modest rental unit based on the following standard criteria: 1) family income (adjusted for family size) amounting to less than 50% of median income for the area; 2) use of the subsidy, in units meeting only minimum standards of liveability; 3) modest rents for the unit, generally within 40% of the median rents for standard units in the area; and 4) no overcrowding in the unit. Low-income families eligible for the vouchers may either stay in their present housing units or move to other units; the vouchers travel with the family.

HOW *See* HOMEOWNER'S WARRANTY PROGRAM.

HMDA *See* HOME MORTGAGE DISCLOSURE ACT.

HTG *See* HONEST-TO-GOD CASH FLOW YIELDS.

HUD *See* DEPARTMENT OF HOUSING AND URBAN DEVELOPMENT (HUD).

HUD HANDBOOKS *See* DEPARTMENT OF HOUSING AND URBAN DEVELOPMENT (HUD).

HUD USER HUD User is the information and research service sponsored by HUD's Office of Policy Development and Research. Established to disseminate the latest research in the fields of housing and urban development, HUD User offers products and services tailored to individual needs. This publication has been prepared to acquaint interested parties with the products available from HUD User. To request more information on how this service can help citizens meet their housing needs or to register and obtain a free subscription to *Recent Research Results,* call the HUD User at 1-800-245-2691 (301/251-3154 in Maryland and Washington, D.C.) or write HUD User at P.O. Box 6091, Rockville, Maryland 20850.

HYPOTHECATE To pledge property as collateral for a debt without giving up title or possession.

I

IBA *See* INDEPENDENT BANKERS ASSOCIATION.

IDENTIFYING RISKS IN PORTFOLIO STRUCTURING Mortgage investments have inherent in them the "mortgage problem" - changes in interest rates affect the nature of the option priced into them. If interest rates rise, prepayments slow down at a time when investors want to capture higher reinvestment rates, but when rates fall, prepayments pick up. To the extent that rates are stable, it is best to go toward the current coupon. When volatility is high, investors should look for higher or lower coupons. A blended portfolio can take advantage of co-variance in types of securities. Complexity risk is the difficulty of identifying an MBS's collateral and simulating its performance. The only way to immunize a portfolio against prepayment risk is through a laborious study of performance history.

Another mortgage investment risk is found in seasoning, which can either be an asset or drawback as premium securities season as well. Statistical risk refers to the difference between a calculated average and actual performance. Finally, there is price risk, which relates to the price that the security will sell when the investor needs cash. The only way to estimate price risk is to examine the performance of securities relative to equal-volatility Treasuries in the past and to assume that this pattern will continue. The end result is that investors must make decisions on the micro level and fine-tune their portfolios and yet maintain a wider perspective of interest rate management.

IMMEDIATE DELIVERY The physical delivery of loans from the seller to the purchaser for immediate underwriting and purchase by the investor. Normally thought to be within 30 days from the date of the commitment letter.

IMMEDIATE-PURCHASE CONTRACT An over-the-counter offer to purchase a group of loans offered for sale in the secondary market. The investor, purchaser of the loans, will perform an initial underwriting. The purchase by the investor and the physical delivery is normally within 30 days from the date of the commitment letter.

IMPOUND *See* ESCROW.

IMPROVED LAND Property that has been developed either partially or fully with installation of utilities, roads, curbs, gutters, and buildings.

IMPROVEMENTS An item permanently attached to raw land. Additions to a building or the building itself can be classified as an improvement.

IMPUTED INTEREST An interest rate that is stated by the Internal Revenue Service because the interest stated in the mortgage is unrealistically low or there is no interest stated.

INCHOATE This term describes something that has begun but is not yet completed. Some examples would be a lien that is going to be recorded but has not yet actually been recorded or a deed that has been signed and acknowledged but has not yet been made a public record.

INCOME ANALYSIS A percentage used to compare a mortgage payment and plus debts to the borrower's income. With conventional loans the sum of the payment for monthly principal, interest, taxes, and insurance (PITI), and any monthly PMI or homeowner or condo association fee, this sum should not exceed 25-28% of the monthly gross income for the purchaser. Furthermore, the sum of the above plus recurring debts with a duration of more than ten months, this total should not exceed 35-38%. For FHA, the debt ratios are 29%/41% and the recurring debts count if they have a duration of more than six months. VA uses the same basic formula as FHA except their emphasis is on the second ratio, 41%, and a residual income chart. If a veteran's debt ratio is more than 41% then the residual income of the veteran must exceed that listed in the VA residual income chart. The worksheet below will many to understand how to pre-qualify applicants.

The "top" ratio is the PITI payment divided by the monthly income of the borrower. If a monthly payment is $686 and the monthly income of the borrower is $2,450, the PITI ratio is 28%, which is an acceptable percentage for most lenders. Currently conventional, FHA, and VA lenders use the borrower's gross income to decide the PITI ratio. An acceptable ratio can vary from 25% to 29% depending on the type of loan.

The "bottom" ratio is the PITI payment plus all recurring debt payments more than six months divided by the monthly income of the borrower. Lenders do not include telephone, utility, and grocery bills as part of debt payments. Some examples of debts used are: as car payments, credit card payments (the minimum payment is used - whether the customer pays in full or does not), and payments for personal and real property.

The worksheets shown in Exhibits 32-34 can be completed in a short time with the help of a calculator. With the help of a computer and selected software programs, the time to complete the worksheets above can be reduced to a very few minutes and the math is always correct. An example of computer

Exhibit 32

Income Analysis—VA

Ratio Calculation

Gross Income			Housing & Debt Payment		
Veteran	$_____		P & I	$_____	
Spouse	$_____		Taxes	$_____	
Other	$_____		Insurance	$_____	
Total	$_____	(A)	Food Ins.	$_____	
			Other	$_____	
			Total	$_____	(B)

Ratio

Divide (D) $\dfrac{\text{debt payment}}{\text{Gross Income}}$

By (A)

Recurring Obligations $_____(C)

=   _____%   Total $_____(D)

Ratio (E)

Residual Income

Total Income	$_____	Net Income	$_____
Less:		Less:	
Income Tax	$_____	Recurring	
SS/Retirement	$_____	Obligations (C)	$_____
Other	$_____	Monthly Paymt. (B)$_____	
Plus		Maint./Util.	$_____
Non-taxable	+_____	Residual Income	$_____(F)
Net Income	$_____		

Ratio (E) should not exceed 41% without compensating factors.

If ratio is higher than 41% the RESIDUAL INCOME MUST BE AT LEAST 20% higher than shown on chart below:

Family Size	N/E	Midwest	South	West
1	411	399	409	443
2	646	627	643	697
3	786	763	781	847
4	873	848	868	941
5	951	924	946	1024
6	1026	999	1021	1099
7	1101	1074	1096	1174

Exhibit 33
Income Analysis—Conventional

Monthly Income			*Monthly Payments*	
a. Borrower's Base Income	$_____		First Mortgage Payments	
			g. P & I	$_____
b. Spouse's Base Income	$_____		h. Taxes	$_____
			i. Haz. Ins.	$_____
			j. PMI	$_____
c. Other	$_____		k. Other	$_____
d. Total Effective Income	$_____		l. Total Mortgage Payment	$_____
e. 25% of Total Income	$_____		m. Total of all other monthly payments extending beyond 10 months, including Alimony/Child Support if applicable	$_____
(Mo. Pmt./Income _____%)				
f. 33% of Total Income	$_____		n. TOTAL ALL PAYMENTS	$_____
(Obligation/Income _____%)				

software in loan underwriting is seen in the definition of COMPUTERIZED LOAN ORIGINATION.

Income used for loan qualification is verifiable income from an employer or from information provided by the self-employed. For an understanding of eligible income for an income analysis, *see* VERIFICATION OF EMPLOYMENT and SELF-EMPLOYED BORROWERS.

See COMPENSATING FACTORS, COMPUTERIZED LOAN ORIGINATION (CLO), SELF-EMPLOYED BORROWERS.

INCOME APPROACH TO VALUE One of three approaches to value used in appraising real property. In the income approach, value is created by the present worth of future income produced by the subject property. The four steps in the income approach are as follows: (1) estimate the annual gross income, (2) decide the effective gross income, (3) decide the net income, and (4) decide the value by using applying a capitalization rate to the net income. Income, Cost and Market are the three approaches to value.

An appraiser may want to use a form like that in Exhibit 35 to estimate the market rent for a property.

See CAPITALIZATION RATE, DEBT COVERAGE RATIO, and EFFECTIVE GROSS INCOME.

Exhibit 34

FHA Prequalifying Worksheet

*Use the factor tables on the next page to calculate the principal and interest and the Mortgage Insurance Premium to be included in the loan amount as well as for the monthly or annual mortgage Insurance payment.

Income Monthly

Borrowers base	$ _____
Other Income	_____
Co-Borrowers Base	_____
Other Income	_____
Total	$ _____

Ratios

Housing Expense divided by
Total Income
(guideline is 29%)   _____ %

Fixed Expense divided by
Total Income
(guideline is 41%)   _____ %

Total Income minus
Fixed Expense = Residual Income
(guideline varies by region)
                                 $ _____

Housing Expense

*Principal & Interest	$ _____
Hazard Insurance	_____
Property Tax	_____
Mortgage Insurance	_____
0.5% of loan divided by	
12 mos. for estimate	
Homeowners Assn. Dues	_____
Total Housing	$ _____

Liabilities

Creditor   Monthly payment

_____   _____
_____   _____
_____   _____
_____   _____
_____   _____
                   _____

Other expenses   _____

Total Liabilities** $ _____   *Use debts with more
                     _____   than 6 months remaining

Plus Housing Expense _____

Total Fixed Expense $ _____

Exhibit 35

SINGLE FAMILY COMPARABLE RENT SCHEDULE

This form is intended to provide the appraiser with a familiar format to estimate the market rent of the subject property. Adjustments should be made only for items of significant difference between the comparables and the subject property.

ITEM	SUBJECT	COMPARABLE NO. 1		COMPARABLE NO. 2		COMPARABLE NO. 3	
Address							
Proximity to Subject							
Date Lease Begins							
Date Lease Expires							
Monthly Rental	If Currently Rented: $	$		$		$	
Less: Utilities							
Furniture	$	$		$		$	
Adjusted Monthly Rent	$	$		$		$	
Data Source							

RENT ADJUSTMENTS	DESCRIPTION	DESCRIPTION	+ (−) $ Adjustment	DESCRIPTION	+ (−) $ Adjustment	DESCRIPTION	+ (−) $ Adjustment
Rent Concessions							
Location/View							
Design and Appeal							
Age/Condition							
Above Grade Room Count	Total Bdrms Baths	Total Bdrms Baths		Total Bdrms Baths		Total Bdrms Baths	
Gross Living Area	Sq. Ft.	Sq. Ft.		Sq. Ft.		Sq. Ft.	
Other (e.g., basement, etc.)							
Other:							
Net Adj. (total)		+ − $		+ − $		+ − $	
Indicated Monthly Market Rent		$		$		$	

Comments on market data, including the range of rents for single family properties, an estimate of vacancy for single family rental properties, the general trend of rents and vacancy, and support for the above adjustments. (Rent concessions should be adjusted to the market, not to the subject property.)

Final Reconciliation of Market Rent:

I (WE) ESTIMATE THE MONTHLY MARKET RENT OF THE SUBJECT AS OF _____, 19 ___ TO BE $ ___

Appraiser(s)   SIGNATURE _____   Review Appraiser SIGNATURE _____
(If applicable)

NAME _____   NAME _____

Freddie Mac Form 1000 (8/88)   **This form must be reproduced by the Seller.**   Fannie Mae Form 1007 (8/88)

 - 33 (8809)   VMP MORTGAGE FORMS • (313)293-8100 • (800)521-7291

INCOME LIMITS Some housing programs are for those families with incomes below established limits. These programs are subsidized in various ways. For housing programs that offer mortgage loans, the subsidy is usually in the form of a lower interest rate. Income limits can pertain to rental property such as housing projects or the Section 8 rent subsidy program. The limits are decided by the family size and the geographic location. *See* HOUSING FINANCE AGENCY.

INCOME PROPERTY Any property to be used for income producing purposes. Income property can be residential, commercial, or industrial. For residential purposes, any housing with more than four units is considered to be an income property. Examples of income properties are: shopping centers, warehouses, and office buildings.

INCOMPETENT In real estate law, a person is deemed incompetent if they cannot fulfill the obligations of a contract due to reasons such as being a minor or mentally ill.

INDEMNIFY The act of insuring or protecting a person against loss or damage.

INDENTURE An executed deed through which two or more parties having interests enter into corresponding grants or obligations to each other.

INDEPENDENT BANKERS ASSOCIATION (IBA) An association whose membership is comprised of medium-sized and small bankers who operate independently in rural areas. Headquartered in Sauk Center, Minnesota, a Washington, D.C. office is also maintained to lobby for applicable independent banking legislation in policy procedures, management, etc.

INDEX The instrument used to serve as a base for the cost of money for Adjustable Rate Mortgages. For example, a one-year adjustable rate mortgage may have a one-year Treasury bill as the index. If the one year T-bill is the index, each yearly adjustment period of the rate will involve the price of a one-year Treasury bill plus the margin. The index will usually be a price decided by a weekly or monthly average over a specified period. For adjustable rate securities, the index is the weekly average yield on U.S. Treasury securities adjusted to a constant maturity of one year as described in GNMA Handbook 5500.2. Normally, the original lending application process is individually indexed as opposed to GNMA, FNMA and FHLMC pools indexed for securities. Primary lenders who sell loans in the secondary marketplace must apply indexes as dictated by the conduits for ARMs. Generally, the indexes used for

ARM adjustments are: 6-month, 1-year, 3-year, 5-year and 7-year Treasuries, 11th District Cost of Funds, FHLB, FNMA, FHLMC, Prime Rate, and various other schedules.

Exhibit 36 presents the indices most often used for adjustable rate loans. A history of the index will help decide what it may do in the future.

See ADJUSTABLE RATE MORTGAGE, and MARGIN.

INDEX LEASE A lease with a rent that adjusts to the movement of an index such as the Consumer Price Index or Cost-of-Living Index.

INEFFICIENT HEDGE A hedge that does not exactly offset the increase or decrease in the value of the hedged loans or securities. An adverse basis move leads to an inefficient hedge and would occur when:

(1) Rates rise but the lender's capital loss on pipeline loans associated with higher yield requirements is not fully offset by the hedge gain. As a result, there is still a net loss, but one that is less than if the pipeline had been unhedged.

(2) Rates fall but the loss on the hedge outweighs the increased value of the pipeline. In this case, a net loss is incurred though the value of the pipeline rose.

(3) In extreme cases, pipeline yields and hedge market rates move in opposite directions, rather than just by unequal amounts. If both moves were adverse, the net loss would encompass the full extent of lost pipeline value plus the full loss on the hedge position.

See HEDGE, HEDGING POSITION.

INFRASTRUCTURE Facilities and services of a community as they relate to providing transportation, water, sewer, and recreation or community services.

INGRESS The right to enter or have access to property is ingress.

INITIAL MARGIN Cash or Treasury securities that must be placed as a *good faith* deposit with a futures exchange or clearing house prior to establishing a futures position.

INJUNCTION A court order requiring a person or a party to perform or to refrain from performing a certain action.

IN PERSONAM A Latin term meaning *against the person*; a court action against a defendant.

Exhibit 36
A Recent History of Several Major Indices

6 Month T-bills (Discount Basis)

	1973	1974	1975	1976	1977	1978	1979	1980
JAN	5.53	7.63	6.53	5.24	4.78	6.69	9.50	11.85
FEB	5.75	6.87	5.67	5.14	4.90	6.74	9.35	12.72
MAR	6.43	7.83	5.64	5.49	4.88	6.64	9.46	15.10
APR	6.53	8.17	6.01	5.20	4.79	6.70	9.50	13.62
MAY	6.62	8.50	5.65	5.60	5.19	7.02	9.53	9.15
JUN	7.23	8.23	5.46	5.78	5.20	7.20	9.06	7.22
JUL	8.08	8.03	6.49	5.60	5.35	7.47	9.19	8.10
AUG	8.70	8.85	6.94	5.42	5.81	7.36	9.45	9.44
SEP	8.54	8.60	6.87	5.31	5.99	7.95	10.13	10.55
OCT	7.26	7.56	6.39	5.07	6.41	8.49	11.34	11.57
NOV	7.82	7.55	5.75	4.94	6.43	9.20	11.86	13.61
DEC	7.44	7.09	5.93	4.51	6.38	9.40	11.85	14.77

	1981	1982	1983	1984	1985	1986	1987	1988
JAN	13.88	12.93	7.90	9.06	8.03	7.13	5.47	6.31
FEB	14.13	13.71	8.23	9.13	8.34	7.08	5.60	5.96
MAR	12.98	12.62	8.33	9.58	8.92	6.60	5.56	5.91
APR	13.43	12.68	8.34	9.83	8.31	6.07	5.93	6.21
MAY	15.33	12.22	8.20	10.31	7.75	6.16	6.11	6.53
JUN	13.95	12.31	8.89	10.55	7.16	6.28	5.99	6.76
JUL	14.40	12.24	9.29	10.58	7.16	5.85	5.86	6.97
AUG	15.55	10.11	9.53	10.65	7.35	5.58	6.14	7.36
SEP	15.06	9.54	9.19	10.51	7.27	5.31	6.57	7.43
OCT	14.01	8.30	8.90	10.05	7.32	5.26	6.86	7.50
NOV	11.53	8.32	8.89	8.99	7.26	5.42	6.23	7.76
DEC	11.47	8.23	9.14	8.36	7.09	5.53	6.36	8.24

1 Year Treasury

	1973	1974	1975	1976	1977	1978	1979	1980
JAN	5.89	7.42	6.83	5.81	5.29	7.28	10.41	12.06
FEB	6.19	6.88	5.98	5.91	5.47	7.34	10.24	13.92
MAR	6.85	7.76	6.11	6.21	5.50	7.31	10.25	15.82
APR	6.85	8.62	6.90	5.92	5.44	7.45	10.12	13.30
MAY	6.89	8.78	6.39	6.40	5.84	7.82	10.12	9.39
JUN	7.31	8.67	6.29	6.52	5.80	8.09	9.57	8.16
JUL	8.39	8.79	7.11	6.20	5.94	8.39	9.64	8.65
AUG	8.82	9.36	7.70	6.00	6.37	8.31	9.98	10.24
SEP	8.31	8.87	7.75	5.84	6.53	8.64	10.84	11.52
OCT	7.40	8.05	6.95	5.50	6.97	9.14	12.44	12.49
NOV	7.57	7.66	6.49	5.29	6.95	10.01	12.39	14.15
DEC	7.27	7.31	6.60	4.89	6.96	10.30	11.98	14.88

	1981	1982	1983	1984	1985	1986	1987	1988
JAN	14.08	14.32	8.62	9.90	9.02	7.73	5.78	6.99
FEB	14.57	14.73	8.92	10.04	9.29	7.61	5.96	6.64
MAR	13.71	13.95	9.04	10.59	9.86	7.03	6.03	6.71
APR	14.32	13.98	8.98	10.90	9.14	6.44	6.50	7.01
MAY	16.20	13.34	8.90	11.66	8.46	6.65	7.00	7.40
JUN	14.86	14.07	9.66	12.08	7.80	6.73	6.80	7.49
JUL	15.72	13.24	10.20	12.03	7.86	6.27	6.68	7.75
AUG	16.72	11.43	10.53	11.82	8.05	5.93	7.03	8.17
SEP	16.52	10.85	10.16	11.58	8.07	5.77	7.67	8.09
OCT	15.38	9.32	9.81	10.90	8.01	5.72	7.59	8.11
NOV	12.41	9.16	9.94	9.82	7.88	5.80	6.96	8.48
DEC	12.85	8.91	10.11	9.33	7.68	5.87	7.17	8.99

Exhibit 36 (continued)

3 Year Treasury

	1973	1974	1975	1976	1977	1978	1979	1980
JAN	6.27	6.96	7.23	6.99	6.22	7.61	9.50	10.88
FEB	6.58	6.76	6.65	7.06	6.44	7.67	9.29	12.84
MAR	6.86	7.35	6.81	7.13	6.47	7.70	9.38	14.05
APR	6.78	8.05	7.76	6.84	6.32	7.85	9.43	12.02
MAY	6.83	8.27	7.39	7.27	6.55	8.07	9.42	9.44
JUN	6.83	8.15	7.17	7.31	6.39	8.30	8.95	8.91
JUL	7.54	8.41	7.72	7.12	6.51	8.54	8.94	9.27
AUG	7.89	8.66	8.16	6.86	6.79	8.33	9.14	10.63
SEP	7.25	8.41	8.29	6.66	6.84	8.41	9.69	11.57
OCT	6.81	8.00	7.81	6.24	7.19	8.62	10.95	12.01
NOV	7.00	7.61	7.46	6.09	7.22	9.04	11.18	13.31
DEC	6.81	7.24	7.44	5.68	7.30	9.33	10.71	13.65

	1981	1982	1983	1984	1985	1986	1987	1988
JAN	13.01	14.64	9.64	10.93	10.43	8.41	6.41	7.87
FEB	13.65	14.73	9.91	11.05	10.55	8.10	6.56	7.38
MAR	13.51	14.13	9.84	11.59	11.05	7.30	6.58	7.50
APR	14.09	14.18	9.76	11.98	10.49	6.86	7.32	7.83
MAY	15.08	13.77	9.66	12.75	9.75	7.27	8.02	8.24
JUN	14.29	14.48	10.32	13.18	9.05	7.41	7.82	8.22
JUL	15.15	14.00	10.90	13.08	9.18	6.86	7.74	8.44
AUG	16.00	12.62	11.30	12.50	9.31	6.49	8.03	8.77
SEP	16.22	12.03	11.07	12.34	9.37	6.62	8.67	8.57
OCT	15.50	10.62	10.87	11.85	9.25	6.56	8.75	8.43
NOV	13.11	9.98	10.96	10.90	8.88	6.46	7.99	8.72
DEC	13.66	9.88	11.13	10.56	8.40	6.43	8.13	9.11

5 Year Treasury

	1973	1974	1975	1976	1977	1978	1979	1980
JAN	6.34	6.95	7.41	7.46	6.58	7.77	9.20	10.74
FEB	6.60	6.82	7.11	7.45	6.83	7.83	9.13	12.60
MAR	6.81	7.31	7.30	7.49	6.93	7.86	9.20	13.47
APR	6.67	7.92	7.99	7.25	6.79	7.98	9.25	11.84
MAY	6.80	8.18	7.72	7.59	6.94	8.18	9.24	9.95
JUN	6.69	8.10	7.51	7.61	6.76	8.36	8.85	9.21
JUL	7.33	8.38	7.92	7.49	6.84	8.54	8.90	9.53
AUG	7.63	8.63	8.33	7.31	7.03	8.33	9.06	10.84
SEP	7.05	8.37	8.37	7.13	7.04	8.43	9.41	11.62
OCT	6.77	7.97	7.97	6.75	7.32	8.61	10.63	11.86
NOV	6.92	7.68	7.80	6.52	7.34	8.84	10.93	12.83
DEC	6.80	7.31	7.76	6.10	7.48	9.08	10.42	13.25

	1981	1982	1983	1984	1985	1986	1987	1988
JAN	12.77	14.65	10.03	11.37	10.93	8.68	6.64	8.18
FEB	13.41	14.54	10.26	11.54	11.13	8.34	6.79	7.71
MAR	13.41	13.98	10.08	12.02	11.52	7.46	6.79	7.83
APR	13.99	14.00	10.02	12.37	11.01	7.05	7.57	8.19
MAY	14.63	13.75	10.03	13.17	10.34	7.52	8.26	8.58
JUN	13.95	14.43	10.63	13.48	9.60	7.64	8.02	8.49
JUL	14.79	14.07	11.21	13.27	9.70	7.06	8.01	8.66
AUG	15.56	13.00	11.63	12.68	9.81	6.80	8.32	8.94
SEP	15.93	12.25	11.43	12.53	9.81	6.92	8.94	8.69
OCT	15.41	10.80	11.28	12.06	9.69	6.83	9.08	8.51
NOV	13.38	10.38	11.41	11.33	9.28	6.76	8.35	8.79
DEC	13.60	10.22	11.54	11.07	8.73	6.67	8.45	9.09

Exhibit 36 (continued)

National Median Cost of Fun

	*1979	1980	1981	1982	1983	1984	1985	1986
JAN	—	8.09	9.50	11.44	10.14	9.89	9.75	8.50
FEB	—	8.29	9.82	11.26	9.75	9.73	9.40	8.29
MAR	—	7.95	10.24	11.37	9.72	9.73	9.36	8.35
APR	—	8.79	10.40	11.35	9.62	9.64	9.29	8.22
MAY	7.35	9.50	10.59	11.39	9.62	9.74	9.19	8.12
JUN	7.27	9.41	10.79	11.38	9.54	9.67	8.95	7.95
JUL	7.44	9.18	10.92	11.54	9.65	9.90	8.87	7.94
AUG	7.49	8.98	10.76	11.50	9.81	10.01	8.77	7.80
SEP	7.38	8.78	11.02	11.17	9.74	9.93	8.63	7.59
OCT	7.47	8.60	11.53	10.91	9.85	10.15	8.59	7.50
NOV	7.77	8.68	11.68	10.62	9.82	10.04	8.50	7.33
DEC	7.87	8.84	11.58	10.43	9.90	9.92	8.48	7.28

	1987	1988
JAN	7.22	7.12
FEB	7.02	7.11
MAR	6.99	7.13
APR	6.93	7.12
MAY	6.92	7.11
JUN	6.90	7.11
JUL	6.96	7.14
AUG	6.95	7.21
SEP	6.93	7.21
OCT	7.03	7.29
NOV	7.04	
DEC	7.11	

11th District Cost of Funds

	*1978	1979	1980	1981	1982	1983	1984	1985
JAN	6.49	7.25	8.76	10.45	11.95	10.46	10.03	10.22
FEB	7.10	7.92	9.65	11.16	12.34	10.42	10.17	10.16
MAR	6.51	7.42	8.86	10.95	12.14	9.87	9.98	9.98
APR	6.68	7.67	9.82	11.14	12.17	9.81	10.14	9.97
MAY	6.61	7.67	10.41	11.43	12.17	9.63	10.26	9.70
JUN	6.75	7.76	10.08	12.14	12.67	9.82	10.43	9.57
JUL	6.69	7.68	9.67	11.85	12.23	9.68	10.71	9.37
AUG	6.71	7.77	9.39	12.03	11.96	9.97	10.86	9.27
SEP	6.89	7.91	9.29	12.33	11.77	10.00	11.04	9.13
OCT	6.83	7.79	9.11	12.29	11.29	10.00	10.99	9.03
NOV	7.11	8.42	9.52	12.47	11.04	10.03	10.89	9.04
DEC	7.04	8.65	9.63	12.18	11.09	10.19	10.52	8.88

	1986	1987	1988
JAN	8.77	7.40	7.615
FEB	8.96	7.45	7.647
MAR	8.74	7.31	7.509
APR	8.59	7.25	7.519
MAY	8.44	7.22	7.497
JUN	8.37	7.27	7.618
JUL	8.20	7.28	7.593
AUG	8.02	7.28	7.659
SEP	7.90	7.39	7.847
OCT	7.72	7.44	7.828
NOV	7.60	7.56	7.914
DEC	7.51	7.65	

Exhibit 36 (continued)

FHLBB Contract Rate

	1973	1974	1975	1976	1977	1978	1979	1980
JAN	7.53	8.47	9.32	9.07	8.84	8.95	10.08	11.78
FEB	7.55	8.53	9.19	9.03	8.80	8.99	10.14	12.30
MAR	7.54	8.47	9.07	8.92	8.76	9.04	10.22	12.56
APR	7.55	8.43	8.92	8.85	8.74	9.14	10.29	13.21
MAY	7.62	8.49	8.85	8.84	8.75	9.17	10.35	13.74
JUN	7.64	8.66	8.86	8.82	8.78	9.27	10.46	12.88
JUL	7.70	8.82	8.89	8.85	8.83	9.41	10.67	12.23
AUG	7.87	8.95	8.95	8.91	8.86	9.55	10.88	11.89
SEP	8.10	9.15	8.93	8.94	8.86	9.62	10.94	12.00
OCT	8.35	9.31	8.97	8.94	8.88	9.68	11.01	12.31
NOV	8.42	9.37	9.09	8.91	8.89	9.74	11.23	12.85
DEC	8.46	9.39	9.09	8.90	8.93	9.85	11.59	13.15

	1981	1982	1983	1984	1985	1986	1987	1988
JAN	13.24	15.37	13.04	11.70	12.09	10.40	9.19	8.92
FEB	13.73	15.22	12.88	11.73	11.90	10.46	8.89	8.84
MAR	13.91	15.07	12.61	11.69	11.72	10.24	8.80	8.84
APR	13.99	15.39	12.42	11.61	11.62	10.00	8.79	8.93
MAY	14.19	15.57	12.36	11.63	11.62	9.80	8.93	8.90
JUN	14.40	15.01	12.21	11.79	11.29	9.83	9.02	8.98
JUL	14.77	14.96	12.18	12.03	11.02	9.88	9.05	8.98
AUG	15.03	15.03	12.25	12.24	11.02	9.88	9.05	9.00
SEP	15.38	14.71	12.38	12.43	10.87	9.71	8.91	8.98
OCT	15.47	14.37	12.19	12.52	10.76	9.59	8.86	9.11
NOV	15.80	13.74	12.11	12.38	10.86	9.48	8.89	9.16
DEC	15.53	13.44	11.94	12.26	10.80	9.29	8.86	9.31

Source: Telerate
*Data not available prior to this date.

IN REM A Latin term meaning *against the thing*; a court action against a property as opposed to an individual.

INSOLVENCY A condition when a debtor is unable to pay his creditors.

INSPECTION CERTIFICATE A lender may require that the collateral used for a loan is the same as described in the loan application. A designated agent can make an inspection and issue a certificate to the lender certifying that a property is one and the same as described to the lender for the loan purposes. The agent or inspector not only certifies to the physical composition of the improvements, but to the land as it pertains to the accuracy of the dimensions and location.

Inspection certificates are also used by appraisers to certify completion of necessary repairs. Lenders may use a form like the one in Exhibit 37 as an inspection certificate.

INSTALLMENT A partial payment of a purchase price of a property or a methodical repayment of a debt.

INSTALLMENT SALE A method of sale that has the property owner accepting a mortgage as part payment. The seller reports the principal collected as income in the taxable year it is received.

INSTITUTIONAL LENDER A financial institution whose lending practices are regulated by law. Examples are: mutual savings banks, life insurance companies, commercial banks, trust and pension funds, and savings and loan associations.

INTERMEDIATE COMBINATION A window type.
See WINDOW.

INSTRUMENT A legal document containing some right or obligation.
See DOCUMENTS.

INSULATION Material made with fiberglass, compressed wood-wool, fiberboard, and other combinations. Insulation retards heat and air loss. You should check for insulation in the attic and inquire about its existence in the walls. Insulation in the wall can be identified by removing a light switch plate and probing the sides to discover the presence and type of insulation. If you discover foam insulation, it is advisable to take a sample to the Health Department to decide if the foam contains any harmful chemicals such as formaldehyde.

Exhibit 37

SATISFACTORY COMPLETION CERTIFICATE

On _____ 19_____, the property situated at

_____

_____

_____

was appraised by me or _____.

The appraisal report was subject to: _____ satisfactory completion, _____ repairs, or _____

_____

I certify that I have reinspected subject property, the requirements or conditions set forth in the appraisal report have been met, and any required repairs or completion items have been done in a workmanlike manner.

Itemized below are substantial changes from the data in the appraisal report, and these changes do not adversely affect any property ratings or final estimate of value in the report:

_____ 19_____   _____

Date   Inspector

FHLMC 442 Rev. 6/78   VMP - 44

CONSOLIDATED BUISNESS FORMS, INC.-MT. CLEMENS, MI 48043 313/792-4700

The capacity of insulation is measured by an "R-value." The higher the "R-value" the greater the insulation capacity.

INSURABLE INTEREST An interest in property either real or personal that would cause a loss if the interest were damaged or destroyed.

INSURED ASSOCIATION A savings association whose accounts are insured by the FSLIC, FDIC or a private deposit insurance company. The FSLIC and FDIC guarantee individual accounts up to $100,000.

INSURED CLOSING AGREEMENT An agreement that insures a closing agent as the agent for the title insurance company, and that the agent will comply with the written instructions from the lender, will not misappropriate settlement funds, and that the lender will not suffer any loss or damage as a result thereof. The closing agent agrees that their willingness to act as the closing agent constitutes an agreement to compensate the lender for all damages the lender may suffer because of the agent's failure to comply with the lender's instructions. Failure to comply with the insured closing agreement gives the lender the right to call upon the title company represented by the closing agent to purchase subject mortgage under the terms of the insured closing letter.

As a rule, the title company will give its approval of an attorney to close loans under one of the following plans:

With a Binder: an Interim Title Binder or Commitment for Insurance must be issued to the lender before settlement funds are transmitted to the approved issuing agent.

Without a Binder: (called "fast closing" or "special insured closing"): the requirement of an Interim Title Binder or Commitment for Insurance can be waived. The attorney is required to file the final certificate with the title company immediately following closing.

To obtain protection by a title insurance company under its Insured Closing Agreement, the lender must name that specific title company as the one to be used, or an Interim Title Binder or Commitment for Insurance must be issued to the lender by the title insurance company prior to closing.

To comply with consumer laws and certain investor requirements, the lender must allow the borrower to select a title company if they wish to do so. If the borrower selects a company, it should be named in the Specific Closing Instructions to the closing agent.

There are cases, because of investor requirements or FHA/VA regulations, where the lender must require a title binder prior to closing not withstanding the fact that the closing agent is approved under the "fast closing" or "special insured closing" provision.

INSURED LOAN For a conventional loan, private mortgage insurance, called PMI, insures a portion of the loan against default. The amount insured depends upon the type of mortgage and the loan-to-value ratio. For example, a fixed-rate loan based on a 95% loan-to-value ratio can be insured on a 25% coverage basis and a 90% loan on a 20% coverage basis. This means that a purchaser's down payment plus the mortgage insurance will reduce the lender's risk down to approximately 70%.

PMI cost depends on the coverage required, type of mortgage, and the premium plan selected. Premium plans offered are usually an annual plan that is paid on a monthly basis, or a single premium plan that can be paid for a varying number of years.

Any premium refund will depend upon the date of loan termination and the PMI company. There are refunds available in certain situations.

Many borrowers assume that the premiums will automatically discontinue once the loan is amortized down to a loan-to-value ratio that a lender does not require PMI coverage, such as 80% or less. This is an erroneous assumption. Any discontinuance of PMI will depend mostly on the investor's (owner of the mortgage) requirements and the payment record of the mortgagor. What seems surprising is that (based on my experience with the public), most applicants do not ask this question and are generally uninformed about PMI.

California was the first state to have a law requiring a lender to notify a borrower as to when PMI can be canceled (Chapter 569, Laws of 1988).

See FHA - INSURED LOAN.

INSURANCE In residential property, the term *insurance* is normally encountered in four roles or types of coverage. (1) Insurance is available for protection against damage to real property that is commonly known as fire or hazard insurance. (2) Insurance is available to cover losses incurred from a foreclosure, called *private mortgage insurance* (PMI) for conventional loans and mortgage insurance premium (MIP) for FHA loans. (3) Insurance is available for payment of the mortgage in full in the event of the death of a mortgagor. (4) Insurance is available for continued payment of the PITI if the borrower becomes disabled.

INTEREST The cost for the use of money. The cost is usually measured in by a percentage rate although it can be in the form of discount points. Interest on a real estate mortgage, unlike rent, is paid in arrears. For example, a home loan monthly payment due on August 1st includes the interest payment for the month of July. Rent due on August 1st is for the month of August. States have laws regulating the maximum interest rate charged on a loan. Any interest rate above a state maximum violates the state usury law. State laws vary on the penalty charged to a usurious lender. At the time of this writing, of the three types of loans (conventional, FHA, and VA), only VA regulates the maximum rate permitted. At the time of this writing, interest on real estate loans is tax deductible.

See ACCRUED INTEREST, AMORTIZATION FACTORS, ANNUAL PERCENTAGE RATE, ADD-ON INTEREST, COMPOUND INTEREST, DEFERRED INTEREST, STANDING INTEREST.

INTEREST ONLY (IO) A security that pays cash flows from the interest paid by an underlying pool of mortgages. An IO is an interest-only security backed by an underlying collateral, a mortgage pool.

See PO.

INTEREST RATE The cost for the use of money expressed as a percentage of the sum of money borrowed or the rate of return from an investment in a mortgage.

INTEREST RATE FUTURES *See* FINANCIAL FUTURES.

INTEREST RATE SWAP An agreement between two parties to exchange payments that are based on specified interest rates - no transfer of principal, however. Swaps are cash flow exchanges that allow parties to change their interest rate exposure. Swaps may be used by some income property lenders (in income property, the lender is an investor who buys the loan) to match the duration of 5-year bullet/3-year lock-out loans with FRMs held in portfolio. Swaps are used in the Federal Home Loan Bank borrowings by many lending sources who specialize in income property origination as well as existing loans. Strategies employed by thrift institutions in interest rate swaps include the exchange of fixed and float payments but do not include an exchange of principal.

Interest rate swaps are an ideal way to agree mutually to convert a succession of cash flows as a means of improving a duration match in asset and liability conditions. Floating rate payables as exchanged for fixed-rate payables can be swapped to the advantage of a company wishing to withhold risk of interest rates as found in fixed-rate loan investments. Lock-outs in multifamily securities guard investors against prepayment risk. Interest rate swaps, however, can be problematic for some lending institutions. Care should be taken when it is evident that decreasing interest rates are threatening. Unless capitalization is strong for the institution's projected endurance, such swaps may cause losses.

INTERIM FINANCING This term is used to express a mortgage that is of a short term and generally used for construction financing. Disbursements are made as levels in the construction are accomplished.

See CONSTRUCTION MORTGAGE LOAN.

INTERMEDIATE-TERM STANDBY (ITS) A four-product addition to Fannie Mae's list of programs available on a negotiated basis and offered to sellers/servicers. It covers only fixed rate mortgages to be purchased for the Fannie Mae portfolio as well as fifteen-year loans that continue to be offered under standard programs. Lenders may sell seven-year, balloon mortgages and ten-year, fully amortizing mortgages to Fannie Mae at steep discounts with no initial fee on the ITS. However, there is a fee of two basis points of any unused amount payable at the end of the six-month term. The seven-year and ten-year balloons will have thirty-year amortizations. Ten- and twenty-year fully amortized loans are expected to increase availability to consumers.

INTERMEDIATION The investment process whereby savers and investors place their funds in financial institutions that appear to pay high rates of return. The institutions who can compete with the rates being paid by others, such as the U.S. government on its Treasury Bills, will then be able to pay higher rates on the depository inflow of the savers and investors.

See DISINTERMEDIATION.

INTERNAL RATE OF RETURN (IRR) Internal rate of return commonly defines a rate of return equal to present value of yields looked for in future income, compared to present value of money invested or the rate that inflows and outflows for a given discounted bond or portfolio exactly offset. Not only the dollars of returns received is considered in the internal rate of return on investment sums, but a duration of periods realized for the return of investment yields is considered. Rating the speed of various investments to the quality and simultaneously measuring their amounts with time lines is the effect.

If a Present Value (PV) table is unavailable, process of elimination can be used: 1) choose a logical return sum of investment or estimate (in theory) a trial rate in a computation of Internal Rate of Return (IRR); 2) choice of the trial balance applied in discounting the PV of future returns closely match a sum of the original investment first chosen, the balance is the correct IRR rate. Conversely, if evidence shows the balance rate does not match this IRR rate, search for a new return rate as a trial rate; 3) repeat such a procedure as this to equate the investment first selected to the present value of future returns in trial rates until PV is achieved as a final calculation. The IRR will then be the last calculation of a trial rate used.

IN-THE-MONEY The hedging of pipelines with "in-the-money" options are best exercised on an expiration date since this classification identifies the intrinsic value of the option that permits the right to buy or sell at higher than market prices, hence the term "in-the-money." A call option is in-the-money when its strike price is less than the value of the underlying security. A put option is in-the-money when the strike price is greater than the value of the security.

INTERSTATE LAND SALES ACT Federal law administered by the Department of Housing and Urban Development requires that promotional and advertising procedures as well as disclosures meet certain minimum requirements when land is sold on an interstate basis.

INTER VIVOS A Latin term meaning between living persons.

INTESTATE Legal condition of a person who dies without a will.

INTRINSIC VALUE (1) The amount by which a put or call option is in-the-money. The value of the option bearing the right to buy or sell the underlying mortgage security for a higher price than the prevailing price in today's market. Thus, a put means that the strike price is less than the security price and a call means that the security price is less than the strike price.

(2) The value of a tangible asset as separated from the intangible word. The value of something in itself. For example: The value of actual silver used in a coin is the intrinsic value as opposed to the value of the coin in the marketplace.

INVENTORY SEGMENT In a mortgage pipeline, the time between a loan closing and delivery of the loan to a secondary market investor.

INVERSE CONDEMNATION Litigation to seek a claim by a property owner against a governmental agency or municipality for damages created to the value of property that was taken by eminent domain proceedings, and for which no compensation was paid.

INVESTOR In real estate, this term has two meanings. Parties investing in real estate are investors. Parties who buy mortgages are investors.

In recent times there has been a lot of press about FHA discontinuing the investor loan. This means FHA will no longer insure loans to people who do not occupy the property as their principal residence. There are at least seven exceptions to the ban on FHA investor loans. *See* FHA - INVESTOR.

When a lender says he cannot make a certain loan because he does not have an investor for the loan, this means the lender cannot sell the loan in the secondary market. There are many loans authorized by FHA and VA that are not made by lenders. FHA and VA may make the rules, but the investor requirements dictates how, when, and why a lender will make a loan.

To understand the relationship between the agency, lender, and the investor, keep the following in mind.

Agency   Lender   Investor

"Agency" refers to FHA, VA, FNMA, or FHLMC; "Lender" refers to the company making the loan; "Investor" refers to supplier of the money for the loan. For FHA and VA loans, the Investor is usually thought of as GNMA - though it is not the ultimate supplier of the money for the loans.

These three entities (Agency, Lender, and Investor) interrelate to one another. FHA or VA guidelines can state a lender can do thus and thus with a loan. The lender must comply with the minimum set forth in the guidelines formed by the agencies, but the lender can require more or the lender can refuse to participate in a program. The principal reason a lender may not offer programs or features available through FHA or VA is the absence of money available from the Investor, the Secondary Market.

For example, FHA guidelines state it is not necessary to round down to the nearest $50 in determining the loan amount, if the MIP is being financed. A lender may require rounding down on all loans to avoid a possible mistake in not rounding down, which is a requirement if the borrower is paying the MIP in cash. The lender may not want to run the risk of having an uninsurable loan because someone in their organization forgot to round down on a loan that required rounding down.

Another example is the 245 program. FHA has guidelines for Plans IV and V, but there is a lack of Investors for these two Plans. Therefore, the only Plans the public usually hears about are Plans I, II, and III.

FHA encourages the 203(k) loan. Lenders have a hard time finding a good Investor for Section 203(k), often the only way the public hears about 203(k) is when a TV "investor guru" skirts over the highlights and advertises a costly tape that will explain "this fascinating new FHA program."

To understand the everyday practice of real estate finance, you must remember the relationship among: 1) the agency, 2) the lender, and 3) the investor. Avoid the trap of thinking a program is available because FHA or VA offers it, or thinking FHA or VA requires certain conditions when the investor is actually the party making the requirements.

INWOOD ORDINARY ANNUITY COEFFICIENT A factor used to show the present worth of a series of payments in the future when discounted at the stated rate of interest. It provides solutions for buying mortgages at a discount, evaluating cash flows, APR, and discounted yield. Refer to the ELLWOOD TABLE.

See HEWLETT-PACKARD 12C (HP-12C).

IO *See* INTEREST ONLY.

IRR *See* INTERNAL RATE OF RETURN.

ISSUE DATE The date when a mortgage-backed securities pool issued under a GNMA I or II program accrues interest. The issue date for such pools is always the first calendar day of the month of issue.

ISSUER A business organization, which having met the criteria established by Ginnie Mae, has received at least one commitment to guarantee securities from Ginnie Mae and has issued securities based upon said commitment. Fannie Mae, Freddie Mac, and some private mortgage insurance companies may establish separate criteria.

ITS *See* INTERMEDIATE-TERM STANDBY.

ITALIAN VILLA

Italian Villa. A massive 2 or 3-story Latin style house of masonry featuring: large overhanging eaves, a heavy cornice line, brackets and decorative iron work. Italian marble is often used for flooring, steps and window seals.

J

JALOUSIES Adjustable glass louvers in windows or doors so that the amount of light and air can be regulated and rain excluded.

JAMB A vertical member or lining of a doorway or window. A door jamb or window jamb supports the horizontal member of the opening.

JERRY-BUILT A slang term meant to imply construction that is of an inferior workmanship or quality.

JOINT In construction, this term means the point that two objects or surfaces join or meet.

JOINT AND SEVERAL LIABILITY An obligation or liability from one or all of the borrowers to their lender. Under joint and several liability, a lender can sue one or all of the borrowers for satisfactory performance.

JOINT TENANCY Ownership of property by two or more parties. Each party owns an undivided interest with the right of survivorship. In the event of death of an owner, the surviving owner(s) inherits the property. In a joint tenancy there is one title that is owned by two or more parties sharing equal ownership. In the event of death, the title is unaffected by an ownership change. The title continues with the remaining owners who now have larger shares. The decedent's interest cannot be transferred by will or descent. There is no probate under a joint tenancy.

JOINT VENTURE An agreement between two or more parties to invest in a business or property.

JOIST The horizontal supporting boards of a floor or a ceiling. This term is commonly used in conjunction with what it supports such as "floor joist" or "ceiling joist."

JOURNEYMAN Skilled worker who has learned the trade through an apprenticeship or a period of on-the-job training.

JUDGEMENT A formal decision by a court of law. A judgment can result in a lien against property or a garnishment of wages so that a creditor can collect a debt. Depending on circumstances involved, a lender who incurs a loss from a a foreclosure can obtain a judgement against the borrower. To collect the lien, the court will be asked to issue a "writ of execution" ordering the sheriff to seize and sell as much property belonging to the borrower as is necessary to satisfy the amount of the lien, which can include the loan plus foreclosure expenses. A judgement differs from a mortgage in that it does not have a specific property used as collateral.

See DEFICIENCY JUDGEMENT.

JUDICIAL FORECLOSURE Court approval to foreclose with its supervision. The court determines an acceptable price based upon an appraisal.

JUMBO LOAN A mortgage loan that has a principal balance greater than the amount eligible for purchase by Fannie Mae or Freddie Mac.

JUMBO POOL Large (jumbo) multiple issuer pools under GNMA II provide investors with geographic diversity and greater prepayment consistency. Loans from many lenders or from a single lender can be included in a jumbo pool. Jumbo pools are custom pools. Other special pool characteristics such as short maturities, below market interest rates, or the single issuer approach are optional. The minimum pool size is $250,000 for a jumbo pool and $1 million for a custom pool under GNMA II. Fannie Mae has set the stage for a broad program by which the individual seller/servicer will market their pro-rated portions of jumbo pools. GNMA II—with its statutory limit of $101,250 for individual FHA/VA purchases—provides an optional approach with their conforming loans: a custom pool classification where loans from a single lender can be included in a jumbo pool. GNMA II prescribes a minimum pool size of $1 million for the custom pool designation and $250,000 for a multiple issuer's pool.

Private conduits may follow this approach to jumbo pools set by the quasi-governmental institutions; however, their pools will exceed federal government balance limitations. Initiating secondary jumbo marketing is natural for private conduits to pursue because the opportunity for large profit potential in mortgage related security issues backed by jumbo loans is great. The non-conforming aspect of secondary jumbo marketing has restrained private conduits from setting the stage for broad programs designed by public agencies such as Fannie Mae's jumbo pool program. However, because the sale of jumbo loans are non-conforming, loans over the dollar amount of $187,450 are considered more risky and call for added points and higher rates. Since the current limitation deters lenders from selling jumbos to Ginnie Mae, Fannie Mae or Freddie Mac, a local system has been adopted by some lenders as an alternative to a jumbo pool program by keeping individual non-conforming loans on their books as a permanent portfolio for the organization.

This does not mean that approved lenders cannot sell their pooled loans into the secondary market to capitalize new loans; it means that conforming loans only are eligible for these particular government-sponsored secondary market conduits for pooling purposes. Lenders can still sell their jumbo loans to investors in heavy pool forms, continue to service the loans by collecting payments from borrowers, and collect fees from investors.

Regardless of the system for marketing jumbo loans into the secondary market, affluent communities often have special financing needs. Some lending institutions offer $350,000 jumbo loans at a fixed rate over 30 years at 80% LTVR while others offer adjustable-rate mortgages up to $750,000. On prime properties it is not considered risky to loan up to $1,000,000 in specific instances with a 60% LTVR applied on market values of $900,000- $1,000,000 with adjustable-rate jumbos; 70% LTVRs are applied on market values from $750,000-$900,000 with jumbo ARMs.

JUNIOR MORTGAGE In general, a mortgage that is subordinate or behind a prior mortgage. A second mortgage would be an example of a junior mortgage. There is more risk with a junior mortgage since foreclosure of a senior mortgage, such as a first mortgage, will eliminate the second mortgage on the subject property. In a foreclosure by a senior mortgage, the debt owed on the junior mortgage is not eliminated — only the existence of the second mortgage on the subject property is eliminated. Foreclosure by a junior mortgage has no effect on the senior mortgage. Some mortgages, however, have restrictions about what types of junior mortgages can be placed on the subject property. Failure to get permission from a first mortgage lender who restricts the type of junior mortgages allowed can result in foreclosure by the first mortgage lender. An example would be a conventional lender with a first mortgage allowing an escalation of the interest rate in the event of a resale of the property. If a buyer obtains a second mortgage from a commercial lender (bank, credit union, finance company, etc.) so that the first mortgage rate will remain unchanged and it is done without the first mortgage lender's consent, foreclosure could result.

JUNK BOND Any high-yielding, non-convertible debt security rated Ba1/ BB+ and below.

The most common securities issued are straight subordinated debt and debt with no equity add-on or equity kicker of warrants or common stock. Junk bonds are a quick and easy way to raise capital compared to the highly restrictive requirements encountered in borrowing from banks. Junk bonds are also called "High Yield Bonds."

K

KEY LOT A lot that enjoys added value because of its strategic location.

KICKBACK Payment made in return for a referral that resulted in business for the payer and the person or business being referred is unaware of the payment. Kickbacks are generally illegal. In general, it is illegal for a real estate agent to collect a referral fee for placing a loan if the buyer is uninformed of the fee, the agent does not perform any lending functions, and the agent collects a commission from the sale of the property.
See COMPUTERIZED LOAN ORIGINATION (CLO), RESPA.

KICKER In real estate financing, this term identifies something more than principal and interest being returned to the lender. Examples of kickers would be equity participation in the ownership of the property or participation in rentals received.

KICKER MORTGAGE LOAN A commercial mortgage loan that is often used with income properties. Office buildings, research and development centers, warehouses, and shopping centers are frequently financed with a kicker loan. A kicker loan is a way of leveraging properties more efficiently than a loan term of 10 years or less will permit on income property. Lenders and borrowers together may be attracted to participation loans and the kicker mortgage when interest rates soar above normal. Shorter term and kicker mortgages, rather than straight debt loans, have coupon rates of smaller values and permit mortgagees to participate in the appreciation of property value in the long or short run.

The period of loan term change is characterized by any sudden spike in 10-year Treasury rates that influence loan terms to shorten to five and three years duration for a mortgagor/developer's mortgage origination by commercial mortgagee lenders. If the commercial lender is a bank or a pension fund, the lender will be susceptible to any possible proposal that will avoid pay off by another permanent lender.

KICK PLATE A metal strip at the lower edge of a door used to protect the finish.

KILN A large, oven-like chamber used to dry or harden materials such as lumber, brick, and lime. This term is heard in connection with the construction industry when one reads that lumber has been kiln-dried.

KILO This term is used to note one thousand such as a kilogram having one thousand grams, a kilovolt having one thousand volts or a kilowatt having one thousand watts.

KING POST The middle post of a truss.

KITING CHECKS Writing a check against funds that are not on deposit on the date the check is written.

KNOLL A small, rounded hill.

L

LACHES The practice of delaying or being negligent in asserting one's legal rights. For example, a property owner watches a neighbor build a garage. The property owner knows that part of the garage is on their property, the neighbor does not know that he/she is encroaching. After the garage is complete, the property owner approaches the neighbor and asks for the removal of the part of the garage that encroaches on their property. If litigated, the issue will involve the laches doctrine.

LAG SCREW A large, heavy, wood screw with a square head without a slot in the head.

LAMINATED Layers of wood or other material bonded together to form a single unit.

LAND The surface of the earth extending down to the center and upward to the sky. In real estate, the term "land" includes surface rights, mineral rights, and air rights.

LAND ACQUISITION LOAN A loan to acquire land that is to be held and "parked" by a commercial developer. The person or enterprise that uses this type of loan is speculating on a future change in the zoning or an alteration in the present use of the land that will make it more valuable. These loans are risky and hard to acquire.

LAND BANKING The practice of acquiring land and holding it for future use.

LAND CONTRACT This term is synonymous with contract for deed and installment land contract. With a land contract, the purchaser is not given title to the property until the full price has been paid. The purchaser enjoys equitable title in that he has the right to possession, but the seller retains legal title. In the event of default, the seller can regain his property more quickly than with a mortgage.

An installment land contract permits a seller to hold onto the below market rate original mortgage while selling the home or land on an installment basis. The installment payments are for a short term and may be for interest only. At the end of the contract the unpaid balance, frequently the full purchase price, must be paid. The seller continues to hold title to the property until all payments are made. Therefore, the buyer acquires no equity until the contract ends. If a buyer fails to make a payment on time the investment is lost.

ments are made. Therefore, the buyer acquires no equity until the contract ends. If a buyer fails to make a payment on time the investment is lost.

These loans are popular because they offer lower payments than market rate loans. Land contracts may be used to avoid due-on-sale clauses. The buyer and seller may assert to the lender who provided the original mortgage that the due-on-sale clause does not apply because the property will not be sold until the end of the contract. Therefore, the low interest rate continues. However, the lender may contend that the contract in fact represents a sale of the property. Consequently, the lender may have the right to accelerate the loan (or call it due) and raise the interest rate to current market levels.

See DUE-ON-SALE CLAUSE.

LAND DEVELOPMENT LOAN A short term loan used primarily by subdivision developers. This loan is for the purposes of acquiring the land and developing it for a specific use that can be either residential, commercial, or industrial. This loan differs from a construction loan in that there are improvements made to the land but no permanent improvements in the form of buildings. A professional developer will use this type of loan to acquire the land and make improvements such as grading, and the installation of streets, curbs, and gutters. Some or all utility services such as, sewer, water, and electricity are made available to each lot.

LAND LEASE A lease of the ground or land and none of the improvements. A lease for use of the land.

See LAND SALE-LEASEBACK.

LAND PURCHASE-LEASEBACK An entity buys the land and leases it back to the seller. The tenant then secures a leasehold mortgage to build permanent improvements to the land. The tenant raises cash from the sale of the land and the mortgage to make permanent improvements to the land in the form of buildings. The owner of the land will usually subordinate their ownership in the land to a construction loan.

LAND RESIDUAL *See* RESIDUAL.

LAND SALE-LEASEBACK An owner of property sells the land and leases it back.

In this arrangement the land may or may not be improved by a building.

LANDLOCKED A lot that does not have access to a public thoroughfare except through an adjacent lot.

LANDLORD A party who rents property. A landlord is a lessor.

LANDMARK An identifying mark or monument serving to indicate the boundary for a tract of land.

LAP JOINT The point of contact between two pieces of wood connected together by lapping one over the other.

LAP SIDING The siding used for exterior finishes of a house or other structure. Each board overlaps another in a fashion similar to clapboard siding.

LASER REPORTING SYSTEM The trademarked name for Fannie Mae's computer communication system between itself and lenders. It is incompatible with Freddie Mac's Midanet II reporting system. Laser works directly from individual loans to all the loans serviced by a lender for the Fannie Mae portfolio while Freddie Mac uses accounting groups — reports on loans purchased from a lender under a particular commitment are handled as a group. The Aggregate Exception System (AES), the Summary Reporting System (SRS), and the Mortgage-Backed Security Reporting System (MRS) have all been converted to a Laser Reporting System. The SRS, MRS and MBS systems are all "summary systems" in that reports on the unpaid balance of principal are of groups of loans, not individual mortgages. In the SRS system, the principal balances are reported every six months; balances are reported every month for the MRS and MBS programs.

The SRS system was designed to be similar to Freddie Mac's system of accounting by reporting in groups in order to appeal to thrift institutions. Laser reporting is an electronic system with an update program from the end of one month to the end of the next month. Laser has full ARM capabilities and may become an industry standard.

LATE CHARGE *See* DELINQUENCY.

LATENT DEFECT A hidden or concealed defect. One that is known by a seller but cannot be seen by a purchaser or easily discovered by an appraiser or property inspector.

LATH Thin strips of wood or metal or other material used as the support or groundwork for slates, tiles, or plaster.

LAW DAY The day a note or a mortgage is due to be paid. In common law, the mortgagor had to pay the debt in full on law day or lose the property to the mortgagee.

LAWFUL INTEREST The maximum interest rate allowed by law. *See* INTEREST.

LEAD-BASED PAINT Houses built before 1978 (per FHA regulations) should be checked for lead-based paint. Applicable surfaces include all interior and exterior surfaces regardless of height. Lead-based paint is hazardous to your health and if found should be either washed, sanded, scraped, or wire-brushed and then replaced with two coats of non-lead based paint. Flakes from lead-based paint can get into the hands of children. The flakes have a sweet taste, similar to sweet pickles, and if eaten they can cause permanent brain damage. Lenders have taken steps to prevent and solve the problems created by lead-based paint.

LEAN-TO A term used to describe a shed or building constructed against an outside wall of another building and having an inclined roof. The structure appears to lean to the attached building. See ROOF.

LEASE An agreement, written or unwritten, involving payment of rent for possession of real estate for a specific period of time. The owner of the property must retain the reversionary right, the property must revert to the owner at the end of the lease. A lease is a conveyance and a contract. Use of the property is conveyed to the tenant and the tenant must fulfill obligations in the lease contract. The rights of the owner or lessor is called the "leased fee estate." The rights of the tenant or lessee is called the "leasehold estate." A lease should be written otherwise the courts will write the lease, as they will for a person who dies without a will (intestate).

LEASE OPTION *See* LEASE PURCHASE.

LEASE PURCHASE A seller and a buyer can enter into an agreement to purchase property with rental payments that apply to the sales price, usually in the form of a downpayment. In residential property, when a purchaser does not have sufficient funds for a minimum downpayment, he can enter into a lease and have a part of the rental payment accumulate into an amount that is sufficient for the required downpayment. Lenders have guidelines for this type of purchase plan. Usually the lender will require that the rent portion of the lease-purchase payment to be a fair market rent and not an artificial, below-the-market rental used to create the required downpayment. If the rent is not a fair market rent, then the lender views the transaction as the seller giving the buyer the downpayment in the form of a reduced rent.

The appraiser making an appraisal on the property, involved in a lease-purchase, will be asked to estimate the fair market rent. If the lease-purchase rental payments are below the fair market rent, the lender will ignore these payments and not credit them as accumulating towards the required downpayment. A lease-purchase is a lease with an option to buy.

A seller, for example, sells a property to a buyer, who lacks the sufficient downpayment, for $80,000. The buyer will be required to make monthly payments of $1,100 per month with $800 as rent and $300 as an accumulating downpayment. At the end of 27 payments the buyer will have accumulated slightly more than a 10% downpayment.

In a lease-purchase, it is advisable that parties enter into two separate agreements, a sales contract and a lease contract. The two contracts are tied to one another, but the agreements and responsibilities are specified for each contract. If the tenant violates the rental agreement, then the matter is treated as a routine breach of a lease contract instead of a breach of a sales contract that can be more cumbersome and expensive to terminate.

See OPTION.

LEASEHOLD The estate or interest that a tenant has in the real estate. It is an exclusive right to property as opposed to a guest in a motel or hotel or a license issued for space in a building. Removal of a tenant is more serious process than removal of a guest or the holder of license. Some tenants, such as in a land lease, may have a leasehold estate that lasts for 99 years.

LEAVES The hinged, sliding, or detachable parts of a sliding door, window, tabletop, or shutters.

LEGACY A gift of money or personal property by will.

LEGAL AGE The age when a person can take title to real estate and is no longer considered a minor.

LEGAL DESCRIPTION A statement acceptable by real estate law for describing real estate.

LEGAL ELIGIBILITY A regulatory provision that governs the investments that life insurance companies, mutual savings banks, and other regulated investors may make under state laws and regulations.

LEGAL NAME That name used by an individual for business purposes. A legal name means a person's full name.

LEGAL NOTICE Notice that conforms to practices required by law.

LEGAL RATE OF INTEREST *See* INTEREST.

LEGAL TENDER Payment that is deemed acceptable by law from a debtor to a creditor.

LENDER OPTION *See* FHA - LENDER OPTION.

LENDER PARTICIPATION *See* EQUITY PARTICIPATION and KICKER MORTGAGE LOAN.

LESSEE A party who rents property from another. A tenant.

LESSOR The party who rents property to a tenant or lessee.

LETTER OF CREDIT (LOC) A written agreement that substitutes a bank's credit for that of an individual or business. The bank issuing the Letter of Credit will honor drafts or other demands for payment upon compliance with conditions specified in the LOC.

In mortgage lending it supports the lending institution's marketing commitment. Commercial banks finance mortgage bankers who warehouse pipelines of uncommitted loans via LOC contracts with banks. This strategy can produce a high credit rating since a letter of credit may either promise to support or substitute any commitment to the secondary market participants. The borrowings are based on the carry between the difference in long-term mortgage rates and short-term borrowing rates during the warehousing cycles. This carry may be negative or positive depending on the borrowing periods used.

LETTER OF INTENT A written agreement outlining how a party intends to perform certain actions connected with real estate. A letter of intent is not binding. It is merely to show the intentions of the parties involved.

LEVEL PAYMENT MORTGAGE A mortgage requiring the same payment each month until the debt is amortized or paid. A constant payment as in a fixed rate mortgage as opposed to a graduated or an adjustable rate mortgage. *See* FIXED RATE MORTGAGE.

LEVERAGE The practice of creating money by borrowing on real estate either by acquiring the subject property or using the subject property as collateral to buy other properties. Real estate offers a classic example of leverage. Someone once said that real estate is the only $100,000+ asset you can buy for a less than 10% cash investment and have 100% control. With a VA loan, you can buy a $184,000 asset for no money down.

Leveraging is attractive because the return on the money is based not on the cash investment, but on the total investment. For example, if you bought a $100,000 house for 10% down, and sold it a year later for $110,000 your return is not 10% (the amount of increase in the value of the house) but it is 100% (based on selling the house at a $10,000 profit plus the return of your initial downpayment of $10,000). The return is even more incredible (or more specifically it is called infinity) if you use the same example and substitute a 100% no-money-down VA loan.

See REVERSE LEVERAGE.

LEVY Assess, collect, or seize.

See ATTACHMENT, WRIT OF EXECUTION.

LIABILITY A debt, financial obligation, or potential loss. Nearly all residential loans require the borrower to be personally liable.

See EXCULPATORY CLAUSE, NON-RECOURSE, RECOURSE, RELEASE OF LIABILITY, SURETY.

LIABILITY INSURANCE Protection against claims by third parties due to damages or injuries caused by the insured on his property.

See HAZARD INSURANCE.

LIABLE Responsible or obligated.

LIBOR *See* LONDON INTERBANK OFFERED RATE.

LICENSEE A person who has a valid real estate license.

LICENSE LAWS Laws enacted by states to grant licenses to people engaged in the sale of real estate and to regulate their practices. The governing authority is the Real Estate Commission for each state. The Commissions carry forth tasks such as enforce the requirements to gain a license - including the successful completion of a real estate exam, investigate violations of licensing laws and recommend appropriate disciplinary action, and supervision of educational courses to take a licensing exam or to keep a license on an active status.

LIEN A claim by one person on the property of another as security for money owed. Such claims may include obligations not satisfied, judgment, unpaid taxes, materials or labor. A lien may be general or specific.

A *general lien* applies to all real and personal property. A *specific lien* applies to a specific property, such as a house.

Liens can be *statutory* or *equitable,* and they can be *voluntary* or *involuntary.* A mortgage on a house is an equitable, voluntary lien. A mechanic's lien is a statutory, involuntary lien. A lien caused by a judgement is a general lien. Liens take priority according to time sequence, excepting tax liens. A first mortgage lender will be very careful to document their first lien priority.

See ENCUMBRANCE.

LIEN THEORY This theory treats the mortgage as a secured debt against property by which the owner retains title. This theory differs from the title theory, which supports the belief that mortgage property is transferred to the lender or his representative, such as a trustee named in a Deed of Trust, and the title is not re-conveyed until the debt has been paid. Unless the mortgage instrument contains a power of sale, the lender must have court approval to foreclose.

See JUDICIAL FORECLOSURE, MORTGAGE, TITLE THEORY.

LIFE The period of time improvements to a property are expected to have physical or economic utility. The term also applies to mortgage lending since the yield is based on the average life of a mortgage.

See DISCOUNTED YIELD, YIELD ON AVERAGE LIFE, YIELD TO MATURITY.

LIFE ESTATE An estate in property that is the duration of the life of the person or party receiving the estate or interest. A grantor of a life estate has a reversionary interest. If the property reverts to a third party, it is considered as a remainderman interest.

For example, if Bill grants Sue a life estate in a property, she is a life tenant and has use of the property for as long as she lives. When Sue dies, the estate will revert back to Bill - this is called a reversion. If the property reverts to Bill's son, he is a remainderman.

A life tenant has certain privileges and limitations. A life tenant (1) is entitled to use the property just as though they were the fee owner; (2) is obligated to take care of the property so that it is left in its original condition; (3) must pay taxes and any interest on mortgages, but is not obligated for principal payments on a mortgage, or to have the property insured; and (4) cannot create any interest in the property beyond the measuring life (the life of the life tenant or a designated third party).

If life tenant purchases the interest of the reversion or the remainderman, the ownership of all interests is merged and the life tenant has a fee simple interest.

Fee simple and a life estate are the only kinds of freehold estates.

See FREEHOLD.

LIFE INSURANCE MORTGAGE RATES Life insurance companies make conventional loans on most types of properties. They supply funds for properties where large loans are required such as large commercial properties (shopping centers, industrial properties, hotels, etc.). Insurance companies essentially invest funds through mortgage companies (when not acting primarily as loan brokers) who, in turn, are appointed as loan correspondents or lend the funds directly. Mortgage companies make mortgage loans in their respective cities and areas and, when completed, deliver these loans to the life insurance companies. Frequently, these companies act as service agencies for such loans on a fee basis.

Insurance mortgage lending operations are governed by individual state laws (the state in which the company is incorporated and the state in which the company does business). There is no state restriction imposed on the loan term. However, company policy will usually hold the term to not more than 25-30 years and will require periodic amortization. For total mortgage investments, including loans on business and large commercial properties, life insurance companies ranked first among institutional lenders for many years. Overall, the long-term nature of life insurance assets make amortized real estate loans a suitable investment for insurance company funds.

In recent years many life insurance companies have been more active in making commercial real estate loans. Their lending policies broaden with their supply of funds available for investment purposes. When the supply of funds is abundant, smaller loans, loans on all types of properties in various locations are considered. It is expected that life insurance companies will become more diversified in their commercial lending policies in the future. Lending (including investment equity, participation in gross profits and secondary financing) is increasingly changing for all lenders, including insurance companies.

The American Council of Life Insurance (ACLI) provides a survey of annual average contract interest rates on commercial mortgage commitments. The following is a survey sample for the years 1966–1987 for mortgage commitments on multi-family and nonresidential mortgages.

Average Contract Interest Rates on Commercial Mortgages
Made by Reporting Life Insurance Companies

Year	Annual Average Contract Interest Rate
1966	6.35%
1967	6.92%
1968	7.65%
1969	8.62%
1970	9.86%
1971	8.99%
1972	8.50%
1973	8.70%
1974	9.47%
1975	10.14%
1976	9.78%
1977	9.31%
1978	9.57%
1979	10.36%
1980	12.53%
1981	13.90%
1982	14.04%
1983	12.46%
1984	12.81%
1985	11.67%
1986	9.53%
1987	9.54%

SOURCE: The American Council of Life Insurance, Investment Bulletin, "Mortgage Commitments on Multifamily and Nonresidential Properties."

LIFE TENANT A tenant who enjoys the use of property for their life. *See* LIFE ESTATE.

LIGHT In appraisal terminology, the word "light" indicates a single window pane.

LIMITED PARTNERSHIP A partnership consisting of one or more parties who serve as general partners and are liable for losses and responsible for the operation of the business. The limited partners are liable only to the extent of their investment and they are passive in their participation in the business operation.

LINE OF CREDIT The maximum dollar amount a bank will lend to one of its credit worthy customers without requiring a new, formal loan submission. An investor dealing in various real estate investments can buy and sell many investments without having to go through a formal loan submission for each property if the total loans on each property is below the line of credit.

LINTEL A horizontal piece of board, stone, or steel positioned above a door or a window. Its purpose is to support the load above the opening.

LIQUIDATED DAMAGES A predetermined amount agreed upon in a contract that one party will pay to another in the event of a breach of the subject contract.

LIQUIDITY The degree of ease that certain assets can be converted into cash. *See* MARKETABILITY.

LIQUID PORTFOLIO A lending institution's assets kept in short term securities (five years or less). Savings and loans under federal charters must keep a percentage of their assets in portfolio for liquidity. The Federal Home Loan Bank Board (FHLBB) mandates the ratio of assets to liabilities. The ratio may be subject to change from time to time.

LIS PENDENS A recorded legal notice indicating that there is a pending suit affecting property within that jurisdiction.

LISTING This term can refer to (1) the written contract between principal and agent, or (2) an agreement between the seller of property and a broker, or (3) a property that a broker has for sale.

There are several types of listings between a seller of property and a broker. The types of listings are as follows: open listings, net listings, oral listing, exclusive agency listings, or an exclusive right-to-sell-listing. The most common listing is the exclusive right-to-sell-listing.

See EXCLUSIVE LISTING.

LITIGATE To dispute or contend in form of law; to settle a dispute or seek relief in a court of law; to carry on a suit.

LITIGATION A lawsuit. Legal action, including all proceedings therein.

LITTORAL Land bordering on a large body of water.

LIVABILITY The quality of property to be used as a home.

LIVE LOAD The weight from people and fixtures that occupy the space in a building or on a structure. For example, the weight of moving traffic over a bridge as opposed to the weight of the bridge itself.

LOAD-BEARING WALL A wall that is built to withstand a supporting weight. A load-bearing wall gives structural support.

LOAN ADMINISTRATION The next step after closing a mortgage loan. The day-to-day operation of a mortgage company that services loans. It involves servicing the loan, i.e., collecting the monthly payment and making proper disbursements to principal, interest, taxes, insurance, and any additional applications. The goals of loan administration should be to (1) give proper service to the borrower, (2) protect the security for the loan, and (3) to earn a profit from the servicing operation.
See LOAN ORIGINATION PROCESS.

LOAN AGREEMENT A written agreement to repay a loan. If the agreement is secured by a mortgage, it serves as a note proving indebtedness and stating the manner in which it shall be paid. The note states the actual amount of the debt that the mortgage secures and renders the mortgagor personally responsible for repayments and the rate of interest charged.

LOAN APPLICATION The standard loan application form used by nearly all lenders is the FHLMC 65/FNMA 1003 form. (See Exhibits 38 and 39.)
   It is important for the applicant to be prepared for a loan application. Many lending experts agree that loan processing time can be drastically reduced if the applicant(s) is prepared. A checklist for a loan applicant is essential.

   (1) Applicants must be ready to show a photo ID and evidence of their Social Security number (an unexpired driver's license, picture ID card issued by the applicant's state of residence, military ID card, alien registration receipt card - form I-151- a valid passport with photograph - issued by any country, employee ID card with picture, or union card with picture). In cases where an acceptable picture identity is not possible, the lender must explain why and state in what manner the identity of the applicant was proven. Evidence of a Social Security number is a required for any person earning or receiving money in the U.S. It is possible for an applicant to have driver's licenses issued in many states, and to have many Social Se-

Exhibit 38

RESIDENTIAL LOAN APPLICATION

MORTGAGE APPLIED FOR	☐ Conventional ☐ FHA ☐■ VA	Amount $	Interest Rate %	No. of Months	Monthly Payment Principal & Interest $	Escrow/Impounds (to be collected monthly) ☐ Taxes ☐ Hazard Ins. ☐ Mtg. Ins. ☐

Prepayment Option

Property Street Address	City	County	State	Zip	No. Units

Legal Description (Attach description if necessary)	Year Built

Subject Property

Purpose of Loan: ☐ Purchase ☐ Construction-Permanent ☐ Construction ☐ Refinance ☐ Other (Explain)					
Complete this line if Construction-Permanent ☐■ or Construction Loan	Lot Value Data Year Acquired $	Original Cost $	Present Value (a) $	Cost of Imps. (b) $	Total (a + b) ☐■	ENTER TOTAL AS PURCHASE PRICE IN DETAILS OF PURCHASE

Complete this line if a Refinance Loan	Purpose of Refinance	Describe Improvements ( ) made ( ) to be made		
Year Acquired	Original Cost $	Amt. Existing Liens $		Cost: $

Title will Be Held in What Name (s)	Manner In Which Title Will Be Held

Source of Down Payment and Settlement Charges

This application is designed to be completed by the borrower(s) with the lender's assistance. The Co-Borrower Section and all other Co-Borrower questions must be completed and the appropriate boxes(es) checked if ☐ another person will be jointly obligated with the Borrower on the loan, or ☐ the Borrower is relying on income from alimony, child support or separate maintenance or on the income or assets of another person as a basis for repayment of the loan, or ☐ the Borrower is married and resides, or the property is located, in a community property state.

Borrower				Co-Borrower			
Name		Age	School Yrs.	Name		Age	School Yrs.
Present Address No. Years	☐ Own	☐ Rent		Present Address No. Years	☐ Own	☐ Rent	
Street				Street			
City/State/Zip				City/State/Zip			
Former address if less than 2 years at present address				Former address if less than 2 years at present address			
Street				Street			
City/State/Zip				City/State/Zip			
Years at former address	☐ Own	☐ Rent		Years at former address	☐ Own	☐ Rent	
Marital Status ☐ Married ☐ Separated ☐ Unmarried (Inc. single, divorced, widowed)		DEPENDENTS OTHER THAN LISTED BY CO-BORROWER NO. AGES		Marital Status ☐ Married ☐ Separated ☐ Unmarried (Inc. single, divorced, widowed)		DEPENDENTS OTHER THAN LISTED BY BORROWER NO. AGES	
Name and Address of Employer		Years employed in this line of work or profession? _____ Years Years on this job _____ ☐ Self Employed*		Name and Address of Employer		Years employed in this line of work or profession? _____ Years Years on this job _____ ☐ Self Employed*	
Position/Title	Type of Business			Position/Title	Type of Business		
Social Security Number***	Home Phone	Business Phone		Social Security Number***	Home Phone	Business Phone	

Gross Monthly Income				Monthly Housing Expense **			Details of Purchase	
Item	Borrower	Co-Borrower	Total		PRESENT	PROPOSED	Do Not Complete if Refinance	
Base Empl. Income	$	$	$	Rent			a. Purchase Price	$
Overtime				First Mortgage (P&I)		$	b. Total Closing Costs (Est.)	
Bonuses				Other Financing (P&I)			c. Prepaid Escrows (Est.)	
Commissions				Hazard Insurance			d. Total (a + b + c)	
Dividends/Interest				Real Estate Taxes			e. Amount This Mortgage	( )
Net Rental Income				Mortgage Insurance			f. Other Financing	( )
Other † (BEFORE COMPLETING, SEE NOTICE UNDER DESCRIBE OTHER INCOME BELOW)				Homeowner Assn. Dues			g. Other Equity	( )
				Other:			h. Amount of Cash Deposit	( )
				Total Monthly Pmt.	$	$	i. Closing Costs Paid by Seller	( )
				Utilities			j. Cash Reqd. For Closing (Est.)	$
Total	$	$	$	Total	$	$		

Describe Other Income		
◇ B – Borrower C – Co-Borrower	NOTICE: † Alimony, child support, or separate maintenance income need not be revealed if the Borrower or Co-Borrower does not choose to have it considered as a basis for repaying this loan.	Monthly Amount $

If Employed In Current Position For Less Than Two Years, Complete the Following						
B/C	Previous Employer/School	City/State	Type of Business	Position/Title	Dates From/To	Monthly Income $

These Questions Apply To Both Borrower and Co-Borrower					
If a "yes" answer is given to a question in this column, please explain on an attached sheet.	Borrower Yes or No	Co-Borrower Yes or No		Borrower Yes or No	Co-Borrower Yes or No
			Are you a U.S. citizen?		
Are there any outstanding judgments against you?			If "no," are you a resident alien?		
Have you been declared bankrupt within the past 7 years?			If "no," are you a non-resident alien?		
Have you had property foreclosed upon or given title or deed in lieu thereof			Explain Other Financing or Other Equity (if any).		
in the last 7 years?					
Are you a party to a law suit?					
Are you obligated to pay alimony, child support, or separate maintenance?					
Is any part of the down payment borrowed?					
Are you a co-maker or endorser on a note?					

*FHLMC/FNMA require business credit report, signed Federal Income Tax returns for last two years; and, if available, audited Profit and Loss Statement plus balance sheet for same period.
**All Present Monthly Housing Expenses of Borrower and Co-Borrower should be listed on a combined basis.
***SSN optional for FHLMC

Freddie Mac Form 65 Rev. 10/86   (VMP) -21H (9001)   VMP MORTGAGE FORMS • (313)293-8100 • (800)521-7291   Fannie Mae Form 1003 Rev. 10/86

Exhibit 38 (continued)

This Statement and any applicable supporting schedules may be completed jointly by both married and unmarried co-borrowers if their assets and liabilities are sufficiently joined so that the Statement can be meaningfully and fairly presented on a combined basis; otherwise separate Statements and Schedules are required (FHLMC 65A/FNMA 1003A). If the co-borrower section was completed about a spouse, this statement and supporting schedules must be completed about that spouse also.

☐ Completed Jointly   ☐ Not Completed Jointly

Assets		Liabilities and Pledged Assets			
Indicate by (*) those liabilities or pledged assets which will be satisfied upon sale of real estate owned or upon refinancing of subject property					
Description	Cash or Market Value	Creditors' Name, Address and Account Number	Acct. Name if Not Borrower's	Mo. Pmt. and Mos. Left to Pay	Unpaid Balance
Cash Deposit Toward Purchase Held By	$	Installment Debts (Include "revolving" charge accounts)		$ Pmt./Mos.	$
		Co. Acct. No.			
Checking and Savings Accounts (Show Names of Institutions (Accounts Numbers) Bank, S & L or Credit Union)		Addr.			
		City		/	
Addr.		Co. Acct. No.			
City		Addr.			
Acct. No.		City		/	
Bank, S & L or Credit Union		Co. Acct. No.			
Addr.		Addr.			
City		Co. Acct. No.		/	
Acct. No.		Addr.			
Bank, S & L or Credit Union		City		/	
Addr.		Co. Acct. No.			
City		Addr.			
Acct. No.		City		/	
Stocks and Bonds (No. Description)		Other Debts including Stock Pledges			
				/	
		Real Estate Loans Acct. No.			
		Co.			
		Addr.			
		City			
Life Insurance Net Cash Value		Co. Acct. No.			
Face Amount $		Addr.			
Subtotal Liquid Assets		City			
Real Estate Owned (Enter Market Value		Automobile Loans Acct. No.			
from Schedule of Real Estate Owned)		Co.			
Vested Interest in Retirement Fund		Addr.			
Net worth of Business Owned (ATTACH FINANCIAL STATEMENT)		City			
		Co. Acct. No.		/	
Automobiles Owned (Make and Year)		Addr.			
		City		/	
Furniture and Personal Property		Alimony/Child Support/Separate Maintenance Payments Owed to			
Other Assets (Itemize)				/	
		Total Monthly Payments			
Total Assets	$	Net Worth (A minus B) $		Total Liabilities	$

SCHEDULE OF REAL ESTATE OWNED (If Additional Properties Owned Attach Separate Schedule)

Address of Property (Indicate S if Sold, PS if Pending Sale or R if Rental being held for income)	Type of Property	Present Market Value	Amount of Mortgages & Liens	Gross Rental Income	Mortgage Payments	Taxes, Ins. Maintenance and Misc.	Net Rental Income
		$	$	$	$	$	$
TOTALS ▶		$	$	$	$	$	$

List Previous Credit References

B–Borrower C–Co-Borrower	Creditor's Name and Address	Account Number	Purpose	Highest Balance	Date Paid
				$	

List any additional names under which credit has previously been received _____

AGREEMENT: The undersigned applies for the loan indicated in this application to be secured by a first mortgage or deed of trust on the property described herein, and represents that the property will not be used for any illegal or restricted purpose, and that all statements made in this application are true and are made for the purpose of obtaining the loan. Verification may be obtained from any source named in the application. The original or a copy of this application will be retained by the lender, even if the loan is not granted. The undersigned ☐ intend or ☐ do not intend to occupy the property as their primary residence.

I/We fully understand that it is a federal crime punishable by fine or imprisonment, or both, to knowingly make any false statements concerning any of the above facts as applicable under the provisions of Title 18, United States Code, Section 1014.

_____ Date _____   _____ Date _____
Borrower's Signature   Co-Borrower's Signature

Information for Government Monitoring Purposes

The following information is requested by the federal government for certain types of loans related to a dwelling in order to monitor the lender's compliance with equal credit opportunity, fair housing, and home mortgage disclosure laws. You are not required to furnish this information, but are encouraged to do so. The law provides that a lender may not discriminate on the basis of this information, or on whether you choose to furnish it. However, if you choose not to furnish the information and you have made this application in person, under federal regulations the lender is required to note race or national origin and sex on the basis of visual observation or surname. If you do not wish to furnish the information, please check below.

Borrower: ☐ I do not wish to furnish this information   Co-Borrower: ☐ I do not wish to furnish this information

Race/National Origin: Race/National Origin:
☐ American Indian, Alaskan Native   ☐ Asian, Pacific Islander   ☐ American Indian, Alaskan Native   ☐ Asian, Pacific Islander
☐ Black   ☐ Hispanic   ☐ White   ☐ Black   ☐ Hispanic   ☐ White
☐ Other (specify):   ☐ Other (specify):
Sex: ☐ Female   ☐ Male   Sex: ☐ Female   ☐ Male

To Be Completed by Interviewer

This application was taken by:
☐ face to face interview
☐ by mail
☐ by telephone

Interviewer _____   Name of Interviewer's Employer _____
Interviewer's Phone Number _____   Address of Interviewer's Employer _____

Exhibit 39

STATEMENT OF ASSETS AND LIABILITIES
(Supplement to Residential Loan Application)

Name_____

The following information is provided to complete and become a part of the application for a mortgage in the amount of $_____
with interest at_____%, for a term of_____months and to be secured by property known as:

Property Street Address:_____

Legal Descriptions:_____

Statement of Assets and Liabilities

Assets		Liabilities and Pledged Assets			
Description	Cash or Market Value	Creditors' Name, Address and Account Number	Acct. Name if Not Borrower's	Mo. Pmt. and Mos. Left to Pay	Unpaid Balance
Cash Deposit Toward Purchase Held By	$	Installment Debt (Include "revolving" charge accounts)		$ Pmt/Mos.	$
		Co.　　　　　　　　Acct. No.			
Checking and Savings Accounts (Show Names of Institutions (Accounts Numbers) Bank, S & L or Credit Union)		Addr.		/	
		City			
		Co.　　　　　　　　Acct. No.			
Addr.		Addr.		/	
City		City			
Acct. No.		Co.　　　　　　　　Acct. No.			
Bank, S & L or Credit Union		Addr.		/	
		City			
Addr.		Co.　　　　　　　　Acct. No.		/	
City		Addr.			
Acct. No.		City			
Bank, S & L or Credit Union		Co.　　　　　　　　Acct. No.		/	
		Addr.			
Addr.		City			
City		Other Debts including Stock Pledges			
Acct. No.					
Stocks and Bonds (No./Description)		Real Estate Loans　　Acct. No. Co.		/	
		Addr.			
		City			
Life Insurance Net Cash Value		Co.　　　　　　　　Acct. No.			
Face Amount $		Addr.			
Subtotal Liquid Assets		City			
Real Estate Owned (Enter Market Value from Schedule of Real Estate Owned)		Automobile Loans　　Acct. No. Co.			
Vested Interest in Retirement Fund		Addr.		/	
Net worth of Business Owned (ATTACH FINANCIAL STATEMENT)		City			
		Co.　　　　　　　　Acct. No.			
Automobiles Owned (Make and Year)		Addr.		/	
		City			
		Alimony/Child Support/Separate Maintenance Payments Owed to			
Furniture and Personal Property				/	
Other Assets (Itemize)		Total Monthly Payments		$	
Total Assets	A $	Net Worth (A minus B) $		Total Liabilities	B $

SCHEDULE OF REAL ESTATE OWNED (If Additional Properties Owned Attach Separate Schedule)

Address of Property (Indicate S if Sold, PS if Pending Sale or R if Rental being held for income)		Type of Property	Present Market Value	Amount of Mortgages & Liens	Gross Rental Income	Mortgage Payments	Taxes, Ins. Maintenance and Misc.	Net Rental Income
	▽		$	$	$	$	$	$
		TOTALS ►	$	$	$	$	$	$

List Previous Credit References

▽ B-Borrower　C-Co Borrower	Creditor's Name and Address	Account Number	Purpose	Highest Balance	Date Paid
				$	

List any additional names under which credit has previously been received_____

I/We fully understand that it is a federal crime punishable by fine or imprisonment, or both; to knowingly make any false statements concerning any of the above facts, as applicable under the provisions of Title 18, United States Code, Section 1014.

_____　Date ___ / ___ / ___　　_____　Date ___ / ___ / ___
Borrower's Signature　　　　　　　　　　　　　　　Co-Borrower's Signature

To be Completed by Interviewer

This application was taken by:
☐ face to face interview　　_____　_____
　　　　　　　　　　　　　Interviewer　　　Name of Interviewer's Employer
☐ by mail
☐ by telephone　　　　　　_____　　_____
　　　　　　　　Interviewer's Phone Number　Address of Interviewer's Employer

curity numbers. Therefore, ask the applicant about additional driver's licenses or Social Security numbers.

(2) An original sales contract or a copy with original signatures or a certified copy. The lender will check the contract for the following:

  (a) Excessive earnest money or good faith deposit;

  (b) The required amendatory language if the date of the contract is prior to the appraisal;

  (c) Sales concessions exceeding of 6% of the total acquisition;

  (d) A statement showing which party will pay for any required repairs. If the sales contract does not specify who is making the repairs, the responsibility for them must be established before submission for approval. Unless stated otherwise in the contract, FHA automatically will assume the buyer is paying for repairs, this will increase the settlement requirements.

(3) A residence history:

  (a) Where the applicant and any co-mortgagor have lived for the past 24 months,

  (b) If the applicant rents,

    1) Landlord's name, address or telephone number, or

    2) Rental agency address and phone number.

  (c) If the applicant owns their present home,

    1) Name of lender, address, phone number and loan account number;

    2) The type of loan, i.e., FHA, VA, or conventional.

(4) An employment history:

  (a) The place of employment for the past 24 months, the position held and whether the employment was full-time, part-time, or temporary, and the monthly income earned upon departure. The applicant should include a history of any unemployment over the past two years. Addresses and zip codes of present and past employers should be furnished.

  (b) Self-employed or fully commissioned people should be prepared to submit a complete and signed tax return (complete with all schedules) for the past two calendar years, plus a year-to-date income and expense statement and a current balance sheet. If the business is a corporation or partnership, copies of signed federal business income tax returns for the last two years with all applicable schedules attached will be required.

(5) A list of assets:

    (a) Names, addresses, and account numbers for all depositories such as banks, savings and loan associations, money market accounts, and credit unions;

    (b) value of one's household goods and personal property;

    (c) Make, model, year, and market value of automobiles;

    (d) Cash and face value of insurance policies;

    (e) Address, description, and value of real estate owned; income properties should have a spread sheet of pertinent facts. See Figure at the end of this definition;

    (f) If a gift is the source of funds for down payment or closing costs or both, the lender will need a letter signed by the donor stating said gift is for the down payment/closing costs and is not to be repaid. A lender may require verification of funds used by the donor.

(6) A list of liabilities:

    (a) Said list should include the creditor's name, balance, monthly payment or method of payment, and the account number. Those creditors that will not furnish above information over the phone to a credit bureau will result in requiring the applicant to prepare a list of such information along with mailing addresses and zip codes. Information usually not given over the phone normally applies to real estate loans, bank, and credit union loans.

    (b) If child support or alimony creates a liability, a signed copy of the divorce decree will be necessary. The signature on said decrees should be one of legal authority.

(7) Additional sources of income:

If source of income is from the following sources:

    (a) military retirement,

    (b) company pensions,

    (c) Social Security or Social Security benefits,

    (d) disability benefits,

    (e) child support or alimony, then a lender will need a statement of benefits from the corresponding source of income. Child support or alimony may require a signed copy of the decree.

(8) For FHA/VA or VA loans:

You must furnish all of the above plus one or more of the following:
    (a) Certificate of Eligibility (VA only);

    (b) Copies of DD214 for all periods of service;

    (c) Statement of service (VA only, active duty personnel);

    (d) DD1747 off-base housing authorization (VA active duty).

(9) If an application involves a sale of present home, the following will be helpful:

    (a) It is important to remember that any funds received from sale of real estate will involve the net proceeds as shown on a settlement statement. Therefore, one should consider the dollar figure given at application to be the net amount after deduction of any sales commission, discount points, closing costs and any other expenses.

    (b) Before loan closing, the lender probably will require a copy of the settlement statement and possibly a certified copy of the warranty deed.

    (c) If a relocation service is acquiring your previous home, the acquisition will most likely be a "skip deed" situation instead of a true sale. If there has not been a final closing with transfer of title, then a lender will find it helpful to have a letter from the relocation service stating that all mortgage payments, taxes, insurance, maintenance, burdens, and responsibilities of subject property are removed from the present owners and assumed by the relocation service.

    (d) If the applicant's relocation is due to a company transfer, and part or all their closing costs will be borne by the employer, a letter from the employer dealing directly with what costs will be paid will be much more helpful than a company manual or policy statement.

(10) Last, but definitely not least, is something that might best be described as a communication gap between lenders and the general public. This gap is something lenders call "verification of settlement requirement." The term "settlement requirement" means funds needed to acquire the property. Funds required can be the down payment, closing costs and prepaid items. The term "funds" can include balances in checking, savings, and money market accounts, stocks, bonds, real estate, and possibly a small amount of cash on hand. These funds must be verifiable. The method used to verify funds is usually a form titled "Verification of Deposit"; other methods can be used such as copies of statements, certificates, or a settlement statement for real estate. The communication gap between lenders and borrowers about this subject usually surfaces at the end of the loan application when the loan officer observes that assets listed for settle-

ment requirement are insufficient. The typical response from the borrower is "Oh, I'll have the money by loan closing." There have been many delays, heartaches, and much frustration created by inadequate verifiable funds for settlement requirement. One of the most important things a borrower can do in preparing for loan application is to have sufficient funds that can be verified for settlement requirement. Nothing but delays and frustration will occur when an applicant lists a total of, say $10,000, in accounts and the verification documents show $8,000, or the depository account is less than two months old. If the account is less than two months old, verification of funds used to open the account must be obtained; or applicants tell the loan officer they will net $18,000 from sale of their residence, but then forget to include sales commission or closing expenses, and the settlement statement shows a net of $16,200. Or worse yet, the house was not actually sold but disposed of by a "skip deed" process to relocation service. This section of the application checklist is very important, because failure to comply with verification of sufficient settlement requirement can definitely delay loan approval or loan closing; - it can easily be conquered with clear communication between lender and borrower.

Credit documents are valid for ninety days. If one, just one, document is missing because of an omitted question at application, or a wrong address or account number is given, it could cause the whole loan application to be reprocessed.

The lender will need to order many verifications, most lenders will ask the applicant to sign a form like the one in Exhibit 40.

LOAN APPROVAL *See* COMPUTERIZED LOAN ORIGINATION, FHA - FIRM COMMITMENT, INCOME ANALYSIS, VA - CERTIFICATE OF COMMITMENT.

LOAN ASSUMPTION *See* ASSUMPTION.

LOAN CLOSER The person who performs the clerical duties related to the conclusion of a real estate transaction, which includes:

(1) preparation of notes, mortgages, deeds and financing statements;

(2) preparation of the settlement statement;

(3) collection of information to satisfy insurance and tax requirements;

(4) obtaining necessary signatures of all parties on the appropriate documents;

(5) disbursements of loan proceeds;

Exhibit 40

BORROWER SIGNATURE AUTHORIZATION

PART I — General Information

1. Borrower(s)	2. Lender Name and Address

3. Date	4. Loan Number	

PART II — Borrower Authorization

I hereby authorize the Lender to verify my past and present employment earnings records, bank accounts, stock holdings and any other asset balances that are needed to process my mortgage loan application. I further authorize the Lender to order a consumer credit report and verify other credit information, including past and present mortgage and landlord references. It is understood that a copy of this form will also serve as authorization.

The information the Lender obtains is only to be used in the processing of my application for a mortgage loan.

Borrower	Date
Borrower	Date
Co-Borrower	Date
Co-Borrower	Date

Privacy Act Notice: This information is to be used by the agency collecting it or its assignees in determining whether you qualify as a prospective mortgagor under its program. It will not be disclosed outside the agency except as required and permitted by law. You do not have to provide this information, but if you do not your application for approval as a prospective mortgagor or borrower may be delayed or rejected. The information requested in this form is authorized by Title 38, USC, Chapter 37 (if VA); by 12 USC, Section 1701 et. seq. (if HUD/FHA); by 42 USC, Section 1452b (if HUD/CPD); and Title 42 USC, 1471 et. seq., or 7 USC, 1921 et. seq. (if USDA/FmHA).

(6) delivery of information for recordation; and

(7) assemblage of documents and preparation of file for entry into system and servicing setup.

Closing may be performed by the originating lender's staff member or may be performed by outside counsel, title company agent, etc.

See ESCROW AGENT.

LOAN COMMITMENT An agreement to lend a specific amount of money over stated terms and conditions, including time.

A lender may use a loan commitment form like the one in Exhibit 41.

LOAN CORRESPONDENT An originator of loans and a servicer of those loans, such as a mortgage banker or an agent for an FHA-approved mortgagee. A lender who originates loans for a later sale to an investor is a loan correspondent of that investor.

LOAN COVERAGE That ratio by which the net operating income before depreciation exceeds the debt service. An example would be net income before depreciation of $400,000 as to debt service of $200,000 would result in a two-to-one loan coverage ratio.

See DEBT COVERAGE RATIO.

LOAN FEE The fee charged by the lender to make a real estate loan. A loan fee is known as an origination fee or a service fee. The lender views the loan fee as a help in defraying the cost of making a loan. Lenders look to servicing fees and premiums on the sale of loans or servicing rights as the real profit makers.

Loan fees are not tax deductible in the year they are paid. Loan fees are considered in the cost basis of a home and therefore will lower the gain on a sale of property.

FHA and VA limit the loan fee to 1% of the loan amount. Conventional lenders usually charge 1% of the loan amount, but they can charge more.

LOAN GUARANTY CERTIFICATE *See* VA - LOAN GUARANTY CERTIFICATE.

LOAN ORIGINATOR/LOAN OFFICER A person who originates mortgage loans. A loan officer is sometimes called an *originator*.

The loan originator's primary responsibility is working with borrowers who seek funds in the form of mortgages secured by real estate. They are responsible for developing such clients by soliciting builders, brokers and other

Exhibit 41

MORTGAGE LOAN COMMITMENT

EQUAL HOUSING LENDER

LENDER

TO:

DATE:
PROPERTY:
ADDRESS:

It is a pleasure to notify you that your application for a first mortgage loan has been approved subject to the following matters set forth below and on the reverse side hereof.

AMOUNT,
TERMS AND
FEES

Amount of Loan ....$
Loan Origination Fee.......$
Loan Discount Fee ....$
Lenders Inspection Fee ......$
Mortgage Insurance
  Application Fee...........$
Assumption Fee ....$

Contract Interest Rate .... %
Annual Percentage Rate ...... %
Appraisal Fee ....$
Credit Report Fee...........$
Non-Refundable Stand-by Fee $

(Please Remit)

Commitment Expires:

REPAYMENT
TERMS

☐ Standard Fixed Payment Mortgage
To be repaid in   equal monthly installments of $ including interest, with the first monthly installment due approximately 30 days after date of settlement.

☐ Renegotiable Rate Mortgage
To be repaid in consecutive equal monthly installments of $ including interest for the Initial Loan Term of   years. The above stated Contract Interest Rate shall be subject to revision at the end of the Initial Loan Term and all subsequent renewal terms, subject to the limitations in the Disclosure you received at application date.

☐ Graduated Payment Mortgage
To be repaid in the manner and amounts as specified in the Disclosure you received at application date.

☐ Adjustable Rate Mortgage
To be repaid in the manner and amounts as specified in the Disclosure you received at application date. The above stated Contract Interest Rate shall be considered the "Initial Interest Rate" only.

EVIDENCE
OF TITLE

The following Evidence of Title is to be provided to the Lender and must indicate no liens, encumbrances, or any adverse convenants or conditions to title unless approved by Lender. The Evidence of Title must be issued from a firm or source, and in a form, acceptable to Lender.

☐ Mortgage Title Guarantee Policy
☐ Torrens Title Guarantee Policy

☐ Abstract of Title
☐ Lawyers Opinion of Title

Borrower will be charged for the cost of providing such title and the cost of recording documents, all of which will be ordered by Lender unless requested otherwise.

ADDITIONAL
REQUIRED
ITEMS OR
CONDITIONS

All Items Checked ☐ Below Apply:
☐ Signed Sales Contract — required
☐ Plat of survey, acceptable to Lender, showing the improvements to be properly within the lot lines and no encroachments on other properties — required.
☐ Copy of present Evidence of Title showing Legal Description needed.
☐ The attached list of repairs is to be completed prior to settlement or an escrow in the amount of $ will be held until the work is satisfactorily completed.
☐ We will pay out on the Loan upon completion of the building, subject to a satisfactory Compliance Inspection Report by our Appraiser and a Certificate of Occupancy from the Governing Municipality.
☐ A Contractor's Statement and Supporting Waivers of Lien are to be provided.
☐ Flood Insurance Mandatory, see reverse
☐
☐
☐

SEE REVERSE

The Continuation of Commitment Conditions is on the reverse and is made a part of this Commitment.

INSTRUCTIONS

Please sign and return Lender's copy of this Commitment, along with any required fees and items requested, to the lender at the: ☐ above address ☐ following address, within   days of date hereof, or at the option of Lender, this Commitment shall become null and void.

I (WE) hereby accept the terms and
Conditions of this Commitment.

_____

_____

Borrower	Date
Borrower	Date
Borrower	Date
Borrower	Date

COMMITMENT ISSUED BY:

_____
Authorized Signature

-96 (8710) 01   VMP MORTGAGE FORMS • (313)293-8100 • (800)521-7291   10/87

Exhibit 41 (continued)

ADDITIONAL REQUIRED ITEMS OR CONDITIONS - (continued)

FIRE AND EXTENDED COVERAGE INSURANCE
At the time of settlement we will require an original insurance policy containing fire and extended coverage insurance in an amount at least equal to that of the mortgage through a company acceptable to Lender, and a receipt showing premiums paid in advance for one year. The insurance policy shall also contain a standard mortgage clause in favor of Lender.

FmHA, FHA OR VA INSURED LOANS
Loan Commitments issued for these types of mortgage loans are subject to all the terms and conditions of the FmHA or FHA commitment; or the VA certificate of reasonable value, as well as the rules and regulations of the Farmers Home Administration or the Department of Veterans Affairs.

FLOOD INSURANCE
If the "Flood Insurance Mandatory" box was checked, this property has been determined to be in an area which has a special flood hazard. Federal law requires that flood insurance, available through any agent, be written in either the maximum amount available or the loan balance, whichever is the lesser. This insurance will be mandatory until this loan is paid in full. By signing and accepting this commitment you acknowledge that the property securing this loan is in an area identified as having a special flood hazard and agree to these insurance requirements.

TAX AND INSURANCE PAYMENTS
Monthly deposits, and initial deposits as determined by Lender, are required to cover the payment of estimated annual real estate taxes, special assessments and, if applicable, FHA or Private Mortgage Insurance Premiums. Lender may also require additional deposits for hazard or other insurance if required for this loan. Such deposits are to be placed in a separate escrow or impound account.

SPECIAL ASSESSMENTS
All unpaid and future special assessment installments must be paid in full prior to, or at time of settlement.

DOCUMENTATION
The mortgage or deed of trust, note and other pertinent loan documents will be provided by Lender and must be signed by all applicants that are to be contractually liable under this obligation. Further, the mortgage or deed of trust, must also be signed by any non-applicant spouses if their signature is required under state law to create a valid lien, pass clear title, or waive inchoate rights to property. Note: Samples of loan documents are available upon request.

CANCELLATION
The Lender reserves the right to terminate this commitment prior to the settlement of the loan in the event of an adverse change in your personal or financial status, or the improvements on the property are damaged by fire or other casualty.

NON-REFUNDABLE STANDBY FEE
This commitment will become effective upon compliance with the terms herein and the receipt of your check in the amount of the nonrefundable standby fee. It is understood and agreed that if this mortgage loan is not settled in accordance with the terms and conditions of this commitment, the Lender shall retain this fee as earned charges for the origination and approval of this loan.

ADDITIONAL CONDITIONS FOR CONSTRUCTION LOANS

CONSTRUCTION LOANS: ONE PAYOUT AND MULTIPLE PAYOUT
Improvements are to be built in a good and workman-like manner in strict accordance with plans and specifications furnished Lender and in compliance with applicable building codes. After completion, said improvements shall be approved by a representative of Lender and an occupancy permit issued by local municipality. Any changes, whether they be additions, deletions, or alterations, of the plans and specifications, must be approved in writing by Lender in order that this loan commitment remain in effect.

CONSTRUCTION LOANS: MULTIPLE PAYOUT
Evidence must be submitted that the net proceeds of our loan are sufficient to complete the construction of the building, free and clear of all claims of Mechanic's Liens for labor and material. All disbursements will be made upon the order of the borrower upon presentment of proper waivers of lien, subject to compliance inspections by the Department of Veterans Affairs, the Federal Housing Administration, or Lender, not to exceed 80% of the value of the work done, and subject to the Lender having in its possession at all times an amount of undisbursed loan proceeds at least equal to the amount required to complete the improvements.

members of the real estate community. The loan originator is generally the person who interviews applicants on behalf of the lending institution, takes the formal written applications and provides potential borrowers with disclosures that meet the compliance requirements of RESPA, ECOA, and Truth-in-Lending.

LOAN ORIGINATION FEE   The fee a lender charges for making a mortgage. The fee is expressed as a percentage. For FHA loans, the origination fee is limited to 1% of the "base" loan (loan amount without the MIP). For VA loans, the origination fee is limited to 1% of the total loan (loan amount with the funding fee) with the exception of a rate reduction refinance where it is limited to 1% of the base loan (loan amount without the funding fee). Conventional loans have no restrictions for the charge for an origination fee. Origination fees are not considered tax-deductible.

See BASE LOAN.

LOAN ORIGINATION PROCESS   Creating a mortgage is an origination. When someone asks a lender how many originations they had for the last month? They are asking the lender for the number of loans made. The origination process is a multi-faceted operation. The process can be broken down into seven steps.

Step 1 Pre-qualification.   Before the preliminary interview the lender may wish to decide if the applicant will qualify for the loan. At prequalification, the lender or the real estate agent should give the applicant an application checklist to prepare for the interview. The use of an income analysis worksheet or a computer software program will be helpful in this process. Pre-qualification will allow a lender to establish the type of mortgage and the maximum loan amount for which the applicant can qualify. This step helps to avoid time wasted in showing the applicants properties they can't afford. If special financing is required, it can help prepare a buyer and a seller to choose the type of financing that will be needed to attain loan approval, e.g., using an ARM loan, using a buydown, paying extra points. *See* LOAN APPLICATION for a checklist.

Step 2 Application.   The lender completes a formal, written loan application that will give detailed data about the loan transaction, the borrower, and the property. This step is the beginning point of the documentation process. A good interview will limit follow up time and effort. It is important to obtain maximum information from the borrower at the time of the application interview. In reviewing loan documents, a lender looks for "red flags" that may indicate fraud. Many of the guidelines in this Quality Control plan are not for labeling a practice or a document as illegal, but are to help the lender recognize signs or "flags" calling for careful examination of the facts.

Normally, there will be a sales contract available at the time of the interview. The sales contract can indicate potential problems. A lender should look for the following "red flags":

(1) Compare signatures on the contract to signatures on other documents.

(2) Be suspicious of a large amount for the earnest money or good faith deposit. Large downpayments on FHA and VA loans are uncommon.

(3) Downpayments normally come from cash savings accumulated from earned income. Other sources for downpayments, such as a gift, sweat equity, trades, should be carefully watched.

(4) Check for any relationship between the seller, purchaser, or real estate agent.

(5) Be careful with non-owner occupant purchasers, there has been much abuse associated with that group.

(6) An excessive real estate commission can signal kickbacks or other violations.

(7) Addendums to the contract should cause you to ask why they were not included in the contract.

(8) Except for pre-qualification purposes, a contract dated after receipt of credit documents is suspicious.

Step 2a Pre-underwriting. If the lender has not completed step 1, then the lender should begin with the income analysis. Pre-underwriting is the process used by the lender to decide, based on the data collected in the preliminary interview, whether the applicant meets the lender's basic criteria for loan approval. The result of this decision will be loan denial or continuation of loan processing.

Review the loan application for the "flags" listed below:

(1) See that the form is complete, the information given makes sense, and is realistic.

(2) Unrealistic commuting distance from subject property to place of employment should be explained.

(3) If the purchaser is buying a home that does not appear to meet the needs nor the lifestyle of the purchaser, you should ask why.

You should be suspicious of the following borrowers:
(1) A high income borrower with little assets.
(2) A high income borrower indebted to unlikely creditors, such as finance companies.
(3) A low income borrower with high assets.
(4) A borrower without any bank accounts.
(5) A borrower who holds stock in the employer company.

Make a general evaluation of the information, not just the dollar amounts. You should ask yourself if the same person appears throughout the file?

Step 2b A deficiency in the loan application. If apparently the applicant fails to meet the minimum requirements needed to qualify for the proposed loan, the lender may decline the loan. Any inability to repay the loan is an acceptable reason for a declination.

Step 3 Loan Processing. During the processing stage the lender verifies the applicants income, credit history, bank deposits, and past mortgage or rental payments. A property appraisal is requested and any additional documentation that will be needed to complete the approval evaluation is obtained. As the loan documents come to the lender, the processor should not simply file them in the loan jacket. (See Exhibit 42.)

Review the **Credit Report** for the following items:
(1) There is credit established.
(2) The accounts and balances are consistent to what was reported at application.
(3) Reasons for any recent credit inquires.
(4) History of court records or bankruptcies.
(5) Personal identification as: "also known as" or "doing business as." Ask the reasons for using different names.

Besides checking for adequate assets and income, review the Verification of Deposit (VOD) or the Verification of Employment (VOE) forms for the following "flags":

(1) The average balance for the past two months does not support the present balance. (VOD)
(2) Round dollar amounts. (VOD & VOE)
(3) The age of the account. (VOD)

Exhibit 42

Schedule of Real Estate

(To be used for loan processing of an individual with multiple ownership of rental properties)

Address	Mkt. Value	Mrtg. Bal.	Equity	Gross Rent	Mrtg. Pay	Income	Mortgagee Name Loan # & Mailing Address	Subdivision Name & Comments

I certify that the above named subdivisions are not "Contiguous" to each other, except as follows

_____

(4) Numbers that are squeezed in to make a higher sum. (VOD & VOE)

(5) A small company that belongs to a credit union. (VOD)

(6) An out of town bank or employer for local resident. (VOD & VOE)

(7) Illegible signatures. (VOE & VOD)

(8) Similarities in names. (VOE & VOD)

(9) The verification is signed by an unauthorized official. (VOE & VOD)

(10) Different type styles on the same form. (VOE & VOD)

(11) White outs or cross outs. (VOE & VOD)

(12) The date of verification being before the date requested. (VOE & VOD)

(13) The VOE or VOD is not folded as it should be when sent by mail.

(14) Information not on the standard VOE or VOD must be on letterhead.

(15) No prior year earnings. (VOE)

(16) Employee is paid monthly. (VOE)

Be suspicious of requests for Verification forms to be mailed to a designated party.

If W-2's are used to verify income, you should be suspicious of the following:

(1) The form is handwritten or typed, not machine printed or computer generated.

(2) The employer's copy is submitted and not the employee's copy.

(3) The amounts for FICA and social security are more than the legal limits.

If payroll check stubs are used to verify income, review for the following:

(1) Check to see if the number sequence makes sense.

(2) The information is consistent to the application.

(3) It is computer or machine generated.

If tax returns are used to establish income, review the following items:

(1) The entries make sense.

(2) Who prepared the returns. If it was a paid preparer, is the information handwritten?

(3) A different paid preparer was used for each year.

(4) A paid preparer signing all copies of the 1040.

(5) A high income borrower who prepares his tax returns.

(6) No interest income reported, but large savings are reported in the application.

(7) No dividends listed, but applicant owns stock.

(8) Depreciation deductions not taken for real estate.

Whenever possible, you should always ask for any supporting information to be on company letterhead, dated, and signed by an authorized person. The information should be then forwarded by mail to the lender. Parties to the loan transaction should never be allowed to hand carry verification documents.

Information or documents that are pertinent to a loan file and cannot be obtained by a traditional source (VOE, VOD, credit report, etc.) should be accompanied by an affidavit from the party supplying the information or document. The affidavit should read: **WARNING:** It is a crime to make knowingly false statements to the United States on this or any other similar form. Penalties upon conviction can include a fine or imprisonment. For details see Title 18 U.S. Code Section 1001 and Section 1010. For FHA loans you may choose to use the following:

SECTION 1010 OF TITLE 18, U.S.C., "FEDERAL HOUSING ADMINISTRATION TRANSACTIONS," PROVIDES: "WHOEVER, FOR THE PURPOSE OF—INFLUENCING IN ANY WAY THE ACTION OF SUCH ADMINISTRATION—MAKES, PASSES, UTTERS, OR PUBLISHES ANY STATEMENT, KNOWING THE SAME TO BE FALSE—SHALL BE FINED NOT MORE THAN $5,000 OR IMPRISONED NOT MORE THAN TWO YEARS, OR BOTH."

Besides looking at the value in the appraisal, review the appraisal for the following items:

(1) Large unjustified adjustments.

(2) Comparables being used are not consistent with the area.

(3) Tenant is shown as the occupant on an owner occupied loan.

(4) Do notes or remarks made by the appraiser make sense?

(5) Do photographs reflect the area as your recall?

(6) Who requested the appraisal?

Step 4 Underwriting. In this step the lender assesses two main factors that are (1) the ability and willingness of the borrower to repay the debt; and (2) the property's ability to serve as collateral for the debt. To insure that loans are marketable in the secondary market these two factors must be considered. The quality of underwriting can affect the price an investor will pay for a loan. Become suspicious when there are significant changes from the handwritten application (taken at the time of the interview) compared to the typed application prepared after all information has been verified.

Every investor has certain minimum requirements for the loans they purchase and many have a terraced price that rises with the quality of the loan. Loans placed in pools for mortgage backed securities must meet specific guidelines related to the type of security issued.

Step 4a Loan Approval. If the loan meets the underwriting requirements, loan approval is granted. The applicant is notified and a closing date is set. In this step the institution typically sends written notice of approval by a commitment letter to the borrower. The commitment letter states the terms of the mortgage and explains the procedures for closing.

Step 4b Loan Declined. If the underwriting results in a loan declination, the institution must provide the applicant with a written notification of the action taken. The declination letter must contain specific reasons for credit denial and the provisions of section 701(a) of the Equal Credit Opportunity Act (see form in ECOA definition) must be sent to the applicant.

Step 4c Pre-Close Audit. The purpose of a pre-close audit is to insure that all documents have been obtained and are properly completed before the closing date. Any conditions of approval imposed by the underwriter must be satisfied or explicit instructions prepared to insure their receipt before funding.

Step 5 Closing. A closing date should never be set until the loan is approved. Closing a loan is the process of executing and delivering all documents required by the lender, the disbursement of the mortgage funds, and recording pertinent instruments. Before disbursement or funding, the lender should perform a brief audit of the file along the guidelines presented above.

In 1990, The Mortgage Bankers Association of America began to promote the use of a uniform format for closing instructions. The MBA chose a closing format developed by the Education Committee of the MBA of the Carolinas (refer to credits in the Preface). The purpose of a uniform format for use by mortgage lenders is to have closing agents quickly locate unusual requirements and be alert to the Specific Closing Instruction of each lender. There are eight sections to the Specific Closing Instructions:

(1) Loan Identification

(2) Loan Terms

(3) Loan Contingencies

(4) Closing, Recording, and Disbursement Procedures

(5) Title Examination

(6) Loan Documents to be Completed by the Attorney

(7) Other Loan Closing Requirements and Documentation

(8) Collection of Fees and Checks to the Lender

1   *Identification of the Loan Transaction:* This section should list all infor-
    mation and identify all parties from whom the agent may need to inter-
    view. For example, the name of the real estate agent and the branch office
    is included in this section and an identification of the type of loan.

2   *Loan Terms:* This section should include a general summary of the loan
    terms agreed upon by the borrower and lender. By repeating the loan
    terms in the closing instruction, the closing agent can check for discrepan-
    cies between the closing instructions and the actual loan documents. It is
    important the agent be aware that the loan must close according to the
    terms of the sales contract, if applicable. He/she must notify the lender of
    any events at closing that are contrary to the Specific Closing Instructions
    and sales contract.

3   *Contingencies:* Lenders should be sensitive to the types of requests made
    of closing agents and contingencies for which the agent is responsible for
    in residential loan closings. Often the real estate agent or the branch of-
    fice should be taking care of these items and not giving the responsibility
    to the closing agent.

4   *Closing, Recording, and Disbursement Procedures:* There are many
    ways mortgage lenders handle their closing requirements. Some lenders
    require binders and a pre-review; others send their loan proceeds check to
    closing. It is anticipated that each lender will include its own language in
    this section.

5   *Title Examination:* This section gives specific requirements to the type of
    mortgage title policy the lender will accept and what endorsements are
    required.

6   *Loan Documents to be Completed by Closing Agent:* This section refers
    to the major legal instruments (the Note and security instrument) that will
    be completed by the closing agent's office. Some lenders complete most
    of their notes and security instruments while others send them in blank to
    the agent's office for the agent and his staff to complete. Since these

documents, especially the Note, are very important for the delivery to the secondary market, the specific requirements of each lender should be noted in this section.

7   *Other Loan Closing Requirements and Documentation to be Obtained by the Closing Agent:* This section lists in alphabetical order every additional required form, documentation, etc. that may be required by a mortgage lender. If a mortgage lender has computerized closings, then the closing instructions would list only those documents required for this specific transaction. By putting them in alphabetical order, the agent has some way of quickly referring to the closing instructions if the agent has a question regarding specific forms.

8   *Collection of Fees, Checks to Lenders:* This section is for a "sample only," to bring to the attention of the lender that they must be specific in giving the closing agent instructions for amounts to be collected, how they should be made payable, and whether separate checks are required if made payable to the lender.

Before closing and disbursement, the lender should instruct the closing agent to not disburse the loan if the following discrepancies are found:

- Any discrepancy between the actual legal description and the legal description furnished in Specific Closing Instructions from the lender;

- Any reduction in lot size shown on the survey greater than 2 percent on the front lot line and 5 percent on the side and rear lot lines;

- Any violation of restrictive covenants, building setback lines shown on survey, or zoning ordinances and regulations;

- Any joint driveway that is not reflected in a recorded joint driveway agreement;

- Any joint agreement not of record;

- Any encroachment from or onto the property, or any easement affecting the property;

- Any water system other than individual well, approved community water system or public water system; and

- Any other exceptions: rights-of-way, water courses, etc., to be shown as exceptions on the title insurance policy.

Below is a list of title policy requirements that nearly all lenders will want satisfied. When a closing agent is used, it the responsibility of the agent to decide if the title policy requirements are met.

(1) The policy should insure that the title is generally acceptable and that the security instrument constitutes a valid first lien on the borrower's fee simple (or lender-approved leasehold) estate in the mortgage premises. The title policy should list any subordinate liens and state that they are subordinate to the lender's first mortgage lien. The lender should be made aware of and approve in advance any subordinate liens.

(2) Most lenders will accept only the American Land Title Association (ALTA) Loan Policy of 1987 or 1970. Most lenders will reject the ALTA Loan Policy of 1970, revised 3/84. Most lenders will not accept alternative ALTA approved forms of mortgagee title insurance such as the ALTA Short Form Residential Loan Policy (10/19/88). The closing agent should refer to closing instructions or call the lender before closing to decide if the lender will accept alternative ALTA forms of mortgagee title insurance or a specific insurer's program.

(3) Most lenders require that insurance be obtained through a title company that is acceptable to the lender. The lender will specify the title company selected by the borrower or their closing agent in the closing instructions. A closing agent should obtain the approval from the lender before closing if the agent wants to use a different title company.

(4) The effective date of the title insurance policy may be no earlier than the later of the date of final disbursement of the loan proceeds or the date of mortgage recordation. The policy should be in effect during the entire loan term.

(5) Unless otherwise advised by the lender, the title insurance policy should insure the lender as follows:

Conventional loans: "_____(lender)_____, its successor and assigns as their respective interest may appear."

FHA loans: _____(lender)_____, and/or the Secretary of Housing and Urban Development of Washington, D.C., their successors and assigns as their respective interest may appear."

VA loans: "_____(lender)_____, and/or the Secretary of Veterans Affairs, their successors and assigns as their respective interest may appear."

(6) The lender will want the borrower to own the property in fee simple, unless the lender approves a leasehold estate. In some states, due to certain conditions, leasehold estates are acceptable.

(7) The amount of title insurance coverage must at least equal the original principal amount of the mortgage. If the principal amount of the loan increases because of negative amortization, the title insurance should cover the maximum possible increase.

(8) If a pre-review of the title commitment or binder is not required by the lender, a "marked-up" binder, final certification, or a copy of the request for title insurance should be included in the closed loan package. The closing agent should request a final title policy immediately after recording the security instrument and forward the final title policy to the lender. The final certificate should not be delayed pending receipt of "satisfied" papers from a holder of a prior mortgage. The title insurance company will normally issue the title policy without exception if the agent furnishes evidence of payment in full from the previous mortgage holder. Any delay in receiving the mortgagee title insurance policy after closing can cause failure to meet delivery dates to investors and can create costly penalties for the lender.

(9) The use of ALTA endorsements should be used for Special Title Coverage requirements. A list of recommended special endorsements are as follows:

Condominiums: ALTA Endorsement Form 4.
Planned Unit Developments (PUDs): ALTA Endorsement Form 5.
Adjustable-Rate Mortgages (no negative amortization): ALTA Endorsement Form 6.1.
Loans having negative amortization: ALTA Endorsement Form 6.2.
Manufactured Housing Units: ALTA Endorsement Form 7.
Environmental Lien Protection (all loans): ALTA Endorsement Form 8.1.

(10) It is not uncommon for a lender to request that the closing agent record an assignment of mortgage and obtain a title policy endorsement.

(11) An individual closing agent should not certify to the title or handle the closing of the loan if the closing attorney is a party to the transaction.

Below is a list of acceptable title exceptions for most lenders:

(1) Easements:

(a) Customary *public utility subsurface* easements (as long as they do not extend under any buildings or other improvements) that were in place and completely covered when the mortgage was originated.

(b) *Above-surface public utility easements* that extend along one or more of the property lines for distribution purposes or along the rear property line for drainage, as long as they do not extend more than 12 feet (10 feet on FHA/VA loans) from the property lines and do not interfere with the use of the buildings or improvements for their intended purpose.

(c) *Mutual easements* for joint driveways and party walls should be recorded, provide unlimited use without restrictions, specify obligations of parties as to maintenance, and be binding upon all heirs and assigns.

NOTE: Any easement or rights-of-way, either recorded or unrecorded, must be specifically identified as to location and purpose and shown on the survey. If the closing agent is unable to provide this service because the easement(s) is non-specific, the closing agent should have the title company provide affirmative coverage against loss. If any easement adversely affects the property, the closing agent should call the lender before closing.

(2) Ad valorem *Real Property Taxes/Assessments* that the policy states are a lien but "not yet due and payable."

(3) *Restrictive covenants,* declarations and conditions, minimum cost, minimum dwelling size, or set back restrictions as long violating them will not result in a forfeiture or reversion of title or lien of any kind for damages, or have an adverse effect on the fair market value of the property. The following language (or similar language having the same meaning) should appear in every binder and final policy:

"THIS POLICY/BINDER SPECIFICALLY GUARANTEES THAT ANY PAST, PRESENT, OR FUTURE VIOLATION OF THE RESTRICTIONS, COVENANTS, BUILDING SETBACK LINES, EASEMENT AREAS, WIDENING STRIPS, PARTITION WALLS OR OTHER LIMITATIONS AND RESTRICTIONS WILL NOT WORK A FORFEITURE OR REVERSION OF THE TITLE OR RESULT IN A LIEN OR CHARGE SUPERIOR TO THE INTER-

EST OF THE MORTGAGEE TO BE INSURED HEREIN, AND THAT THE SAME HAVE BEEN VIOLATED AS OF THE DATE OF THIS POLICY/BINDER."

(a) For the District of Columbia and Virginia, in all cases where any rights of *dower or curtesy* may affect the taking of title to the property, the policy is to provide affirmative title insurance that the lien of the lender's security instrument has priority over any statutory rights of dower or curtesy. In those situations the following language is to be included in the policy/binder:

"THIS POLICY/BINDER INSURES, UP TO THE FACE AMOUNT HEREOF, THAT THE INSURED SHALL INCUR NO LOSS OR DAMAGE AS A RESULT OF THE EXERCISE OR ATTEMPTED EXERCISE, OF DOWER OR CURTESY RIGHTS."

If there is a violation, the closing agent should include in the title policy/binder a statement describing the nature of the violation and provide specific, affirmative insurance for the lender against any loss or damage resulting from the violation.

(b) The closing agent should be able to insure in the final title policy that the covenant, codes, conditions, and restrictions in the commitments or in any *condominium or PUD* constituent documents have not been violated and that future violations thereof will not cause a forfeiture or reversion of title.

(4) Encroachments:

(a) *Encroachments* of one foot or less on adjoining property by eaves or other overhanging projections or by driveways, as long as there is at least a 10-foot clearance (8 feet on FHA/VA loans) between the buildings on the security property and the property line affected by the encroachment.

(b) *Encroachments* on adjoining properties by hedges or removable fences.

NOTE: The lender will want express affirmative coverage against "any loss or damage" concerning each exception to any and all minor encroachments, violations of restrictions, common walls, overhangs of eaves, porches, decks, roofs, etc. When ordering the title policy, the closing agent should specifically request the title company provide affirmative coverage. If the main body of the house or improvements encroach upon adjoining property, the closing agent *should not close the loan* even if affirmative coverage is available. The closing agent should call the lender before closing.

(5) *Outstanding oil, water, or mineral rights,* as long as they do not materially alter the contour of the property or impair its value or usefulness for its intended purposes. The policy must affirmatively insure that the exercise of such rights will not result in damage to the property or impairment of the use of the property for residential purposes.

In addition, a certification as follows will be required from the closing agent:
"The known facts do not import exercise, or impending exercise, or such outstanding rights in such manner as to materially alter the contour of the mortgaged property or impair its value or usefulness for its intended purpose, and generally that such outstanding rights are similar to those customarily acceptable to prudent lending institutions, informed buyers, and lending attorneys in the community."

(6) *Lot dimension variations* between the appraisal report and the survey regarding the length of the property lines as long as the variations do not interfere with the current use of the improvements and are within an acceptable range (for front property lines, a 2 percent variation is acceptable; for all other property lines, 5 percent is acceptable).

(7) *Rights of lawful parties in possession* as long as such rights do not include the right of first refusal to purchase the property. No rights of parties in possession (including the term of a tenant's lease) may have a duration of more than two years. The title policy must affirmatively insure as to the above facts. Any other exceptions regarding rights of parties in possession for recorded or unrecorded leases are generally unacceptable unless prior approval is obtained from the lender and the tenant's rights or lease is fully subordinated to the mortgage and the title policy gives affirmative coverage against all loss or damage resulting from the exercise of any rights under the lease.

(8) Minor discrepancies in the *legal description* as long as the policy provides affirmative title insurance against all loss or damage resulting from the discrepancies.

(9) Exceptions to *Indian claims* as long as the policy provides affirmative coverage against all loss and damage from such claims. The

closing agent should call the lender before closing to obtain the specific affirmative language that is required by the investor.

Below is a list of unacceptable title exceptions for most lenders:

(1) Any exception for *unpaid real estate taxes, special or supplemental taxes, assessments,* or other charges that are considered "due and payable."

(2) General exceptions *about matters of survey,* including unrecorded easements or rights of way. Most lenders will require survey coverage on all estates in land that are security for the loan, whether owned in fee simple or as an easement.

(3) Any exception for *mechanics or materialmens's liens.*

(4) General exceptions about *unrecorded rights or claims* of parties in possession.

(5) For *party walls* unless such exception affirmatively insures the rights of the titleholder in and to the use of said party walls in common with others.

(6) The dower, curtesy, homestead, community property, or other *statutory marital rights* if any, of the spouse of any individual insured.

(7) Any *items appearing in the public records* or attaching subsequent to the effective date of the Title Commitment, but before the date the lender perfects their security interest in the property and that were not specifically excepted in the Title Commitment or approved by the lender.

UNIFORM CLOSING PACKAGE REQUIREMENTS

The following items should be completed or complied with before closing:

1. INSURED CLOSING AGREEMENT from the title company named in the Specific Closing Instructions.

2. TITLE EXAMINATION: to obtain an insured first lien position without objectionable exception from the title company named in the Specific Closing Instructions.

3. HAZARD INSURANCE: original policy with paid receipt for the first year's premium.

4. FLOOD INSURANCE: if applicable, must be obtained.

5. TERMITE/INSECT INSPECTION: satisfactory report with non indication of the need for treatment or repairs.

6. SURVEY: matches the legal description and no encroachments indicated.
7. CONTINGENCY REQUIREMENTS: must be met.
8. CLOSING COSTS: must be paid according to the sales contract at closing.

The closing agent should contact the lender before loan closing in the following circumstances:

•   If you are unable to close the loan by the date specified in the Specific Closing Instructions.

•   If you are unable to obtain an insured first lien position without any unusual objections or exceptions to title except as allowed in the General Closing Instructions.

•   If the title company used is different from the one named in the Specific Closing Instructions.

•   If there is any change or discrepancy in the sales contract.

•   If information provided in the closing package is incorrect.

•   If the termite report indicates infestation or damage that has not been treated or repaired, or further inspections are recommended.

•   To receive approval to escrow funds for completion of improvements.

•   To verify the acceptability of a hazard insurance company that is rated, except for what is specified in the General Closing Instructions or the Specific Closing Instructions (see "Hazard Insurance").

•   If you must close the loan with a Power of Attorney, or intend to close by mail.

•   If secondary financing is intended, that is not specifically indicated or approved in the specific closing instructions.

•   If there is any discrepancy in the survey (see "Survey" in the general closing instructions).

•   To confirm that the lender has set up a master file that includes declarations and restrictions, if the security property is a condominium or in a PUD.

•   To receive approval for a leasehold estate.

•   If you have any questions regarding the General Closing Instructions, Specific Closing Instructions, or documents in the closing package.

•   If you are unable to comply with any of the requirements set forth in the General Closing Instructions or Specific Closing Instructions.

Step 5a Post Close Audit. The purpose of a post close audit is to insure that the loan is closed according to the lender's closing instructions, that all computations were made correctly, and that all required documents were prepared and executed properly. Closing packages must comply with requirements of the investor and any state requirements. After the loan has been funded it should be returned to the audit department to continue the post close quality control process. The institution must designate an individual who has not been involved in the originating, processing, or underwriting of the loan to perform these audits. Here a systematic check of all figures that should be made to insure proper funding and a follow up of recording information initiated. The auditor reviews the closing package for compliance with closing instructions of the lender.

Review the preliminary title evidence for the following items:

(1) The seller is listed on the title.

(2) The length of time the seller was on the title.

(3) The date and amounts of existing encumbrances.

(4) Is the buyer, relatives of the buyer, buyer owned entities, or the real estate agent listed in the "chain of title?"

Review the closing documents, primarily the HUD-1 settlement statement, for the following items:

(1) Improper credits from the seller.

(2) Any "flip clause," right of assignment, or power of attorney used.

(3) Improper fees charged.

(4) Excessive real estate commission paid.

(5) Any "zero down" scheme used.

The hazard insurance policy should be investigated for the following:

(1) A tenant policy issued, instead of a homeowner's policy on an owner occupied loan.

(2) A "dwelling only" policy was used.

(3) The address on the billing matches information on application.

Step 5b Funding. The final step in closing, after all documents have been executed and witnessed, is the disbursement of funds as instructed by the lender.

Step 5c Management Review. To reap the benefits of audits, the results must be reviewed by management on a regular basis. A random percentage of all loans should be selected for reverification of origination data to insure compliance with investor criteria and detect evidence of negligence or fraud.

Management must act on any deficiencies discovered. Form letters in this section will help in management review.

Step 5d Servicing Set up. Once the loan file has been funded, it may be set up on a computer system. This may include coding of the loan to identify the amounts to be transferred from the clearing account to each investor custodial bank accounts and preparation of escrow accounts.

Step 6 Marketing. The principal responsibilities of the marketing functions are to arrange for the sale of mortgages produced by the institution to the secondary market. This includes management of the pricing risk associated with the pipeline before delivery to a prospective investor.

Step 7 Shipping to Investor. After the loan has been priced and a commitment obtained, the file is packaged and forwarded for purchase. It is important to package the loan according to investor procedures and to transmit all final documents such as recorded mortgages or title policies within the time allotted by the investor.

The term "origination" applies to the process that a mortgage-backed security certificate secured by a pool of approved mortgage loans is produced. Mortgage bankers originate MBSs and issue the securities by seeking applications for loans. Builders, brokers and others buy MBSs. Primary portfolio lenders originate mortgages for borrowers and then service the loans.

See FIDELITY OR SURETY BOND, TITLE INSURANCE.

LOAN ORIGINATIONS See Exhibits 44-51.

LOAN PACKAGE An assemblage of eligible mortgages for inclusion in a GNMA II multiple-issuer pool, formed in connection with a commitment to guarantee from Ginnie Mae.

LOAN PROCESSOR The person who prepares the application and supporting documents for underwriting. Processors are responsible for completing the credit investigation of the applicants based on information contained in the written application, for ordering appraisals, and for packaging the loan for Underwriting.

Quality Control Status Sheet

Borrower(s) _____ Loan # _____ QC Inception Date _____

Property Address _____

Lender Name _____ Commitment # _____ Investor _____

Lender Contact _____ Phone # _____

Review Appraiser _____ Phone # _____

Projected QC Completion Date _____ QC Review Complete _____

	Ordered	Rec'd	Re-Ordered	Charges
Appraisal (If Applicable)_____				
Review Appraisal _____				
Credit Report _____				
Verification of Employment: *Borrower*				
1)_____				
2)_____				
3)_____				
Co-Borrower				
1)_____				
2)_____				
3)_____				
Verification of Deposit:				
1)_____				
2)_____				
3)_____				
Verification of Mortgage:				
1)_____				
2)_____				
3)_____				
Gift Letter _____				
Verification of Gift Funds _____				

Existence & Accuracy of Documents:

_____ Note	_____ Good Faith Estimate
_____ Mod	_____ Survey
_____ Mortgage/Deed	_____ Truth-in-Lending
_____ Rider	_____ Right of Rescission
_____ Assignment(s)	_____ HUD-1
_____ Title Policy	_____ Clear Termite
_____ MI Certificate	_____ Sales Contract
_____ Hazard Insurance	_____ Power of Attorney
_____ Flood Insurance	

Quality Control Monthly Audit Control Log

Month of _____

Loan #	Branch	Originator	Underwriter	Loan Type	Purpose	LTV	Loan Amount	Audit Initiated	Audit Completed	Audit Type

Audit Type Codes: D = Document Review Only
C = Compliance Audit Only
R = Reverification Audit (includes infile credit & review appraisal)
F = Full Audit (includes new credit & appraisal reports)
S = Servicing Audit Only

Exhibit 43

Steps in the Origination Process

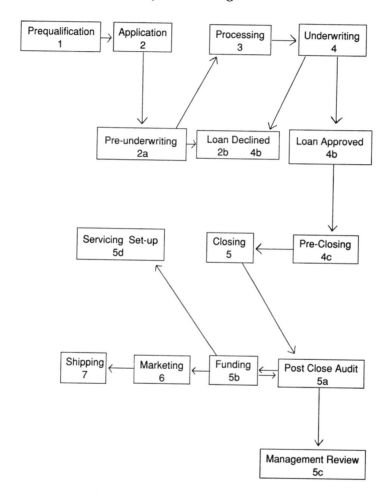

Exhibit 44

Actual Number of 1-4 Unit
Residential Mortgage Loans Originated

	Conventional Rixed-Rate	Conventional Adjustable-Rate	FHA	VA
1984	1,051	1,667	306	187
1985	1,441	1,464	486	231
1986	3,204	1,367	1,005	432
1987	2,498	1,737	826	296
1988	1,431	1,976	518	170

Source: Mortgage Bankers Association

Exhibit 45
Actual Dollar Volume of 1-4 Unit
Residential Mortgage Loans
(in Millions of Dollars)

	Total	Private	FHA-Insured	VA Guaranteed
1980	$133,761	$106,704	$14,955	$12,102
1981	98,213	80,141	10,538	7,534
1982	96,951	77,782	11,482	7,687
1983	201,863	154,229	28,753	18,880
1984	203,705	175,081	16,600	12,024
1985	243,075	199,058	28,436	15,082
1986	454,050	361,121	62,038	30,891
1987	449,544	376,441	51,220	21,882
1988	374,401	329,492	31,933	12,977

Source: U.S. Department of Housing and Urban Development

Exhibit 46

Originations of FHA, VA, and Conventional Loans by Mortgage Companies

Percentage Distribution

	Total	FHA	VA	Conventional
1980	100.0	41.3	32.5	26.1
1981	100.0	36.5	25.2	38.3
1982	100.0	35.0	22.0	43.0
1983	100.0	38.4	23.7	37.9
1984	100.0	26.3	18.0	55.7
1985	100.0	36.5	18.1	45.4
1986	100.0	40.2	19.9	39.9
1987	100.0	33.8	13.9	52.3
1988	100.0	27.5	11.2	61.3

Source: U.S. Department of Housing and Urban Development

Exhibit 47

Originations of FHA, VA, and Conventional Loans by Savings and Loans

Percentage Distribution

	Total	FHA	VA	Conventional
1980	100.0	3.5	2.6	94.0
1981	100.0	3.8	1.9	94.3
1982	100.0	4.0	3.6	92.4
1983	100.0	8.3	5.6	86.0
1984	100.0	5.6	4.0	90.4
1985	100.0	6.1	4.6	89.3
1986	100.0	4.6	2.6	92.8
1987	100.0	2.9	1.3	95.8
1988	100.0	2.0	1.0	97.0

Source: U.S. Department of Housing and Urban Development

Exhibit 48

Originations of FHA, VA, and Conventional Loans
by Commercial Banks

Percentage Distribution

	Total	FHA	VA	Conventional
1980	100.0	3.5	2.6	94.0
1981	100.0	3.8	1.9	94.3
1982	100.0	4.0	3.6	92.4
1983	100.0	8.3	5.6	86.0
1984	100.0	5.6	4.0	90.4
1985	100.0	6.1	4.6	89.3
1986	100.0	4.6	2.6	92.8
1987	100.0	4.6	1.5	93.9
1988	100.0	4.6	1.5	93.9

Source: U.S. Department of Housing and Urban Development

Exhibit 49

Originations of FHA Loans
by Mortgage Companies, S&L's, and Commercial Banks

Percentage Distribution

	Mortgage Companies	S&L's	Commercial Banks
1980	81.3	8.4	6.7
1981	82.9	7.2	7.9
1982	85.4	3.4	8.8
1983	79.8	4.9	13.0
1984	75.5	8.1	14.1
1985	81.2	4.7	12.3
1986	85.2	5.5	7.9
1987	72.7	9.8	15.8
1988	73.6	9.9	13.7

* Adding the three percentages across from each year will not add to 100%. The tables reflect the originations by Mortgage Companies, Savings & Loans, and Commercial Banks. There are more than three types of FHA, VA, and conventional lenders.

Exhibit 50
Originations of VA Loans
by Mortgage Companies, S&L's, and Commercial Banks

Percentage Distribution

	Mortgage Companies	S&L's	Commercial Banks
1980	79.1	12.5	6.2
1981	80.2	12.2	5.4
1982	80.1	5.8	11.9
1983	74.9	10.2	13.4
1984	71.1	12.8	13.9
1985	76.1	8.5	17.2
1986	85.0	4.8	9.0
1987	69.9	10.3	18.6
1988	73.5	13.1	11.0

* Adding the three percentages across from each year will not add to 100%. The tables reflect the originations by Mortgage Companies, Savings & Loans, and Commercial Banks. There are more than three types of FHA, VA, and conventional lenders.

Source: U.S. Department of Housing and Urban Development

Exhibit 51

Originations of Conventional Loans
by Mortgage Companies, S&L's, and Commercial Banks

Percentage Distribution

	Mortgage Companies	S&L's	Commercial Banks
1980	7.2	54.7	25.3
1981	11.5	50.3	25.5
1982	15.5	43.6	29.9
1983	14.7	50.7	25.0
1984	15.1	53.3	21.7
1985	14.4	53.6	25.6
1986	14.5	47.4	27.7
1987	15.3	44.2	29.9
1988	15.9	47.3	27.2

* Adding the three percentages across from each year will not add to 100%. The tables reflect the originations by Mortgage Companies, Savings & Loans, and Commercial Banks. There are more than three types of FHA, VA, and conventional lenders.

Source: U.S. Department of Housing and Urban Development

LOAN QUALIFICATION The phrase used to signify that the loan applicant has been approved. For FHA, *see* FHA - LOAN APPROVAL, THE FIRM COMMITMENT. For VA, *see* VA - CERTIFICATE OF COMMITMENT.

LOAN SHIPPER The shipping of loans is the preparation, completion and packaging of loan documents after closing to be delivered to an investor. The shipper and the post close auditor may, in smaller institutions, be the same individual. This person's responsibilities usually include follow-up on recorded documents, or insurance certificates for final transmission to an investor.

LOAN SUBMISSION A package of documents received by the lender regarding a certain property or properties that the mortgagor or his agent delivers to the mortgagee for review and qualification for a loan. The package includes the note, mortgage or trust, policy of title insurance, and a certificate of insurance or guarantee (if an FHA, VA or FmHA loan is involved).

LOAN-TO-VALUE RATIO (LTV) The percentage amount borrowed in the acquisition or refinancing of property. An 80% loan-to-value ratio would require the loan to be no more than 80% of the lesser of the purchase price or the appraised value.

Risk rate is the property's appraised value versus the mortgage's principal amount. It is closely akin to an underwriting process that establishes risks determined in individual ownership, including terms and size of a potential mortgage loan. Various types of loans call for exact procedures and underwriting factors. On the other hand, an estimate of value and the actual worth of real property made per current market pricing by real estate appraisers who have professional training is based initially by on-the-site inspections.

The quality of the appraisal can not be overstated for the individual portfolio lender and seller/servicers who are active in secondary market trading. An 80% loan is basic for many lending institutions operating in conventional mortgages; but, if the lender's risk is limited, the institution may require only 95% government-insured loans or limited private mortgage insurance. LTV provisions are commonly made for determining a borrower's default in the ratio of the borrower's current payment to disposable income and a current loan-to-value ratio that statistically influence the borrower's incentive and ability to cure delinquencies before default occurs.

The LTV is treated differently for conventional and government-insured loans. Conventional loans are not insured or guaranteed by a government agency. They are generally privately insured.

Private mortgage insurance is unlimited by appraised values. Actual yearly payments are made by the borrower for private mortgage insurance according to the LTV ratio balance, while yearly payments thereafter are based on per month accruals at .29%. Low-to-moderate income homebuyers may not meet present MI underwriting criteria, however.

LOAN UNDERWRITER A person who makes an analysis of a submission as to the risk involved. Underwriters can be used in the insurance industry, by mortgage companies, and in the securities business (see UNDERWRITER). In the mortgage business, an underwriter is one who approves or rejects loan submissions. Loan underwriting can be described as "an exercise in the art of judgement." An underwriter is charged with the responsibility of analyzing risk based on credit and property documentation and terms of credit requested. This function may be performed by an individual or by committee. The underwriting decisions determine:

(1) if a loan is in compliance with investor criteria;

(2) the creditworthiness of borrower;

(3) the acceptability of collateral; and

(4) establishing conditions that must be satisfied before closing.

An underwriter completes a form similar to that in Exhibit 52.

LOC *See* LETTER OF CREDIT.

LOCK BOX A metal box put on the door of a listed property by the listing agent so showings can occur without the listing agent being required to be at the property. REALTORS have a key to the box, which contains a key to the house.

LOCK-IN LEGISLATION Consumer complaints about lock-in interest rates initially applied for that were increased at settlement has been an issue between borrowers and lenders that has reached several state lawmaking bodies. Traditionally, a fairly stable interest rate environment has existed. Volatility increased during the refinancing rush by mortgagors who hurried to their lending institutions to take advantage of the sudden drop in interest rates.

LOCK-IN PERIOD A period of time that the interest rate and discount quoted on specific loan is protected or guaranteed. It is common for lenders to quote rates and discount points. If a lender quotes an interest rate of 10% on a $100,000 loan with a discount of 2% for 45 days, and if the quote is locked in, the customer is assured of getting the loan quoted if the loan is approved and closed within the stated time. Lock-in agreements should be in writing. A loan quote does not have to be locked in, it can be quoted on a "market" basis

Exhibit 52

 FannieMae

Transmittal Summary

Lender Name	Lender Address

Borrower Name	Lender Number	Lender Loan Number

Property Address	Contract Number	Fannie Mae Loan No.

Section 1 — Loan Characteristics (Check all Applicable Categories)

Loan Type

☐ FHA	☐ 1st Mort.	☐ Fixed Rate	☐ Buydown	
☐ VA	☐ 2nd Mort.	☐ ARM Plan		
☐ Conv.		No.		

Loan Purpose

☐ Purchase
☐ Refinance

If Refinance, Purpose

Occupancy

☐ Primary Single-Family

Owner-Occupied

☐ Second Home
☐ S.F. Investment
☐ 2-4 Family Investment
☐ 2-4 Family Owner-Occupied

Loan Terms

Original Loan Amount	Initial Note Rate	Initial Monthly Installment	Date of Note	Term (months)
$	%	$		

Section 2 — Underwriting Information

Sales Price	Appraised Value	Loan to Value
$	$	%

Does Fannie Mae have an interest in the first mortgage? ☐ Yes ☐ No

What is combined Loan-to-Value Ratio? _____ %

Appraiser Name & Company Name

Property Type

☐ Condominium Project Type _____   ☐ De Minimus PUD
☐ PUD Project Type _____   ☐ Other
☐ Cooperative Project Type _____

Underwriter Name

Stable Monthly Income

	Borrower	Co-Borrower	Total
Base Income	$	$	$
Other Income	$	$	$
Positive Cash Flow (Subject Property)	$	$	$
Total Income	$	$	$

Ratios

Primary Housing Expense/Income _____ %

Total Obligation/Income _____ %

Investment Property Only

Debt Service Coverage Ratio _____ %

Proposed Monthly Payments

Borrower's Primary Residence

First Mortgage P&I	$
Second Mortgage P&I	$
Hazard Insurance	$
Taxes	$
Mortgage Insurance	$
Home Owner Association Fees	$
Other:	$
Total Primary Housing Expense	$
Other Obligations	
Negative Cash Flow (Subject Property)	$
All Other Monthly Payments	$
Total All Monthly Payments	$

Section 3—Lender's Underwriting Comments

Section 4—Exhibits Submitted in Addition to Fannie Mae Standard Document Requirements

1.	4.
2.	5.
3.	6.

Section 5—Lender's Contact (Person to Whom Correspondence Should Be Directed)

Name	Title	Telephone No.
Signature		Date

Fannie Mae
Form 1008 Oct. 85

VMP·25 (8801)   VMP MORTGAGE FORMS • (313)293-8100 • (800)521-7291 which means the loan will close at the going rate and points. Some lenders will allow a market quote to be converted to a locked quote. Terms and conditions can vary with lenders. Even if the quote is at market, it is best to get the quote in writing. A customer or broker should carefully read the loan quote agreement so that the conditions are understood. A lock-in agreement is not a mortgage or a loan commitment.

LOCK-OUT PROTECTION A period during which prepayments on a mortgage may not be made. Typical to multifamily lending, investors in multifamily securities are usually provided with this provision as a means of allowing some degree of call protection. An investor's strategy relies on principal repayment scheduling that depends partly on a pool's lock-out guarantee of such security investment. The undivided interest in the purchase will stand for an assurance that the mortgage's prepayment does not occur after the established date according to the issuer's multifamily lock-out terms. Freddie Mac multifamily security lock-outs call for 4 1/2 years as of a delivery date to the agency. Lock-outs currently have no single-family application similar to multifamily mortgages.

LOFT An upper room with open space. The term can refer to any open space that is not finished and can be used for storage.

LOG CABIN

Log Cabin. This is a house built of unfinished logs.

LONDON INTER-BANK OFFER RATE (LIBOR) An average of daily lending rates from several major London banks. LIBOR has been used as an index for Adjustable Rate Mortgages.

A traditional lender's strategy may include the purchase of FHLB advances that can be financed relatively inexpensively but are subject to regulations. Particular finance alternatives include Certificates of Deposits (CDs), including a one-year CD, interest rate swaps, and interest rate caps. By buying an interest rate cap that pays a one-year LIBOR rate if it should exceed, for example, a nine percent rate, the traditional lender can benefit from lower funding costs as rates decline while limiting the cost of funds to nine percent if interest rates increase.

Interest rate swaps, for example, will lower basis risk, therefore permitting thrifts to swap short-term, variable-interest liabilities for their long-term fixed rate pledges or commitments. The usual type of swap is the exchange of short-term LIBOR for long-term Treasury-based rates. Basis risk is reduced by allowing institutions to commit to pay fixed spreads exceeding three-year, five-year or any long-term Treasury index for one-year LIBOR rates since an institution may efficiently issue long-term debts, net of insurance and reserve expenses - inasmuch as LIBOR approaches the equality of CD rates.

A Eurobond issue uses this floating rate LIBOR index; but, when interest rates increase and fall during times of volatility, a spread will occur indicating some widening between LIBOR and Treasury securities of corresponding maturities. Interest rate LIBOR quotes for quarterly, semi-annual, and annual deposits are available on a daily basis that shows the average rates at several London financial institutions that measures the international cost of money.

LONG-TERM LEASE A lease of ten years or more in duration.

LOSS DRAFT The payment by an insurance company for a loss insured by a hazard insurance policy. The check is normally made out to the homeowner and the mortgage company, if there is a loss payable clause in the policy.

LOSS PAYABLE CLAUSE An endorsement to the property insurance policy specifying the lender as a payee in the event of property damage. This endorsement protects the lender's interest in the property in proportionate value to the loan outstanding. With a loss payable clause the homeowner can endorse the loss draft to the lender who then ensures that repairs are made in workman like fashion or that the loan is paid off in the event of a complete loss from fire.

LOT A distinct portion of land.

LOT AND BLOCK A method for describing or finding a parcel of land.

LOUVER Horizontal slats or fins over an opening allowing ventilation with the exclusion of rain or snow.

LOUVER WINDOW *See* WINDOW.

LTV *See* LOAN-TO-VALUE RATIO.

LUMINOUS CEILING A ceiling of translucent materials emitting light throughout its entire surface from fluorescent tubes above the ceiling. Usually made of glass or plastic.

M

M ROOF *See* ROOF.

MAINTENANCE The work required to keep a building in its proper operating condition.

MAJORITY The age at that an individual is no longer deemed a minor for conducting business affairs or a term used to describe more than half.

MANDATORY COMMITMENT An agreement requiring the buyer and seller to perform, neither having the option to not perform. If performance is not possible, there are usually severe penalties to be paid by the defaulting party.

MANSARD ROOF A roof with two slopes on all four sides.
See ROOF.

MANTEL Usually and ornamental shelf over a fireplace.

MANUAL AWNING A window type.
See WINDOW.

MANUFACTURED (OR FACTORY BUILT) HOUSING A residential unit that is constructed in sections in a factory. The house is built in two sections. Some manufactured housing operations use converted aircraft hangers. In the factory there are usually two production lines, one for each half of the house. When the sections come off the assembly line they are carried to the building site by a flat-bed truck. At the building site, the foundation has been laid (either a slab or a crawl space foundation) and the plumbing, wiring, and any heating and air conditioning ducts are in place. The sections are then placed onto the foundation and joined together for the finished product. Manufactured housing is often called *modular housing.*
　　The quality of construction and the materials used for manufactured housing is very similar to a house built by conventional methods; therefore, it is distinguished from a mobile home. When the unit is permanently affixed to a foundation, it assumes the characteristics of a site-built residential dwelling and can be legally classified as real property. When a mortgage loan is issued on a manufactured house, an ALTA 7 endorsement is usually required if loan closing instructions indicate that the secured property is improved by a manufactured housing unit.

See PRE-FABRICATED HOUSING.

MARGIN (1) For adjustable rate loans, it is the spread between the index and the rate. One could say a margin is the lender's profit. Margin is what is added to the index to decide the interest rate for adjustable rate loans. Example: Assuming the index is 10 percent and the margin is 2.5 percent, the rate would be 12.5 percent. One word of caution: do not assume that the lower the margin, the lower the lender's profit. A lender may charge a low margin, but have a high measure for an index or have shorter adjustment periods. Adjustable rate mortgages must be looked at in their entirety; what a lender gives on one feature may be more than taken back by another.

(2) In future trading, it is the specific amount set by each exchange that buyers and sellers are required to deposit as a guarantee assuring successful performance of a commitment to take delivery during a designated period of time. The funds are held by the clearing organization of the exchange.

(3) The down payment required when borrowing funds for stock purchase. The Federal Reserve Board sets margins in stock purchases and the down payment is expressed as a percentage of the purchase price or market value.

MARGIN CALL The requirement for additional funds or collateral to serve as security for trading losses on outstanding positions that are subject to margin. An investor will receive a variation of a margin call if the equity position falls below the requirements set by the National Association of Securities Dealers, the exchanges, or the brokerage firm.

MARK If it is necessary for a person to sign a legal document with a mark, the signatures of two witnesses is usually required.

MARK-TO-THE-MARKET The daily adjustment of margin accounts to reflect the market gain or loss on the position relative to the daily settlement price. The change must be settled each day through the posting of a "variation margin." If the futures position has made money, one receives cash from the clearinghouse. However, if the position has lost money, one must pay on the market movement. This process revalues the commodity or futures contract on a daily basis and adjusts margin accounts to reflect the market gain or loss on a position relative to the daily settlement price.

See MARGIN.

MARKETABILITY Market capacity of Ginnie Mae, Fannie Mae or Freddie Mac in their individual security types to engage reasonable price changes in buying and selling is essential to the marketplace. The volume of mortgage-backed securities traded is fundamental to their value. Liquidity is an inherent

quality due to marketability. MBSs cause a relative intensity of marketability due to the influence of the active primary loan sources and secondary trading activity. This is a form of negotiable security.
See NEGOTIABLE SECURITY.

MARKETABLE TITLE A title that is free and clear of objectionable liens, clouds or other title defects. Title that enables an owner to sell property freely to others and others will accept without objection. Marketability is considered extremely important in the primary origination of mortgage loans.

MARKET APPROACH TO VALUE The evaluation of property based on actual sales of comparable properties. It is one of three approaches to value, the other two being cost and income. This approach to value is the most often used for an existing residential property. In this approach the appraiser uses information from other comparable properties such as the sales price, the proximity to one another, and the dates of the sale. The word "comparable" is the key to an effective market approach to value. In making sure the properties are comparable, the appraiser obtains information as to the total square footage of heated living area, the story height, type of construction, the age and condition of the building, the total number of rooms, number of bedrooms, number of bathrooms, the type of heating and air conditioning, whether there is a garage or a carport and how many cars it will accommodate, and the appraiser will consider any special amenities. Depending on the availability of information about comparable sales, the appraiser will use properties that are truly comparable to one another, are located within two blocks of the subject property, and have sold within the past six months.

Real estate agents are sometimes prone to using a square foot price as a general rule of thumb to decide values of homes. With this method, the price of a home will be very close to a dollar value of homes. With this method, the price of a home will be very close to a dollar value decided by multiplying the heated square footage by a dollar amount. For example, a 2,000 square foot home with a $40 square foot price should be valued at $80,000. To decide a square foot price, simply divide the sales price by the heated square footage ($80,000 + 200 = $40). Heated area should be used so that even comparisons of square feet can be made between homes that have carports or garages to homes that have none. The drawback to this rule of thumb is that it gives a false implication that houses are valued solely by square footage. A home with three bedrooms, two baths, den, living room, dining room, and kitchen will not appraise automatically for more than a comparable home with the same components solely because each room in the subject property is one foot and six inches larger than the comparable property. Houses of similar room composi-

tion and locations will most likely appraise for the same value regardless of small differences in the square footage created by rooms being slightly longer or wider than comparable rooms of another house.
See APPRAISED VALUE.

MARKETING SEQUENCE FOR MORTGAGE BANKING COMPANIES
See LOAN ORIGINATION PROCESS and SECONDARY MARKETING.

MARKET ORDER An order to buy or sell a security at the highest and best price available.

MARKET PRICE The market price is the last reported selling price at which a security is sold.

MARKET RENT Rent attributable to a unit if it were leased to the public. Contract rent is the actual rent paid for a unit.

MARKET STUDY A projection of future demand for a specific property (residential, commercial, or industrial) with a recommendation pertaining to volume, size, square footage, sales price or rental. The term has become generic and can mean any study of a market, a project, or an enterprise, to decide the probability of success.
See FEASIBILITY STUDY.

MARKET VALUE The price at which a willing seller will sell and a willing buyer will buy, neither being under duress.
See FAIR MARKET VALUE.

MASONRY Walls built of brick, stone, concrete, tile, or similar materials.

MASTER DEED The conveyance document used for the sale of condominiums. The master deed along with a declaration must be submitted when public record is made of the condominium. Recording requirements may vary according to state laws.
See CONDOMINIUM.

MASTER LEASE A controlling lease that governs subsequent leases. A master lease can apply to an office building with subsequent leases pertaining to individual spaces in the building.

Exhibit 53

Comparable Sales Chart
(For requesting increase in appraised value)

Address of Comparable Properties	Area (Square Feet)	Number of Stories	Number of Rooms	Number of Bedrooms	Number of Baths	Type of Heat & Air Conditioning (if any)	Type of Construction	Age	Sales Price	Date of Sale (Month & Year)	Type of Financing	Other Amenities (if necessary list in Remarks)	Number of Fireplaces	Garage or Carport
Subject Property														
Sale #1 (address)														
Sale #2 (address)														
Sale #2 (address)														
REMARKS:														

Address of Comparable Properties	Area (Square Feet)	Number of Stories	Number of Rooms	Number of Bedrooms	Number of Baths	Type of Heat & Air Conditioning (if any)	Type of Construction	Age	Sales Price	Date of Sale (Month & Year)	Type of Financing	Other Amenities (if necessary list in Remarks)	Number of Fireplaces	Garage or Carport
Subject Property														
Sale #1 (address)														
Sale #2 (address)														

MASTER MORTGAGE A standard mortgage form designed to reduce the cost of recording future mortgages. The master mortgage is then used as a referral for subsequent mortgages; pages from the mortgages are eliminated and recording fees are less.

MASTER PLAN Usually pertains to a zoning matter that a developer submits a plan for the overall, long-term development of a property.

MASTER SERVICING The collecting of monthly mortgage payments on the collateral of a structured financing from several servicers. Master servicing occurs when the issuing institution contracts with other primary lenders/services to buy mortgages in order to arrange a pool of loans that will constitute the mortgage-backed security. This type of agency relationship between originators of primary loans and the certificate issuer as the "master services" results in a payment being transmitted to the investor after the security is made a surety. The MBS is made a surety when customer payments are collected from primary servicers, formed into an aggregate sum for the transmittal, and a master-servicer fee of 25 to 50 basis points levied. In consideration for the pass-through rate to the final investor, the additional basis points result in the net rate of 11.1% (if and when the pool consists of 12% mortgages). Regardless of the fact that the underlying first mortgages reflect much protection for the master services as he or she passes through a private MBS, a pool mortgage insurance policy is necessary for a stop-loss enhancement tool demanded by rating agencies.

MATRIX QUALITY CONTROL MONITORING SYSTEM A system proposed to be used by Freddie Mac for early detection of potential problems.

MATURITY (1) The date when the principal or stated value of a debt security becomes due and payable in full to the holder. MBSs, bonds, drafts or notes that contain an expiration date (for the instrument of indebtedness) that then becomes due and payable increases their marketability. The limiting dates of pooled MBSs, or maturity dates on Freddie Mac and Fannie Mae pools are based on the underlying mortgages. The pool maturity date may be confusing to investors. For example, 90% of the loans may be due for maturity at the end of 15 years while 10% of the loans may be due for maturity at the end of 30 years. The latest maturity date of the mortgages representing the pool is in 30-years.
    (2) The date a loan is due to be paid in full.

MBB *See* MORTGAGE-BACKED BONDS.

MBS See MORTGAGE-BACKED SECURITY.

MECHANIC'S LIEN A lien given by law to protect and secure the payment for labor or materials. It is a lawful claim that secures priority payment for work performed and material furnished by a contractor or other person for the construction or repair of a building; these claims are attached to the land, buildings and improvements. Mechanics liens vary by state law. In some states, foreclosure by a loan recorded before a mechanics liens will eliminate all mechanics liens. The rest of this definition follows the procedure for mechanics liens in many states, and, particularly, in the state of California.

Mechanic's liens may cause expensive legal costs and loan delays. In construction loans it is anticipated that a lien not previously recorded may still be valid; therefore, on the date of consummation, the lender must show some evidence of building starts in order to guarantee constructive notice in public records. Lenders assure themselves of no mechanic's liens by paying bills or assuring the payment of all bills for construction work and improvements for labor and materials.

Mechanic's liens, in some states, precede over a mortgage when any work has begun on a property before the construction loan is recorded. A pre-construction affidavit or certification usually assures the lender that his first lien is protected. The contractor and prospective mortgagor must verify that up to a certain date no initial labor has begun on the property, including the delivery of materials. A mechanic's lien is evident when it is obvious that material is on the building site, whether it is recorded or not. It is for this reason that lenders gather all the information they can at the time of recording the mortgage. If there is no evidence of a lien on the record, no material delivered to the property and no prevailing questions or contract doubts, the construction loan will be recorded.

Because mechanic's liens are automatic when actually recorded or when other official notice is made, there must be a period of time specified after the materials have been delivered or the labor provided that notice must be served on the owner. This is a separate and distinct requirement that should not be confused with the time that the contract is valid. State statutes vary on the notice period, but it is most commonly 60 days. The preconstruction affidavit precludes this 60-day notification period.

An additional safety provision may be included in the building construction contract pertaining to sub-contractor liens. This can be subject to negotiation with the contractor. Some state statutes demand that this type of contract be recorded before sub-contractors begin work; in this way the agreement may avoid their rights to a lien.

Escrow will close in the same way as other residential mortgages are closed, aside from a construction loan, in that required documents must be signed by the borrowers and contractors. It is then that the proper documents can be recorded in public records for inspection by interested parties. A mortgagor's deposit is duly credited for accounts in process unless there is evidence of ownership without claimants on the land, in which case the equity is sufficient to waive a required deposit to the construction lender.

A covered insurance policy is then obtained by the lender, the land inspected, and the borrower informed (with the contractor) to begin construction. Engineers, architects and superintendents may claim a mechanic's lien against the borrower. In most states a mechanic's lien arises, but may not actually exist, at the moment a contract is consummated through either an express or implied initial agreement. Of course, the debt must be proven to exist at the moment of such agreement and must have a legal expiration. Mortgages or trust deeds must be executed and recorded before commencement of construction in order to insure their priority over the mechanic's lien.

Persons having priority may, by agreement, waive their rights in favor of others. An agreement to do this is called a "subordination agreement." These agreements are often executed in connection with deeds of trust or mortgage to subordinate a landowner's purchase money deed of trust to a construction loan. Without such priority of claim for payments against the real property, the building contractor might refuse to expend time and materials on the project. In addition, a preliminary notice must contain a statement that if all bills are not paid in full for labor, service equipment or materials furnished, the improved property may still be subject to a mechanic's lien. The construction lender's copy of the preliminary notice must contain an estimate of the total price of labor, service, equipment or materials to be furnished to the project. Failure to give the preliminary notice within 20 days of the furnishing of labor, service, equipment or materials to the construction lender does not preclude the right to give a preliminary notice later, but claim rights may thus be subordinated.

The holder of the mortgage or deed of trust, which otherwise would be inferior to the mechanic's lien, may be prioritized by filing an appropriate bond with the county recorder. The bond must be in an amount of not less than 75 percent of the principal amount of the mortgage or trust deed. Thereupon, the lien of the mortgage or trust deed is prior and paramount to any mechanic's liens for work done or materials furnished subsequent to the time such bond was filed for record. The purpose of the bond is to assure payment in suits that may be brought to foreclose mechanic's liens on the property.

In regard to recordation, when all instructions have been complied with, the escrow department or loan closer will send the documents to be recorded at the county recorder's office - usually through a title company. The time of recordation will be specified. If new construction is involved, care must be taken that no work of any kind has commenced at the site before the loan is recorded. Otherwise, any mechanic's liens filed will have priority over the construction loan. Some lenders require the title company or one of its appraisers take a photograph of the site after the loan papers have been recorded to establish that no work had started or materials delivered before recordation. In conclusion, the escrow department may do almost anything and everything that is required and authorized to close and record the loan. At the conclusion of the escrow, the loan file is turned over to the lender or the lender's representative or correspondent for loan servicing.

See PRE-CONSTRUCTION AFFIDAVIT.

MEDIAN SALES PRICES *See* Exhibits 54 and 55.

MEETING OF THE MINDS A consent or agreement between parties of a contract.

MERCHANTABLE TITLE *See* MARKETABLE TITLE.

MERIDIAN LINE A surveyor's term used to indicate a north-south line.

METES AND BOUNDS A description of property by identifying boundaries through their terminal points and angles.

MI *See* MORTGAGE INSURANCE.

MIC *See* MORTGAGE INSURANCE CERTIFICATE.

MIDANET Mortgage Information Direct Access Network. Freddie Mac's automated system that electronically transfers loan data and accounting reports. This system operates progressively for the standard fixed rate and ARM single-family programs or the posted spread for the Guarantor program. The posted required net yields for Freddie Mac's MIDANET delivery operations on mandatory delivery commitments for purchasing whole loans and intermediate term or participations are facilitated by MIDANET for 15-year and 30-year fixed rate and ARM mortgage loans. These loans have mandatory delivery periods of 30, 60-91, and 91-120 days. Delivery is obtainable exclusively for 30-year fixed rate mortgages in a ten-day period of time.

Lenders can obtain MIDANET loan delivery period information with the use of personal computer systems; accounting procedures and rate are available with IBM-compatible computers. An operator's handbook and software instructions are furnished to lenders who sign up for the personal computer MIDANET.

Exhibit 54

Median Sale Prices of New Single Family Houses Sold

	U.S.	Northeast	Midwest	South	West
1980	$64,600	$69,500	$63,400	$59,600	$72,300
1981	68,900	76,000	65,900	64,400	77,800
1982	69,300	78,200	68,900	66,100	75,000
1983	75,300	82,200	79,500	70,900	80,100
1984	79,900	88,600	85,400	72,000	87,300
1985	84,300	103,300	80,300	75,000	92,600
1986	92,000	125,000	88,300	80,200	95,700
1987	104,500	140,000	95,000	88,000	111,000
1988	112,500	149,900	100,100	92,000	126,000

Source: U.S. Department of Commerce, The Bureau of the Census and the U.S. Department of Housing and Urban Development

Exhibit 55

Median Sales Prices of Existing Single Family Houses Sold

	U.S.	Northeast	Midwest	South	West
1980	$62,200	$60,800	$51,900	$58,300	$89,300
1981	66,400	63,700	54,300	64,400	96,200
1982	67,800	63,500	55,100	67,100	98,900
1983	70,300	72,200	56,600	69,200	94,900
1984	72,400	78,700	57,100	71,300	95,800
1985	75,500	88,900	58,900	75,200	95,400
1986	80,300	104,800	63,500	78,200	100,900
1987	85,600	133,300	66,000	80,400	113,200
1988	89,300	143,000	68,400	82,200	124,900

Source: The National Association of Realtors®

MIDGETS Short maturity fixed-rate, single-family loans spanning a 15-year period have been securitized by Ginnie Mae pools since 1982. Realized as affordable by some borrowers, a common mortgage-backed security program has been added to other fixed rate pools. The Freddie Mac pass-through security PC program called "Gnomes" has been added to its product line under a standard MBS issue. Similarly, a Fannie Mae pass-through security with a 15-year maturity in individual pools are a part of Fannie Mae's portfolio or issued by single or multiple issuers.

MILITARY CLAUSE A clause found in a lease allowing a military tenant to terminate the lease in the event of transfer, discharge, or other circumstances requiring the transfer of their residence.

MILL One tenth of a cent. This term normally is used for tax rate purposes. One hundred mills would be a tax of ten cents per dollar of assessed valuation.

MINERAL RIGHTS Those rights associated with the sale of resources such as oil or gas coming from the subject property.

MINIMUM LOT AREA The smallest lot allowed in a subdivision for a building site.

MINI-WAREHOUSE A one-story building subdivided into cubicles for storage purposes.

MINOR A person who is not of legal age as specified by law. A person who has not reached their majority. In most cases, a minor cannot be a grantor (seller of property) but can be a grantee by gift or inheritance. A legal requirement for conveying property with clear title is that the seller is competent. Minority is viewed as not being competent. There are circumstances where a obstacle due to minority can be removed or waived - state laws vary on this issue. Courts sometimes establish a guardian for a minor.

MIP *See* FHA - INSURED LOAN.

MISDEMEANOR A crime usually punishable by imprisonment for one year or less. A misdemeanor is less serious than a felony.

MISNOMER A mistake in a name. If such a mistake occurs in a deed, it must be corrected.

MISREPRESENTATION A representation either unintended or deliberate of an untrue set of facts. Misrepresentation may be failure to disclose a set of facts that would have caused another party to act differently or to make a different decision.

MITER In usage by carpenters, a miter is the ends of two pieces of boards that are cut in such a way that when they are joined together an angular shape is produced.

MITIGATION OF DAMAGES A reduction in damages. For example, a landlord may have a duty to find a replacement tenant for a tenant who has breached the lease unlawfully.

MIXED USE A combination of uses such as commercial and residential on one subject property or an area, sometimes known as mixed zoning.

MLS *See* MULTIPLE LISTING SERVICE.

MMI *See* MUTUAL MORTGAGE INSURANCE FUND.

MOBILE HOME A prefabricated residential building that are semi-permanently attached to a pad (designated lot). Although these buildings may not be very mobile after they have been attached to the pad, by nature they are mobile to the site. FHA and VA have financing programs for mobile homes.

MODE The most frequent value in an array of numbers or a manner or method of doing something.

MODIFIED PASS-THROUGH The required passing through of principal and interest collected by the investor of a mortgage-backed security. In a modified pass-through, principal and interest are paid to the investor regardless of whether or not the mortgage payment is made by the borrower.

MODULAR HOUSING *See* MANUFACTURED HOUSING.

MOISTURE BARRIER Treated material used to retard or prevent moisture or water vapor from seeping into or through walls or floors of a building.

MOLD A strip of decorative material usually required to cover gaps at wall junctions.

MONEY SUPPLY The total circulation of currency as a medium of exchange, including deposits in savings and checking accounts (federal government and bank holdings are excluded). This total represents the nation's money supply. Inflation and prices have a tendency to increase when there is an excess of money relative to the supply of goods. Conversely, a reduction in amounts of money may decrease prices and trigger unemployment. The Federal Reserve System reports on the money supply weekly and monthly.

MONTEREY ARCHITECTURE

Monterey Architecture. A two-story house, often made of stucco with a balcony across the front made of very plain wood or iron. The roof is usually made of tile.

MONTH-TO-MONTH TENANCY In absence of any written agreement, a lease, either written or oral, is deemed to be on a month-to-month tenancy. When the landlord accepts payment for rent from a tenant, the lease is extended for one more month. The lease contains until either party gives a thirty day notice of termination.

MONEY MARKET A market for assets with maturities of less than one year. Examples of money market instruments are federal funds, Treasury bills, bankers' acceptances, commercial paper, certificates of deposit, federal agency discount paper, and repurchase agreements.

MONEY MARKET FUND A mutual fund that invests in money market instruments.

MONUMENT A visible marker, either natural or artificial, set at a point to determine boundaries for a survey of property.
See LANDMARK.

MOODY'S A U.S. credit rating agency that defines its rating categories as follows:

Aaa - Bonds that are judged to be of the best quality. They carry the smallest degree of investment risk. Interest payments are protected by a large or exceptionally stable margin and principal is secure. While the various protective elements are likely to change, such changes are unlikely to impair the fundamentally strong position of such issues.

Aa - Bonds that are judged to be of high quality by all standards. Together with the Aaa group, they comprise what are generally known as high grade bonds. They are rated lower than Aaa bonds because protection may not be as great, fluctuation of protective elements may be of greater amplitude or there may be other elements that make the long-term risks appear larger.

A - Bonds that possess many favorable investment attributes, considered upper medium grade obligations. Factors giving security to principal and interest are considered adequate but elements may be present that suggest a susceptibility to impairment.

Baa - Bonds that are considered medium grade obligations they are neither highly protected nor poorly secured. Interest payments and principal security appear adequate for the present but certain protective elements may be lacking or may be characteristically unreliable over any great length of time. Such bonds lack outstanding investment characteristics and have speculative characteristics. Bonds rated below Baa are not considered investment grade.

Ba - Bonds that are judged to have speculative elements; their future cannot be considered well assured. Often the protection of interest and principal payments may be very moderate and therefore not well safeguarded.

B - Bonds that generally lack the characteristics of desirable investments. Assurance of interest and principal payments or maintenance of other terms of the contract over any long period of time may be small.

Caa - Bonds of poor standing. Such issues may be in default or there may be elements of danger with respect to principal or interest.

Ca - Bonds that are highly speculative. Such issues are often in default.

C - The lowest rated class of bonds. Issues so rated can be regarded as having extremely poor prospects of ever attaining any real investment standing.

MORATORIUM A period of time during which certain activity is not allowed or required. FHA may have an active loan program in all parts of the country except an isolated area where they declare a moratorium pending investigation of abuse or fraud - such was the case with the investor loan.

MORE OR LESS A phrase used to indicate a slight variation in the true size of real property. Indicates that a measurement is not exact. For example, a description of farm might be 756 acres, more or less. The description of the farm is that the acreage may be more or less by one acre.

MORNET An electronic mailbox service for communications between lenders and Fannie Mae via personal computer. Mornet is similar to the Computerized Loan Origination (CLO), MIDANET and Laser systems used by Freddie Mac and Fannie Mae.

MORTAR A paste-like material made of lime and cement mixed with sand and water. Mortar is used as a bonding material for brick or stone.

MORTGAGE A written instrument creating a lien upon real estate used for the security of payment for a specified debt. Some states use a Deed of Trust or a Trust Deed in lieu of a Mortgage as the evidence of a real estate loan. In both cases, Mortgage or Deed of Trust, there is a signature of a note. The purpose of the note is to create a personal liability, the purpose of the Mortgage or Deed of Trust is to create a lien.

In states that use a Mortgage, the homeowner is looked upon as the owner of the title to property encumbered by a loan. States that use a Mortgage as the lien instrument are called "lien theory states." States that use a Deed of Trust or Trust Deed are called "title theory states." The Trustee in a Deed of Trust is considered to be the owner of the property until the debt is paid.

See CO-MORTGAGOR, CO-SIGNER, RELEASE, SATISFACTION OF A MORTGAGE, SURETY.

MORTGAGE-BACKED BONDS (MBB) A bond that is backed by a pool of mortgages. The bond is a general obligation of the issuing institution. It is a non-pay-through security secured by the mortgage collateral that is owned by the issuer. Bond issuers retain cash flows but have a general obligation to make bond payments to investors. Mortgage bonds are similar to traditional corporate bonds but without the pass-through feature. The cash flows are not relevant to cash flows on the underlying mortgage security; therefore, they are not "passed through" to investors. The investor buys a bond but does not own shares of the collateral. The pool of mortgages securing the mortgage-backed bonds, as issued in the secondary markets, are simply mortgage collateral owned by issuers. It was the success of pass-through securities issued by Ginnie Mae and Freddie Mac PCs that led to the expansion of the pay-through bond and the rise of conduits as issuers who market mortgage-backed securities backed by loans that were originated and serviced by a substantial number of lenders.

MORTGAGE-BACKED SECURITY (MBS) Securities or investments that represent an undivided interest in a pool of loans secured by mortgages or deed of trusts. Principal reductions from the underlying mortgages is used to pay off the bond or securities. Ginnie Mae, Fannie Mae, Freddie Mac and private conduits qualified to deal in the secondary market are active in trading mortgage-backed securities. Conventional mortgage-backed securities are currently issued in two separate program classes by Fannie Mae and Freddie Mac. These two secondary market agencies assemble loan pools involving the first program class from their portfolios and issue the MBSs to dealers who, in turn, distribute them to investors. A second program class is assembled by lenders who establish pools of mortgages and, in turn, swap or otherwise exchange for MBSs issued by either Fannie Mae or Freddie Mac. The securities may be held in the lender's portfolio temporarily or as a permanent asset or sold into the capital markets.

MORTGAGE-BACKED SECURITIES CLEARING CORPORATION (MBSCC) The central depository for certificates guaranteed by Ginnie Mae. The key function of the MBSCC is to operate an electronic book-entry safekeeping system that verifies the trading of Ginnie Mae securities (without paper). In addition, this book-entry registration can be used to immobilize Ginnie Maes used for repos and reverse repos. All GNMA I and II investors and issuers must follow the MBSCC book-entry procedure as of February 1987. The SEC oversees the MBSCC. Ginnie Mae MBS issuers, dealers and sellers who participate in the MBSCC depository assign Ginnie Maes over to the depository, thus making the clearing house the registered security holder.

MORTGAGE BANKER A party who originates, sells, and services mortgages. A mortgage banker retains servicing rights to loans and acts as a correspondent between lenders and borrowers. A mortgage banker can later sell servicing rights and earn a premium. Mortgage bankers have always enjoyed a large percentage of all FHA and VA loan originations, as compared to S&Ls, banks, and credit unions. In the past the term "mortgage banker" was almost synonymous with "mortgage company." Today most banks and thrifts operate their real estate loan department as a mortgage banking operation. *See* LOAN ORIGINATIONS.

MORTGAGE BANKERS ASSOCIATION A nationwide association devoted exclusively to the field of mortgage and real estate finance. The MBA represents nearly 3,000 member firms and corporations comprised of mortgage companies, commercial banks, savings and loan associations, mutual savings banks, mortgage brokers, life insurance companies and other businesses engaged in various aspects of real estate finance. The Association runs a School of Mort-

of Mortgage Banking and a Certified Mortgage Banker program, besides other educational services. The address for the MBA is: Mortgage Bankers Association, 1125 15th St. NW, Washington, D.C. 20005. The MBA was originally formed as a trade association in 1914 and was known as the Farm Mortgage Bankers Association. The name of "Mortgage Bankers Association" began in 1923.

MORTGAGE BANKING Many Savings and Loans, banks, and credit unions now operate their real estate loan department in mortgage banking manner that means they are very active in the secondary market. These institutions no longer look at making residential loans for their portfolio. A lender who sells loans to investors and has the ability to retain the loan servicing rights, has a mortgage banking business.

MORTGAGE BROKER A party who originates and sells mortgages but does not service the loan. Many states have or are considering laws to license mortgage brokers. In Missouri a newly enacted law (House Bill 1788, Laws of 1990) will require licensing of mortgage brokers by the director of the division of savings and loan supervision. The law became effective August 28, 1990. In the endeavor to license mortgage brokers, the Missouri law gives a good definition of a mortgage broker.

A mortgage broker is defined as any person who does not service loans secured by liens or mortgages on real property or who does not maintain a real property mortgage loan servicing portfolio and who directly or indirectly: (1) holds himself out for hire to serve as an agent for any person in an attempt to obtain a loan that will be secured by a lien or mortgage on real property; (2) Holds himself out for hire to serve as an agent for any person who has money to loan, where the loan is or will be secured by a lien or mortgage on real property; (3) holds himself out as being able to make, purchase, place, sell or exchange loans secured by liens or mortgages on real property; or (4) holds himself out to be a mortgage broker.

The Missouri law exempts the following entities, among others form its provisions: (1) A person doing business under the laws of Missouri or the U.S. relating to banks, trust companies, savings and loan associations, credit unions, small business investment corporations or real investment trusts, or any person servicing loans secured by liens or mortgages on real property or maintaining a servicing portfolio for such loans; (2) An attorney rendering services in the performance of his duties as an attorney; (3) A Missouri licensed real estate broker rendering services in the performance of his duties as a real estate broker who obtains financing for real estate transaction if the real estate broker: (a) does not act as a loan broker in more than five transactions during any twelve-month period; (b) does not receive a fee for his activities as a loan broker until after financing is actually obtained; and (c) files a disclosure statement describing the transaction with the director of the division of savings and loan supervision within 30 days of each transaction; (4) A mortgage loan company subject to licensing, supervision or audition by FNMA, FHLMC, VA GNMA, or HUD as an approved seller or servicer; (5) A natural person who provides funds for investment in loans secured by a lien on real property on his own account, who does not charge a fee or cause a fee to be paid for any service other than the normal and scheduled rates for escrow, title insurance and recording services, and who does not collect funds to be used for the payment of any taxes or insurance premiums on the property securing any such loans; and (6) a person doing business under the laws of Missouri or the U.S. relating to any broker-dealer, agent or investment adviser.

Mortgage brokers are gaining acceptance throughout the country. Many lenders are now recognize mortgage brokers as providing a genuine service and will pay them a fee that is not recaptured by an offsetting fee tacked on to the list of charges paid by the loan applicant. A mortgage broker can reduce the time it takes to shop through the maze of mortgages offered to the typical home mortgage loan applicant. A good mortgage broker should be able to tell what loan is best for the loan applicant and recommend the lender with the best service and price. Their future seems to hinge upon two important points: (1) the performance of a service that is a unique benefit to the loan applicant, and (2) the cost of their service being absorbed by the lender and it not being a simple referral fee that the loan applicant eventually pays.

MORTGAGE COMMITMENT An agreement to lend a specific amount of money over stated terms and conditions, including time. Mortgage commitments are usually conditional on approval of various segments of a loan application. Some of the more common conditions for approval that are incorporated into the mortgage commitment are: acceptable income and credit for the borrower, an appraisal supporting the value and approving the condition of the property, sufficient funds to close the loan, good title to the property used for collateral. A mortgage commitment can be issued on what is sometimes advertised as a "24 hour approval" with all or nearly all conditions listed or a mortgage commitment can be issued after loan processing with only good title listed.

MORTGAGE COMPANY OPERATIONS Mortgage companies operate primarily as mortgage loan correspondents or brokers. Their source of money for residential lending is closely tied to GNMA, FNMA, FHLMC, and private investors. Before the use of mortgage-backed securities, the source of money for a mortgage company was almost exclusively made up of, life insurance companies, mutual savings institutions, pension funds and other financial institutions.

companies, mutual savings institutions, pension funds and other financial institutions.

Mortgage companies essentially act as middlemen and are a primary source for mortgage loans. They make FHA, VA, and conventional mortgage loans. Some mortgage companies are very active in income property loans since they are accustomed to acting as loan correspondents for the traditional sources for these loan, i.e., life insurance companies, pension funds, and thrifts. Some companies are very diversified and engage in property rentals, leases, property management and insurance activities. Some may operate as real estate intermediaries for a commission.

Mortgage companies are usually regulated by state law; their operations will therefore vary from state-to-state. Depending on the state and other business conditions, they may operate under minimum supervision and have a wide latitude of powers. Most companies, however, secure their funds from commercial sources, operating on lines of credit or arranging for advances against loans until they are sold to investors.

Mortgage companies are generally free from the sort of lending restrictions and limitations placed on institutional lenders. Mortgage companies are fairly active in construction lending. Such loans are made with their funds, borrowed funds, or with the funds of the institutional companies they represent. These funds, upon the sale of the home, are converted to long- term mortgage loans. Most mortgage companies will only deal in mortgages that can be readily sold to the secondary market. As a result, these lenders prefer government-insured or guaranteed mortgages or conventional or uninsured mortgages that have advance purchase commitments.

Generally, after the mortgage banker originates a loan and channels it to the institutional buyer, the institution will contract with the mortgage banker to service the loan for a fee. This fee is negotiable generally from three-eights to one-half of one percent of the outstanding balance of the mortgage. The lender's service consists of collecting payments due on the mortgage, paying taxes, seeing that the property is insured and, when necessary, foreclosing.

Mortgage companies throughout the country have played a significant role in making mortgage funds available to individuals and institutions. Acting as mortgage loan correspondents they have pioneered the way to modern mortgage banking.

MORTGAGE CONSTANT The percentage ratio between annual debt service and the principal loan amount. Dividing of the annual debt service by the principal loan amount will equal the mortgage constant.

MORTGAGE CORRESPONDENT See LOAN CORRESPONDENT.

MORTGAGE CREDIT CERTIFICATE (MCC) A non-refundable tax credit bearing from 10% to 50% of the interest paid on a home mortgage loan. There are qualifying restrictions such as limiting the program to first-time homebuyers with restricted income limits and sales prices.

MORTGAGE CREDIT CONDITION (MC) *See* FHA - MORTGAGE CREDIT CONDITION.

MORTGAGE GUARANTY INSURANCE CORPORATION (MGIC)
MGIC is a private mortgage insurance firm that has a program that permits borrowers to include one-time premiums for mortgage insurance on 15-year mortgage loans with a 90% LTV or less. This program was created in response to the enthusiasm of the FHA one-time premium on the part of lenders. The program saves lenders the trouble of renewing the premiums and may slightly add to servicing and secondary market income streams. Other private insurance companies have considered programs very much like the MGIC's.

MGIC initiated the first MBSs issued by a private entity and created an auxiliary called Maggie Mae in 1978. Maggie Mae has almost 1,400 authorized seller/servicers who package mortgages for investors. This conduit has assembled packages of first and second mortgages and, in turn, has issued mortgage-related securities, including assembled mortgages, on homes built with all union labor in specific states, counties and cities; 3- and 5-year price level ARMs; and 30-year and shorter maturities.

MORTGAGE INDIVIDUAL FINANCING Individuals and non-financial institutions who act as lenders make more individual mortgages from month-to-month than any other class of mortgagees. Accounting for less than one-fourth of total mortgage debt, they rank second as the source of prime mortgage funds and are, by far, the largest source of junior mortgage loans. The great majority of such loans are those made on one-to-four unit properties.

Individuals and other non-financial institutions obtain mortgage loan funds from title insurance companies, mortgage companies and real estate brokers. Some of these mortgages are subsequently sold to institutions and trusts. Individual mortgage financing practices are not uniform and, in general, are not subject to national or state licensing laws or other regulations. As a result, these lenders can take greater investment risks and often accept extremely high loan-to-value ratios. They typically do not use the standard credit analysis procedures that guide institutional lenders. In fact, many of the loans they make would not be acceptable to institutional lenders. However, individual mortgage financing tends to be made at higher interest rates. The individual cannot compete with institutional lenders in securing prime mortgages. Due to large scale operations, institutions can supply funds at lower costs, hence lower interest rates than the individual can offer.

Often, a professional appraiser is employed to value the property or the individual lender will appraise the property personally. Of course, if the loan will be FHA-insured or VA- guaranteed, agency procedures must be followed; however, most individual mortgages are made on conventional loans as these lenders may not become FHA-approved.

Individual lenders may insist on a "straight loan," with full payment made at the maturity date. A lender who grants a renewal is likely to require additional servicing and closing cost fees on the renewal. The maximum loan term is typically 15 years and have a maturity ranging from five to ten years. Interest rates will vary but tend to increase with the security risk involved. The maximum rate charged, however, will be subject to state usury laws. In California, for example, the rate cannot exceed the higher of 10% per annum or 5% plus the prevailing Federal Reserve discount rate of interest. Thus, if the discount rate is 10%, the individual lender's rate can be as high as 15%.

MORTGAGE INSTRUMENT Any document related to the making of a mortgage. It can refer to the mortgage, note, Deed of Trust, or the Trust Deed.

MORTGAGE INSURANCE (MI) This term has a double meaning. The FHA insurance on a loan is mortgage insurance and is called MI or MIP (mortgage insurance premium). The FHA mortgage insurance protects the lender in the event of foreclosure. For FHA loans, see FHA - INSURED LOAN. For conventional loans see PRIVATE MORTGAGE INSURANCE.

The second meaning of mortgage insurance is the insurance sold to a homeowner that pays off the mortgage in the event of the death of an owner. This insurance is common decreasing-term but it has taken on the term, mortgage insurance. Disability insurance is offered to homeowners and the benefits can vary from paying off the loan to making payments while the homeowner is disabled.

MORTGAGE INSURANCE CERTIFICATE (MIC) A certificate issued by HUD/FHA as evidence that the mortgage has been insured. This certificate is evidence that a contract of mortgage insurance exists between HUD/FHA and the lender. Without this document, HUD/FHA will not honor any claims. If the MIC has been lost, you should search for HUD Mortgagee Letter 88-36 or attain a copy of the FHA Compendium from HUD.

11/09/88   Mortgagee Letter 88-36 establishes a new procedure for obtaining a duplicate MIC. Request for duplicate MICs must be made in writing to the Chief of Mortgage Credit in the HUD Field Office having jurisdiction over the property. The request must be accompanied by a copy of the mortgage note, a completed but unsigned Mortgage Insurance Certificate, Form HUD - 59100 (attached to the back side of Mortgagee Letter 88-36) and a self addressed, stamped envelope. Letter finishes with instructions on how to complete Form 59100 and what actions Field Office will take.

MORTGAGE INSURANCE COMPANIES OF AMERICA (MICA)
MICA is a mortgage insurance group comprised mostly of private insurance companies (PMIs) or their subsidiaries, called *conduits*. Any private mortgage insurance company who will insure a mortgage against homeowner default can become a member. PMIs issue mortgage insurance that reimburses the financial institution for its costs and losses after foreclosure has been finalized.

MORTGAGE INSURANCE PREMIUM (MIP) An amount paid by the borrower/mortgagor to FHA for mortgage insurance protection for the lender.
See FHA -MORTGAGE INSURANCE PREMIUM.

MORTGAGE INVESTMENT STRATEGIES Fixed income research should include assured immunization strategies using dedicated mortgage portfolios where pension funds are investing in mortgage investment operations. The key strategies include identifying factors important to performance and being able to measure them, identifying and itemizing the risks in a portfolio investment strategy, and then tying the two together. The investment strategy should include the selection of an evaluation period based on overall goals and timetables. For example, when benefits must be paid out to a given number of retirees, is the cash available? Secondly, eligible investments must be identified and each sector must be divided into alternatives with the appropriate risk-return characteristics. In order to realize high returns, investors must assume higher risks.

MORTGAGE LOAN SCHEDULE A listing giving information of each mortgage originated by a lender. Such a listing is helpful to an investor and should include

(1) the name of each mortgagor,

(2) the address and zip code of each mortgaged property and the type of dwelling,

(3) the original principal amount of each mortgage loan,

(4) the investor loan number,

(5) the unpaid principal balance outstanding at loan closing,

(6) the interest rate,

(7) the required monthly payment of principal and interest,

(8) original loan-to-value ratio,

(9) number of units,

(10) seller's loan number,

(11) occupancy code,

(12) first payment date,

(13) date to which interest is paid,

(14) date of the mortgage note,

(15) maturity date of the mortgage note,

(16) the purpose of the mortgage loan,

(17) the appraised value of the mortgage property, and

(18) if the dwelling is a condominium or in a PUD, the investor may request information relative to the master deed, bylaws, or association.

MORTGAGEE The lender. For newcomers to the lending industry, an easy way to remember mortgagee and mortgagor is to visualize the word mortgagee and see the two "e's" in it, just like the word "lender," then think of the word mortgagor and how it has two "o's," just like the word "borrower."

MORTGAGEE LETTERS *See* FHA - COMPENDIUM.

MORTGAGE LIFE INSURANCE *See* MORTGAGE INSURANCE.

MORTGAGE NOTE The original note or bond or other evidence of indebtedness executed by a mortgagor.

MORTGAGE RECORDS All papers and documents relative to a mortgage loan that might include, but not limited to, the following: tax receipts, insurance policies, insurance premium receipts, stock certificates, ledger sheets, payment records, title insurance policies, insurance claim files and correspondence, foreclosure files, and current and historical computerized data files.

MORTGAGE REDEMPTION *See* REDEMPTION PERIOD.

MORTGAGE-RELATED SECURITY (MRS) A generic term used to describe a variety of mortgage related securities. A reference used by investors in the capital markets to distinguish types of investment securities from each other. A MRS is based on mortgage collateral while Treasury bonds are government-related securities. Investors closely inspect quality spreads between a "target Treasury bond" and MRS investments if there exists competitive values between the two.

MORTGAGE REVENUE BONDS (MRB) Bonds issued by a public agency to create funds for housing. The bonds are retired by payments generated by the mortgage loans. These bonds are typically tax-exempt securities sold by state or municipal authorities for raising capital for low interest rate mortgage loans to qualified individuals.

MORTGAGE SERVICING Mortgage bankers and financial institutions who operate like mortgage bankers and retain the contractual rights to collect mortgage payments (including principal and interest) from individuals who borrow money for real estate purchases perform the function of mortgage servicing. This specific function may include the packaging of individual mortgage loans into a larger pool of debt that is more suitable to investors. This servicing function is for and on behalf of the investors who cannot or do not wish to service the mortgages.

Investors then pay the mortgage banker to collect the payments, remit the principal and interest to the investor, obtain escrow payments for taxes and insurance, and fund disbursement on payment due dates. The investor expects the servicer to maintain appropriate administrative records on the loans as well as handle delinquencies. The mortgage banker's servicing fee is usually the difference between the coupon rate of the mortgage and the investor's yield.

See SERVICING AGREEMENT.

MORTGAGE SERVICING MARKETPLACE A development in the secondary mortgage markets for mortgage servicing transferring activities. With the exception of a dependable market value facing buyers and sellers in this type of trading, it is becoming a quick way to raise additional cash in order to recover losses suffered when borrowers rush to seize low interest rate opportunities.

When rates increase, borrowers with lock-in loans either refinance or obtain new loans on their properties which causes new servicing problems for lenders. The volume increases to a point where secondary market operations do not pay off and hedging procedures are not very efficient for offsetting losses. Therefore, buyers and sellers of loan servicing are forced to re-evaluate pricing methods for an efficient yield for both parties.

MORTGAGE WHOLESALER *See* WHOLESALER.

MORTGAGED PROPERTY The real property or other interest in real property with all the improvements, hereditaments, and appurtenances that is security for a mortgage loan.

MORTGAGING OUT To obtain 100% or more financing for the acquisition of and any construction involved in the subject property. For example, an owner occupant builds their home and after completion closes an FHA permanent loan. According to the latest FHA regulations there is no cost certification for an owner constructing their home. If the owner obtained an FHA mortgage for $85,000 and the total project cost was $75,000, the owner "mortgaged out" - which for bottom line purposes - they received some cash for their sweat equity.

MORTGAGOR The borrower.

MOSAIC A combination of colored stones and/or glass arranged to form a decorative design.

MOST-FAVORED TENANT CLAUSE A provision in a lease assuring a tenant that any negotiating concessions given to other tenants will be given to him.

MOTHER HUBBARD CLAUSE A provision in a mortgage allowing a mortgagee not only to foreclose on a mortgage in default but to foreclose on the mortgagor for any other loans that are owed to the mortgagee.
See ANACONDA MORTGAGE, DRAGNET CLAUSE.

M ROOF A twin, double-pitch roof.
See ROOF TYPES.

MULLION That framing that divides the lights or panes of windows.

MULTI-FAMILY HOUSING A residential structure with more than one dwelling unit. Apartments, high-rise apartments, and townhouses are all categorized as multi-family properties.
    A lender can use a form like that in Exhibit 56 to take a loan application on a multi-family project.

MULTIPLE ISSUER POOL A mortgage-backed securities pool formed under the GNMA II program that normally consists of more than one loan package

Exhibit 56

MULTIFAMILY LOAN APPLICATION

LOAN APPLIED FOR ▶	Amount	Interest Rate	Monthly Payment Principal & Interest	Amortization Basis	Term	Escrow/Impounds (to be collected monthly)	
	$		%	$	Mos.	Mos.	Taxes ☐ Hazard Ins. ☐

Prepayment Option

PURPOSE OF LOAN

☐ **PURCHASE SUBJECT PROPERTY** — Settlement Date _____ per sales agreement (attach copy)

Sales Price	Cash Down Paymt.	Source of Equity Funds (cash down and/or other - explain)
$	$	

Secondary Financing	Interest Rate	Monthly Payment Principal & Interest	Term	To Be Payable To:
$	%	$	Mos.	

☐ **REFINANCE SUBJECT PROPERTY**

Describe Significant Improvements Made.

FUNDS TO BE USED TO PAY: ▼	Date Acquired	Purchase Price		
		$	Cost $ _____	

First Lien Balance	Maturity Date	Payable To:	(name & address)	Account No.
$				

Second Lien Balance
$

Remaining Funds to be used to

☐ **CONSTRUCT NEW MULTIFAMILY BUILDING(S)**

Estimated time to complete construction _____ mos.

Date Property Acquired	Cost	Existing Lien(s)	Payable to:	(Name & Address)
	$	$		

USE OF FUNDS: ▼		SOURCE OF FUNDS: ▼	
Pay Existing Lien(s)	$	Loan Applied For	$
Land Dev. Costs	$	Funds Invested by Owner	$
Direct Constr. Costs	$	Other:	$
Indirect Constr. Costs	$		$
TOTAL:	$	TOTAL:	$

Attach copies of plans; specifications; site plan; construction contract (if applicable); detailed breakdown of estimate of land development, direct & indirect construction costs; and, if applicable, details of performance and payment bonds or completion bond.

General Contractor (name & address)

Explain source of funds to be invested by owner and/or other.

SUBJECT PROPERTY

Street Address		City	County	State	ZIP Code

Legal Description (attach separate sheet, if necessary)	Site/Lot Size	No. Bldgs.	No. Stories	No. Units	No. Pkg Spaces	Yr. Built

Title is in ☐ Fee Simple

☐ Leasehold (attach copy of ground lease)

Brief Description of Improvements, incl. type structural frame, exterior walls, heat & A/C system recreation facilities.

☐ Annualized estimates based on present levels of income & expenses — OR ☐ Pro-forma estimates for:

Gross Rental Income from apartments	$ _____
Other gross rental income _____	$ _____
Less vacancy (_____ %)	(_____)
Other income (explain) _____	$ _____
Less operating expenses	(_____)
Net effect income before debt services and depreciation	$ _____

No. Apts. Vacant	Is project subject to rent control? ☐ No ☐ Yes If yes, attach copy of Rent Control Law	Name of current resident manager	Telephone No. ( )

Management will be by: (individual or firm's name & address)

Apts. are rented	☐ Furnished No. _____
	☐ Unfurnished No. _____

Individual or firm manages following multifamily buildings:

Utilities incl. in rent. ☐ Water ☐ Gas ☐ Elec. ☐ Heat ☐ A/C	(Address)	(No. Units)

Attach signed, certified current income and expense statement and balance sheet for subject property as well as statements for the previous two calendar or fiscal years (pro-forma statements are required for new properties). Attach signed, certified current rent schedule showing occupant's name (if vacant, so indicate); apartment no. and type, monthly rent and lease expiration date; whether rented furnished or unfurnished; and type of utilities furnished by owner. Expense statements should itemize expenditures for repairs and/or replacements.

BORROWER(S) TYPE

BORROWER(S) WILL BE ☐ Individual(s) ☐ Partnership ☐ Corporation ☐

Name of Borrower(s) (name of individual[s], partnership, corp.)	Title Will Be Vested in: (name of individual[s], partnership, corp.)

PARTNERSHIP TYPE ☐ General ☐ Limited ☐ Joint Venture (Attach partnership agreement)

Principal Business of Partnership	Partnership Address	Telephone No. ( )

CORPORATION	Corporation Address	Telephone No. ( )	Date of Incorp.	State of Incorp.

VMP MORTGAGE FORMS • (313)293-8100 • (800)521-7291

FNMA Form 1053 Jan. 84

Exhibit 56 (continued)

List below names of: Individual borrowers; general partners, if partnership; or officers, if corporation. Under "Title," indicate "Indiv.," "Gen'l Ptnr," "Pres.," "V. Pres.," "Treas.," etc. "Stockholder," as appropriate.

PERSONAL INFORMATION

	Name	Phone	Age	Home Address		Title	Ownership
A							%
B							%
C							%
D							%

ENTER INFORMATION BELOW ON LINES WITH LETTER CORRESPONDING TO THE PERSON NAMED ABOVE

EMPLOYMENT SUMMARY

	Primary Employer (name & address)	Type Business	Position	Years in this Business	Social Security No.
A					
B					
C					
D					

NAME OF GUARANTORS OF LOAN (If none, so state) ▶ _____

FINANCIAL STATEMENTS. Satisfactory financial statements are required to be submitted with this application. Use of FHLMC Form 75A/FNMA Form 1053A as a form of **personal financial statement** is optional.

ATTACHMENTS

CHECK ITEMS ATTACHED TO THIS APPLICATION

☐ Sales agreement (if purchase)
☐ Ground lease (if leasehold)
☐ Partnership agreement (if partnership)
☐ Recorded plat or survey
☐ Area map with arrow to site
☐ Copy of rent control laws or ordinances (if applicable)

☐ Construction contract or breakdown of est. costs; plans, specs., & site plan (if construction)
☐ Property income & exp. statements for previous 2 years (or pro-forma, if new or proposed)
☐ Description of repairs; replacements (if indicated in expense statement)

☐ Current income & expense statement and balance sheet regarding subject property.
☐ Current rent schedule, per instructions on front (unless construction)
☐ Financial Statements
☐ Statement of management plan
☐ Statement of borrower's experience in owning, managing or building multifamily buildings
☐ Other _____

FOR LENDER'S USE

INFORMATION FOR GOVERNMENT MONITORING PURPOSES (complete if borrower[s] are individual[s])

Instructions: Lenders must insert in this space, or on an attached addendum, a provision for furnishing the monitoring information required or requested under present Federal and/or present state law or regulation. For most lenders, the inserts provided in FHLMC Form 65-B/FNMA Form 1003-B may be used.

AGREEMENT: The undersigned applies for the loan indicated in this application to be secured by a first mortgage or deed of trust on the property described herein, and represents that the property will not be used for any illegal or restricted purpose, and that all statements made in this application and the attachments, are true and are made for the purpose of obtaining the loan. Verification may be obtained from any source named in this application and/or attachments.

I/we fully understand that it is a federal crime punishable by fine or imprisonment, or both, to knowingly make any false statements concerning any of the above facts as applicable under the provisions of Title 18, United States Code, Section 1014.

_____ Date _____   _____ Date _____

_____ Date _____   _____ Date _____

REVERSE   FNMA Form 1053 Jan. 84

package having similar characteristics (see *GNMA Handbook 5500.2* for more information).

MULTIPLE LISTING SERVICE (MLS) A joint effort by real estate brokers to pool together their listings so that all members of the Multiple Listing Service will have an opportunity to sell the listings. A multiple listing is an exclusive right to sell with an additional obligation of listing the property in a Multiple Listing Service.

MUNICIPAL TRI-PARTY PARTICIPATION A leveraged participation plan involving Fannie Mae. The agency's approved lender and a third-party local government agency, corporation, or home builder may use subsidiaries for buying down interest rates to affordable levels for low and moderate income families seeking to purchase either new or rehabilitated housing. Fannie Mae's participation plan can be from 50% to 95% interests in 5% increments. The agency will pool conventional fixed-rate second mortgages while the remaining portion is shared by the lender and the third party.

MUTUAL CAPITAL CERTIFICATE (MCC) Equity certificates issued by mutual savings and loan banks and used to satisfy net worth and reserve requirements.

MUTUAL FUND An investment vehicle where many investors pool their money to act as a single investor. A management fee is always charged; one-time sales fees (loads) may or may not be charged. A mutual fund may be a short-term money market security public investment that may include the selling of shares in low minimum amounts. An important factor in a mutual fund's returns is the basing of funds against results of the past performances of the fund, but not necessarily against future performance projections. Mutual funds may fluctuate in their returns and net asset value of shares sold.

Ginnie Mae MBSs are popular investments due to their guaranteed backing by the U.S. government. *Equity mutual funds* and *fixed-income mutual funds* differ in that the former invests primarily in stocks while the latter may invest in debt securities insured by corporations or by the federal government or its agencies. Additionally, a fund that may invest in any combination of stocks and bonds is called a balanced mutual fund. In all cases, a bondholder is a creditor, not a part owner as in shareholding.

The key strategy of the mutual fund is diversification through various investments in industry, stocks, bonds or money markets. Money market investments are short-term debt obligations that reflect maturities short of one year. U.S. Treasury bills and commercial paper are examples of these short-term instruments.

A fund's share is based upon market value computed by determining a market value of ownership of the total securities held. The security assets held include cash; all liabilities are deducted before dividing the difference between the outstanding number of shares. The outstanding total could conceivably be influenced by purchase and redemption activity as well as the market value volatility of interest rates. Fund shares are redeemable by selling back the shares to a fund investor at their then current net asset value. The redemption of funds may be more or less than the original price. Most fund shares are redeemable on any business day.

The fund portfolio manager is probably the most important person in any mutual fund organization as he or she manages the fund's assets. Portfolio management calls for determining what stocks, bonds, or other investments will most likely increase the fund's profits under its investment goals and risk management policies. The three types of risk are (1) economic risk or changes in the pulse of the economy; (2) the market risk or the volatility of interest rates affecting the price of mortgage-backed securities, stocks, etc. bought and sold; (3) the credit risk of the security issuer indicating assurance that payments will be made.

Economic risks include depressions, recessions, and any other global economic change in financial affairs that would affect a mutual fund organization's price of stock to shareholders. The capacity to pay regular dividends to shareholders could suffer because of economic disasters. The "pulse" of national politics is important to the fund.

Market risk is best described using an example: where a long-term bond is purchased at $1,000 par value and pays 12% it will continue paying this rate as long as it is held by the investor. At maturity, the bond will then produce the full purchase price or $1,000. In the event the investor sees fit to sell the bond before maturity, it may pay an increase or decrease on the original $1,000. A decrease in value occurs when and if interest rates increase to more than the original 12% market price. On the other hand, an increase in value will be experienced if interest rates decrease to less than the original 12% market price.

The ability to pay regular dividends to shareholders is credit risk. Security issuers with weak credit worthiness call for relatively low credit ratings but will have higher interest rates. Debt securities insured or guaranteed by the federal government, of course, have extremely high credit ratings.

MUTUAL MORTGAGE INSURANCE FUND (MMI) The FHA Insurance fund in which all mortgage insurance premiums are deposited and by which all losses are met. Business income for and insurance claims against the Section 203(b) single-family home mortgage program is a "reserve fund" for MMIF. The premiums are transferred from loss reserves to income according to the same formula by which FHA pays refunds of the up-front mortgage insurance premium (MIP) on prepaid loans.

See FHA - INSURED MORTGAGE.

MUTUAL SAVINGS BANKS State-chartered savings institutions that are mutually owned by their investors. These institutions invest mainly in mortgages. They operate just like a savings and loan association are located primarily in the northeast.

See SAVINGS BANK.

N

NAHB See NATIONAL ASSOCIATION OF HOME BUILDERS.

NAME AFFIDAVIT In conveying property a name must be established if the current name of the seller is different from the name the seller used to acquired title. A "Name Affidavit" or a "One and the Same" will be required to avoid a title defect. For example, if Mary Sue (a single person) acquired property, then became married to John Doe, there will be a title defect is Mary sells her property as just Mary Sue. A Name Affidavit avoids the title defect by declaring that Mary Sue and Mary Doe are "one and the same."

Lenders are very sensitive to any name variations in loan processing documents. If name variations exist the lender will want an executed "Name Affidavit." The lender wants names and signatures in the Note and Security Instrument to be uniform in all instances.

NAMED-PERIL INSURANCE Protects those risks and perils as set forth in the insurance policy and no other as distinguished from an all-risk policy.

NAR See NATIONAL ASSOCIATION OF REALTORS.

NAREB See NATIONAL ASSOCIATION OF REAL ESTATE BROKERS.

NATIONAL APARTMENT ASSOCIATION (NAA) An organization for owners, builders, and others involved in the multi-family housing industry. Address: National Apartment Association, 1825 K Street NW, Washington, DC 20006.

NATIONAL ASSOCIATION OF CORPORATE REAL ESTATE EXECU-TIVES (NACORE) Organization composed of parties dealing with buying, selling, and management of real estate owned by corporations. Address: National Association of Corporate Real Estate Executives, 7799 SW 62nd Avenue NW, South Miami, Florida 33143.

NATIONAL ASSOCIATION OF HOME BUILDERS (NAHB) A national trade association for builders and housing authorities interested in single-family and multi-family types of construction. The membership covers contractors, builders, architects, engineers, mortgage lenders and others with such interests. The NAHB offers educational programs and information on low-rent public housing. The association is based in Washington, D.C.

NAHB administers the Home Owners Warranty Program that provides warranties on new homes. Builders who register with local or state Home Owners Warranty Councils may apply for an insured warranty good for a period of ten years.

The NAHB address is: National Association of Home Builders, 15th and M Street NW, Washington, DC 20005.

NATIONAL ASSOCIATION OF REAL ESTATE BROKERS (NAREB) An organization for minority real estate brokers and salespeople. This organization is composed of black real estate brokers who subscribe to a code of ethics and who work for fair and better housing opportunities. Members are known as "realtist." Address: National Association of Real Estate Brokers, 1629 K Street NW, Washington, DC 20006.

NATIONAL ASSOCIATION OF REALTORS (NAR) An organization composed of REALTORS and Realtor-Associates representing all divisions of the real estate industry. This organization has more than 700,000 members. The working process is done through local boards and through state associations. Address: National Association of REALTORS, 430 North Michigan Avenue, Chicago, Illinois 60611.

NATIONAL COUNCIL OF SAVINGS INSTITUTIONS (NCSI) Savings institutions (banks without stockholders, chartered and supervised by states), such as mutual savings banks, that distribute to depositors earnings from investments in mortgages in homes, U.S. government bonds, corporate securities and municipal bonds make up this assemblage of savings bankers whose headquarters are in Washington, D.C.

NATIONAL CREDIT UNION ASSOCIATION (NCUA) The federal regulatory agency for federally-chartered and insured credit unions. The NCUA administers the National Credit Union Share Insurance Fund. Under the Secondary Mortgage Market Enhancement Act (SMMEA), credit unions were given powers similar to thrift institutions and may now purchase mortgage-backed securities as investments.

NATIONAL LEAGUE OF CITIES The National League of Cities is a group comprised of cities with populations over 30,000. Closely affiliated with the U.S. Conference of Mayors, this organization works with the federal government to implement programs and enforce standard policies across the U.S.

NCSI *See* NATIONAL COUNCIL OF SAVINGS INSTITUTIONS.

NCUA *See* NATIONAL CREDIT UNION ASSOCIATION.

NEGATIVE AMORTIZATION In simple terms, negative amortization will result in a mortgage loan balance increasing instead of decreasing. Negative amortization can occur if the loan is repaid in level monthly payments that are lower than what is required to amortize a mortgage based on the note rate. For example, an individual obtains a $90,000 mortgage at 12-1/2% interest with a provision for payments based on 10% for the first 3 years. The negative amortization will be the sum accumulated by the difference in payments at 12-1/2% and those at 10%, plus in all probability, interest on the interest accrued at the note rate of 12 1/2%.

There is usually a limit to the extent of negative amortization. An industry-wide answer would be 125% of the original loan balance. Keep in mind that conventional loans are not as regulated as the FHA and VA loans. It is extremely important to read and understand the disclosure information that is normally passed out at loan application.

Besides the interest expense caused by negative amortization, there are other costs caused by loans with negative amortization as compared with regularly amortized loans. Since there is a possibility of a loan balance increasing to 125% of its original amount, a lender will most likely require title insurance equal to 125% of the original mortgage balance. Mortgage insurance premiums for ARM loans with the possibility of negative amortization is more costly when compared to other ARM loans. Mortgage insurance premiums are based on risk. Adjustable rate loans with the possibility of negative amortization have a higher delinquency ratio when compared to other ARM loans without it. Of course, if negative amortization occurs, the loan balance will increase causing increases in the mortgage insurance and hazard insurance coverage.

One may wonder if there is anything "positive" about loans with negative amortization. The major benefit of these loans is their ability to qualify purchasers who would normally have no chance of buying the home of their choice. Since most negatively amortized loans involve adjustable rate mortgages, there is a possibility that one could purchase a higher priced home than one would normally qualify for, and have an improving interest rate cost by virtue of a lowering index in the future. This scenario plus the possibility of the home increasing in value and an increasing family income is what lures most purchasers into negatively amortized loans. Is this type of thinking bad? Only the future can tell. Negatively amortized loans are a risk, but just as one can pull down the lever of a one-arm bandit in Las Vegas, one could have the following things occur: (a) loan qualification as opposed to rejection; (b) lower interest rates in the future through an adjustable rate mortgage; (c) paper equity created by increasing value of the home; (d) increasing family income in the future - if all of these images appear on the screen, then it's jackpot!

One final point, since there is no prepayment penalty with most of these mortgages, one can avoid negative amortization by prepaying in an amount equal to the negative amortization.

The following is an example of how negative amortization works during one year:

On an adjustable rate mortgage of $65,000 at 12%, the first twelve payments of $668.60 paid the balance down to $64,764.11. At the end of the first year, the rate increases to 14%, but because of a 7 1/2% payment cap, the payments are not high enough to cover all of the interest. This interest shortage is added to the debt (with interest on it), which produces a negative amortization of $471.47 during the second year. ARMs that cannot be converted to fixed rate mortgages, therefore, are inherently risk prone.

EXAMPLE OF NEGATIVE AMORTIZATION
FROM BEGINNING LOAN
(NON-CONFORMING ARM)

Beginning Loan Amount = $65,000 @ 12% (or $668.60 per month).

Loan Amount at end of first year = $64,764.11 after 12 months.

Negative Amortization during second year = $471.47 @14%

Loan amount at end of second year = $65,235.58 ($64,764.11 + $471.47). All the 14% interest is not covered due to the 7 1/2% payment cap. (If the borrower sold at this point, he or she would owe almost $236 more than the amount originally borrowed on the property.)

In conclusion, the payment cap limits increases in the monthly payment by deferring some of the increase in interest. Eventually, the borrower must repay the higher remaining loan balance at the ARM rate then in effect. When this occurs, there may be a substantial increase in monthly payments with interest shortages added to the debt. Some mortgages contain a cap on negative amortization. The cap typically limits the total amount owned to 125% of the original loan amount. When that point is reached, monthly payments may be set to repay fully the loan over the remaining term with the payment cap no longer applying. Negative amortization may be limited by voluntarily increasing the monthly payment.

Some agreements may require the borrower to pay special fees or penalties if the ARM is paid early. Many ARMs allow the borrower to pay the loan in full or in part without penalty whenever the rate is adjusted. Prepayment conditions are, however, often negotiable.

The ARM loan may contain a provision that allows the borrower to convert to a fixed rate mortgage at designated times. If and when the conversion takes place, the new rate is generally set at current market rates for fixed rate mortgages. Interest rates or up-front fees for convertible ARMs may be higher; additionally, a special fee at the time of conversion may be required. Federal regulations require certain disclosures about ARMs in advertising such as the index rate, margin, cap, etc. Lenders must furnish this information upon request.

NEGATIVE CARRY In mortgage banking, lenders sell loans in the secondary market. It takes time to get the loan sold into the secondary market. While the loan is still with the lender, it is said to be in the warehouse. The primary source for supporting loans in the warehouse is borrowed money, primarily through a line of credit. If the average interest rate for the loans held in warehouse is below the rate paid for a line of credit (or any other method used to borrow money), then the lender has a negative carry. It is sometimes called *negative spread.*

NEGATIVE CASH FLOW The net loss after all operating expenses and debt service are paid.
See CASH FLOW.

NEGOTIABLE INSTRUMENT Any money instrument (check, CD, stock, promissory note) that is transferable from one person to another. Some notes or CDs may not be transferable; if not, they are not negotiable instruments.

NEGOTIABLE ORDER OF WITHDRAWAL (NOW) An instrument that represents a withdrawal from a savings account.

NEGOTIABLE SECURITY As described under the Uniform Commercial Code (UCC), a negotiable security is a credit document that meets certain legal requirements and can be transferred by endorsement or delivery. A mortgage-backed security is assignable and transferable, thus, a negotiable security.

NEGOTIATED TRANSACTION A transaction where the terms and offerings are decided by negotiation between the issuers and the underwriter. For example, Fannie Mae will consider purchasing FHA/VA buydowns that vary from normal Fannie Mae standards on a negotiated basis.

NET LEASABLE AREA Floor space that may be used by tenants for conducting their business. Usually excludes such areas as lobbies and space needed to house heating, cooling, or other equipment of a building.

NET LEASE A lease that requires the tenant to pay such items as real estate taxes, hazard insurance premiums, and maintenance. A net lease is described as "net-net" if the tenant is required to pay taxes and insurance premiums. A net lease is described as "net-net-net" or a "triple net lease" if the tenant is required to pay the real estate taxes, insurance premiums, and maintenance costs.

NET LISTING A listing that bases the broker's commission on the excess of the sales price over a net price agreed by the seller. This practice is illegal in some states.

NET NET *See* NET LEASE.

NET NET NET *See* NET LEASE.

NET OPERATING INCOME (NOI) Income after operating expenses have been deducted but before income taxes and debt service (principal and interest payments) have been deducted. This term is preferred over the term "net income" in reference to business operations.

NET PRESENT VALUE ANALYSIS *See* INWOOD ORDINARY ANNUITY CO-EFFICIENT and REVERSION FACTOR.

NET RATE The interest rate an investor receives after a servicing fee is deducted.

NET RETURN The net cash received for an investment. It is a rate of interest based on a "cash-on-cash" method. When an investor deducts all costs and expenses associated with making an investment from what is received from the investment, the investor is looking at the net return.

NET WORTH The excess of assets over liabilities. When an investor or a company lists all their assets and then subtracts what is owed on loans, what is left is the net worth. The form used to decide net worth is commonly called a balance sheet. The net worth is very important for income property loans. The primary concern for residential loans is the earning power of the borrower and not the net worth.

NET YIELD The return on investment after subtracting all expenses.

NET YIELD REPORTING The servicer of loans passes through principal as collected, and interest on a scheduled basis; the principal portion of a mortgage payment is remitted if these payments have been made.

NEWEL An upright post at the top or bottom of a stairway or at the landing turn or at a point that a circular stairway winds. A newel supports the handrail.

NEW ENGLAND FARM HOUSE

New England Farm House. An Early American style which is usually made of clapboard siding and is box-shaped.

NEW ORLEANS HOME STYLE

New Orleans. This house hugs the ground and has distinctive and varying roof planes. There will be many long windows across the front with shutters that open and close to protect the home from hurricanes. If the house has columns, they will be narrow and round. Dormers will have a French influence, being rounded at the top.

NEXT OF KIN Persons who are related by blood.

NICHE A recess in a wall, usually for some decorative object.

NO-BIDS Upon foreclosure, VA, unlike FHA, does not necessarily pay the loan off and accept the property. In cases where VA does not accept the property it is called a "no-bid" and VA pays the guaranty to the lender who then becomes the owner of the foreclosed property. Declining real estate values in some areas have caused an increase of no-bids by VA. Lenders in these areas have been hit hard with VA no-bids and they have caused lenders to incur substantial losses.

VA No-Bids
Fiscal Year through June 30,1990

State	City	Foreclosures	No-Bids	Percent of No-Bids
AL	Montgomery	429	1	0.2
AK	Anchorage	362	279	77.1
AZ	Phoenix	1,575	54	3.4
AR	Little Rock	321	19	5.9
CA	Los Angeles	588	24	4.1
	San Francisco	175	12	6.9
CO	Denver	2,948	467	15.8
CT	Hartford	7	0	0.0
DE	Delaware (PA)	16	0	0.0
DC	Washington	33	1	3.0
FL	St. Pete.	1,961	89	4.5
GA	Atlanta	894	2	0.2
HI	Honolulu	2	0	0.0
ID	Boise	142	6	4.2
IL	Chicago	837	102	12.2
IN	Indianapolis	477	47	9.9
IA	Des Moines	145	23	15.9
KS	Witchita	358	23	6.4
KY	Louisville	250	1	0.4
LA	New Orleans	861	166	19.3
ME	Togus	18	2	11.1
MD	Maryland (DC)	116	2	1.7
	Baltimore	107	1	0.9
MA	Boston	19	4	21.1
MI	Detroit	466	30	6.4

MN	St. Paul	512	24	4.7
MS	Jackson	258	9	3.5
MO	St. Louis	358	4	1.1
MT	Ft. Harrison	137	29	21.2
NE	Lincoln	199	8	4.0
NV	Nevada (LA)	193	10	5.2
	Nevada (SF)	41	5	12.2
NH	Manchester	25	0	0.0
NJ	Newark	104	4	3.8
NM	Albuquerque	214	19	8.9
NY	Buffalo	33	2	6.1
	New York	40	2	5.0
NC	Winston-Salem	695	5	0.7
ND	North Dakota (MN)	84	21	25.0
OH	Clevelend	903	68	7.5
OK	Muskogee	1,577	388	24.6
OR	Portland	72	12	16.7
PA	Philadelphia	198	15	7.6
	Pittsburgh	181	35	19.3
RI	Rhode Island (MA)	3	0	0.0
SC	Columbia	426	9	2.1
SD	South Dakota (MN)	74	6	8.1
TN	Nashville	480	2	0.4
TX	Texas (AR)	7	2	28.6
	Houston	3,422	903	26.4
	Waco	3,305	573	17.3
UT	Salt Lake City	373	37	9.9
VT	White River Jct.	2	0	0.0
VA	Virginia (DC)	48	0	0.0
WA	Washington (OR)	29	3	10.3
	Seattle	590	60	10.2
WV	West Virginia	2	0	0.0
	Hungtinton	91	3	3.3
WI	Milwaukee	300	16	5.3
WY	Wyoming (CO)	319	85	26.6
PR	San Juan	26	0	0.0
	TOTAL	29,688	3,721	12.5

Source: Department of Veterans' Affairs.

See LOAN GUARANTY.

NOMINAL LOAN RATE Face rate of interest.

NOMINEE An entity or individual designated to represent another entity or individual.

NON-BEARING WALL A wall that does not help to support the structure of a building.

NON-CONFORMING LOAN Normally usage of the word "nonconforming" implies loan amounts and underwriting practices that are outside those used by Freddie Mac and Fannie Mae guidelines.

NON-CONFORMING USE Usage that violates zoning regulations but is allowed to continue because it predates regulation it violates.

NON-DISTURBANCE CLAUSE OR AGREEMENT (1) An agreement with the mortgagee allowing the lessee to continue occupancy under a lease in the event there is foreclosure of the mortgage. A non-disturbance agreement is effective providing the mortgage lien is recorded before the lease in question. (2) A clause describing the right of a seller to obtain mineral rights provided that the exploration of minerals will not conflict with surface operations or development.

NON-JUDICIAL FORECLOSURE Power to sell property at foreclosure without court procedure. This foreclosure proceeding can be used by a trustee named in a deed of trust.
See TITLE THEORY.

NON-NEGOTIABLE INSTRUMENT An instrument, such as a mortgage, that must be transferred by assignment.

NON-OWNER OCCUPIED A property that is not occupied by the owner is said to be non-owner occupied.
See FHA - INVESTOR LOAN.

NON-PERFORMANCE Failure or refusal to act as agreed in a contract or other form of agreement.
See DAMAGES, FORFEITURE.

NON-RECOURSE LOAN A loan secured by property only. The holder of the note cannot seek liability from the debtor. Non-recourse loans are used in commercial or income property lending. The lender considers all aspects for the success of the project and the "track record" of the borrower.

In commercial lending the appraisal is much more detailed than a residential appraisal. Often there is a detailed feasibility study required for a commercial loan. Besides the lender making an independent decision about the merits of the property used for collateral, the lender will lean heavily on the experience of the developer or borrower. The experience of the borrower is called the "track record."

Competition and the large debt involved in commercial or income property loans forces lenders to make many of these loans on a non-recourse basis. The property stands alone and the lender cannot look for other assets from the borrower if the loan goes into foreclosure.

NON-SUPERVISED LENDER *See* SUPERVISED LENDER.

NOOK Commonly used to describe an obscure corner of a room or a portion of a house or a parcel of land.

NORMAL WEAR AND TEAR Deterioration or depreciation caused by the age and use of the property. A tenant is not responsible for damage caused by normal use.

NOTARIZE The act of a Notary Public in witnessing the authenticity of a signature.

NOTARY PUBLIC A person authorized to acknowledge certain documents such as contracts, mortgages, deeds, and affidavits, attest to the authenticity of signatures, and administer oaths.

NOTE A written instrument that acknowledges a debt. A note is the document that creates the liability of the borrower. A note is usually an additional instrument or it is incorporated into a mortgage or a Deed of Trust. The note states the loan amount, interest rate, term of the loan, and the acknowledgement of the borrower of the obligation to pay the loan.

Lenders normally provide the Note form to be used and it should be the latest revised Note form issued by the respective governmental agencies, investors, or the lender. In relationship to the term of the loan, the maturity date should be the calendar month before the calendar month that the first payment is due. Lenders are very sensitive to any alterations or corrections to a note. If the lender allows any alterations, e.g., lift-offs, corrections, and erasures, they should be initialled by all borrowers.

NOTE RATE The true rate of interest is the note rate. The term "note rate" can be traced to the interest rate stated on the mortgage note or a similar type of instrument. "Accrual rate" is another term used to express what the term note rate means, the true interest rate or the rate of interest being accrued on the mortgage.

NOTICE Official proclamation of a legal action or intent to take action.

NOTICE OF DEFAULT A notice to a borrower that the lender now considers that the property can be foreclosed. The lender notifies the borrower that they consider the terms of the mortgage to be in violation. In the notice of default, there is usually a time limit, a grace period, the borrower can use to cure or remedy the violation that caused the lender to issue a notice. The borrower may be three months past due on the monthly payment or the property can be in severe disrepair. If the borrower cures the violation within the grace period, the lender will normally not proceed with foreclosure. If the same violation continues on a frequent basis the lender may not accept whatever action is taken by the borrower.

In mortgage banking a notice of default is a standard notice required by all mortgage insurance companies, FHA and VA. The Notice of Delinquency has been standardized by the Mortgage Bankers Association and the Mortgage Insurance Companies Association. In an effort to streamline servicers' reporting duties and information collected on defaults, most MIs now accept the form as general procedure. Servicers may choose to use either their individual company forms or the standard Notice. Early reporting of defaults should not interfere with the terms of the master policy of individual companies.

NOTICE TO QUIT A phrase that can mean that a landlord wants a tenant to vacate or a tenant intends to vacate by a certain date.

NOTORIOUS POSSESSION Openly occupying real estate owned by another and a requirement for gaining ownership of the real estate by adverse possession.
See ADVERSE POSSESSION.

NOVATION A substitution of a debt or a debtor based on the agreement of all parties.
See FHA - RELEASE OF LIABILITY, VA - RELEASE OF LIABILITY.

NUISANCE Land usage that unreasonably interferes with the surrounding land activities.

NULL AND VOID A phrase used to describe something that cannot be legally enforced.

O

OBLIGATION BOND A bond executed by the borrower for more than the loan amount. The bond serves as security for the lender against nonpayment of taxes, insurance premiums, or any unpaid interest.

OBLIGEE A note holder, bondholder, mortgagee, creditor.

OBLIGOR The debtor or mortgagor.

OBSOLESCENCE Loss of value due to circumstances other than normal wear and tear, such as functional utility or economic or social changes.

OCCUPANCY AGREEMENT An agreement to permit a purchaser to occupy before closing. Rent usually is prorated on a daily basis.

OCCUPANCY RATE OR LEVEL A percentage of rental units that are occupied.

OCTAGON HOME STYLE

Octagon. A house built in the shape of an octagon and usually made of wood with a wood shingle roof.

OFFER An agreement, promise, or expression of willingness to perform in a specific manner in relationship to entering a contract for the purchase of property.

OFFER AND ACCEPTANCE The required ingredients of a valid contract. A meeting of the minds on purchase price and terms.
See CONTRACT OF SALE.

OFFERING SHEET A one-page summary listing of mortgages offered to investors in the secondary market. A sample offering sheet will be similar to the following:

OFFERING SHEET FOR ARM LOANS

Seller/Servicer:	A Chicago Mortgage Banker
Product:	1) $3,567,350 1yr ARM without conversion feature
	2) $3,352,500 1yr ARM with conversion feature
	3) $4,464,800 5yr Fixed 1yr ARM thereafter
	4) $3,069,350 3yr Fixed 1yr ARM thereafter
Index:	1yr T-bill constant
Margin:	275 gross
Caps:	2% annual, 6% life.
Weighted Average Coupon:	Product #1) 7.448% #2) 7.996% #3) 9.570% #4 9.70%
Loan Sizes:	All conforming loan amounts.
Property Location:	Chicago area.
Underwriting:	FNMA/FHLMC guidelines.
General information:	Seller is flexible, *will sell servicing released or retained.*
Fee:	1/4% to selling broker.

OFFICE OF EQUAL OPPORTUNITY (OEO) The HUD office in charge of administrating the regulations of the Fair Housing Act.
See FAIR HOUSING ACT.

OFFICE OF INTERSTATE LAND SALES REGISTRATION (OILSR) This office is a division of HUD and is responsible for accepting registrations of certain subdivisions sold in interstate commerce.
See PROPERTY REPORT.

OFFICE OF THE INSPECTOR GENERAL The Office of the Inspector General is an independent federal office authorized to audit and investigate HUD programs to decide inefficiencies and prevent fraud and abuse through early detection. Mortgagees who fail to produce their record upon request of the Office will be subject to subpoenas, enforced through the federal district court system.

OFF-RECORD TITLE DEFECT A defect in the title that is not found in an ordinary title search. A deed that is recorded but has a fraudulent signature is an example of an off-record title defect. The best protection from an off-record title defect is title insurance.

OFF-SITE COST Expenses related to construction that are incurred away from the site of construction. Examples would be extending roads, sewers, and water lines to the site.
Off-site costs are sometimes called *off-site improvements.*

OHM The resistance of a circuit with a potential difference of one volt producing a current of one ampere. The practical unit of electrical resistance.

OID *See* ORIGINAL ISSUE DISCOUNT.

ONE-YEAR TREASURY INDEX The index value of a "constant maturity" one-year Treasury bill that is calculated weekly and published on the H-15 report produced by the Federal Reserve. It is the current rate for a one-year Treasury bill (normalized to represent a full 52-week yield) that is calculated weekly. This index is generally used as the base rate for one-year adjustable-rate mortgages.

OPEN AND NOTORIOUS *See* NOTORIOUS POSSESSION.

OPEN-END COMMITMENT A commitment to advance construction loan funds where there is no permanent mortgage takeout. With this type of commitment, the lender is exercising a lot of faith in the success of the project. The lender will have an open mind about successive extensions of the construction loan until it is paid off by the sale of the project or through a permanent loan.

OPEN-END MORTGAGE A mortgage that allows future advances of principal upon agreement of the mortgagor and mortgagee. The mortgage can be either a construction loan or a permanent loan. The borrower is given a limit of the total outstanding balance. This loan is very similar to having a line of credit.

OPEN HOUSE The practice of showing a listing during hours that have been advertised to the public.

OPEN LISTING A listing allowing many brokers to sell the property. A listing that does not give the real estate agent an exclusive agency or an exclusive right to sell.
See LISTING, EXCLUSIVE LISTING.

OPERATING EXPENSES Expenses, such as taxes, insurance, and utilities, incurred in the maintenance of properties. Operating expenses do not include debt service or depreciation.

OPERATING RATIO The percentage relationship between operating expenses and effective gross income. For example if the operating expenses of an apartment complex total $65,187, and the effective gross income (gross income minus a vacancy allowance) is $217,290, the operating ratio is 30 percent.

OPINION OF TITLE A written opinion as to the validity of title, generally prepared by an attorney.
See ABSTRACT OF TITLE, CERTIFICATE OF TITLE.

OPPORTUNITY COSTS Before an investor will make an investment they should consider an alternative use of the money that is to be invested. The return on the money in an alternative investment is called an "opportunity cost." If an investment will yield a 10% return and an alternative investment of equal risk and value will yield 11%, the opportunity cost is 1% to make the investment.

OPTION An agreement to purchase or lease subject property for a specific period and specific terms within a specified time. A consideration is given to the owner who agrees to give this right for the specified time.
An option creates a contractual right, it does not create an estate. An option to buy is called a *call,* and option to sell is called a *put.*

An experienced real estate attorney should be used in executing an option. If all the significant terms and subject matter are not disclosed in an option, a court will rule that the option is unenforceable.

The difference between a sales contract and an option is the obligation to perform. If the seller and buyer are obligated to perform, it constitutes a sales contract. If only one party is obligated to perform, it is an option. Therefore, an option can be described as a unilateral contract.

A person offering the option might or might not purchase the property or perform. There is usually a clause giving the party accepting the option the right to keep the option money if the person who offered the option does not perform.

A clause can be inserted in the option allowing the person who is submitting the option the right to assign it to another party. A person dealing in buying and selling options should have a real estate license.

See LEASE PURCHASE.

OPTIONAL DELIVERY An option of delivering loans under a loan purchase program.

ORAL CONTRACT An unwritten contract. Contract to purchase real estate must be in writing. Contracts to lease property for a period of one year or less need not be in writing. However, it is strongly recommended that all real estate contracts or leases be in writing.

ORDINANCES Rules written by municipalities for governing the uses of land.

ORDINARY AND NECESSARY BUSINESS EXPENSE Acceptable deductions for federal income tax purposes. Expenses incurred through the normal operation of a business.

ORDINARY INCOME For federal income tax purposes, this income can be in the form of salaries, fees, commissions, dividends, interest, and other items not classified as capital gain.

ORDINARY INTEREST Interest calculated on a 360-day year.
See EXACT INTEREST.

ORDINARY LOSS Loss that can be deducted against ordinary income.

ORIENTAL STYLE

Oriental. This house is typically a long oblong design with a pagoda-styled roof.

ORIENTATION The positioning of a structure on a site relative to prevailing winds, exposure to the sun, and privacy from neighboring structures or traffic.

ORIGINAL FACE The original principal amount of a mortgage-backed instrument.

ORIGINAL-ISSUE DISCOUNT (OID) A debt instrument that is issued for less than its stated redemption price at maturity. The discount must be greater than 1/4 point per year at maturity. The IRS treats the accretion of this discount over the life of the security as current income. This is a fairly new approach to the accounting procedure applied by original issuers in compliance with REMICs. According to REMIC rules, a sale of assets rather than debt liabilities may be applied in original issue discount MBSs for collateral mortgage obligations. In REMICs, original issuers analyze the OID rule with care. In stripped mortgage securities, the tax treatment is complex. Investors do not have the OID income calculations burden, only the issuer is concerned with reporting OID income information in stripped mortgage securities prepayment scenarios.

See REAL ESTATE MORTGAGE INVESTMENT CONDUITS.

ORIGINATION (1) Making a single family mortgage. (2) A process whereby a mortgage-backed security certificate secured by a pool of approved mortgage loans is produced. Mortgage bankers originate MBSs and issue the securities by seeking applications for loans.

See LOAN ORIGINATION PROCESS.

ORIGINATION FEE *See* LOAN ORIGINATION FEE.

ORIGINATION PROCESS *See* LOAN ORIGINATION PROCESS.

ORIGINATOR *See* LOAN ORIGINATOR.

OTC *See* OVER THE COUNTER (OTC) MARKET.

OUT-OF-THE-MONEY Standby commitment or option contracts that do not offer as favorable a price as is available in the market. A call option is out of the money when the underlying security is worth less than the exercise price; a put option is out of the money when the underlying security is worth more than the exercise price. An option with no intrinsic value. The holder of an option that is out of the money on the expiration date will avoid exercising such option. Options are priced relative to striking prices "In, At or Out-of-the-Money"; thus, an option that bears the right to buy or sell at the "in" price to the holder carries a higher cost when exercising the option.

OVERAGE For leasing purposes, it is the amount of rent over the base rent based on gross sales revenue. In mortgage origination, it is the discount points that exceed the amount required to sell the loan in the secondary market without a loss.
See OVERRIDE, PERCENTAGE LEASE.

OVERALL CAPITALIZATION RATE *See* OVERALL RATE OF RETURN.

OVERALL RATE OF RETURN Net operating income divided by the purchase price of property. It is sometimes called the "overall capitalization rate."

OVER-COLLATERALIZATION Providing more collateralization than is needed to support the principal amount of bonds. A form of a rating agency's determination of an issuer's standing includes over-collateralization. A rank held in the ownership of this added insurance against insufficient funds from principal and interest payments is important to rating agencies in all mortgage-related issuances. Mortgage-backed bonds and pay-through bonds are subject to an issuer's standing on over-collateralization as one qualification among other factors considered. These other factors are as follows: (1) credit integrity of the servicer, (2) outside insurance guarantees income sufficiency is adequate, (3) cash flow schedules are maintained, and (4) reinvestment risks in declining interest rate environments.

OVERHANG Extension of a roof beyond the exterior wall.

OVER-IMPROVEMENT Improvement to property that exceeds necessary level for the property to achieve its highest and best return.

OVERRIDE Commission or fee paid to a managerial person, rental for more than a face amount, or a provision in a listing agreement protecting the listing broker's right to a commission, for a specified of time, that is more than the initial agreement (in the event the owner sells property to a customer the broker had worked with during the time of the listing).

OVER-THE-COUNTER (OTC) MARKET A market in which securities dealers trade among themselves, acting as principals or brokers for customers. They not only deal in mortgage-backed securities, but other securities as well, in non-exchange deals called "over the counter." For example, MBS warrants give purchasers (by agreement) MBSs sold at a stated strike price. The strike price is to be delivered at a specified date in the future. If the strike price can be held as low as possible, warrants are justified.

OWNER-OCCUPANT A person who lives in property he owns.

OWNERSHIP FORM Type of ownership of real estate such as a partnership, corporation, limited partnership, joint tenancy, tenancy in common, sub-chapter s corporation, tenancy in severalty, tenancy by the entireties, community property, and trust.

OWNER TRUST An entity established to issue collateralized mortgage obligations (CMOs). Ownership of the trust may be sold in shares of beneficial interest.

The current accounting treatment permitted by the IRS for sale-of-assets—as a preferred off balance sheet approach for CMO issuers and as ownership interests—differs from the former viewpoint taken by tax authorities, which did not allow the performance of a treatment called "sale-of-assets" accounting. CMO issuers had to combine the underlying mortgage pool and CMO bonds as assets on balance sheets. Originators of mortgage pools as collateral and CMOs as bonds were assets of issuers as far as the IRS was concerned. Due to REMIC provisions, however, the rule changed.

Whether the Tax Reform Act of 1986 (that created the Real Estate Mortgage Investment Conduit or REMIC) or the earlier development responding to tax intricacies produced by the grantor trust led to the provisions, or whether efforts made to advance the capital markets through secondary market investments were the cause, is not clear. What is clear, however, is that REMIC, as a tax device, is used to convey an effect if an issuer so chooses for a particular structure, such as a CMO. In other words, the REMIC is not an MBS device, but a tax innovation conceived by the IRS from congressional legislation.

Since the owner trust is now a legal issuing procedure, there is a limiting requirement for this privilege of avoiding a necessity to enter the CMO assets and liabilities to the financial statements. Unlike the grantor trust that merely passed through the principal and interest to the investor, the owner trust sells an amount of ownership interests or equity in an owner trust thereby a sale predominates as an accounting treatment for mortgage loans. An off-balance sheet approach is subject to 50% or more of the beneficial interest shown as "owner trust." This justifies a residual cash flow to the owner from a CMO issue. A market for mortgage loan residual investment therefore was created by the REMIC legislation which separated regular interests from residual interests and through stripping mortgage cash flows.

P

PAC *See* PLAN AMORTIZATION CLASS.

PACKAGE LOAN/MORTGAGE A mortgage that includes personal property. Such items as a washer, dryer, refrigerator, drapes, free-standing carpet are made a part of the security on a package mortgage.

PACKAGING The assembling of groups of mortgages for sustaining a foundation for mortgage-related securities, such as mortgage-backed securities, collateralized by fixed or adjustable rate mortgage pools.

PAD A graded site for a residential use or the site for a mobile home with utility connections.

PAIROFF A transaction designed to liquidate a forward contract by allowing the lender to buy back what was originally sold at a cost to be decided by the degree of market movement experienced.

PAM *See* PLEDGED ACCOUNT MORTGAGE.

PAR A price of 100% or the price where the principal equals the sales price. It is the price of a mortgage without a discount charged.
See DISCOUNTED YIELD.

PARITY For a convertible bond it is the comparison of market price of the underlying stock to the assumed value of the convertible bond. To reach parity the convertible bond must sell at a price equal to the value of the underlying stock. An option is said to be trading at parity if its value is equal to underlying security.
See CONVERTIBLE BOND.

PARITY CLAUSE A provision in a mortgage allowing more than one note to serve as security for the loan. All notes have the same priority, with no one note having a priority over another. All notes have a parity status to each other.

PARKING INDEX A ratio indicating the number of parking spaces to the gross leasable area or to the number of leasable units.

PARQUET FLOOR Hardwood floor in short pieces laid in a design or pattern.

PARTIAL RELEASE A provision in a mortgage that allows some of the property pledged as collateral to be free provided specific payment is made. For example, a five-acre tract of land serves as collateral for a mortgage and the owner wishes to pay one-half the balance owed on the mortgagee. The mortgagee can accept the payment and grant a partial release for one-half of the mortgaged property, or two and one-half acres. The released property is then free and clear of the mortgage.

PARTICIPATION CERTIFICATE (PC): The Federal Home Loan Mortgage Corporation issues PC's that represent ownership in residential mortgages to add flexibility for the investor. They are mortgage-backed securities that identify the participating interest in a block or pool of loans. The mortgages are conventional loans. The purchaser of a PC is guaranteed a pro-rata share of principal and interest. Principal is paid as collected.

PARTICIPATION INTEREST PURCHASE (PIP) The participation pools wherein Fannie Mae will purchase 50% to 95% interests, in 5% increments, in pools of conventional fixed rate or adjustable-rate first mortgages and conventional fixed rate second mortgages. The lender may retain or sell all or part of his retained interest to one other qualified investor. If the lender sells its retained interest, the following guidelines apply:

(1) Besides Fannie Mae and the originating Fannie Mae lender, only one other investor may hold an interest in the pool;

(2) the third party investor may not be an individual and must acknowledge in writing that the loans are subject to the terms of Fannie Mae's selling and servicing contract;

(3) the lender's obligations under the selling and servicing contract may be assigned, after Fannie Mae's approval, if the third party assumes the warranties and responsibilities of the lender.

PARTICIPATION LOAN (1) A mortgage wherein one lender (or more) has a share in a mortgage with the lead or originating lender. (2) A mortgage where a lender shares in part of the income generated from the property or the proceeds resulting from a sale of the property.

PARTICIPATION LOAN WITH SUBORDINATION The lead lender exposes the participants' positions to all of the losses from a foreclosure to the extent of the participant's ownership in the mortgage.

PARTITION Division of real property into separate parcels according to the owners' proportionate shares. Before a partition, two owners could own property together as tenants in common. After the partition, each owner could own one portion of the property.

PARTITION SALE The sale of property according to a court decree so there will be a partition of real estate.

PARTNERSHIP An association of two or more persons for business purposes. There are two forms of a partnership: general and limited.

A *general partnership* is a form of business where two or more owners, or partners, conduct a business for a profit. All owners share fully in the profits or losses of the business. A general partnership is subject to dissolution if a partners dies, withdraws, or files bankruptcy.

A *limited partnership* consists of one or more parties who serve as general partners and are liable for losses and responsible for the operation of the business. The limited partners are liable only to the extent of their investment and they are passive in their participation in the business operation.

See GENERAL PARTNER.

PART PERFORMANCE Performance of a contract that is less than the full performance required.

PARTY WALL A wall built between two properties. The wall serves as an exterior wall for each property. Each owner or party has a right to use the wall, and it serves as an easement on each adjoining property covered by the wall.

PASSIVE INVESTOR One who invests money and has no active role in the business or property.

See LIMITED PARTNERSHIP.

PASS-THROUGH CERTIFICATE A certificate that gives ownership in a pool of mortgages.

PASS-THROUGH SECURITY A mortgage-backed security representing an interest in an underlying pool of mortgages. Payments that are received from the underlying pool are passed through to the security investor. GNMA is not a security issuer, only the guarantor.

PATENT An instrument used by the government to convey title of its land to an individual.

PAYMENT-CAPPED ADJUSTABLE-RATE MORTGAGE In the early stages of the development of adjustable rate mortgages, "payment caps" were used instead of the now popular "rate cap." Occasionally, you will still find ARM loans with payment caps, but not very often. FNMA offered three standard plans an interest rate index for 1-year ARMs, 3-year ARMs and 5-year ARMs. All three were indexed to the Treasury Securities (weekly average). The interest rate and payment adjustment intervals followed a 1-year, 3-year and 5-year adjustment intervals according to identical Treasury securities interest rate intervals. Payment caps were according to the borrower's election to limit payment increase to 7% annually on the 1-year ARM. Payment caps on a 3-year and 5-year ARM were the same with the borrower electing to limit a payment increase to 7% at each adjustment period. If a loan was not fully amortized following a 7% payment increase, the payments would increase annually by no more than 7% until the full amortization payment was reached.

All adjustable rate mortgages that Fannie Mae purchases must have either an interest rate cap, a payment cap (to be exercised at the borrower's option) or both. Lenders must notify mortgagors of their option to invoke the payment cap. Lenders should review Fannie Mae's standards for any buy-downs on ARM loans.

See NEGATIVE AMORTIZATION.

PAYMENT SHOCK An unexpected increase in the monthly payment in an adjustable rate mortgage that causes a homeowner to panic because of financial inability to pay the new payment. To avoid payment shock, lenders began using payment caps, then later, rate caps. Payment caps cured payment shock; but, there was one terrible side effect - it caused negative amortization. Finally, the lenders came up with the right medicine for ARM loans - rate caps. Rate caps prevent payment shock and they do not cause the dreaded side effect of negative amortization.

PAY-THROUGH BOND Freddie Mac issues multi-class pay-through bonds (CMOs), guaranteed mortgage certificates (GMCs), and pass-through securities (PCs). These bonds are like corporate sinking-fund bonds.

See SINKING FUND.

PC *See* PARTICIPATION CERTIFICATE.

PD *See* FHA - PROPERTY DISPOSITION.

PENSION FUND Money accumulated by an institution for the future retirement needs of its contributors. Pension funds are authorized to buy long-term assets such as mortgages and high-grade stocks and bonds.

PER DIEM Daily.

PER DIEM INTEREST Interest calculated on a daily basis. Normally heard at closing when the interest on the mortgage is charged on a daily or per diem basis.
See EXACT INTEREST.

PERCENTAGE LEASE A lease providing for a percentage of sales payable to the lessor.
See OVERAGE, RECAPTURE CLAUSE.

PERCOLATION TEST A test that measures the drainage characteristics of soil. A lender will normally require a perculation test whenever a septic tank will be used as a waste disposal method for a home.

PERFECT HEDGE A hedge that protects a lender against risk without creating additional risk. Such an instrument would protect the lender from price, product and fallout risk on specific loans.

PERFECTING TITLE The action of a court to eliminate any clouds or encumbrances upon a title. There are many reasons for taking this course of action but all center around a central theme of it being impossible to clean the title by private and voluntary action.

PERFORMANCE BOND A bond issued by an insurance company to guarantee the performance of certain work. If said work is not performed, the insurer either will complete the work or pay damages according to the amount of the bond.

PERMANENT FINANCING Financing that is not interim, short-term, or temporary in nature. Any long-term mortgage used to finance real estate. Most permanent home loans are for either 15 or 30 years; although, there is no general restriction of the term in years. A permanent mortgage does not have to be for a minimum term, such as 30 years. It can be a mortgage amortized over 30 years but with a balloon in five years. Lenders dictate the term for permanent financing but many are more flexible than what the public perceives.

PERMANENT LENDER Those institutions providing permanent mortgage financing as opposed to interim lending. Mortgage companies, banks, savings and loan association, and more recently, credit unions, are all examples of permanent investors.

PERMISSIVE USE The right to use property with the express or implied permission of the owner.

PERSONAL LIABILITY A recourse allowing a lender to ask the mortgagor, who has failed to repay a mortgage according to the terms, for compensation on any loss from a loan due to foreclosure. Nearly all residential loans are made on a personal liability basis. For commercial loans, the lender is not as successful in obtaining personal liability as compared to residential loans.

Seasoned commercial developers expect the lender to carefully judge the loan on the feasibility of the project and to make an underwriting decision based upon the merits of the collateral and the past performance record of the developer.

See EXCULPATORY CLAUSE, LIABILITY, NON-RECOURSE.

PERSONAL PROPERTY Property that is not classified as real property or real estate. Examples are securities, cash, furniture, and household items. Appliances not permanently attached to a structure are viewed as personal property. Real property is transferred by a deed, most personal property is transferred by a bill of sale or by endorsement.

PERSONAL RESTRICTION A restrictive covenant may be personal between the original seller and buyer. The determination whether a covenant runs with the land or is personal is governed by the language of the covenant, the intent of the parties, and state law. Restrictive covenants that run with the land are encumbrances that may affect the value and marketability of title. Restrictive covenants created by a deed may limit the density of buildings per acre, regulate size, style, or price range of buildings to be erected, or prevent particular businesses from operating.

See DEED RESTRICTION.

PHYSICAL APPROACH TO VALUE *See* COST APPROACH TO VALUE.

PHYSICAL DETERIORATION A loss in value due to age and use. For example, cracks in the walls or ceilings due to settling in the foundation.

See DEPRECIATION.

P&I CUSTODIAL ACCOUNT The non-interest bearing account that an issuer maintains with a financial institution. In the account, the issuer deposits principal and interest collected from individual mortgagors for loans included in Ginnie Mae pools.

PIGGYBACK LOAN Normally, two lenders participating in the same loan. The mortgage has one lender with a senior position and another lender with a junior interest. A lender who's specialty is in underwriting 80% LTV first mortgage loans and a lender who's specialty is in second mortgages with a combined LTV of 95%, can join together in originating loans. The loan product is called a *piggyback mortgage*. It is two loans, a first and a second, originated and closed simultaneously.

PILASTER A column or projection used to support a floor girder or stiffen a wall.

PIP *See* PARTICIPATION INTEREST PURCHASE.

PIPELINE A term used by lenders to inventory the dollar amount of loan applications in process. The various stages a loan passes through beginning with an application from a prospective borrower and ending with the sale and delivery of the loan in the secondary mortgage market. A pipeline can be broken down into the production and inventory segments. A lender needs to inventory its pipeline for decisions pertaining to commitment coverage.

PITCH The angle of the slope of a roof.

PITI *See* PRINCIPAL, INTEREST, TAXES AND INSURANCE.

PITI RATIO *See* INCOME ANALYSIS.

PL The designation for a GNMA I pool of project loans featuring level payments.

PLACEMENT FEE A fee paid to a mortgage broker for referring a lender. The fee can be paid by either the broker or the lender (in certain cases).
See COMPUTERIZED LOAN ORIGINATION, MORTGAGE BROKER, REAL ESTATE SETTLEMENT PROCEDURE (RESPA).

PLAINTIFF A person who initiates a lawsuit.
See LITIGATION.

PLAM *See* PRICE LEVEL ADJUSTED MORTGAGE.

PLANNED AMORTIZATION CLASS BOND (PAC BOND) A tranche of a CMO used to retire a CMO by a predetermined amortization schedule independent of the prepayment rate on the underlying collateral. The amortization of the other tranches may have to slowed down or accelerated to met the PAC schedule. The schedule is fixed amortization applying many forms of prepayment occurrence, whereas all other classes acquire full payments or principal before the planned amortization class claims its first amortization date. These other CMO classes will, in turn, claim their principal payments as they come due because of prepayment. The scheduled principal payments are due to the planned amortization class as the PAC attains the declared amortization date.

PLANNED UNIT DEVELOPMENT (PUD) A zoning classification to allow development of a planned community. A PUD usually contains a mixture of land uses such as office and residential as well as common open spaces. It is a planned development that offers flexibility in the design of a subdivision. A PUD must contain some or all of the following units: single-family houses, semi-detached houses, row dwellings, and privately owned common property. It may include rental apartments, cooperatives or condominiums in combination with single-family dwellings. Stores, schools, and open recreation spaces (utility of open space) in a carefully planned arrangement with varied types of housing constitute a PUD. If the privately owned common property is a minor element of the development or if there is no common property at all, the development is not a PUD.

In a PUD, the common property must include major and essential elements of the development other than streets, sewers, street lighting, and water facilities. The major commonly owned elements must enhance the value of the properties in the development. A homeowners' membership association by virtue of a PUD containing the major and essential community-owned facilities must mandate its own assessments. The homeowners' association typically enters into a maintenance/management contract with a PUD manager.

Finally, an evaluation procedure details improvements to the land or valuation appraisals of the dwellings after complete market studies are made. A lending commitment for a loan upon final sale of the various types of housing in the PUD will call for extensive underwriting. Supporting an estimated marketing value is, of course, an appraisal report showing adequate value for recapturing an institution's investment in a possible default of the PUD. The individual unit and the entire complex should be studied as to its weighted value in a preparation for sale in the marketing of said unit. Applicable valuation approaches should rely on market data rather than cost approach or income approach unless the prospective mortgagor's plan is to lease-out the individual units to others.

A DeMinimus PUD is distinguished from a PUD by the increased quality and quantity of the common area amenities. Units in a DeMinimus PUD have part of their value tied to the amenities available in the common areas.

See the last paragraph to the definition of Condominium for specific information pertaining to closing a loan transaction with a PUD as the secured property.

See FIDELITY OR SURETY BOND.

PLASTERBOARD Drywall, sheetrock, or gypsum board used for construction as a substitute for plaster.

PLAT A map or chart of a specific land area. A plat shows property with its precise location and boundaries.

PLAT BOOK A book containing plats of properties according to public records.

PLATES Pieces of wood placed on wall surfaces as fastening devices. The bottom member of a wall is the sole plate and the top member of a wall is the rafter plate.

PLEDGED ACCOUNT MORTGAGE (PAM) A home mortgage with cash paid by the mortgagor into an account and pledged to the lender. Money is drawn periodically from the account to supplement the mortgage payments. The mortgage is a graduated payment mortgage and is sometimes called a "FLIP" mortgage.

Another variation of the ARM is the pledged account buy-down mortgage. In this plan (initially introduced by Fannie Mae) a large initial payment is made to the lender at the time the loan is made. The payment can be made by the buyer, builder or anyone else willing to subsidize the loan. The payment is placed in an account with the lender where it earns interest. The borrower's interest is then lowered for the first year. For instance, if $50,000 was borrowed at 17%, an initial deposit could reduce the rate to 13% and the monthly payments to $553.10. Over the next five years, the interest rate would increase by one point each year at most. After the five-year period, the borrower's mortgage would become a ARM with interest rate and payment changes every five years, based on the index.

This plan does not include any payment or rate caps other than those in the first five years. But, there can be no negative amortization so possible increases in the total debt are limited. Because of the buy-down feature, some borrowers who may otherwise not be eligible for financing, may be able to qualify for this loan.

See FLEXIBLE LOAN INSURANCE PLAN (FLIP).

PLENUM A chamber serving as a distribution area for heating or cooling systems.

PLOT PLAN A drawing showing the placement of a building on a site with precise locations, dimensions, and elevations.

PLOTTAGE VALUE The increase of value in land by assembling smaller properties into one large site.

PLUMB A term implying a true vertical position or a perpendicular position. A door or window frame with side members in a true vertical position is *plumb*, one not in true vertical position is *out of plumb*.

PLUMBING SYSTEM A plumbing system can be inspected in many ways. **Water pressure** can be checked by turning the kitchen faucets on full force and then going to the bathroom that is the farthest distance away and turning on the faucets. The result should be a strong flow of water and not a trickle.

Check the **condition of the water** by filling the tub and sink to see if the water is clear and not rusty and then notice how fast the water drains.

Check the operation of the toilets by dropping a piece of tissue in the bowl and then flushing to see if it drains completely, refills, and shuts off properly. When checking the bathroom, put your foot behind the toilet and exert pressure. If the floor gives, it is most likely rotted because of a water leak from the toilet.

Plumbing **leaks** that are in the slab or under a house can be discovered by shutting off all plumbing and then observing the water meter for two to three minutes to verify that there is no water flow.

Water pipes can be signs of age and past problems. The older houses will have brass, lead, or iron pipes, newer houses will have copper or PVC plastic piping. The type of material used in the plumbing system will indicate the age and if you notice a mixture of pipe materials, it is an indication of plumbing problems that have occurred in the past.

PMI *See* PRIVATE MORTGAGE INSURANCE.

PMM *See* PURCHASE-MONEY MORTGAGE.

PN The designation for a GNMA I pool of project loans featuring non-level payments.

PO *See* PRINCIPAL ONLY.

POINT The dollar amount equal to one percent of the principal balance of a mortgage. Discount points are a one-time charge assessed by the lender so that the yield or net interest of the mortgage will increase.

See DISCOUNT, DISCOUNT POINTS, DISCOUNT YIELD.

POINTING The filling up of joints in a masonry wall such as brick so that the appearance is more attractive and the wall has more support.
See RAKED JOINT.

POLICE POWER The right of any governmental body to enforce laws that promote the public health, morals, and safety and the welfare of the community. Examples of police power are condemnation, zoning, rent controls, housing codes, licensing requirements, and subdivision regulations.

POOL Under the GNMA II program, an assemblage of loans brought together to form multiple-issuer pools or custom pools. An assemblage of loans brought together or an assemblage of loan packages brought together will be two separate units. When the phrase "pool and loan package" is used, the term pool generally denotes a custom pool under the GNMA II program, but in certain contexts includes a pool of mortgages backing an issuance of securities under the GNMA I program. In general, the term "pool" is applied in Fannie Mae and Freddie Mac assemblages with a coupon or pass-through rate.

POOL FACTOR A factoring process can be decided for pass-through investors when a part of the pool is the only investment held. In order to establish a factoring balance of the certificate owned, a pool factor is found when the remaining principal is divided by the original principal.

As an example, an original $200,000 certificate owned at face value in a secondary market pool that has an original $2 million principal and this principal is paid down to $1,903,678.02, a pool factor is then 0.95183901. The $200,000 certificate owned (at face value) by an investor will then amount to $190,367.80 remaining principal balance after the original certificate is multiplied by the pool factor.

POOL INSURANCE Besides the mortgage insurance that gives some protection to mortgage lenders against defaults that cause a loss to the mortgagee (often shelters 25% of the original balance), there is extra insurance called pool insurance. This pool insurance assures private issuers a 100% shield against default on an individual loan in the mortgage pool extending to limits called stop loss on a principal sum of the mortgage.

The stop loss limit comes into play upon failure of the mortgage insurer's payoff on the full loss of the loan. In this case, the pool insurance, which usually is based upon the composition of principal balances, remains in a mortgage pool on a 10% stop loss. Private insurers are charged a per annum fee according to the collective sum of principal mortgage balance of the pool and the pool insurance payment is evidence of their rating status in this issuance of mortgage securities. A 10% limit on a stop loss of a $2,000,000 mortgage pool is therefore $200,000. Pool insurance upholds private issuers of MBSs.

PORCHES A covered entrance to a house that normally extends from the exterior wall. Check porches to make sure there is no wood resting on the ground. Ideally, wood should have a clearance of at least 6 inches from the ground. Wood porches and decks that are too close to the ground will eventually water rot and must be replaced or torn down. If the portion below the floor level of a porch is enclosed down to the ground with non-wood material, make sure it is properly ventilated.

PORTFOLIO A listing or distribution of mortgage loans or MBS income called the mortgage loan portfolio. Primary portfolio lenders/investors sell loans in secondary markets as a supplementary advantage.

PORTFOLIO LENDER A bank, savings and loan, mortgage company or other entity who originates or services their loans, thereby accounting for their individual profits, are known as portfolio lenders. Primary mortgage operators who carry specific portfolios (as opposed to secondary market participation) find it increasingly difficult to continue as private lenders in the primary market due to government sponsored enterprises growing in importance in secondary marketing.

By increasing the funding activities, lenders participating in the secondary market tend to lower interest rates (as a result) which exerts pressure on the portfolio lender's margin or profit. A portfolio lender pays their premiums on deposit insurance or special assessments while the secondary markets which have government support do not have to pay user fees for the official status. Risk taking is avoided by use of government guarantees instead of capital by the use of leverage that may further weaken interest rate profit margins to portfolio lending.

POSITION The relationship between the dollar amount of mortgages in the pipeline or in production to the dollar amount of commitments from investors to purchase the mortgages.

POSITIVE CARRY In mortgage banking lenders sell loans in the secondary market. It takes time to get the loan sold into the secondary market. While the loan is still with the lender, it is said to be in the warehouse. The primary source for supporting loans in the warehouse is borrowed money, primarily through a line of credit. If the average interest rate for the loans held in warehouse is above the rate paid for a line of credit (or any other method used to borrow money), then the lender has a positive carry. It is sometimes called a *positive spread.*

See NEGATIVE CARRY.

POSSESSION The holding, control, and occupancy of property.

POST MODERN VICTORIAN HOME STYLE

Post Modern Victorian. This home is massive with many different roof angles, much gingerbread woodwork, arched windows, flat windows, decorative half timbers and a double wide chimney with a decorative cap.

POWER OF ATTORNEY A written agreement giving authority to a person to act as an agent on behalf of another to the extent of the powers listed in the agreement. To be used for closing a loan transaction, the Power of Attorney should be specific and grant the authority to endorse checks, purchase property, execute a note, and encumber real estate, preferably naming a specific property. When the Power of Attorney is used in the execution of a security instrument, it must be recorded before recording the security instrument. A lender will want a copy of the Power of Attorney with a receipt showing it has been recorded.

The Attorney-in-Fact should sign all required signatures. The signature should reflect the name of the principal first followed by the signature of the Attorney-in-Fact and the signature should specify that capacity. For example, *John E. Doe by Susan A. Smith, Attorney-in-Fact.*

See VA - POWER OF ATTORNEY.

POWER OF SALE Authority given to a trustee under a deed of trust to sell property in the event of default or nonpayment by the mortgagor.

See TITLE THEORY.

PRE-CLOSING A meeting to review and sign documents but transfer of title is pending satisfaction of a condition. For example, a condition of the appraisal - such as a satisfactory final inspection, or the arrival of verifiable cash needed to close, or the sale of a previous home. This type of closing is sometimes called a *dry closing.*

PRE-CONSTRUCTION AFFIDAVIT Before construction, loan documents are recorded. The sworn statement from the owner and contractor, called a preconstruction affidavit, shown below, certifies that no work has been done or materials delivered to the site that would permit a lien to be filed, before the recording of the lender's construction loan mortgage or trust deed.

Joint Preconstruction Affidavit

Owner:_____

State of:_____

County of:_____

The undersigned being duly sworn, say that he/they: _____ is/are fee simple owner of the premises known as _____ that has been mortgaged to _____ for the sole purpose of securing a construction loan on said premises. The undersigned deponent states that to his/their knowledge there has been no work started, materials delivered, or labor begun either directly or indirectly up to and including this date.

Deponent further says there are no pending suits against him/them in any court or any judgements in any court remaining unpaid; and that no person has any contract for the purpose of, or claim to or against said premises with the exception of the following:

_____

_____

Further affiant saith naught.

_____Owner

_____Owner

Sworn to and subscribed before me this_____day of_____19_____

My commission expires_____

_____
                                                    Notary Public

PRE-FABRICATED HOUSING Portions of a house that are constructed in a factory for assemblage on a building lot. The sections of the house are transported by a truck to the building site. Walls, doors, windows, and trusses are built in a factory and then delivered to a building site for assemblage into the final product. At the building site, the foundation has been laid (either a slab or a crawl space foundation) and the plumbing, wiring, and any heating and air conditioning ducts are in place. The sections are then erected onto the foundation. The assemblage begins with the wall sections and ends with the truss sections for the roof. Pre-fabricated houses are sometimes called *pre-fabs*.
See MANUFACTURED HOUSING.

PREFERRED DEBT A senior or first mortgage. Any debt that has priority over other debts.

PREMISES Land and improvements.
See PROPERTY.

PREMIUM An amount for which a security sells above face value. In new issues a premium is an amount that a market price rises over the original selling price. Premium sometimes refers to charges made whenever securities are borrowed to make deliveries on short sales. Premium sometimes refers to the redemption price of a security if that price is higher than the security's face value or a fee paid by buyer's option.

PREPAID INTEREST Interest that is paid before it is earned.
See PREPAID ITEMS.

PREPAID ITEMS OR EXPENSES Obligations that are paid in advance at a real estate closing. Examples of prepaid items include but are not limited to the first annual premium for hazard, flood, and private mortgage insurance, initial deposits for real estate taxes and insurance, and any prepaid or interim mortgage interest. Per diem interest is classified as prepaid or interim interest. All other costs at closing are considered to be closing costs.

PREPAYMENT An advanced payment on a mortgage. A mortgage prepayment can be the result of a lender's inducement to a borrower on their mortgage balance at a discount. To pay off a low interest loan at a discount may appear to be an advantage to a multitude of mortgagors while not accounting for the consequences of such discounts. The discounted pay-off savings rate realized by some low-interest recipients may not offset the gain.

As far as the IRS is concerned, the discount is income received in the same year the discount was accepted. This may be money that would be better invested in other markets yielding a higher return, after taxes. This refinancing syndrome occurred in 1983 as interest rates dropped to 11.5% reflecting this reaction by lender.

On the other hand, prepayments can be a savings advantage to some borrowers who find ways to make affordable prepayments from time to time. Some lenders recommend to borrowers that a tremendous savings can be realized upon paying a little extra each month as loan installments are made. This additional amount will be applied to a borrower's principal on the mortgage. The less principal remaining on the mortgage, the less interest is paid during the mortgage's duration.

A borrower who refinances or begins a payment on a new mortgage may request a complete report, as an example, to study to help decide on an actual amount of expense.

Here are some helpful points to remember about prepaying a mortgage.

(1) A borrower can save thousands of dollars by prepaying a mortgage.

(2) A borrower is obligated to pay the monthly principal and interest each and every month.

(3) After the borrower pays the required monthly payment they are free to apply whatever they can afford to the principal portion.

(4) It is a good idea to put the payment numbers on your check, but it is even a better idea to write two separate checks when you prepay so their can be a paper trail (the canceled checks) verifying the prepayment.

(5) Nearly all loans will allow prepayments in any amount. The speed of a prepayment (when the loan will be paid off) can be determined with software programs (demonstrated in the CLO definition) for personal computers. If you do not have a computer, you can use a HP-12C calculator or a loan amortization table to select a shortened term you need. For example, a $125,000 loan amortized on a 15-year term will have payments of $1,343.26. The borrower can begin sending in prepayments of approximately $250 and the loan will prepay in 179 months.

(6) If you choose a permanent loan with a shorter term, such as a 15 year term, you are obligated to make monthly payments based on the shorter term. If you choose a longer term, such as a 30 year term, the option is yours about increasing your payments to shorten the loan term.

(7) Prepaying your loan will increase the equity in your home and it will make a future sale based on an equity assumption more difficult.

Prepayment is a matter of personal preference. Below are some points to consider to help you decide when prepayment is right and when it is wrong.

Right to prepay (1) Your goal is to own your home debt-free. (2) You cannot earn more interest on your money than what you are paying on your home mortgage.

See OPPORTUNITY COSTS.

Wrong to prepay (1) At this point in time, owning your present home debt-free is not a primary goal. (2) You can safely earn more interest in alternative investments than what you are paying on your home mortgage. (3) You have a FHA or a VA loan with a low interest rate (less than 10%) and it will not escalate upon loan assumption.

The 1990 Housing Bill requires loan servicers to provide mortgagors, at least annually, a written notice of the outstanding balance remaining to prepay the mortgage and any requirements the mortgagor must meet to prevent the accrual of any interest after the date of prepayment.

PREPAYMENT CLAUSE A clause in a mortgage giving the borrower the right to pay a mortgage off before it is due. The prepayment clause should be carefully read to discover any prepayment penalty.

PREPAYMENT PENALTY A fee imposed by a lender for the prepayment of a mortgage, usually a percentage of the balance paid. Some prepayment penalties call for a penalty if any portion of the loan is prepaid, others allow up to a certain amount of the balance to be prepaid during a period, before invoking a penalty.

PRE-SALE The sale of a proposed project before construction begins.
See CUSTOM BUILDER.

PRESCRIPTION Rights to property by adverse possession. A continued use of another person's property can result in adverse possession. The continued use is termed a "prescription."

PRESENT VALUE *See* NET PRESENT VALUE ANALYSIS.

PRICE In mortgage and bonds, price refers to the amount paid relative to the face value of the instrument. If the price is less than the face value of the instrument, then the instrument is sold or purchased at a discount. If the instrument is sold at the face value, then it is sold or purchased at par.
See DISCOUNTED YIELD.

PRICE LEVEL ADJUSTED MORTGAGE (PLAM) A mortgage with the balance and monthly payment increasing or decreasing in direct relationship to an index, such as the Consumer Price Index or Cost-of-Living Index.

PRICE RISK The risk that because of a rise in the general level of market interest rates, a loan will decrease in value between the time of commitment to originate and the time of commitment to sell.

PRICING EXCEPTION An adjustment to the price paid for a mortgage by the investor due to the characteristics of the loan that do not meet requirements outlined in a commitment.

PRIMARY FINANCING A loan that is secured by a first mortgage. A mortgage loan is created by lending funds to a borrower who gives the lender a document called a *mortgage* as security. Primary financing is sometimes called a *primary mortgage.*

PRIMARY MARKET Originating new mortgages is an activity of the primary market. Buying and selling mortgages is an activity of the secondary market. Lenders are normally active in both markets.

PRIMARY MORTGAGE LOAN *See* PRIMARY FINANCING.

PRIME RATE The lowest rate charged to the largest and strongest customers of a bank for a short term loan. The prime rate is often used as measure of the cost of short term credit. The prime rate is primarily controlled by the laws of supply and demand for money and the cost to the lender of the money to be loaned. The prime rate is often used as an index for a loan. Nearly all construction loans are made on a prime rate or prime rate plus basis. If a construction lender makes a loan commitment to a builder based on "prime plus 2," the lender has just committed to lend money based on the bank's prime rate plus an additional 2% of interest.

PRIMARY RESIDENCE *See* PRINCIPAL RESIDENCE.

PRINCIPAL (1) The loan balance of a mortgage. (2) A party to a transaction, such as a buyer or a seller. (3) In an agency relationship, the principal is the party who hires an agent to represent him in a sale.

PRINCIPAL, INTEREST, TAXES AND INSURANCE (PITI) A monthly payment on a real estate loan that includes a payment to amortize the loan balance (P), interest on the outstanding loan balance for that month (I), 1/12th of the annual real estate taxes (T), 1/12th of the annual insurance premium (I).

PRINCIPAL ONLY (PO) A security that pays cash flows from the principal paid by an underlying pool of mortgages. A PO is a principal-only security backed by an underlying collateral, a mortgage pool.
See IO.

PRINCIPAL RESIDENCE The dwelling that one uses most of the time as a residence. The place one classifies as one's home. FHA defines principal residence as "the dwelling where the borrower maintains, or will maintain, a permanent place of abode and typically spends, or will spend, the majority of the calendar year. A borrower can have only one principal residence."
    Proof of a principal residence can be established by a person's permanent mailing address, the address shown as the service site for utilities and telephone service.

PRINCIPAL TRANSACTION A sale wherein one or both of the principals act independently for their account. A principal transaction is a sale of real estate, mortgage loans, or securities, without a broker or agent involved.

PRIORITY *See* RECORDING.

PRIVATE CONDUIT A purchaser of loans that do not meet the guidelines (nonconforming) for a government related agency such as FHA, VA, FNMA, and FHLMC. The loans usually exceed the maximum loan amounts (jumbo) loans. The word private means that the buyer is not government related. The word conduit means that it is a safe passage or a pipeline into the secondary market for these non-conforming loans.

PRIVATE MORTGAGE INSURANCE (PMI) Commonly called "PMI," private mortgage insurance insures a portion of the loan against default. The amount insured depends upon the type of mortgage and the loan-to-value ratio.

For example, a fixed-rate loan based on a 95% loan-to-value ratio could be insured on a 25% coverage basis and a 90% loan on a 20% coverage basis. This means that a purchaser's down payment plus the mortgage insurance will reduce the lender's risk down to approximately 70%.

PMI costs depends on the coverage required, the type of mortgage, and the premium plan selected. Premium plans offered are usually an annual plan that is paid on a monthly basis, or a single premium plan that can be paid for a varying number of years.

Under conventional financing terms, a borrower may have an option of selecting private mortgage insurance suitable to their plans for the duration of the mortgage. Currently, there are two choices for financing the premium: a customary premium financing method or a newly conceived premium financing plan can be selected. In comparing the two choices, lenders can calculate for the borrower, in present values, the actual dollar costs between two conventional loans of equivalent value.

CONVENTIONAL LOAN PLAN OPTIONS

The following transaction is a model for calculating premium financing in mortgage insurance costs.

Price Paid	$100,000 (Customary method)
Down Payment	$ 10,000
Mortgage Loan	$ 90,000
Interest Rate	10%
Loan to Value	90%

Customary Plan $450 upon loan closing (0.5% of the mortgage) plus a monthly fee of $21.75 (0.29% annually) for the life of the loan (if planning to carry the loan for five years).

The borrower can choose, at their discretion, the one-time, up-front premium payment of two percent - a similar option to the FHA program. This adds to the balance of the loan which will increase the total debt owed on the mortgage. This premium may or may not be refundable depending on the insurance company. Now calculated on the newly conceived premium financing option

Adjusted Mortgage Loan	$91,800 (New Method)
Interest Rate	10%
Loan to Adjusted Value	92%

New Plan for Premium $1,800 upon loan closing (.02% additional points) or $360 upon loan closing resulting in present value costs of $2,160 upon loan closing resulting in monthly installments of $15.80 (if for 15 years).

HP12C OPTIMUM PMI PLAN

The customary plan tends to be a more conservative practical approach to mortgage insurance, the new method should not be discounted if the borrower intends to own the property (thus hold the mortgage) for at least 15 years. Under the customary plan, the borrower's total cost is $2,474 for 15 years. Under the new plan, the borrower's cost decreases by $1,000 if the loan term is for 15 years or more.

BORROWER'S OPTIMUM MORTGAGE INSURANCE PREMIUM PLANS
(with HP12c Key Strokes)

	Key Strokes	Display	Explanation
Step 1	(f)CLEAR(REG)	0.00	Clears storage register
Step 2	21.75 (CHS)(PMT)	–21.75	Minus sign stores monthly premium MI payment
Step 3	10 (g) (i)	0.83	Calculates annual interest rate and converts to months
Step 4	15 (g) (n)	180.00	Stores pay-off in months assuming a 15-year period
Step 5	(PV)	2,024.00	Calculates present value of monthly premium MI pmt
Step 6	450 (=)	2,474.00	Plus sign calculates total PV cost of pay-off in 15 years (if customary $450 mortgage balance is premium paid)

NOTE The actual dollar costs that the lender can point out to the borrower is the $5.95 "out-of-the-pocket" savings on the loan at a 10% rate ($21.75-$15.80) when choosing the new plan on a 15- year monthly basis at the same 10% rate. Larger tax breaks are possible in 15 years; a mortgagor will have a larger balance on the loan. If the PMI refunds part of the premium, this cost will be less when the mortgage reaches maturity.

Many people assume that the premiums will automatically discontinue once the loan is amortized down to a loan-to-value ratio where a lender does not require PMI coverage, such as 80% or less. This is an erroneous assumption. Any discontinuance of PMI will depend mostly on the investor's (owner of the mortgage) requirements and the payment record of the mortgagor. What seems surprising is that, based on my experience with the public, most applicants do not ask this question and are generally uninformed about PMI.

Any premium refund will depend upon the date of loan termination and the PMI company. There are refunds available in certain situations. Due to the difference in the initial cost, a conventional mortgage premium refund will not be as high as compared to the FHA one-time premium. If one borrows the FHA one-time premium, the initial and final cost is 3.8% of the loan amount as compared to an initial cost of approximately .65% plus 1/4 of 1% per month for a 90% fixed-rate conventional loan.

California has a new law requiring the lender to notify the borrower when the PMI can be canceled (Chapter 569, Laws of 1988).

PRIVATE OFFERING A real estate investment offered to a limited group of investors. This type of offering or sale normally is without the benefit of advertising or general promotion and is exempt from registration with the Securities and Exchange Commission and State Securities Registration laws.

PROBATE Proving that a will is valid. This term can be used to describe any action over which probate court has jurisdiction.
See ADMINISTRATOR, EXECUTOR, INTESTATE, TESTATOR, WILL.

PROCEEDS (1) The net sum of cash realized from sale of property, or (2) the net sum of cash given to a borrower by the lender in a loan transaction.

PROCESSING After a loan application is taken, loan processing begins. Processing is the segment between loan application and before loan closing. All procedures and documentation to support what the applicant told the lender at loan application is called *loan processing.* Employees in mortgage companies who work on the verifying and assembling the paperwork necessary in processing are called *processors.*
See LOAN ORIGINATION PROCESS, LOAN PROCESSOR.

PROCURING CAUSE In real estate sales, this term is used to decide whether a real estate salesperson is the procuring cause of the sale, entitling him or her to a commission.

PRODUCTION SEGMENT In a mortgage pipeline, the time between the taking of the loan application from a borrower and loan closing.
See MORTGAGE PIPELINE.

PRODUCT RISK A corollary of fall-out risk. Product risk reflects the uncertainty of whether or not the actual closing percentage will be greater or smaller than the anticipated closing percentage.

PRO FORMA STATEMENT A statement forecasting future income, expenses, net income, and cash flow.
See PROSPECTUS.

PROJECTED INTERMEDIATE A window type.
See WINDOW.

PROMISSORY NOTE A written promise to pay a specified sum to a specified person for specified terms.

PROPERTY In legal definition, it is the right to possession, enjoyment, and disposition of all things subject to ownership.
See PREMISES.

PROPERTY LINE The recorded boundary of a parcel of land.

PROPERTY MANAGEMENT The management of property used as a business such as an apartment complex. The person in charge of the property management is the property manager. If the property manager resides in the property managed, they are called a *resident manager.*

PROPERTY REPORT A disclosure required by the Interstate Land Sales Act for the sale of subdivisions consisting of 50 lots or more unless exempted. The report is filed with HUD's Office of Interstate Land Sales Registration.
See OFFICE OF INTERSTATE LAND SALES REGISTRATION.

PROPERTY TAX (AD VALOREM) Tax questions are likely to be raised in most real estate transactions as to the amount of taxes and assessments to be charged in property transfers. This important issue can become a prerequisite that covers a variety of tax bases and their effect on property ownership. Real estate brokers and agents engaged in the real property listing and sales promotion should be aware of a controlling device adjusted for estimates of value. Land taxation or Ad Valorem (according to value) taxes based on the owner's ability to pay on his agricultural holds were originally an index to charge made by levying authorities since income was obtained from agricultural products. Land taxation is considered justified in that it is easily assessable due to land's obvious existence.

Property tax liens, therefore, are liens against real property. Personally owned tax liens are liens against real property if assessed on the secured assessment roll. The real property securing them is that listed on the roll that is cross-referenced. Whether locally assessed personal property is assessed on the secured roll or on the unsecured roll depends upon certain facts and judgements. If the personal property is owned by the owner of the land on the lien date and the assessor believes that the real property at this location is sufficient security for the tax, the personal property is assessed on the secured roll. The secured property taxes become liens on personal property of the same owner located elsewhere in the county when the taxpayer so requests and the assessor issues a certificate that is recorded with the country recorded on or before the lien date. The personal property and the securing real property are cross-referenced in such cases. This rule represents the criteria of systems followed in many states.

See AD VALOREM.

PRORATE To allocate between seller and purchaser their proportionate shares of expenses or obligations such as real estate taxes or property insurance.

See CLOSING, CLOSING COSTS, ESCROW AGENT, PREPAID ITEMS.

PROSPECTUS A descriptive statement disclosing the details of a proposed investment. A prospectus would give information that is contained in a pro forma statement. If a prospectus has yet to be approved by the SEC, it is a red *herring*. If a prospectus need not be approved, it is a *descriptive memorandum*.

See PRO FORMA.

PROXY A person who represents another or a document granting representation to another.

PSA *See* PUBLIC SECURITIES ASSOCIATION.

PUBLIC SECURITIES ASSOCIATION (PSA) An organization that recently declared a formula standardizing a prepayment assumption for CMO's collateral. Since all CMOs existing were formed by unpredictable prepayment assumptions, a disadvantage was apparent in the development of a capable secondary market in trading, pricing, and the arrangement for consistency in dealing in CMOs.

Now mandatory for any future issues of CMOs (effective July 1, 1985), the trading of CMOs will use a .2% pre-payment rate on mortgage collateral for the 1st month, increasing by 2/10 of 1% up to the 30th month. The constant annual rate of a 6% (prepayment) monthly rate will begin on the 31st month and for the balance of the mortgage collateral. This is now known as "PSA experience."

A new settlement date system for mortgage securities has been established by PSA for its membership based upon an analysis of the association's thirty-six primary government securities dealers involved in MBSs. No official legal

six primary government securities dealers involved in MBSs. No official legal weight is carried by these guidelines. They are accepted as industry standards, as a general recommendation including PSAs reduction of delivery tolerances from 4.999999% to 2.499999% for investors in mortgage securities regarding settlement for investors effective December 1, 1986 for trades settling on or after April 1, 1987.

PUBLIC OFFERING The solicitation of the general public to buy investment units. The solicitation usually requires approval by the SEC.

PUD *See* PLANNED UNIT DEVELOPMENT.

PUNCH LIST A list of unfinished repairs to a building. A purchaser, appraiser, or a lender may list repair items to be corrected before a closing can take place. The repair list is termed a punch list.

PURCHASE AGREEMENT *See* CONTRACT OF SALE.

PURCHASE-MONEY MORTGAGE (PMM) Any mortgage that is given by an owner of property to a purchaser of same property to help finance a sale. A first or second mortgage is a purchase-money mortgage if it is given by the owner to the buyer. Depending on state law, deficiency judgements may or may not be given in purchase money mortgage transactions.

PUT *See* OPTION.

PYRAMID ROOF *See* ROOF.

Q

QUADRUPLEX Four-unit building.

QUALIFICATION *See* LOAN QUALIFICATION.

QUALITY CONTROL A written plan to evaluate the operations of a lender. The need for a Quality Control system is not unique to the mortgage industry. Nearly every successful business has a set of written policies and procedures. "Written" is the key word. Every business has a plan or a purpose, but nearly every successful business has a written purpose and the procedures needed to accomplish that purpose. A Quality Control system varies according to the 1) purpose, 2) size, and 3) complexity of the business.

Quality Control for lending institutions must consider services performed by individuals not under the direct supervision of the lender. Examples of services over which lenders may not exercise direct control are credit reports, employers and depositors completing verification forms, appraisals, surveys, title insurance, closings, mortgage insurance, hazard insurance, and loans originated by correspondent lenders.

The very nature of a successful lending business today is to match what is available in the secondary market to 1) the people and system you have selected for your operation, and 2) the appetite of your market location. Many lenders operate in reverse; they find out what loans their markets demand and they originate those loans - even if it means jamming a few square pegs into round holes along the way. Once a lender has a formula for a successful operation, a good Quality Control plan is essential in insuring a success.

Although the selection of loan products available in the secondary market should follow a plan, this part of the lending business is normally not included in a written Quality Control plan. Fannie Mae describes the purpose of a lender's Quality Control system as follows:

An effective quality control system verifies the existence and accuracy of legal documents and credit documentation and the quality of property appraisals and underwriting decisions.

The lender's system must assure that mortgages conform to the lender's policies; are of a quality acceptable to institutional and secondary market investors; comply with insurer and guarantor requirements; and meet specific Fannie Mae requirements. The quality control system must be capable of evaluating and monitoring the overall quality of loan production.

Freddie Mac identifies quality control as:

A specific set of internal procedures designed to insure that all mortgages delivered to Freddie Mac are of investment quality and adhere to their underwriting guidelines. In addition, Freddie Mac believes that this process simply helps a lender identify the Higher Risk loans that historically have resulted in greater default risk.

Much of quality control is review of the loan processing work. For understanding how quality control is helpful in the origination process, *see* LOAN ORIGINATION PROCESS.

QUARTER ROUND Mold used to cover a joint. A cross-section of a quarter round mold will equal approximately one-fourth of a circle.

QUEEN ANNE HOME STYLE

Queen Anne. A nineteenth century style home of many surface textures, materials and colors. Other characteristics are: various window designs, multistories, irregular in shape, turrets or towers, bay windows, projecting upper stories and much ornate fine detailing.

QUIET ENJOYMENT The uninterrupted use and possession of property given to an owner or a tenant.

QUIET TITLE ACTION Court action to eliminate any claims or clouds on a title that an owner or a lender views as an unjust or invalid hinderance to its marketability. In a quiet title action the title can be "cleaned-up" and become marketable. When a title is said to be marketable it can be sold freely at fair market value or the owner can freely use it as collateral for a loan.

See CLOUD ON TITLE.

QUITCLAIM DEED A deed that conveys only the grantor's rights in the property without disclosing the nature of the rights and with no warranties of ownership. A deed the grantor uses to release to the grantee any interest or title in the property that the grantor possesses. A quit claim deed is often given to clear the title when the grantor's interest in a property is questionable. By accepting such a deed, the buyer assumes all the risks.

See CLOUD ON TITLE, REMISE.

QUOTATION A quotation is a bid to buy and an offer to sell a security in a specific market at a specific time.

See BID AND ASKED PRICE.

R

RADIANT HEATING Heating by the use of coils, pipes, or panels recessed in the ceilings, walls, or floors. The power source for the coils can be electricity, hot water, steam, or hot air.

RADON Radon is a gas trapped in a closed space, such as a house. As accumulated trapped gas inside a home, radon is believed to cause lung cancer. Radon comes from the natural breakdown of uranium. It has always been present in nature mainly in rocks containing uranium, granite, shale, phosphate and pitch-blende.

You can test your home for radon gas by purchasing a charcoal canister that can be bought for $10 to $25. Experts have said that lenders will soon require a home to be tested for radon gas. Some relocation companies are requiring homes to be tested for radon gas. The cure for radon gas can be relatively simple and inexpensive.

If the house is built on a conventional foundation, the usual cure is to install a vapor proof covering in the crawl space along with a suction system that draws the air out of the area before it gets into the living spaces. The average cost to cure radon gas problems is normally between $200 to $1,000, with many homes being cured for only $100.

The Environmental Protection Agency has more information on radon gas, write to Consumer Information Center, Pueblo, CO. 81009. There are two booklets offered: *A Citizen's Guide to Radon* (item 139T, $1) and *Removal of Radon from Household Water* (item 472T, 50 cents).

RAFTER A structural roof member spanning from an exterior wall to a center ridge board. Rafters are used to support the roof.

RAKED JOINT Wet mortar between brick joints is scraped or raked out to give a more pronounced look to the brick. The raked joint makes brick veneer look more appealing, but it has a draw back in colder climates. If moisture in the joints freezes, the resultant expansion from the freezing will make the brick brittle and cause hairline cracks throughout the wall.

RAM *See* REVERSE ANNUITY MORTGAGE.

RANGE LINES Parallel lines marking out land into six-mile strips known as ranges. Range lines are parallel to a principal meridian and are numbered east or west of the meridian in a Government Rectangular Survey.

RAP *See* REGULATORY ACCOUNTING PRINCIPALS.

RAR *See* RESIDENTIAL APPRAISAL REPORT.

RATABLE PROPERTY OR ESTATE Real or personal property that is subject to being taxed by a governing body.

RATE CAP Rate caps limit the increase or decrease in the interest rate of the mortgage. There can be rate caps for each adjustment period and rate caps for the life of the loan.

Assume an initial rate of 7%, annual rate caps of 2%, a lifetime cap of 5%, a margin of 2.75%, the one year T-bill as the index and the T-bill is 6.5%. Assuming the T-bill rate in the second year is 7.5%, the new rate should be 10.25% (the total of the index plus the margin) but the rate is 9% because of the 2% cap limitation. Assuming a T-bill rate of 8.5% in the third year, the new rate should be 11.25 (8.5 + 2.75), but the rate is 11% because of the 2% cap. Assuming a T-bill rate of 9.5% in the fourth year, the rate should be 12.25%, but the rate is capped at 12% because of the 5% lifetime cap. Assuming a T-bill rate of 7% in the fifth year, the rate should be 9.75%, but it is 10% because of the 2% cap in the upward or downward adjustment in the rate.

The following offers a summary of the above numbers:

Year	Index Rate	Margin	Index Rate + Margin	Rate
1	6.5%	2.75	9.25%	7%
2	7.5%	2.75	10.25%	9%
3	8.5%	2.75	11.25%	11%
4	9.5%	2.75	12.25%	12%
5	7.0%	2.75	9.75%	10%

See ADJUSTABLE RATE MORTGAGE.

RATE GUARANTEE An upfront fee type of guarantee permitting Fannie Mae approved lenders the option to guarantee a price on mortgages sold to this secondary conduit.

See RATE-LOCK STANDBY (RLS).

RATE-LOCK STANDBY (RLS) A Fannie Mae program that allows lenders to guaranty the price/yield at which they can sell mortgages to Fannie Mae over a specified period (currently two or four months). This optional commitment is paid for in an upfront fee.

RATE OF CONDITIONAL PREPAYMENT (RCP) The constant ratio of monthly prepayment gauging of current outstanding mortgages that will prepay as predicted such as FHA prepayment experience.

RATE OF INTEREST Annual interest rate in a pool is the coupon rate but not necessarily the yield.

RATE OF RETURN The return of an investment measured in a percentage. A 6% Certificate of Deposit has a rate of return of 6% interest.
See CASH-ON-CASH RETURN, YIELD.

RATIO ANALYSIS *See* COMPUTERIZED LOAN ORIGINATION SYSTEM, INCOME ANALYSIS.

RCP *See* RATE OF CONDITIONAL PREPAYMENT.

READY, WILLING, AND ABLE Description of a buyer who is legally capable and financially able to consummate a purchase.
See CONTRACT OF SALE.

REAL ESTATE Physical land and its permanently attached improvements.
See REAL PROPERTY.

REAL ESTATE BROKER *See* BROKER.

REAL ESTATE INVESTMENT TRUST (REIT) A trust that invests at least 75% of its money in real estate or mortgages. If the trust meets certain requirements, it is exempt from corporate income tax. When a trust distributes a minimum of 95% of its income to its shareholders, it is exempt from corporate tax, but the shareholders must include the income in their personal tax returns.

An equity trust is essentially a landlord, investing in equities in income-producing real estate. Income is derived primarily from rents of the properties. The mortgage REIT, on the other hand, either provides short-term (interim) financing on large construction and development projects or makes or buys permanent mortgage loans.

To qualify as an REIT, the entity must (1) be a cooperation, trust, or association, (2) have at least 100 owners and 50% or more of the shares cannot be owned by five or less shareholders, (3) have trustees that operate the REIT, (4)

owned by five or less shareholders, (3) have trustees that operate the REIT, (4) have limited liability to the shareholders and shares that can be freely transferred, (5) have income that is passive and from rents or mortgage interest. The principal advantage of a REIT is the avoidance of corporate tax. The principal disadvantage of an REIT is that because of the organizational requirements for the start up and maintaining the structure, they are usually restricted to large investments.

REAL ESTATE MORTGAGE INVESTMENT CONDUIT A REMIC is a tax selection that can be used for mortgage-backed securities, CMO's, commercial-backed financing, and other mortgage-related securities. In comparison to a CMO, a REMIC has the following advantages:

1) Clarification of tax treatment;

2) Ability to treat a REMIC as a sale instead of a borrowing; and

3) Thrift institutions such as savings and loan associations can count REMIC investments as meeting their tax and regulatory requirements.

In summary, mortgages sold though the REMIC method could bring better prices that could result in lower yields to the public.

REAL ESTATE MORTGAGE TRUST (REMT) *See* REAL ESTATE INVESTMENT TRUST.

REAL ESTATE OWNED (REO) A term that implies real estate owned by a lending institution for investment purposes or property acquired through foreclosure or deed-in-lieu of foreclosure.

REAL ESTATE SECURITIES AND SYNDICATION INSTITUTE (RESSI) An institution of syndicators affiliated with the National Association of REALTORS.

REAL ESTATE SETTLEMENT PROCEDURE ACT (RESPA) A Federal law that governs mortgage applications for federally-related real estate loans on one-to-four family dwelling properties. Regulation X implements the Act. There are four principal stipulations of the act.

(1) An informational booklet about closing costs must be given to the parties at loan application. The booklet is titled *Settlement Costs and You.* It gives information about closing costs, explains the provisions of the Act, and gives a line-by-line explanation of the HUD-1 settlement statement.

(2) The borrower must be provided with a "good faith estimate" of closing costs. Prepaid items are not required in the estimate.

(3) Lenders are required to use a uniform settlement statement, called a
HUD-1 form.

(4) The Act, as amended, includes a provision of the Housing and Urban
Development (HUD) ruling that continues to oppose referral fees
paid by mortgage lenders.

HUD has interpreted RESPA to forbid compensatory loan referrals in connection with federally related mortgages bearing no direct identity to actual services performed. The difference seems to lie somewhere between commission
and fees then as a matter of course assigning vested rights in a contract to the
actual lender according to the Section 3(3) of RESPA without including funds
paid out. The controversy continues as two separate Federal court findings differ in their decisions leaving HUD to reason out both cases. In the interim,
mortgage lenders while paying the referral fees could be violating Section 8 of
RESPA.

In September of 1990 the MBA issued a memo about the referral subject.

The memo states

> Section 8 (a) of RESPA prohibits giving and accepting "any fee,
> kickback, or thing of value" for the referral of business. Section 8 (b)
> prohibits giving and accepting any portion of any charge made or
> received for a settlement service "other than for services actually per-
> formed." Since the enactment of RESPA, HUD has interpreted Sec-
> tion 8 of the statute to include the making of a mortgage loan as a
> settlement service. However, in 1984 the 6th Circuit Court of Appeals
> ruled in *U.S. v. Graham Mortgage Corp.* that for the purposes of a
> criminal prosecution under RESPA, the making of a mortgage loan
> was not a settlement service and did not fall under RESPA. This issue
> has not yet been resolved by statute or regulation.

> HUD intends to eliminate regulatory and legal impediments created
> by the *Graham* decision. MBA supports this decision. HUD believes
> it is necessary to amend the RESPA regulations to define real estate
> settlement services in a way that includes CLOs.

All charges in connection with closing, including prepaid items and closing
costs, must be included in the Settlement Statement. The statement must show
all parties to the transactions, and the amounts they paid or received. The

charges should agree with the sales contract and the lender's schedules and they must be acceptable under FHA/VA regulations, if applicable. The signature of the borrower(s), seller(s), and settlement agent, in addition to all certifications required by HUD or the FHA is required on, or attached to, the HUD-1 form.

One such certification for FHA loans is the "First Lien Letter."

FIRST LIEN LETTER

DATE:_____

COMMITMENT NO._____

BORROWERS:_____

_____

TITLE COMPANY:_____

In connection with property covered by the captioned title insurance commitment, we wish to advise that the first mortgage in the amount of $_____ has been closed and completely disbursed (FHA funds).

This mortgage is a valid first lien on the property, subject only to those encumbrances shown in Schedule B of the captioned commitment. All taxes and special assessments that presently constitute a valid lien on the subject property have been paid in full.

BY_____

The Tax Reform Act of 1986 requires that the gross proceeds from real estate transactions be reported to the IRS. If the lender does not close the transaction, then it becomes the closing agent who is responsible for complying with all IRS regulations concerning this reporting requirement. It is wise for the lender to have the following statement in the closing instructions "The lender is NOT responsible for closing any residential mortgage loans and hereby disclaims any and all responsibility for preparing or filing any required forms."

See COMPUTERIZED LOAN ORIGINATION SYSTEM (CLO).

REAL ESTATE SYNDICATE A syndicate is not a form of ownership. It is a term to describe a ownership by two or more people. The form of ownership can be a partnership, joint tenancy, tenancy in common, etc.

REAL PROPERTY The rights and interests stemming from the ownership of real estate. This term often is used to mean the same as real estate.

REALTIST A member of the National Association of Real Estate Brokers.
See NATIONAL ASSOCIATION OF REAL ESTATE BROKERS.

REALTOR® A registered trade name that may be used only by members of state and local boards that are affiliated with the National Association of Realtors.® Members are professionals in real estate who subscribe to a Code of Ethics established by the National Association of REALTORS.®
See NATIONAL ASSOCIATION OF REALTORS.®

REAPPRAISAL LEASE A lease with the rental reappraised or revalued at periodic intervals by independent appraisers. If a lease stipulates that the annual rent will be 10% of the property value, the lease most likely will have a reappraisal provision at periodic intervals.

REASSESSMENT The revaluation of property for ad valorem tax purposes.
See CADASTRAL MAP.

RECAPTURE For Federal Income Tax purposes, it is the recovering of depreciation deductions taken for more than the straight-line basis and counting the excess as ordinary income. When income is classified as ordinary income it is taxed at a higher rate than capital gains. The recapture provision prohibits a taxpayer from having a dual benefit of accelerated depreciation and capital gain treatment.
See DEPRECIATION.

RECAPTURE CLAUSE A clause in a contract permitting the grantor of an instrument the right to take that interest back under certain conditions. This clause normally is found in percentage leases. In percentage leases, the recapture clause allows the lessor to regain the premises if sales are below a certain minimum amount.

RECAPTURE RATE In appraising, this term is used to describe the rate that investment capital will be returned over a period of time.
See CAPITALIZATION RATE.

RECASTING The process of changing the term of a mortgage. An existing mortgage with a 10-year remaining term could be recast by extending the term to 20 years. Extending the term reduces the monthly payment. Recasting is not refinancing. In recasting, the original loan is not paid off, it is changed.

RECIPROCITY A mutual agreement to exchange privileges. Two states may agree to allow a person to sell real estate in either state if the licensee has a valid license in either state.

RECISSION OR RIGHT OF RECISSION A three-day business period (72 hours) that allows the borrower to cancel the transaction. During the recission period, funds are withheld pending the decision of the borrower. This regulation is part of the Truth in Lending Act, Regulation Z. Under certain emergency circumstances, this requirement can be waived.
The recission period is explained in detail in TRUTH IN LENDING ACT.

RECLAIM To convert previously uncultivated areas such as swamps or low-lying areas into suitable land for cultivation purposes.

RECOGNIZED GAIN Economic gain that is recognizable for tax purposes.
See CAPITAL GAIN.

RECONCILIATION In appraising, reconciliation is the final step of adjusting the three approaches to value (market, cost, and income) to arrive at the final estimate of value. Reconciliation is the same as the correlation process. (2) The process of remitting to security holders.
See APPRAISED VALUE, REMITTANCE.

RECONVEYANCE The conveying of title back to the original owner. When a mortgage is paid in full under a deed of trust, title is reconveyed from the trustee to the equity owner.
See TITLE THEORY.

RECORDING Making written instruments a part of public record. Items that are often recorded are deeds, mortgages, options, sales contracts, and assignments. Generally, when an instrument is recorded it affects the title to a property and its priority in relationship to other recorded instruments is established by the time of recording. An exception to the time rule is a government tax lien.
See REGISTRAR.

RECOURSE (1) The right of a lender to claim assets from a mortgagor in default, in addition to the subject property's serving as security. A lender has recourse against a borrower if he is personally liable for the loan.

(2) A loan sale can be made with full recourse, without recourse, or with partial recourse. A purchaser of loans with full recourse has the right to full reimbursement from the seller for any losses resulting from the loans or other items purchased. In a loan purchase without recourse the buyer abrogates the right to reimbursement from the seller. A buyer of loans with partial recourse shares any losses with the seller.

See LIABILITY.

RECOVERY FUND A fund set up by a state real estate commission for reimbursing wronged persons who are unable to get compensation from brokers for fraudulent acts or misrepresentation. A fund to assure payment of uncollectible court judgments against parties with a real estate license.

See FRAUD.

REDEMPTION The right of a mortgagor in default to redeem their property by currying or paying off the mortgage in default before foreclosure. Depending upon state law, a mortgagor who has lost their property by foreclosure might be able to redeem it by a right of redemption. The redemption period is established by state law, therefore, it is called a *statutory right of redemption*. The right of redemption has an old history. Unlike most laws stemming from Roman or English law, the right of redemption is mentioned in one of the first books in the Bible. Quoting from Leviticus "If a man sells a house in a walled city, he retains the right of redemption a full year after its sale." Lev 25:29 NIV.

See DEFAULT, EQUITY OF REDEMPTION, FORECLOSURE, REINSTATEMENT.

REDEMPTION PERIOD A period that a former owner can reclaim foreclosed property or property that has been sold for taxes. The redemption period varies among the states. The originator or issuer of mortgage-backed securities is charged with maintaining proper monthly payments during redemption periods.

RED HERRING A preliminary prospectus that has not been approved by the Securities and Exchange Commission.

See PROSPECTUS.

REDISCOUNT RATE The rate of interest charged by the Federal Reserve Bank for loans to its member banks. It is commonly called the discount rate. The rediscount rate indicates the position of the Federal government in terms of a "tight" money or vice versa position. It affects interest rates for all loans, consumer and real estate loans.

See FEDERAL RESERVE SYSTEM.

REDLINING The illegal practice of lending institutions of restricting the number of loans or the loan-to-value ratio in certain neighborhoods because of race or ethnic background. A lending policy of denying real estate loans on properties in older, changing areas, usually with large minority populations, because of alleged higher lending risks without considering the credit worthiness of individual loan applicants. The Fair Housing Act, and the Home Mortgage Disclosure Act forbids redlining.

See FAIR HOUSING ACT, HOME MORTGAGE DISCLOSURE ACT.

REDUCTION CERTIFICATE An instrument wherein the lender acknowledges the remaining balance, rate of interest, and date of maturity for a mortgage.

See ESTOPPEL.

REFERRAL The act of recommending the use of a certain broker. The person making the recommendation may receive a referral fee if he is properly licensed.

See BIRD DOG.

REFERENCE DATE The date of the published index that is used for calculating payment adjustments for adjustable payment mortgage pools.

See GNMA Handbook 5500.2 for more information.

REFINANCE To pay off an existing loan with a new loan. Reasons for refinancing can be many. However, in most cases it is either to raise capital or to replace a mortgage with a new mortgage that provides a better rate of interest and possibly better terms.

When the reason for refinancing is to achieve a lower interest rate, a common rule of thumb is that if the new loan is at least 2% lower than the old rate (the loan that will be paid off) then it will be of financial benefit to refinance. There are more accurate ways of deciding the financial gain or loss of refinancing. In Exhibit 57, you can use a calculator to find the answer.

Since refinancing is a new loan, normally there will be an origination fee and discount points incurred. Some lenders offer refinance loans at an interest rate slightly above the market. Above market rate loans can be sold at a premium. If a lender receives enough premium for a loan, they can close a loan without charging an origination fee or discount points. As you can tell from the refinance figure above and the refinance printout in the CLO definition, elimi-

Exhibit 57

Should You Refinance That Costly Mortgage?

A rule of thumb is a 2% to 3% lower interest rate makes financing worthwhile. Eliminate guess work by using this formula for a more exact cost savings.

Refinance Worksheet

Present monthly payments .... $_____
*Number of months to pay .... ×_____
   Total payments .... $_____A

Payments at alternative
   lower rate .... $_____
*Number of months to pay........... ×_____
   Total payments .... $_____B

   Difference in total payments
   (A minus B) .... $_____C

Refinance costs:
   Any prepayment penalty .... $_____D
   Closing costs of new mortgage,
     including any "points" .... $_____E
   Added income taxes over term
     of mortgage because of
     reduced deduction from
     lower interest rate .... $_____F

   Total (D plus E plus F) .... $_____G

   Net savings over life
   of mortgage (C minus G) .... $_____

*NOTE: Number of months to pay should be for the period of time you expect to own the property and not the number of months required to retire the loan.

This worksheet can also be used in deciding which new loan is best for your needs.

nating front end costs will make a big difference in deciding if refinancing is worthwhile.

See COMPUTERIZED LOAN ORIGINATION (CLO), FHA - REFINANCE, VA - REFINANCE.

REFORMATION A legal remedy that can correct mistakes in written instruments so that the corrected instrument will set forth what the parties intended.

REGENCY HOME STYLE

Regency. This is a 2 or 3-story, symmetrical house with a hip roof. A small octagonal window over the front door is traditional.

REGISTRAR The person responsible for maintaining accurate, efficient records of instruments that can be recorded.

See RECORDING.

REGULATION A Special exemption from normal SEC registration of a security issue when the amount of the offering is less than $1,500,000.

REGULATION D A regulation of the Securities and Exchange Commission that outlines necessary conditions or requirements for a private offering exemption.

REGULATION Q Regulation that allows certain federal agencies to offer different interest rates on savings accounts in banks and savings and loan associations. This legislation is responsible for the gradual deregulation of federally regulated banks and savings institutions. Deregulations include phasing out of deposit interest rates, authorization for interest-bearing checking accounts, and allowing savings and loan associations to become involved in consumer loans to a greater degree.

REGULATION Z *See* TRUTH IN LENDING.

REGULATORY ACCOUNTING PRINCIPLES (RAP) Accounting principles required by regulation that allows savings institutions to elect annually to defer gains or losses on the sale of assets and amortize these deferrals over the average life of each loan group or the stated life of each security sold.

REHABILITATION To modernize a house with work on such items as plumbing, heating and air conditioning, electrical, kitchen equipment. Normally rehabilitation may involve new construction but the floor plan is left untouched.
See EFFECTIVE AGE.

REINFORCING RODS *See* SLAB.

REINSTATEMENT To bring back or restore a past-due loan to a current status. The lender recognizes that the acceleration clause was exercised but the loan is now current.
See REDEMPTION.

REINSURANCE The practice of an original insurer gaining additional insurance from another insurer.
See COINSURANCE.

REINVESTMENT RISK Reinvestment risk is a precarious risk within mortgage related pass-through uncertainties that MBS investors must anticipate.
A pass-through problem is the inclination to produce considerable returns in the early years of the mortgage maturity. MBS pass-throughs are notorious in that their returns influence reinvestments negatively unless the cash flow return is matched to a high capital market interest rate.
To receive returns that the investor cannot control in such negative conditions as prepayments (where he or she obtains a larger cash flow) from pass-throughs but where the changes for reinvestment may or may not average a same (or higher) rate of return, is a risk found in reinvestment cases.

RISER The part of a step that is vertical. The vertical board after the tread is a riser.

See STAIRWAY, TREAD.

REISSUE RATE A reduced charge by a title insurance company if another policy had recently been issued on the same property.

REIT *See* REAL ESTATE INVESTMENT TRUST.

RELEASE The act of freeing real estate from a mortgage, lien, or other encumbrance.

RELEASE CLAUSE A clause permitting a mortgagor to pay off a portion of a mortgage and have that portion of the secured property released from the mortgage.

RELEASE OF LIABILITY The act of releasing a mortgagor from personal liability. The procedure varies as to whether the loan is a Conventional, FHA, or VA loan. For Conventional loans the requirement for release of liability is established by the investor or the lender or both. If a lender informs a borrower that they can be released from liability, it is the lender's responsibility to process the file so that the release can be obtained.

Except in states that have laws to the contrary, lenders are not required to contact the endangered sellers and inform them of the possible consequences involving foreclosure of their previous home loan. Some veterans have experienced an unpleasant surprise about a loss from a previous foreclosure they never knew about.

See FHA - RELEASE OF LIABILITY, GUARANTY PERFORMANCE, VA - RELEASE OF LIABILITY, and SURETY.

RELICTION Gradual withdrawal of water leaving dry land exposed.

RELOCATION CLAUSE A provision in a lease giving the landlord the right to move a tenant within the building.

REMAINDER In estate and real property, the time that takes effect after the expiration of a preceding estate. After a life estate has expired, the remaining estate would be termed a remainder.

REMAINDER MAN That person who is entitled to receive possession of property after the death of a life tenant.

See LIFE ESTATE.

REMAINING BALANCE FACTORS To use the remaining balance tables (Exhibit 58), start with the top line under the appropriate original term of the loan and then go down the table to the age of the loan for which you want the remaining balance.

All factors in the remaining balance tables are per a $100.00 loan amount, so that a 30-year loan at a rate of 11 1/2% interest would have a remaining balance of $92.86 at the end of 25 years and, of course, -0- at the end of 30 years. For a $10,000.00 loan, simply multiply the factor by 100, a $100,000.00 loan, multiply by 1,000, etc.

The factors also represent a percentage of the loan, so that a $100.00 loan has 92.86% remaining at the end of 10 years, 84.77% at the end of 15 years and 45.03% at the end of 25 years.

A remaining balance at the end of 10 years for a $100.00 loan has 92.86% remaining, 84.77% at the end of 25 years.

A remaining balance at the end of 10 years for a loan of $72,450.00 at 11.75% interest for a 30-year term would be $67,479.93, which is 724.50 × 93.14 or $72,450.00 × 93.14%. The factor of 724.50 was known by dividing $72,450.00 by 100. All factors are per $100.00 loan amounts.

REMIC *See* REAL ESTATE MORTGAGE INVESTMENT CONDUIT.

REMISE To give up, release, or quitclaim interest in a property.
See QUITCLAIM.

REMITTANCE The accounting sent each month to a securities holder that specifies the cash distribution, by scheduled principal, interest and unscheduled recoveries of principal, being made that month on each GNMA I certificate. In general, remittance is a report on a specific cycle or period for loan servicing purposes.

RENDERING A perspective drawing of a project. The drawings in this book showing the various architectural styles are renderings.

RENEGOTIABLE RATE MORTGAGE (RRM) A mortgage with the interest rate readjusted at specified adjustment periods. The mortgage balance is not due on the adjustment dates, only the rate is renegotiated.
See CANADIAN ROLLOVER MORTGAGE.

RENT-ROLL A list of leases for a project with details of the tenant's lease periods and security deposits. Rent-roll is known as rent schedule.

Exhibit 58

Remaining Balance Factors
Original Term In Years

9.00%

Age of Loan	1	2	3	4	5	6	7	8	9	10	15	20	25	30
1	0.	52.24	69.61	78.26	83.42	86.84	89.26	91.06	92.44	93.54	96.69	98.13	98.88	99.32
2		0.	36.36	54.47	65.28	72.44	77.51	81.27	84.17	86.47	93.08	96.08	97.66	98.57
3			0.	28.46	45.44	56.68	64.65	70.57	75.13	78.73	89.12	93.84	96.33	97.75
4				0.	23.74	39.46	50.60	58.87	65.24	70.28	84.80	91.39	94.87	96.86
5					0.	20.61	35.22	46.07	54.42	61.02	80.07	88.71	93.27	95.88
6						0.	18.40	32.07	42.59	50.90	74.89	85.77	91.53	94.81
7							0.	16.75	29.64	39.84	69.23	82.57	89.62	93.64
8								0.	15.49	27.73	63.04	79.06	87.53	92.36
9									0.	14.49	56.27	75.22	85.24	90.94
10										0.	48.86	71.03	82.74	89.43
11										0.	40.76	66.44	80.00	87.75
12										0.	31.90	61.41	77.01	85.92
13										0.	22.20	55.92	73.74	83.92
14										0.	11.60	49.91	70.16	81.73
15											0.	43.34	66.25	79.33
16											0.	36.16	61.97	76.71
17											0.	28.29	57.28	73.84
18											0.	19.69	52.16	70.70
19											0.	10.29	46.56	67.27
20												0.	40.43	63.52
21												0.	33.72	59.41
22												0.	26.39	54.92
23												0.	18.37	50.01
24												0.	9.60	44.64
25													0.	38.76
26													0.	32.33
27													0.	25.30
28													0.	17.61
29													0.	9.20
30														0.
35														
40														

9.25%

Age of Loan	1	2	3	4	5	6	7	8	9	10	15	20	25	30
1	0.	52.30	69.69	78.34	83.51	86.93	89.35	91.14	92.53	93.62	96.76	98.18	98.93	99.35
2		0.	36.45	54.59	65.42	72.59	77.66	81.43	84.33	86.62	93.22	96.19	97.75	98.64
3			0.	28.55	45.59	56.87	64.85	70.79	75.35	78.95	89.33	94.01	96.47	97.86
4				0.	23.84	39.63	50.81	59.11	65.50	70.54	85.06	91.61	95.05	97.00
5					0.	20.73	35.41	46.31	54.69	61.32	80.39	88.99	93.51	96.06
6						0.	18.52	32.27	42.85	51.21	75.26	86.11	91.81	95.04
7							0.	16.88	29.86	40.12	69.63	82.95	89.94	93.91
8								0.	15.62	27.96	63.47	79.49	87.90	92.67
9									0.	14.62	56.71	75.70	85.66	91.31
10										0.	49.29	71.53	83.21	89.82
11										0.	41.16	66.97	80.52	88.19
12										0.	32.25	61.97	77.57	86.40
13										0.	22.47	56.48	74.33	84.44
14										0.	11.75	50.46	70.78	82.29
15											0.	43.86	66.89	79.93
16											0.	36.63	62.62	77.35
17											0.	28.70	57.94	74.51
18											0.	20.00	52.81	71.40
19											0.	10.46	47.18	67.99
20												0.	41.01	64.26
21												0.	34.25	60.16
22												0.	26.83	55.66
23												0.	18.70	50.73
24												0.	9.78	45.33
25													0.	39.40
26													0.	32.90
27													0.	25.78
28													0.	17.96
29													0.	9.39
30														0.
35														
40														

Exhibit 58 (continued)

Remaining Balance Factors
Original Term In Years

9.50%

Age of Loan	1	2	3	4	5	6	7	8	9	10	15	20	25	30
1	0.	52.36	69.77	78.43	83.60	87.01	89.44	91.23	92.61	93.70	96.83	98.24	98.97	99.38
2		0.	36.53	54.72	65.56	72.74	77.82	81.59	84.49	86.78	93.35	96.30	97.84	98.71
3			0.	28.65	45.74	57.05	65.06	71.00	75.57	79.17	89.53	94.18	96.60	97.96
4				0.	23.95	39.80	51.02	59.35	65.75	70.81	85.32	91.84	95.23	97.14
5					0.	20.84	35.60	46.55	54.97	61.61	80.70	89.27	93.73	96.24
6						0.	18.64	32.48	43.11	51.51	75.62	86.44	92.08	95.25
7							0.	17.01	30.08	40.40	70.03	83.33	90.27	94.16
8								0.	15.75	28.18	63.89	79.92	88.27	92.97
9									0.	14.76	57.14	76.16	86.08	91.65
10										0.	49.72	72.04	83.67	90.21
11										0.	41.56	67.50	81.02	88.62
12										0.	32.60	62.51	78.11	86.87
13										0.	22.74	57.03	74.91	84.95
14										0.	11.91	51.01	71.39	82.84
15											0.	44.38	67.52	80.52
16											0.	37.10	63.27	77.97
17											0.	29.10	58.59	75.17
18											0.	20.30	53.46	72.09
19											0.	10.63	47.81	68.70
20												0.	41.60	64.98
21												0.	34.78	60.89
22												0.	27.27	56.39
23												0.	19.03	51.45
24												0.	9.96	46.01
25													0.	40.04
26													0.	33.47
27													0.	26.25
28													0.	18.31
29													0.	9.59
30														0.
35														
40														

9.75%

Age of Loan	1	2	3	4	5	6	7	8	9	10	15	20	25	30
1	0.	52.43	69.85	78.52	83.68	87.10	89.52	91.32	92.70	93.78	96.90	98.29	99.01	99.41
2		0.	36.62	54.84	65.71	72.89	77.98	81.75	84.65	86.94	93.49	96.41	97.93	98.77
3			0.	28.75	45.89	57.23	65.26	71.21	75.78	79.39	89.72	94.34	96.73	98.06
4				0.	24.06	39.97	51.24	59.59	66.01	71.07	85.58	92.05	95.41	97.27
5					0.	20.96	35.79	46.79	55.24	61.91	81.01	89.54	93.95	96.41
6						0.	18.76	32.68	43.37	51.81	75.97	86.76	92.35	95.46
7							0.	17.13	30.29	40.68	70.43	83.71	90.58	94.41
8								0.	15.88	28.41	64.31	80.34	88.63	93.26
9									0.	14.89	57.57	76.62	86.49	91.98
10										0.	50.15	72.53	84.12	90.58
11										0.	41.97	68.02	81.51	89.03
12										0.	32.95	63.06	78.64	87.33
13										0.	23.01	57.58	75.48	85.45
14										0.	12.07	51.55	71.99	83.38
15											0.	44.90	68.15	81.10
16											0.	37.58	63.91	78.59
17											0.	29.50	59.24	75.82
18											0.	20.61	54.10	72.77
19											0.	10.80	48.43	69.41
20												0.	42.19	65.70
21												0.	35.30	61.62
22												0.	27.72	57.12
23												0.	19.36	52.16
24												0.	10.15	46.69
25													0.	40.67
26													0.	34.04
27													0.	26.72
28													0.	18.67
29													0.	9.79
30														0.
35														
40														

Exhibit 58 (continued)

Remaining Balance Factors
Original Term In Years

10.00%

Age of Loan	1	2	3	4	5	6	7	8	9	10	15	20	25	30
1	0.	52.49	69.93	78.60	83.77	87.19	89.61	91.40	92.78	93.87	96.97	98.35	99.05	99.44
2		0.	36.70	54.96	65.85	73.04	78.13	81.91	84.81	87.09	93.62	96.52	98.01	98.83
3			0.	28.85	46.04	57.41	65.46	71.42	75.99	79.60	89.92	94.50	96.85	98.15
4				0.	24.17	40.15	51.45	59.83	66.26	71.33	85.83	92.27	95.57	97.40
5					0.	21.07	35.98	47.03	55.51	62.20	81.32	89.80	94.16	96.57
6						0.	18.88	32.88	43.63	52.10	76.33	87.08	92.61	95.66
7							0.	17.26	30.51	40.96	70.82	84.07	90.88	94.65
8								0.	16.01	28.64	64.73	80.75	88.98	93.53
9									0.	15.03	58.01	77.08	86.88	92.30
10										0.	50.58	73.02	84.56	90.94
11										0.	42.37	68.54	82.00	89.43
12										0.	33.30	63.60	79.17	87.77
13										0.	23.29	58.13	76.04	85.93
14										0.	12.22	52.09	72.58	83.91
15											0.	45.42	68.76	81.66
16											0.	38.05	64.54	79.19
17											0.	29.91	59.88	76.45
18											0.	20.91	54.74	73.43
19											0.	10.98	49.05	70.09
20												0.	42.77	66.41
21												0.	35.83	62.33
22												0.	28.16	57.83
23												0.	19.69	52.86
24												0.	10.34	47.37
25													0.	41.30
26													0.	34.60
27													0.	27.20
28													0.	19.02
29													0.	9.98
30														0.
35														
40														

10.25%

Age of Loan	1	2	3	4	5	6	7	8	9	10	15	20	25	30
1	0.	52.55	70.01	78.69	83.86	87.28	89.70	91.49	92.86	93.95	97.03	98.40	99.09	99.47
2		0.	36.79	55.09	65.99	73.20	78.29	82.06	84.96	87.24	93.75	96.62	98.09	98.89
3			0.	28.95	46.20	57.60	65.65	71.63	76.21	79.82	90.11	94.65	96.97	98.24
4				0.	24.28	40.32	51.66	60.07	66.51	71.59	86.08	92.48	95.74	97.52
5					0.	21.19	36.17	47.27	55.78	62.49	81.62	90.06	94.37	96.73
6						0.	19.01	33.09	43.89	52.40	76.68	87.39	92.86	95.85
7							0.	17.39	30.73	41.24	71.21	84.43	91.18	94.88
8								0.	16.15	28.87	65.15	81.16	89.33	93.80
9									0.	15.17	58.44	77.53	87.27	92.61
10										0.	51.00	73.51	84.99	91.29
11										0.	42.77	69.06	82.47	89.82
12										0.	33.66	64.13	79.68	88.20
13										0.	23.56	58.67	76.59	86.41
14										0.	12.38	52.63	73.16	84.42
15											0.	45.94	69.37	82.21
16											0.	38.52	65.17	79.78
17											0.	30.31	60.52	77.08
18											0.	21.22	55.37	74.08
19											0.	11.15	49.67	70.77
20												0.	43.35	67.10
21												0.	36.35	63.04
22												0.	28.61	58.54
23												0.	20.03	53.56
24												0.	10.52	48.04
25													0.	41.93
26													0.	35.16
27													0.	27.67
28													0.	19.37
29													0.	10.18
30														0.
35														
40														

Exhibit 58 (continued)

Remaining Balance Factors
Original Term In Years

10.50%

Age of Loan	1	2	3	4	5	6	7	8	9	10	15	20	25	30
1	0.	52.61	70.08	78.77	83.95	87.37	89.78	91.57	92.95	94.03	97.10	98.45	99.13	99.50
2		0.	36.87	55.21	66.13	73.35	78.44	82.22	85.11	87.39	93.88	96.72	98.16	98.94
3			0.	29.05	46.35	57.78	65.85	71.83	76.42	80.03	90.30	94.81	97.09	98.33
4				0.	24.38	40.49	51.88	60.30	66.77	71.85	86.33	92.68	95.90	97.64
5					0.	21.30	36.36	47.50	56.05	62.78	81.92	90.32	94.57	96.88
6						0.	19.13	33.29	44.15	52.70	77.03	87.70	93.10	96.04
7							0.	17.52	30.94	41.52	71.59	84.79	91.47	95.10
8								0.	16.28	29.10	65.56	81.56	89.66	94.06
9									0.	15.43	58.86	77.97	87.65	92.90
10										0.	51.43	73.99	85.42	91.62
11										0.	43.17	69.57	82.94	90.20
12										0.	34.01	64.66	80.19	88.62
13										0.	23.84	59.21	77.13	86.86
14										0.	12.54	53.16	73.74	84.91
15											0.	46.45	69.97	82.75
16											0.	38.99	65.79	80.35
17											0.	30.72	61.15	77.68
18											0.	21.53	56.00	74.73
19											0.	11.33	50.28	71.44
20												0.	43.93	67.79
21												0.	36.88	63.74
22												0.	29.05	59.24
23												0.	20.36	54.25
24												0.	10.71	48.71
25													0.	42.56
26													0.	35.73
27													0.	28.14
28													0.	19.72
29													0.	10.58
30														0.
35														
40														

10.75%

Age of Loan	1	2	3	4	5	6	7	8	9	10	15	20	25	30
1	0.	52.67	70.16	78.86	84.04	87.46	89.87	91.66	93.03	94.10	97.16	98.49	99.16	99.53
2		0.	36.96	55.33	66.27	73.50	78.60	82.37	85.27	87.54	94.00	96.82	98.23	99.00
3			0.	29.14	46.50	57.96	66.05	72.04	76.63	80.24	90.49	94.95	97.20	98.41
4				0.	24.49	40.67	52.09	60.54	67.02	72.11	86.57	92.88	96.05	97.75
5					0.	21.42	36.55	47.74	56.32	63.07	82.22	90.57	94.77	97.03
6						0.	19.25	33.50	44.41	53.00	77.37	88.00	93.34	96.22
7							0.	17.64	31.16	41.80	71.98	85.14	91.75	95.31
8								0.	16.41	29.33	65.97	81.95	89.98	94.31
9									0.	15.45	59.29	78.41	88.02	93.19
10										0.	51.85	74.46	85.83	91.95
11										0.	43.58	70.07	83.39	90.56
12										0.	34.36	65.19	80.68	89.02
13										0.	24.11	59.75	77.66	87.31
14										0.	12.70	53.70	74.30	85.40
15											0.	46.96	70.57	83.28
16											0.	39.47	66.41	80.91
17											0.	31.12	61.78	78.28
18											0.	21.84	56.62	75.35
19											0.	11.50	50.89	72.09
20												0.	44.50	68.47
21												0.	37.40	64.43
22												0.	29.49	59.94
23												0.	20.69	54.94
24												0.	10.90	49.37
25													0.	43.18
26													0.	34.29
27													0.	28.62
28													0.	20.08
29													0.	10.58
30														0.
35														
40														

Exhibit 58 (continued)

Remaining Balance Factors
Original Term In Years

11.00%

Age of Loan	1	2	3	4	5	6	7	8	9	10	15	20	25	30
1	0.	52.73	70.24	78.94	84.12	87.54	89.96	91.74	93.11	94.18	97.22	98.54	99.20	99.55
2		0.	37.04	55.45	66.41	73.65	78.75	82.53	85.42	87.69	94.13	96.91	98.31	99.05
3			0.	29.24	46.65	58.14	66.25	72.25	76.84	80.45	90.67	95.10	97.31	98.49
4				0.	24.60	40.84	52.30	60.78	67.27	72.37	86.81	93.07	96.20	97.86
5					0.	21.54	36.74	47.98	56.59	63.36	82.51	90.81	94.95	97.16
6						0.	19.37	33.70	44.67	53.30	77.71	88.29	93.57	96.39
7							0.	17.77	31.38	42.08	72.36	85.48	92.03	95.52
8								0.	16.55	29.56	66.38	82.34	90.30	94.55
9									0.	15.59	59.71	78.84	88.38	93.47
10										0.	52.28	74.93	86.23	92.26
11										0.	43.98	70.57	83.84	90.92
12										0.	34.72	65.71	81.17	89.42
13										0.	24.39	60.28	78.19	87.74
14										0.	12.86	54.23	74.86	85.87
15											0.	47.47	71.15	83.79
16											0.	39.94	67.01	81.46
17											0.	31.53	62.39	78.87
18											0.	22.15	57.24	75.97
19											0.	11.68	51.49	72.74
20												0.	45.08	69.13
21												0.	37.92	65.11
22												0.	29.94	60.63
23												0.	21.03	55.62
24												0.	11.09	50.03
25													0.	43.80
26													0.	36.85
27													0.	29.09
28													0.	20.43
29													0.	10.78
30														0.
35														
40														

11.25%

Age of Loan	1	2	3	4	5	6	7	8	9	10	15	20	25	30
1	0.	52.80	70.32	79.03	84.21	87.63	90.04	91.82	93.19	94.26	97.28	98.59	99.23	99.57
2		0.	37.13	55.58	66.55	73.79	78.90	82.68	85.57	87.84	94.25	97.01	98.37	99.10
3			0.	29.34	46.80	58.32	66.45	72.45	77.05	80.66	90.85	95.24	97.41	98.56
4				0.	24.71	41.01	52.51	61.01	67.52	72.63	87.05	93.26	96.34	97.97
5					0.	21.65	36.93	48.22	56.86	63.64	82.80	91.05	95.14	97.30
6						0.	19.50	33.91	44.94	53.59	78.05	88.58	93.79	96.55
7							0.	17.90	31.60	42.36	72.73	85.82	92.29	95.72
8								0.	16.68	29.79	66.79	82.72	90.61	94.78
9									0.	15.73	60.14	79.26	88.73	93.74
10										0.	52.70	75.39	86.63	92.57
11										0.	44.38	71.07	84.27	91.26
12										0.	35.07	66.23	81.64	89.80
13										0.	24.66	60.81	78.70	88.16
14										0.	13.02	54.76	75.41	86.33
15											0.	47.98	71.73	84.29
16											0.	40.41	67.61	82.00
17											0.	31.93	63.01	79.44
18											0.	22.46	57.85	76.57
19											0.	11.86	52.09	73.37
20												0.	45.65	69.79
21												0.	38.44	65.78
22												0.	30.38	61.30
23												0.	21.36	56.29
24												0.	11.28	50.69
25													0.	44.42
26													0.	37.40
27													0.	29.56
28													0.	20.79
29													0.	10.97
30														0.
35														
40														

Exhibit 58 (continued)

Remaining Balance Factors
Original Term In Years

11.50%

Age of Loan	1	2	3	4	5	6	7	8	9	10	15	20	25	30
1	0.	52.86	70.40	79.12	84.30	87.72	90.13	91.91	93.27	94.34	97.34	98.63	99.26	99.60
2		0.	37.21	55.70	66.69	73.94	79.06	82.83	85.72	87.99	94.37	97.10	98.44	99.14
3			0.	29.44	46.95	58.50	66.64	72.66	77.26	80.86	91.03	95.38	97.51	98.63
4				0.	24.82	41.18	52.72	61.25	67.77	72.88	87.29	93.45	96.48	98.06
5					0.	21.77	37.12	48.46	57.13	63.93	83.09	91.29	95.32	97.42
6						0.	19.62	34.11	45.20	53.89	78.38	88.87	94.01	96.71
7							0.	18.03	31.82	42.64	73.11	86.15	92.55	95.90
8								0.	16.82	30.02	67.19	83.10	90.91	95.00
9									0.	15.87	60.56	79.68	89.07	93.99
10										0.	53.12	75.85	87.01	92.86
11										0.	44.78	71.55	84.70	91.59
12										0.	35.43	66.74	82.11	90.17
13										0.	24.94	61.34	79.21	88.57
14										0.	13.18	55.28	75.95	86.78
15											0.	48.49	72.30	84.77
16											0.	40.88	68.20	82.52
17											0.	32.34	63.61	80.00
18											0.	22.77	58.46	77.17
19											0.	12.03	52.69	73.99
20												0.	46.22	70.44
21												0.	38.96	66.45
22												0.	30.82	61.97
23												0.	21.70	56.96
24												0.	11.47	51.33
25													0.	45.03
26													0.	37.96
27													0.	30.03
28													0.	21.14
29													0.	11.18
30														0.
35														
40														

11.75%

Age of Loan	1	2	3	4	5	6	7	8	9	10	15	20	25	30
1	0.	52.92	70.48	79.20	84.38	87.80	90.21	91.99	93.35	94.41	97.40	98.68	99.30	99.62
2		0.	37.30	55.82	66.83	74.09	79.21	82.98	85.87	88.13	94.49	97.19	98.50	99.19
3			0.	29.54	47.10	58.68	66.84	72.86	77.46	81.07	91.20	95.51	97.61	98.70
4				0.	24.93	41.36	52.94	61.48	68.01	73.13	87.52	93.63	96.61	98.16
5					0.	21.89	37.31	48.70	57.39	64.21	83.37	91.52	95.49	97.55
6						0.	19.74	34.32	45.46	54.19	78.71	89.14	94.22	96.86
7							0.	18.16	32.04	42.92	73.48	86.47	92.80	96.09
8								0.	16.95	30.25	67.59	83.47	91.20	95.22
9									0.	16.01	60.97	80.09	89.41	94.24
10										0.	53.54	76.30	87.39	93.14
11										0.	45.18	72.04	85.12	91.91
12										0.	35.78	67.25	82.57	90.52
13										0.	25.22	61.86	79.70	88.97
14										0.	13.35	55.80	76.48	87.21
15											0.	49.00	72.86	85.24
16											0.	41.35	68.79	83.03
17											0.	32.75	64.21	80.54
18											0.	23.08	59.07	77.75
19											0.	12.21	53.28	74.60
20												0.	46.78	71.07
21												0.	39.48	67.10
22												0.	31.27	62.63
23												0.	22.04	57.62
24												0.	11.66	51.98
25													0.	45.64
26													0.	38.51
27													0.	30.50
28													0.	21.50
29													0.	11.38
30														0.
35														
40														

RENT-UP The amount of time for leasing all of a new project.

REO *See* REAL ESTATE OWNED.

REPO *See* REPURCHASE AGREEMENT.

REPLEVIN A legal procedure to recover personal property that has been unlawfully taken or withheld. If a landlord has taken a tenant's property unlawfully, the tenant can file a procedure known as a replevin to repossess the property taken.
See DISTRAINT.

REPURCHASE AGREEMENT A simultaneous agreement between the seller and purchaser of mortgage-backed security that the seller agrees to repurchase the securities at a specified future date and price.

REQUEST FOR DETERMINATION OF REASONABLE VALUE *See* VA - REQUEST FOR DETERMINATION OF REASONABLE VALUE.

REQUIRED NET YIELD (RNY) The purchasers of mortgages including lenders and investors who buy from originators, secondary market conduits buying from originators, and pension funds buying from those who loan on real estate, all have a common goal called the required net yield.
Conditions in secondary marketing trades dictate prices that loan originators receive for these mortgages at RNY requirements that can be subject to many factors, such as loan seasoning, weighted average coupon, the weighted average remaining maturity, the anticipated loan life, delivery date, and type of mortgage loan characteristics affecting the collateral. Sensitive time periods are important as to originating the loan and its sale in secondary markets since market prices do change from par to discount to premium depending upon the above qualities controlling the cash flow.

RESCIND The act of withdrawing an offer or a contract. Cancellation of a transaction or contract by operation of law or mutual consent.

RESCISSION Regulation Z requires a three-day rescission period that the consumer can rescind the transaction. The three days are known as a rescission period. The recission period is explained in detail in TRUTH IN LENDING ACT.

RESIDENTIAL APPRAISAL REPORT (RAR) The mortgage underwriting process calls for a complete, thoroughly analyzed valuation of the subject residential real estate by a competent appraiser who is not only price-wise, but market-wise as well. The RAR of the professional appraiser outlines the factors covering the market value of the property as it stands on the day the estimate was certified. The RAR must include the following statements: (1) the specific purpose for which the fair market value is being estimated; (2) the subject property's identification with a description of the property rights; (3) a complete explanation of the steps taken to arrive at a final conclusion of the value estimate; and (4) the date the estimate was made.

According to R-41c, clarification 3, it is not intended for the appraiser to become enmeshed in aspects of the underwriting process other than those necessary to perform the appraisal.

A difficult task an appraiser must face is price vs. value. Price is an actual amount of money that the subject property was sold, not necessarily fair market value in the comparable sense as found in recently bought properties (indicating the same quality). A grass roots estimation of value cannot be made without access to reliable information such as the reason for the transaction in the first place. This is obviously an impossible determination in the estimate of value because of the incentives involved such as, desiring to live near a relative who has strongly influenced the purchase of an overpriced home or the affluent medical physician who is anxious to lower the listed price in return for a quick sale thereby liquidating assets for the purchase of a more expensive home. Price vs. value studies show prices paid for like residences, not the buyer's down payment, is the key along with the amortization of the mortgage on a loan-to-value basis. To decide equity of buyers at the point of down payment is more of a problem for appraisers than comparing prices paid for comparables for the subject property being purchased.

For portfolio lenders the market data approach was successful as long as a good cross-section of sales was available along with details of the home purchase and the terms used. The non-portfolio lender (or the secondary market originator) who immediately sells the loan to investors is not as affected by the market analysis system. The non-portfolio lender's appraiser is nearly always a fee appraiser who (although a trained professional) is an entrepreneur, just as the mortgage company that hires him is an enterprising mortgage lender anxious to market a loan. What does this suggest? An appraiser, in efforts to please the lender, is aware that the fair market value is being estimated and will bring a report that the loan originator (contractor) finds favorable. The R-41c clarification number (3) makes it clear that adjustments to the objective appraised value does not include underwriting influences that may bias the final valuation. Residential Appraisal Report side #1 and 2 follow (a Freddie Mac and Fannie Mae standard form report represents the current form available).

A lender will probably want the appraisal done on forms like those shown in Exhibits 59-61.

Exhibit 59

Property Description & Analysis **UNIFORM RESIDENTIAL APPRAISAL REPORT**   File No.

SUBJECT
Property Address	Census Tract	LENDER DISCRETIONARY USE
City	County	State	Zip Code	Sale Price $
Legal Description	Date
Owner/Occupant	Map Reference	Mortgage Amount $
Sale Price $ Date of Sale	PROPERTY RIGHTS APPRAISED	Mortgage Type
Loan charges/concessions to be paid by seller $	Fee Simple	Discount Points and Other Concessions
R.E. Taxes $ Tax Year HOA $/Mo.	Leasehold	Paid by Seller $
Lender/Client	Condominium (HUD/VA)
	De Minimis PUD	Source

NEIGHBORHOOD
LOCATION	Urban	Suburban	Rural	NEIGHBORHOOD ANALYSIS	Good	Avg.	Fair	Poor
BUILT UP	Over 75%	25-75%	Under 25%	Employment Stability				
GROWTH RATE	Rapid	Stable	Slow *	Convenience to Employment				
PROPERTY VALUES	Increasing	Stable	Declining	Convenience to Shopping				
DEMAND/SUPPLY	Shortage	In Balance	Over Supply	Convenience to Schools				
MARKETING TIME	Under 3 Mos.	3-6 Mos.	Over 6 Mos.	Adequacy of Public Transportation				

PRESENT LAND USE % LAND USE CHANGE PREDOMINANT SINGLE FAMILY HOUSING
Single Family — Not Likely — OCCUPANCY — PRICE $(000) AGE (yrs)
2-4 Family — Likely — Owner — Recreation Facilities / Adequacy of Utilities / Property Compatibility / Protection from Detrimental Cond. / Police & Fire Protection / General Appearance of Properties / Appeal to Market

Note: Race or the racial composition of the neighborhood are not considered reliable appraisal factors.
COMMENTS:

SITE
Dimensions ___ Topography ___
Site Area ___ Corner Lot ___ Size ___
Zoning Classification ___ Zoning Compliance ___ Shape ___
HIGHEST & BEST USE: Present Use ___ Other Use ___ Drainage ___
UTILITIES Public Other SITE IMPROVEMENTS Type Public Private View ___
Electricity — Street — Landscaping
Gas — Curb/Gutter — Driveway
Water — Sidewalk — Apparent Easements
Sanitary Sewer — Street Lights — FEMA Flood Hazard Yes* ___ No ___
Storm Sewer — Alley — FEMA* Map/Zone
COMMENTS (Apparent adverse easements, encroachments, special assessments, slide areas, etc.)

IMPROVEMENTS
GENERAL DESCRIPTION	EXTERIOR DESCRIPTION	FOUNDATION	BASEMENT	INSULATION
Units	Foundation	Slab	Area Sq. Ft.	Roof
Stories	Exterior Walls	Crawl Space	% Finished	Ceiling
Type (Det./Att.)	Roof Surface	Basement	Ceiling	Walls
Design (Style)	Gutters & Dwnspts	Sump Pump	Walls	Floor
Existing	Window Type	Dampness	Floor	None
Proposed	Storm Sash	Settlement	Outside Entry	Adequacy
Under Construction	Screens	Infestation		Energy Efficient Items
Age (Yrs.)	Manufactured House			
Effective Age (Yrs.)				

ROOMS | Foyer | Living | Dining | Kitchen | Den | Family Rm. | Rec. Rm. | Bedrooms | # Baths | Laundry | Other | Area Sq. Ft.
Basement / Level 1 / Level 2

Finished area above grade contains: Rooms; Bedroom(s); Bath(s); Square Feet of Gross Living Area

INTERIOR
SURFACES Materials/Condition	HEATING	KITCHEN EQUIP.	ATTIC	IMPROVEMENT ANALYSIS	Good	Avg.	Fair	Poor
Floors	Type	Refrigerator	None	Quality of Construction				
Walls	Fuel	Range/Oven	Stairs	Condition of Improvements				
Trim/Finish	Condition	Disposal	Drop Stair	Room Sizes/Layout				
Bath Floor	Adequacy	Dishwasher	Scuttle	Closets and Storage				
Bath Wainscot	COOLING	Fan/Hood	Floor	Energy Efficiency				
Doors	Central	Compactor	Heated	Plumbing-Adequacy & Condition				
	Other	Washer/Dryer	Finished	Electrical-Adequacy & Condition				
	Condition	Microwave		Kitchen Cabinets Adequacy & Cond.				
Fireplace(s) #	Adequacy	Intercom		Compatibility to Neighborhood				

AUTOS
CAR STORAGE Garage ___ Attached Adequate House Entry Appeal & Marketability
No. Cars ___ Carport ___ Detached Inadequate Outside Entry Estimated Remaining Economic Life ___ Yrs.
Condition ___ None Built-In Electric Door Basement Entry Estimated Remaining Physical Life ___ Yrs.
Additional Features:

COMMENTS
Depreciation (Physical, functional and external inadequacies, repairs needed, modernization, etc.):

General market conditions and prevalence and impact in subject/market area regarding loan discounts, interest buydowns and concessions:

Freddie Mac Form 70 10/86   Fannie Mae Form 1004 10/86
VMP-22F (8810) 01   VMP MORTGAGE FORMS • (313)293-8100 • (800)521-7291

Exhibit 59 (continued)

Valuation Section   **UNIFORM RESIDENTIAL APPRAISAL REPORT**   File No. _____

Purpose of Appraisal is to estimate Market Value as defined in the Certification & Statement of Limiting Conditions.

COST APPROACH

BUILDING SKETCH (SHOW GROSS LIVING AREA ABOVE GRADE)
If for Freddie Mac or Fannie Mae, show only square foot calculations and cost approach comments in this space

ESTIMATED REPRODUCTION COST-NEW-OF IMPROVEMENTS:

Dwelling _____	Sq. Ft. @ $ _____	= $ _____
	Sq. Ft. @ $ _____	= _____
Extras _____		= _____
		= _____
Special Energy Efficient Items _____		= _____
Porches, Patios, etc. _____		= _____
Garage/Carport _____	Sq. Ft. @ $ _____	= _____
Total Estimated Cost New		= $ _____

	Physical	Functional	External
Less			

Depreciation _____ = $ _____
Depreciated Value of Improvements .... = $ _____
Site Imp. "as is" (driveway, landscaping, etc.) = $ _____
ESTIMATED SITE VALUE .... = $ _____
(If leasehold, show only leasehold value.)
INDICATED VALUE BY COST APPROACH = $ _____

(Not Required by Freddie Mac and Fannie Mae)
Does property conform to applicable HUD/VA property standards? ☐ Yes ☐ No
If No, explain: _____

Construction Warranty ☐ Yes ☐ No
Name of Warranty Program _____
Warranty Coverage Expires _____

SALES COMPARISON ANALYSIS

The undersigned has recited three recent sales of properties most similar and proximate to subject and has considered these in the market analysis. The description includes a dollar adjustment, reflecting market reaction to those items of significant variation between the subject and comparable properties. If a significant item in the comparable property is superior to, or more favorable than, the subject property, a minus (−) adjustment is made, thus reducing the indicated value of subject; if a significant item in the comparable is inferior to, or less favorable than, the subject property, a plus (+) adjustment is made, thus increasing the indicated value of the subject.

ITEM	SUBJECT	COMPARABLE NO. 1		COMPARABLE NO. 2		COMPARABLE NO. 3	
Address							
Proximity to Subject							
Sales Price	$		$		$		$
Price/Gross Liv. Area	$	$		$		$	
Data Source							
VALUE ADJUSTMENTS	DESCRIPTION	DESCRIPTION	+ (−) $ Adjustment	DESCRIPTION	+ (−) $ Adjustment	DESCRIPTION	+ (−) $ Adjustment
Sales or Financing							
Concessions							
Date of Sale/Time							
Location							
Site/View							
Design and Appeal							
Quality of Construction							
Age							
Condition							
Above Grade	Total / Bdrms / Baths	Total / Bdrms / Baths		Total / Bdrms / Baths		Total / Bdrms / Baths	
Room Count							
Gross Living Area	Sq. Ft.	Sq. Ft.		Sq. Ft.		Sq. Ft.	
Basement & Finished							
Rooms Below Grade							
Functional Utility							
Heating/Cooling							
Garage/Carport							
Porches, Patio,							
Pools, etc.							
Special Energy Efficient Items							
Fireplace(s)							
Other (e.g. kitchen) equip., remodeling)							
Net Adj. (total)		+ / − $		+ / − $		+ / − $	
Indicated Value of Subject		$		$		$	

Comments on Sales Comparison: _____

INDICATED VALUE BY SALES COMPARISON APPROACH .... $ _____
INDICATED VALUE BY INCOME APPROACH (If Applicable) Estimated Market Rent $ _____ /Mo. x Gross Rent Multiplier _____ = $ _____
This appraisal is made ☐ "as is" ☐ subject to the repairs, alterations, inspections or conditions listed below ☐ completion per plans and specifications.
Comments and Conditions of Appraisal: _____

Final Reconciliation: _____

RECONCILIATION

This appraisal is based upon the above requirements, the certification, contingent and limiting conditions, and Market Value definition that are stated in
☐ FmHA, HUD &/or VA instructions.
☐ Freddie Mac Form 439 (Rev. 7/86)/Fannie Mae Form 1004B (Rev. 7/86) filed with client _____ 19 _____ ☐ attached.
I (We) ESTIMATE THE MARKET VALUE, AS DEFINED, OF THE SUBJECT PROPERTY AS OF _____ 19 _____ to be $ _____
I (We) certify: that to the best of my (our) knowledge and belief the facts and data used herein are true and correct; that I (we) personally inspected the subject property, both inside and out, and have made an exterior inspection of all comparable sales cited in this report; and that I (we) have no undisclosed interest, present or prospective therein.

Appraiser(s) SIGNATURE _____   Review Appraiser SIGNATURE _____ ☐ Did ☐ Did Not
NAME _____   (If applicable) NAME _____ Inspect Property

Freddie Mac Form 70   10/86   Fannie Mae Form 1004   10/86

Exhibit 60

[X]

PROPERTY DESCRIPTION & ANALYSIS   **SMALL RESIDENTIAL INCOME PROPERTY APPRAISAL REPORT**   File No. _____

Subject

Property address					**Lender discretionary use**
City	County	State	Zip code		Sale price $
Legal description					Gross monthly rent $
Owner/occupant			Tax year	R.E. taxes $	Closing date
Sale price $	Date of sale	Census tract	Map reference		Mortgage amount $
Property rights appraised [ ] Fee simple [ ] Leasehold [ ] Condominium or [ ] PUD HOA $ /Mo.					Mortgage type
Borrower		Project Name			Discount points and other concessions
Loan charges/concessions to be paid by seller $					Paid by seller $
Lender/client					Source
Appraiser					

Neighborhood

Location	[ ] Urban	[ ] Suburban	[ ] Rural	**Predominant occupancy**	**Single family housing**	**Neighborhood analysis**	Good Avg. Fair Poor	
Built up	[ ] Over 75%	[ ] 25-75%	[ ] Under 25%		PRICE $(000) AGE (yrs.)	Employment stability		
Growth rate	[ ] Rapid	[ ] Stable	[ ] Slow	[ ] Owner	Low	Convenience to employment		
Property values	[ ] Increasing	[ ] Stable	[ ] Declining	[ ] Tenant	High	Convenience to shopping		
Demand/supply	[ ] Shortage	[ ] In balance	[ ] Over supply	[ ] Vacant (0-5%)	Predominant	Convenience to schools		
Marketing time	[ ] Under 3 mos.	[ ] 3-6 mos.	[ ] Over 6 mos.	[ ] Vacant (over 5%)		Adequacy of public transportation		

Typical 2-4 family bldg. Type_____	**Present land use %**	**Land use change**	**2-4 family housing**
No. stories_____ No. units_____	One family _____	[ ] Not likely	PRICE $(000) AGE (yrs)
Age_____ yrs. Condition _____	2-4 family _____	[ ] Likely	Low
Typical rents $_____ to $_____	Multifamily _____	[ ] In process	High
[ ]Increasing [ ]Stable [ ]Declining	Commercial _____	To:	Predominant
Est. neighborhood apt. vacancy_____%	Industrial _____		Adequacy of utilities
[ ]Increasing [ ]Stable [ ]Declining	Vacant _____	Rent controls [ ] Yes* [ ] No [ ] Likely*	Property compatibility

Neighborhood analysis continued: Recreation facilities / Adequacy of utilities / Property compatibility / Protection from detrimental cond. / Police & fire protection / General appearance of properties / Appeal to market

Note: Race and the racial composition of the neighborhood are not considered reliable appraisal factors.

Description of neighborhood boundaries: _____

Description of those factors, favorable or unfavorable, that affect marketability (including neighborhood stability, appeal, property conditions, vacancies, * rent control, etc.). _____

The following available listings represent the most current, similar, and proximate competitive properties to the subject property in the subject neighborhood. This analysis is intended to evaluate the inventory currently on the market competing with the subject property in the subject neighborhood and recent price and marketing time trends affecting the subject property. (Listings outside the subject neighborhood are not considered applicable). The listing comparables can be the rental or sale comparables if they are currently for sale.

ITEM	SUBJECT	COMPARABLE LISTING NO. 1	COMPARABLE LISTING NO. 2	COMPARABLE LISTING NO. 3
Address				
Proximity to subject				
Listing price	$	[ ] Unf. [ ] Furn. $	[ ] Unf. [ ] Furn. $	[ ] Unf. [ ] Furn. $
Approximate GBA				
Data source				
# Units/Tot. rms./BR/BA				
Approximate year built				
Approx. days on market				

Comparison of listings to subject property: _____

Reconciliation: Description and analysis of the general market conditions that affect 2-4 family properties in the subject neighborhood (including the above neighborhood indicators of growth rate, property values, demand/supply, and marketing time) and the prevalence and impact in the subject market area regarding loan discounts, interest buydowns, and concessions; and identification of trends in listing prices, average days on market and any change over past year, etc.:_____

Site

Dimensions _____		Topography _____
Site area _____ Corner lot [ ] No [ ] Yes		Size _____
Specific zoning classification and description _____		Shape _____
Zoning compliance [ ] Legal [ ] Legal nonconforming (Grandfathered use) [ ] Illegal [ ] No zoning		Drainage _____
Highest & best use as improved: [ ] Present use [ ] Other use (explain)_____		View _____
		Landscaping _____

Utilities	Public	Other	Off-site Improvements	Type	Public	Private	Driveway _____
Electricity			Street				Apparent easements _____
Gas			Curb/gutter				
Water			Sidewalk				FEMA Special flood hazard area [ ] Yes* [ ] No
Sanitary sewer			Street lights				*FEMA Zone/Map Date_____
Storm sewer			Alley				*FEMA Map No.

Comments (apparent adverse easements, encroachments, special assessments, slide areas, illegal or legal nonconforming zoning, use, etc.): _____

Exhibit 60 (continued)

[X]

PROPERTY DESCRIPTION & ANALYSIS, continued   **SMALL RESIDENTIAL INCOME PROPERTY APPRAISAL REPORT**

Description of Improvements

General description	Exterior description	(Materials/condition)	Foundation		Insulation	(R value if known)
Units/bldgs. _____ / _____	Foundation		Slab		[ ] Roof	
Stories	Exterior walls		Crawl space		[ ] Ceiling	
Type (det./att.)	Roof surface		Sump Pump		[ ] Walls	
Design (style)	Gutters & dwnspts.		Dampness		[ ] Floor	
Existing/proposed	Window type		Settlement		[ ] None	
Under construction	Storm sash/Screens		Infestation		Adequacy	
Year Built	Manufactured housing* [ ] Yes [ ] No		Basement _____ % of 1st floor area		Energy efficient items:	
Effective age (yrs.)	*(Complies with the HUD Manufactured Housing Construction and Safety Standards.)		Basement finish			

Units	Level(s)	Foyer	Living	Dining	Kitchen	Den	Family rm.	# Bedrooms	# Baths	Laundry	Other	Sq. ft./unit	Total (☑)

Improvements contain: _____ Rooms; _____ Bedroom(s); _____ Bath(s); _____ Square feet of GROSS BUILDING AREA

GROSS BUILDING AREA (GBA) IS DEFINED AS THE TOTAL FINISHED AREA (INCLUDING COMMON AREAS) OF THE IMPROVEMENTS BASED UPON EXTERIOR MEASUREMENTS.

Surfaces	(Materials/condition)	Heating		Kitchen equip. (#/unit-cond.)	Attic		Improvement analysis	Good	Avg.	Fair	Poor
Floors		Type		Refrigerator	[ ] None		Quality of construction	[ ]	[ ]	[ ]	[ ]
Walls		Fuel		Range/oven	[ ] Stairs		Condition of improvements	[ ]	[ ]	[ ]	[ ]
Trim/finish		Condition		Disposal	[ ] Drop stair		Room sizes/layout	[ ]	[ ]	[ ]	[ ]
Bath floor		Adequacy		Dishwasher	[ ] Scuttle		Closets and storage	[ ]	[ ]	[ ]	[ ]
Bath wainscot		**Cooling**		Fan/hood	[ ] Floor		Energy efficiency	[ ]	[ ]	[ ]	[ ]
Doors		Central		Compactor	[ ] Heated		Plumbing—adequacy & condition	[ ]	[ ]	[ ]	[ ]
		Other		Washer/dryer	[ ] Finished		Electrical—adequacy & condition	[ ]	[ ]	[ ]	[ ]
		Condition		Microwave	[ ] Unfinished		Kitchen cabinets—adequacy & cond.	[ ]	[ ]	[ ]	[ ]
Fireplace(s)	#	Adequacy		Intercom			Compatibility to neighborhood	[ ]	[ ]	[ ]	[ ]
Car storage:	[ ] Garage	[ ] Attached	[ ] Adequate	[ ] None			Appeal & marketability	[ ]	[ ]	[ ]	[ ]
No. cars:	[ ] Carport	[ ] Detached	[ ] Inadequate	[ ] Offstreet			Estimated remaining economic life				years

Comments on repairs needed, additional features, modernization, etc.: _____

Additional comments on neighborhood, site and description of improvements

Depreciation (physical, functional, and external inadequacies, etc.): _____

Environmental conditions observed by or known to the appraiser: _____

VALUATION ANALYSIS
Purpose of Appraisal is to estimate Market Value as defined in the Certification & Statement of Limiting Conditions.

Cost approach

Comments on cost approach, accrued depreciation, and estimated site value:

ESTIMATED REPRODUCTION COST—NEW—OF IMPROVEMENTS:
_____ Sq. Ft.@ $ _____ = $ _____
_____ Sq. Ft.@ $ _____ = _____
_____ Sq. Ft.@ $ _____ = _____
_____ Sq. Ft.@ $ _____ = _____
Extras _____ = _____
_____ = _____
_____ = _____
Special Energy Efficient Items _____ = _____
Porches, Patios, etc. _____ = _____
Total Estimated Cost New .... = $ _____

	Physical	Functional	External
Less			

Depreciation _____ = $ _____
Depreciated Value of Improvements .... = $ _____
Site Imp. "as is" (driveway, landscaping, etc.) ..... = $ _____
ESTIMATED SITE VALUE .... = $ _____
(If leasehold, show only leasehold value.)

INDICATED VALUE BY COST APPROACH .... = $ _____

Freddie Mac Form 72 10/89 2-4 units 10CH.   PAGE 2 OF 4   Fannie Mae Form 1025 2-4 units 10/89

Exhibit 60 (continued)

[X]

VALUATION ANALYSIS, continued   **SMALL RESIDENTIAL INCOME PROPERTY APPRAISAL REPORT**

Comparable rental data

At least three rental comparables should be reported and analyzed in this section. The rental comparables should represent the most current rental information on properties as similar and proximate to the subject property as possible. (This comparison is based on current rental data, therefore, the rental comparables typically are not the same comparables used in the sales comparison analysis.) The appraisal report should assure the reader that the units and properties selected as comparables are comparable to the subject property (both the units and the overall property) and accurately represent the rental market for the subject property (unless otherwise stated within the report).

ITEM	SUBJECT	COMPARABLE RENTAL NO. 1	COMPARABLE RENTAL NO. 2	COMPARABLE RENTAL NO. 3
Address				
Proximity to subject				
Lease dates (if available)				
Rent survey date				
Data source				
Rent concessions				

Description of property—units, design, appeal, age, vacancies, and conditions	No. Units No. Vac. Yr. Blt.:	No. Units No. Vac. Yr. Blt.:	No. Units No. Vac. Yr. Blt.:	No. Units No. Vac. Yr. Blt.:

	Rm. Count Tot / Br / Ba	Size Sq. Ft.	Rm. Count Tot / Br / Ba	Size Sq. Ft.	Total Monthly Rent	Rm. Count Tot / Br / Ba	Size Sq. Ft.	Total Monthly Rent	Rm. Count Tot / Br / Ba	Size Sq. Ft.	Total Monthly Rent
Individual unit breakdown					$			$			$

Utilities, furniture, and amenities included in rent				

Functional utility, basement, heating/cooling, project amenities, etc.				

Reconciliation of rental data and support for estimated market rents for the individual subject units (including the adjustments used, the adequacy of comparables, rental concessions, etc.) _____

Subject's rent schedule   The rent schedule reconciles the applicable indicated monthly market rents to the appropriate subject unit, and provides the estimated rents for the subject property. The appraiser must review the rent characteristics of the comparable sales to determine whether estimated rents should reflect actual or market rents. For example, if actual rents were available on the sales comparables and used to derive the gross rent multiplier (GRM), actual rents for the subject should be used. If market rents were used to construct the comparables' rents and derive the GRM, market rents should be used. The total gross estimated rent must represent rent characteristics consistent with the sales comparison data used to derive the GRM. The total gross estimated rent is not adjusted for vacancy.

Unit	Lease Date		No. Units Vacant	ACTUAL RENTS			ESTIMATED RENTS		
	Begin	End		Per Unit Unfurnished	Furnished	Total Rents	Per Unit Unfurnished	Furnished	Total Rents
				$	$	$	$	$	$
						$			$

Other monthly income (itemize) _____ $ _____
Vacancy: Actual last year _____ % Previous year _____ % Estimated: _____ % $ _____ Annually   **Total gross estimated rent** $ _____
Utilities included in estimated rents: [ ] Electric [ ] Water [ ] Sewer [ ] Gas [ ] Oil [ ] Trash collection

Comments on the rent schedule, actual rents, estimated rents (especially regarding differences between actual and estimated rents), utilities, etc.: _____

Exhibit 60 (continued)

[X]

VALUATION ANALYSIS, continued   **SMALL RESIDENTIAL INCOME PROPERTY APPRAISAL REPORT**

Sales comparison analysis

The undersigned has recited three recent sales of properties most similar and proximate to the subject property and has described and analyzed these in this analysis. If there is a significant variation between the subject and comparable properties, the analysis includes a dollar adjustment reflecting the market reaction to those items or an explanation supported by the market data. If a significant item in the comparable property is superior to, or more favorable than, the subject property, a minus (−) adjustment is made, thus reducing the indicated value of subject; if a significant item in the comparable is inferior to, or less favorable than, the subject property, a plus (+) adjustment is made, thus increasing the indicated value of the subject. [(1) **Sales Price ÷ Gross Monthly Rent**]

ITEM	SUBJECT	COMPARABLE SALE NO. 1	COMPARABLE SALE NO. 2	COMPARABLE SALE NO. 3
Address				
Proximity to subject				
Sales Price	$	☐ Unf. ☐ Furn. $	☐ Unf. ☐ Furn. $	☐ Unf. ☐ Furn. $
Sales price per GBA	$	$	$	$
Gross monthly rent	$	$	$	$
Gross mo. rent mult. (1)				
Sales price per unit	$	$	$	$
Sales price per room	$	$	$	$
Data source				

ADJUSTMENTS	DESCRIPTION	DESCRIPTION	+ (−) $ Adjustment	DESCRIPTION	+ (−) $ Adjustment	DESCRIPTION	+ (−) $ Adjustment
Sales or financing concessions							
Date of sale/time							
Location							
Site/view							
Design and appeal							
Quality of construction							
Year built							
Condition							
Gross Building Area	Sq. ft.	Sq. ft.		Sq. ft.		Sq. ft.	
Unit breakdown	No. of units / Rm. count Tot·Br·Ba / No. Vac.	No. of units / Rm. count Tot·Br·Ba / No. Vac.		No. of units / Rm. count Tot·Br·Ba / No. Vac.		No. of units / Rm. count Tot·Br·Ba / No. Vac.	
Basement description							
Functional utility							
Heating/cooling							
Parking on/off site							
Project amenities and fee (if applicable)							
Other							
Net Adj. (total)		☐ + ☐ − $		☐ + ☐ − $		☐ + ☐ − $	
Adj. sales price of comparables		$		$		$	

Comments on sales comparison (including reconciliation of all indicators of value as to consistency and relative strength and evaluation of the typical investors'/purchasers' motivation in that market):

INDICATED VALUE BY SALES COMPARISON APPROACH $

Analysis of any current agreement of sale, option, or listing of the subject property and analysis of any prior sales of subject and comparables within one year of the date of appraisal:

Income Approach

Total gross monthly estimated rent $ _____ x gross rent multiplier (GRM) _____ = $ _____ INDICATED VALUE BY INCOME APPROACH

Comments on income approach (including expense ratios, if available, and reconciliation of the GRM)

Reconciliation

INDICATED VALUE BY SALES COMPARISON APPROACH .... $ _____

INDICATED VALUE BY INCOME APPROACH .... $ _____

INDICATED VALUE BY COST APPROACH .... $ _____

This appraisal is made ☐ "as is" ☐ subject to the repairs, alterations, inspections or conditions listed below ☐ subject to completion per plans and specifications.

Comments and conditions of appraisal: _____

Final reconciliation: _____

This appraisal is based upon the above conditions and the certification, contingent and limiting conditions, and Market Value definition that are stated in

Freddie Mac Form 439/Fannie Mae Form 1004B (Rev. _____) ☐ attached or ☐ filed with client on _____ or ☐ other attached.

I (WE) ESTIMATE THE MARKET VALUE, AS DEFINED, OF THE SUBJECT PROPERTY AS OF _____ to be $ _____

I (We) certify that to the best of my (our) knowledge and belief the facts and data used herein are true and correct; that I (we) personally inspected the subject property, both inside and out, and have personally made an exterior inspection of all comparables cited in this report; and that I (we) have no undisclosed interest, present or prospective therein.

APPRAISER(S)	REVIEW APPRAISER (if applicable)	
SIGNATURE	SIGNATURE	☐ Did ☐ Did not
NAME	NAME	inspect property

Freddie Mac Form 72 10/89 2-4 units 10CH.   PAGE 4 OF 4   Fannie Mae Form 1025 2-4 units 10/89

Exhibit 61

APPRAISAL REPORT – INDIVIDUAL ☐ CONDOMINIUM OR ☐ PUD UNIT   File No.

To be completed by Lender

Borrower _____ Census Tract _____ Map Reference _____
Unit No. _____ Address _____ Project Name/Phase No. _____
City _____ County _____ State _____ Zip Code _____
Actual Real Estate Taxes $ _____ (yr.) Sales Price $ _____ Property Rights Appraised ☐ Fee ☐ Leasehold
Loan Charges to be Paid by Seller $ _____ Other Sales Concessions _____
Lender/Client _____ Lender's Address _____
Occupant _____ Appraiser _____ Instructions to Appraiser _____
                              ☐ FNMA 1073A required   ☐ FHLMC 465 Addendum A required   ☐ FHLMC 465 Addendum B required

NEIGHBORHOOD

				NEIGHBORHOOD RATING	Good Avg. Fair Poor
Location	☐ Urban	☐ Suburban	☐ Rural		
Built Up	☐ Over 75%	☐ 25% to 75%	☐ Under 25%	Adequacy of Shopping	☐ ☐ ☐ ☐
Growth Rate ☐ Fully Developed	☐ Rapid	☐ Steady	☐ Slow	Employment Opportunities	☐ ☐ ☐ ☐
Property Values	☐ Increasing	☐ Stable	☐ Declining	Recreational Facilities	☐ ☐ ☐ ☐
Demand/Supply	☐ Shortage	☐ In Balance	☐ Oversupply	Adequacy of Utilities	☐ ☐ ☐ ☐
Marketing Time	☐ Under 3 Mos.	☐ 4-6 Mos.	☐ Over 6 Mos.	Property Compatibility	☐ ☐ ☐ ☐

Present Land Use _____ % 1 Family _____ % 2 - 4 Family _____ % Apts. _____ % Condo   Protection from Detrimental Cond.
            _____ % Commercial _____ % Industrial _____ % Vacant   Police and Fire Protection
Change in Present Land Use ☐ Not Likely ☐ Likely* ☐ Taking Place*   General Appearance of Properties
            *From _____ To _____   Appeal to Market

Predominant Occupancy	☐ Owner	☐ Tenant	_____ % Vacant		Distance	Access or Convenience
Condominium Price Range $ _____ to $ _____ Predominant $ _____				Public Transportation		
Age _____ yrs. to _____ yrs. Predominant _____ yrs.				Employment Centers		
Single Family Price Range $ _____ to $ _____ Predominant $ _____				Neighborhood Shopping		
Age _____ yrs. to _____ yrs. Predominant $ _____ yrs.				Grammar Schools		
Describe potential for additional Condo/PUD units in nearby area				Freeway Access		

Note: FHLMC/FNMA do not consider race or the racial composition of the neighborhood to be reliable appraisal factors.
Describe those factors, favorable or unfavorable, affecting marketability (e.g. public parks, schools, noise, view, mkt. area population size & financial ability)

SITE

Lot Dimensions (if PUD) _____ Sq. Ft.   ☐ Corner Lot Project Density When Completed as Planned _____ Units/Acre
Zoning Classification _____   Present Improvements ☐ do ☐ do not conform to zoning regulations
Highest and Best Use ☐ Present Use ☐ Other (specify) _____

		OFF SITE IMPROVEMENTS	
	Public Other (describe)		Project Ingress/Egress (adequacy) _____
Elec.		Street Access ☐ Public ☐ Private	Topo _____
Gas		Surface _____	Size/Shape _____
Water		Maintenance ☐ Public ☐ Private	View Amenity _____
San. Sew.		☐ Storm Sewer ☐ Curb/Gutter	Drainage/Flood Conditions _____
	☐ Underground Elec. & Tel.	☐ Sidewalk ☐ Street Lights	Is property located in a HUD Identified Special Flood Hazard Area? ☐ No ☐ Yes

COMMENTS (including any easements, encroachments or adverse conditions) _____

PROJECT IMPROVEMENTS

Existing Approx. Year Built 19_____ Original Use _____

TYPE	☐ Condo ☐ PUD	☐ Converted (19_____)	PROJECT RATING	Good Avg. Fair Poor
PROJECT	☐ Proposed	☐ Under Construction	Location	☐ ☐ ☐ ☐
	☐ Elevator	☐ Walk-up No. of Stories _____	General Appearance	☐ ☐ ☐ ☐
	☐ Row or Town House	☐ Other (specify) _____	Amenities & Recreational Facilities	☐ ☐ ☐ ☐
	☐ Primary Residence	☐ Second Home or Recreational	Density (units per acre)	☐ ☐ ☐ ☐

If Completed   No. Phases _____ No. Units _____ No. Sold _____   Unit Mix _____ ... ☐ ☐ ☐ ☐
If Incomplete Planned No. Phases _____ No. Units _____ No. Sold _____   Quality of Constr. (mat'l. & finish) ☐ ☐ ☐ ☐
Units in Subject Phase: Total _____ Completed _____ Sold _____ Rented _____   Condition of Exterior ☐ ☐ ☐ ☐
Approx. No. Units for Sale: Subject Project _____ Subject Phase _____   Condition of Interior ☐ ☐ ☐ ☐
Exterior Wall _____ Roof Covering _____ Security Features _____   Appeal to Market ☐ ☐ ☐ ☐
Elevator: No. _____ Adequacy & Condition _____ Soundproofing: Vertical _____ Horizontal _____
Parking: Total No. Spaces _____ Ratio _____ Spaces/Unit _____ Type _____ No. Spaces for Guest Parking _____
Describe common elements or recreational facilities _____
Are any common elements, rec. facilities or parking leased to Owners Assoc.? _____   If yes, attach addendum describing rental terms and options

SUBJECT UNIT

☐ Existing ☐ Proposed ☐ Under Constr. Floor No. _____ Unit Livable Area _____   ☐ Basement _____ % Finished _____
Parking for Unit: No. _____ Type _____ ☐ Assigned ☐ Owned   Convenience to Unit _____

Room List	Foyer	Liv	Din	Kit	Bdrm	Bath	Fam	Rec	Lndry	Other		UNIT RATING	Good Avg. Fair Poor
Basement												Condition of Improvements	☐ ☐ ☐ ☐
1st Level												Room Sizes and Layout	☐ ☐ ☐ ☐
2nd Level												Adequacy of Closets and Storage	☐ ☐ ☐ ☐

			Kit. Equip., Cabinets & Workspace	☐ ☐ ☐ ☐
Floors	☐ Hardwood	☐ Carpet over _____ ☐	Plumbing Adequacy and Condition	☐ ☐ ☐ ☐
Int. Walls	☐ Drywall	☐ Plaster	Electrical Adequacy and Condition	☐ ☐ ☐ ☐
Trim/Finish	☐ Good	☐ Average ☐ Fair ☐ Poor	Adequacy of Soundproofing	☐ ☐ ☐ ☐
Bath Floor	☐ Ceramic	☐ _____ Wainscot: ☐ Ceramic ☐	Adequacy of Insulation	☐ ☐ ☐ ☐
Windows (type):		☐ Storm Sash ☐ Screens ☐ Combo	Location within Project or View	☐ ☐ ☐ ☐
Kitchen Equip: ☐ Refrig.	☐ Range/Oven ☐ Fan/Hood ☐ Washer ☐ Dryer		Overall Livability	☐ ☐ ☐ ☐
☐ Intercom ☐ Disposal	☐ Dishwasher ☐ Microwave ☐ Compactor		Appeal and Marketability	☐ ☐ ☐ ☐

HEAT: Type _____ Fuel _____ Cond. _____   Est. Effective Age _____ to _____ yrs.
AIR COND. ☐ Central ☐ Other _____ ☐ Adequate ☐ Inadequate   Est. Remaining Economic Life _____ to _____ yrs.
☐ Earth Sheltered Housing Design ☐ Solar Design/Landscape   ☐ Solar Space Heat/Air Cond. ☐ Solar Hot Water
☐ Flue Damper ☐ Elec./Mech. Gas Furn. Ignition   ☐ Auto Setback Thermostat ☐ Dble./Triple Glazed Windows ☐ Caulk/Weatherstrip
INSULATION (stateR Factor if known) ☐ Walls _____ ☐ Ceiling _____ ☐ Floor _____ ☐ Roof/Attic _____ ☐ Water Heater
If rehab proposed, do plans and specs provide for adequate energy conservation? _____ If no, attach description of modification needed.
ENERGY EFFICIENCY APPEARS: ☐ High ☐ Adequate ☐ Low   Energy Audit ☐ Yes (attach, if available) ☐ No
COMMENTS (special features, functional or physical inadequacies, modernization or repairs needed, etc.) _____

FHLMC Form 465 9/80   ATTACH DESCRIPTIVE PHOTOGRAPHS OF SUBJECT PROPERTY AND STREET SCENE   FNMA Form 1073 9/80
17 (6/04)   VMP MORTGAGE FORMS • (313)293-8100 • (800)521-7291

Exhibit 61 (continued)

BUDGET ANALYSIS

Unit Charge $_____ /Mo. x 12 = $_____ /yr. ($_____ /Sq. Ft./year of livable area). Ground Rent (if any) $_____ /yr.

Utilities included in unit charge: ☐ None ☐ Heat ☐ Air Cond. ☐ Electricity ☐ Gas ☐ Water ☐ Sewer

Note any fees, other than regular Condo/PUD charges, for use of facilities_____

To properly maintain the project and provide the services anticipated, the budget appears: ☐ High ☐ Adequate ☐ Inadequate

Compared to other competitive projects of similar quality and design subject unit charge appears: ☐ High ☐ Reasonable ☐ Low

Management Group: ☐ Owners Association ☐ Developer ☐ Management Agent (identify)_____

Quality of Management and its enforcement of Rules and Regulations appears: ☐ Superior ☐ Good ☐ Adequate ☐ Inadequate

Special or unusual characteristics in the Condo/PUD Documents or otherwise known to the appraiser, that would affect marketability (if none, so state)

Comments

NOTE: FHLMC does not require the cost approach in the appraisal of condominium or PUD units.

COST APPROACH

Cost Approach (to be used only for detached, semi-detached, and town house units):

Reproduction Cost New_____ Sq. Ft. @ $_____ per Sq. Ft. = _____ $_____

Less Depreciation: Physical $_____ Functional $_____ Economic $_____ (_____)

Depreciated Value of Improvements: _____

Add Land Value (if leasehold, show only leasehold value- attach calculations) _____

Pro-rata Share of Value of Amenities _____ $_____

Total Indicated Value: ☐ FEE SIMPLE ☐ LEASEHOLD _____ $_____

Comments regarding estimate of depreciation and value of land and amenity package

MARKET DATA ANALYSIS

The appraiser, whenever possible, should analyze two comparable sales from within the subject project. However, when appraising a unit in a new or newly converted project, at least two comparables should be selected from outside the subject project. In the following analysis, the comparable should always be adjusted to the subject unit and not vice versa. If a significant feature of the comparable is superior to the subject unit, a minus ( ) adjustment should be made to the comparable, if such a feature of the comparable is inferior to the subject, a plus (+) adjustment should be made to the comparable.

LIST ONLY THOSE ITEMS THAT REQUIRE ADJUSTMENT

ITEM	SUBJECT PROPERTY	COMPARABLE NO. 1		COMPARABLE NO. 2		COMPARABLE NO. 3	
Address Unit No. Project Name							
Proximity to Subj.							
Sales Price	$		$		$		$
Price/Living Area	$		$		$		$
Data Source							
Date of Sale and Time Adjustment	DESCRIPTION	DESCRIPTION	+ (-) $ Adjustment	DESCRIPTION	+ (-) $ Adjustment	DESCRIPTION	+ (-) $ Adjustment
Location							
Site/View							
Design and Appeal							
Quality of Constr.							
Age							
Condition							
Living Area, Room Count and Total	Total B-rms Baths	Total B-rms Baths		Total B-rms Baths		Total B-rms Baths	
Gross Living Area	Sq. ft.	Sq. ft.		Sq. ft.		Sq. ft.	
Basement & Bsmt. Finished Rooms							
Functional Utility							
Air Conditioning							
Storage							
Parking Facilities							
Common Elements and Recreation Facilities							
Mo. Assessment							
Leasehold/Fee							
Special Energy Efficient Items							
Other (e.g. fire-places, kitchen equip., remodeling)							
Sales or Financing Concessions							
Net Adj. (total)		☐ Plus ☐ Minus $		☐ Plus ☐ Minus $		☐ Plus ☐ Minus $	
Indicated Value of Subject		$		$		$	

Comments on Market Data Analysis

INDICATED VALUE BY MARKET DATA APPROACH .... $_____

INDICATED VALUE BY INCOME APPROACH (If applicable) Economic Market Rent $_____ /Mo. x Gross Rent Multiplier_____ = $_____

This appraisal is made ☐ "as is". ☐ subject to the repairs, alterations, or conditions listed below. ☐ subject to completion per plans and specifications.

Comments and Conditions of Appraisal_____

Final Reconciliation_____

Construction Warranty ☐ Yes ☐ No Name of Warranty Program_____ Warranty Coverage Expires_____

This appraisal is based upon the above requirements, the certification, contingent and limiting conditions, and Market Value definition that are stated in

☐ FHLMC Form 439 (Rev. 10/78)/FNMA Form 1004B (Rev. 10/78) filed with client_____, 19____ ☐ attached

I ESTIMATE THE MARKET VALUE, AS DEFINED, OF SUBJECT PROPERTY AS OF_____, 19____ to be $_____

Appraiser(s)_____ Review Appraiser (if applicable)_____

Date Report Signed_____, 19____ ☐ Did ☐ Did Not Physically Inspect Property

FHLMC Form 465 9/80   REVERSE   FNMA Form 1073 9/80

Lenders will use forms like those in Exhibits 62-65.

For second mortgages, lenders may want to use the form shown in Exhibit 66.

See APPRAISAL REPORT.

RESIDENTIAL HOUSING STARTS Housing starts are watched closely by investors since changes in the business cycle is predicted by the increase or decrease of residential construction reports issued by the Federal Reserve Board in the second or third week of the month. The Federal Reserve System and the Department of Commerce remain active in the nation's housing starts.

RESIDENTIAL MEMBER (RM) A designation formerly given to an appraiser who was a member of the American Institute of Real Estate Appraisers.

See APPRAISAL INSTITUTE.

RESIDUAL (1) the remaining income after deducting fixed obligations (see INCOME ANALYSIS); (2) the value of property that is left after its economic life is finished; (3) in the income approach to value, it is the value given to the land; (4) commissions earned but deferred to a later date.

RESIDUAL CLASS OF MORTGAGE-BACKED SECURITIES (MBSR)
The residual class of an MBS is the last class to be paid as a residual piece of a CMO. Residuals can be created from excess debt service and expenses of CMOs which can be combined with stripped MBSs for hedging on interest rates, thereby leveling out prepayments. This last tranche should be attractive to insurance companies or savings and loan companies that excel in the marketplace as keen observers of prepayments where interest rates increase or decrease by 300 basis points. It is most valuable at high rates when few prepayments exist.

RESOLUTION TRUST CORPORATION (RTC) The Resolution Trust Corporation (RTC) and the Oversight Board of the Resolution Trust Corporation (Oversight Board) were established as instrumentalities of the United States on August 9, 1989, by the enactment of Section 21A of the Federal Home Loan Bank Act (12 U.S.C. 1441a) as added thereto by Section 501(a) of the Financial Institutions Reform, Recovery, and Enforcement Act of 1989 (FIRREA) (Pub. L. No. 101-73, Section 501(a), 103 Stat. 183, 363-393). Throughout this definition, all references to Section 21A are to Section 21A of the Federal Home Loan Bank Act as amended by Section 501(a) of FIRREA.

The mission of the RTC is to carry out a program, under the general oversight of the Oversight Board, to manage and resolve institutions that come under its jurisdiction and to dispose of any residual assets in a manner that

- maximizes return and minimizes loss;

Exhibit 62

RESIDENTIAL APPRAISAL REVIEW FORM

Lending Institution _____
Lender's Address _____
Name of Borrower _____
Property Address _____
Loan Number _____
Appraised Value $ _____ Date _____
Lender's Appraiser _____ Phone _____
Appraiser's Address _____
Review Appraiser _____ Phone _____
Reviewer's Address _____

FORMAT AND PRESENTATION

	Yes	No	N/A
1. Is the Appraisal format in conformance with company appraisal requirements?	☐	☐	☐

LENDER SECTION

	Yes	No	N/A
2. Is the lender section of the report complete and accurate?	☐	☐	☐

NEIGHBORHOOD SECTION

	Yes	No	N/A
3. Does the neighborhood section provide the reviewer an adequate understanding with respect to locational factors, growth rate and economic trends, property values, housing supply, marketing time, land use, price ranges, convenience to employment and amenities, adequacy of utilities and recreational facilities, property compatibility, appearance of properties, detrimental conditions and marketability?	☐	☐	☐
4. Does the appraisal report enable the reviewer to spot healthy growth patterns or trends that may indicate a deteriorating neighborhood with limited market appeal?	☐	☐	☐

	Yes	No	N/A
5. Are comments in the neighborhood section relevant and do they give insight into those conditions which positively or negatively affect the appraised properties value and marketability?	☐	☐	☐
6. Have all fair and poor ratings in the neighborhood section been explained?	☐	☐	☐
7. If marketing time is over six months, has the appraiser commented on the reasons for slow market conditions in the subject area?	☐	☐	☐
8. If the market is slow, has the appraiser indicated whether or not this has resulted in a decline in values?	☐	☐	☐
9. Is the neighborhood section of the report completed and accurate?	☐	☐	☐

Reviewer's Comments _____

SITE SECTION

	Yes	No	N/A
10. Has the appraiser commented on unfavorable site factors?	☐	☐	☐
11. Does the appraiser indicate whether or not the subject property meets all the criteria for a desirable lot in the area?	☐	☐	☐
12. Has the appraiser addressed and commented on problems relating to poor drainage, flood conditions, adverse easements, encroachments or other detrimental factors?	☐	☐	☐

	Yes	No	N/A
13. Does the appraiser indicate the subject's zoning and whether or not the subject conforms with present zoning requirements?	☐	☐	☐
14. Has the appraiser accurately indicated the dimensions and size of the subject lot?	☐	☐	☐
15. Does the appraisal report reveal whether or not site improvements and services to the site are adequate and acceptable in the market place?	☐	☐	☐
16. Is the site section of the appraisal report complete and accurate?	☐	☐	☐

Reviewer's Comments _____

IMPROVEMENTS SECTION

	Yes	No	N/A
17. If the subject property is a condominium, are the project improvements and project rating sections complete and accurate?	☐	☐	☐
18. Did the appraiser comment on physical and functional inadequacies and indicate whether or not repairs and modernization are needed?	☐	☐	☐
19. Has the appraiser explained fair or poor improvement ratings?	☐	☐	☐
20. Does the appraiser indicate whether or not factors receiving poor or fair ratings, adversely affect the property's marketability?	☐	☐	☐
21. Have factor's relating to age, condition, quality or construction, finish and equipment, as well as size and utility been properly handled?	☐	☐	☐
22. Has the appraiser given serious attention to structural problems?	☐	☐	☐
23. Did the appraiser comment on unusual layouts, peculiar floor plans, inadequate equipment and amenities?	☐	☐	☐
24. Has the appraiser indicated whether or not factors relating to			

	Yes	No	N/A
unusual layouts, peculiar floor plans, inadequate equipment and amenities affect the value and market appeal of the subject?	☐	☐	☐
25. If there is evidence of dampness, termites or settlement, did the appraiser comment on these factors?	☐	☐	☐
26. Has the appraiser provided the reviewer with a clear and accurate understanding of the physical and functioning attributes of the subject property?	☐	☐	☐
27. Is the property rating section accurate as well as consistent with other data contained in the report?	☐	☐	☐
28. Has the appraiser presented information on construction features in a manner that gives an accurate and adequate view of the subject property?	☐	☐	☐
29. Has information relating to the improvements been well handled?	☐	☐	☐
30. In the reviewer's opinion, is the descriptive section of the appraisal report (page one) acceptable?	☐	☐	☐
31. Has appraiser required all needed repairs?	☐	☐	☐
32. Is the improvement section of the report complete and accurate?	☐	☐	☐

Reviewer's Comments _____

COST SECTION

	Yes	No	N/A
33. Are the appraiser's measurements for gross living area correct?	☐	☐	☐
34. Has the appraiser commented on functional and economic obsolescence?	☐	☐	☐
35. In estimating reproduction costs, has the appraiser used cost figures that are appropriate for the local market?	☐	☐	☐

	Yes	No	N/A
36. Do figures for physical, functional and economic depreciation appear reasonable in light of the subject's age, condition, state of modernization, size, utility, and location?	☐	☐	☐
37. Is the estimate of land value appropriate?	☐	☐	☐
38. Are the appraiser's mathematical calculations accurate?	☐	☐	☐
39. Is the budget analysis section accurate and complete (if condo)?	☐	☐	☐
40. Is the cost section complete and accurate?	☐	☐	☐

Reviewer's Comments _____

Review Form No. 2002
Revised 1/88

VMP - 22G (8812)

VMP MORTGAGE FORMS • (313)293-8100 • (800)521-7291

Exhibit 62 (continued)

MARKET ANALYSIS SECTION

Yes No N/A

41. Has the appraiser selected his or her comparables from the subject neighborhood? ☐ ☐ ☐

42. If not, has the appraiser explained why comparables were selected from a different neighborhood? ☐ ☐ ☐

43. In your opinion, are the comparables really similar with respect to location, site, design and style, quality and amenities, as well as size and utility? ☐ ☐ ☐

If no, Comp. # _____ needs to be replaced.

44. Are all of the comparables recent sales of similar properties from the subject neighborhood? ☐ ☐ ☐

45. If the comparables are over three months old, has the appraiser explained why he or she failed to use recent sales? ☐ ☐ ☐

46. Are room counts and square foot areas of the subject and comparables similar? ☐ ☐ ☐

47. Do the sale prices of the comparables correlate and indicate comparability? ☐ ☐ ☐

48. Do the prices per square foot of the comparables correlate and indicate comparability? ☐ ☐ ☐

49. Has the appraiser bracketed his or her sales data (before making adjustments?) ☐ ☐ ☐

50. Do time adjustments, for date of sale, appear reasonable in light of market trends and current market conditions? ☐ ☐ ☐

51. Has the appraiser avoided numerous adjustments? ☐ ☐ ☐

52. Has the appraiser adjusted all three comparables in a reasonable and consistent manner? ☐ ☐ ☐

53. Are total gross adjustments exceeding 25% of the comparable's sales price and individual line adjustments exceeding 10% of the comparable's sales price adequately explained and justified? ☐ ☐ ☐

54. Are the appraiser's mathematical calculations accurate? ☐ ☐ ☐

55. Is there a convincing value range with respect to the three adjusted comparables — In brief, are the adjusted value conclusions reasonably similar? ☐ ☐ ☐

Reviewer's Comments _____

Yes No N/A

56. Does the appraiser's final value conclusion relate for the adjusted comparables? ☐ ☐ ☐

57. Has the appraiser selected good market data and handled it well? ☐ ☐ ☐

58. Has the appraiser commented on the subject's marketability? ☐ ☐ ☐

59. Does the appraiser's marketability information appear to be accurate? ☐ ☐ ☐

60. Has the appraiser avoided the appearance of backing into any or all of the approaches to value? ☐ ☐ ☐

61. Is there clarity with respect to the appraiser's reasoning? ☐ ☐ ☐

62. Can you read the appraisal report, step by step, and arrive at the same conclusion of value as the appraiser? ☐ ☐ ☐

63. Does the appraiser appear to be an individual offering an independent and impartial third party opinion of value rather than an advocate? ☐ ☐ ☐

64. Are all the required photographs attached and do they adequately show the subject and surrounding properties? ☐ ☐ ☐

65. Is other needed illustrative material attached and properly completed? ☐ ☐ ☐

66. If the appraiser is using computer generated data, are the facts and comments in the report accurate and applicable to the subject and comparable properties? ☐ ☐ ☐

67. Does it appear that the appraiser has clearly thought through this process rather than using a computer as a substitute? ☐ ☐ ☐

68. Has the appraiser identified which comparable(s) are the most relevant? ☐ ☐ ☐

69. Is the market analysis section complete and accurate? ☐ ☐ ☐

INCOME APPROACH SECTION

Yes No N/A

70. Has the income approach been completed? ☐ ☐ ☐

71. Has supporting data been submitted? ☐ ☐ ☐

Yes No N/A

72. Is supporting data valid and correctly analyzed? ☐ ☐ ☐

Reviewer's Comments _____

RECONCILIATION SECTION

Yes No N/A

73. In your opinion, has the appraiser proven his or her case? ☐ ☐ ☐

74. Do you concur with the value conclusion of the appraiser, based upon data contained within the report? ☐ ☐ ☐

75. Are the appraiser's comments and final reconciliation of value adequate and does the appraisal give insight into the value and marketability of the subject property? ☐ ☐ ☐

Yes No N/A

76. Is it clear which approach to value was given the most weight in the final estimate of value? ☐ ☐ ☐

77. Is the final estimate of value weighted by the most appropriate approach to value? ☐ ☐ ☐

78. Is the appraiser's value conclusion reasonable? ☐ ☐ ☐

79. Has the appraiser signed the report and typed his or her name under the signature? ☐ ☐ ☐

80. Is there a phone number on the report and/or cover letter which would enable the reviewer to contact the appraiser and clarify a questionable appraisal report? ☐ ☐ ☐

Reviewer's Comments _____

REVIEWER'S SUMMARY

Appraisal report was: Good ☐   Fair ☐   Poor ☐

Recommendation:

☐ Accept as is

☐ Have another appraisal prepared by someone else

☐ Accept when revised-See Items # _____

☐ Other

Comments: _____

Field Review was made   ☐ Yes   ☐ No

Sales price $ _____   Appraisers Value $ _____   Reviewers Recommendation $ _____

Reviewer's Signature _____   Title _____   Date of Review _____

Reviewer's Signature _____   Title _____   Date of Review _____

See Attached ☐

Review Form No. 2002
Revised 1/88

Exhibit 63

RESIDENTIAL APPRAISAL REVIEW SHORT FORM

Lending Institution _____
Lender's Address _____

Name of Borrower _____
Property Address _____

Loan Number _____
Appraised Value $ _____ Date _____
Lender's Appraiser _____ Phone _____
Appraiser's Address_____
Review Appraiser _____ Phone _____
Reviewer's Address_____

REVIEW ANALYSIS

DESCRIPTION	Acceptable	Unacceptable	N/A		Acceptable	Unacceptable	N/A
1. Legal Description (verify)	☐	☐	☐	5. Improvements	☐	☐	☐
2. Census Tract	☐	☐	☐	6. Subject Unit	☐	☐	☐
3. Neighborhood	☐	☐	☐	7. Comment Section	☐	☐	☐
4. Site	☐	☐	☐				

Remarks: _____

COST ANALYSIS SECTION:							
8. Physical Depreciation	☐	☐	☐	12. Adjustments & Calculations			
9. Functional Depreciation	☐	☐	☐	(verify)	☐	☐	☐
10. External Depreciation	☐	☐	☐	13. Comments	☐	☐	☐
11. Land to Improvement							
Ratio (verify)	☐	☐	☐				

Remarks: _____

MARKET DATA ANALYSIS SECTION:							
14. Documentation Numbers				21. Math Calculations (verify)	☐	☐	☐
(verified)	☐	☐	☐	22. Comments Section	☐	☐	☐
15. Location Adjustments	☐	☐	☐	23. Net Adjustment Ratio			
16. Site and View Adjustments	☐	☐	☐	1) ___ % 2) ___ % 3) ___ %	☐	☐	☐
17. Quality/Design and				24. Gross Adjustment Ratio			
Appeal Adjustments	☐	☐	☐	1) ___ % 2) ___ % 3) ___ %	☐	☐	☐
18. Condition Adjustments	☐	☐	☐				
19. Room Count and Square				25. Comparable Data Sections	☐	☐	☐
feet Adjustments	☐	☐	☐	26. Income Approach (if App.)	☐	☐	☐
20. Amenities Adjustments	☐	☐	☐	27. Condo Project Addenda	☐	☐	☐

Remarks: _____

ADDENDA REQUIRED				CONDOMINIUM			
28. Plat Map	☐	☐	☐	37. No. of Units Not Complete	☐	☐	☐
29. Building Sketch	☐	☐	☐	38. Presale Requirements Not Met	☐	☐	☐
30. Comparable Map	☐	☐	☐	39. Sale(s) From Project Needed	☐	☐	☐
31. Photo Pages	☐	☐	☐	40. Sale(s) Out of Project			
32. Statement Limiting				Needed	☐	☐	☐
Conditions	☐	☐	☐	41. Addendum A	☐	☐	☐
33. Purchase Agreement	☐	☐	☐	42. Addendum B	☐	☐	☐
34. Original Signature	☐	☐	☐	UNITS			
35. 442 Certification of				43. Rental Survey	☐	☐	☐
Completion	☐	☐	☐	44. Operating Income Statement	☐	☐	☐
36. Copy of Permit for							
Addition/Conversion	☐	☐	☐				

Remarks: _____

REVIEW SUMMARY

Appraisal report was: Good ☐   Fair ☐   Poor ☐
Recommendation:
☐ Accept as is   ☐ Accept when revised-See Items # _____
☐ Have another appraisal prepared by someone else ☐ Other
Comments:_____

Field Review was made   ☐ Yes   ☐ No
Sales price $ _____ Appraisers Value $ _____ Reviewers Recommendation $ _____

Reviewer's Signature _____ Title _____ Date of Review _____

Reviewer's Signature _____ Title _____ Date of Review _____

See Attached ☐

205 (8901)

Exhibit 63 (continued)

SUPPLEMENTARY DATA

ITEM	SUBJECT	COMPARABLE NO. 1		COMPARABLE NO. 2		COMPARABLE NO. 3	
Address							
Proximity to Subject							
Sales Price	$		$		$		$
Price/Gross Liv. Area	$	/	$	/	$	/	$
Data Source							
VALUE ADJUSTMENTS	DESCRIPTION	DESCRIPTION	+ (−) $ Adjustment	DESCRIPTION	+ (−) $ Adjustment	DESCRIPTION	+ (−) $ Adjustment
Sales or Financing							
Concessions							
Date of Sales/Time							
Location							
Site/View							
Design and Appeal							
Quality of Construction							
Age							
Condition							
Above Grade	Total Bdrms Baths	Total Bdrms Baths		Total Bdrms Baths		Total Bdrms Baths	
Room Count							
Gross Living Area	Sq. Ft.	Sq. Ft.		Sq. Ft.		Sq. Ft.	
Basement & Finished							
Rooms Below Grade							
Functional Utility							
Heating/Cooling							
Garage/Carport							
Porches, Patio							
Pools, etc.							
Special Energy							
Efficient Items							
Fireplace(s)							
Other (e.g. kitchen equip., remodeling)							
Net Adj. (total)		+ − $		+ − $		+ − $	
Indicated Value of Subject		$		$		$	

Comments on Sales Comparison _____

_____

_____

_____

_____

_____

REVIEWER'S SUMMARY COMMENTS

_____

_____

_____

_____

_____

_____

_____

_____

_____

_____

_____

_____

_____

_____

_____

_____

_____

_____

_____

_____

_____

_____

_____

_____

Review Form No. 2006
Developed 1/88

Exhibit 64

Residential Appraisal Field Review Report

The purpose of this review is to determine the completeness and accuracy of the data in an appraisal report and to verify the accuracy of the market value estimate as of the effective date of the original appraisal. The appraisal review must address all factual, judgmental, and appraisal technique discrepancies. This field review is a spot check on the original appraisal report as part of a mortgage quality review. It is not intended to be used as a new appraisal. (Please attach a copy of the original appraisal report to this report.)

Property Address	City	State	Zip Code
Legal Description			
Property Rights Appraised	Client Reference Number		
Effective Date of Original Appraisal and Field Review			
Borrower			
Review Appraiser	Company Name		
Address			
Telephone Number	Soc. Sec. or Tax ID. Number		

Instructions: The review appraiser must personally inspect (by, at least, driving by) the exterior of the subject property and the comparables used in the analysis. Photographs are required for: the front of the comparables; the front of the subject; and a street scene of the subject property. Additional photographs are suggested if any adverse conditions that were not noted in the original appraisal report are observed. (NOTE: The review appraiser is not required to inspect the interior of the subject property. The review appraiser should verify the data in the original appraisal report, using the assessment records, the real estate broker, or any other data source that he or she considers to be reliable and reasonably available.) Based on the exterior inspection of the subject and the comparables, a thorough desk review of the appraisal report, and a review of the relevant market data for the subject market area, respond to the following questions, form an opinion about the appropriateness of the appraisal methods and techniques that were used, and indicate any areas of disagreement (giving reasons for the differences). Do not limit your responses to the space provided; attach an addendum, if necessary.

1. Provide a sales and refinance history for the subject property for the last three years (if it is reasonably available from a data source that the review appraiser considers to be reliable.)

Conveyance Recordation Date	Sales Price	Asking Price	Mortgage Amount	Grantor/Grantee	Data Source

2. Is the appraiser's overall description of the neighborhood complete and accurate (location, general market conditions (i.e., plant closings, crop failures, etc.), property values, demand/supply, marketing time, general appearance of properties, appeal to market, etc.)? ☐ Yes ☐ No

(If no, explain.) _____

3. Is the appraiser's overall description of the site complete and accurate (zoning compliance, apparent adverse conditions, apparent environmental hazards, size, flood hazard, etc.)? ☐ Yes ☐ No (If no, explain.) _____

4. Is the appraiser's overall description of the improvements complete and accurate (property description, depreciation, condition, apparent environmental hazards, etc.)? ☐ Yes ☐ No (If no, explain.) _____

5. Are the design and appeal, quality of construction, and size of the subject property similar to others in this area? ☐ Yes ☐ No (If no, how is the subject different?) _____

6. Are the comparables used in the analysis truly comparable to the subject property, representative of the subject market, and were they the best ones available as of the effective date of the appraisal? ☐ Yes ☐ No (If no, explain and provide an adjustment grid with the appropriate comparables and adjustments on an addendum.) _____

7. (a) Can the date of sale (contract date and/or closing/settlement date), sales price, and sales or financing concessions for the comparables be confirmed through the data source that the appraiser indicated? ☐ Yes ☐ No (If no, explain.) _____

(b) Were the comparables actual closed or settled sales as of the effective date of the original appraisal? ☐ Yes ☐ No (If no, explain.) _____

Freddie Mac Form 1032 11/89
1-4 Family Properties
VMP-36 (9001)

Page 1 of 2

Fannie Mae Form 2000 11/89
1-4 Family Properties

VMP MORTGAGE FORMS • (313)293-8100 • (800)521-7291

Exhibit 64 (continued)

Residential Appraisal Field Review Report

8. Is the specific data for the comparables accurate (time, location, design and appeal, quality of construction, age, condition, size, sales or financing concessions, etc.)? ☐ Yes ☐ No (If no, explain.) _____

9. Are the individual adjustments to the comparables reasonable and supported (time, location, design and appeal, quality of construction, age, condition, size, sales or financing concessions, etc.)? ☐ Yes ☐ No (If no, explain.) _____

10. If the subject property is a small residential income property (2-4 unit) or a single-family investment property, are the comparable rental and expense data accurate and reasonable? ☐ Yes ☐ No ☐ N/A (If no, explain.) _____

11. If the subject property is an individual unit in a condominium or PUD project, is the project description complete and accurate?
☐ Yes ☐ No ☐ N/A (If no, explain.) _____

12. Is the estimate of market value for the subject property reasonable as of the effective date of the appraisal? ☐ Yes ☐ No (If no, provide an appropriate estimate of market value for the subject property and state the assumptions (exterior inspection only, property description and condition, etc.) that the opinion is subject to.) _____

13. Has there been a substantial change in the base economy in the area since the effective date of the appraisal? ☐ Yes ☐ No (If yes, please explain.) _____

14. If the subject property is a cooperative unit, the review appraiser must address the completeness and accuracy of the original appraiser's description and analysis of the cooperative project and specifically comment on the accuracy of: (a) the number of shares attributable to the unit; (b) the pro-rata share of the blanket mortgage payments; and (c) the treatment of the monthly assessments of the comparable sales.

I certify that, to the best of my knowledge and belief, the facts and data used herein are true and correct; that I personally inspected the exterior of the subject property and the comparables used in the report; that the reported analyses, opinions, and conclusions are limited only by the reported assumptions and limiting conditions, and are my personal, unbiased professional analyses, opinions, and conclusions; that I have no present or prospective interest in the property that is the subject of this report, and I have no personal interest in or bias with respect to the parties involved; that my compensation is not contingent on any action or event resulting from the analyses, opinions, or conclusions in, or the use of, this report; and that my analyses, opinions, and conclusions were developed, and this report was prepared, in conformity with the Uniform Standards of Professional Appraisal Practice.

Signature of Review Appraiser | Date

Client Use Only

Review Underwriter's Comments _____

Signature of Review Underwriter | Date

Exhibit 65

RESIDENTIAL APPRAISAL REVIEW NARRATIVE FORM

Lending Institution _____

Lender's Address _____

Name of Borrower _____

Property Address _____

Loan Number _____

Appraised Value $ _____ Date _____

Lender's Appraiser _____ Phone _____

Appraiser's Address _____

Review Appraiser_____ Phone _____

Reviewer's Address _____

REVIEW ANALYSIS

1. Does the appraisal report present a consistent and convincing analysis? _____

2. Are there serious omissions, false information, faulty reasoning or the possibility of calculated deception? _____

3. Comment on the report's quality, completeness, consistency and accuracy. _____

4. Do you agree with the appraiser's value conclusion? Comment on the adequacy of the appraiser's value analysis as well as the soundness of the value conclusion. _____

5. If there is a difference between your opinion and that of the appraiser, what is the reason for the difference? _____

6. Does it appear that the subject property has been over appraised? Comment on your opinion of value and the appraiser's opinion of value.

7. How would you rate the appraisal report with respect to overall quality (poor, fair, good, very good, excellent)? _____

REVIEWER'S SUMMARY

Recommendation: ☐ Accept as is   ☐ Accept when revised-See items # _____
                 ☐ Have another appraisal prepared by someone else   ☐ Other

Comments: _____

Field Review was made ☐ Yes ☐ No

Sales Price $ _____ Appraiser's Value $ _____ Reviewer's Recommendation $ _____

Reviewer's Signature_____ Title _____ Date of Review _____

Reviewer's Signature_____ Title _____ Date of Review _____

See Attached ☐

Review Form No. 2004
Revised 1/88

-206 (8901)   VMP MORTGAGE FORMS • (313)293-8100 • (800)521-7291

Exhibit 65 (continued)

SUPPLEMENTARY DATA

ITEM	SUBJECT	COMPARABLE NO. 1	COMPARABLE NO. 2	COMPARABLE NO. 3
Address				
Proximity to Subject				
Sales Price	$	$	$	$
Price/Gross Liv. Area	$ /	$ /	$ /	$ /
Data Source				
VALUE ADJUSTMENTS	DESCRIPTION	DESCRIPTION + (−) $ Adjustment	DESCRIPTION + (−) $ Adjustment	DESCRIPTION + (−) $ Adjustment
Sales or Financing				
Concessions				
Date of Sales/Time				
Location				
Site/View				
Design and Appeal				
Quality of Construction				
Age				
Condition				
Above Grade	Total Bdrms Baths	Total Bdrms Baths	Total Bdrms Baths	Total Bdrms Baths
Room Count				
Gross Living Area	Sq. Ft.	Sq. Ft.	Sq. Ft.	Sq. Ft.
Basement & Finished				
Rooms Below Grade				
Functional Utility				
Heating/Cooling				
Garage/Carport				
Porches, Patio				
Pools, etc.				
Special Energy				
Efficient Items				
Fireplace(s)				
Other (e.g. kitchen				
equip., remodeling)				
Net Adj. (total)		+ − $	+ − $	+ − $
Indicated Value				
of Subject		$	$	$

Comments on Sales Comparison _____

_____

_____

_____

_____

REVIEWER'S SUMMARY COMMENTS

_____

_____

_____

_____

_____

_____

_____

_____

_____

_____

_____

_____

_____

_____

_____

_____

_____

_____

_____

_____

_____

_____

Review Form No. 2004
Revised 1/88

Exhibit 66

Freddie Mac
Federal
Home Loan
Mortgage
Corporation

Owned by America's
Savings Institutions

Second Mortgage
Property Value Analysis Report

(This form may be used if the second mortgage will not exceed $15,000 and value is based on "as is" condition.)

Borrower/Subject Property Information

Borrower	CensusTract _____ Map Reference _____
Property Address	Check one ☐ SF ☐ PUD ☐ CONDO ☐ 2-4 Units
City _____ County _____	State _____ Zip Code _____
Phone No. Res _____ Loan Amount Requested $_____ Term _____ Mos	Owner's Estimate of Value $_____

No. of Bedrooms	No. of Baths	Family room or den Yes / No	Gross Living Area Sq Ft	Garage/Carport (specify type & no)	Porches, Patio or Pool (specify)	Central Air Yes / No

---

Field Report

NEIGHBORHOOD

Location	Urban	Suburban	Rural		Good Avg Fair Poor
Built Up	Over 75%	25% to 75%	Under 25%	Property Compatibility	
Growth Rate	Fully Dev	Rapid	Steady	Slow	General Appearance of Properties
Property Values	Increasing	Stable	Declining	Appeal to Market
Demand Supply	Shortage	In Balance	Over Supply	
Marketing Time	Under 3 Mos	4-6 Mos	Over 6 Mos	

Present Land Use ___ % 1 Family ___ % 2-4 Family ___ % Apts ___ % Condo ___ % Commercial ___ % Industrial ___ % Vacant ___ %

Change in Present Land Use   Not Likely   Likely   Taking Place From   To

Predominant Occupants   Owner   Tenant   % Vacant

Single Family Price Range $_____ to $_____   Predominant Value $_____

Single Family Age _____ yrs to _____ yrs   Predominant Age _____ yrs

Note: Freddie Mac does not consider race or the racial composition of the neighborhood to be reliable appraisal factors

Comments including those factors, favorable or unfavorable, affecting marketability (e.g. public parks, schools, view, noise)

SUBJECT PROPERTY

Approx Year Built 19___   No. Units ___   No. Stories ___

Type detached, duplex, semi-det, etc.

Design (rambler, split level, etc.)

Exterior Wall Material _____ Roof Material _____

Is the property located in a HUD Identified Special Flood Hazard Area?   No   Yes

Special Energy Efficient Items

Comments (favorable or unfavorable including any deferred maintenance)

PROPERTY RATING	Good	Avg	Fair	Poor
Condition of Exterior				
Compatibility to Neighborhood				
Appeal and Marketability				

Market Comparable Analysis Prior To Improvement

Item	Subject Property	Comparable No. 1		Comparable No. 2		Comparable No. 3	
Address							
Proximity to Sub							
Sales Price			$		$		$
Date of Sales (mi)	Description	Description	+/- $ Adjustment	Description	+/- $ Adjustment	Description	+/- $ Adjustment
Time Adjustment							
Location							
Site/View							
Age							
Condition							
Living Area Rm	Total / B rms / Baths	Total / B rms / Baths		Total / B rms / Baths		Total / B rms / Baths	
Count and Total							
Gross Living Area	Sq Ft	Sq Ft		Sq Ft		Sq Ft	
Air Conditioning							
Garage/Carport							
Porches, Patio							
Pools, etc							
Special Energy							
Efficient Items							
Other							
Net Adjust (Total)		Plus / Minus	$	Plus / Minus	$	☐ Plus ☐ Minus	$
Indicated Value			$		$		$
of Subject							

General Comments

The information shown on this report is derived from an inspection of the neighborhood and exterior inspection of the subject property and market comparables. The estimated market value is based upon this information and the knowledge of the undersigned. This report is not to be construed as an appraisal report.

Estimated Market Value $_____ as of _____ 19___

Completed By _____	Title _____
Signature _____	Date _____ 19___

ATTACH CURRENT DESCRIPTIVE PHOTOGRAPHS OF SUBJECT PROPERTY AND STREET SCENE

Freddie Mac 704 1/86 (FMP)-72 (8703)   VMP MORTGAGE FORMS • (313)293-8100 • (800)521-7291

- minimizes the impact on local real estate and financial markets; and
- maximizes the preservation of the availability and affordability of residential property for low- and moderate-income individuals.

The duties of the Oversight Board are to oversee and be accountable for the RTC. The Oversight Board is required, in consultation with the RTC, to develop and establish overall strategies, policies, and goals for the RTC's activities, including the RTC's overall financial goals, plans and budgets. The Oversight Board is required to review the overall performance of the RTC on a periodic basis, including its work, management activities, and internal controls and the performance of the RTC relative to approved budget plans pursuant to the terms of FIRREA.

RTC operates according to a strategic plan. The purpose of the strategic plan is to set forth the RTC's goals, objectives, and implementing procedures in support of its mission. FIRREA establishes the minimum contents that the plan and the implementing guidelines and procedures must contain. The strategic plan's goals establish broad, general direction for the RTC in six areas: case resolution, asset disposition, affordable housing, conflicts of interest and ethical standards, external relations, and administration.

1   CASE RESOLUTION. Manage and resolve institutions under RTC jurisdiction in a timely and cost effective manner, while minimizing the negative effects on local financial and real estate markets.

2   ASSET DISPOSITION. To dispose of real estate and other assets in such a way as to maximize the net present value to the RTC while minimizing the effect of these transactions on local real estate and financial markets.

3   AFFORDABLE HOUSING PROVISIONS. To dispose of eligible single- and multi-family residential properties in a way that maximizes the preservation of the availability and affordability of residential real property for low- and moderate-income individuals.

4   CONFLICTS OF INTEREST AND ETHICAL STANDARDS. Adopt conflicts of interest and ethical standards for RTC employees, officers, advisory board members, contractors, and agents.

5   EXTERNAL RELATIONS. Establish and maintain open communications with the Congress, other government offices, and the public to increase understanding of RTC policies and actions.

6   ADMINISTRATION. Assure that the RTC has sufficient and effectively managed human and financial resources to achieve the mission and the goals of the agency.

The strategic plan's objectives provide more specific statements with respect to the goals set forth. Subject to the review of the Oversight Board, the RTC is responsible for amending the FDIC's policies and procedures and, where necessary, adopting its own set of rules, regulations, standards, policies, procedures, guidelines, and statements necessary to implement the strategic plan established by the Oversight Board.

Consistent with FIRREA, the strategic plan generally relies on the RTC to develop the specific guidelines and procedures for implementing the general guidance provided in the strategic plan. Until such specific procedures are developed by the RTC, the Oversight Board has directed the RTC to operate, consistent with Oversight Board policies, according to existing FDIC procedures.

The challenges facing the RTC, and thus the Oversight Board, in terms of magnitude and complexity, are unparalleled in recent history. It is anticipated that a significant portion of the assets of thrift institutions in the Southwest will come under the jurisdiction of the RTC, and thus, must be disposed of either through case resolutions or outright asset sales. In the interim, the RTC will become a major holder of real estate in this market. There is no historical model for a task of this magnitude to which the Oversight Board can turn as it develops policies for the RTC which are designed to ensure that the RTC's actions are consistent with FIRREA's statutory objectives.

As the Oversight Board and the RTC develop more experience, issues will arise that will require new policies and directions. As a result, it is expected that the strategic plan will be reined and strengthened on a periodic basis, based on the experience gained by the Oversight Board and RTC. Additionally, as the National and Regional Advisory Boards begin operating, they will provide a new source of input for the policies and procedures developed by the Oversight Board and RTC regarding the sale and disposition of real property assets.

The strategic plan was developed by Oversight Board staff in consultation with staff of the Treasury Department, the Department of Housing and Urban Development, the Federal Reserve Board, and the RTC. The strategic plan incorporates individual policies that have been adopted by the Oversight Board and, to the extent appropriate, comments received during the public comment period.

The following reporting requirements are from Title V of the Financial Institutions Reform, Recovery, and Enforcement Act of 1989 (Pub. L. No. 101-73, Section 501, 103 Stat. 183, 363-94) ("FIRREA"). All references to Section 21A, are to Section 21A of the Federal Home Loan Bank Act (12 U.S.C. 1441a), as added by Section 501(a) of FIRREA.

1.   The RTC shall make available to the public:

- any agreement by the RTC relating to a transaction that provides assistance pursuant to section 13(c) of the Federal Deposit Insurance Act ("section 13(c)"), not later than 30 days after the first meeting of the Oversight Board after such agreement is entered into; and

- all agreements relating to the RTC's review of prior cases pursuant to subsection (b)(11)(B) of 21A.

"Agreement" includes a) all documents that effectuate the terms and conditions of the assisted transaction; b) a comparison by the RTC of the estimated cost of the transaction with the estimated cost of liquidating the insured institution; and c) a description of any economic or statistical assumptions on which such estimates are based.

The Oversight Board may withhold public disclosure if it decides by a unanimous vote that disclosure would be contrary to the public interest. A written report explaining the reasons for such a determination must be published in the Federal Register and transmitted to the House and Senate Banking Committees.

Section 21A (k)(2)(A), (B), and (C)

2. The RTC shall make available to the House and Senate Banking Committees any agreement by the RTC relating to a transaction that the RTC provides section 13(c) assistance not later than 25 days after the first meeting of the Oversight Board after such agreement is entered into. This requirement is in addition to the RTC's obligation to make such agreements publicly available.

Section 21A (k)(3)(A)

3. The RTC shall submit a report to the Oversight Board and the Congress containing the results and conclusions of the review of 1988 and 1989 FSLIC transactions (pursuant to subsection (b) (11)(B) of 21A) and recommendations for legislative action that the RTC may determine to be appropriate.

Section 21A (k)(3)(B)

4. The RTC's Real Estate Asset Division shall publish before January 1, 1990 an inventory of real property assets of institutions subject to the jurisdiction of the RTC. The inventory must be updated semiannually and must identify properties with natural, cultural, recreational, or scientific values of special significance.

5. Annually, the Comptroller General shall audit the financial statements of the RTC unless the Comptroller General notifies the Oversight Board not later than 180 days before the close of a fiscal year that it will not perform an audit for that fiscal year. In that event, the Oversight Board must contract with an independent certified public accountant to perform the annual audit. All books, records, accounts, reports, files, and property belonging to or used by the RTC, or the Oversight Board, or by an independent certified public accountant retained to audit the RTC's financial statement, shall be made available to the Comptroller General.

Sections 21A (k)(1)(A) and (B)

6. The Inspector General of the RTC shall comply with the reporting requirements imposed on the Inspector General pursuant to the Inspector General Act of 1978, as amended.

Section 501 (b) of FIRREA

7. The RTC shall a) document decisions made in the solicitation and selection process and the reasons for the decisions; and b) maintain such documentation in the offices of the RTC, as well as any other documentation relating to the solicitation and selection process.

Section 21A (b)(12)(C)

8. The Oversight Board and the RTC shall annually submit a full report of their respective operations, activities, budgets, receipts, and expenditures for the preceding 12-month period. The RTC shall submit the annual report to Congress and the President as soon as practicable after the end of the calendar year that the report is made, but not later than June 30 of the year following that calendar year. The report shall include audited statements and such information as is necessary to make known the financial condition and operations of the RTC according to generally accepted accounting principles; the RTC's financial operating plans and forecasts (including budgets, estimates of actual and future spending and cash obligations) taking into account the Corporation's financial commitments, guarantees, and other contingent liabilities; the number of minority and women investors participating in the bidding process for assisted acquisitions and the disposition of assets and the number of successful bids by such investors; and a list of the properties sold to state housing finance authorities (as such term is defined in section 1301 of FIRREA), the indi-

vidual purchase prices of such properties, and an estimate of the premium paid by such authorities for such properties.

Sections 21A (k)(4)(A),(B), and (C)

9. The Oversight Board and the RTC shall submit to Congress not later than April 30 and October 31 of each calendar year, a semiannual report on the activities and efforts of the RTC, the FDIC, and the Oversight Board for the 6-month period ending on the last day of the month before the month that such report is required to be submitted. The report shall include the following information with respect to the RTC's assets and liabilities and to the assets and liabilities of institutions that the RTC is or has been the conservator or receiver:

- the total book value of all assets held or managed by the RTC at the beginning and end of the reporting period;

- the total book value of assets that are under contract to be managed by private persons and entities at the beginning and end of the reporting period;

- the number of employees of the Corporation, the Federal Deposit Insurance Corporation, and the Oversight Board at the beginning and end of the reporting period;

- the total amounts expended on employee wages, salaries, and overhead, during such period that are attributable to a) contracting with, supervising, or reviewing the performance of private contractors, or b) managing or disposing of such assets;

- the total amount expended on private contractors for the management of such assets;

- the efforts of the RTC to maximize the efficient utilization of the resources of the private sector during the reporting period and in future reporting periods and a description of the guidelines and procedures adopted to ensure adequate competition and fair and consistent treatment of qualified third parties seeking to provide services to the RTC or the Federal Deposit Insurance Corporation;

- the total book value and total proceeds from such assets disposed of during the reporting period;

- summary data on discounts from book value that assets were sold or otherwise disposed of during the reporting period;

- a list of all of the areas that carried a distressed area designation during the reporting period (including a justification for removal of areas from or addition of areas to the list of distressed areas);

- an evaluation of market conditions in distressed areas and a description of any changes in conditions during the reporting period;
- any change adopted by the Oversight Board in the minimum disposition price and the reasons for such change; and,
- the valuation method or methods adopted by the Oversight Board or the RTC to value assets and thereasons for selecting such methods.

Sections 21A (k)(5)(A) and (B)

10. Before January 31, 1990, the Oversight Board and the RTC shall appear before the House and Senate Banking Committees to:

- describe the strategic plan established for the operations of the RTC;
- describe the guidelines and procedures established or proposed to be established for the RTC, including specific measures taken to avoid political favoritism or undue influence with respect to the activities of the RTC;
- provide any regulation proposed to be prescribed by the RTC; and
- provide the proposed case resolution schedule.

Sections 21A (k) (7) (A) and (B).

Detail information about the RTC is available by contacting:

Resolution Trust Corporation
Reading Room
801 17th Street, N.W.
Suite 100
Washington, D.C. 20006
202-416-6940

Exhibit 67
Organization Overview

```
┌─────────────────────────┐
│           RTC           │
│     Oversight  Board    │
└─────────────────────────┘
             │
             │
┌─────────────────────────┐
│           RTC           │
│    Board  of  Directors │
└─────────────────────────┘
             │
             │
┌─────────────────────────┐
│           RTC           │
│                         │
└─────────────────────────┘
```

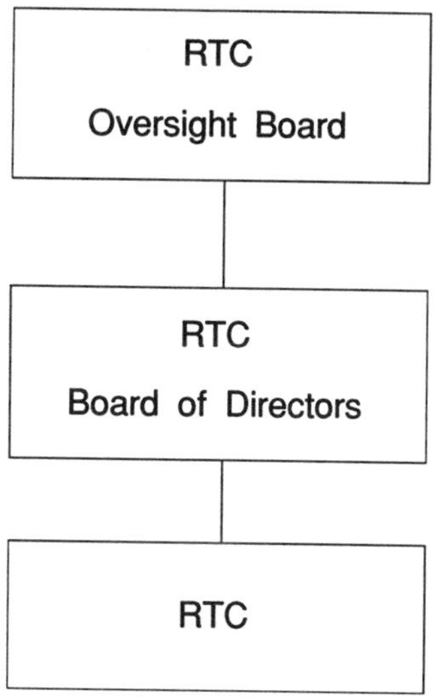

Exhibit 68

RTC
Organization Overview

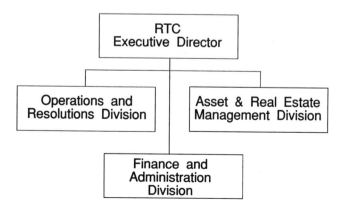

Exhibit 69

RTC Regional Office
Organization

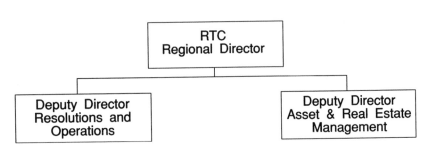

Exhibit 70

RTC REGIONS

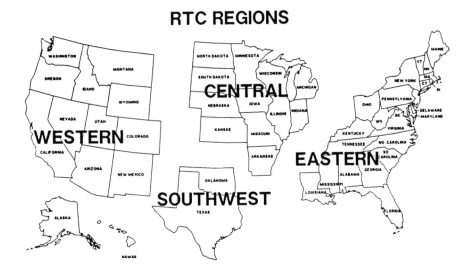

EAST REGION
William M. Dudley, Director
Resolution Trust Corporation
Marquis One Tower, Suite 1100
245 Peachtree Center Avenue, NE
Atlanta, GA 30303
1-800-234-3342
404-522-1145

Bayou Consolidated Office
James R. Hambric, III
Acting Director
Resolution Trust Corporation
10725 Perkins Road
Baton Rouge, LA 70810
504-769-8860

Louisiana,
Mississippi

Northeast Consolidated Office
Stephen W. Wood, Director
Resolution Trust Corporation
East Sixth Street
Red Hill, PA 18076
215-679-9515

Maine, Vermont, New
Hampshire, Connecticut,
Massachusetts, Rhode Island,
New York, New Jersey, Ohio,
Pennsylvania, Delaware,
Maryland

Southeast Consolidated Office
Jimmy R. Caldwell, Acting Director
Resolution Trust Corporation
Freedom Savings & Loan Association
220 E. Madison Street, Suite 302
Tampa, FL 33602
813-870-5000

Florida

Mid-Atlantic Consolidated Office
William C. Thomas, Director
Resolution Trust Corporation
Colony Square
Building 400, Suite 900
Atlanta, GA 30361
404-881-4840
1-800-628-4362

District of Columbia,
Virginia, West Virginia
Kentucky, Tennessee
North Carolina, South Carolina
Georgia, Alabama

CENTRAL REGION
Michael J. Martinelli, Director
Resolution Trust Corporation
Board of Trade Building II
4900 Main Street
Kansas City, MO 64112
1-800-365-3342
(816) 531-2212

Mid-Central Consolidated Office
Dennis Cavinaw, Director
Resolution Trust Corporation
Board of Trade Building II
4900 Main Street
Kansas City, MO 64112
(816) 531-2212
1-800-365-3342

Kansas, Missouri, Arkansas

Lake Central Consolidated Office
Joseph Minitti, Director
Resolution Trust Corporation
2100 East Golf Road
West Building, Suite 300
Rolling Meadows, IL 60008
(708) 806-7750
1-800-526-7521

Illinois, Indiana, Michigan

North Central Consolidated Office
Donaldson Wickens, Director
Resolution Trust Corporation
501 East Highway 13
Burnsville, MN 55337
(612) 894-0800
1-800-338-8098

South Dakota, North Dakota,
Minnesota, Nebraska,
Wisconsin, Iowa

NOTE This office will move to Eagan, MN, in June 1990.

SOUTHWEST REGION
Carmen J. Sullivan, Director
Resolution Trust Corporation
300 N. Ervay, 23rd Floor
Dallas, TX 75201
(214) 953-2300

Metroplex Consolidated Office   Northeast Texas
Jim Messec, Director
Resolution Trust Corporation
300 N. Ervay
22nd Floor
Dallas, TX 75201
(214) 953-2300

Gulf Coast Consolidated Office   Southeast Texas
Timothy Putman, Acting Director
Resolution Trust Corporation
Commonwealth Federal Savings
    Association
10000 Memorial Drive
Houston, TX 77024
(713) 683-3476

Southern Consolidated Office   West Texas
James Forrestal, Acting Director
Resolution Trust Corporation
Bexar Savings Association
1777 NE Loop 410
San Antonio, TX 78217
(512) 820-8164

Northern Consolidated Office   Oklahoma
Virginia Kingsley, Director
Resolution Trust Corporation
4606 S. Garnett
Tulsa, OK 74146
(918) 627-9000

WEST REGION
Anthony Scalzi, Director
1515 Arapahoe Street
Tower 3, Suite 800
Denver, CO 80202
(303) 556-6500

Central Western Consolidated Office Virginia Juedes, Acting Director Resolution Trust Corporation 2910 N. 44th Street Phoenix, AZ 85018 (602) 224-1100	Arizona, Nevada
Coastal Consolidated Office James G. Klingensmith, Acting Director Resolution Trust Corporation 1901 Newport Boulevard 3rd Floor, East Wing Costa Mesa, CA 92627 (714) 631-8380, ext. 4239	Alaska, California, Hawaii, Oregon, Washington, Guam
Intermountain Consolidated Office Keith Carson, Director Resolution Trust Corporation 1515 Arapahoe Street Tower 3, Suite 800 Denver, CO 80202 (303) 556-6500	Colorado, Idaho, Montana, New Mexico, Utah, Wyoming

RESPA See REAL ESTATE SETTLEMENT PROCEDURES ACT.

RESPONDEAT SUPERIOR The doctrine of law which states that a principal is liable and responsible for the acts of an agent. For the principal to be liable, the actions of the agent must be within powers granted in a principal/agency relationship. This author (Santi) was subpoenaed as an expert witness, for FHA/VA matters, at the trial of a personal friend. The friend was under prosecution by HUD for misappropriation of earnest monies given on several contract of sale involving FHA financing.

Exhibit 71

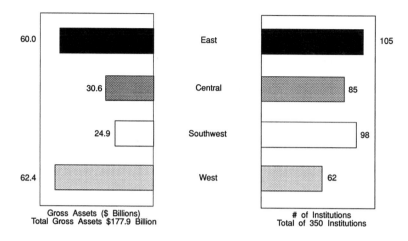

Conservatorship Operations
(As of March 16, 1990)

Region

60.0	East	105
30.6	Central	85
24.9	Southwest	98
62.4	West	62

Gross Assets ($ Billions)
Total Gross Assets $177.9 Billion

# of Institutions
Total of 350 Institutions

Exhibit 72

Resolved Institutions
(As of March 16, 1990)

Region

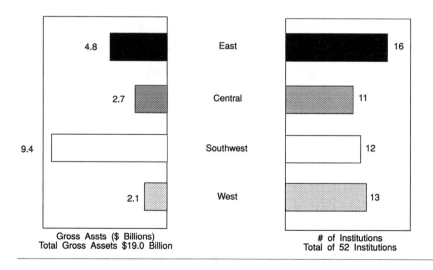

4.8	East	16
2.7	Central	11
9.4	Southwest	12
2.1	West	13

Gross Assts ($ Billions)
Total Gross Assets $19.0 Billion

# of Institutions
Total of 52 Institutions

Exhibit 73

of Institutions

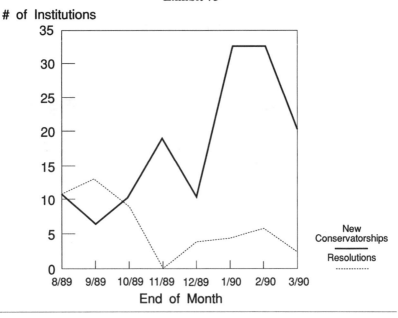

End of Month

New Conservatorships

Resolutions
....

Exhibit 74

Source and Use of Funds
(As of March 26, 1990)

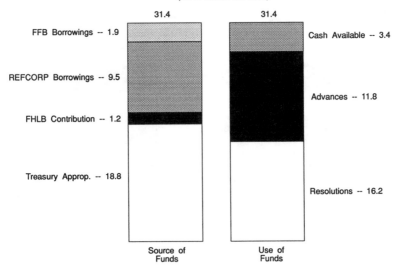

31.4   31.4

FFB Borrowings -- 1.9   Cash Available -- 3.4

REFCORP Borrowings -- 9.5

Advances -- 11.8

FHLB Contribution -- 1.2

Treasury Approp. -- 18.8

Resolutions -- 16.2

Source of
Funds

Use of
Funds

Exhibit 75
Profile of 247 Conservatorship Institutions
Second Quarter 1990

Assets (Gross)	$125.6 Billion
Liabilities	$138.2 Billion
Tangible Capital	–$22.7 Billion
Operating Loss	$1.0 Billion
Net Loss	$2.6 Billion

Note: June 30, 1990 data excludes two institutions which were resolved in early July 1990 and did not report second quarter data. On March 31, 1990 these institutions had combined assets of $187 million.

Exhibit 76
Change in Conservatorship Institutions
July 1, 1990 - September 24, 1990*

	Number	Assets (Gross) $ Billions	Net Loss $ Millions	Operating Loss $ Millions
Conservatorships II/90**	247	125.6	2,622	1,025
New Cons., III/90	36	8.0	169	37
Resolutions, III/90***	63	20.7	855	141
Conservatorships III/90	220	112.9	1,936	921

*Asset and income data are for second quarter 1990.
**June 30, 1990 data excludes two institutions which were resolved in early July 1990 and did not report second quarter data. On March 31, 1990 these institutions had combined assets of $187 million.
***Conservatorship resolutions only, two cases resolved without going into conservatorship not included. Also excluded is one resolution which involved the partial sale of branches with the retention of remaining branches in conservatorship.

The monetary consequences for my friend were a small fine and placement on the FHA suspension list. The entire case was won on the respondeat superior doctrine. It was proven in court that my friend knew nothing about the misappropriation of the escrow monies. The unlawful acts were done by agents working for other brokers who were selling rehabilitated properties my friend owned.

RESTRAINT ON ALIENATION A restriction or condition on the right to transfer property.

RESTRICTION OR RESTRICTION COVENANT A limitation to the use of the property that normally is conveyed in the deed. Subdivision restrictions and zoning ordinances are examples.
See DEED RESTRICTION.

RETAIL EXCHANGE ESTIMATE The volume of retail sales reported by retail establishments and estimated to be amount of consumption taking place in the nation and the personal savings habits of consumers. The Federal Reserve System reports are made the second week of the month.

RETAINAGE Money that has been earned by a contractor, but is withheld or retained until the project is completed and all obligations discharged by the contractor.
See CONSTRUCTION LOAN.

RETIRE To pay off a debt.

REVERSE LEVERAGE Negative cash flow. The payments for a mortgage on an investment property exceeds the cash flow.
See LEVERAGE.

REVERSE PRICE RISK (RPR) The risk that occurs when a commitment to sell a loan to an investor has been made before making a loan commitment to a borrower. In this situation, a decrease in rates requires that loans be delivered at an unexpected discount.

REVERSE REPURCHASE AGREEMENT (REVERSE REPO) The   purchase of mortgage-backed securities by a dealer from his customer while at the same time that customer enters into an agreement to repurchase the MBSs from a dealer on a delayed settlement basis, a securitized borrowing.

REVERSION The act of property reverting to the lessor, grantor, or owner after the estate period has expired. A reversion in a lease would be that the property reverts to the landlord after the lease has expired.

REVERSIONARY INTEREST *See* LIFE ESTATE.

REVOCATION The act of recalling or terminating power of authority given to another through such acts as Power of Attorney, Agency, or Licensing Privileges.

REVOLVING LOAN FUND A pool of money set aside for making loans. As the loans are paid back, the pool is replenished.

RICH Overpriced in relationship to another security in called rich in terms of an historical price relationship.
See CHEAP.

RIDER An addendum or amendment to a contract.

RIDGE The peak or top horizontal edge of a roof.

RIDGEBOARD The top horizontal board of a roof. Rafters are attached to it.

RIGHT OF FIRST REFUSAL The right of a party to match or equal the terms of a proposed contract before the contract is executed. The party owning a first right of refusal has the first opportunity either to purchase or lease the property.

RIGHT OF RECISSION The recission period is explained in detail in TRUTH-IN-LENDING ACT.

RIGHT OF SURVIVORSHIP The right of a surviving joint tenant to the property of a deceased joint tenant.
See JOINT TENANCY.

RIGHT-OF-WAY The usage of property that is similar to an easement. A right-of-way can be a trail, driveway, public road, overhead or underground utility lines, or any type of access to the property.
See ACCESS RIGHTS.

RIGHT TO PRIVACY ACT The Right to Financial Privacy Act of 1978 became effective on March 10, 1979. It was enacted because customers of financial institutions have a right to expect that their financial activities have a reasonable amount of privacy from federal government scrutiny.

The act establishes specific procedures for government authorities that seek information about a customer's financial records.

The act requires that the customer receive the following:

(1) a written notice of the agency's intent to obtain financial records;

(2) the reason why the records are being sought; and

(3) a statement describing procedures to use if the customer does not wish such information to be made available.

Before the act, customers of financial institutions could not challenge government access to their financial records, nor did they have any idea their records were being turned over to a government authority.

To obtain access to the financial records of the customer, the act requires that the government authority must first obtain one of the following:

(1) an authorization, signed and dated by the customer, that identifies the records being sought, the reasons the records are being requested, and the customer's rights under the act;

(2) an administrative subpoena or summons;

(3) a search warrant;

(4) a judicial subpoena;

(5) a formal written request by a government agency.

It is necessary for the financial institution to maintain a record of all instances that a customer's record is disclosed to a government authority.

RIPARIAN The rights of an owner of property located next to a body of water such as a lake or a river.

RISK OF LOSS In contract law, it is the exposure to chances of loss or injury to either buyer or seller.

RISK RATE Generally the rate of return required to attract capital to an investment.

RISK/REWARD RATIO The relationship between the degree of risk involved in an investment to the anticipated return.

RLS *See* RATE-LOCK STANDBY.

RNY *See* REQUIRED NET YIELD.

ROLLOVER 1) Renewal of loan at time of maturity. 2) Reinvestment of proceeds from sale of one housing unit into another.

The term "rollover" applies to an Adjustable Rate Mortgage. ARM loan terms may have a fixed interest rate for a period of time, generally three to five years, with the understanding that the interest rate will then be renegotiated. Loans with periodically renegotiated rates are called rollover mortgages. With these loans, monthly payments are more predictable as the interest rate is fixed for a longer period of time.

ROOF The covering on a building. There are several roof types. (See Exhibit 77.)

To make an inspection of a roof, use the information in this paragraph. The average life of a roof is based on the material used. Asphalt roofs will last 15 to 20 years; wood shingles, 30 to 35 years; and slate should last 40 or more years. Asphalt roofs that have granules missing in spots and shingles that are beginning to buckle will soon need replacing. In most cases, a good pair of binoculars will uncover these tell-tale signs as well as would climbing up on the roof. Look for inadequate flashing and tar around chimneys and vent pipes. Check for sags in the roof that can be a sign of problems with the framing structure supporting the roof. If there are any valleys in the roof, check for signs of patching caused by roof leaks. Ask the owner about roof leaks and check for any water stain marks on the ceiling.

If a home has more than three layers of roofing, it is most likely violates a housing code. Normally FHA, VA, and housing codes stipulate that no more than three layers of roofing can be applied to a home. If you encounter a house that already has three layers of roofing, you must keep in mind the cost of having the old layer removed and hauled away before a new layer can be installed.

ROOF SHEATHING *See* SHEATHING.

ROT Deterioration of wood in a structure, such as a house, garage, or deck. There are generally two types of rot. Dry rot is caused by a fungus that decays

Exhibit 77

Roof Types

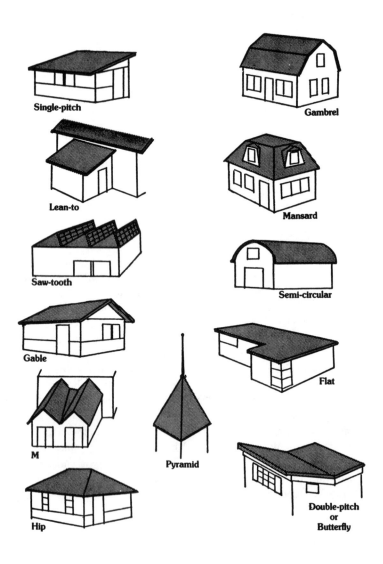

Single-pitch

Lean-to

Saw-tooth

Gable

M

Hip

Gambrel

Mansard

Semi-circular

Flat

Pyramid

Double-pitch
or
Butterfly

the wood. Water rot is usually caused by non-treated wood or wood that is too close to the foundation or ground (closer than 18 inches).

ROTUNDA A circular room or building that usually is topped with a domed roof.

ROW HOUSES Dwelling units that are attached by common walls, sometimes known as townhouses.

ROYALTY Money paid to an owner of property for the extraction of natural resources such as gas or oil. Royalty can mean a franchise fee.

RPR *See* REVERSE PRICE RISK.

RRM *See* RENEGOTIABLE RATE MORTGAGE.

RULE OF 72 A method of calculating the amount of time it takes for money to double itself when compound interest is applied. Divide 72 by your interest rate. The result is the number of years it will take for your money to double.

RULE OF 78s A method used by a lender for deciding an interest rebate for an early pay off of a loan. This method is used primarily for personal or installment loans.

RUN WITH THE LAND An expression affecting the present and future use of a subject property.

RURBAN Land that is on the fringe of urban development. Land in between urban and rural area.

R-VALUE A measure of insulating value; the type and thickness of insulation in attics, walls, floors, doors, windows, or roofs can be measured by an R-value. The "R" refers to resistance to the flow of heat.

S

SAFE HARBOR RULE An expression that generally means an area of safety from legislation or regulation pertaining to income tax. Without the word "rule" it can be used to express an area of safety, such as FHA and VA loans are a safe harbor for having a fixed rate of interest that will not increase upon an ordinary loan assumption.

SALE-BUYBACK A lending institution buys the property from the developer and then sells it back on a long term contract. The seller generates cash, as much as 100%, and since this transaction is normally involved with real property, the seller gets to deduct the interest portion in the installments paid to the purchaser. The purchaser is viewed as having an equitable title and is allowed depreciation deductions. The intent of a sale-leaseback is to use it as a financing strategy to maximize cash in the hands of the developer, similar to a high loan-to-value-ratio loan. Another advantage is the term (number of years), it is usually longer than the term for a mortgage - at least ten years longer.

Advantages for the lending institution are usually a higher interest rate and a "kicker" in the form of a percentage of the net profits earned by the developer. The lending institution will normally have a provision in the contract prohibiting a prepayment.

See KICKER MORTGAGE LOAN, EQUITY PARTICIPATION.

SALE-LEASEBACK Real estate that is sold to a buyer who simultaneously leases the property back to the seller. Identical to "sale-buyback" except that the lending institution is a lessor instead of a grantor or seller.

SALES CONTRACT *See* CONTRACT OF SALE.

SALT BOX COLONIAL HOME STYLE

Salt Box Colonial. An Early American style two-story house which is square or rectangular and features a steep gable roof extending down to the first floor in the rear.

SALVAGE VALUE The value an asset will have at the end of its useful life.

SAM SHARED APPRECIATION MORTGAGE.

SANDWICH LEASE A lease held by a lessee who has subsequently leased to a tenant. For example: Owner A leases to Lessee B; and Lessee B subleases to Lessee C. Lessee B is the owner of a sandwich lease.

SASH The movable part of a window. The framework containing glass in a window or door.

SATELLITE TENANT A tenant in a shopping center who is relatively small and dependent on the larger or anchor tenant to attract business.
See ANCHOR TENANT.

SATISFACTION Payment of a debt such as a judgment.

SATISFACTION OF A MORTGAGE A written instrument acknowledging the full payment of a mortgage. When recorded, this document shows satisfaction of the mortgage debt.
See RELEASE.

SAVINGS ASSOCIATION A state chartered or federally chartered financial intermediary that accepts deposits from the public and invests those funds primarily in residential mortgage loans. It is sometimes called a savings and loan association, a cooperative bank, a homestead society, or a building and loan association.

SAVINGS BANK A state chartered or federally chartered financial intermediary that accepts deposits from the public and invests those funds in a variety of secure investments, mainly mortgage loans, sometimes called a mutual savings bank. Mutual savings banks have investment powers more extensive than savings and loan associations in as much as depositors mutually own the benefits.
See MUTUAL SAVINGS BANK.

SAW-TOOTH ROOF *See* ROOF.

SCENIC EASEMENT An easement to preserve the property in its natural or undeveloped state.

SCHEMATICS Preliminary drawings and sketches prepared for the planning stages of a project.

SEASONED LOAN A loan that has been outstanding for a period of time. FHA requires a loan to be seasoned for twelve months before it is eligible to be considered for refinancing with "cash out" to the borrower at loan closing. Secondary marketing people normally refer to loans that are over 1 year ago old as "seasoned production".

SEC *See* SECURITIES AND EXCHANGE COMMISSION.

SECOND MORTGAGE A real estate mortgage that is second or junior to a first or senior mortgage. A second mortgage has all the rights of a first mortgage with one big exception. Foreclosure by the first mortgage will eliminate a second mortgage. The balance of the second mortgage is not eliminated by foreclosure of the first, but the second mortgage no longer has the property as security for the loan. Second mortgages have more risk than first mortgages because of the possibility of elimination by foreclosure of a first mortgage; therefore, they are normally made at a higher rate of interest and for a shorter term as compared to first mortgages.

A second mortgage automatically becomes a first mortgage if the first mortgage is paid in full. In some cases, parties to a mortgaged property may not want the second to become a first mortgage. For example, there exists an opportunity to refinance a first mortgage with an interest rate of 13% with a loan of an identical balance but with a rate of 9% interest. All parties to the mortgaged property, the first and second mortgagees and the mortgagor, feel they will benefit from the refinancing. In this case the second mortgage will sign a subordination agreement allowing a substitution of first mortgages without disturbing the priority of mortgages.

There is some protection for a second mortgage on a foreclosure by a first mortgage because of a default. If the mortgagor becomes in default on the first mortgage, the second mortgage can foreclose. This process prevents the second mortgage from being eliminated by foreclosure of the first. It is of no consequence if the mortgagor is not delinquent on the second mortgage. A default of the second or the first gives an owner of a second mortgage the right to foreclose.

A lender may use a loan application like the one in Exhibit 78 for second mortgages and home improvement loans.

See GUARANTY PERFORMANCE, PRIORITY, SUBORDINATION.

SECONDARY FINANCING Second mortgages or junior liens.

Exhibit 78

Second Mortgage or Home Improvement Loan Application

TYPE LOAN APPLIED FOR	Amount	Interest Rate	No. of mos.	Monthly payment Principal & Interest	Property type
☐ Conventional ☐ FHA ☐ VA ☐ Secured ☐ Unsecured	$	☐ Simple Int. ☐ Add-on %			☐ Single Family Dwelling ☐ Condo ☐ 2-4 Family Dwelling ☐ PUD ☐ Other _____

Address of property to be improved		Date purchased	Cash down payment	Purchase price $	Present value of home $

Title in name of	Address of title holder	Mortgage Type: Is your present first mortgage a conventional graduated payment mortgage or an FHA 245 mortgage loan? ☐ No ☐ Yes If yes, attach payment schedule

Yr. house built	No. of rooms	No. of bed-rooms	No. of baths	Family room or den ☐ Yes ☐ No	Gross living area sq. ft.	Garage/Carport (Specify type & no.)	Central air ☐ Yes ☐ No

If this is a new residential structure, has it been completed and occupied for 90 days or longer? ☐ Yes ☐ No

Improvements Planned (copied estimate or itemized cost breakdown must be attached)	Type of Improvement
	☐ Property Improvement ☐ Rehabilitation/Modernization ☐ Additions ☐ Energy Conservation ☐ Solar Installation

The Co-Borrower Section and all other Co-Borrower questions must be completed and the appropriate boxes(es) checked if ☐ another person will be jointly obligated with the Borrower on the loan, or ☐ the Borrower is relying on income from alimony, child support or separate maintenance or on the income or assets of another person as a basis for repayment of the loan, or ☐ the Borrower is married and resides, or the property is located in a community property state.

Borrower		Co-Borrower	
Name	Age	Name	Age
Present Address (if different from above) No. Years _____ ☐ Own ☐ Rent		Present Address (if different from above) No. Years _____ ☐ Own ☐ Rent	
Street		Street	
City/State/Zip		City/State/Zip	
Former address if less than 2 years at present address		Former address if less than 2 years at present address	
Street		Street	
City/State/Zip		City/State/Zip	
Years at former address ☐ Own ☐ Rent		Years at former address ☐ Own ☐ Rent	
Complete for Secured Loans Only	Dep. other than listed by Co-Borrower	Complete for Secured Loans Only	Dep. other than listed by Borrower
☐ Married ☐ Separated ☐ Unmarried (incl. single, divorced, widowed)	No. ___ Ages	☐ Married ☐ Separated ☐ Unmarried (incl. single, divorced, widowed)	No. ___ Ages
Name and Address of Employer	Years employed in this line of work or profession? _____ Years Years on this job _____ ☐ Self Employed*	Name and Address of Employer	Years employed in this line of work or profession? _____ Years Years on this job _____ ☐ Self Employed*
Position/Title	Type of Business	Position/Title	Type of Business
Social Security Number**	Home Phone	Business Phone	Social Security Number**	Home Phone	Business Phone
Name & Address of nearest relative not living with you	Relationship	Home Phone	Name & Address of nearest relative not living with you	Relationship	Home Phone

Gross Monthly Income				Bank	Account No.	Name & Address of Depository
Item	Borrower	Co-Borrower	Total	Checking		
Empl. Income	$	$	$	☐ Yes ☐ No		
Other 1 (Before completing, see notice under Describe Other Income below.)				Savings		
Total	$	$	$	☐ Yes ☐ No		

Describe Other Income

B-Borrower	NOTICE: 1 Alimony, child support, or separate maintenance income need not be revealed if the Borrower or Co-Borrower does not choose to have it considered as a basis for repaying this loan.	Monthly Amount $

If Employed In Current Position For Less Than Two Years, Complete the Following

B/C	Previous Employer/School	City/State	Type of Business	Position/Title	Dates From/To	Monthly Income

These Questions Apply To Both Borrower and Co-Borrower

If a "yes" answer is given to a question in this column, please explain on an attached sheet.	Borrower Yes or No	Co-Borrower Yes or No		Borrower Yes or No	Co-Borrower Yes or No
Are there any outstanding judgments against you?	___	___	Are you a co-maker or endorser on a note?	___	___
Have you been declared bankrupt within the past 7 years?	___	___			
Have you had property foreclosed upon or given title or deed in lieu thereof in the last 7 years?	___	___	Do you have any past due obligations owed to or insured by any agency of the federal government?	___	___
Are you a party to a law suit?	___	___	Are you a U.S. citizen?	___	___
			If "no," are you a resident alien?	___	___
Are you obligated to pay alimony, child support, or separate maintenance?	___	___	If "no," are you a non-resident alien?	___	___

*FHLMC/FNMA require business credit report, signed Federal Income Tax returns for last two years; and, if available, audited Profit and Loss Statement plus balance sheet for same period.
** Required only FHA or VA home improvement loan.

Freddie Mac Form 703 Rev. 10/86   VMP-71 (8901)01   VMP MORTGAGE FORMS • (313)293-8100 • (800)521-7291   Fannie Mae 1012 Rev. 10/86

Exhibit 78 (continued)

DEBTS: List all fixed obligations and installment accounts (if more space is needed list on attached sheets.)*
If no outstanding debt, list three previous credit references.

B-Borrower C-Co-Borrower	Creditor's Name and Address	Account No.	Date Incurred	Original Amount	Present Balance	Monthly Payment	Amount Past Due
				$	$	$	$

Auto

Lien Holder:	Year and Make					
Lien Holder:	Year and Make					

Real Estate

Name & Address of First Lien Holder of Security Property						
Name & Address of Subordinate Lien Holder(s) of Security Property						
List Debts On Other Real Estate Owned						

List any additional names under which credit has previously been received:	If not included in monthly mortgage payment enter the following:		
	Monthly payment for Tax and Insurance ▶		
	Monthly payment for Home Owner Association dues ▶		
	Total Monthly Obligations ▶		

IMPORTANT — APPLICANT READ BEFORE SIGNING

I/We apply for the loan indicated in this application which may be secured by a mortgage or deed of trust on the property described herein and represent that the property will not be used for any illegal or restricted purpose, and that all statements made in this application are true and are made for the purpose of obtaining the loan. Verification may be obtained from any source named in this application. The original or a copy of this application will be retained by the lender, even if the loan is not granted. I/We hereby consent to and authorize the lender, HUD-FHA, FNMA or FHLMC, after the giving of reasonable notice, to enter the improved property for the sole purpose of determining that the improvements specified in this application have been completed.

I/WE UNDERSTAND THAT THE SELECTION OF A CONTRACTOR OR DEALER, ACCEPTANCE OF MATERIAL USED AND WORK PERFORMED IS MY/OUR RESPONSIBILITY. NEITHER THE LENDER, HUD-FHA, FNMA NOR FHLMC GUARANTEES THE MATERIAL OR WORKMANSHIP.

I/We ☐ : do or ☐ do not intend to occupy the property as my/our primary residence.

I/We understand that it may be a federal crime punishable by fine or imprisonment, or both, to knowingly make any false statements concerning any of the above facts as applicable under the provisions of the United States Criminal Code.

_____ Date _____ _____ Date _____
Borrower's Signature   Co-Borrower's Signature

Information For Government Monitoring Purposes

The following information is requested by the Federal Government for certain types of loans related to a dwelling, in order to monitor the lender's compliance with equal credit opportunity and fair housing laws. You are not required to furnish this information, but are encouraged to do so. The law provides that a lender may neither discriminate on the basis of this information, nor on whether you choose to furnish it. However, if you choose not to furnish it, under Federal regulations this lender is required to note race and sex on the basis of visual observation or surname. If you do not wish to furnish the above information, please check the box below. [Lender must review the above material to assure that the disclosures satisfy all requirements to which the Lender is subject under applicable state law for the particular type of loan applied for.]

Borrower: ☐ I do not wish to furnish this information   **Co-Borrower:** ☐ I do not wish to furnish this information

Race/National Origin: **Race/National Origin:**

☐ American Indian, Alaskan Native   ☐ Asian, Pacific Islander   ☐ American Indian, Alaskan Native   ☐ Asian, Pacific Islander
☐ Black   ☐ Hispanic   ☐ White   ☐ Black   ☐ Hispanic   ☐ White
☐ Other (specify): _____   ☐ Other (specify): _____
Sex: ☐ Female   ☐ Male   **Sex:** ☐ Female   ☐ Male

This application was taken by:
☐ face to face interview
☐ by mail   _____   _____
☐ by telephone   Interviewer   Name of Interviewer's Employer

                                   _____   _____
                                   Interviewer's Phone Number   Address of Interviewer's Employer

Freddie Mac Form 703 Rev. 10/86   * Indicate by asterisk all FHA and Government Agency Loans.   Fannie Mae Form 1012 Rev. 10/86

SECONDARY MORTGAGE MARKET A market for the sale and purchase of real estate mortgages and mortgage-backed securities. It is a resale market for GNMA, FNMA, and FHLMC mortgage-backed securities. Whole loans are resold in the secondary mortgage market by primary lenders.

This market buys, sells, and trades existing mortgage loans and participations in such mortgages. The primary mortgage originations can be offered to any entities in the secondary market qualified to purchase originations. The secondary mortgage markets create new capital for primary mortgage lenders so that more mortgage loans can be originated.

See PRIMARY MARKET.

SECONDARY MORTGAGE MARKETING The process of selling closed mortgage loans to investors in the secondary market, obtaining commitments, pricing, and establishing rates. This process incorporates the assurance that mortgages originated are saleable products.

SECOND HOME A vacation home. The IRS defines a second home as a residence used by the taxpayer for personal residence purposes for at least 14 days of the year or 10% of the number of days that property is rented at fair market value, whichever is the greater.

The FHA second home loan is for those who intend to occupy a home for only recreation or vacation purposes. The loan is restricted to only one loan per mortgagor and the maximum LTV is 85%. The intent of the mortgagor will be a key issue in originating these loans.

The 1990 Housing Bill prohibits FHA insurance on second homes, except in extraordinary, hardship cases.

SECTION 8 PROGRAM A rental subsidy program. Eligible families receive a certificate that entitles them to seek housing in the community and to have much of the rent paid either by HUD or a Public Housing Authority.

SECTOR SPREAD The difference in yields/prices between mortgages and securities as hedging tools such as Treasury Bills, Notes, Bonds and Ginnie Mae instruments. The two major reasons for this price difference are (1) changing expectations of mortgage prepayments that vary with loan coupon and market conditions and (2) supply factors in the Treasury and the mortgage securities markets.

SECURED PARTY A party having a secured interest in an asset. For example, a lender is a secured party when the property is named in the mortgage as collateral for the loan.

SECURITIES AND EXCHANGE COMMISSION (SEC) A U.S. government regulatory and enforcement agency that supervises investment trading activities and registers public investments and those securities that fall under its jurisdiction. The SEC administers statutes to enforce disclosure requirements that were designated to protect investors in securities offerings. Government Sponsored Enterprises (GSEs such as Fannie Mae) currently enjoys several exemptions from securities laws.

SECURITY (1) Real estate that serves as collateral for a debt. (2) The debt instrument proving the right a party has in a property.

SECURITY DEPOSIT A deposit paid as good faith for completing the terms of a lease.

SECURITY INSTRUMENTS Documents that show evidence of ownership and can be traded for value, e.g., bonds, stocks, certificates, and mortgages. Fixed annuities, life insurance policies, IRA or Keogh plans, commodity futures contracts, and shares issued by a non-profit organization are not classified as securities.

Lenders can use the form in Exhibit 79 to help verify securities that applicants own.

SECURITY INTEREST The interest in real estate serving as collateral.

SEED MONEY Front-end funds that are required for a real estate transaction. Examples of front-end cost would be feasibility studies, appraisals, loan commitment fees, attorney fees, and accountant fees.

SETTLING Movement of the foundation of a building that can cause cracks in interior and exterior walls and various other structural problems. There are many causes for shifts in a foundation. Earthquakes, unstable soil such as sandy loam soil, are examples of causes by nature. Failure to comply with the way the foundation should have been built, or failure to build the proper foundation, such as a reinforced foundation, are examples of causes by man. Homeowners victimized by settling, especially by natural causes, should contact their lender, or FHA or VA. The lender or an agency (FHA/VA) will advise the homeowner of their alternatives.
See FROST LINE.

SEISIN The actual possession of real estate and its rights as if it were a freehold estate. Seisin is synonymous with ownership.
See FREEHOLD.

Exhibit 79

VMP MORTGAGE FORMS • (313)293-8100 • (800)521-7291

VMP -24S (9007)

INSTRUCTIONS TO LENDER:
1. FILL OUT PART I - REQUEST
2. HAVE APPLICANT(S) SIGN EACH COPY (No Carbon Signatures)
3. FORWARD TO SECURITIES DEALER

INSTRUCTION TO SECURITIES DEALER:
1. COMPLETE PART II AND III
2. RETURN BOTH COMPLETED COPIES TO LENDER

70,411 H

Request for Verification of Securities

Privacy Act Notice: This information is to be used by the agency collecting it or its assignees in determining whether you qualify as a prospective mortgagor under its program. It will not be disclosed outside the agency except as required and permitted by law. You do not have to provide this information, but if you do not your application for approval as a prospective mortgagor or borrower may be delayed or rejected. The information requested in this form is authorized by Title 38, USC, Chapter 37 (if VA); by 12 USC, Section 1701 et. seq. (if HUD/FHA), by 42 USC, Section 1452b (if HUD/CPD); and Title 42 USC, 1471 et. seq., or 7 USC, 1921 et. seq. (if USDA/FmHA).

Instructions: Lender - Complete items 1 through 8. Have applicant(s) complete item 9. Forward directly to securities dealer named in item 1.
Securities Dealer - Please complete items 10 through 16 and return directly to lender named in item 2.
The form is to be transmitted directly to the lender named in item 2 and is not to be transmitted through the applicant(s) or any other party.

Part I - Request

1. To (Name and address of securities dealer)	2. From (Name and address of lender)

I certify that this verification has been sent directly to the bank or securities dealer and has not passed through the hands of the applicant or any other party.

3. Signature of Lender	4. Title	5. Date	6. Lender's Number (Optional)

7. Information To Be Verified

Account in the Name of				Account Number	

# Shares	Type/Series	Issuer	Div. Income	Market Value
			$	$

TO SECURITIES DEALER: I/We have applied for a loan and stated in my financial statement that the current balance with you is as shown above. You are authorized to verify this information and to supply the lender identified above with the information requested in items 10 and 11. Your response is solely a matter of courtesy for which no responsibility is attached to your institution or any of your officers.

8. Name and Address of Applicant(s)	9. Signature of Applicant(s)
	X
	X

Part II - To be Completed by Securities Dealer

10. Account in the Name of				Account Number	

# Shares	Type/Series	Issuer	Div. Income	Market Value
			$	$

11. Additional information which may be of assistance in determination of credit worthiness.

Part III - Authorized Signature - Federal statutes provide severe penalties for any fraud, intentional misrepresentation, or criminal connivance or conspiracy purposed to influence the issuance of any guaranty or insurance by the VA Secretary, the USDA, FmHA/FHA Commissioner, or the HUD/CPD Assistant Secretary.

12. Signature of Securities Dealer Representative	13. Title (Please print or type)	14. Date

15. Print or type name signed in item 12

16. Phone No.

7/90

SECURITIES DEALER-RETURN BOTH COPIES TO LENDER
LENDER-DETACH THIS COPY AND FILE FOR FOLLOW-UP

SELF-EMPLOYED BORROWERS Lenders usually classify a borrower as self-employed if he/she owns 25% or more of a business.

Lenders will normally consider income from a self-employed borrower if there is at least a two-year history. An applicant who has between one to two years of self-employment may be considered if there is a previous history of employment or education in a related field. Lenders will usually not consider income from self-employed borrowers with a business less than one-year old.

When a borrower's income is from a business that he/she owns or is a principal owner and the income will be used for loan qualification, the amount of income considered will be either: (1) the total net profit, (2) the amount of the draw or bonus taken form the capital account, if the business is a partnership, plus the borrower's share of the net profit, or (3) the amount of wage or salary as shown on the W - 2, if the business is a corporation, plus any bonus or other compensation. Since Federal Tax returns will be used in verifying income, a lender will allow a self-employed borrower to add back to the net income: (1) all depreciation, (2) depletion, and (3) IRA/Keough contributions. Retained earnings do not normally count as income. A self-employed borrower cannot use withdrawals from capital accounts as income.

Consistency of income is important. Income that has been level or increasing is acceptable. A decline in income over an extended period of time will require explanation. It may be that the decline is small compared to the applicant's net profit. Furthermore, any decline in income may be due to a temporary industry change.

An average monthly income is calculated for self-employed borrowers because the income is subject to fluctuations. An average figure is a better way to decide the long-term earning ability of the borrower. A minimum of two year's income must be verified. When a year-to-date income statement is used, the income on the statement should be averaged with the previous two year's tax returns. If the borrower provides the lender with tax returns for the past three years, the income from each return should be averaged.

Self-employed or fully commissioned people should be prepared to submit a complete and signed tax return (complete with all schedules) for the past two calendar years, plus a year-to-date income and expense statement and a current balance sheet. If the business is a corporation or partnership, copies of signed federal business income tax returns for the last two years with all applicable schedules attached will be required.

Lenders may want to use the forms in Exhibits 80-82 to help in underwriting self-employed applicants.

See INCOME ANALYSIS.

SELLER-SERVICER A lender approved to sell and service mortgages. Approval to sell and service loans is granted by the investor. See Servicing Agreement.

Exhibit 80

Self-Employed Income Analysis

Borrower Name
_____

Property Address
_____

General Instructions: This form is to be used as a guide in Underwriting the Self-employed borrower. The underwriter has a choice in analyzing the Individual Tax return by either the Schedule Analysis Method or the Adjusted Gross Income (AGI) Method.

The AGI Method begins with adjusted gross income from the individual tax returns and either increases or decreases that figure after analyzing specific lines and schedules of the return.

Adjusted Gross Income (AGI) Method

A. Individual Tax Return (1040)   19 _____   19 _____   19 _____

   1. Adjusted Gross Income   _____   _____   _____

Income Section:

   2. Wages, salary considered elsewhere . . . . (−) _____   _____   _____
   3. Taxable Interest Income . . . . (−) _____   _____   _____
   4. Tax-exempt Interest Income . . . . (+) _____   _____   _____
   5. Dividend Income . . . . (−) _____   _____   _____
   6. Taxable Refunds . . . . (−) _____   _____   _____
   7. Alimony . . . . (−) _____   _____   _____
   8. Business Income or Loss - Schedule C
      a. Depletion . . . . (+) _____   _____   _____
      b. Depreciation . . . . (+) _____   _____   _____
      c. 20% Meals and Entertainment Exclusion . . . . (−) _____   _____   _____
   9. (−) Capital Gain or (+) Capital Loss - Schedule D . . .   _____   _____   _____
  10. IRA Distributions (non-taxable) . . . . (+) _____   _____   _____
  11. Pensions and Annuities (non-taxable) . . . . (+) _____   _____   _____
  12. Schedule E - Depreciation . . . . (+) _____   _____   _____
  13. Schedule F - Depreciation . . . . (+) _____   _____   _____
  14. Unemployment Compensation . . . . (−) _____   _____   _____
  15. Social Security Benefits (non-taxable) . . . . (+) _____   _____   _____
  16. Other _____   _____   _____   _____
       _____   _____   _____   _____

Adjustment Section:

  17. IRA Deduction . . . . (+) _____   _____   _____
  18. Self-Employed Health Insurance . . . . (+) _____   _____   _____
  19. Keogh Retirement Plan . . . . (+) _____   _____   _____
  20. Penalty for Early Withdrawal . . . . (+) _____   _____   _____
  21. Alimony . . . . (+) _____   _____   _____

Additional Schedules:

  22. Form 2106 Unreimbursed expenses (not fully deductible) . . (−) _____   _____   _____
  23. Form 4562 Amortization . . . . (+) _____   _____   _____
  24. Form 8582*
      a. Unallowed Losses . . . . (−) _____   _____   _____
      b. Carryovers . . . . (+) _____   _____   _____
  25. Total . . . .   _____   _____   _____

Unallowed Losses or Carryover Losses (From Form 8582) = (Net loss for active participation activities acquired before 10/23/86) + (Net loss for active participation activities acquired after 10/22/86) + (Net loss for passive activities acquired before 10/23/86) + (Net loss for passive activities acquired after 10/22/86) − (Total losses allowed for all passive activities for tax year) **Treat numbers as if they were all positive.**
For the 1987 and 1988 Tax Year Unallowed Losses or Carryover Losses (From Form 8582) = (Line 1b + Line 1e + Line 2b + Line 2e) − Line 19

Exhibit 80 (continued)

Self-Employed Income Analysis

B. Corporate Tax Return Form (1120) - Corporate Income to qualify the borrower will be considered only if the borrower can provide evidence of access to the funds.

	19 _____	19 _____	19 _____
1. Taxable Income (Tax and Payments Section)	(+) _____	_____	_____
2. Total Tax (Tax and Payments Section)	(−) _____	_____	_____
3. Depreciation (Deductions Section)	(+) _____	_____	_____
4. Depletion (Deductions Section)	(+) _____	_____	_____
5. Mortgages, notes, bonds payable in less than one year (Balance Sheets Section)	(−) _____	_____	_____
6. Subtotal	_____	_____	_____
7. Times individual percentage of ownership	X _____ %	X _____ %	X _____ %
8. Subtotal	_____	_____	_____
9. Dividend Income reflected on borrower's individual income tax returns	(−) _____	_____	_____
10. Total Income available to borrower	_____	_____	_____

C. S Corporation Tax Returns (Form 1120s) or Partnership Tax Returns (Form 1065) - Partnership or S Corporation income to qualify the borrower will be considered only if the borrower can provide evidence of access to the funds.

	19 _____	19 _____	19 _____
1. Depreciation (Deductions Section)	(+) _____	_____	_____
2. Depletion (Deductions Section)	(+) _____	_____	_____
3. Mortgages, notes, bonds payable in less than one year (Balance Sheets Section)	(−) _____	_____	_____
4. Subtotal	_____	_____	_____
5. Times individual percentage of ownership	X _____ %	X _____ %	X _____ %
6. Total income available to borrower	_____	_____	_____
Total Income Available (add A, B, C)	I _____	II _____	III _____

D. Year-to-Date Profit and Loss

Year-to-date income to qualify the borrower will be considered only if that income is in line with the previous year's earnings or if audited financial statements are provided.

1. Salary/Draws to Individual . . . . $ _____

2. Total Allowable add back $ _____ X _____ % of individual ownership = $ _____

3. Total net profit $ _____ X _____ % of individual ownership = $ _____

4. Total . . . . $ _____

Combined Total I, II, III, YTD = $ _____ divided by _____ months = $ _____ Monthly Average

This form is only a reference to help organize information from the tax returns. You must refer to the selling guide for our complete underwriting requirements on the self-employed.

Fannie Mae
Form 1084B Dec. 89

Exhibit 81

 FannieMae

Comparative Income Analysis

Borrower Name

Company Name

General Instructions: This form is to be used to compare the borrower's company over a period of years. Each item is defined as follows:

  Gross Income = Gross receipts or Sales (–) Returns and Allowances

  Expenses = Cost of goods sold (+) Total Deductions

  Taxable Income on
   Schedule C = Net Profit or loss (Sole Proprietorship)
   Form 1065 = Ordinary Income or Loss (Partnership)
   Form 1120 = Taxable Income (Corporation)
   Form 1120(s) = Taxable Income (S Corporation)

	19 _____	19 _____	19 _____
Gross Income	_____ 100%	_____ 100%	_____ 100%
% Change	(+) (–)_____ % **	(+) (–)_____ % **	
Expenses	_____ % *	_____ % *	_____ % *
% Change	(+) (–)_____ % **	(+) (–)_____ % **	
Taxable Income	_____ % *	_____ % *	_____ % *
% Change	(+) (–)_____ % **	(+) (–)_____ % **	

* The expenses and taxable income each period as a percentage of gross income for that period.

** The percentage change for each item from the previous period.

The Taxable Income Trend is _____ increasing _____ level _____ decreasing.

Exhibit 82

Operating Income Statement
One-to Four-Family Investment Property and Two-to Four-Family Owner-Occupied Property

Property Address

Street	City	State	Zip Code

General Instructions: This form is to be prepared jointly by the loan applicant, the appraiser, and the lender's underwriter. The applicant must complete the following schedule indicating each unit's rental status, lease expiration date, current rent, market rent, and the responsibility for utility expenses. Rental figures must be based on the rent for an "unfurnished" unit.

	Currently Rented	Expiration Date	Current Rent Per Month	Market Rent Per Month		Paid By-Owner	Paid By Tenant
Unit No. 1	Yes ____ No ____	_____	$ _____	$ _____	Electricity	☐	☐
Unit No. 2	Yes ____ No ____	_____	$ _____	$ _____	Gas	☐	☐
Unit No. 3	Yes ____ No ____	_____	$ _____	$ _____	Fuel Oil	☐	☐
Unit No. 4	Yes ____ No ____	_____	$ _____	$ _____	Fuel (Other)	☐	☐
Total			$ _____	$ _____	Water/Sewer	☐	☐
					Trash Removal	☐	☐

The applicant should complete all of the income and expense projections and for existing properties provide actual year-end operating statements for the past two years *(for new properties the applicant's projected income and expenses must be provided)*. This Operating Income Statement and any previous operating statements the applicant provides must then be sent to the appraiser for review, comment, and/or adjustments next to the applicant's figures *(e.g., Applicant/Appraiser 288/300)*. If the appraiser is retained to complete the form instead of the applicant, the lender must provide to the appraiser the aforementioned operating statements, mortgage insurance premium, HOA dues, leasehold payments, subordinate financing, and/or any other relevant information as to the income and expenses of the subject property received from the applicant to substantiate the projections. The underwriter should carefully review the applicant's/appraiser's projections and the appraiser's comments concerning those projections. The underwriter should make any final adjustments that are necessary to more accurately reflect any income or expense items that appear unreasonable for the market. *(Real estate taxes and insurance on these types of properties are included in PITI and not calculated as an annual expense item.)*
Income should be based on current rents, but should not exceed market rents. When there are no current rents because the property is proposed, new, or currently vacant, market rents should be used.

Annual Income and Expense Projection for Next 12 months

	By Applicant/Appraiser	Adjustments by Lender's Underwriter
Income *(Do no include income for owner-occupied units)*		
Gross Annual Rental *(from unit(s) to be rented)*	$ _____	$ _____
Other Income *(include sources)*	+ _____	+ _____
Total	$ _____	$ _____
Less Vacancy/Rent Loss	− _____ (___ %)	− _____ (___ %)
Effective Gross Income	$ _____	$ _____
Expenses *(Do not include expenses for owner-occupied units)*		
Electricity	_____	_____
Gas	_____	_____
Fuel Oil	_____	_____
Fuel .... (Type _____)	_____	_____
Water/Sewer	_____	_____
Trash Removal	_____	_____
Pest Control	_____	_____
Other Taxes or Licenses	_____	_____
Casual Labor	_____	_____
This includes the costs for public area cleaning, snow removal, etc., even though the applicant may not elect to contract for such services.		
Interior Paint/Decorating	_____	_____
This includes the costs of contract labor and materials that are required to maintain the interiors of the living units.		
General Repairs/Maintenance	_____	_____
This includes the costs of contract labor and materials that are required to maintain the public corridors, stairways, roofs, mechanical systems, grounds, etc.		
Management Expenses	_____	_____
These are the customary expenses that a professional management company would charge to manage the property.		
Supplies	_____	_____
This includes the costs of items like light bulbs, janitorial supplies, etc.		
Total Replacement Reserves - See Schedule on Pg. 2	_____	_____
Miscellaneous	_____	_____
....	_____	_____
....	_____	_____
....	_____	_____
....	_____	_____
....	_____	_____
....	_____	_____
Total Operating Expenses	$ _____	$ _____

Freddie Mac
Form 998 Aug 88
VMP -97 (8809)

This Form Must Be Reproduced By Seller
Page 1 of 2
VMP MORTGAGE FORMS • (313)293-8100 • (800)521-7291

Fannie Mae
Form 216 Aug 88

Exhibit 82 (continued)

Replacement Reserve Schedule

Adequate replacement reserves must be calculated regardless of whether actual reserves are provided for on the owner's operating statements or are customary in the local market. This represents the total average yearly reserves. Generally, all equipment and components that have a remaining life of more than one year - such as refrigerators, stoves, clothes washers/dryers, trash compactors, furnaces, roofs, and carpeting, etc. - should be expensed on a replacement cost basis.

Equipment	Replacement Cost	Remaining Life	By Applicant/ Appraiser	Lender Adjustments
Stoves/Ranges	@$ _____ ea. ÷	_____ Yrs. x _____ Units = $	_____	$ _____
Refrigerators	@$ _____ ea. ÷	_____ Yrs. x _____ Units = $	_____	$ _____
Dishwashers	@$ _____ ea. ÷	_____ Yrs. x _____ Units = $	_____	$ _____
A/C Units	@$ _____ ea. ÷	_____ Yrs. x _____ Units = $	_____	$ _____
C. Washer/Dryers ..	@$ _____ ea. ÷	_____ Yrs. x _____ Units = $	_____	$ _____
HW Heaters	@$ _____ ea. ÷	_____ Yrs. x _____ Units = $	_____	$ _____
Furnace(s)	@$ _____ ea. ÷	_____ Yrs. x _____ Units = $	_____	$ _____
(Other)	@$ _____ ea. ÷	_____ Yrs. x _____ Units = $	_____	$ _____
Roof	@$ _____ ÷	_____ Yrs. x One Bldg. =	$ _____	$ _____

Carpeting (Wall to Wall)

		Remaining Life		
(Units)	_____ Total Sq. Yds. @$ _____ Per Sq. Yd. ÷	_____ Yrs. = $	_____	$ _____
(Public Areas)	_____ Total Sq. Yds. @$ _____ Per Sq. Yd. ÷	_____ Yrs. = $	_____	$ _____

Total Replacement Reserves. (Enter on Pg. 1) $ _____ $ _____

Operating Income Reconciliation

$ _____ − $ _____ = $ _____ ÷ 12 = $ _____
Effective Gross Income   Total Operating Expenses   Operating Income   Monthly Operating Income

$ _____ − $ _____ = $ _____
Monthly Operating Income   Monthly Housing Expense   Net Cash Flow

(Note: Monthly Housing Expense includes principal and interest on the mortgage, hazard insurance premiums, real estate taxes, mortgage insurance premiums, HOA dues, leasehold payments, and subordinate financing payments.)

Underwriter's instructions for 2-4 Family Owner-Occupied Properties

- If Monthly Operating Income is a positive number, enter as "Net Rental Income" in the "Gross Monthly Income" section of Freddie Mac Form 65/ Fannie Mae Form 1003. If Monthly Operating Income is a negative number, it must be included as a liability for qualification purposes.

- The borrower's monthly housing expense-to-income ratio must be calculated by comparing the total Monthly Housing Expense for the **subject property** to the borrower's stable monthly income.

Underwriter's instructions for 1-4 Family Investment Properties

- If Net Cash Flow is a positive number, enter as "Net Rental Income" in the "Gross Monthly Income" section of Freddie Mac Form 65/Fannie Mae Form 1003. If Net Cash Flow is a negative number, it must be included as a liability for qualification purposes.

- The borrower's monthly housing expense-to-income ratio must be calculated by comparing the total monthly housing expense for the borrower's **primary residence** to the borrower's stable monthly income.

Appraiser's Comments (Including sources for data and rationale for the projections)

_____   _____   _____
Appraiser Name   Appraiser Signature   Date

Underwriter's Comments and Rationale for Adjustments

_____   _____   _____
Underwriter Name   Underwriter Signature   Date

SELLER'S MARKET Economic conditions with demand for housing at a peak level. Seller's usually dictate the terms in a contract of sale in a seller's market.

SEMI-CIRCULAR ROOF *See* ROOF.

SEMI-DETACHED DWELLING A dwelling that is attached to one wall of an adjoining dwelling. A townhouse is a good example of a semi-detached dwelling.
See PARTY WALL.

SENIOR MORTGAGE A first mortgage is normally a senior mortgage. The priority of mortgages can be compared to rungs on a ladder. A first mortgage is the top rung, a second mortgage is the second rung, and it continues for each subsequent or junior mortgage. If the first mortgage matures or is refinanced and if there is an outstanding second mortgage, it will become a senior mortgage when the first mortgage is paid, unless there is a subordination agreement.
See SUBORDINATION AGREEMENT.

SENIOR/SUBORDINATED MORTGAGE SECURITIES Developed in 1986 and used heavily by California S&Ls; the private pool mortgage issuers may structure a senior/subordinated pool of mortgages into two subpools. These subpools are divided into pieces therefore passing the income earned from the pieces separately to investors. The senior loan pool usually consists of approximately 90% of the pooled loans. It is a so-called senior pool since any loss through foreclosure will be subtracted from income stream being received by the holders of the junior piece or subpool.

   Mortgage pool insurance was avoidable on the senior piece due to the high pricing of the 90% separation of a full pool. A tax disadvantage was realized on the junior piece when it was sold to investors so it was naturally retained by issuers except, when and if, the issuers adapt a strategy of declaring the senior/sub mortgage security as a REMIC under new tax laws thereby avoiding this disadvantage. The senior/sub securities are expected to be used by conduits of the secondary markets under the REMIC legislation.
See REAL ESTATE MORTGAGE INVESTMENT CONDUITS.

SEPTIC TANK An underground private sewage disposal system. The waste is converted to gas and liquids before sinking into the ground (called a disposal field) from field lines that extend out from the tank.

   Lenders normally require a percolation test from a county health authority to certify that the septic tank is in proper working condition. Septic tanks are best used in low density population areas and in soil that is porus enough to accept the seepage from the field lines.

SEQUESTRATION ORDER A court order authorizing the seizing of land, rents, or profits from a defendant who is in contempt of court. The sequestration order assists in the proper execution of rulings from a court.

SERVICING Lenders that collect mortgage payments and then disperse principal, interest, and in most cases, taxes and insurance.

SERVICING AGREEMENT OR SALE AND SERVICING AGREEMENT An agreement setting forth the requirements of the seller, who sells loans and retains servicing, and the investor, who purchases the loans. Major items addressed in an servicing agreement are as follows:

- Proof that the seller is authorized and is capable of servicing mortgage loans.
- What is to be in a mortgage file, how they will be maintained, and the custody of the files.
- What type of reports are required and when they are due. The types of reports fall into two broad categories: reports to the investor and reports to the mortgagor. The fiscal responsibilities of the accounting and the type of accounting records.
- The type of amortization method used. The application of payment for a deficiency, a mortgage paid in full, and a partial payments. Reapplication of prior payments are normally prohibited.
- The establishment and treatment of escrows.
- The timely payment of taxes and assessments.
- The type of insurance required, hazard and any flood insurance required.
- Any private mortgage insurance requirements.
- Guidelines for Partial Release, Eminent Domain, or any other changes that affect the mortgaged property.
- What happens when properties are transferred.
- The method of treating delinquencies. The schedule of late charges.
- How abandoned properties are to be treated.
- How adverse events to the property are to be treated, e.g., liens, vacancy, and waste.

- Stipulations against modifications and releases of the mortgage documents except as outlined by the investor.
- Conditions requiring the repurchase of a loan by the seller/servicer.
- The servicing compensation.
- Other servicing agreements, such as a subservicing agreement.
- Auditing procedures and requirements.
- What happens in the event of a financial change to the servicer, such as bankruptcy.
- How the investor will be indemnified against any adverse actions caused by the servicer, e.g., fraud, any breach of the servicing agreement.
- How the servicing agreement can be terminated.
- Under what conditions and how servicing can be transferred by the seller or the investor.

The 1990 Housing Bill requires lenders to disclose on all home mortgages, at the time of origination, (1) whether they have the capacity to service the loan, (2) the probability (to the nearest 25%) that the servicing on the loan will be transferred in the first year, and (3) the percentage (to the nearest 25%) of their loans made during the previous complete calendar year where the servicing was transferred.

The bill requires certain actions that previously existed only as informal industry standards. Specifically, all servicers of any type of home mortgages must notify borrowers in writing of any transfer of servicing rights at least 15 days before the next mortgage payment is due. Servicers are prohibited from charging late fees for 60 days following a servicing transfer to borrowers who have made payments to the wrong servicer.

See DELINQUENCY RATIO.

SERVICING INCOME The gross fee paid to a mortgage banking enterprise for servicing a loan. The fee is deducted from the gross interest rate the investor receives for a loan. If the interest rate for a loan is 10% and the lender charges the investor 1% for servicing the loan, the investor receives a net interest of 9% for the loan.

GNMA allows a servicing fee of up to 3/8ths of one percent. Servicing fees for conventional loans can be whatever the servicer negotiates with the investor.

SERVICING RELEASED The lender sells the loan to the investor and lender is released from servicing responsibilities according to a Purchase Agreement.

The relinquishment of servicing is documented by the execution of an Assignment of Servicing.

SERVICING RETAINED The lender sells the loan to the investor according to the Purchase Agreement and retains the responsibilities and income related to servicing the loan according to the SALE AND SERVICING AGREEMENT.

SERVICING RIGHTS Servicing rights may be retained by the originating (primary) lender/servicer of the mortgage as an asset. This annuity is therefore realized through servicing fees.

The mechanics of issuing MBSs encompasses the need for many loans great enough to arrange pools for the security. In agreeing for such arrangement, the issuing institution and the primary lender reach a purchase price for the pool of loans originated by the lender/servicer of 12% loans, for example. But the lender continues to service the mortgages. Under such contract, the originator is declared the permanent primary servicer.

The issuing institution will commit itself to the payment of 40 basis points annually as a servicing fee to the primary lender/servicer. The net pass-through percentage rate becomes 11.6 to the issuing institution in return for the necessary service function that the primary servicer performs.

SERVICING RUNOFF Loans are being paid off faster than loans are being originated. It is a net reduction in the outstanding principal balance of the servicing portfolio.

SERVICING TRANSFER The sale of the right to service mortgage loans. *See* SERVICING AGREEMENT OR SALE AND SERVICING AGREEMENT.

SERVIENT ESTATE Land that has an easement in support of an adjacent property. If parcel A has an access easement to parcel B, parcel A is the servient estate.

SETBACK The minimum distance required for a dwelling to be built from a curb or street.

SETTLEMENT For real estate sales it is synonymous with "closing." For secondary marketing it is the purchase of a loan by an investor.

SETTLEMENT COSTS *See* REAL ESTATE SETTLEMENT PROCEDURES ACT.

SETTLEMENT DATE The date that settlement is made.

SETTLEMENT REQUIREMENTS The dollar amount of certified funds required to close a loan, or any conditions before disbursement of funds at settlement, or closing. For example, a final inspection, proof of verified cash for closing, documents to be delivered, etc., are all settlement requirements.

SETTLEMENT STATEMENT An accounting of the debits and credits incurred at closing. All FHA, VA, and most conventional financing loans use a uniform closing or settlement statement commonly called "the HUD-1." This standard closing form was introduced by the Real Estate Settlement Procedures Act.

See REAL ESTATE SETTLEMENT PROCEDURES ACT.

SEVERALTY Ownership of real property by an individual entity.

See TENANCY IN SEVERALTY.

SEVERANCE DAMAGES The loss in value caused by a condemnation procedure. The property is not as valuable or useful after condemnation as it was before. The drop in value is directly attributed to a partial taking by condemnation.

See DAMAGES.

SFHA *See* FLOOD INSURANCE.

SHAKES Refers to individual shingles on a roof. Shakes can be used as roofing or siding material and are composed of split wood, preferably cedar.

SHARED APPRECIATION MORTGAGE (SAM) A residential loan with a favorable interest rate that entitles the lender to a share of the appreciation in property value.

SHARED EQUITY In general, shared equity is the use of a related co-mortgagor's income and assets so that an owner/-occupant purchaser can qualify for a loan. There are many variations in a Conventional shared equity loan. The various types will depend upon the requirements of the lender and the investor (purchaser of the loan). FHA, however, has standard guidelines for shared equity loans and they apply throughout the country.

With FHA, the co-mortgagor helps the buyer gain loan approval and in return they receive an ownership or a share of the equity in the home. Present guidelines call for a co-mortgagor to have at least a 20% but no more than a 45% share of the equity. The percentage of sharing in the monthly payment decides the percentage of ownership, regardless of the down payment contribution. Maximum LTV for shared equity is the same as Section 203 (97% of the first $25,000 and 95% above $25,000 - see FHA 203 if cost to acquire price is less than $50,000). Refinances cannot exceed a 75% LTV with no cash out, except refinancing by an occupant mortgagor for the purposes of buying out an investor co-mortgagor. Some other basic guidelines are:

- A written Shared Equity Agreement must be approved by FHA.

- The occupant mortgagor must qualify for at least 55% of the monthly payment plus any rental payments to the investor.

- The co-mortgagor may charge a fair market rent for their share of the ownership.

- Either party may sell their interest in the property by providing a 30-day written option to purchase to the other shared equity party.

- The co-mortgagor must sell to the occupant mortgagor after being notified by a 30-day written notice.

- Sales price will be decided by a HUD approved appraiser.

- The co-mortgagor may not force a sale except to prevent foreclosure.

- The co-mortgagor liability for loan underwriting purposes is equal to the percentage of ownership and not viewed as potentially wholly liable as in the case of a straight co-mortgagor case. Furthermore, the 7 unit rule (*see* FHA INVESTOR LOAN) does not apply to shared equity.

- Co-mortgagors must be related.

After repeated cases involving abuse of shared equity, FHA began to limit the options available to investors. Finally, on 27 June 1988 FHA issued Mortgagee Letter 88-24 that eliminated investor participation in the shared equity program. Investors are no longer eligible, only related co-mortgagors can obtain a shared equity mortgage.

SHEATHING Wide boards, usually 4x8's that are nailed to studding or roofing rafters to serve as a base for the outer covering of the walls or roof.

SHEETROCK *See* DRYWALL.

SHELF REGISTRATION A term used for an established inventory of securities for possible hedging purposes that may be re-evaluated by investors based on changing conditions in the marketplace or prepayment expectations. However, futures represent an overhead cost, the possibility of margin calls.

SHERIFF'S DEED Deed for property that is sold by court order in connection with satisfaction of delinquent taxes or a judgment.

SHIM Thin piece of wood used for leveling or tightening a stair, window, etc.

SHIPPING The process of sending a complete mortgage package to the investor.
See LOAN SHIPPER.

SHOE MOLDING A thin strip of wood or quarter round located at the junction of the baseboard and floor board. Shoe molding is used to conceal joints and prevent drafts.

SHORTFALL The negative difference between the net note rate and the net yield required by the investor. It generally refers to adjustable rate mortgages with interest rate or payment caps that might cause the loans to fall short of required market rates. An upfront discount can be required to compensate the investor for foregone income in the initial period. Additional upfront discounts may be required for a loan with interest rate caps for possible income deficiencies after the loan rate is due for adjustment.

SHORT RATE The calculation of the refund of unearned premium or the premium earned on a hazard insurance policy canceled between anniversary dates based on a higher rate to compensate for the short term of the policy.

SIDING See VENEER.

SIGNS AND SYMBOLS The reader will often encounter certain signs and symbols (as shown on the next page) on blueprints and appraisals.

SILENT PARTNER A partner who is not active in the management of a partnership.
See LIMITED PARTNERSHIP.

SILL PLATE The lowest member of the house framing that sits on top of the foundation wall. The lowest horizontal element of a frame such as a window or door frame.

SINGLE DEBIT An accounting system used in servicing mortgage loans. The servicer reports paid installments as a single item, furnishing detail only on uncollected installments and on collection of items other than current monthly installments.

SINGLE FAMILY DETACHED (SFD) A dwelling with no adjoining walls or common areas with another dwelling.

Signs and Symbols

The reader will often encounter the following signs and symbols on blueprints and appraisals.

⸬ geometrical proportion	——W——	water line
▭ identical with	——G——	gas line
± plus or minus	——·—·—	center line
∠ angle	—x—x—	fence line
L right angle	Lˢ	lengths
⌐ or ⟩ greater than	Lˡ	lineal foot
⌐ or ⟩ greater than	▨ ⏦	per square foot
⌐ or ⟨ less than	ϕ	diameter
⌐ or ⟨ less than	℞	plate
⊥ perpendicular	℄	center line
⌢ difference	P—	direction of pressure
∫ integration	A———A / ᴬ___ᴬ	{ indicates cross section of a drawing
⊏⊐ equivalent	▨▨▨▨▨	{ indicates exposed surface of a section cut
∶∶ proportion	#	{ pounds after a number / number before a number
⁻∶ difference, excess	▭	stadia station
∴ therefore	△	triangulation station
∵ because	⊙	transit traverse station
∞ infinity	⊕	indicates elevation point
∞ varies as	⊢—3 ½—⊣	{ dimension line. Number indicates distance between lines.
√ radical		{ indicates that a section of a drawing, identical to the sections on either side of the symbol, has been omitted to reduce size.
° degree		
′ minute or foot		
″ second or inch	20° / 5′	{ indicates dimensions of rise and span of a roof pitch.

SINGLE PITCH ROOF See ROOF.

SINKING FUND A fund set aside to provide for the payment of a long-term debt such as a bond. For income property, the term "sinking fund" applies to a special fund set aside from earnings for future replacements required to maintain the improvements.
See ELLWOOD TABLE, HEWLETT-PACKARD 12C (HP-12C).

SITE DEVELOPMENT COST Engineering, architectural, and legal fees associated with a real estate project; they are sometimes called *soft costs*. Site development costs are in contrast to land and construction costs that are called *hard cost*.

SIX FUNCTIONS OF A DOLLAR See ELLWOOD TABLE, HP-12C.

SKIP DEED PROCESS Obtaining a signed deed transferring title to an eventual purchaser. The Deed is not recorded until a new purchaser becomes available. This process is often used by relocation service companies.

SLAB Concrete floor or roof, any flat, horizontal concrete area. A called slab is a reinforced slab if there are steel rods (called reinforcing rods) or metal fabric inside the slab.

SMALL BUSINESS INVESTMENT COMPANIES (SBIC) Private compa- nies that are licensed and regulated by the Small Business Administration to provide small businesses with equity, capital, and long-term financing.

SMSA See STANDARD METROPOLITAN STATISTICAL AREA.

SOCIETY OF REAL ESTATE APPRAISERS (SREA) A former appraisal organization that awarded the designations of Senior Real Estate Analyst, Se- nior Real Property Appraiser, and Senior Residential Appraiser. The Society was formed in 1935 and has 20,000 members. At the end of 1990, the Society merged with the American Institute of Real Estate Appraisers (AIREA).

On January 1, 1991, THE APPRAISAL INSTITUTE became the new appraisal organization consisting of the former SREA and AIREA. The surviving desig- nation for the SREA will be the Senior Residential Appraiser.

SOFFIT The underside of any part of a structure, especially roofs or eaves.

SOFT COSTS See SITE DEVELOPMENT COST.

SOFT DOLLARS   The amount of investment in real estate that qualifies for tax deductions in the year paid. Prepaid interest and any fees that are deductible in the year they are paid would qualify as soft dollars.

SOLDIERS' AND SAILORS' CIVIL RELIEF ACT OF 1940   A rather obscure Act until the Middle East crisis involving Iraq. For the conflict with Iraq, the person most affected by this Act is the reservist called to active duty. The Act applies to military service persons whose ability to meet financial and other obligations (incurred before military service) is impaired by reason of military service. Section 501 seems to support the fact that servicemen can take advantage of the Act upon proving that their interest has been affected by military action. Debts incurred by a reservist after the call to active duty are not covered by this Act. Examples of debts covered by this Act are: mortgage obligations, credit card debt, and installment loan obligations (car loans, etc.).

Section 526 provides that "no obligation or liability bearing interest at a rate *in excess of 6 per centum per annum* incurred by a person in military service . . . bear interest at a rate in excess of *6 per centum per annum* unless, in the opinion of the court, *upon application thereto by the creditor*, the ability of such person in military service to pay interest upon such obligation or liability at a rate in excess of 6 per centrum per annum is not materially affected by reason of such service . . . The term 'interest' includes service charges, renewal charges, fees, or other charges (except bona fide insurance) in respect of the obligation or liability." In essence the military person cannot be charged more than 6 percent on eligible debts, and cannot be charged late fees - unless a creditor can show that the call to duty does not materially affect the military person's ability to pay the loan. The 6 percent limit starts upon the date the military person is called to active duty. The interest rate limit is retroactive in the event a lender is notified after the call to active duty. It is the duty of the reservist to notify the lender. A lender is not obligated to notify the reservist of eligibility for an interest rate reduction. Each branch of military service is obligated to notify the reservists called to active duty about the benefits of this Act.

A lender must forgive the lost interest caused by reducing the interest rate - it cannot be deferred. See FHLMC and FNMA in this definition for interest rate reimbursement to the lender.

The purpose as stated in the act is: "In order to provide for, strengthen, and expedite the national defense under the emergent conditions that are threatening the peace and security of the United States and to enable the United States the more successfully to fulfill the requirements of the national defense, provision is made to suspend enforcement of civil liabilities, in certain cases, of persons in the military service of the United States in order to enable such persons to devote their entire energy to the defense needs of the Nation, and to this end provisions are made for the temporary suspension of legal proceedings and transactions which may prejudice the civil rights of persons in such service . . ." Section 510.

"The military persons eligible include all members of the Army of the United States, The United States Navy, the Marine Corps, the Coast Guard, and all officers of the Public Health Service detailed by proper authority for duty either with the Army or the Navy." Section 511(1). (At the time the Acct was enacted, the Air Corps was part of the Army, so the current United States Air Force would be included by implication, as well as the reserve forces of each of the above branches.) Although there is mention of a "certificate" in the Act, it is not defined. Lenders should check with their investor as to what is required for proof of a reservist being called to active duty, military orders or a letter from military headquarters may be enough evidence.

The term 'military service,' . . . shall signify Federal service on *active duty* with any branch of service heretofore referred to or mentioned as well as training or education under the supervision of the United States preliminary to induction into the military service. The terms 'active service' or 'active duty' shall include the period during which a person in military service is absent from duty on account of sickness, wounds, leave, or other lawful cause. Section 511(1).

Subject to court interpretation, the Act may also apply to persons or actions related to an eligible military person, e.g., dependents and co-makers of a debt.

Also subject to court interpretation, a reservist who is not materially affected by the call to active duty is not affected by the Act. Reservist who continue to get their normal pay from their employer while on active duty, or the reservist who is independently wealthy, may not be eligible for relief under this Act.

"The term 'period of military service,' . . . shall include the time between the following dates: . . . for persons entering active service after the date of this Act (Oct. 17, 1940), with the date of entering active service. It shall terminate with the date of discharge from active service or death while in active service . . . " Section 511(2).

Section 532 applies only to obligations secured by a mortgage, trust deed, or other security in the nature of a mortgage upon real or personal property owned by a person in military service at the start of the period of military service. The section further provides that in any lawsuit brought in any court during the period of military service to enforce obligations arising out of non-payment of any sum due under the obligation or out of any other breach of the terms occurring prior to or during the period of such service the court *may* on its own motion or *shall* after application to it by the service person or a person on their behalf, (1) stay the proceeding, or (2) make such other disposition of the case as may be equitable to conserve the interests of all parties. The court will take the above action *unless* in the opinion of the court the ability of the defendant to comply with the terms of the obligation is *not materially affected* by reason of the military service.

In addition, no sale, foreclosure, or seizure of property for nonpayment of any sum due under any such obligation, or for any other breach of the terms, whether under a power of sale, under a judgement entered upon warrant of attorney or to confess judgement contained therein, or otherwise, shall be valid during the period of military service or within three months' thereafter, except pursuant to an agreement between the creditor and service person, unless upon an order previously granted by the court and a return thereto made and approved by the court. A Contract for Deed or Land Contract is also covered by this Act.

Any person who knowingly makes or causes to be made any sale, foreclosure, or seizure of property defined as invalid, or attempts to do so, shall be guilty of a misdemeanor and shall be punished by imprisonment not to exceed one year or fine not to exceed $1,000 or both.

In a foreclosure action by a mortgage company under power of sale against a mortgagor in the service, the court stayed the foreclosure, thought the mortgagor had not made mortgage payments in nine months. The court ruled that the past due payments and the military person being in default when he entered service, these facts were not enough to deprive him of relief under the Act. *Federal National Mortgage Association*, 136 F. Suppl. 859 (E.D. Mich. 1956). The Act is "friendly to those who dropped their affairs to answer their country's call." *Le Maistre v. Leffers*, 333 U.S. 1,6 (1948).

The FHA's interpretation of the Act is expressed in 24 CFR 203.345, 203.346. the FHA regulation provides two special relief measures for persons called to active military service. One provision provides that the lender may, by written agreement, delay part of all of the monthly P&I payment for the period of military service and for three months thereafter. The other provision excludes, for loans in default, the period of military service from the one year period that the lender must commence foreclosure or acquire the property by other means. HUD Handbook 4330.1, Paragraph 124, discusses forbearance relief provisions for service persons.

At the time of this writing, FHA underwrites a loan application from a reservist called to active duty at the reservist's civilian pay, if the military pay is lower. You should ask FHA for the current status for qualifying a low application from a reservist called to active duty.

For loans owned by FHLMC, the servicer must request permission from FHLMC for interest reduction. The servicer submits a recommendation detailing the facts. Section 6514 authorizes the servicer to grant appropriate relief to an eligible borrower. Servicers must contact the borrower at least semiannually during the period of active military service to decide whether the reduction in monthly payments should be revised in view of the borrower's current financial ability. On August 30, 1990, FHLMC announced that it will absorb the loss of interest caused by reducing the interest rate for eligible reservists.

For FNMA, Sections II, 102.05 and IV, 401.04,05 authorize the servicer to grant military indulgence for eligible borrowers. FNMA has announced that it will reimburse lenders for the loss of interest caused by reducing the interest rate for eligible reservists. FNMA has further said that lenders need not verify if a reservist has been materially affected by the call to active duty.

VA has prepared a circular outlining their position. Quoting from page 2, paragraph 6: "VA is not charged with enforcement of the Act, but will perform its mission of serving veterans by making every effort to ensure that they re ceive the protections to which they are entitled. Moreover, it is not VA's responsibility to provide legal advice to veterans or loan holders with respect to requirements of the Act." In addressing the 6 percent rate limitation, quoting from the circular, page 2, paragraph 6, subparagraph a, (1): "the Act is silent a to any actions that the veteran must take to begin payments at the lower rate. Absent a specific requirement, veterans (or their spouses, other co-obligor or legal representatives) should, however, be encouraged to notify their loan holder before beginning payments at the reduced rate. Veterans should be encouraged to co-operate with their loan holders by providing information that will help demonstrate their eligibility for benefits available under the Act. Loan holders are cautioned to review their payment processing procedures in order to ensure that payments in the amount allowable under the Act are not inappropriately returned to borrowers as insufficient, even though no prior notice may have been received. Loan holders should be prepared to respond to inquiries from veterans as to the amount of monthly installment payment which would be required at a 6% interest rate and to provide revised payment cards or coupon books when appropriate . . . "

At the time of this writing, VA underwrites a loan application from a reservist called to active duty at the reservist's military pay. you should ask VA for the current status for qualifying a low application from a reservist called to active duty.

At the time of this writing, the only real benefit to an eligible reservist is the right to break a long-term lease with a one-month notice. Because of when the Act was written (1940), there is the mention of a landlord being prohibited from evicting an eligible reservist-tenant if the monthly rental is less than $150 per month. Efforts are being made to increase the $150 limit.

SOLE PROPRIETORSHIP A business owned by an individual. In a sole proprietorship, the profits or losses are reported directly to the individual's tax return as personal income or loss.

SOLVENT A financial position of being able to meet one's current financial obligations.

SOUTHERN COLONIAL HOME STYLE

Southern Colonial. A two or three-story early American style frame house with a colonnade. The roof extends over the colonnade.

SPANISH RANCH HOME STYLE

Spanish Ranch. A one-story ranch-style house with decorative arches, wrought iron window guards. This house is often made of stucco or brick.

SPANISH VILLA HOME STYLE

Spanish Villa. A Spanish style house featuring stucco exterior, a tile roof and an arched entry-way.

SPEC HOUSE A term referring to a newly-constructed house that was not custom-built or pre-sold. The house is constructed on the speculation that someone will purchase it.

SPECIAL FLOOD HAZARD AREAS (SFHA) *See* FLOOD INSURANCE.

SPECIAL WARRANTY DEED A deed conveying special warranty of the title as compared to general warranties. In a special warranty deed, the grantor warrants title against claims held "by, through, or under the grantor." The grantor does not warrant against title defects occurring before he owned the property.
See WARRANTY DEED.

SPECIFIC LIEN *See* LIEN.

SPECIFIC PERFORMANCE Court action requiring the completion of a contract according to its terms.

SPOT LOANS Single-family loans that are solicited on an individual basis vs. a package basis. Loans on individual existing residential dwellings are normally called *spot loans*. Loans from builders who have taken commitments for tracts of houses are not classified as spot loan business.

SPOT ZONING Zoning of a parcel of land on a specialized basis as opposed to a general or master plan.

SPREAD (1) The difference between the cost of money and the average rate that it can be loaned. (2) The profit made in the difference of interest rates, such as in a wraparound mortgage. (3) The difference between bid price and asking price. (4) The extension of a lien or an existing mortgage with additional real estate serving as collateral.
See ARBITRAGE, WRAPAROUND MORTGAGE.

SPLIT-FEE FINANCING A joint venture between a lender and a developer. The lender purchases the land, leases it to the developer, and finances the improvements.
See SALE-LEASEBACK.

SQUARE FOOTAGE An area measured in square feet. Square footage as applied to residential real estate is the number of heated and livable square feet as measured by the outside walls.

SQUARE FOOT PRICE See MARKET APPROACH TO VALUE.

SREA See SOCIETY OF REAL ESTATE APPRAISERS.

STAIRWAY All stairways with four or more steps should have a handrail installed.
See BALUSTER, NEWEL, RISER, TREAD.

STAFF APPRAISER An appraiser who is part of the staff of an institution, such as a bank, mortgage company, FHA and VA, is called a *staff appraiser*. The 1990 Housing Bill makes employees of corporate appraisal firms eligible for inclusion on HUD fee panels.
See FEE APPRAISER.

STANDARD METROPOLITAN STATISTICAL AREA (SMSA) A designation given by the federal Office of Management and Budget (OMB) to counties containing at least one central city of 50,000 or more residents. It is the area of a central city and its surrounding suburbs including small jurisdictions.

STANDBY COMMITMENT A commitment to purchase loans on specified terms with the understanding that the commitment will not be exercised unless there is no alternative.

STANDBY CONTRACT An option to sell mortgage-backed securities for a specified amount of mortgages by or upon a specific date at a specific price.

STANDBY FEE A fee charged by a lender to provide a standby loan commitment. The standby fee is forfeited if the loan is not closed by a specified time.

STANDING MORTGAGE A mortgage without amortization payments and requiring the entire loan balance due at maturity. Interest is paid at periodic intervals.
See STRAIGHT MORTGAGE.

START RATE The rate of interest for the first year on an Adjustable Rate Mortgage.
See ADJUSTABLE RATE MORTGAGE.

STARTS The number of residential dwelling units on which construction has started within a specific period of time.

STATUTE OF FRAUDS Old English law requiring certain contracts to be in writing before they are considered enforceable. Real estate contracts must be in writing to be considered enforceable.

STATUTE OF LIMITATIONS A statutory period of time that a claim can be enforced by a suit.

STEP-DOWN LEASE A lease providing for specific decreases in rent at certain intervals.

STEP-UP LEASE A lease providing for specific increases in rent at certain intervals.

STIPULATION The terms of a written contract.

STRAIGHT MORTGAGE Sometimes called a "straight note," it is a mortgage that is not amortized. There may be periods requiring interest payments, or it may be structured for all the principal and interest to paid on a maturity or "balloon" date.
See STANDING MORTGAGE.

STRAIGHT PASS-THROUGH A practice of passing through the principal and interest collected to the investor of a mortgage-backed security. The payment in a straight pass-through is contingent upon the borrower's remitting the principal and interest.

STRAW MAN A person who purchases property for another so that the eventual owner's identity is concealed.

STRIKE RATE The contract yield that the lender and secondary market investor agree that the lender can deliver the loan to an investor under the terms of an optional commitment.

STRICT FORECLOSURE A foreclosure proceeding without a sale of the mortgaged property.
See FORECLOSURE.

STUD A term used in construction for boards (usually 2" × 4") or framing materials that are vertical with horizontal pieces attached. Studs usually are placed either 16" or 24" apart.

SUBCHAPTER S An Internal Revenue code allowing small corporations to eliminate income tax at the corporate level by electing to be treated as a partnership. The shareholders pay the income tax.

SUBCONTRACTOR A person or a company that contracts work under a developer or a general contractor.

SUBDIVISION Land divided into many parcels and held for sale or lease.

SUBFLOORING Boards or sheets of plywood that are nailed directly to floor joists and serve as a base for the finished covering such as carpet or hardwood flooring.

SUBJECT PROPERTY That property that is the subject of an appraisal, sale, lease, option, or loan. The property in question. The term is most often used in appraising.

SUBJECT TO An assumption of an existing mortgage without personal liability. The seller of the original mortgagor is held liable for any deficiency resulting from a foreclosure. The owner of property purchased with "subject to the mortgage" is still liable to loss of the property through foreclosure.

SUBLEASE A lessee executing a lease to a third part for the remaining portion of the original lease.
See SANDWICH LEASE.

SUBMORTGAGE The use of a mortgage as security for obtaining another mortgage. A mortgage can be an asset, therefore, it can be used as collateral for a loan.

SUBORDINATION AGREEMENT The act of moving a prior or senior mortgage into a secondary position subject to agreement with the owner of the prior mortgage. An example would be a first mortgage becoming a second mortgage. A clause allowing a holder of a prior encumbrance to become junior to an existing or anticipated encumbrance.
    For example, a homeowner wishes to refinance a 13% first mortgage with a 9% first mortgage. There is a problem, the homeowner has a second mortgage on the property. When the 13% first mortgage is paid off, the second mortgage will become a first mortgage. The lender will make the new 9% mortgage only if it is recorded as a first mortgage. The solution is to have the owner of the second mortgage sign a subordination agreement so the second

will stay in it's second position - it will subordinate or allow the upcoming 9% mortgage to be a first mortgage.

Subordination can apply to leases, other debt instruments, and other real estate rights.

See SECOND MORTGAGE.

SUBROGATION The substitution of one person for another in reference to a claim or right for a debt. A homeowner who has an owner's title policy can look to the title company to subrogate for them in the event of a debt from a claim. The title company becomes responsible for the claim.

SUBSIDY Funds to lower the cost of housing by granting below-market interest loans or the reduction in the cost of land, labor, or material. For example, the FHA Section 235 was an interest subsidy mortgage. The homeowner paid a portion of the interest, as little as 1% in the beginning of the program, and HUD paid the differential.

SUBSTITUTE SALE An alternative to a forward sale by which a lender sells for future delivery something that he or she does not own. The price of the instrument sold should be expected to move with changes in interest rates in a similar manner to the value of the loans hedged with the substitute sale. A lender generally will offset his substitute sale with a purchase of the security sold in conjunction with an actual sale of loans into the secondary market.

SUBSTITUTION OF ENTITLEMENT *See* VA - RESTORATION OF ELIGIBILITY OR ENTITLEMENT.

SUBSTITUTION OF LIABILITY *See* FHA - RELEASE OF LIABILITY, NOVATION, RELEASE OF LIABILITY, VA - RELEASE OF LIABILITY, VA - RESTORATION OF ELIGIBILITY OR ENTITLEMENT, SURETY.

SUCCESSORS AND ASSIGNS Phrase meaning to succeed to the rights of ownership by corporation as assigned by said corporation.

SUMP PUMP A pump used to dispose of moisture and liquids collected in a basement.

SUPERVISED LENDERS Any lender subject to inspection by a government agency, such as FDIC and FSLIC. Supervised lenders can automatically participate in the FHA Direct Endorsement Program (DE) and the VA Automatic

Approval process. Non-supervised lenders, such as mortgage companies, must apply to FHA and VA for "DE" or "automatic" approval.

SURCHARGE Additional rental for utility services such as lights, gas, or water. People also use the term surcharge as a descriptive word for any additional charge to offset extra costs for performing a service or to charge a penalty.

SURETY One who guarantees or underwrites the performance of another. Although surety is commonly thought of as volunteering to pay a debt if the primary borrower fails to repay the obligation, such is not always the case.

For example, if a homeowner sells their home by loan assumption (any cash received for the equity does not matter) without being released of liability by the mortgagee, the homeowner is now surety for the person who assumed their mortgage.

See CO-MORTGAGOR.

SURRENDER To give up rights in a lease by mutual agreement between lessor and lessee.

SURVEY A drawing by a licensed surveyor showing the measurements of a parcel of land as well as the improvements to the land and the process by which the land is measured and its boundary lines ascertained. A survey shows the relationship of the land surveyed to other surrounding tracts. A survey is often required by lenders to assure them that a building is actually sited on the land according to its legal description.

If the survey is needed for a loan transaction the lender will want the survey to be dated no more than ninety (90) days before the closing of the loan. It must contain a registered land surveyor's certification (or that of a licensed engineer, as permitted by state law) as to the completeness and accuracy of the legal description, which certification should carry the surveyor's seal of authority or registration number.

A survey should include the information below:

- Owner or Prospective Owner
- Address (street number/lot/block)
- Subdivision (section/phase)
- Location (township, county, state)
- Date of Survey
- Scale

- Recorded map reference, if any
- Certifications required by applicable state statue
- North Arrow
- Beginning point, course and distance of all boundary lines
- Standard curve data (radius, intersection angle, chord distance and chord bearing)
- Adjoining property owners or lot numbers
- Names of streets and highways
- Encroachments onto adjoining property
- Encroachments from adjoining property
- Improvements and distances from each lot line, side street line and front lot line
- Visible utilities above ground
- Apparent underground utilities
- Subdivision plat set-back or minimum building lines
- Subdivision plat easements reserved
- Access to public right-of-way
- Rights of way widths
- Physical features other than improvements
- Flood Hazard determination
- Apparent evidence of new construction on property or adjacent public ways
- Disposal sites
- Waterways named

A borrower may be able to use an existing survey or such information or affidavits acceptable to the title company as long as the title company is willing to afford full coverage with no broad exceptions as matters of survey. The lender will need a copy of the existing survey and other documentation that may be required by a title company.

SURVIVORSHIP The special feature in ownership of property as joint tenants. Survivorship stipulates that in the event of a death a joint tenant, all the rights of the deceased joint tenant owner passes on to the surviving joint tenants.

See JOINT TENANCY, TENANCY BY THE ENTIRETY.

SWEAT EQUITY This term applies to labor or materials supplied by a purchaser and used as a credit for settlement requirements. The scope of the work or materials furnished cannot go beyond what is listed on the appraisal. The value of the sweat equity can be decided by the purchaser; however, the lender reserves the right to set a value if said value given by purchaser seems unreasonable (for FHA loans, the HUD cost analyst sets the value if there is disagreement as to what the sweat equity is worth). For example, a purchaser is short of settlement requirements by a total of $400 and the subject property is in need of painting. A purchaser could do the labor required for painting and if $400 is a figure acceptable to the lender, that amount would go towards the settlement requirements. The person providing the sweat equity must be qualified to perform the work.

Work not eligible for sweat equity is clean-up, debris removal, general maintenance requirements, and delayed work (on-site escrow). Work on other properties (other than the subject property) should be handled on a cash payment basis and is not eligible for sweat equity.

Subject to interpretation by lenders, sweat equity should not constitute the entire settlement requirements and should never cause a reduction in the maximum loan-to-value. There can be no cash back to the borrower for sweat equity. FHA readily accepts the use of sweat equity as a form of downpayment.

SWING LOAN *See* BRIDGE FINANCING.

SYNDICATION *See* REAL ESTATE SYNDICATE.

T

TACKING The practice of adding or combining periods in making a claim to squatter's rights to land. The periods are combined to satisfy statutory requirements for a claim by adverse possession. The only periods allowed are those that are continuous and uninterrupted. The parties must have been in succession of interest, e.g., seller and buyer, landlord and tenant, predecessor and successor of an estate.

TAIL What GNMA will allow in terms of contract deliveries that are above or below the agreed upon principal balance. The balance that is over or under the agreed upon principal balance.

TAKEDOWN The drawing of funds that are committed by a lender per a previous agreement.

TAKEOUT BID An active secondary market in "whole loans" exists, and major transactions are often arranged by the same investment bankers who, one would normally think, restrict their activities to security placements. Therefore securities dealer often agree to purchase MBSs in whole loan form rather than in a block, or pool, for a designated price, from a mortgage banker. This agreement is subject to a successful bid for mortgages sold in an auction.

This takeout or "back-up bid" allows the same mortgage banker to bid on the purchase of mortgages at the whole loan auction. The dealer's back-up bid permits the mortgage banker to supplement a purchase of mortgages in bulk, acquired form secondary mortgage market agencies, to add to his servicing portfolio. This agreement between the mortgage banker and the securities dealer assists the secondary market agencies to coordinate their management and liquidation activity. In affect, the mortgage banker purchased mortgage collateral that is backed financially by securities dealers.

TAKEOUT COMMITMENT A commitment from a lending institutions can be essential in gaining a short-term construction loan for a development. The preceding statement is especially true for commercial developments.

Construction lenders will want to be assured what will be "taken out" by a permanent mortgage when construction of the development is completed. A takeout commitment is sometimes called *takeout financing.*

TANDEM MORTGAGE DISPOSITION PROGRAMS The sale by GNMA of mortgages pursuant to its Special Assistance function, emergency home purchase assistance program or management and liquidation function.

TANDEM PROGRAMS Special assistance programs offered through GNMA. Under these programs GNMA enters into commitments to buy mortgages at less than market yields in the expectation that they later may be sold to other investors. The rationale is to stimulate the housing market by providing an advance commitment to purchase a mortgage at a specified price.

TAX DEED Deed that conveys property repossessed by the government for nonpayment of taxes. The usual method of sale is with sealed bids submitted at a tax sale. Nearly all properties purchased at a tax sale have a redemption period. The taxpayer whose property was seized is allowed to redeem the property by paying the winning bid plus costs of the sale and interest.

TAX ESCALATION CLAUSE The provision in a lease requiring the tenant to absorb any increase in real estate taxes.

TAX-EXEMPT BOND FINANCING Periods of a mortgage credit shortage has caused the innovation of tax-exempt bond financing as a finance conduit. It is another finance system that has experienced increased investor interest for tax-exempt bond issues of state and local governments. It is the primary source of funds for state and local housing agencies. The tax-exempt bond financing represents an alternative to Federal support.

TAX-INCREMENT FINANCING The financing of urban renewal by a bond issue that will be serviced from anticipated additional tax revenues generated from the redevelopment or renewal project.

TAX LIEN A lien against property for the amount of unpaid taxes. There are two types of tax liens, federal and state.

A federal tax lien can be caused by failure to pay Internal Revenue tax, estate, and payroll tax. Federal tax liens are *general liens*. The lien(s) apply to property and rights to property. The priority of the lien is dependent upon any lien previously recorded, just the same as with a mortgage.

A state tax lien can be caused by failure to pay real property taxes. A state tax lien is usually a *specific lien* against a property on which taxes have not been paid.

TAX PARTICIPATION CLAUSE *See* TAX ESCALATION CLAUSE.

TAX RATE *See* AD VALOREM, PROPERTY TAX.

TAX REPORT Tax bills are obtained from information on the tax report or tax record form. The following information is needed for the lender to have the proper information to service the loan:

- Permanent Tax Office Identifying Number (Tax code, TMS number, parcel or identifying number) should be listed exactly as shown on the security deed:
- Tax map, lot, and block should be shown exactly as listed on the tax records;
- Property address;
- Sanitary district should be listed only if an assessment will be paid from escrow;
- County and city taxing authorities must always be shown though city taxes may not be applicable;
- Estimated amount of tax bill and property value must be shown for the current and subsequent years; and
- The form should be signed by the closing attorney certifying the due date and the date that taxes have been paid.

TAX ROLL Public records showing all property within a governmental jurisdiction, the party billed for taxes, assessed valuation, and the taxes levied.

TAX SALE *See* TAX DEED.

TAX STAMPS A State tax, in the form of stamps, required on deeds and mortgages when real estate title passes from one owner to another. The amount of stamps required varies with each State. When the Federal government abolished the tax stamp revenue in January, 1968, various states, counties and local jurisdictions instituted a tax on real estate transfers.

The total cost is normally decided by applying a formula of the cost of the stamps to the value of the property being transferred. The following is an example of how tax stamps required is decided:

Valuation	Tax Stamps
$ 100 to $ 500	$ .55
501 to 1,000	1.10
1,001 to 1,500	1.65

TAX STOP CLAUSE *See* TAX ESCALATION CLAUSE.

TBA (TO BE ANNOUNCED) The term used in the securities industry when trading occurs in pools not yet formed and yet to be assigned a pool number. A participation certificate for instance when traded TBA must have information such as pool prefix number, the original face value, and date of maturity in an exchange of pool information between purchasers and the sellers. The Public Securities Association (PSA) requires a seller (being customers or dealers in TBA transactions) to furnish pool information to purchasers verbally before 3 p.m., two days before scheduled settlement date.

TEASER RATE A low initial rate on an Adjustable Rate Mortgage. The low rate is used to attract or "tease" the borrower into accepting a ARM mortgage. An ARM loan transfers risk from the lender to the borrower. Some lenders are very anxious to make ARM loans. Lenders will sometimes offer a very low rate for the first year, in hopes that the public will accept ARM loans and the rates will go up as adjustments are made.

TENANCY The holding of real estate by either lease or title.

TENANCY AT SUFFERANCE Tenancy established when a tenant wrongfully holds over after the expiration of a lease. The tenant remains without a direct consent from the landlord. By allowing the tenant to stay, the landlord implies consent.

TENANCY AT WILL Tenancy created when a person holds or occupies real estate with the permission of the owner for an indefinite period of time. It can be canceled at any time by the landlord or the tenant.

TENANCY BY THE ENTIRETY Ownership of real estate by a married couple that limits one from selling real estate without the consent of the other and maintains that, upon the death of a spouse, the real estate is then owned by the surviving spouse.

Upon the death of one spouse, the survivor owns the property without considering the rights of heirs or creditors of the deceased spouse. The surviving spouse owns the property without any need for probate. Normally, a borrower will be asked at loan application if title is to be held in tenancy by the entirety or tenancy in common.

TENANCY FOR LIFE *See* LIFE ESTATE.

TENANCY FOR YEARS Tenancy that is created by a lease for a fixed term.

TENANCY IN COMMON Ownership in real estate by two or more persons each owning an undivided interest without right of survivorship. This form of ownership is normally the result of property given by descent or a will.

A tenant in common may sell their interest without the consent of the other tenants. But no co-tenant can attempt to sell the entire property without the consent of the other co-tenants. If the other tenants refuse to cooperate in a sale of the property, the co-tenant wanting to sell can bring an action for partition, divide the property among the co-tenants, and have the property sold at auction.

A tenant in common cannot affect the future rights of the other co-tenants without all of them agreeing. All co-tenants must agree to an encumbrance.

TENANCY IN SEVERALTY Ownership of property vested in one person or one legal entity.

See SEVERALTY.

TENANT (1) One who is commonly called the *lessee* under a lease. (2) One who holds exclusive possession of property such as a life tenant or tenant for years.

TENANT MIX The selection of tenants in a complex, such as a mall or a shopping center. Care is used to not only prevent tenants in the same business from being in close proximity to each other, but to assure that the flow of pedestrian traffic will pass by all of the stores. For example, locating two anchor tenants at separate ends of a mall or shopping center is a good tenant mix.

TENDER (1) An unconditional offer by a contracting party to perform their part of a contract. (2) Payment or deliverance of an amount due a creditor (sometimes called *legal tender*).

TENEMENTS Items that are permanently affixed such as buildings and improvements.

TENURE The manner that ownership rights are possessed such as an owner of property or a tenant in property. Holding or possessing anything; the right to possess and use property.

TERM The period of time between a borrowing date and a due date. Term is used in such instruments as a mortgage or a lease. For example, a thirty year mortgage has a term of thirty years.

TERMITE/INSECT REPORT A Wood Destroying Insect Information Report (Termite Report) is required for FHA/VA and nearly all Conventional loans.

The Report is for existing homes. The Report should be dated within 60 days of closing. The lender should be allowed to review the Report to insure that it is completed properly and will be acceptable in all respects to the FHA, VA, or the investor for the particular loan being closed.

Requirements by FHA and VA can vary for each state. The borrower(s) should sign the report accepting and acknowledging receipt of the Report. If termite infestation or damage of any type is indicated, the property should be treated and repairs completed before closing. For VA loans, the cost of the Report and any necessary repairs or treatment must be paid by the seller.

For newly constructed homes (those less than one year old) a Soil Guarantee (FHA form 2052/VA form 26-8375) is required. The form must be completed in detail and signed by the builder and exterminator. The lender will want the original copy of the Report.

TERMS The conditions and obligations of a mortgage, a lease, or other contract.

TESTATE Leaving a valid will at death.

TESTATOR A man who makes a valid will.

TESTATRIX A woman who makes a valid will.

T&I The abbreviation for tax and insurance, normally referring to escrows used to pay taxes on real estate and hazard insurance premiums on mortgages included in pools and loan packages.

T&I CUSTODIAL ACCOUNT An account that an issuer maintains with a financial institution FOR escrowed funds used to pay real estate taxes and hazard insurance premiums on property pledged as collateral for mortgages included in pools and loan packages.

THIRD PARTY (1) A person who is not a direct party to a contract but is affected by it, such as a real estate agent. (2) A lender who was not the originating party in a loan transaction. A lender who accumulates loans from correspondents for a later sale to an investor is a third-party lender.

TIME IS OF THE ESSENCE Phrase in a contract that means delays are unacceptable and performance must be completed by specific dates as set forth in the contract.

TIME SHARE Multiple ownership of a unit in a development whereby use of the ownership is for a specific period.

TIME VALUE When quantity of the option differs form its intrinsic value to that of an existing market price, it is called a time value of the option. When hedging a mortgage pipeline, a buyer of an option exercises the option (at expiration) only when time value equals intrinsic value or, in-the-money conditions.

TIME VALUE OF MONEY An economic principle that supports the belief that money is worth more today than in the future.
See INWOOD ORDINARY ANNUITY COEFFICIENT and REVERSION FACTOR.

TITLE Documentation as to the rightful ownership of real property.

TITLE I LOANS FHA loans that are second mortgages.

TITLE II LOANS FHA loans that are first mortgages.

TITLE BINDER Written evidence of temporary title insurance that must be replaced by a permanent title insurance policy after a limited time.

TITLE DEFECT A claim against property that clouds the title to the property and prohibits clear title.

TITLE EXCEPTION A condition of the property that title policy will not insure, sometimes called *uninsured exclusions*.
For a list of customary title exceptions, *see* LOAN ORIGINATION PROCESS, Step 5. Look for: **Below is a list of acceptable title exceptions for most lenders:**

TITLE INSURANCE (1) The insurance, called a *lender's policy*, protecting a loan institution against loss resulting from any defects in the title or claims against the real property that were not uncovered in the title search or that were not listed as exemptions to the scope of the insurance policy. All secondary mortgage markets require safe and marketable title. (2) The insurance, called an *owner's policy*, protecting owners from a defect in the title that was not disclosed at the time of closing. Usually a defect that went unnoticed in the title search.

A list of possible hidden defects are as follows:

    1.   documents that are fraudulent, e.g., forged deeds, mortgages, releases of dower;

2. a minority that was not removed (under the legal age);
3. confusion in names, lack of a "one and the same" certification;
4. mental incompetence;
5. marital status that was incorrect, spouse was not incorporated as part of a transaction;
6. missing documents;
7. incorrect interpretation of a will; and
8. unauthorized acknowledgements.

For a list of title policy requirements *see* LOAN ORIGINATION PROCESS, Step 5. *See* OFF RECORD TITLE DEFECT, REISSUE RATE.

TITLE OPINION *See* OPINION OF TITLE.

TITLE REPORT The current status of title as it pertains to any defects, liens, easements, or covenants. A title report is not the chain of title. *See* CERTIFICATE OF TITLE, TITLE INSURANCE.

TITLE SEARCH OR EXAMINATION Investigation of public records to discover anything that might affect a title. It is a check of the title records, generally at the local courthouse, to make sure the buyer is purchasing a house from the legal owner and there are no liens, overdue special assessments, or other claims or outstanding restrictive covenants filed in the record, that would adversely affect the marketability or value of title. *See* ABSTRACT OF TITLE, CERTIFICATE OF TITLE.

TITLE THEORY Doctrine that says the mortgagee holds legal title until the debt is paid in full. The borrower is said to have equitable title. States that adopt the title theory doctrine are called *title theory states*. In title theory states a Deed of Trust is used in the mortgage process. *See* DEED OF TRUST, DEFEASANCE, FORECLOSURE, LIEN THEORY, MORTGAGE, RECONVEYANCE.

TOENAIL Method of driving nails at an angle into corners or joints so they will bond together.

TONGUE-AND-GROOVE Method of joining similar boards together. The jutting edge of one board fits into a grooved edge of another board.

TOPOGRAPHY The contour of the land. A topography map shows land elevations.

TORRENS SYSTEM Title registration used to verify the ownership and en-cumbrances (except tax liens) without requiring an additional search of the public records.

TORT A civil wrong or negligent act that is neither a crime nor a breach of contract, but creates damages to the wronged party. For example, a closing attorney who fails to comply with closing instructions may be liable for tort action for damages caused by negligence.

TOTAL ACQUISITION *See* FHA TOTAL ACQUISITION.

TOTAL LOAN-TO-VALUE (TLTV) A percentage decided by dividing debt by the value of the mortgaged property. The sum of the debt is the outstanding loan balance of a first mortgage plus any balances from junior financing (second mortgage). The value used is the current market value of the mortgage property.
See LOAN TO VALUE.

TOTAL OBLIGATION The summation of obligations that can include PITI, maintenance expense, insurance, Social Security, and obligations that exceed a defined repayment period, such as six months.

TOWNHOUSE HOME STYLE

Townhouse. Typically a two or more story unit attached to other like-units by a party wall. Most townhouses are in planned unit developments or condominium developments. Theycan also be found in cluster housing, row house, or brownstones.

TRACK RECORD A phrase used to describe the past record of success for a borrower. In commercial lending, the development and the track record of the developer are of utmost importance.

TRACT A parcel of land. Usually refers to a large piece of land which might be subdivided.

TRACT HOUSES Houses that are in a large-scale development and are similar in design.

TRACT LOAN A mortgage to a developer for land that is being subdivided.

TRADE DATE The date when parties enter into an agreement to purchase or sell mortgage-backed securities.

TRADER *See* WRITER.

TRADES A term applied to either purchases or sales of securities in a securities market.

TRADING INCOME Income realized from trading of portfolios of MBSs.

TRADING PROFITS OR LOSSES Results of trading portfolios (profits or losses) of MBSs.

TRANSFER AGENTS Transfer agents keep records of names of all registered shareholders, their addresses and number of certificates they own. Transfer agents see that transferred certificates are properly canceled and are reissued in the name of the transferee.

TRANSFER TAX Tax imposed by state or local governments when real estate is transferred from seller to purchaser.
See TAX STAMPS.

TRANSOM WINDOW *See* WINDOW.

TRAP A bend in a water pipe that traps water so that gases will not escape from the plumbing system into the house.

TRAVERSE WINDOW *See* WINDOW.

TREAD Horizontal portion of a step in a stairway.

See STAIRWAY, RISER.

TRIM Interior finishing pieces such as moldings, window casings, and hardware.

TRIPLE NET LEASE *See* NET LEASE.

TRIPLEX Three-unit dwelling.

TRUSS A rigid framework for spanning over load-bearing walls. It is formed by assembling various units and its purpose is to carry a load (such as floor truss and roof truss).

See PRE-FABRICATED HOUSING.

TRUST The fiduciary relationship with legal title held by a person or entity who wants the property to be administered by a trustee for the benefit of another who is termed the beneficiary and who holds equitable title to the property.

TRUST DEED *See* DEED OF TRUST.

TRUSTEE An individual who holds title to property in trust for another as security for performance of an obligation. The trustee is placed in a position of responsibility for another, a responsibility enforceable in a court of law.

TRUTH-IN-LENDING ACT Regulation that requires full disclosure in writing of all costs connected with the credit portion of a purchase, including the APR. The law became effective in July 1969 as part of the Consumer Credit Protection Act. It is implemented by the Federal Reserve Board's Regulation Z.

Lenders must comply with Regulation Z if a loan is made to a natural person and is not for business, commercial, or agricultural use. The loan must have more than four payments. The Federal Trade Commission is responsible for enforcement of Regulation Z.

Under the Truth in Lending Act, a lender is required within three working days of receiving an application to give or mail to the borrower a "Truth-in-Lending Disclosure Statement" disclosing "Annual Percentage Rate" and "Finance Charge" as well as a schedule of payments, late charge assessments and prepayment penalties.

If the estimated APR on disclosures at application differs by more than .125% for fixed rate loans, to the actual APR, a new Truth in Lending disclosure must be made available to the purchaser no later than closing.

Disclosures must be in a reasonably understandable form. They must be legible, whether typewritten, handwritten, or printed by computer. The disclosures may be grouped together and segregated from other information in a variety of ways. The disclosures must be in writing and in a form that the applicant may keep.

Terms like "Finance Charge" and "Annual Percentage Rate," must be more conspicuous than any other disclosure. The lenders identity may be more prominently displayed than the finance charge and the annual percentage rate.

The Truth in Lending Act states that when a lien is to be placed on real estate that is the principal residence of the customer, the customer has the right to rescind or cancel the transaction until midnight of the third business day following the date of consummation of the transaction. The creation of a first lien or equivalent security interest to finance the acquisition of a dwelling in which the consumer resides or expects to reside is exempt from the right of rescission. Exempt is a loan committed before completion of the construction of the residence to satisfy the construction loan and provide permanent financing of the residence, whether or not the consumer previously owned the land on which the residence was constructed. A loan to refinance or a loan being placed on property unencumbered at the time of the transaction is subject to the right of the consumer to rescind the transaction.

Every person who has an ownership interest in the property to be held as security must be given two copies of the notice of the right to rescind. One copy may be used to rescind the transaction. The notice of one holder of an interest in the security intending to rescind the transaction has the effect of rescinding the entire transaction.

Business days are defined by Regulation Z as any calendar day except Sunday and the following legal holidays: New Years' Day, Martin Luther King's Birthday, Washington's Birthday, Memorial Day, Independence Day, Labor Day, Columbus Day, Veterans Day, Thanksgiving Day, and Christmas Day. The day of the transaction is not a business day in counting elapsed time.

As an example, in a week when there is no legal holiday, the loan should be closed as follows:

<u>Monday</u>

April 15 (1) All loan documents will be signed, notarized, etc.

(2) Each borrower holding an interest in the security property will be given two copies of the notice of the right to rescind.

(3) Borrowers will be given a copy of the completed Truth-in-Lending Disclosure except for the date of disbursement (that will be

unknown at this point), or the lender will have previously provided the borrower with a Disclosure showing the estimated Date of Disbursement.

Tuesday
April 16   No action permitted.

Wednesday
April 17   No action permitted.

Thursday
April 18   No action permitted.

Friday
April 19   Upon receipt of the Certification of Confirmation signed by all borrowers no earlier than the fourth business day following execution of the loan documents:

(1) Complete Truth-in-Lending Disclosure with the date of disbursement and give a copy to the borrower, if the lender has not already given the disclosure with the estimated date of disbursement;

(2) Record documents; and

(3) Disburse funds.

In the example above, Friday is the earliest day that the transaction could be completed. Had the example included a Sunday or Legal Holiday, or both, the elapsed time would have been greater. The closing agent should have the borrower(s) sign two copies of the disclosure statements before the execution of any other documents and should return one copy to the lender with the closing documents. An original must be given to the borrower(s). The disclosure should not be altered without the proper approval of the lender or used in preparation of closing documents.

The only time a customer may waive the right to rescind is if the customer decides that the extension of credit is needed to meet a bona fide personal financial emergency.

If the customer decides to rescind, the following information is needed:

(1) a dated written statement that describes the emergency;

(2) a statement that specifically waives or modifies the right to rescind; and bears the signatures of each consumer entitled to rescind.

See GOOD FAITH ESTIMATE, LOAN ORIGINATION PROCESS Step 5, RECISSION, REGULATION Z.

TUCK-POINTING *See* VENEER.

TURNKEY PROJECT A phrase meaning the contractor will completely finish a building project on behalf of the owner or purchaser. The only participation by the owner to begin operational use of the building is to wait until the building is completely finished and then insert a key in the front door lock and turn it.

U

UCC *See* UNIFORM COMMERCIAL CODE.

ULTRA VIRES Any act or conduct of a corporation that is beyond the its legal powers as set forth in the articles of incorporation, i.e., the corporate charter or certificate of incorporation.

UNDERLYING MORTGAGE A mortgage that takes priority over other mortgages or subsequent liens.

UNDER-IMPROVEMENT A development or building that represents less than the best and most profitable use for the property location.

UNDERLYING SECURITY (1) The characteristics of the underlying mortgage pipeline is the security that is considered in the purchasing or selling of the option being exercised.

(2) In the valuing of options, it is the difference between "price of the underlying security and the exercise price" of the option.

UNDERWRITER Securities dealers use this term for identifying an originator of all MBSs. The underwriter is the firm that agrees to buy an issue of securities on a given date at a specific price, or agrees to buy the unsubscribed securities of an issue. The issuer can be given assurance of all anticipated proceeds from the sale by the underwriter.

See LOAN UNDERWRITER.

UNDIVIDED INTEREST Interest in property that has not been divided or segregated. The undivided interest may or may not be equal. If ownership is by joint tenancy the share of ownership will be equal. If ownership is by tenancy in common the ownership interest can be unequal. An undivided interest is a fractional ownership of the whole and not specified part.

See JOINT TENANCY and TENANCY IN COMMON.

UNEARNED INCREMENT Increase in the value of real estate through an unrelated effort by the property owner. Examples would be population growth, commercial development, and other occurrences that increase the value of property.

UNEARNED INCOME Income that is not earned from personal services. Income from rents, dividends, and royalties is unearned income.

UNEARNED INTEREST Interest on a loan that has previously been collected but that has not yet been earned because the principal has not been outstanding long enough.

UNENCUMBERED PROPERTY Property that is free and clear of any liens or claims.

UNIFORM COMMERCIAL CODE (UCC) A code that attempts to unify all law related to commercial transactions.

UNIFORM SETTLEMENT STATEMENT Standard closing statement required by Housing Urban Development, sometimes called a "HUD-1."
See REAL ESTATE SETTLEMENT PROCEDURES ACT.

UNILATERAL CONTRACT A contract that binds only one party.

UNIMPROVED PROPERTY Raw land that has not been developed.

UNIT A residential dwelling. A house is a single family unit. A duplex is a two family unit dwelling. A residence in an apartment is a unit.

UNITED STATES LEAGUE OF SAVINGS ASSOCIATIONS A national trade organization for savings associations, organized in 1892. The U.S. League offers a broadly based program having the following objectives: the support of thrift promotion; the encouragement of private investment in the purchase of homes; the development of safe operating methods for member institutions; and the improvement of statutes and regulations affecting the savings association business and the public interest.

UP/ON Refers to a commitment fee that is divided into two parts. A portion of the fee is paid upon execution of the commitment, the rest is paid upon delivery of the loans to the investor.

UPSET PRICE The minimum asking price for property that is auctioned. The property being auctioned will not be sold at any price below the upset price.

USEFUL LIFE *See* ECONOMIC LIFE.

USUFRUCTUARY RIGHTS Rights and interests to use without damaging the property that belongs to another.
See EASEMENT.

USURY The act of charging an interest rate greater than is permitted by state law. FHA and VA loans are exempt from state usury laws.

V

VA - AUTOMATIC APPROVAL Certain lenders designated by VA may approve or reject VA home loan applications. The advantage of being an automatic lender is a reduction in loan processing time, since the file does not have to be forwarded to the VA Regional Office for approval of the loan. The automatic authority may not apply to all loans, such as multi-family loans, joint mortgagor, or disabled veterans.

Furthermore, any VA loan sent to a Regional Office for review cannot later be approved on an automatic basis. Supervised lenders may use the automatic approval system. Non-supervised lenders must apply for VA approval to act as an automatic lender.

VA - CERTIFICATE OF COMMITMENT Approval for a VA loan is officially termed a "Certificate of Commitment." It is valid for six months for existing and proposed dwellings. Certificates of Commitments can be extended if it is for a proposed dwelling. The extension period is six months. The commitment will not be extended for an existing dwelling.

VA - CERTIFICATE OF ELIGIBILITY This certificate is a VA Form 26-8320 and contains the following information: name of veteran, service serial number/social security number, entitlement code, branch of service, date of birth, date issued, signature of Authorized Agent, and issuing office. The reverse side of this form shows the amount of entitlement or guaranty used and the amount available for real estate loan purposes.

See VA - ELIGIBILITY for time in service required for a VA loan.

VA - CERTIFICATE OF REASONABLE VALUE The name given for a VA appraisal. The term "appraisal" implies a judgement or an opinion. Judgments and opinions may vary. Variations in appraisals, appraisers, and appraisal policies may vary for the VA Regional Offices. Simply stated, properties are different, appraisers are different, and appraisal policies from the various VA Regional Offices differ; however, all attempt to do what is best for the various parts of the country.

Uniform guidelines regarding appraisals are as follows:

(1) A VA appraisal is known as a CRV (Certificate of Reasonable Value).

(2) A CRV is valid for 6 months for existing construction, and 12 months for proposed construction.

(3) A CRV may not be extended.

(4) With a few exceptions, proposed construction should be prior-approved by a submission of plans and specifications to VA. Periodic inspections will then be made by VA. A few exceptions to the above would be:

    (a) if the dwelling has been prior-approved and inspected by FHA (Federal Housing Administration);

    (b) the new dwelling has been substantially completed for more than 12 months;

    (c) the new dwelling will be insured by an acceptable homeowners warranty program or a similar insurance program;

    (d) the home is in a rural area, making routine inspections an impossibility or extremely difficult; and

    (e) in certain cases, the VA Regional Office may consider new construction without VA or FHA inspections, if the veteran agrees in writing to waive the VA warranty required of a builder.

(5) A VA Regional Office maintains a very small staff of appraisers. Appraisers are used primarily for review of appraisals done by VA designated fee appraisers. A VA designated fee appraiser is a private individual who has satisfactorily met certain VA requirements of character and experience, and is authorized to make appraisals on behalf of the VA.

(6) A veteran cannot be charged for the appraisal unless the appraisal is ordered in their name.

(7) A requested value is necessary.

(8) A VA Regional Office may change or adjust the value or conditions outlined by the VA appraiser.

(9) An appraisal cannot be made by a fee appraiser if that individual is an officer, director, trustee, employer or employee of the lender, contractor or vendor, unless the appraisal is for alterations, improvements, or repairs costing less than $2,500.

(10) VA will now accept FHA appraisals.

VA will allow the veteran to pay more than the VA appraised value, if the veteran pays the excess in cash which has not been borrowed. The sales contract must contain the VA amendatory language if it is written before the appraisal.

VA - CLOSING COSTS *See* CLOSING COSTS.

VA - COMPROMISE SALES AGREEMENT (CSA) *See*   COMPROMISE
SALES AGREEMENT (CSA) and DEED-IN-LIEU OF FORECLOSURE.

VA - DVB CIRCULARS A method the VA Central Office uses to communicate new programs or changes in existing loan programs to the Regional Offices. DVB stands for Department of Veterans Benefits. A first-time-ever list and brief summary of DVB circulars is available in a book titled *Mortgage Lending* written by Albert Santi and published by Probus Publishing. If you want to research the subjects condominium and credit reports, turn to page 219 of *Mortgage Lending* and you will find the information below.

Condominium

08-15-80	26-80-32	Uniform Condominium Act
08-27-80	26-80-34	Processing Planned-Unit Developments (Other than Condominiums)
10-16-81		(Change 2)
07-27-83		(Change 3)
04-07-82	26-82-11	Suggested Duties Statement and Classification Guidance for Condominium Specialist Position in Loan Guaranty Divisions
12-12-84	26-84-55	Confirming the Recent Hotline Item-HUD/FHA Acceptance of Conversion Condominiums
04-01-85	26-85-10	Insurance on Portfolio Condominium Loans
09-29-86		(Change 2)
06-25-85	26-85-27	Policies and Procedures - Condominium Loans Under 38 U.S.C. 1810(a)(6)
07-17-85		(Erratum)

Credit Reports

09-16-81	26-81-30	Credit Report Terminals

07-21-82		(Change 2)
06-30-83		(Change 4)
12-10-84		(Change 5)
09-27-82	26-82-33	Credit Reports
03-23-88	26-88-17	Residential Mortgage Credit Report Standards.

VA - ELIGIBILITY Many people are eligible for a VA loan. Most veterans must have served in the United States Armed Forces for more than 180 days of continuous active duty service (not as a reservist), and were not dishonorably discharged. The following is a more specific answer predicated on the veteran not being a reservist nor dishonorably discharged:

(1) Veterans who served more than 90 days of continuous service during:

(a) World War II era - 16 September 1940 through 25 July 1947; (b) Korean Conflict - 27 June 1950 through 31 January 1955; (c) Vietnam Conflict-August 5, 1964 through 7 May 1975.

(2) Service people not on active duty "for training purposes" and who have served for more than 180 days of continuous service, (reservists) including the "Cold War" veterans,

(3) Individuals who enlisted after 7 September 1980 or entered on active duty after 16 October 1981 must have completed 24 months of active duty service or the full period that the person was called or ordered to active duty. (Note: VA does list certain exceptions to this general guideline.)

(4) A veteran discharged for a service-related injury that occurred during service other than "for training purposes" (reservist); no minimum period required. A veteran entering service after 7 September 1980 would be eligible if discharged for disability, whether or not service-connected. If the disability was service connected, it could not have been from willful misconduct or incurred during an unauthorized absence. Additionally, these veterans can be eligible if discharged for hardship.

(5) Veterans entering service before 8 September 1980 can be considered eligible if discharged for hardship and if they completed 181 days of service.

(6) Unmarried surviving spouses. Specifically, a widow or widower of a veteran whose death was caused by a service-connected injury or ailment. To be eligible for loans, an unmarried surviving spouse cannot have acquired eligibility by reason of their own active military service. Eligibility as an unmarried surviving spouse is complete and distant from the eligibility of the deceased veteran, and any benefit the deceased veteran may have used in no way affects the benefits available to the eligible unmarried surviving spouse.

(7) Allies. Any United States citizen who served in the Armed Forces of a country allied with the United States in World War II.

(8) Hospitalized veterans. A person who has completed all the basic requirements but is hospitalized pending final discharge.

(9) Spouses of Service Personnel Missing in Action or Prisoners of War. If an individual has been either missing in action, captured, or interned in the line of duty for more than 90 days, their spouse is eligible for one VA home loan.

The word "eligibility" is explained in VA LOAN GUARANTY.

VA - ENTITLEMENT *See* VA LOAN GUARANTY.

VA - FUNDING FEE A fee VA uses to offset the cost of their operations, similar to the charge FHA uses for mortgage insurance. For years the fee was 1% of the loan amount. But on 18 December 1989, VA changed the structure of the fee.

The Veteran Home Loan Indemnity and Restructuring Act of 1989 changed the funding fee as follows:

(1) 1.25% for purchase or construction loans with less than a 5% downpayment (a LTV ratio of between 96-100%) and for any refinance loans, without regard to the LTV ratio;

(2) .75% for purchase or construction loans with at least a 5% but less than a 10% downpayment (91-95% LTV ratio); and

(3) .50% for purchase or construction loans with a 10% or more downpayment (90% or less LTV ratio).

For loan assumptions the funding fee is .50%. Vendee loans will have a 1% funding fee. DVB 26-89-39. The funding fee may be financed or paid in cash. If financed, the seller may not contribute or reimburse the veteran for any portion of the financed VA funding fee.

The Budget Reconciliation of 1990 increased the funding fee again. Effective for all loans closed on or after 1 November 1990, fees for all loans under the VA home loan guaranty program will be increased by .625 percent, as follows:

(1) For purchase or construction loans with less than a 5% downpayment (a LTV ratio of between 96-100%) and for any refinance loans, without regard to the LTV ratio, the funding fee is raised from 1.25% to 1.875%;

(2) For purchase or construction loans with at least a 5% but less than a 10% downpayment (91-95% LTV ratio), the funding fee is raised from .75% to 1.375%; and

(3) For purchase or construction loans with a 10% or more downpayment (90% or less LTV ratio), the funding fee is raised from .50% to 1.125%.

VA - GRADUATED PAYMENT MORTGAGE (GPM) The VA GPM mortgage is the same as the FHA 245 Plan III.

See FHA - GRADUATED PAYMENT MORTGAGE.

VA - LOAN A real estate mortgage available to qualified veterans for (a) buying a single-family home, which could include condominiums, zero-lot-line housing, co-ops, and any other acceptable form of housing by the VA; (b) refinancing an existing mortgage. VA loans are fixed rate amortized loans with either a level or graduated monthly payment.

There are several features of a VA loan.

(1) A 100% loan is available and the seller can pay all or part of the veteran's closing costs including any escrow requirements. If the seller pays all of the veteran's closing expenses, this will allow the veteran to purchase a home with a zero investment.

(2) Usually the veteran is assured a market or below market interest rate in comparison to conventional loans.

(3) There is no mortgage insurance premium charged on a VA loan. FHA loans normally have a one-time premium or a 1% monthly premium for mortgage insurance in addition to the interest rate. Usually, conventional loans that have a loan-to-value ratio higher than 80%

will have a front-end premium and a minimum of 1% private mortgage insurance added to the interest rate.

(4) When veterans sell their property, the original loan terms of the mortgage will remain the same and cannot be changed by loan assumption. (Note: there may be rare exceptions to the above statement, such as below market rate VA loans financed by tax-free bonds and later escalated due to income of assumptors being over statutory limits).

(5) For loans closed after 1 March 1988, VA requires pre-qualification for loan assumptions. Loans originated before the March date do not require pre-qualification except as noted in the paragraph. But, the interest rate will remain unchanged regardless of the origination date, except those financed by housing agency bonds.

(6) Anyone can prepay part or all of a VA loan without penalty.

(7) Other mortgages can be placed behind a VA first mortgage, i.e., second mortgages and wrap-around mortgages. Because of the many VA features, the marketability of a home can increase with a VA mortgage.

For more detail information on VA loans, please refer to one of two books written by Albert Santi: *The Mortgage Manual* and *Mortgage Lending*. Both books are published by Probus Publishing.

VA - LOAN AMOUNT A widely misunderstood VA principle is what many call the maximum VA loan amount. THERE IS NO MAXIMUM VA LOAN AMOUNT! To understand this principle, consider the following question and the differing answers.

QUESTION: What is the VA maximum loan amount?

ANSWER FROM MOST ANY LENDER: "$184,000."

ANSWER FROM VA: "We do not set a maximum loan limit, we only set the maximum guaranty."

On 1 March 1990, GNMA began to guaranty pools with VA loans up to $184,000. Since nearly all VA loans are placed in GNMA pools, lenders are quick to give the practical response, which is the maximum VA loan that can be placed in a GNMA pool ($184,000). The author, Santi, as a lender made several VA loans in the mid $200,000 range in the '70s.

See INVESTOR.

VA - LOAN GUARANTY The words "entitlement," "eligibility," and "guaranty" have a similar meaning. These terms are used in reference to the dollar amount of guaranty or entitlement available on each VA loan. The dollar amount of guaranty or entitlement decides the amount of VA loan available. "Guaranty" is used more in VA's relationship with the lender; "entitlement" or "eligibility" is used in VA's relationship to the veteran.

Originally, the maximum entitlement available for home loan purposes was $2,000. The maximum was raised to $4,000 on 28 December 1945; to $7,500 on 12 July 1950; to $12,500 on 7 May 1968; to $17,500 on 31 December 1974; to $25,000 on 1 October 1978; to $27,500 on 1 October 1980; and was further raised to $36,000 on 21 December 1987. On 18 December 1989 the President signed Public Law 101-237, *Veterans Home Loan Indemnity and Restructuring Act of 1989.* This new law established a new higher tier of guaranty for home purchase and construction and condominium loans. The maximum amount of entitlement was raised to the lesser of $46,000 or 25% of the loan when the loan amount exceeds $144,000. Entitlement of more than $36,000 may not be used for any refinancing. The new guaranty provisions are as follows:

(1) For loans of $45,000 or less, 50% of the loan is guaranteed.

(2) For loans of more than $45,000 and not more than $56,250, $22,500 of the loan is guaranteed.

(3) For loans of more than $56,250 and not more than $144,000, the lesser of $36,000 or 40% of the loan is guaranteed.

(4) For loans of more than $144,000 made for the purchase or construction of a home or farm residence or to purchase a residential unit in a condominium, the lesser of $46,000 or 25% of the loan is guaranteed.

Except for loans more than $144,000, the maximum amount of guaranty remains at $36,000. If a proposed VA loan is $144,000 or less, the guaranty or any remaining guaranty is based on $36,000 as being the maximum guaranty. If a veteran applies for any home loan in an amount of $144,000 or less, the maximum guaranty is based on $36,000. Examples: John Veteran applies for a $125,000 loan and has never used his eligibility, maximum guaranty on his loan would be $36,000. If Susie Veteran applies for a $125,000 loan and she has previously used $10,000 of her guaranty, her guaranty would be $26,000 ($36,000 minus the $10,000 she previously used). If a loan is less than the amounts given in 1) and 2) above, the guarantees would be calculated as stated in those sentences.

For loans more than of $144,000, the maximum amount of guaranty is based on $46,000 except on *refinance* **cases where the guaranty remains at $36,000.**

If a veteran has a copy of the Certificate of Eligibility, the reverse side of said Certificate should state the available eligibility and any previously used. To decide remaining entitlement, simply subtract amount previously used from the amount available.

Many veterans do not have a copy of their Certificate of Eligibility and are unsure of the exact entitlement previously used. A veteran can decide a minimum entitlement available by simply subtracting the maximum available at time of loan closing from the present maximum entitlement. For example, a veteran used their VA entitlement for a home loan purchase in 1971; to decide minimum remaining entitlement, subtract $12,500 (maximum entitlement at that time) from $36,000 (current maximum if loan amount is $144,00 or less). The remaining entitlement would be $23,500. Of course, the remaining entitlement might be slightly more if the veteran did not use the maximum available in 1971.

GNMA is the agency that shapes guidelines for lenders making VA loans. To understand how GNMA decides a VA maximum loan amount, let us assume the following: sales price and CRV is $75,000 and the veteran's used entitlement is $20,000. Always use the lower of the sales price or the CRV (Certificate of Reasonable Value - VA appraisal). When you read, sales price and CRV, this means both have the same dollar amount.

(1) We decide the remaining or unused guaranty (entitlement) as follows:

$36,000 maximum guaranty (entitlement)
−$20,000 used guaranty (entitlement)
$16,000 remaining guaranty

(2) We decide the percentage of guaranty as follows:

$16,000 divided by $75,000 = 21.33% guaranty

(3) GNMA requires a 25% dollar coverage. To decide the GNMA coverage required, we do the following:

$75,000 sales price and CRV
× .25
$18,750 minimum dollar coverage required by GNMA

(4) We meet the GNMA minimum dollar coverage as follows:

> $18,750 minimum dollar coverage required by GNMA
> $16,000 remaining guaranty
> $ 2,750 cash required to meet GNMA dollar coverage.

(5) We decide the VA loan amount, eligible for purchase by GNMA, as follows:

> $75,000 sales price and CRV
>   –$ 2,750 cash requirement
> $72,250 VA loan

The cash required is paid in the form of a downpayment.

To make sure we meet the 25% minimum GNMA dollar coverage for the loan, we do the following:

> $16,000 divided by $75,000 =   21.33% guaranty
> $2,750 divided by $75,000 =   + 3.67% downpayment
>   25.00% GNMA coverage

To obtain the maximum guaranty for this loan, you choose between the lesser of 60% of the loan amount ($43,350) or the remaining guaranty ($16,000). The guaranty for the above loan is $16,000.

The above example is the formula used by GNMA to decide the eligibility of a VA loan placed into a GNMA pool. There is a faster and easier formula to decide the loan amount acceptable to GNMA. The formula is as follows:

>   Sales Price and CRV × 75% + unused guaranty = loan amount

Using the numbers from the GNMA example above, determining the maximum loan amount with the shortcut formula would be as follows:

> $75,000 × 75% = $56,250 + unused guaranty ($16,000) = $72,250

Another useful formula to decide a 100% VA loan amount is as follows:

>   unused guaranty × 4 = 100% VA loan

Using numbers from the GNMA example above, we decide the 100% VA loan as follows:

> $16,000 × 4 = $64,000

As you can see, for a $2,750 cash downpayment, the veteran can increase their loan amount to $72,250, an additional $8,250.

Many people, including loan officers and loan processors, think a VA loan is limited to 4 times the guaranty, and there are probably an equal amount who think VA sets the maximum loan amount. If you ask VA for the maximum loan amount, they will be quick to tell you there is no maximum VA loan. VA limits the amount of loan guaranty, not the loan amount (*see* VA - LOAN AMOUNT).

A word of caution, there is a unique relationship between agency, lender, and investor. Some lenders in the COLT states (Colorado, Oklahoma, Louisiana, and Texas) and other real estate depressed areas, may require the 25% dollar coverage to be in the form of a VA guaranty and not guaranty plus cash. Upon foreclosure, VA, unlike FHA, does not necessarily pay the loan off and accept the property. In cases where VA does not accept the property, called a "no-bid," the VA pays the guaranty to the lender who then becomes the owner. Declining real estate values and an increase in foreclosures have caused lenders in the COLT states to loose money on homes they own due to VA foreclosures.

Guaranty serves a two-fold purpose. Guaranty primarily decides the dollar amount of a VA loan. For example, most lenders will lend at least an amount equal to four times the guaranty or entitlement.

Guaranty is additionally involved in the event of foreclosure. After foreclosure, the lender often becomes the owner of the foreclosed property. VA can accept the property in question from the lender by reimbursement of the outstanding loan balance plus foreclosure expenses; or VA can instruct the lender to keep title to the foreclosed property (this situation is called a *no-bid*) and accept a check equal to the remaining balance times the guaranty percentage originally issued when the loan was originated.

VA - POWER OF ATTORNEY Loan application may be made by the veteran's spouse or a member of the veteran's immediate family. Closing and loan documents can be forwarded to a veteran for signature in front of a notary. A power of attorney can be used in the absence of a veteran. If the veteran is available to sign loan application papers, only a general power of attorney is needed. If the veteran is unable to sign the loan application, then a specific power of attorney will be required. All powers of attorney should be recorded. Power of attorney can be used for loan closing provided:

(1) The donor's power of attorney is valid and legally adequate to enable the attorney in fact to act for the veteran. The power of attorney must have the authority to use the veteran's entitlement.

(2) The veteran has consented, in writing, to the specific transaction. The written consent must express a clear understanding of what is involved with the veteran's eligibility. It must express that the veteran's intends to occupy the property as a home upon the veteran's return or upon occupancy by the veteran's immediate family during the term of absence, and the veteran's signature must be attested by the Commanding Officer, Adjutant, or other person acting in a representative capacity. However, if the power of attorney expressly represents that the veteran intends to acquire the property as a home and adequately identifies the property and the terms of the proposed transaction, a separate written statement by the veteran is not necessary.

(3) There must be an affidavit that the veteran is alive at the time of loan closing. A Certificate of Guaranty will not be issued, if at the time of loan closing, the veteran was reported as missing in action or deceased. Proof of the veteran's status can be done by letter or cable dated subsequent to the loan closing from the veteran, or by a statement from the veteran's Commanding Officer that the veteran is alive and not missing-in-action on the date of loan closing. The Red Cross is often the fastest means of obtaining such verification if the absent borrower is out of the country.

See POWER OF ATTORNEY.

VA - REFINANCE Many experts call the VA refinance loan the "best loan in US." An eligible veteran can refinance their home and invest the funds for whatever reason(s) deemed worthy by the veteran. In comparing forms of refinancing, VA has the best program available. The refinance loan can be equal to 100% of the appraised value if there is no cash out. In general, if refinancing involves cash out, the loan will be limited to a 90% LTV and the veteran must occupy the property being refinanced. There are three allowances for a refinancing loan to be greater than 90% of the CRV (VA appraisal). First, refinancing a construction loan. Second, refinancing an installment land sale contract. Third, refinancing an existing loan assumed by a veteran with a new VA loan at a lower interest rate. These types of refinancing loans may not exceed the lesser of the VA appraised value or the sum of the outstanding balance on the loan being refinanced plus closing costs (which may include discount points) paid by the veteran. If there is no cash out from the refinance, the veteran does not have to occupy the property, however, the veteran must certify they previously occupied the property. Investment in a business, buying a farm, acquiring rental property, educational expenses for the veteran or children, home improvement or any other worthy reason may be acceptable to VA.

At the present time, 1990, the VA guaranty for refinancing is limited to $36,000. A veteran cannot use the higher guaranty, $46,000, for refinancing purposes. DVB 26-89-39.

VA - RELEASE OF LIABILITY For VA loans originated after March 1, 1988 all assumptors must pre-qualify before the VA loan can be assumed. If the assumptor is approved to assume the loan, the veteran is released from liability. But, this regulation only applies to loans originated after the March 1 date.

For all the VA loans assumed before the March date, the veteran must apply for a release of liability. VA is particular about reminding the veteran that the release can only be granted by the VA. A real estate agent or lender can be helpful in assisting the veteran; however, the veteran is cautioned that for VA guaranteed loans, a "release of liability" can only be granted by the VA. When application is made for the "release," the following conditions must be met:

(1) The loan must be current;

(2) The income and credit of the purchaser must be acceptable to VA;

(3) The purchaser must assume the VA loan and the indemnity obligation.

Owner occupancy is not required and the assumptor does not have to be a veteran. The release process can be lengthy.

For a veteran who doesn't want to wait, they can sell on a loan assumption and then later apply for a release of liability. For VA to grant a release of liability after a sale, the Deed transferring the property must contain an Assumption Clause, or the parties must sign an Indemnity Agreement, the instrument used must be recorded, the loan current, and the purchaser's income and credit must be acceptable to VA. The veteran-seller should insist that an assumption clause be inserted in the deed conveying the property to the assumptor. The assumption clause will give the veteran two benefits. First, the clause will permit VA to consider a release upon the veteran's application after the property has been conveyed. Secondly, the clause will afford the veteran a right of action against the assumptor if the loan is foreclosed. The following is a sample assumption clause.

SAMPLE ASSUMPTION CLAUSE

For and in consideration of Ten Dollars ($10.00) cash in hand paid, the receipt of which is hereby acknowledged, and other good and valuable consid-

eration, a part of which is the assumption of one certain trust deed dated
_____, 19___, and filed for record_____,
19___, in the office of the recorder of deeds of _____County,
Tennessee, in Book_____, Page____, and note of even date thereby secured, in the original principal amount of $_____
payable to _____,
which debt the grantee herein assumes and agrees to pay as part payment of
the purchase price.

The grantee further hereby assumes the obligations of _____
under the terms of the instruments creating the loan to indemnify the Veterans
Administration to the extent of any claim payment arising from the guaranty or
insurance of the indebtedness above mentioned.

If the Assumption Clause is not incorporated in the Deed, the veteran-seller
and the assumptor may sign an Indemnity Agreement that must be recorded.
The Indemnity Agreement has wording similar to the Assumption Clause. **If
neither the Assumption Clause nor the Indemnity Agreement is executed,
VA will not grant a release of liability.**

If a release of liability is not obtained, there are some general guidelines a
seller can use to help prevent a loss created from a loan that they still remain
liable for.

(1) The seller is free to write the lender and ask for written notification
of any pending foreclosure of the previous home loan. The seller
should make sure the lender is supplied with a current mailing address.

(2) The seller may obtain a large cash equity from the assumptor. For
example, a sale of a home with a loan balance of $40,000 and accept
a $15,000 cash equity from the assumptor will lessen the chances of
a foreclosure because of the investment by the buyer. The numbers
may vary from case-to-case, but it would be safe to assume that the
larger the cash equity involved, the less a chance of foreclosure, particularly foreclosure with a deficiency.

(3) The seller could require a guaranty performance agreement to be executed by the assumptor and secured by a second mortgage. A guaranty agreement can serve as sufficient collateral for a second
mortgage; money would not have to be lent by the seller to the purchaser. Foreclosure by the owner of the second mortgage may occur
if the obligations of the first mortgage are not being fulfilled. The
owner of the second mortgage would then have a legal right to buy
the property back by foreclosing the second mortgage. Most state

laws require the owner of a second mortgage to be put on notice of any pending foreclosure by the owner of the first mortgage. *See* GUARANTY PERFORMANCE for explaining this procedure in detail.

Some veterans have received an unpleasant surprise when they are unexpectantly advised that they owe the VA thousands of dollars plus interest for a deficiency judgement that occurred on a home they purchased with a VA loan years ago. One may ask if a VA loan is assumed but later foreclosed with a loss incurred, is the original veteran-borrower liable for a loss caused by someone else? The answer is, Yes! Furthermore, if a veteran will not indemnify VA for their loss, VA is entitled but not limited to the standard course of action our judicial system provides. Courses of action outside the courts could come from claims by the VA to the veteran's pension, social security income, or by withholding any subsequent VA benefits until the loss is paid.

> Under the governing law, a veteran who obtains from a private lender a loan which is guaranteed or insured by the Veterans Administration is legally obligated to indemnify the United States Government for the net amount of any guaranty or insurance claim the VA may thereafter be required to pay to the holder of the loan. This right of indemnity has been upheld by the Supreme Court of the United States, notwithstanding that a deficiency judgment was not obtained or was not obtainable by the mortgage holder under local state law. (U.S. v. Shimer, 367 U.S. 374, 1961)

See SURETY.

VA - RESTORATION OF ELIGIBILITY OR ENTITLEMENT The general requirement for restoration is that the loan must be paid in full, and the real property that served as security for the loan must have either (a) been disposed of by the veteran or (b) been destroyed by fire or other natural hazard. A veteran's entitlement can now, as of December 1989, be fully restored by having a prior VA loan paid off. A veteran no longer has to dispose of the property acquired by the use of their entitlement. Such restoration would be for the sole purpose of obtaining a new VA loan on the *same property,* and the veteran must meet all qualifying criteria including occupancy of the property being refinanced.

A veteran's entitlement may be restored by what is known as "substitution of entitlement." A new veteran purchaser assumes the outstanding indebtedness and (a) qualifies for the existing loan based on their income and credit; (b) has sufficient available entitlement to replace the amount of entitlement used by the seller in originally obtaining the loan; (c) and certifies that he or she does or will occupy the property as a home.

The VA Regional Office that originally guaranteed the loan should be contacted for details, processing, and instructions. (Note: An exception to this general guideline would be veterans who enlisted after 7 September 1980 or entered active duty after 16 October 1981. These veterans could have obtained a VA home loan while in service by completing 181 days of active duty, but without completing 2 years of service. These veterans, barring an approved exception, will not be eligible for restoration of entitlement.) DVB 26-89-39.

VA - SUBSTITUTION OF ENTITLEMENT *See* VA - RESTORATION OF ELIGIBILITY.

VACANCY RATE A rate or factor expressed in a percentage that estimates the vacancies for a rental project. If a vacancy rate is 5%, this implies that in a 100-unit apartment project, there will be five vacant units at all times.

VACATION HOME *See* SECOND HOME.

VALUABLE CONSIDERATION Items, including money, that can support a contract.

VALUATION CONDITION (VC) *See* FHA - VALUATION CONDITION.

VAPOR BARRIER Material used to prevent vapor or moisture (condensation) from penetrating walls in a building.
See CONDENSATION, VENEER, WEEP HOLE.

VARIABLE RATE MORTGAGE (VRM) *See* ADJUSTABLE RATE MORTGAGE.

VARIANCE Permission granted from a governing authority to construct or conduct a usage of improvements that is contrary to code or law.

VENDEE A purchaser, usually of real estate.

VENDOR A seller, usually of real estate.

VENEER Brick, thin sheets of wood, or other material serving as a cover for less expensive material on the outside walls. For example, a wall is described as a "brick wall" if the brick extends from the outside into the inside of the wall. It is a "brick veneer wall" if it is brick on the outside but wood and drywall on the inside.

The exterior veneer should be checked for its condition and the original workmanship involved in the installation. Wood siding and windows should be checked for rotting and all wood should be at least 6 to 8 inches above the ground as a precautionary measure against termite infestation and water rot. Veneer such as brick or stone should be checked for tuck-pointing and for cracks. Tuck-pointing is a term indicating the need to fill in the gaps between the brick or stone due to insufficient mortar that is normally caused by erosion. Excessive cracking in the brick, stone, or stucco can indicate settling or foundation problems.

VERIFICATION OF DEPOSIT (VOD) and VERIFICATION OF EMPLOYMENT (VOE) A standard form used by lenders for FHA, VA, and Conventional loans. The lender completes PART I and sends it to the depository or the employer. The depository or employer completes PART II and sends it back to the lender. There are severe penalties for falsifying information in the forms and for interfering in the direct handling of the forms from the lender to the depository or employer and back to the lender. Interested parties such as a real estate agent or the loan applicant are to never handle any loan verification forms.

The primary reason for the forms is to verify what the applicant has stated at loan application. These forms are sometimes a source of important but unpleasant surprises for all parties involved with the loan.

For the Verification of Deposit, the items the lender will scrutinize will be: in block #10, is the current balance much less than what the applicant stated at loan application? Is the balance high enough for the settlement requirements? Does the average balance for the past two months support the current balance? If not, the lender must verify where the money came from. Has the account been open for more than two months (or any period the lender may use)? If not, the lender will require proof of previous deposit accounts. Does block #11 contain any surprises, such as unreported loans? Are there any adverse credit remarks in block #12?

For the Verification of Employment, the items the lender will scrutinize will be: for one or all the VOEs, is the length of employment covered for a two year term? There must be a two year history, this can include being a student or being unemployed. Blocks 10-16 are self-explanatory, do they match up to what was given at loan application? Is there any surprise in block 17 for a previous employment?

VERIFICATION OF RENT OR MORTGAGE *See* DELINQUENCY.

VERTICAL INTEGRATION The theory expounded by large-scale firms that advocates integrating all mortgage transactions into one process. Larger compa-

Exhibit 83

VMP MORTGAGE FORMS • (313)293-8100 • (800)521-7291

VMP-24 (9007)

INSTRUCTIONS TO LENDER:
1 FILL OUT PART I REQUEST
2 HAVE APPLICANT(S) SIGN EACH COPY (No Carbon Signatures)
3 PULL YELLOW COPY AND FILE FOR FOLLOW-UP
4 FORWARD OTHER 2 COPIES (CARBON INTACT) TO DEPOSITORY

INSTRUCTIONS TO DEPOSITORY:
1. COMPLETE PART II
2. RETURN BOTH COMPLETED COPIES TO LENDER

70,136-10

FannieMae

Request for Verification of Deposit

Privacy Act Notice: This information is to be used by the agency collecting it or its assignees in determining whether you qualify as a prospective mortgagor under its program. It will not be disclosed outside the agency except as required and permitted by law. You do not have to provide this information, but if you do not your application for approval as a prospective mortgagor or borrower may be delayed or rejected. The information requested in this form is authorized by Title 38, USC, Chapter 37 (if VA); by 12 USC, Section 1701 et. seq. (if HUD/FHA); by 42 USC, Section 1452b (if HUD/CPD); and Title 42 USC, 1471 et. seq., or 7 USC, 1921 et. seq. (if USDA/FmHA).

Instructions: Lender - Complete items 1 through 8. Have applicant(s) complete item 9. Forward directly to depository named in item 1.
Depository - Please complete items 10 through 18 and return directly to lender named in item 2.
The form is to be transmitted directly to the lender and is not to be transmitted through the applicant(s) or any other party.

Part I - Request

1. To (Name and address of depository)	2. From (Name and address of lender)

I certify that this verification has been sent directly to the bank or depository and has not passed through the hands of the applicant or any other party.

3. Signature of Lender	4. Title	5. Date	6. Lender's No. (Optional)

7. Information To Be Verified

Type of Account	Account in Name of	Account Number	Balance
			$
			$
			$
			$

To Depository: I/We have applied for a mortgage loan and stated in my financial statement that the balance on deposit with you is as shown above. You are authorized to verify this information and to supply the lender identified above with the information requested in items 10 through 13. Your response is solely a matter of courtesy for which no responsibility is attached to your institution or any of your officers.

8. Name and Address of Applicant(s)	9. Signature of Applicant(s)
	X
	X

To Be Completed by Depository

Part II - Verification of Depository

10. Deposit Accounts of Applicant(s)

Type of Account	Account Number	Current Balance	Average Balance For Previous Two Months	Date Opened
		$	$	
		$	$	
		$	$	
		$	$	

11. Loans Outstanding To Applicant(s)

Loan Number	Date of Loan	Original Amount	Current Balance	Installments (Monthly/Quarterly)	Secured By	No. of Late Pymts.
		$	$	$ per		
		$	$	$ per		
		$	$	$ per		

12. Please include any additional information which may be of assistance in determination of credit worthiness. (Please include information on loans paid-in-full in item 11 above.)

13. If the name(s) on the account(s) differ from those listed in item 7, please supply the name(s) on the account(s) as reflected by your records.

Part III — Authorized Signature - Federal statutes provide severe penalties for any fraud, intentional misrepresentation, or criminal connivance or conspiracy purposed to influence the issuance of any guaranty or insurance by the VA Secretary, the USDA, FmHA/FHA Commissioner, or the HUD/CPD Assistant Secretary.

14. Signature of Depository Representative	15. Title (Please print or type)	16. Date

17. Please print or type name signed in item 14

18. Phone No.

Fannie Mae
Form 1006 Mar. 90

VMP-24 (9007) VMP MORTGAGE FORMS • (313)293-8100 • (800)521-7291

DEPOSITORY-RETURN BOTH COPIES TO LENDER
LENDER-DETACH THIS COPY AND FILE FOR FOLLOW-UP

Exhibit 84

INSTRUCTIONS TO LENDER:
1. FILL OUT PART I REQUEST
2. HAVE APPLICANT(S) SIGN EACH COPY (No Carbon Signatures)
3. PULL YELLOW COPY AND FILE FOR FOLLOW-UP
4. FORWARD OTHER 2 COPIES (CARBON INTACT) TO EMPLOYER

INSTRUCTIONS TO EMPLOYER:
1. COMPLETE PART II - VERIFICATION
2. RETURN BOTH COMPLETED COPIES TO LENDER

VMP-23 (9007)

76,136-A

FannieMae — Request for Verification of Employment

Privacy Act Notice: This information is to be used by the agency collecting it or its assignees in determining whether you qualify as a prospective mortgagor under its program. It will not be disclosed outside the agency except as required and permitted by law. You do not have to provide this information, but if you do not your application for approval as a prospective mortgagor or borrower may be delayed or rejected. The information requested in this form is authorized by Title 38, USC, Chapter 37 (if VA); by 12 USC, Section 1701 et. seq. (if HUD/FHA); by 42 USC, Section 1452b (if HUD/CPD); and Title 42 USC, 1471 et. seq., or 7 USC, 1921 et. seq. (if USDA/FmHA).

Instructions: Lender - Complete items 1 through 7. Have applicant complete item 8. Forward directly to employer named in item 1. Employer - Please complete either Part II or Part III as applicable. Complete Part IV and return directly to lender named in item 2. The form is to be transmitted directly to the lender and is not to be transmitted through the applicant or any other party.

Part I - Request

1. To (Name and address of employer)	2. From (Name and address of lender)

I certify that this verification has been sent directly to the employer and has not passed through the hands of the applicant or any other interested party.

3. Signature of Lender	4. Title	5. Date	6. Lender's Number (Optional)

I have applied for a mortgage loan and stated that I am now or was formerly employed by you. My signature below authorizes verification of this information.

7. Name and Address of Applicant (include employee or badge number)	8. Signature of Applicant
	X

Part II - Verification

9. Applicant's Date of Employment	10. Present Position	11. Probability of Continued Employment

12A. Current Gross Base Pay (Enter Amount and Check Period)
☐ Annual ☐ Weekly ☐ Other (Specify)
☐ Monthly ☐ Hourly
$ _____

13. For Military Personnel Only		14. If Overtime or Bonus is Applicable, Is Its Continuance Likely?
Pay Grade		Overtime / Bonus
Type	Monthly Amount	☐ Yes ☐ No ☐ Yes ☐ No

12B. Gross Earnings

Type	Year To Date	Past Year 19____	Past Year 19____
Base Pay	Thru ____ 19____ $	$	$
Overtime	$	$	$
Commissions	$	$	$
Bonus	$	$	$
Total	$	$	$

	Monthly Amount
Base Pay	$
Rations	$
Flight or Hazard	$
Clothing	$
Quarters	$
Pro Pay	$
Overseas or Combat	$
Variable Housing Allowance	$

15. If paid hourly — average hrs. per wk.

16. Date of applicant's next pay increase

17. Projected amount of next pay increase

18. Date of applicant's last pay increase

19. Amount of last pay increase

20. Remarks (If employee was off work for any length of time, please indicate time period and reason)

Part III - Verification of Previous Employment

21. Date Hired	23. Salary/Wage at Termination Per (Year) (Month) (Week)
22. Date Terminated	Base_____ Overtime_____ Commissions_____ Bonus_____
24. Reason for Leaving	25. Position Held

Part IV - Authorized Signature
Federal statutes provide severe penalties for any fraud, intentional misrepresentation, or criminal connivence or conspiracy purposed to influence the issuance of any guaranty or insurance by the VA Secretary, the USDA, FmHA/FHA Commissioner, or the HUD/CPD Assistant Secretary.

26. Signature of Employer	27. Title (Please print or type)	28. Date

29. Print or type name signed in Item 26

30. Phone No.

Fannie Mae
Form 1005 Mar. 90

EMPLOYER-RETURN BOTH COMPLETED COPIES TO LENDER
LENDER-DETACH THIS COPY AND FILE FOR FOLLOW-UP

nies that are already involved in financial services anticipate further growth in acquisition of mortgage banking companies. The mortgage banking companies are incorporated as subsidiaries or integrating mortgage finance service companies. Firms aspire to eliminate part, or all layers, of services necessary for a typical "separate" institution that charges a separate fee for its individual services such as brokerages, mortgage originators, appraisers, loan servicers, etc.

As *mortgage bankers,* they hold the mortgage instrument in a pool for sale to the secondary mortgage market. As a *conduit* they make available primary mortgages for creation and issue of MBSs in all permitted forms. As *investment bankers* they sell mortgage-backed securities to the final purchaser who holds a mortgage-related security, or securities, within their portfolio, or on behalf of an institution.

VETERANS ADMINISTRATION *See* VA.

VICTORIAN HOME STYLE

Victorian. A nineteenth century style house with three different designs of window arches. It has symmetrical bays and an entrance way with columns supporting an entablature.

VOD *See* VERIFICATION OF DEPOSIT and VERIFICATION OF EMPLOYMENT.

VOE *See* VERIFICATION OF DEPOSIT and VERIFICATION OF EMPLOYMENT.

VOLT Electromotive force that when steadily applied to a conductor whose resistance is one ohm will produce a current of one ampere.

VOLUNTARY CONVEYANCE *See* DEED IN LIEU OF FORECLOSURE.

VRM VARIABLE RATE MORTGAGE.
See ADJUSTABLE RATE MORTGAGE.

W

WAC *See* WEIGHTED AVERAGE COUPON.

WAINSCOTING Wood or other material different from the wall that is used to line the lower three or four feet of an interior wall.

WAIVER To give up or voluntarily abandon a claim, right, or privilege. A waiver is a unilateral act that leaves all parties where they were originally.

WALLBOARD *See* DRYWALL.

WALL SHEATHING *See* SHEATHING.

WAM *See* WEIGHTED AVERAGE MATURITY.

WAREHOUSE LINE Credit used by a lender to close loans and hold them until the mortgages are sold to the investor.

WAREHOUSING The practice of gathering real estate mortgages for later resale in the secondary market. A line of credit at a commercial bank is established on a short term basis using permanent mortgages as collateral for borrowing. This is a form of interim financing and is used until the mortgages are sold to permanent investors.
See NEGATIVE CARRY, POSITIVE CARRY.

WARRANTY A promise that certain facts or statements are true.

WARRANTY DEED A deed conveying title and containing a covenant from the grantor to the grantee that title is free and clear of encumbrances other than any stated in the contract or deed. There are two types of warranty deeds, general and special.

A general warranty deed conveys not only all the grantor's interest and title to the property to the grantee, but warrants that if the title is defective or has a "cloud" on it, such as mortgage claims, tax liens, title claims, judgements, or mechanic's liens, the grantee may hold the grantor liable.

A special warranty deed on the other hand, conveys title to the grantee and agrees to protect the grantee against title defects or claims asserted by the grantor and those persons whose right to assert a claim against the title arising during the period the grantor held title to the property. In a special warranty deed the grantor guarantees to the grantee that he or she has done nothing during the time title was held to the property that in the future might impair the grantee's title.

WARRANTY OF COMPLETION OF CONSTRUCTION If the FHA or VA approves plans and specifications before the beginning of construction and inspects the property during construction, then "Warranty of Completion of Construction in Substantial Conformity with Approved Plans and Specifications" (VA form 26-1859, HUD Form 92544) will be required. The name of the builder should be entered in the warranty form.

WATER TABLE The distance from natural ground water to the ground surface.

WATER ROT *See* ROT.

WATT A measure of electrical power that is equal to the flow of one ampere caused by the pressure of one volt.

WATT-HOUR A unit used to decide the basis of electric bills. A 75-watt light bulb burning for one hour will use 75 watts of electricity.

WEATHER STRIPPING Insulation by means of felt or metal placed around the interior opening of a door or window to keep out wind and rain.

WEEP HOLE One of a series of small holes in a retaining or foundation wall for permitting excess water to drain.

WEIGHTED AVERAGE COUPON The Weighted Average Coupon (WAC) of Mortgage Loans is calculated by multiplying the unpaid Principal Balance of each Mortgage Loan by the Coupon of such Mortgage Loan (resulting in a "product" for each Mortgage Loan). The sum of the products divided by the sum of the unpaid Principal Balances equals the WAC. The WAC means the weighted average coupon of mortgage loans as a group. The WAC and the WAM are used for mortgage-backed pool optimization of present market conditions.

WEIGHTED AVERAGE MATURITY The Weighted Average Remaining Maturity of a group of Mortgage Loans is calculated by multiplying the unpaid principal balance of each mortgage loan by the number of months remaining to maturity of such mortgage loan (resulting in a "product" for each mortgage loan), adding the products so obtained for all of the mortgage loans, and dividing the sum of all the products by the aggregate unpaid principal balance of all the mortgage loans. The WAM is the weighted average remaining maturity of the applicable mortgage loans as a group.

WHOLE LOAN SALE The sale or purchase of an entire loan as opposed to the sale or purchase in a participation or share of the loan or a mortgage-backed security. Whole loans are not as liquid as mortgage-backed securities.

WILL A formal written statement of the disposition of property upon the death of a testator or testatrix (man or woman). The person who made the will must be of sound mind and of age. Most states require the will to be in writing and witnessed by at least two people, three is preferred.

See CODICIL, DESCENT, DEVISE, EXECUTOR, HOLOGRAPHIC WILL.

WILLIAMSBURG HOME STYLE

Williamsburg. English style house named after houses built in Williamsburg, VA. This house features simple exterior lines, windows with small panes, a hip or gable roof, large and high chimneys and simple front doors. It has symmetrical windows with the front door centered between the windows.

WILLIAMSBURG GEORGIAN HOME STYLE

Williamsburg Georgian. Williamsburg style with a Georgian influence. The house will have two chimneys, arches and decorative brick work.

WINDOW There are several types of windows (see Exhibit 85).

WIRING *See* ELECTRICAL SYSTEM.

WITHOUT RECOURSE (1) A mortgage that says the lender will not pursue personal liability against the borrower. The lender's security is the real estate being financed. (2) A sale of loans without obligating the seller to buy them back under certain conditions. An example of a condition is the sale being subject to review appraisals. If the buyer of the mortgages is not satisfied with some of the appraisals, the seller must buy back the mortgages the buyer specifies.

See EXCULPATORY CLAUSE, NON-RECOURSE, SUBJECT TO.

WOMEN'S COUNCIL OF REALTORS (WCR) An organization affiliated with the National Association of REALTORS(R). It is said to be the largest women's retail organization in America.

WORKOUT A mutual attempt by the mortgagee and mortgagor to help in avoiding foreclosure or bankruptcy.

WRAP-AROUND MORTGAGE A financing arrangement allowing a new junior mortgage to be treated as a prior mortgage or senior mortgage. It is a mortgage loan in the amount equal to the principal balance due under the existing un-retired loan, plus an additional sum advanced by a lender who will hold the mortgage called a wrap-around (commonly called a "wrap"). The wrap-around mortgage payment is a combination of all mortgage payments. A third mortgage can be used for an example of a wrap-around mortgage. The mortga-

Exhibit 85

Window Types

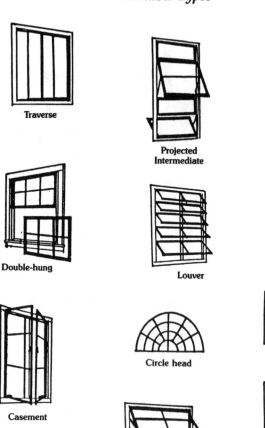

Traverse

Projected
Intermediate

Details

Double-hung

Louver

Details

Casement

Circle head

Basement

Transom

Manual Awning

Intermediate
Combination

Fixed bow

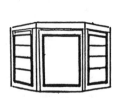

Fixed bay

gor makes one payment to the wrap-around mortgagee who then pays the mortgage payment owed to the first and second mortgages and then keeps the rest.

The wrap-around mortgage has three advantages: (1) it is valuable as a creative financing tool, it gives a certain element of safety to a junior mortgage holder, and it can be used to earn a spread on interest rates. Using the example above, the seller feels comfortable about owner-financing with a third mortgage and can therefore extend credit to a buyer. The buyer has less front end cash required to purchase the property because of the third mortgage that might not be available if it were not for the advantages to a wrap. (2) The owner of the "wrap" knows that the first and second mortgage payment are kept current, because they are being paid by the owner of the third mortgage or wrap. (3) The wrap lender is most likely going to charge a higher rate of interest on the wrap as compared to the first and second mortgages, therefore, making a *spread* on the interest rates. For example, the interest rate on the first is 8%, the interest rate on the second is 10%, and the interest rate on the wrap is 12%. The owner of the wrap makes a spread of 4% on the first and 2% on the second. Remember, the mortgagor makes one payment to the wrap-around mortgagee who then keeps the proportionate payment and pays the mortgage payment owed to the first and second mortgagees.

A wraparound mortgage is a junior or subordinate mortgage, but it includes all of the senior mortgages.

See ALL-INCLUSIVE TRUST DEED, ARBITRAGE, SPREAD.

WRIT OF EXECUTION A court order authorizing an official to execute a decision such as eviction of a tenant or selling property. A writ to carry out the judgment or decree of a court.

WRITER The mortgage "trader" is typically the writer, or seller of over-the-counter (OTC) mortgage related securities (MRSs) options. Mortgage related options are over-the-counter options representing contracts made as buyer and seller only. These contracts are a two-party agreement as opposed to trading in options standardized on the exchange.

Mortgage lenders are the buyers (or holders) of options who then pay the writer (or seller) an advance fee to compensate for possible price adjustment risks in the underlying mortgage security. This is the same as insurance for the holder of the option, against volatility of interest rates.

The holder of an option has bought a guarantee for the selling of MRSs at an agreed price regardless of rising interest rates. Since mortgage pipelines are vulnerable to change in interest rates after a lender's commitment to borrowers, the OTC option provides effective hedges at minimum costs.

Y

YIELD (1) The amount of income returned from an investment expressed as a percentage. For example, discount points plus interest rates will equal the yield. Yields on bonds are the annual percentage of returns that mortgage and bonds pay. Yield refers to the effective annual amount of interest income that accrues on an investment. (2) The productivity of farm lands.

See DISCOUNTED YIELD, ELLWOOD TABLE, and INWOOD ORDINARY ANNUITY COEFFICIENT.

YIELD ON AVERAGE LIFE A 30-year mortgage yield and a mortgage-backed security yield with 30-year mortgages are based on a single loan being prepaid in twelve years. This yield calculation represents a fair estimate on a pool of loans wherein the average mortgage loan life is assumed to be twelve years. This is an accepted practice for trading MBSs and whole loan mortgages in the secondary market.

YIELD SPREADS RELATIVE TO TREASURIES The evaluation of mortgage pass-through securities in comparison to U.S. 10-year Treasury Yield curve spreads are based on three factors assigned to the MBSs. These three factors are (1) the average life, (2) the security credit rating, and (3) the coupon rates. However, the delicate supply and demand conditions control the spread amounts. As a matter of fact, the FNMA pass-through and the FHLMC pass-through are issued at a larger spread to 10 year Treasury yields than the GNMA pass-through. Fannie and Freddie are limited to integrity rather than full faith and credit of the U.S. Government, not to mention the larger payment delays inherent in the pass-through of the former corporate entities. A narrower spread to Treasuries can be attributed to the government backing of Ginnies or a short delay in payments on GNMA's.

YIELD TO MATURITY (YTM) The percentage return of an investment based on the loan's reaching its maturity. Yield to maturity disregards the average life concept. The yield to maturity is based on the assumption that the loan will be due and payable, in full, at maturity.

See DISCOUNT YIELD.

YTM *See* YIELD TO MATURITY.

Z

ZERO-COUPON BONDS AND HEDGING SERVICING PORTFOLIOS
A hedging strategy employed by some is purchasing servicing portfolios and zero coupon bonds of similar increments simultaneously. Zero-coupon bonds rise in value as the interest rates decrease, therefore adjusting for loss in income from the prepayments in servicing portfolios. On the other hand, as interest rates increase prepayments slow down in the servicing portfolio, yielding dollar amounts that overcome decreased value produced by zero-coupon bonds. The holder of bonds can then retain zero-coupons until maturity at face value. This hedging strategy experiences an upside risk rather than a downside risk. To promote and expand the growth of servicing securities much like mortgage-backed bonds is anticipated as a normal trade function by portfolio servicers. The stripping of Treasury securities creating interest-only securities and zero-coupon bonds started with investment bankers in 1982.

ZERO LOT LINES A structure with at least one side resting directly on the lot's boundary line.

ZERO RATE AND LOW RATE MORTGAGE A unique mortgage in that it appears to be completely, or almost interest free. The buyer makes a large down payment, usually one third of the sale price, and makes the remaining installments over a short term.

For example, a prospect wants to buy a $90,000 home but discovers the market interest unacceptable. The buyer opts to use their savings to make the downpayment, say $30,000, on a zero rate (or no-interest) mortgage. Then a front-end finance charge is made, say 12% of the money needed in financing, or about $7,200. An agreement is made to repay the principal ($60,000) in 84 monthly installments of $714.29 In seven years the loan will be paid off.

In these mortgages, the sales price may be increased to reflect the loan costs. Thus, the buyer could be exchanging lower interest costs for a higher purchase price. Partly because of this, they may be able to deduct the prepaid finance charge and a percentage (for example, 10%) of the payments from income taxes as if it were interest. Before going ahead with these plans, however, the prospect may want to check with the IRS through an attorney, to decide if the mortgage qualifies for the tax treatment.

ZONING ORDINANCES The acts of an authorized local government establishing building codes, and setting forth regulations for property land usage.

ORDER FORM
Other fine products from Albert Santi

To order simply fill out this order form and mail or call 901-755-8728.
Yes! Please send the following:

____ *Mortgage Lending*   **$24.95 ea.**
Hardcover, 700 pages, 4th edition of Q & A's for FHA, VA, & Conventional Loans. Also includes a Quality Control Section, and an FHA & VA Compendium of Handbooks, Mortgagee Letters, and DVB Circulars.

____ *The Mortgage Manual*   **$19.95 ea.**
Paperback, 500 pages, 4th edition of Q & A's for FHA, VA & Conventional Loans.

____ *The HP-12C Real Estate Solutions Manual*   **$9.95 ea.**
This book is 100% guaranteed to turn a novice into a real estate math wizard.

____ **The 90-Minute Mortgage Manual Finance Seminar**   **$14.95**
On two cassette tapes.

Reader Service Program (RSP©) Keep your books updated!
____ For *The Mortgage Manual*   **$15.95 (2 annual updates)**
____ For *Mortgage Lending*   **$20.95 (2 annual updates)**
____ *The Mortgage Financing Mystery*   **Call for price**
New off press

Computer Software

For computer software, please specify disk size (3.5" for 5.25").

____ *Qualification Commander*   **$295.00**
Refer to the definition of: Computerized Loan Origination (CLO) for a demonstration of this program. First annual update is included with your purchase.

____ *Mortgage Blaster*   **Available on shareware basis for $15.00!**
Complete Refinancing Analysis • Loan Amortization Schedules • Prepayment Analysis • Find out which loan is best • Compare three loans at the same time • Income Analysis • Amortization Schedules • Net Payment Analysis • Loan Calculator.

____ *Broker Ledger*   **$65.00**
A simplified broker/agent cashflow program, mo.-to-mo., year-to-date expense/income statement.

____ *EscroTrac*   **$75.00**
For tracking and recording completion of all events from offer acceptance to date of close.

____ *NewBasis*   **$25.00**
A program for determining the realized gain, new IRS basis for an exchange.

____ *PropVest*   **$75.00**
Income property analysis program.

____ *ProSpect*   **$75.00**
Database program for prospective sellers and buyers.

____ *MailSpec*   **$65.00**
A mailing list program for generating, storing, retrieving and printing names, addresses, phone numbers.

____ *UnitBoss*   **$125.00**
Residential income property management program, capable of managing up to 160 properties.

Call 901-755-8728 or mail your order, along with a check, to: Mortgage Techniques, P.O. Box 17214, Memphis, TN, 38187-0214. (Please add $3.50 for first item ordered and .50 for each additional for shipping!)